Stiglitz and Walsh

PRINCIPLES OF MACROECONOMICS
Fourth Edition

The Most Modern Text for Principles of Macroeconomics

Accessible and Student-friendly

Two of the most innovative researchers and educators in the field of economics, Joseph Stiglitz and Carl Walsh, have written the most relevant, student-friendly Principles of Macroeconomics text available. How? By giving students a text that is . . .

- Teeming with **applications and examples** from the New Economy, an economy in which students are active participants.

- **Accessible and interesting** in every paragraph.

- Always focused on the **five key fundamentals**: trade-offs, incentives, exchange, information, and distribution.

- Filled with thorough coverage of newsworthy topics such as economic growth, technological change, Fed policy and inflation targeting, and globalization.

Accurate and Contemporary

Stiglitz and Walsh have also written the most satisfying text for instructors. How? By giving them a text that more accurately reflects their exciting and innovative field while never losing sight of the importance of student readability and satisfaction, a text that . . .

- Treats the **long run first.**

- **Integrates** financial markets with the goods and labor markets.

- Thoroughly covers **economic growth.**

- Uses the **inflation targeting/ADI approach** to discuss monetary policy.

- Consistently emphasizes the importance of **finance markets and financial issues** in today's interconnected world economy.

Modern Organization and Approach

Stiglitz/Walsh has long been recognized for bringing a modern perspective to the Principles of Macroeconomics course. The new Fourth Edition continues that practice. A few of the key characteristics of the text that reflect its modern, realistic, and relevant approach include:

Presenting the Long-Run/Full-Employment Model first.

Integrating financial markets with Goods and Labor in the Long-Run/Full-Employment model.

Dedicating a full chapter to the key topic of Economic Growth in the Long-Run/Full-Employment section.

Featuring the Inflation Targeting/ADI approach in the Short-Run/Fluctuations section for understanding monetary policy and the role of the Fed in the macroeconomy.

Devoting an entire part to Globalization, a topic that many students are eager to learn about, given its inherent importance and the attention that it receives from today's popular-culture opinion makers.

Contents in Brief

Riveting Boxes That Highlight the New Economy Being Created by the Internet and Information Revolution

From Google to eBay, StubHub, Napster, and online poker, the manifestations of the New Economy are changing the way we live, travel, spend our leisure time, shop, and work. Though the fundamentals of economics have remained constant, how those fundamentals are utilized is changing at an ever-quickening pace. Stiglitz/Walsh Fourth Edition recognizes this fact.

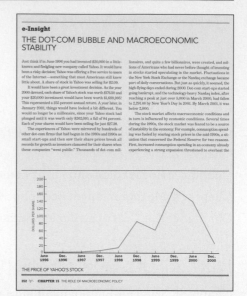

e-Insight

THE DOT-COM BUBBLE AND MACROECONOMIC STABILITY

Just think if in June 1996 you had invested $20,000 in a little-known and fledgling new company called Yahoo. It would have been a risky decision; Yahoo was offering a free service to users of the Internet—something that most Americans still knew little about. A share of stock in Yahoo was selling for $21.09.

It would have been a great investment decision. As the year 2000 dawned, each share of Yahoo's stock was worth $476.50 and your $20,000 investment would have been worth $1,688,966! This represented a 256 percent annual return. A year later, in January 2001, things would have looked a bit different. You would no longer be a millionaire, since your Yahoo stock had plunged until it was worth only $262,010, a fall of 84 percent. Each of your shares would have been selling for just $27.38.

The experiences of Yahoo were mirrored by hundreds of other dot-com firms that had begun in the 1980s and 1990s as small start-ups and then saw their share prices break all records for growth as investors clamored for their shares when these companies "went public." Thousands of dot-com mil-

lionaires, and quite a few billionaires, were created, and millions of Americans who had never before thought of investing in stocks started speculating in the market. Fluctuations in the New York Stock Exchange or the Nasdaq exchange became part of daily conversations. But just as quickly, it seemed, the high-flying days ended during 2000. Dot-com start-ups started going bankrupt, and the technology-heavy Nasdaq index, after reaching a peak at just over 5,000 in March 2000, had fallen to 2,291.46 by New Year's Day in 2001. By March 2001, it was below 2,000.

The stock market affects macroeconomic conditions and in turn is influenced by economic conditions. Several times during the 1990s, the stock market was feared to be a source of instability in the economy. For example, consumption spending was fueled by soaring stock prices in the mid-1990s, a situation that concerned the Federal Reserve for two reasons. First, increased consumption spending in an economy already experiencing a strong expansion threatened to overheat the

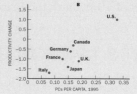

THE PRICE OF YAHOO'S STOCK

352   **CHAPTER 15** THE ROLE OF MACROECONOMIC POLICY

Internet Connection

PRESENT VALUE CALCULATIONS

The Internet provides several sites that you can use to make present discounted value calculations. If you want to know the present value of a future payment, the calculator at www.unb.ca/web/transpo/mynet/npv.htm allows you to specify the amount, the future date, and the interest rate. It then gives you the present discounted value of the future amount.

The Web site http://learningforlife.fsu.edu/course/fp101/search_frameset.htm provides a convenient table that lets you determine how much you need to discount future dollar amounts. For example, if the interest rate is 5 percent, the table shows that a dollar in 10 years' time is worth 61 cents today and a dollar in 15 years is worth 48 cents today.

does not use the funds to purchase the car today. This is approximately a monthly interest rate of 0.83 percent (10 percent divided by 12), so the first $300 payment in one month has a present discounted value of $300/(1 + 0.0083) = $297.52. The $300 payment in two months is worth $300/(1 + 0.0083)² = $295.06, while the final $5,000 payment at the end of three years is worth $3,756.57 ($5,000/(1 + 0.1)³). When we add up the present discounted value of all the payments under the lease plan, we find they total $15,506 in current dollars. Since Sarah can purchase the car today for $15,000, she saves $506 by buying rather than leasing.

This comparison depends on the interest rate. If the interest rate rises to 15 percent, the present discounted value of the lease payments falls to $14,351; now it makes sense to take out the lease. A good way to test your understanding of present discounted value is to see if you can explain why the present discounted value of the lease falls as the interest rate rises. When is it better to try to postpone payments, when the interest rate is high or low?

Calculating present discounted values can be complicated when many payments over several periods are involved, as in our car lease example. Spreadsheet programs have built-in functions that enable you to do these calculations quickly. (To obtain the present discounted value of the lease using Excel, for example, simply enter = 2500−pv(10%/12,36,300,5000).)

Inflation and the Real Rate of Interest The interest rate, as we have seen, is a price. It tells how many dollars we can get at a future time if we give up one dollar today. But except for misers like Scrooge or Silas Marner who store money for its own sake, dollars are of value only because of the goods that can be bought with them. Owing to inflation—the increase in prices over time—dollars in the future buy fewer goods than dollars today. In deciding whether to borrow or whether to lend, individuals want to know how much *consumption* they will get tomorrow if they give up a dollar's worth of consumption today. The answer is given by the **real rate of interest.** This is distinguished from the **nominal rate of interest,** the rate one sees posted at a bank or reported in the newspaper, which simply describes the number of dollars one gets next year in exchange for a dollar today.

---

e-Insight

COMPUTERS AND INCREASED PRODUCTIVITY GROWTH

If the recent increases in productivity growth are due to new information and computer technologies, then we might expect that all the major industrialized economies would be benefiting from them. Panel A shows average labor productivity growth for the seven advanced economies known since 1976 as the "Group of Seven," or the G-7 (the G-7 became the G-8 with the addition of the Russian Federation in 1998). As the chart shows, only the United States has seen labor productivity increase in recent years. For all the other members of the group, productivity growth was higher from 1980 to 1995 than it has been since. Yet the new information and computer technologies are available to all these countries; so why hasn't growth increased in all of them? Should we conclude that the new technologies are not the source of America's increased productivity growth?

Perhaps the acceleration in U.S. productivity growth has not been matched in these other industrialized economies

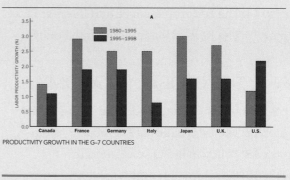

PCs AND PRODUCTIVITY GROWTH

PRODUCTIVITY GROWTH IN THE G–7 COUNTRIES

Internet Connection boxes provide useful links to Web resources and home pages.

e-Insight boxes apply economic principles to new developments in information technology and the Internet.

Additional Features to Heighten Student Understanding

Thinking Like an Economist boxes reinforce the core ideas emphasized throughout the book: Trade-offs, Incentives, Exchange, Information, and Distribution.

Case in Point vignettes highlight real-world applications in each chapter.

International Perspective boxes present applications to international issues.

Stiglitz/Walsh uses techniques designed to assist retention . . .

"Fundamentals of . . ." sections distill the essence of particularly important and tricky topics.

"Wrap-Ups" provide a short summary of the key points presented in a section.

"Five Core Ideas" are emphasized throughout the book.

Emphasis throughout the text on the five core ideas in Economics:

Trade-offs

Incentives

Exchange

Information

Distribution

---

market. Once this has happened, the level of employment, potential output, the real rate of interest, and the price level are determined as the full-employment model of Part Two explained. Because it takes time for wages and prices to adjust fully, we often refer to the full-employment model as describing the economy in the **long run**—a length of time sufficient to allow wages and prices to adjust to equilibrate supply and demand.

When wages or prices adjust sluggishly, the basic price mechanism that leads to equilibrium can't function effectively. The **short run** is that period during which wages or prices have failed to keep demand and supply in balance. In the short run, the level of employment can diverge from the full-employment level, and wages and prices will not respond quickly enough to move the economy back to full employment. But as noted above, once wages and prices have had enough time to adjust, the economy does return to full employment and the model of Part Two holds sway.

The third and fourth of our fundamental ideas entail simplifying assumptions about how individuals, firms, and economic policymakers behave. They will play an important role in clarifying the implications of the slow adjustment of wages and prices for short-run economic fluctuations.

STICKY WAGES

Our first key concept is one we have already discussed: the fundamental explanation for cyclical unemployment is that wages do not adjust quickly enough when either the demand or the supply for labor shifts. *At least for a while, and sometimes for extended periods of time*, the demand for labor at market wages can differ from the supply of labor. Because this is such a crucial assumption in macroeconomics, some of the reasons for the slow adjustment of wages have already been discussed in this chapter.

Fundamentals of Fluctuations 1

STICKY WAGES

In the short run, shifts in labor supply or demand often result in labor surpluses (high unemployment) or shortages (very low unemployment) because nominal wages tend to adjust slowly.

STICKY PRICES

Like nominal wages, many prices are also sticky. And just as shifts in labor demand lead to fluctuations in unemployment when wages fail to adjust, so shifts in product demand will lead to fluctuations in production. When demand for a firm's product falls, the firm might respond by lowering its price or by reducing production. Our analysis of economic fluctuations is based on a fundamental insight:

Internet Connection

DATING BUSINESS CYCLE PEAKS AND TR

Almost all the data that economists use to study the economy are produced by the government. In the United States, the Department of Commerce and the Bureau of Labor Statistics within the Department of Labor collect much of the data economists use, such as the statistics on unemployment and GDP. The widely accepted dates for the peaks and troughs of business cycles, however, are determined by the members of the Business Cycle Dating Committee of the National Bureau of Economic Research (NBER), a private, nonprofit research

organization. The NBER...
back to 1854; the entire...
(www.nber.org/cycles.h...
"a recurring period of decline in total output, income, employment, and trade, usually lasting from six months to a year, and marked by widespread contractions in many sectors of the economy." In popular usage, the economy is usually considered to be in a recession if real GDP declines for two consecutive quarters.

Wrap-Up

ECONOMIC FLUCTUATIONS

Recessions: periods of significant decline in real GDP.

Expansions: periods of growth in real GDP.

Output gap: the deviation (a percentage) of observed real GDP from potential real GDP.

Case in Point

ESTIMATING THE OUTPUT COSTS OF A RECESSION

Recessions are periods when workers suffer from higher than normal levels of unemployment. By using the output gap and Okun's Law, economists have developed a way to estimate the opportunity cost of idle workers who are willing and able to work at the going wage. For example, Figure 11.1 shows that the output gap reached –8 percent during the 1982 recession. Since potential GDP in 1982 was approximately $5.2 trillion (in 2000 dollars), the cost of the recession in 1982 was about $420 billion (8 percent of $5.2 trillion) in lost income. The gap fell to only –3.2 percent in the recession of 1991; by then potential GDP had risen to $7.1 trillion, so a 3.2 percent shortfall represented a loss of $218 billion in 1991. These figures agree with most observers' view that the recession of 1982 was much more severe. Yet even a relatively mild recession is serious; to provide some perspective, in 1991 the total real value of expenditures by the federal government for all nondefense programs was only $183 billion.

...alth, there remains considerable unease among ...ets distribute that wealth and about the effects ...ike bidders at an auction, what market participants are willing and able to pay depends on their income. Incomes differ markedly across occupations. Some groups of individuals—including those without skills that are valued by the market—may receive such a low income that they cannot feed and educate their children without outside assistance. Government provides the assistance by taking steps to increase income equality.

Steps that soften the distributional impact of markets may blunt economic incentives. While welfare payments provide an important safety net for the poor, the taxation required to finance them may discourage people from working and saving. If the government takes one out of every two or three dollars that an individual earns, that individual may not be inclined to work as much. And if the government takes one out of every two or three dollars a person earns from interest on savings, the person may decide to spend more and save less. Thus, efforts by the government to redistribute income may come at the cost of reduced economic efficiency.

The primary reliance on private decision making in the United States reflects economists' beliefs that this reliance is appropriate and necessary for economic efficiency. But economists also believe that certain interventions by government are desirable. Like the appropriate balance between public and private sectors, the appropriate balance between concerns about equality (often referred to as *equity concerns*) and efficiency is a central issue of modern economies. As elsewhere, trade-offs must be made.

Wrap-Up

FIVE CORE IDEAS

1. *Trade-offs:* resources are scarce, so trade-offs are a basic fact of life.
2. *Incentives:* in making choices, decision makers respond to incentives.
3. *Exchange:* people benefit from voluntary exchange, and in market economies, market exchanges lead to the efficient use of resources.
4. *Information:* the structure that markets take and how well they can function depend critically on the information available to decision makers.
5. *Distribution:* markets determine how the goods and services produced by the economy are allocated to members of society.

The Three Major Markets

The market economy revolves around exchange between individuals (or households) who buy goods and services from firms and those firms, which take *inputs*, the various materials of production, and produce *outputs*, the goods and services that they

[1] Alan Greenspan, speech at the Federal Reserve Bank of Kansas City Jackson Hole Conference, August 25, 2000.

An Unmatched Media Package

Norton's innovative multimedia package provides everything instructors and students need to teach and learn essential economic concepts. Features include SmartWork (our new online homework management system), a Student Web site designed for quick review, and ready-to-go solutions for WebCT, BlackBoard, and in-class multimedia presentations.

NEW! SMARTWORK: NORTON'S INNOVATIVE HOMEWORK MANAGEMENT SYSTEM

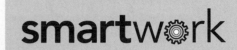

SmartWork has three main advantages:

1. *SmartWork allows professors to assign smarter homework*—questions and exercises that go beyond multiple choice. For every chapter, the instructor will be provided with three ready-made assignments. (You can either use these as-is, or customize them.) The three types of ready-made assignments are

   - **Graphing Tutorials** that allow students to move lines, curves and points and see the implications instantly.

   - **Audio Graphs** allow students to experience the material in a unique way. Students are taken through a lesson and see economic equations worked out and graphs manipulated while hearing an audio presentation of the lesson.

   - **Conceptual Quizzes** pair questions with thought-provoking feedback. This feature asks students to reconsider their answer after they respond to a question.

2. *SmartWork gives students smarter feedback.* SmartWork's interactive feedback gives students the help they need, right when they need it.

3. SmartWork provides professors with a smarter way to customize assignments, write their own assignments, and track student progress.

FREE STUDENT WEB SITE

All students have instant access to the powerful review materials on the Stiglitz and Walsh student Web site. Features include:

1 **Practice Quizzes with NEW! Diagnostic Feedback.** These multiple-choice review questions give students feedback about which sections of the chapter they should review.

2 **Chapter Reviews**—each Web chapter will open with a brief summary of the major points covered in the corresponding text chapter.

3 **Glossary**—taken from the book's glossary

4 **NEW! Economics Newsfeed**—updated daily and often hourly with new articles, this feature gives students examples of how the concepts taught in this course are applied in the real world.

e-BOOK AVAILABLE FROM NORTONeBOOKS.COM

An affordable and convenient alternative to the print textbook, *Principles of Macroeconomics*, Fourth Edition is also available as an e-book. The Norton e-book format retains the content of the print book and replicates actual book pages for a pleasant reading experience.

Principles of

MACROECONOMICS

FOURTH EDITION

Joseph E. Stiglitz
COLUMBIA UNIVERSITY

Carl E. Walsh
UNIVERSITY OF CALIFORNIA, SANTA CRUZ

Principles of
MACROECONOMICS

FOURTH EDITION

W. W. Norton & Company
NEW YORK · LONDON

W. W. Norton & Company has been independent since its founding in 1923, when William Warder Norton and Mary D. Herter Norton first published lectures delivered at the People's Institute, the adult education division of New York City's Cooper Union. The Nortons soon expanded their program beyond the Institute, publishing books by celebrated academics from America and abroad. By mid-century, the two major pillars of Norton's publishing program—trade books and college texts—were firmly established. In the 1950s, the Norton family transferred control of the company to its employees, and today—with a staff of four hundred and a comparable number of trade, college, and professional titles published each year— W. W. Norton & Company stands as the largest and oldest publishing house owned wholly by its employees.

Editor: Jack Repcheck

Managing Editor, College: Marian Johnson

Director of Manufacturing—College: Roy Tedoff

Manuscript Editor: Alice Falk

Project Editor: Lory A. Frenkel

Editorial Assistants: Sarah Solomon, Mik Awake

Book Designer: Rubina Yeh

Photo Researcher: Kelly Mitchell

PRINTED IN THE UNITED STATES OF AMERICA.

Fourth Edition.

Composition by TSI Graphics

Page layout by Cathy Lombardi

Manufacturing by R.R. Donnelley

Library of Congress Cataloging-in-Publication Data

Stiglitz, Joseph E.

   Principles of macroeconomics / Joseph E. Stiglitz, Carl E. Walsh—4th ed.

     p. cm.

   Includes index.

   ISBN 0-393-92624-9 (pbk.)

    1. Macroeconomics. I. Walsh, Carl E. II. Title

   HB172.5.S753   2005

339—dc22

2005040184

W. W. Norton & Company, Inc., 500 Fifth Avenue, New York, N. Y. 10110

www.wwnorton.com

W. W. Norton & Company Ltd., Castle House, 75/76 Wells Street, London WIT 3QT

1 2 3 4 5 6 7 8 9 0

ABOUT THE AUTHORS

Joseph E. Stiglitz is professor of economics, business, and international and public affairs at Columbia University. Before joining the Columbia faculty, he held appointments at Yale, Oxford, Princeton, and Stanford. Internationally recognized as one of the leading economists of his generation, Professor Stiglitz has made important contributions to virtually all of the major subfields of economics, in particular the economics of information, one of the key topics highlighted in this text. He was a co-recipient of the Nobel Prize in Economic Science in 2001, and earlier in his career received the American Economic Association's John Bates Clark Medal, which is given every two years to the most outstanding economist under the age of forty. Professor Stiglitz is the author and editor of hundreds of scholarly articles and books, including the best-selling undergraduate textbook *Economics of the Public Sector* (Norton) and, with Anthony Atkinson, the classic graduate textbook *Lectures in Public Economics*. He is the author of two influential popular books as well: *Globalization and Its Discontents* and *The Roaring Nineties*. In addition, he was the founding editor of the *Journal of Economic Perspectives*. Professor Stiglitz has also played a prominent role at the highest levels of economic policy making. He was a member and chairman of President Clinton's Council of Economic Advisers and later served as Senior Vice President and Chief Economist of the World Bank.

Carl E. Walsh is professor of economics at the University of California, Santa Cruz, where he teaches principles of economics. He previously held faculty appointments at Princeton and the University of Auckland, New Zealand, and has been a visiting professor at Stanford. He is widely known for his research in monetary economics and is the author of a leading graduate text, *Monetary Theory and Policy* (MIT Press). Before joining the Santa Cruz faculty, Professor Walsh was senior economist at the Federal Reserve Bank of San Francisco, where he continues to serve as a visiting scholar. He has also been a visiting scholar at the Federal Reserve Banks of Kansas City, Philadelphia, and at the Board of Governors. He has taught courses in monetary economics to the research department and staff economists at the central banks of Hong Kong, Norway, Portugal, Spain, and the United Kingdom, and at the International Monetary Fund. He is a past member of the board of editors of the *American Economic Review* and is currently an associate editor of the *Journal of Money, Credit, and Banking* and the *Journal of Economics and Business*. He is also on the editorial board of the *Journal of Macroeconomics*.

ABOUT THE AUTHORS

CONTENTS IN BRIEF

CONTENTS

CHAPTER 3   HOUSEHOLDS AND FIRMS IN THE MACROECONOMY   71

CHAPTER 4   MEASURING OUTPUT AND UNEMPLOYMENT   93

PART 3 MACROECONOMIC FLUCTUATIONS 243

CHAPTER 11 INTRODUCTION TO MACROECONOMIC FLUCTUATIONS 244

PART 4   THE GLOBAL ECONOMY 363

CHAPTER 17 THE INTERNATIONAL FINANCIAL SYSTEM 394

CHAPTER 18 POLICY IN THE OPEN ECONOMY 416

PART 5   FURTHER TOPICS IN MACROECONOMICS   455

PREFACE

The study of economics has always been fascinating, yet it is difficult to remember a more exciting or important time in the discipline. Think of today's major economic issues—the huge American trade and budget deficits, global warming, the debate between proponents of conservation and energy exploration, ensuring adequate health care, ending global poverty, reforming Social Security, outsourcing, rethinking the nature of competition and regulation in the Internet age, and copyright protection in a digital, "downloadable" world. The list goes on and on. To understand these issues, the core insights of economics are invaluable.

Exciting new theoretical advances are allowing economists to understand better how individuals, families, and businesses make decisions about what to buy, what to sell, how much to save, and how to invest their savings. These advances affect the way governments design policies to protect the environment, to promote educational opportunities, and to deal with the changes in our economy brought about by technological innovations and the increasingly global economic marketplace in which we all participate.

There has never been a time when the need to be informed about economic issues has been more acute. Nor is it any less critical for students to acquire the tools that will enable them to think critically about the economic decisions they face in their personal lives and the issues they must decide on as engaged citizens. Even something as basic to the study of economics as the concept of trade-offs helps provide students with a tool that can inform the way they think about issues at the personal, local, state, national, and even global levels. Whereas the Principles of Economics course has always been popular among business students, now most students realize that *everyone* should be conversant with the fundamentals of economics. We have written our book, and revised it for the Fourth Edition, keeping this concept of the politically engaged student in mind.

Preparing the Fourth Edition of this textbook has provided us with the opportunity to make several fundamental improvements over the previous edition. We still emphasize the five core concepts of modern economics, which are the importance of **trade-offs, incentives, exchange, information,** and **distribution.** Yet economic research is continuously yielding new, interesting, and important insights, and we believe that these exciting new developments should be conveyed to students in introductory courses. While the textbook has always offered the most integrated coverage of information economics, in this new edition we introduce students to new research in behavioral economics. We have also made several changes to the organization of the book that will give instructors increased flexibility in structuring their courses.

Mission Statement for the Fourth Edition

Our text has always strived for two goals: One, to be transparently accessible and interesting, dare we say a "good read," for the student reader; and two, to not shy away from teaching students the latest exciting insights of the discipline, to teach them the substance of economics as a field of study. Many books seem to take the stance that students cannot "handle" the new topics—we believe that it just a matter of explaining the ideas simply and clearly.

To achieve these goals, the four main objectives of the previous editions continued to guide us. These objectives are to provide students with a clear presentation of the basic competitive model; to present macroeconomics in its modern form, consistent with the way active researchers and economists in policy making institutions analyze the economy; to structure the textbook in ways that are conducive to good teaching and student learning; and to ensure that the textbook reflects the contemporary scene, stressing the core insights economics provides for understanding the ever-changing economy.

Changes to the Fourth Edition—Macroeconomics

The new edition maintains the modern approach to macroeconomics, which recognizes that the Federal Reserve and other central banks implement monetary policy through interest rates rather than the explicit control of the money supply. By providing a more realistic treatment of monetary policy, the modern approach also allows students to quickly understand and discuss the types of policy actions they read about in newspapers. While the general approach developed in the Third Edition is maintained, our treatment of macroeconomics in the new edition aims to streamline the presentation, moving the more advanced material into the "Topics" section of *Principles of Macroeconomics*.

KEY CHANGES FOR THE FOURTH EDITION:

Important changes to *Principles of Macroeconomics* include:

- Updating the opening chapter to reflect new developments since the Third Edition.

- Shortening the introductory review material on microeconomics.

- Discussing price indices and the measurement of inflation in a separate chapter (Chapter 5).

- Reorganizing Part 2, on Full-Employment Macroeconomics. Separate chapters are now devoted to government finance (Chapter 7) and the open economy (Chapter 8). These two important topics can now be treated individually, allowing instructors greater choice in deciding how to organize their course, and reducing the number of new concepts introduced in each chapter.

- Combining the important material on government deficits and surpluses in Chapter 7 rather than splitting it between Part 2 and Part 4 as in the previous edition.

- Moving the material on money, prices, and the Federal Reserve to the end of Part 2 (Chapter 10) to improve the flow of the full-employment section. Chapter 6 provides the basic framework for the determination of real output, real wages, and the real interest rate; Chapter 7 adds the government; Chapter 8 extends the results to the case of the open economy; and Chapter 9 provides a discussion of economic growth. The material on money and prices then follows in Chapter 10.

- Extensively rewriting Part 3 on Macroeconomic Fluctuations to improve the exposition. Many users of the Third Edition felt too much material was introduced in the chapters on the aggregate demand–inflation relationship and the short-run inflation adjustment relationship. To address this concern, we have moved the extended discussion of inflation and unemployment into Part 4 (The Global Economy). Part 3 begins with an overview (Chapter 11), covers the basics of aggregate expenditures (Chapter 12), and then develops the aggregate demand–inflation relationship in Chapter 13.

- Consolidating the material on the international economy into a new Part 4, with chapters dealing with international trade (Chapter 16), the international financial system (Chapter 17), policy in the open economy (Chapter 18), and economic development and transition (Chapter 19).

In making these changes, we have continued to be motivated by the desire to write a modern, student-friendly textbook that reflects the way economists approach their subject today.

The Organization of the Text

The text is organized to work for both the student and the instructor. For students, we utilize the five core concepts of trade-offs, incentives, exchange, information, and distribution throughout the text. These concepts anchor the wide range of topics we cover, linking them all to a core set of basic principles to which students can always refer. For students, we provide a firm grounding in basic concepts, but we do not stop there. We also ensure that students are able to understand both the tremendous insights offered by the basic economic model of competitive markets, and its limitations. This prepares students to understand the lessons offered by modern economics for studying imperfect competition, information, growth, and economic fluctuations. We show how these modern insights help one understand economic phenomena that classical economics cannot. By exposing students to modern economics—from the economics of information and innovation to behavioral economics—they obtain a sense of the richness of the discipline and its value for understanding the world around them.

The text is designed to offer solid coverage of traditional topics, combined with a flexible structure that allows it to be tailored to fit with the individual needs of the instructor. The basic material of competitive markets and the full-employment economy are presented first. Then, the section dealing with fluctuations begins with an overview chapter that allows students to gain insight into the basic intuition and key issues that are addressed in detail in subsequent chapters. This structure also allows an instructor who does not wish to devote too much time to a topic such as imperfect information to give students a sense of its importance and the lessons economists have learned about it. There is also a new and expanded treatment of the international economy. Finally, the "Topics" chapters offer additional flexibility for the instructor in fine-tuning the readings from the text to the context of his or her course structure.

Learning Tools

We have developed a clutch of Learning Tools that will help our student readers relate to the principles being described and better retain the information.

① RIVETING BOXES THAT HIGHLIGHT THE NEW ECONOMY BEING CREATED BY THE INTERNET AND INFORMATION REVOLUTION

From Google, to eBay, Expedia, StubHub, Napster, and online poker, the manifestations of the New Economy are changing the way we live, work, shop, travel, and spend our leisure time. Though the fundamentals of economics have not and will not change, how those fundamentals are utilized can and is changing, at an ever-quickening pace. Stiglitz/Walsh Fourth Edition recognizes this fact.

e-INSIGHT BOXES apply economic principles to new developments in information technology and the Internet.

INTERNET CONNECTION BOXES provide useful links to Web resources and home pages.

② ADDITIONAL TOOLS TO HEIGHTEN STUDENT UNDERSTANDING

THINKING LIKE AN ECONOMIST boxes reinforce the core ideas emphasized throughout the book: Trade-offs, Incentives, Exchange, Information, and Distribution.

CASE IN POINT vignettes highlight real-world applications in each chapter.

INTERNATIONAL PERSPECTIVE boxes present applications to international issues.

"FUNDAMENTALS OF . . ." sections distill the essence of particularly important and tricky topics.

"WRAP-UPS" provide a short summary of the key points presented in a section.

PRINCIPLES OF MACROECONOMICS, FOURTH EDITION e-BOOK

Same Great Content, Half the Price   The e-book version of *Principles of Macroeconomics*, Fourth Edition, offers the full content of the print version, at half the price. A variety of features make the e-book a powerful tool for study and review.

- **Zoomable images** allow students to get a closer look at the figures and photographs.

- **Clear text**, designed specifically for screen use, makes reading easy.

- A **search function** facilitates study and review.

- A **print function** permits individual pages to be printed as needed.

- **Sticky notes** allow students to add their own notes to the text.

Online and cross-platform software works on both Macs and PCs and allows students to access the e-book from home, school, or anywhere with an Internet connection. Visit NORTONeBOOKS.com for more information.

Ancillary Package

An assortment of valuable supplements are available to students and teachers who use the textbook.

SmartWork Homework Management System   Developed in coordination with Science Technologies, SmartWork is an innovative online homework management system. SmartWork requires active learning from students and provides smart, interactive feedback. Instructors can choose from three types of ready-made assignments:

- *Interactive Graphing Exercises* allow students to manipulate points, lines, and curves, see the implications instantly, and then answer questions about them.

- *Audio Graphs* guide students step-by-step through a slide show presenting core concepts. On screen, students see economic equations worked out and graphs manipulated while hearing an audio presentation of the lesson.

- *Conceptual Quizzes* pair questions with thought-provoking feedback. Students are asked to reconsider their answers after they respond to each question.

With SmartWork's intuitive interface, instructors can also customize Norton's ready-made assignments or write their own exercises with remarkable ease. Access to SmartWork is free to all students who purchase a new textbook or e-book.

Student Web site   This free companion Web site offers students powerful review materials. Practice quizzes feature diagnostic feedback indicating which sections in the chapter the student should review. The student Web site also provides chapter reviews, a glossary, and a daily economics newsfeed.

NORTON MEDIA LIBRARY

This instructor's CD-ROM includes PowerPoint lecture slides (corresponding to the lecture modules in the *Instructor's Manual*) as well as all the graphs and tables from the book. New **lecture-launcher audiovisual slide shows** provide brief segments on each chapter's material as it relates to imperfect markets or the new economy.

NORTON RESOURCE LIBARY

(WWNORTON.COM/NRL)

The Norton Resource Library provides comprehensive instructor resources in one centralized online location. In the library, instructors can download ready-to-use, one-stop solutions for online courses, such as WebCT e-packs and BlackBoard course cartridges, or can tailor these premade course packs to suit their own needs. The library's exceptional resources include PowerPoint lecture slides, graphs and tables from the book, and a computerized test-item file.

TRANSPARENCIES

A set of color transparencies is available to qualified adopters.

STUDY GUIDE

BY LAWRENCE W. MARTIN, *MICHIGAN STATE UNIVERSITY*
0-393-92827-6 • PAPER

This innovative study guide reinforces the key concepts of each chapter through reviews, practice exams, and problem sets designed to help students apply what they've learned. "Doing Economics" sections are structured around a series of "Tool Kits" in which students learn a problem-solving technique through its step-by-step application. Each "Tool Kit" is followed by worked examples and practice problems that apply the relevant technique.

INSTRUCTOR'S MANUAL

BY GERALD McINTYRE, *OCCIDENTAL COLLEGE*
0-393-92821-7 • PAPER

For each chapter of the textbook, the *Instructor's Manual* contains lecture advice, lecture modules, lecture applications, problem sets, and solutions. The extensive lecture modules can be used with a set of PowerPoint slides prepared by Gerald McIntyre. These lecture notes are far more extensive than what other publishers offer, and will be extremely valuable to the first time instructor.

TEST-ITEM FILE AND COMPUTERIZED TEST-ITEM FILE

BY DAVID GILLETTE, *TRUMAN STATE UNIVERSITY*
0-393-10727-2 • PAPER

The Fourth Edition *Test-Item File* includes over 4,000 questions, a 15 percent increase over the previous edition. In addition, each chapter includes a subset of questions covering the boxed inserts (such as e-Insights), that professors can use in their exams, thereby encouraging students to read these discussions.

Acknowledgments

The book's first three editions were improved immeasurably by the input of numerous reviewers. In particular, we thank Robert T. Averitt, Smith College; Mohsen Bahmani-Oskoose, University of Wisconsin, Milwaukee; Richard Barret, University of Montana; H. Scott Bierman, Carleton College; John Payne Bigelow, University of Missouri; Howard Bodenhorn, Lafayette College; Bruce R. Bolnick, Northeastern University; Adhip Chaudhuri, Georgetown University; Michael D. Curley, Kennesaw State College; John Devereus, University of Miami; Stephen Erfle, Dickinson College; Rudy Fichtenbaum, Wright State University; Kevin Forbes, Catholic University; K. K. Fung, Memphis State; Christopher Georges, Hamilton College; Ronald D. Gilbert, Texas Tech University; Robert E. Graf, Jr., United States Military Academy; Glenn W. Harrison, University of South Carolina; Marc Hayford, Loyola University; Yutaka Horiba, Tulane University; Charles How, University of Colorado; Sheng Cheng Hu, Purdue University; Glenn Hubbard, Columbia University; Nancy Jianakopolos, Colorado State University; Allen C. Kelley, Duke University; Lori Kletzer, University of California, Santa Cruz; Michael M. Knetter, Dartmouth College; Kevin Lang, Boston University; William Lastrapes, University of Georgia; John Leahy, Boston University; Eric Leeper, Indiana University; Colin Linsley, St. John Fisher College; Stefan Lutz, Purdue University; Mark J. Machina, University of California, San Diego; Burton G. Malkiel, Princeton University; Lawrence Martin, Michigan State University; Thomas Mayer, University of California, Davis; Craig J. McCann, University of South Carolina; Henry N. McCarl, University of Alabama, Birmingham; John McDermott, University of South Carolina; Marshall H. Medoff, University of California, Irving; Peter Mieszkowski, Rice University; Myra Moore, University of Georgia; W. Douglas Morgan, University of California, Santa Barbara; John S. Murphy, Canisius College; Michael Nelson, University of Akron; William Nielson, Texas A & M University; Neil B. Niman, University of New Hampshire; David H. Papell, University of Houston; Douglas Pearce, North Carolina State University; Jerrold Peterson, University of Minnesota, Duluth; James E. Price, Syracuse University; Daniel M. Raff, Harvard Business School; Christina D. Romer, University of California, Berkeley; Richard Rosenberg, Pennsylvania State University; Rosemary Rossiter, Ohio University; David F. Ruccio, University of Notre Dame; Christopher J. Ruhm, Boston University; Suzanna A. Scotchmer, University of California, Berkeley; Richard Selden, University of Virginia; Andrei Shleifer, Harvard University; Nirvikar Singh, University of California, Santa Cruz; John L. Solow, University of Iowa; George Spiva, University of Tennessee; Mark Sproul, University of California, Los Angeles; Frank P. Stafford, University of Michigan; Raghu Sundaram, University of Rochester; Hal R. Varian, University of California, Berkeley; Franklin V. Walker, State University of New York at Albany; James M. Walker, Indiana University; Andrew Weiss, Boston University; Mark Wohar, University of Nebraska, Omaha; and Gilbert R. Yochum, Old Dominion University.

Many additional reviewers provided suggestions that help guide us in preparing the Fourth Edition. Our thanks to John Nader, Grand Valley State University;

Timothy A. Duy, University of Oregon; Richard Fox, Madonna University; Dale Cloninger, University of Houston, Clear Lake; Gavin Wright, Stanford University; Richard Stahnke, Hamilton College; Maristella Botticini, Boston University; Chris Niggle, University of Redlands; Santanu Roy, Southern Methodist University; Roger White, Franklin and Marshall College; Geoffrey Carliner, Boston University; Robert L. Pennington, University of Central Florida; Roger A. McCain, Drexel University; Nancy A. Jianakoplos, Colorado State University; Sudeshna C. Bandyopadhyay, West Virginia University; Jennifer Thacher, University of New Mexico; Alan Gummerson, Florida International University; Nejat Anbarci, Florida International University; Samuel Allen, University of California, Davis; Robert G. Bise, Orange Coast College; Sarah L. Stafford, College of William and Mary; Catherine Krause, University of New Mexico; Ariel Belasen, Binghamton University; Alina Luca, Drexel University; S. Abu Turab Rizvi, University of Vermont; Nivedita Mukherji, Oakland University; Faik A. Koray, Louisiana State University; Mehdi Haririan, Bloomsburg University; F. G. Hank Hilton, Loyola College; Michael Margolis, Oberlin College; Joseph K. Cavanaugh, Wright State University; Lisa Gundersen, Iowa State University; Eva Toth Szalvai, Bowling Green State University; Maya Federman, Pitzer College; Annie Fang Yang, University of Minnesota, Twin Cities; Molly Espey, Clemson University; Nora Underwood, University of California, Davis; Mary Schranz, University of Wisconsin, Madison; Scott Cunningham, University of Georgia; Ehsan Ahmed, James Madison University; Lee van Scyoc, University of Wisconsin, Oshkosh; Parker Wheatley, Carleton College; Daniel Rubenson, Southern Oregon University; Elliott Parker, University of Nevada, Reno; Peter Murrell, University of Maryland; Abdulhamid Sukar, Cameron University; Philip S. Heap, James Madison University; Erik D. Craft, University of Richmond; Sharmila King, University of the Pacific; Linus Yamane, Pitzer College; Cathleen Leue, University of Oregon; Daniel Monchuk, University of Southern Mississippi; Rik W. Hafer, Southern Illinois University, Edwardsville; and Ben Young, University of Missouri, Kansas City.

A particular note of appreciation is due Mary Schranz, University of Wisconsin, Madison, who provided detailed, thoughtful, and extremely helpful comments on draft chapters of the macroeconomics material. Her insights significantly improved the end product.

The major changes in the Fourth Edition and the improvements they represent are due in no small measure to the constant encouragement, advice, and enthusiasm of our editor, Jack Repcheck. Jack provided the perfect blend of critical feedback and positive reinforcement to encourage us at each stage of the process to strive toward our goals of accessibility and modernity, and to incorporate the latest insights from the forefront of economics in a manner that is accessible to students getting their first introduction to the field.

A special note of thanks continues to be owed Judy Walsh. Judy's knowledge of economics and her willingness to discuss ideas, make suggestions, and offer examples and encouragement have all contributed greatly to the improvements made to the Fourth Edition.

Alternative Course Outline

In the Fourth Edition, we have further improved the flexibility of the book, allowing it to be easily adapted to courses of varying length and objectives. **Part 5, Further Topics in Macroeconomics**, contains chapters that can be covered at the end of a course, time permitting, or integrated with the core discussion of macroeconomics. **Part 4, The Global Economy**, provides instructors with the option of constructing a more internationally focused introductory course, covering international trade, finance, and development. Alternatively, instructors can selectively choose from among these topics and include them in a more traditional organized course. The following outlines, which represent only a small subset of those that might be devised, reflect the flexibility the Fourth Edition offers.

OUTLINE FOR A ONE-SEMESTER COURSE IN MACROECONOMICS

CHAPTER	TITLE
1	Macroeconomics and the Economic Perspective

Introductory chapters if necessary

2	The Price System
3	Households and Firms in the Labor and Capital Markets

Core macroeconomics presentation

4	Measuring Economic Output and Unemployment
5	The Cost of Living and Inflation
6	The Full-Employment Model
7	Government Finance at Full Employment
8	The Open Economy at Full Employment
9	Economic Growth
10	Money, the Price Level, and the Federal Reserve
11	Introduction to Macroeconomic Fluctuations
12	Aggregate Expenditures and Income
13	Aggregate Demand and Inflation
14	The Federal Reserve and Interest Rates
15	The Role of Macroeconomic Policy

Plus any of the optional chapters comprising Parts 4 and 5

16	International Trade and Trade Policy
17	The International Financial System
18	Policy in the Open Economy
19	Economic Development and Transition
20	Inflation and Unemployment
21	Controversies in Macroeconomic Policy
22	A Student's Guide to Investing

OUTLINE FOR A SHORT COURSE IN MACROECONOMICS

Part 1

INTRODUCTION

Learning Goals

In this chapter, you will learn

1 How important historical events such as the Great Depression have shaped the field of macroeconomics

2 The three important goals of macroeconomic performance

3 What the key concepts that define core ideas in economics are

4 What markets are, and which are the principal markets that make up the economy

5 Why economics is called a science, and why economists often disagree

Chapter 1

MACROECONOMICS AND THE ECONOMIC PERSPECTIVE

Macroeconomics is the study of the overall economy—not the study of employment levels and prices in a particular industry but the study of total employment and unemployment and the general level of prices throughout the economy. It is also concerned with the effects on the overall economy of government policies. Macroeconomics deals with the *aggregate* economy. To begin to get a sense of the field of macroeconomics, it is useful to start with a brief history of the macroeconomy. The episodes described in this brief history have been important in shaping the field of macroeconomics, and we will use them throughout the following chapters to illustrate macroeconomic topics.

Imagine the world in 1929, three-quarters of a century ago. The stock market was booming, and no end to the good times was in sight. True, some commentators were saying the market was overvalued, that a crash was sure to come, but most investors were optimistic about the future. Unemployment was low, and the general level of prices was stable.

Only one year later, the world had changed forever. The October 1929 stock market crash wiped out almost a quarter of the value of the New York stock market; similar crashes occurred in other countries. The Dow industrial average (the precursor of today's Dow Jones industrial average, a measure of stock market prices), which had hit a high of 381 in September 1929, fell to 41 in July 1932. Unemployment rose to previously unseen levels throughout the world economy. By 1933, one of every four workers in the United States was unemployed. The United States and other industrialized economies still had the same buildings, plants, and equipment as before, the same labor force was available and apparently willing to work, yet many of these resources lay idle. This period, the 1930s—now indelibly linked with hardship and depressed economic conditions—is commonly called the **Great Depression.**

Out of this catastrophe, macroeconomics was born. While the science of economics can be dated to the publication in 1776 of Adam Smith's *The Wealth of Nations,* the birth of macroeconomics as a separate branch within economics can be dated to the publication in 1936 of John Maynard Keynes's *The General Theory of Employment, Interest, and Prices.* Prior to Keynes's time, economists had studied the behavior of the entire economy and placed special emphasis on understanding the role of money and the general level of prices. But the modern field of macroeconomics, with its stress on understanding why economies experience episodes like the Great Depression and why employment and production grow and fluctuate over time, begins with Keynes. Our understanding of the forces influencing aggregate economies has evolved dramatically since Keynes wrote, but his work helped define the field and has had lasting impacts (both good and bad) on economic policy.

Not just macroeconomics, but many of the government policies and programs we take for granted today, such as Social Security and federal insurance for bank deposits, grew out of the experience of the 1930s. Perhaps its most important legacy is the general acceptance of the notion that governments are responsible for ensuring that periods like the Great Depression never reoccur. In the United States, the Employment Act of 1946 requires the federal government to cultivate "conditions under which there will be afforded useful employment opportunities . . . for those able, willing, and seeking to work, and to promote maximum employment, production, and purchasing power."

The impact that the Great Depression has had on the subsequent history of the United States and other major economies can teach us a great deal about macroeconomics and important government policies.

The Commitment to Full Employment and Growth

Before the Great Depression, the United States and other industrialized economies had gone through frequent periods of rapid economic growth followed by declines in production. These declines were often accompanied by financial panics in which banks were forced to close their doors, refusing to let depositors withdraw their funds.[1] The Roaring Twenties was one period associated in the popular mind with a booming economy. This pattern of periods of rapid growth alternating with periods of decline has continued to today, although the fluctuations in economic activity since World War II have generally been milder than those experienced before the war (see Figure 1.1). Looking back over the most recent fifteen years, we see that the 1990s was a period of rapid growth, high employment, and rising incomes in the United States. In early 2001, the boom times of the 1990s came to an end. The stock market collapsed as the dot-com bubble burst. Unemployment began to rise. By most measures, the downturn was short and mild, with the economy growing again by the end of 2001. Yet unemployment remained stubbornly high and many

---

[1]Each Christmas season, the movie *It's a Wonderful Life* is shown on television. A central event in the movie is the threatened failure of the bank owned by the character played by Jimmy Stewart.

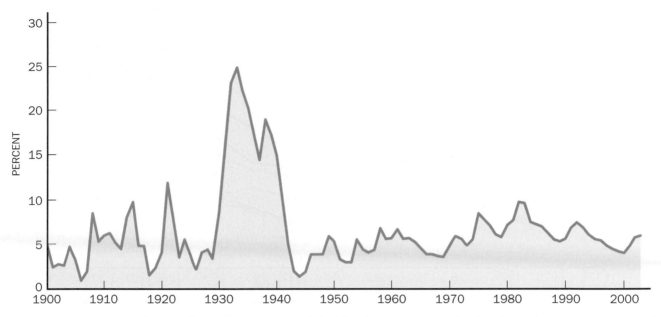

Figure 1.1

UNEMPLOYMENT, 1900–2003

The proportion of the labor force unemployed and seeking jobs rose to 25 percent during the Great Depression. Since 1960, unemployment has fluctuated around an average of about 6 percent, but it has risen to almost 10 percent (in 1983) and fallen to as low as 3.5 percent (in 1969). After reaching 7.5 percent in 1992, the unemployment rate fell steadily over the rest of the 1990s and was at 4.0 percent in 2000. It then rose to 6.0 percent in 2003.

SOURCE: *Economic Report of the President* (2004), Table B-42.

talked of a "jobless recovery." It was not until 2004 that employment growth fully recovered.

When the Great Depression hit, it was not confined to the United States. Figure 1.2 shows that production declined in all the major industrial economies, with the United States and Germany being hit the hardest. We often think of the "global economy" and the close international linkages we have today as uniquely characteristic of the modern world, but the economies of Europe and North America were also linked in the 1920s, and economic crises took on a global dimension, just as they can today.

The world economy recovered slowly from the dramatic depths of the Great Depression. The United States produced less in 1936 than it had in 1929. And in 1937 another decline occurred, helping to solidify our view of the 1930s as an entire decade of hardship. Only with the increased production associated with the advent of World War II did incomes in the United States significantly surpass earlier levels and unemployment return to more normal levels. The massive increase in orders to factories for war materials stimulated firms to expand production and hire workers. By 1944, the unemployment rate had fallen to 1.2 percent of those willing to work.

The end of World War II brought new worries that the economy would lapse back into recession and the hard times of the 1930s. The fear was that when the strong demand for production arising from the wartime needs of the government ended, firms would again be idle and the era of massive unemployment would return. Fortunately, while production declined from its wartime peaks, the economy did not

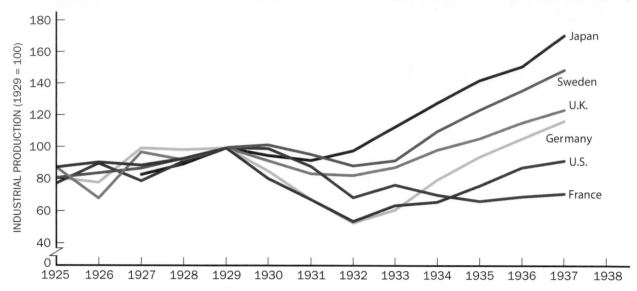

Figure 1.2

INDUSTRIAL PRODUCTION

The Great Depression was not limited to the United States. All industrial economies suffered declines in economic activity and production in the 1930s. The index of industrial production for each country is scaled so that all the indexes equal 100 for the year 1929.

SOURCES: League of Nations, *World Production and Prices* (Geneva: League of Nations, 1936), Appendix II, p. 142; and *World Production and Prices* (Geneva: League of Nations, 1938), Table 1, p. 44.

revert to the conditions of the Great Depression. The late 1940s saw strong growth in economic activity, in part fueled by household spending as Americans moved to the suburbs, built homes, and had children. During the war years, few consumer goods had been available, purchases of some goods had been rationed, and households had been urged to save by buying war bonds to help finance the war effort. Americans wanted to enjoy the return of peace and prosperity by using the incomes they had earned during the war to buy new cars, homes, and appliances.

The shift from wartime production and the demands for military goods to peacetime production and the demands for civilian goods represented a tremendous change in what the economy produced. Assembly lines that had been making tanks for the government shifted to making automobiles for consumers. Construction boomed as it met the demand for new homes. Resources—workers and capital—had to be shifted from what they had been producing to meet the new needs and desires of Americans. Jobs had to be created for the millions of soldiers returning from the war.

The end of the war also saw the government accepting responsibility for preventing a recurrence of the Great Depression, an acceptance formalized when the U.S. Congress passed the Employment Act in 1946. Among its provisions was the establishment of the president's Council of Economic Advisors, a three-member committee of economists who advise the president.[2] While economists have debated how much power the government actually has to influence macroeconomic developments, the voting public often shows that it expects the president to ensure continued economic growth, low inflation, and low unemployment.

---

[2]Professor Stiglitz was chair of President Clinton's Council of Economic Advisors from 1995 to 1996.

Today, a slight rise in the unemployment rate brings demands for the government to do something to "get the economy moving again." And for good reason: In today's economy, when an extra 1 percent of the labor force becomes unemployed, incomes in the economy fall by about $160 billion. A commitment to maintaining full employment was absent in the 1930s, or at least there was much less agreement over whether the government could (as well as whether it should) stimulate the economy.

GETTING THE COUNTRY MOVING AGAIN

The attempts by government to pursue the goals established by the Employment Act have helped economists learn about how the economy operates.

The 1960s saw the first active use of government policy to try to reduce overall unemployment. During the 1960 presidential election, John F. Kennedy narrowly defeated Richard Nixon in what had been the closest presidential race in U.S. history until the contest between George W. Bush and Al Gore in 2000. In part, Nixon's defeat was due to the slowdown in economic activity and rise in unemployment that the country experienced in 1959. During the six years from 1958 through 1963, the unemployment rate averaged almost 6 percent; ten years before it had been 2.8 percent. Kennedy's Council of Economic Advisors proposed a policy based on the ideas of John Maynard Keynes that was designed to stimulate the economy and bring the unemployment rate down to 4 percent, a level that at the time was believed to be consistent with "full employment." The policy called for a major tax cut. Those who opposed the cut argued that it would be fiscally irresponsible and lead to a deficit, with the government spending more than it received in taxes. They contended that inflation would rise and the cost of lower unemployment would be higher inflation. The government would need to decide how much inflation it was willing to tolerate to get unemployment down.

In what is perhaps the most famous macroeconomic policy experiment, the federal government did cut taxes in 1964. At the same time, federal government expenditures rose because of the Vietnam War and President Lyndon Johnson's War on Poverty programs. The unemployment rate did subsequently fall; in fact, it fell below 4 percent, reaching as low as 3.5 percent by 1969. Unfortunately, this fall in unemployment was accompanied by rising inflation; the general level of prices in the United States rose by only 1 percent in 1963, but by 1969 prices were rising at an annual rate of 6.2 percent. To some extent, policymakers at the time thought that higher inflation was simply the price they had to pay to maintain lower unemployment. They saw this as a trade-off: lower unemployment required accepting higher inflation, but inflation could always be reduced again, they believed, by letting average unemployment return to the levels of the late 1950s and early 1960s.

STAGFLATION

During the 1970s, policymakers discovered that the trade-off between unemployment and inflation they thought they were facing had somehow disappeared. Instead, the 1970s saw unemployment and inflation both rise. During the first half of the 1970s, unemployment averaged 5.4 percent, essentially the same level as before the Kennedy tax cut; yet as unemployment rose from the low levels of the late 1960s, inflation remained high. Chapter 13 will explain why the unemployment–inflation trade-off seemed to disappear in the 1970s. Policymakers found themselves confronting very different economic situations from those in the previous decade.

One new situation was caused by a disruption of oil supplies and a rise in oil prices. In the 1970s, the members of the Organization of Petroleum Exporting Countries (OPEC) were able to raise the world price of oil significantly. This action both contributed to the general increase in prices in oil-importing countries and changed the behavior of households and firms. Higher gas prices created incentives for consumers to economize on gas, and households started buying smaller, more fuel-efficient automobiles. In the United States, many of these cars were produced in other countries, particularly Japan, because U.S. automakers were slow to alter the products they made to respond to changes in consumer demand. Firms also needed to adjust their production techniques to conserve energy and adopt more energy-efficient equipment, as well as to produce the more energy-efficient goods that consumers now desired.

During the 1970s, unemployment averaged more than 6 percent, while inflation averaged more than 7 percent per year. This experience with high inflation *and* high unemployment was called **stagflation.** Numerous attempts to control inflation were made without success. In 1971, President Nixon imposed price and wage controls. These temporarily reduced inflation but failed to address the underlying causes, described in Chapter 13. As soon as the controls were lifted, inflation reappeared.

THE CONQUEST OF INFLATION

At the end of the 1970s, most industrial economies continued to suffer unacceptably high rates of inflation. The last big oil price increase of the decade occurred in 1979 and helped push inflation rates to new highs in many countries.

The turning point in the battle against inflation actually occurred in October 1979, when Paul Volker, President Jimmy Carter's newly appointed chairman of the Federal Reserve System, shifted economic policy. Under Volker, the Federal Reserve adopted policies designed to reduce inflation. Chapter 14 will describe how the Federal Reserve is able to affect the economy. As part of its policy changes, the Federal Reserve began to focus more on controlling the money supply. Interest rates rose to record highs, but Volker's policies succeeded in getting inflation down. Reducing inflation wasn't costless, however. By 1982, unemployment reached 10 percent, the highest level in the post–World War II era. President Ronald Reagan's ratings in the polls sank to low levels. Many Democrats thought Reagan was sure to be defeated when new elections were held in 1984.

But during 1984 the economy expanded. Chapter 6 will explain why increases in unemployment tend to be temporary, with the economy eventually returning to full employment. By the time of the presidential election, the unemployment rate had fallen to 7.2 percent, yet inflation remained relatively low. With the macroeconomy improving, Reagan coasted to a landslide reelection victory.

GOVERNMENT DEFICITS AND TRADE DEFICITS

The economy continued to expand during the rest of the 1980s, and inflation remained under control. New macroeconomic issues emerged, however, and the last half of the 1980s and much of the 1990s were dominated by concern over two deficits. One was the federal government's budget deficit. Tax cuts and increases in defense spending under President Reagan helped push the budget into deficit, as federal spending exceeded tax revenues. Little success was achieved in the 1980s in reducing this deficit, and the gap between what the federal government spent and what it collected in taxes reached a peak of $290 billion in 1992. When the government spends more than it receives in taxes, it must borrow, just as you would if you spent more than your income. The total amount the government owed rose from about $700 billion in 1980 to $3.7 trillion in 1997—that is, $3,700,000,000,000, or about $13,500 for every man, woman, and child in the United States. Ours was not the only country showing an imbalance between government spending and tax revenues. Other countries faced the difficult task of balancing spending desires with available tax revenues. Germany, France, Italy, Japan, and the United Kingdom all had deficits in the second half of the 1990s that were larger, relative to the size of their economies, than the deficit of the U.S. federal government. Each government had to make trade-offs, deciding which programs to scale back or which taxes to increase.

The second focus of attention in the 1980s and 1990s was the trade deficit, the difference between what the United States purchases from other countries (our imports) and what we sell to other countries (our exports). Some argued that the trade deficit was costing American workers their jobs and that we should "buy American." Others pointed out that trade provided access to new markets for American producers and more product choices for American consumers. They also argued that international capital markets allowed firms and the government to borrow from foreign lenders, increasing the availability of credit needed to build the new plants and equipment that contribute to future economic growth.

GETTING THE ECONOMY MOVING (AGAIN)

In the presidential election of 1992, Bill Clinton's campaign slogan, "It's the economy, stupid!" struck a responsive chord among voters. After almost eight years of economic growth, the U.S. economy had stalled during the summer of 1990. The overall level of production in the economy declined throughout the rest of 1990 and into 1991. With firms producing less, they needed fewer workers; the unemployment rate rose. This was enough to sink President George H. W. Bush's reelection bid. Strong economic growth in the second half of the 1990s, with low unemployment and low inflation, contributed significantly to President Clinton's reelection in 1996.

As the century ended, the United States was enjoying its strongest economic performance in decades. Unemployment had fallen to the lowest level since the 1970s, and inflation remained low. American workers were becoming more productive, perhaps owing to the computer and technological revolution that was changing the way the economy operates, and their productivity was improving prospects for long-term growth in living standards.

Rising unemployment played a role in Bill Clinton's defeat of George H. W. Bush in the 1992 presidential election.

The information technology revolution was also having an impact on the distribution of income. New technologies increased the demand for better-educated workers, which helped increase the incomes of college-educated workers. At the same time, many manufacturing jobs—jobs that had provided decent wages for workers with less education—moved overseas as competition forced firms to shift production to lower-cost locations. The 1990s saw a widening of the income gap between college-educated workers and those with only a high school diploma.

The last half of the 1990s also saw a tremendous swing in the government's budget outlook. In 1998, the federal government ran its first surplus since 1969, and by 2000, the federal government surplus had grown to more than $200 billion. At the time, the outlook was for years of future surpluses. The turnaround in the budget was due to a combination of factors. Congress had agreed to some tax increases and to restraints on the growth of spending. The booming economy of the 1990s led to higher incomes, which in turn led wage earners to pay more in taxes. Likewise, the stock market boom boosted tax revenues from capital gains.

Meanwhile, many other major economies were experiencing quite different macroeconomic conditions. Asia had been wracked by financial crises, rising unemployment, and stagnating growth, while many European countries found that their unemployment rates remained stubbornly high through most of the 1990s.

As the year 2000 ended, the boom times of the 1990s in the United States also came to a close. High-tech firms were scaling back operations or even going out of business. When President George W. Bush took office in 2001, the macroeconomy was already slowing and unemployment, which was only 4.2 percent at the end of 2000, rose throughout 2001, reaching 5.8 percent by December. A recession officially began in March 2001. Bush had promised tax cuts as he campaigned during 2000, and once in office he pushed them through Congress. At the time, he argued that lower taxes would encourage households to spend more, helping to boost the economy.

NEW CHALLENGES

The first years of the twenty-first century saw heated debates over unemployment, the fiscal deficit, and the risks of deflation. The economic slump that began in early 2001 was over by late 2001, yet the subsequent economic recovery seemed unable to produce lasting employment gains. The unemployment rate remained stubbornly high, beginning to fall only at the end of 2003. The growth in overall economic output while employment remained weak raised concerns about a "jobless recovery" in which firms take advantage of new production techniques and of longer hours put in by employees to gain increases in production without adding new workers.

The tax cuts introduced by President Bush, the rise in expenditures associated with the war on terrorism, and the fall in tax revenues caused by the sluggish economy all served to push the federal budget back into deficit. The federal deficit for 2004 was $412 billion. Many state and local governments also found their budget situation worsening, forcing major reductions in expenditures. Just as in the early 1990s, large budget deficits now loom for the foreseeable future.

A new concern surfaced during 2003 as **deflation**—a situation in which overall prices actually fall—seemed possible. The United States had not experienced significant periods of deflation since the Great Depression of the 1930s, and many were concerned that falling prices would again be associated with depressed economic conditions. Many pointed to the experience of Japan, where deflation had accompanied a decade-long recession during the 1990s. The Federal Reserve under Alan Greenspan had shifted policy in early 2001 to help stimulate economic growth by lowering interest rates, but by 2003, interest rates were almost down to zero, and some feared that the Federal Reserve would be unable to provide further stimulus.

Concerns lessened during 2004 as the economy continued to grow, unemployment edged downward, and fears of deflation disappeared. With the economy expanding, Federal Reserve policymakers gradually began to raise interest rates as they focused on preventing an upswing in inflation.

As this book goes to press in 2005, two major macroeconomic issues are dominating the news. President Bush has made Social Security reform a major part of his domestic agenda. Both Democrats and Republicans agree that some changes must be made to the Social Security program to ensure its future financial health, but the two parties differ significantly in the ways they want to change the program. Some of the issues at the heart of this debate will be discussed in Chapter 21. The second major issue is the federal government's budget deficit. Tax cuts and spending increases since 2000 have led to massive deficits. The impact of government deficits on the economy will be studied in Chapter 7.

"Deflation" was a concern that occupied policymakers in the first years of the twenty-first century. The U.S. economy had not experienced severe deflation since the Great Depression of the 1930s.

THE THREE KEY GOALS OF MACROECONOMIC PERFORMANCE

For more than half a century, the American government has been formally committed to achieving a number of important macroeconomic goals. As the Employment Act of 1946 states, the "Congress hereby declares that it is the continuing policy and responsibility of the Federal Government . . . to promote maximum employment, production, and purchasing power." These goals were further defined in the Full Employment and Balanced Growth Act of 1978, better known as the Humphrey-Hawkins Act, after the bill's chief authors, Senator Hubert Humphrey (D-Minn.) and Representative Augustus Hawkins (D-Calif.). The Humphrey-Hawkins Act formally makes it the policy of the federal government to "promote full employment and production, increased real income, balanced growth, a balanced Federal budget, adequate productivity growth, proper attention to national priorities, achievement of an improved trade balance through increased exports and improvement in the international competitiveness of agriculture, business, and industry, and reasonable price stability."

Three of these aims have come to represent the key goals of macroeconomic policies—full employment, economic growth, and price stability. Full employment ensures that all those willing and able to work can find jobs; economic growth ensures that material standards of living will rise; and a low and stable rate of inflation aids individuals in planning for the future. Macroeconomists are constantly studying the causes of slow growth, unemployment, and inflation. Understanding the causes of these problems is the first step toward designing policies to improve macroeconomic performance.

THREE GOALS OF MACROECONOMIC POLICY

Rapid growth
Full employment
Low inflation

What Is Economics?

Headlines can illustrate many of the important issues with which economics deals, but now a definition of our subject is in order. *Economics* studies how individuals, firms, government, and other organizations within our society make *choices,* and how these choices determine society's use of its resources. Why did consumers choose to buy small, energy-efficient cars in the 1970s and large sports utility vehicles in the 1990s? What determines how many individuals work in health care industries and how many work in the computer industry? Why did the income gap between rich and poor rise in the 1980s? To understand how choices are made and how these choices affect the use of society's resources, we must examine five concepts that play an important role: trade-offs, incentives, exchange, information, and distribution:

1. Choice involves **trade-offs**—deciding to spend more on one thing leaves less to spend on something else; devoting more time to studying economics leaves less time to study physics.
2. In making choices, individuals respond to **incentives.** If the price of Zen MP3 players falls relative to the price of iPods, there is a greater incentive to buy a Zen. If the salaries of engineers rise relative to the salaries of people with MBAs, there is an increased incentive to choose to study for an engineering degree rather than a business degree.
3. When we **exchange** with others, our range of choices becomes larger.
4. Making intelligent choices requires that we have, and utilize, **information.**
5. Finally, the choices we make—about how much education to get, what occupation to enter, and what goods and services to buy—determine the **distribution** of wealth and income in our society.

These five concepts define the core ideas that are critical to understanding economics. They also guide how economists think about issues and problems. Learning to "think like an economist" means learning how to discover the trade-offs and incentives faced, the implications of exchange, the role of information, and the consequences for distribution. These key concepts are emphasized throughout the text in "Thinking Like an Economist" boxes.

TRADE-OFFS

Each of us is constantly making choices—students decide to study at the library rather than in the dorm, to have pizza rather than sushi, to go to college rather than work full-time. Societies, too, make choices—to preserve open spaces rather than provide more housing, to produce computers and import televisions rather than produce televisions and import computers, to cut taxes rather than increase government expenditures. In some cases, individuals or governments explicitly make these choices. You decided to study economics rather than some other subject. The government decides each year whether to cut taxes or to increase spending. In other cases, however, the choices were the result of the uncoordinated actions of millions of individuals. Neither the government nor any one individual decided that the United States would import cars from Japan and export wheat to India. But in each case, choice involves trade-offs—to get more of one thing involves having less of something else. We are forced to make trade-offs because of **scarcity.**

Scarcity figures prominently in economics; choices matter because resources are scarce. For most of us, our limited income forces us to make choices. We cannot afford everything we might want. Spending more on rent leaves less available for clothes and entertainment. Getting a sunroof on a new car may mean forgoing leather seats to stay within a fixed budget. Limited income is not the only reason we are forced to make trade-offs. Time is also a scarce resource, and even the wealthiest individual must decide what expensive toy to play with each day. When we take time into account, we realize scarcity is a fact of life for everyone.

One of the most important points on which economists agree concerns the critical role of scarcity. We can summarize this point as follows: *There is no free lunch. Having more of one thing requires giving up something else. Scarcity means that* trade-offs *are a basic fact of life.*

INCENTIVES

It is one thing to say we all face trade-offs in the choices we make. It is quite another to understand how individuals and firms make choices and how those choices might change as economic circumstances change. If new technologies are developed, will firms decide to increase or decrease the amount of labor they employ? If the price of gasoline rises, will individuals decide to buy different types of automobiles?

When faced with a choice, people evaluate the pros and cons of the different options. In deciding what to eat for dinner tonight, you and your roommates might weigh the advantages and disadvantages of having a frozen pizza again over going out for sushi. Similarly, a firm evaluates the pros and cons of its alternatives in terms of the effects different choices will have on its profits. For example, a retail chain deciding on the location for a new store must weigh the relative advantages of different locations. One location might have more foot traffic but also higher rent. Another location might be less desirable but have lower rent.

Thinking Like an Economist

INCENTIVES AND THE PRICE OF AOL

Today, most online services such as AOL charge their customers a fixed monthly fee for Internet access. In the earlier days of the Internet, the access charge was commonly based on how many minutes the member was connected to the Internet. In 1997, AOL announced that it would change its pricing policy and move to a flat monthly fee with unlimited minutes of connect time. AOL's servers were quickly overwhelmed and members found it almost impossible to log on. Why? Because charges were no longer based on the number of minutes a member was logged on, many customers never logged off. Once connected, they simply left AOL running, tying up its modem capacity. When members had to pay on a per-minute basis, they had an incentive to log off when the service was not being used. The flat fee left no incentive to economize on connect time. Thinking about incentives would have shown AOL that it needed to increase its modem capacity greatly *before* announcing the new pricing plan.

When decision makers systematically weigh the pros and cons of their alternatives, we can predict how they will respond to changing economic conditions. Higher gas prices raise the cost of driving, but the cost of driving a fuel-efficient car rises less than the cost of driving a sports utility vehicle. Therefore, households weighing a car purchase have a greater incentive to choose the fuel-efficient car. If a firm starts selling more of its goods through the Internet, it will rely less on foot traffic into its retail store. This shift reduces its incentive to pay a high rent for a good location.

Economists analyze choices by focusing on incentives. In an economic context, incentives are benefits (including reduced costs) that motivate a decision maker in favor of a particular choice. Many things can affect incentives, but among the most important are *prices*. If the price of gasoline rises, people have a greater incentive to drive less. If the price of MP3 players falls, people have a greater incentive to buy one. When the price of a good rises, firms are induced to produce more of that good, in order to increase their profits. If a resource used in production, such as labor or equipment, becomes more expensive, firms have an incentive to find new methods of production that economize on that resource. Incentives also are affected by the return people expect to earn from different activities. If the income of college graduates rises relative to that of people with only a high school diploma, people have a greater incentive to attend college.

When economists study the behavior of people or firms, they look at the incentives being faced. Sometimes these incentives are straightforward. Increasing the number of courses required to major in biology reduces the incentive to pick that major. In other circumstances, they may not be so obvious. For example, building safer cars may create incentives to drive faster. Identifying the incentives, and disincentives, to take different actions is one of the first things economists do when they want to understand the choices individuals or firms make.

Decision makers respond to incentives; for understanding choices, incentives matter.

EXCHANGE

Somehow, decisions that are made—by individuals, households, firms, and the government as they face trade-offs and respond to incentives—together determine how the economy's limited resources, including its land, labor, machines, oil, and other natural resources, are used. The key to understanding how this happens lies in the role of *voluntary* exchange in *markets*.

Long before the rise of modern industrial societies, the benefits of exchange were well understood. Coastal societies with access to fishing resources, for example, would trade some of their fish to inland societies in return for meat and furs. The coastal group sought meat and furs that were worth more to them than the fish they gave up; the inland group likewise exchanged meat and furs for fish. Both groups benefited from voluntary exchange.

In modern societies, millions of exchanges take place. Few individuals produce any of the goods and services they themselves want to consume. Instead, teachers, police officers, lawyers, and construction workers sell their labor services to a school district, a city, a client, or a home builder and then exchange the income they earn for all the various goods and services produced by others that they wish to consume. An important insight in economics is the recognition that *both* parties in a voluntary exchange gain. Whether it is voluntary exchange between two individuals, between an individual and a firm, or between residents of two different countries, exchange can improve the well-being of both parties.

Economists describe any situation in which exchange takes place as a *market*. For thousands of years, societies have established physical locations such as village markets or periodic trading fairs where people have brought their products, haggled over the terms of exchange, and reaped the benefits of trade. The economic concept of markets covers any situation in which exchange takes place, though this exchange may not necessarily resemble a traditional village market or a modern stock exchange. In department stores and shopping malls, customers rarely haggle over the price. When manufacturers purchase the materials they need for production, they give in exchange money, not other goods. Most goods, from cameras to

Internet Connection
AUCTION SITES

An auction is one form of market that used to require potential buyers to be physically present in a single location. Now, auctions are held over the Internet and can involve participants from around the world. Some sites, such as eBay (www.ebay.com), offer just about everything for sale. Other sites specialize. For instance, Heritage Coins (www.heritagecoins.

com) provides an auction site for rare coins. Even the U.S. government has gotten into the act. The U.S. Treasury does not actually auction items online, but it uses the Web to publicize the locations at which confiscated property will be auctioned (www.treas.gov/auctions/customs).

Today's consumers shop at both traditional markets and online markets such as eBay.com.

clothes, are not sold directly from producers to consumers. Instead they are sold from producers to distributors, from distributors to retailers, and from retailers to consumers. All of these transactions are embraced by the concept of markets and a **market economy.**

In a market economy like that of the United States, most exchanges take place through markets, and these exchanges are guided by the prices of the goods and services involved. The goods and services that are scarcer, or require more resources for their production, come at a higher price. Automobiles are more expensive than paper cups; lawyers charge more than janitors. As a result, markets enable consumers and firms to make choices that reflect scarcity, and therefore lead to efficient uses of resources.

Market economies thus rely primarily on market exchanges to resolve the most basic economic questions: What and how much is produced? How is it produced? For whom is it produced? And who makes the economic decisions? Individuals and firms make the decisions. Individuals make decisions that reflect their own desires as they respond to the incentives they face. Firms make decisions that maximize their profits, and to do so they strive to produce the goods that consumers want at the lowest possible cost. This process determines what is produced, how it is produced, and for whom it is produced. As firms compete in the quest for profits, consumers benefit, both from the kinds of goods available and from the prices at which they are supplied. On the whole, markets ensure that society's resources are used efficiently.

In some areas, however, markets lead to outcomes that society may find inadequate. There may be too much pollution, too much inequality, and too little concern about education, health, and safety. When the market is not perceived to be working well, people often turn to government. An economy such as in the United States is often called a *mixed economy*—one that relies primarily but not exclusively on the free interaction of producers and consumers to determine what is produced, how, and for whom. In some areas, the government makes the decisions, in others it imposes regulations that affect the incentives confronting firms and households, and in many areas, both the *private sector* (households and businesses) and the *public sector* (local, state, and federal governments) are involved (education is a good example).

Governments play a critical role in all market economies. For example, governments provide the legal structure within which private firms and individuals operate. No one would open a store if others could simply steal things off the shelf with impunity; the store owner needs to know there is a legal system that she can use to prosecute theft. No bank would lend money to a family to buy a home if it could not legally require the family to repay the loan. Governments also regulate businesses in many ways, ensuring, for example, that firms do not discriminate by race or sex, do not mislead consumers, and are careful about the safety of their workers. In some industries, such as education and mail service, the government is a major supplier of services. In other industries, such as the defense industry, government is the major purchaser.

The government also supplies goods and services that the private sector does not, such as the national defense, roads, and currency. Government programs provide for the elderly through Social Security (which pays income to retired individuals) and Medicare (which funds the medical needs of the aged). The government helps those who have suffered economic dislocation, through unemployment insurance for those temporarily unemployed and disability insurance for those who are no longer able to work. The government also provides a safety net of support for the poor, particularly children, through various welfare programs.

One can easily imagine the government controlling the economy more directly. In countries where decision making is centralized and concentrated in the government, government bureaucrats might decide what and how much a factory should produce and set the wages that should be paid. At least until recently, governments in countries such as the former Soviet Union and China attempted to control practically all major decisions regarding resource allocation. Even in Europe, not long ago many governments ran oil companies, coal mines, and the telephone system. Increasingly, however, governments have sold these enterprises to the private sector, a process called *privatization*.

Market economies in which individuals and firms make the decisions about what to produce and how much to pay have proven adept at developing new technologies and products. It is hard to imagine government bureaucrats developing MP3 players or iMacs in neon colors. Markets also generally ensure that resources are used efficiently.

Exchange in markets is a key to understanding how resources are allocated, what is produced, and who earns what.

INFORMATION

Making informed choices requires information. After all, it is hard to weigh the costs and benefits of alternatives if you do not know what they are! A firm that is contemplating the purchase of a new software system needs to know not only the costs of the various alternatives but also the capabilities and limitations of each. Information is, in many ways, like other goods and services. Firms and individuals are willing to purchase information, and specialized institutions develop to sell it. In many areas, separate organizations are designed solely to provide information to consumers. *Consumer Reports* is a prime example. The Internet also serves as a major source of independent information for buyers. But there are some fundamental ways in which information differs from other goods. A car seller will let you test-drive a vehicle, but a seller of information cannot let you see the information before you buy. Once you have seen the information, you have no incentive to pay for it. Another way information differs from other goods is that unlike a can of soda or a bagel, information can be freely shared. When I tell you something, it does not subtract from what I know (though it may subtract from the profits I might earn from that information).

In some key areas of the economy, the role of information is so critical that it affects the nature of the market. In the used-car market, buyers and sellers negotiating over the price of a vehicle may have quite different information about its quality. The seller may have better information about the quality of the car but also has an incentive to misrepresent its condition since better-quality cars command higher prices. As a result, the buyer will be reluctant to trust claims that the car is in perfect shape.

When consumers lack adequate information to make informed choices, governments frequently intervene to require that firms provide information. In the United States, we are all familiar with the mandatory nutritional information placed on food products. The Securities and Exchange Commission (SEC) that oversees American stock markets compels firms to meet certain reporting requirements before their stock can be listed on exchanges such as the New York Stock Exchange. Such reporting helps ensure that private investors have reliable information on which to base their investment decisions. Often, however, these regulations do not work adequately, as the Enron scandal in 2001 clearly illustrates. The oil trading company Enron had cooked its books to overstate its profitability in its mandated reports. One outcome of Enron's subsequent financial collapse was the introduction of new regulations designed to improve the reliability of the information that companies must provide to the public.

Governments also regulate the safety of products. In the United States, the Food and Drug Administration (FDA) must approve new pharmaceuticals before they can be sold. The need for such oversight was driven home in 2005 when the drug manufacturer Merck had to pull its pain relief drug Vioxx off the market after studies suggested that it increased the risk of heart attacks and strokes. Critics of the FDA argued that the agency is not adequately monitoring the safety of drugs once they are approved, and proposals have been made to establish a new government review board whose job it will be to decide when new information warrants removing a drug from the market.

Even in the absence of regulation, firms have incentives to signal to buyers that their products are of high quality. One way they do this is to offer guarantees that a producer of low-quality goods could not afford to offer. Individuals are often willing to pay to reduce the risk that arises when information is imperfect. Buying goods over the Internet can be risky if you do not know the seller, so companies like eBay are able to make a profit by offering both information about sellers and insurance to the buyer that protects the buyer in case the seller has misrepresented the item for sale or fails to deliver it.

Imperfect information also can interfere with incentives. Employers want to create incentives for employees to work hard. One way to do this is to base pay on a measure of how productive each worker is. Often, however, it is difficult to measure a worker's productivity. Under such conditions, it is difficult to link pay to performance. For example, a major debate in the United States concerns tying teacher salaries to performance. Because it is hard to measure teaching performance, the pay of most teachers is based primarily on how long they have been teaching.

Information, or its absence, plays a key role in determining the shape of markets and the ability of private markets to ensure that the economy's scarce resources are used efficiently.

DISTRIBUTION

The market economy determines not only what goods are produced and how they are produced but also for whom they are produced. Many people find unacceptable the way the market distributes goods among households. "While recognizing the efficacy of capitalism to produce wealth, there remains considerable unease among some segments about the way markets distribute that wealth and about the effects of raw competition on society."[3] Like bidders at an auction, what market participants are willing and able to pay depends on their income. Incomes differ markedly across occupations. Some groups of individuals—including those without skills that are valued by the market—may receive such a low income that they cannot feed and educate their children without outside assistance. Government provides the assistance by taking steps to increase income equality.

Steps that soften the distributional impact of markets may blunt economic incentives. While welfare payments provide an important safety net for the poor, the taxation required to finance them may discourage people from working and saving. If the government takes one out of every two or three dollars that an individual earns, that individual may not be inclined to work as much. And if the government takes one out of every two or three dollars a person earns from interest on savings, the person may decide to spend more and save less. Thus, efforts by the government to redistribute income may come at the cost of reduced economic efficiency.

The primary reliance on private decision making in the United States reflects economists' beliefs that this reliance is appropriate and necessary for economic efficiency. But economists also believe that certain interventions by government are desirable. Like the appropriate balance between public and private sectors, the appropriate balance between concerns about equality (often referred to as *equity concerns*) and efficiency is a central issue of modern economies. As elsewhere, trade-offs must be made.

Wrap-Up

FIVE CORE IDEAS

1. *Trade-offs:* resources are scarce, so trade-offs are a basic fact of life.
2. *Incentives:* in making choices, decision makers respond to incentives.
3. *Exchange:* people benefit from voluntary exchange, and in market economies, market exchanges lead to the efficient use of resources.
4. *Information:* the structure that markets take and how well they can function depend critically on the information available to decision makers.
5. *Distribution:* markets determine how the goods and services produced by the economy are allocated to members of society.

The Three Major Markets

The market economy revolves around exchange between individuals (or households) who buy goods and services from firms and those firms, which take *inputs,* the various materials of production, and produce *outputs,* the goods and services that they

[3]Alan Greenspan, speech at the Federal Reserve Bank of Kansas City Jackson Hole Conference, August 25, 2000.

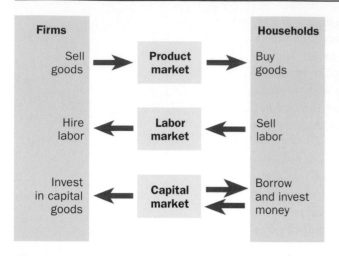

Figure 1.3

THE THREE MARKETS

To economists, people wear different hats. They are usually consumers in the product market, workers in the labor market, and borrowers or lenders in the capital market.

sell. In thinking about a market economy, economists focus their attention on three broad categories of markets in which individuals and firms interact. The markets in which firms sell their outputs to households are referred to collectively as the **product market.** Many firms also sell goods to other firms; the output of the first firm becomes the input of the second. These transactions too are said to occur in the product market.

On the input side, firms need (besides the materials they buy in the product market) some combination of labor and machinery to produce their output. They purchase the services of workers in the **labor market.** They raise funds to buy inputs in the **capital market.** Traditionally, economists also have highlighted the importance of a third input, land, but in modern industrial economies land is of a secondary importance. For most purposes, it suffices to focus attention on the three major markets—product, labor, and capital—and this text will follow that pattern.

As Figure 1.3 shows, individuals participate in all three markets. When individuals buy goods and services, they act as *consumers* in the product market. When people act as *workers,* economists say they "sell their labor services" in the labor market. When people buy shares of stock in a firm, deposit money in a savings account, or lend money to a business, they are participating in the capital market as *investors.*

KEEPING TRACK OF TRICKY TERMS

Terms in economics often are similar to terms in ordinary usage, but they can have special meanings. The terms *markets* and *capital* illustrate this problem.

Though the term *market* is used to conjure up an image of a busy *marketplace,* there is no formal marketplace for most goods and services. There are buyers and sellers, and economists analyze the outcomes *as if* there were a single marketplace in which all transactions occur. For example, economists analyze the "market for books," even though the buyers and sellers in the market for books interact in thousands of individual bookstores and online selling locations.

Moreover, economists often talk about the "market for labor" as if all workers were identical. But workers differ in countless ways. In some cases, these differences are important. We might then talk about the "market for skilled workers" or the "market for computer engineers." In other cases—such as when we are talking about the overall state of the economy and focusing on the overall unemployment rate (the proportion of workers who are looking for jobs but cannot find them)—these differences can be ignored.

When newspapers refer to the *capital market,* they mean the bond traders and stockbrokers and the companies they work for on Wall Street and in other financial districts. When economists use the term *capital market,* they have in mind a broader concept that includes all the institutions concerned with raising funds (and, as we will see later, sharing and insuring risk), including banks and insurance companies.

The term *capital* is used in still another way—to refer to the machines and buildings used in production. To distinguish that particular usage, in this book we refer to machines and buildings as **capital goods.** The term *capital markets* thus refers to the markets in which funds are raised, borrowed, and lent. *Capital goods markets* refers to the markets in which capital goods are bought and sold.

THE THREE MAJOR MARKETS

1. *The product market:* the market in which firms sell the goods they produce.
2. *The labor market:* the market in which households sell labor services and firms buy labor services.
3. *The capital market:* the market in which funds are borrowed and lent.

Microeconomics and Macroeconomics: The Two Branches of Economics

Economists have developed two different ways to look at the economy. The detailed study of the decisions of firms and households, and of prices and production in specific industries, is called **microeconomics.** Microeconomics (*micro* is derived from the Greek word meaning "small") focuses on the behavior of the units—the firms, households, and individuals—that make up the economy. It is concerned with how the individual units make decisions and what affects those decisions.

By contrast, **macroeconomics** (*macro* is derived from the Greek word meaning "large") looks at the behavior of the economy as a whole, in particular the behavior of such aggregate measures as the overall rates of unemployment, inflation, and economic growth and the balance of trade. The aggregate numbers do not tell us what any one firm or household is doing. They tell us what is happening in total, or on average. In a dynamic economy, there are always some industries expanding and others contracting. For instance, the economic expansion of the late 1990s saw rapid growth in Internet-related industries, while oil firms in Texas contracted. But there are times when overall growth in an economy slows, and times when the level of economic activity actually declines, not just in an isolated industry but seemingly across all or almost all industries.

In macroeconomics, we also look at the behavior of the general level of prices, interest rates, and exchange rates. Why do prices of almost all goods and services seem to rise at rapid rates during some periods, while at other times they remain stable? Why do interest rates fluctuate? And what determines the value of the dollar relative to other currencies?

In approaching these questions, it is important to remember that the behavior of the economy as a whole is dependent on the decisions made by millions of households and firms in the economy, as well as the decisions made by the government. Micro and macro perspectives are simply two ways of looking at the same thing. Microeconomics is the bottom-up view of the economy; macroeconomics is the top-down view.

THE BRANCHES OF ECONOMICS

Microeconomics: focuses on the decisions of households and firms and the detailed study of prices and production in specific industries.

Macroeconomics: focuses on the behavior of the economy as a whole and the behavior of aggregate variables such as overall employment, output, economic growth, the price level, and inflation.

The Science of Economics

Economics is a *social science.* It studies the social problem of choice from a scientific viewpoint, which means that it is built on a systematic exploration of the problem of choice. This systematic exploration involves both formulating theories and examining data.

A **theory** consists of a set of assumptions (or hypotheses) and conclusions derived from those assumptions. Theories are logical exercises: *if* the assumptions are correct, *then* the results follow. If all college graduates have a better chance of getting jobs and Ellen is a college graduate, then Ellen has a better chance of getting a job than a nongraduate. Economists make predictions with their theories. They might use their theory to predict what would happen if a tax is increased or if imports of foreign cars are limited. The predictions of a theory are of the form "If a tax is increased and if the market is competitive, then output will decrease and prices will increase."

In developing their theories, economists use *models.* To understand how models are used in economics, consider a modern car manufacturer trying to design a new automobile. It is extremely expensive to construct a new car. Rather than creating a separate, fully developed car for every conception of what engineers or designers would like the new car to be, the company uses models. The designers might use a plastic model to study the general shape of the vehicle and to assess reactions to the car's aesthetics. The engineers might use a computer model to study air resistance and then calculate fuel consumption.

Just as engineers construct different models to study particular features of a car, economists construct different models of the economy—in words or equations—to depict particular features of the economy. An economic model might describe a general relationship ("When incomes rise, the number of cars purchased increases"), describe a quantitative relationship ("When incomes rise by 10 percent, the number of cars purchased rises, on average, by 12 percent"), or make a general prediction ("An increase in the tax on gasoline will decrease the demand for cars").

DISCOVERING AND INTERPRETING RELATIONSHIPS

A *variable* is any item that can be measured and that changes. Prices, wages, interest rates, and quantities bought and sold are variables. What interests economists is the connection between variables. When economists see what appears to be a systematic relationship among variables, they ask, Could it have arisen by chance or is there indeed a relationship? This is the question of **correlation.**

Economists use statistical tests to measure and test correlations. Consider the problem of deciding whether a coin is biased. If you flip the coin 10 times and get 6 heads and 4 tails, is the coin a fair one? Or is it weighted toward heads? Statistical tests will show that the result of 6 heads and 4 tails easily could have happened by chance, so the evidence does not prove that the coin is weighted. It also does not prove that the coin is *not* weighted. The evidence is not strong enough for either conclusion. But if you flip the coin 100 times and get 80 heads, statistical tests will tell you that the possibility of this happening by blind chance with a fair coin is extremely small. The evidence supports the assertion that the coin is weighted.

A similar logic can be used on correlations among economic variables. People with more education tend to earn higher wages. Is the connection merely chance? Statistical tests support the existence of a systematic relationship between education and wages.

CAUSATION AND CORRELATION

Economists want to accomplish more than just asserting that different variables are indeed correlated. They would like to conclude that changes in one variable *cause* the changes in another variable. This distinction between correlation and **causation** is important. If one variable "causes" the other, then changing the first variable necessarily will change the other. If the relationship is just a correlation, this may not be true.

During the 1970s, imports of Japanese cars into the United States increased while sales of U.S.-produced cars decreased. The two variables were negatively correlated. But did increased Japanese car sales *cause* the decrease in sales of American-made cars? Perhaps both were responding to a common factor that was the true cause of the rise in Japanese car sales as well as the decline in sales of American cars. In fact, that is just what was happening—the huge increase in oil prices after 1973 caused consumers to shift their purchases away from gas-guzzling American cars and toward more fuel-efficient Japanese cars.

Why Economists Disagree

Economists are frequently called on to make judgments on matters of public policy. Should the government cut taxes? How should Social Security be reformed? Should Internet commerce be taxed? In these public policy discussions, economists often disagree. These disagreements arise for two reasons. First, economists can differ in their views on the consequences of a proposed policy. Second, they can differ in how they evaluate those consequences.

When economists describe the economy and construct models that predict how the economy will be affected by different policies, they are engaged in what is called **positive economics.** When they evaluate alternative policies, weighing the various benefits and costs, they are engaged in **normative economics.**

Consider the positive and normative aspects of a proposal to restrict imports of textiles produced in developing countries. Positive economics would describe the consequences: the increased prices American consumers would have to pay for clothes, the increased sales of American textiles, the increased employment and profits of U.S. textile manufacturers, and the reduced employment among textile workers in developing countries. Economists might disagree over the consequences of restricting imports because they disagree over the magnitudes of the effects, perhaps agreeing that prices to consumers would rise but disagreeing over the size of that rise.

In the end, though, the policy question is, *Should there be restraints on textile imports?* This is a normative question. Normative economics would weigh these various effects—the losses to consumers, the gains to U.S. textile workers, the increased profits—to reach an overall judgment. Normative economics develops frameworks within which these complicated judgments can be systematically made. Good normative economics also tries to make explicit precisely which values or objectives it is incorporating. It tries to couch its statements in the form "If these are your values, then this is the best policy."

Economists, like members of any other profession, often have different values. Two economists might agree that a particular tax change would increase saving but would benefit the wealthy more than the poor. However, they might reach different conclusions about the desirability of that tax change. One might oppose it because it increases income inequality; the other might support it because it promotes saving. They differ in the values they place on the effects of the policy change, so they reach different conclusions even when they agree on the positive analysis of the proposed policy.

While economists may seem often to differ greatly among themselves, in fact they agree more than they disagree. When they do disagree, economists try to be clear about the source of their disagreement: (1) to what extent does it arise out of differences in models, (2) to what extent does it arise out of differences in estimates of quantitative relationships, and (3) to what extent does it arise out of differences in values? Clarifying the source of and reasons for disagreement can be a very productive way of learning more about an issue.

A Look Ahead

Our first task, taken up in the next three chapters, is to understand how economists measure the aggregate economy's performance. How do we measure the aggregate output of the entire economy? How do we measure unemployment? How do we measure the general level of prices and inflation?

In Parts Two to Five, we will learn about the factors that account for growth, inflation, and economic fluctuations. We also will learn how government policies affect the economy, and how these policies can be used to achieve macroeconomic goals. What happens to the aggregate economy depends not only on government policies but also on the individual decisions made by thousands of firms and millions of households. Microeconomics helps economists understand how firms and households make choices—what trade-offs they face, how they respond to incentives, the effects of information on their choices, and the role markets and exchange play in determining what is produced and how income is distributed. Macroeconomics helps economists understand how the choices of firms and households, together with government policies, affect the aggregate economy.

Review and Practice

SUMMARY

1. The three major goals of macroeconomic policy are high and sustainable economic growth, full employment, and low inflation.
2. Economics is the study of how individuals, firms, and governments within our society make choices. Choices and therefore trade-offs are unavoidable, because desired goods, services, and resources are inevitably scarce.
3. Economists study how individuals, firms, and governments within our society make choices by focusing on incentives. People respond to changes in incentives by altering the decisions they make.
4. Exchange occurs in markets. Voluntary exchange can benefit both parties.
5. Making choices requires information. Limited or imperfect information can interfere with incentives and affect the ability of the private market to ensure an efficient use of society's scarce resources.
6. The incomes people receive are determined by the market economy. Concerns over the equitable distribution of wealth and income in the economy lead to government programs that increase income equality.
7. The United States has a mixed economy, one in which there is a mix of public and private decision making. The economy relies primarily on the private interaction of individuals and firms to determine how resources are allocated, but government plays a large role as well. A central question for any mixed economy is the balance between the private and public sectors.
8. The term *market* is used to describe any situation where exchange takes place. In the U.S. market economy, individuals, firms, and government interact in product markets, labor markets, and capital markets.
9. The two major branches of economics are microeconomics and macroeconomics. Microeconomics focuses on the behavior of the firms, households, and individuals that make up the economy. Macroeconomics focuses on the behavior of the economy as a whole.
10. A correlation exists when two variables tend to change together in a predictable way. However, the simple existence of a correlation does not prove that one factor causes the other to change. Additional outside factors may be influencing both.
11. Positive economics is the study of how the economy works. Disagreements in positive economics center on the appropriate model of the economy or market and the quantitative magnitudes characterizing the models.
12. Normative economics deals with the desirability of various actions. Disagreements in normative economics center on differences in the values placed on the various costs and benefits of different actions.

KEY TERMS

Great Depression
stagflation
deflation
trade-offs
incentives
exchange
information
distribution
scarcity
market economy
product market
labor market
capital market
capital goods
microeconomics
macroeconomics
theory
correlation
causation
positive economics
normative economics

REVIEW QUESTIONS

1. What trade-off between inflation and unemployment did President Kennedy's Council of Economic Advisors believe they faced? What happened to inflation and unemployment after the 1964 tax cut?
2. What is stagflation? When has the United States experienced stagflation?

3. When has the United States experienced the combination of low inflation *and* low unemployment?

4. What are the key goals of macroeconomic policy?

5. Why are trade-offs unavoidable? Why are incentives important in understanding choices?

6. After a voluntary exchange, why are both parties better off?

7. As a commodity, how does information differ from standard goods? How do information imperfections affect markets?

8. Why might there be a trade-off between equity and efficiency?

9. Name the three main economic markets, and describe how an individual might participate in each one as a buyer or a seller.

10. Give two examples of economic issues that are primarily microeconomic and two examples that are primarily macroeconomic. What is the general difference between microeconomics and macroeconomics?

PROBLEMS

1. Look at the front pages of a newspaper this week. What macroeconomic issues are in the news?

2. What is the current unemployment rate in the United States? What is the current rate of inflation? (Go to the Web site of the Bureau of Labor Statistics at www.bls.gov to find this information.)

3. Which two deficits were of concern in the 1980s and 1990s? What happened to these two deficits in the 1990s? What has happened to them during the past five years?

4. How does each of the following affect the incentive to go to college?
   (a) An increase in tuition costs
   (b) A fall in the interest rate on student loans
   (c) A rise in wages for unskilled jobs
   (d) An increase in incomes of college graduates

5. Characterize the following events as microeconomic, macroeconomic, or both.
   (a) Unemployment increases this month.
   (b) A drug company invents and begins to market a new medicine.
   (c) A bank lends money to a large company but turns down a small business.
   (d) Interest rates decline for all borrowers.
   (e) A union negotiates for higher pay and better health insurance.
   (f) The price of oil increases.

6. Characterize the following events as part of the labor market, the capital market, or the product market.
   (a) An investor tries to decide which company to invest in.
   (b) With practice, the workers on an assembly line become more efficient.
   (c) The opening up of economies in eastern Europe offers new markets for American products.
   (d) A big company that is losing money decides to offer its workers special incentives to retire early, hoping to reduce its costs.
   (e) A consumer roams around a shopping mall looking for birthday gifts.
   (f) The federal government uses a surplus to pay off some of its debt.

7. The back of a bag of cat litter claims, "Cats that use cat litter live three years longer than cats that don't." Do you think that cat litter actually causes an increased life expectancy for cats, or can you think of some other factors to explain this correlation? What evidence might you collect to test your explanation?

8. Life expectancy in Sweden is almost eighty years; life expectancy in India is close to sixty years. Does this prove that if an Indian moved to Sweden, he would live longer? That is, does this prove that living in Sweden causes an increase in life expectancy, or can you think of some other factors to explain these facts? What evidence might you collect to test your explanation?

9. During 2004, some economists argued that the Federal Reserve should undertake policies to slow the economic expansion in the United States in order to ensure low inflation. Other economists opposed such policies, arguing that the dangers of inflation were exaggerated and attempts by the Federal Reserve to slow the economy would lead to higher unemployment. Is this a disagreement about positive economics or about normative economics? Explain.

Learning Goals

In this chapter, you will learn

1. What economists mean by the "basic competitive model"

2. How economists analyze choices made by households and firms

3. The role that prices play in a market economy

4. The limitations of the basic competitive model

5. How prices are determined by demand and supply

Chapter 2

THE PRICE SYSTEM

Every day, millions of people take part in thousands of exchanges in hundreds of different markets. Somehow, out of all these exchanges, computers are produced and end up in student dorm rooms, food is grown and ends up on the dinner tables of households, and electricity is delivered to millions of homes and offices at a flick of a switch. In an economy like that of the United States, markets play a critical role in ensuring that workers find jobs, things get produced, and firms sell their products. Exchange and the role of markets are important, but what makes them work? How can you be sure that your local grocery store will have bread in the morning or that your favorite café will have milk and espresso for your morning latte? And how can you be sure that the grocery store won't charge you $20 for that loaf of bread or that your espresso won't cost $10?

The answer can be given in one word—*competition*. So that you can understand what economists mean by competition and why it is so important in market economies, this chapter introduces you to a basic model of the economy and some of the key tools that economists use. You will learn about the important role that prices and competition play in a market economy, and how the concepts of demand and supply can help us understand how the economy works.

The Basic Competitive Model

When firms compete with one another for customers, they will offer customers the desired products at the lowest possible price. Consumers also compete with one another. Only a limited number of goods are available, and they come at a price. Consumers who are willing to pay that price can enjoy the goods, but others are left empty-handed. This picture of competitive markets, which economists call the **basic competitive model,** provides the point of departure for studying the economy. It consists of three parts: assumptions about how consumers behave, assumptions about how firms behave, and assumptions about the markets in which these consumers and firms interact. Consumers are assumed to be *rational,* firms are assumed to be *profit maximizing,* and the markets in which they interact are assumed to be highly *competitive.* The model ignores the government, because we need to see how an economy without a government might function before we can understand the role of the government.

CHOICE

In trying to understand how the economy functions, economists focus on the choices made by households and firms. These choices range from a household deciding which goods to purchase, how much to save, what types of careers to follow, and how much to work, to firms deciding what to produce, how much to produce, and how much labor to hire and capital to purchase in order to produce it. So our first task is to examine how economists analyze choices.

Opportunity sets and budget constraints For a rational individual or a profit-maximizing firm, the first step in the economic analysis of choice is to identify what is possible—what economists call the **opportunity set,** which is simply the group of available options. If your MP3 player contains only the collected songs of Bruce Springsteen and Britney Spears, listening to Alicia Keys or Tim McGraw is out of the question. You can listen to a Springsteen song or a Spears song, but you can't listen to a song that is not on your player. So the starting point for analyzing choice is to determine what is within the opportunity set.

The opportunity set is defined by the constraints that limit choice. In many economic situations, the constraints that are most relevant are time and money. Opportunity sets whose constraints are imposed by money are referred to as **budget constraints;** opportunity sets whose constraints are imposed by time are called **time constraints.** A budget constraint is something most of us are very aware of. If we have to spend more on our rent, we have less money available to spend on other things. Budget constraints define the trade-offs we face. If Michelle has $120 to spend on either CDs or DVDs, and if a CD costs $10 while a DVD costs $20, she can buy 12 CDs *or* 6 DVDs; or she can buy 10 CDs and 1 DVD; or 4 CDs and 4 DVDs. If Michelle decides to buy more DVDs, she will have to settle for fewer CDs.

Individuals also face time constraints. The most common time constraint simply says that the sum of what an individual spends her time on each day—including sleep—must add up to 24 hours. Spending more time surfing means that less time is available for some other activity, like homework. Time and budget constraints limit individuals' opportunity sets and force trade-offs to be made.

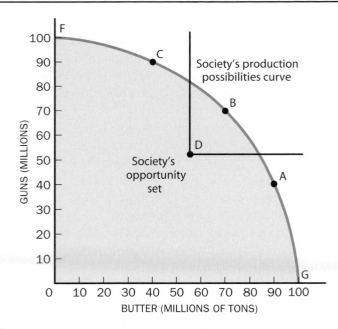

Figure 2.1

THE GUNS AND BUTTER TRADE-OFF

A production possibilities curve can show society's opportunity set. This one describes the trade-off between military spending ("guns") and civilian spending ("butter"). Points *F* and *G* show the extreme choices, where the economy produces all guns or all butter.

OPPORTUNITY SETS AND TRADE-OFFS

Opportunity sets consist of the group of available options. Budget constraints and time constraints limit choices and serve to define opportunity sets. Making choices involves making trade-offs among alternatives in the opportunity set.

The Production Possibilities Curve Business firms and whole societies also face constraints. They too face choices that are limited to opportunity sets. The amount of goods a firm or society can produce, given a fixed amount of land, labor, and other inputs, is referred to as its *production possibilities.*

A commonly used example considers a society in which all economic production is divided into two categories, military spending and civilian spending. For the sake of simplicity, Figure 2.1 refers to military spending as "guns" and civilian spending as "butter."[1] The production of guns is given along the vertical axis, the

---

[1]See the chapter appendix for help in reading graphs. Economists have found graphs to be extremely useful, and they will be employed throughout this book. It is important that you learn to read and understand graphs.

Table 2.1

PRODUCTION
POSSIBILITIES FOR THE
ECONOMY

Guns (millions)	Butter (millions of tons)
100	0
90	40
70	70
40	90
0	100

production of butter along the horizontal. The possible combinations of military and civilian spending—of guns and butter—is the opportunity set. Table 2.1 sets out some of the possible combinations: 90 million guns and 40 million tons of butter, or 40 million guns and 90 million tons of butter. These possibilities are depicted in Figure 2.1. In production decisions, the boundary of the opportunity set—the maximum amount of guns that can be produced for each amount of butter and vice versa—is called the **production possibilities curve.**

Notice that we have drawn the production possibilities curve so that it bows outward. If a society produces only a few guns, it will use those resources—the workers and machines—that are best equipped for gun making. But as society tries to produce more and more guns, doing so becomes more difficult; it will increasingly depend on resources that are less good at producing guns. It will be drawing these resources out of the production of other goods—in this case, butter. Thus, when the economy increases its production of guns from 40 million a year (point *A*) to 70 million (*B*), butter production falls by 20 million tons, from 90 million tons to 70 million tons. But if production of guns is increased further, to 90 million (*C*), an increase of only 20 million, butter production has to decrease by 30 million tons, to only 40 million tons. For each increase in the number of guns, the reduction in the number of tons of butter produced gets larger. That is why the production possibilities curve is curved.

In another example, assume that a firm owns land that can be used for growing wheat but not corn, and land that can grow corn but not wheat. In this case, the only way to increase wheat production is to move workers from the cornfields to the wheat fields. As more and more workers are put into the wheat fields, production of wheat goes up, but each successive worker increases production less. The first workers might pick the largest and most destructive weeds. Additional workers lead to better weeding, and better weeding leads to higher output. But the additional weeds removed are smaller and less destructive, so output is increased by a correspondingly smaller amount. This is an example of the general principle of **diminishing returns.** Adding successive units of any input such as fertilizer, labor, or machines to a fixed amount of other inputs—seeds or land—increases the output, or amount produced, but by less and less.

Inefficiencies: Being off the Production Possibilities Curve

Economies (and firms) will not always be on the production possibilities curve. One of the major quests of economists is to look for instances in which the economy is inefficient in this way.

Whenever the economy is operating below the production possibilities curve, we can have more of every good—more wheat and more corn, more guns and more butter. No matter what goods we like, we can have more of them. That is why we can unambiguously say that points below the production possibilities curve are undesirable. But this does not mean that every point on the curve is better than any point below it. Compare points *C* and *D* in Figure 2.1. Gun production is higher at *C*, but butter production is lower. If people prefer butter, the increased gun production may not adequately compensate them for the decreased butter production.

Costs

Making trade-offs always involves weighing costs and benefits. Often, the benefits depend on an individual's preferences—some people would gladly skip a tennis game to go play golf, and others would just as gladly make the opposite choice. Economists generally do not try to explain why people have different preferences; instead, they focus on costs. An opportunity set, like the budget constraint, the time constraint, or the production possibilities curve, specifies the cost of one option in terms of another. If the individual, the firm, or society is operating on the constraint or curve, then it is possible to get more of one thing only by sacrificing some of another. The "cost" of one more unit of one good is how much you have to give up of the other.

Economists think about costs in terms of trade-offs within opportunity sets. Let's go back to Michelle choosing between CDs and DVDs. The trade-off is given by the **relative price,** the ratio of the prices of CDs and DVDs. In our example, a CD costs $10, and a DVD $20. The relative price is $20/$10 = 2. For every DVD Michelle gives up, she can buy 2 CDs. Likewise, societies and firms face trade-offs along the production possibilities curve, like the one shown in Figure 2.1. There, point A is the choice where 40 million guns and 90 million tons of butter are produced. The trade-off can be calculated by comparing points A and B. Society can have 30 million more guns by giving up 20 million tons of butter.

Trade-offs are necessary because resources are scarce. If you want something, you have to pay for it—you have to give up something. If you want to go to the library tomorrow night, you have to give up going to the movies. If a sawmill wants to make more two-by-four beams from its stock of wood, it will not be able to make as many one-by-four boards.

OPPORTUNITY COSTS

If someone were to ask you right now what it costs to go to a movie, you would probably answer, "Ten dollars," or whatever you last paid for a ticket. But the concept of trade-offs suggests that a *full* answer is not that simple. To begin with, the cost is not the $10 but what that $10 could otherwise buy. Furthermore, your time is a scarce resource that must be figured into the calculation. Both the money and the time represent opportunities forgone in favor of going to the movie, or what economists refer to as the **opportunity cost** of the movie. To apply a resource to one use means that it cannot be put to any other use. Thus, we should consider the next-best, alternative use of any resource when we think about putting it to any particular use. This next-best use is the formal measurement of opportunity cost.

Some examples will help clarify the idea of opportunity cost. Consider a college student, Sarah, who works during the summer. She has a chance to go surfing in Costa Rica with friends, but to do so she has to quit her summer job two weeks early. The friends have found a cheap airfare and place to stay, and they tell Sarah the trip will cost only $1,000. To the economist, $1,000 is not the total cost of the trip for Sarah. Since she would have continued working in her summer job for an extra two weeks if she had not gone to Costa Rica, the income she would have earned is part

Thinking Like an Economist
TRADE-OFFS

Whenever you see an opportunity set, a budget or time constraint, or a production possibilities curve, think *trade-off*. The variables on the two axes identify the objects of the trade-offs, whether those are CDs and DVDs, guns and butter, or something else. The line or curve drawn from one axis to the other provides quantities for the trade-off. The opportunity set shows the choices that are available. The budget constraint illustrates the trade-offs that must be made because of limited money to spend, while the time constraint reflects the limited time we all have. The production possibilities curve gives the trade-offs faced in deciding what to produce when the amount of land, labor, and other inputs is limited. All three focus attention on the necessity of making trade-offs.

Many people think economists study only situations that involve money and budget constraints, but time constraints are often very important in defining trade-offs. Political elections provide a good example of the importance of time constraints. As the 2004 presidential election campaign entered its final stages, each candidate faced tough choices because of the time constraint. The election date was fixed, leaving only so much time for campaigning. Ohio was one of the critical states for both John Kerry and George W. Bush, and both candidates visited it frequently in the months leading up to the election. But time spent in Ohio was time that could not be spent in the other toss-up states. Each candidate had to decide how best to allocate the time remaining before the election.

President George W. Bush greets well-wishers.

Economists find it useful to distinguish between budget constraints and time constraints, but often we study trade-offs that involve both time *and* money. Choosing how to spend your Saturday evening usually involves both. You might decide to go to a movie that lasts for 2 hours and costs $10 or go to a concert that lasts 4 hours and costs $40. Both your budget and time constraints are important for defining your opportunity set.

of the opportunity cost of her time. This forgone income must be added to the airfare and hotel costs in calculating the total economic cost of the surfing trip.

Now consider a business firm that has bought a building for its headquarters that is bigger than necessary. If the firm could receive $3 per month in rent for each square foot of space that is not needed, then that is the opportunity cost of leaving the space idle.

The analysis can be applied to the government as well. The federal government owns a vast amount of wilderness. In deciding whether it is worthwhile to convert some of the land into a national park, the government needs to take into account the opportunity cost of the land. The land might be used for growing timber or for grazing sheep. Whatever the value of the land in its next-best use, this is the economic cost of the national park. The fact that the government does not have to buy the land does not mean that the land should be treated as a free good.

Thus, in the economist's view, when rational firms and individuals make decisions—whether to undertake one investment project rather than another, whether to buy one product rather than another—they take into account *all* of the costs (the full opportunity costs), not just the direct expenditures.

THE OPPORTUNITY COST OF ATTENDING COLLEGE

Opportunity cost is a key concept in economics. It is the correct measure of the cost of everything we do. As a college student, what is your opportunity cost of attending college? If you (or your parents) are asked how much your college costs, you probably think of the tuition, room and board, and books as major costs. But a consideration of opportunity cost suggests that such a list includes both too much and too little.

Since you would need a place to live, and you would need to eat, even if you were not in school, these costs do not represent part of the opportunity cost of attending college. Only if your college charges higher rent than you would otherwise pay would your dorm costs be part of your opportunity cost.

To correctly evaluate opportunity cost, you need to think about what you would be doing if you had decided not to continue in school. The economist's mind immediately turns to the job you might have had if you had not enrolled in college and the income you could have earned. That amount will vary from student to student; but in 2004, eighteen-to-twenty-four-year-olds with a high school diploma who were working full-time earned just under $15,000 per year.[2] This *forgone income* must be added to the direct costs such as tuition to obtain the opportunity cost of attending school. For most students, this forgone income is a major component of the opportunity cost of college.

Test your understanding: Use the concept of opportunity cost to explain why great college basketball players often fail to complete four years of college.

SUNK COSTS

Economic cost includes costs, as we have just seen, that noneconomists often exclude, but it also ignores costs that noneconomists include. If an expenditure has already been made and cannot be recovered no matter what choice is made, a rational person would ignore it. Such expenditures are called **sunk costs.**

---

[2]U.S. Census Bureau, Annual Demographic Survey, Table PINC-04, March 2004 (http://pubdb3.census.gov/macro/032004/perinc/new04_001.htm).

To understand sunk costs, let's go back to the movies, assuming now that you have spent $10 to buy a ticket. You were skeptical about whether the movie was worth $10. Half an hour into the movie, your worst suspicions are realized: the movie is a disaster. Should you leave the movie theater? In making that decision, the $10 should be ignored. It is a sunk cost; your money is gone whether you stay or leave. The only relevant choice now is how to spend the next 60 minutes of your time: watch a terrible movie or go do something else.

Or assume you have just purchased a fancy laptop computer for $2,000. But the next week, the manufacturer announces a new computer with twice the power for $1,000; you can trade in your old computer for the new one by paying an additional $400. You are angry. You feel you have just paid $2,000 for a computer that is now almost worthless, and you have gotten hardly any use out of it. You decide not to buy the new computer for another year, until you have gotten at least some return for your investment. Again, an economist would say that you are not approaching the question rationally. The past decision is a sunk cost. The only question you should ask yourself is whether the extra power of the fancier computer is worth the additional $400. If it is, buy it. If not, don't.

MARGINAL COSTS

The third aspect of cost that economists emphasize is the extra costs of doing something, what they call the **marginal costs.** These are weighed against the (additional) **marginal benefits** of doing it. The most difficult decisions we make are not whether to do something or not. They are whether to do a little more or a little less of something. Few of us waste much time deciding whether or not to work. We have to work; the decision is whether to work a few more or a few less hours. A country does not consider whether or not to have an army; it decides whether to have a larger or smaller army.

Polly is considering flying to Colorado for a ski weekend. She has three days off from work. The airfare is $200, the hotel room costs $100 a night, and the ski ticket costs $35 a day. Food costs the same as at home. She is trying to decide whether to go for two or three days. The *marginal* cost of the third day is $135, the hotel cost plus the cost of the ski ticket. There are no additional transportation costs involved in staying the third day. She needs to compare the marginal cost with the additional enjoyment she will have from the third day.

Internet Connection

THE ECONOMISTS' VOICE

One way to start thinking like an economist is to read what economists have to say about current events. The Economists' Voice at www.bepress.com/ev/ provides articles about current economic issues.

People, consciously or not, think about the trade-offs at the margin in most of their decisions. Economists, however, bring them into the foreground. Like opportunity costs and sunk costs, marginal analysis is one of the critical concepts that enable economists to think systematically about the costs of alternative choices.

This kind of marginal analysis has come to play an increasingly important role in policy discussions. For instance, the key issue in various environmental regulations and safety standards is not whether there should be such regulations, but how tight they should be. Higher standards have both marginal benefits and marginal costs. From an economic standpoint, justification of higher standards hinges on whether the marginal benefits outweigh the marginal costs. Consider, for instance, auto safety. For the past three decades, the government has taken an active role in ensuring auto safety. It sets standards that all automobiles must meet. For example, an automobile must be able to withstand a side collision of a particular velocity. One of the most difficult problems the government faces is deciding what those standards should be. When it considered tightening standards for withstanding side collisions on trucks, the government calculated that the higher standards would result on average in 79 fewer deaths per year. It calculated that meeting the higher standards would increase the cost of each vehicle by $81. (In addition, the heavier trucks would use more fuel.) In deciding whether to impose the higher standard, it used marginal analysis. It looked at the *additional* lives saved and at the *additional* costs.

BASIC STEPS OF RATIONAL CHOICE

Identify the opportunity sets.
Define the trade-offs.
Calculate the costs correctly, ignoring sunk costs and taking into account opportunity costs and marginal costs.

Competitive Markets

Understanding the choices made by rational consumers and profit-maximizing firms is the starting point for economists' basic competitive model. To complete the model, economists make assumptions about the places where self-interested consumers and profit-maximizing firms meet—markets. Economists begin by focusing on the case in which there are many buyers and sellers, all buying and selling the same thing. You might picture a crowded farmers' market—except that you have to picture everyone buying and selling just one good. Let's say we are in Florida and the booths are full of oranges.

Each farmer would like to raise his price. That way, if he can still sell his oranges, his profits go up. Yet with a large number of sellers, each is forced to charge close to the same price, since if any farmer charged much more, he would lose business to the farmer next door. Profit-maximizing firms are in the same position. In an extreme case, if a firm charged any more than the going price, it would lose all its sales. Economists label this case **perfect competition.** In perfect competition, each firm is a *price taker,* which simply means that because it cannot influence the market price, it must accept that price. The firm takes the market price as given because it cannot raise its price without losing all sales, and at the market price it can sell as much as it wishes. Markets for agricultural goods would be, in the absence of government intervention, perfectly competitive. There are so many wheat farmers, for instance, that each farmer believes he can grow and sell as much wheat as he wishes and have no effect on the price of wheat.

On the other side of our farmers' market are rational individuals, each of whom would like to pay as little as possible for oranges. Why can't any consumer pay less than the going price? Because the seller sees another buyer in the crowd who will pay the going price. Thus, the consumers also have to compete against each other for the limited number of oranges in the market, and as a result each takes the market price as given.

While a farmers' market provides one illustration of what economists mean by a market, most markets do not take this form. The modern-day market is more likely to involve buyers and sellers interacting over the Internet than at a farmer's market. But the same basic principles apply. When there are lots of buyers and sellers, each will take the price as given in deciding how much to buy or sell.

THE EFFICIENCY OF COMPETITIVE MARKETS

An important issue in economics is understanding whether a market system can function efficiently. Do the uncoordinated actions of millions of households and firms, interacting in competitive markets, manage to produce the goods and services that consumers want and to produce them in ways that do not waste society's scarce resources? One of the most fundamental, and perhaps surprising, ideas in economics is that competitive markets are efficient. Firms have an incentive to lower costs to the minimum level possible and to produce the goods the consumers want.

Adam Smith argued that in competitive economies, the public interest is best served by individuals pursuing their own self-interest. As he put it:

> Man has almost constant occasion for the help of his brethren, and it is in vain for him to expect it from their benevolence only. He will be more likely to prevail if he can interest their self-love in his favour, and shew them that it is for their own advantage to do for him what he requires of them. . . . It is not from the benevolence of the butcher, the brewer, or the baker, that we expect our dinner, but from their regard to their own interest. We . . . never talk to them of our own necessities but of their advantages.[3]

Smith's insight was that individuals work hardest to help the overall economic production of society when their efforts help themselves. He argued that an "obvious and simple system of liberty" provided the greatest opportunities for people to help themselves and thus, by extension, to create the greatest wealth for a society.

Smith used the metaphor of the "invisible hand" to describe how self-interest led to social good: "He intends only his own gain, and he is in this as in many other cases led by an invisible hand to promote an end which was no part of his intention. . . . By pursuing his own interest he frequently promotes that of the society more effectually than when he really intends to promote it."

Adam Smith's fundamental argument still has great appeal. Competitive markets ensure that the economy produces the goods that consumers want. Production simultaneously takes into account the trade-offs individuals are willing to make (how many DVDs they are *willing* to give up to get one more iPod) and the trade-offs the production possibilities curve gives the economy (how many DVDs *have* to be given up to get one more iPod).

Moreover, competitive markets ensure that goods get to the right people. If individuals do not like the particular mix of goods they have, they can trade; exchange will continue until no further mutually advantageous trades are feasible. In competitive markets, all the possible trades that benefit both parties to the trade will be made. Any further trades or rearrangements of goods would have to leave one of the parties to the trade worse off. Such trades would not take place in a competitive market, since the party that is disadvantaged by a potential trade would not agree to it. As a consequence, in competitive markets, no rearrangement of goods can

---

[3]*The Wealth of Nations* (1776), Book One, Chapter II.

be made that would succeed in leaving someone better off and everyone else no worse off. An economy in which no one can be made better off without someone else being made worse off is said to be **Pareto efficient**—a term named after the great Italian economist of the early twentieth century, Vilfredo Pareto.

Competitive markets also determine the distribution of goods—who gets to consume how much of the goods that are available. High levels of competition for the services of an individual with a rare and valuable skill will result in a very high income for that individual. On the other hand, competition among suppliers of unskilled labor may result in these workers facing very low wages, so low that even long workdays fail to achieve a decent standard of living. This raises the question of the fairness of competitive distribution. Though efficiency is a desirable property of any economic system, the question of fairness is a separate issue. Later in this book we will discuss how economists and policymakers think about the inequalities that inevitably emerge from the workings of the competitive market.

THE BASIC COMPETITIVE MODEL AS A BENCHMARK

Virtually all economists recognize that the competitive model is not a *perfect* representation of actual economies, but most economists still use it as a convenient benchmark—as we will throughout this book. After all, as you learned in Chapter 1, a *model* is never a complete and accurate description—it is not meant to be—but instead is designed to highlight critical aspects of the economy that provide insight and help us understand particular features of the economy. We will point out important differences between the predictions of the basic competitive model and observed outcomes, and these differences can help guide us to other models that provide a better understanding of particular markets and situations. While the basic competitive model may not provide a *perfect* description of some markets, most economists believe that the basic competitive model gives us tremendous insights into a wide range of economic issues; for that reason, it is the foundation on which economists build.

Wrap-Up

INGREDIENTS IN THE BASIC COMPETITIVE MODEL

1. Rational, self-interested consumers
2. Rational, profit-maximizing firms
3. Competitive markets with price-taking behavior

Incentives and Information: Prices, Property Rights, and Profits

For market economies to work efficiently, firms and individuals must be informed and have incentives to act on available information. Indeed, incentives can be viewed as at the heart of economics. Without incentives, why would individuals go to work in the morning? Who would risk bringing out new products? Who would put aside savings for a rainy day? There is an old expression about the importance of having someone "mind the store." But without incentives, why would anyone bother?

Market economies provide information and incentives through *prices, profits,* and *property rights.* Prices provide information about the relative scarcity of different goods. The **price system** ensures that goods go to those individuals and firms that are most willing and able to pay for them. Prices convey information to consumers about scarcity, and consumers respond by adjusting their consumption. Similarly, prices convey information to firms about how individuals value different goods.

The desire for profits motivates firms to respond to the information provided by prices. By producing what consumers want in the most efficient way, in ways that least use scarce resources, they increase their profits. Similarly, rational individuals' pursuit of self-interest induces them to respond to prices. They buy goods that are more expensive—in a sense, relatively more scarce—only if they provide commensurately greater benefits. If a good such as oil becomes scarcer, its price rises. In order to make rational decisions about how much heating oil to use, consumers do not need to know why the price of oil has risen. Perhaps a particularly cold winter has increased demand. Or perhaps trouble in the Middle East has decreased supply. In either case, the higher price signals consumers to reduce their purchases of oil products. If the price of home heating oil rises, that signals to oil refineries to produce more heating oil. Prices provide the information individuals and firms need to make rational decisions.

For the profit motive to be effective there must be **private property,** with its attendant **property rights.** Under a system of private property, firms and individuals are able to own and use (or sell if they choose) factories, land, and buildings. Without private property, firms would not have an incentive to invest in new factories or new technologies, hire employees, produce goods and services that consumers want to buy, and earn profits. Even if the profits to be earned from building a new factory are huge, no firms will build the factory unless they are confident it cannot be arbitrarily taken away from them. They need to be able to keep at least some of their profits to use as they see fit. Similarly, households need to be able to keep at least some of what they receive as a return to their investments. (The return on their investment is simply what they receive back in excess of what they invested.) Property rights include both the right of the owner to use the property as she sees fit and the right to sell.

These two attributes of property rights give individuals the incentive to use property under their control efficiently. The owner of a piece of land tries to figure out

The existence of private property creates incentives for business owners to invest in new buildings and factories.

the most profitable use of the land; for example, whether to build a store or a restaurant. If he makes a mistake and opens a restaurant when he should have opened a store, he bears the consequences: the loss in income. The profits he earns if he makes the right decisions—and the losses he bears if he makes the wrong ones—give him an incentive to think carefully about the decision and do the requisite research. The owner of a store tries to make sure that her customers get the kind of merchandise and the quality of service they want. She has an incentive to establish a good reputation, because if she does so, she will do more business and earn more profits.

The store owner will also want to maintain her property—which is not just the land anymore, but includes the store as well—because she will get more for it when the time comes to sell her business to someone else. Similarly, the owner of a house has an incentive to maintain his property, so that he can sell it for more when he wishes to move. Again, the profit motive combines with private property to provide incentives.

INCENTIVES VERSUS EQUALITY

While incentives are at the heart of market economies, they come with a cost: inequality. Any system of incentives must link compensation with performance. Whether through differences in luck or ability, the performances of different individuals will differ. In many cases, it will not be possible to identify why performance is high. The salesperson may claim that the reason his sales are high is superior skill and effort, while his colleague may argue that it is luck.

If pay is tied to performance, there will inevitably be some inequality. And the more closely compensation is tied to performance, the greater the inequality. The fact that the greater the incentives, the greater the resulting inequality is called the *incentive-equality trade-off.* If society provides greater incentives, total income is likely to be higher, but there will also probably be greater inequality.

One of the basic questions facing society in the choice of tax rates and welfare systems is, How much would incentives be diminished by an increase in tax rates to finance a better welfare system and thus reduce inequality? What would be the results of those reduced incentives?

Incentives, prices, profits, and property rights are central features of any economy, and highlight an important area of consensus among economists: *Providing appropriate incentives is a fundamental economic problem. In modern market economies, profits provide incentives for firms to produce the goods that individuals want, and wages provide incentives for individuals to work. Property rights also provide people with important incentives, not only to invest and to save but also to put their assets to the best possible use.*

Wrap-Up

HOW THE PROFIT MOTIVE DRIVES THE MARKET SYSTEM

In market economies, incentives are supplied to individuals and firms by prices, profits, and property rights.

ALTERNATIVES TO THE PRICE SYSTEM

The price system is only one way of allocating resources, and a comparison with other systems will help clarify the advantages of markets. When individuals get less of a good than they would like at the terms being offered, the good is said to be *rationed*. Different *rationing systems* are different ways of deciding who gets society's scarce resources.

Rationing by Queues Rather than supplying goods to those willing and able to pay the most for them, a society could give them instead to those most willing to wait in line. This system is called *rationing by queues,* after the British term for lines. Tickets are often allocated by queues, whether they are for movies, sporting events, or rock concerts. A price is set, and it will not change no matter how many people line up to buy at that price. (The high price that scalpers can get for hot tickets is a good indication of how much more than the ticket price people would be willing to pay.)[4]

Rationing by queues is thought by many to be a more desirable way of supplying medical services than the price system. Why, it is argued, should the rich—who are most able to pay for medical services—be the ones to get better or more medical care? Using this reasoning, Britain provides free medical care to everyone on its soil. To see a doctor there, all you have to do is wait in line. Rationing medicine by queues turns the allocation problem around: since the value of time for low-wage workers is lower, they are more willing to wait, and therefore they get a disproportionate share of (government-supplied) medical services.

In general, rationing by queues is an inefficient way of distributing resources, because the time spent in line is a wasted resource. There are usually ways of achieving the same goal within a price system that can make everyone better off. Returning to the medical example: if some individuals were allowed to pay for doctors' services instead of waiting in line, more doctors could be hired with the proceeds, and the lines for those unable or unwilling to pay could actually be reduced.

Rationing by Lotteries *Lotteries* allocate goods by a random process, such as picking a name from a hat. University dormitory rooms are usually assigned by lottery. So are seats in popular courses; when more students want to enroll in a section of a principles of economics course than the size of the section allows, there may be a lottery to determine who gets to enroll. Like queue systems, lotteries are thought to be fair because everyone has an equal chance. However, they are also inefficient, because the scarce resources do not go to the individual or firm that is willing and able to pay (and therefore values them) the most.

---

[4]So why are concert tickets rationed by queues rather than by price? The musicians and concert promoters could increase their profits by raising the ticket price, but consider the situation of a popular musician who is concerned about both concert income and income from CD sales. Allocating tickets by queue favors those with the most free time and helps ensure that tickets go to the musician's core fans, particularly those who are younger and have less money to spend. These fans may be most likely to buy CDs, and CD sales depend heavily on word-of-mouth advertising. So by ensuring that her core fans are not priced out of concerts, a musician may actually end up increasing her profits.

Rationing by Coupons Most governments in wartime use *coupon rationing.* People are allowed so many gallons of gasoline, so many pounds of sugar, and so much flour each month. To get the good, you have to pay the market price *and* produce a coupon.

Coupon systems take two forms, depending on whether coupons are tradable or not. Coupons that are not tradable give rise to the same inefficiency that occurs with most of the other nonprice systems—goods do not in general go to the individuals who are willing and able to pay the most. When coupons cannot be legally traded, there are strong incentives for the establishment of a *black market,* an illegal market in which the goods or the coupons for goods are traded.

Limitations of the Basic Competitive Model

If the real world matched up to the assumptions of the basic model of perfectly competitive markets, then markets could be given free rein. They would supply efficient outcomes. If an outcome seemed inequitable, society simply would redistribute initial wealth and let markets take care of the rest.

In the two centuries since Adam Smith first enunciated the view that markets ensure economic efficiency, economists have investigated the model with great care. Nothing they have discovered has shaken their belief that markets are, by and large, the most efficient way to coordinate the millions of individual decisions and actions that make up the economy. However, they also have found significant departures between modern economies and the competitive model. The insights of the basic competitive model remain extremely powerful, and most economists use the model as the starting point for building a richer, more complete model that has extended the power and insights that economics provides to a wide range of situations not dealt with in the basic competitive model. Among the most important areas modern economists have studied are imperfect competition, imperfect information, and technological change.

IMPERFECT COMPETITION

The basic competitive model begins with the assumption that there are so many buyers and sellers in each market that each firm and each individual believes that it has no effect on the equilibrium price. We say that firms and households are *price takers.* In particular, the amount produced by any firm has a negligible effect on the market price.

In many markets, firms do seem to have an effect on the price. They are *price makers.* This is true of many of the goods we buy—from automobiles to film, brand-name cereals, beer, and soft drinks. The production decision of a price maker determines the price it receives; alternatively, such a firm picks a price, and the price it picks determines how much it can sell.

Adam Smith was the first person to describe the fundamentals of the basic competitive model.

In most markets in modern economies, competition is not perfect. A firm that raises its price does not lose all of its customers, as would be the case in the perfectly competitive model. There are several reasons for this, the most important being that the products of different firms are slightly different from one another. There is *product differentiation*. The automobile made by Ford is slightly different from the one made by General Motors, and likewise throughout most of the major industries in the United States. The differences may be real or simply perceived. They may be as simple as the differences in location of several gasoline stations, or as complex as the differences between two separate computers. The differences may be related to differences in the quality of products, or they may arise from brand loyalty or firm reputations.

In labor markets, competition is also often limited. In many industries, workers do not compete actively against one another but rather work together, through unions. Together, they threaten to refuse to work for a firm unless the firm raises its wages; that is, they use their market power to extract higher wages by threatening a strike. Of course, their market power is limited by the fact that the employer may turn to nonunion workers.

The role of unions has been declining markedly in the United States for the past forty years. In fact, within the private sector, the decline has been even more evident; the major area of growth of unionization is among public employees. Part of this decline is attributed to the increased competition faced by such traditionally highly unionized sectors as automobiles and steel. And employment in these sectors has declined, some claim, partly as a result of the high wages the unions have won for their workers. In most European countries, however, unions remain powerful and play a major role in setting wages.

IMPERFECT INFORMATION

An important assumption of the basic competitive model is that households are well-informed. They have good information about the products they buy. They know the prices at which they can acquire each item at each store. They have good information about the firms in which they invest. Similarly, firms have good information about potential employees. Firms know each worker's abilities. They can costlessly monitor what workers are doing and ensure that they do as they are told. It is clear that these assumptions are not quite correct; both households and firms face limited or, as economists say, **imperfect information.** This fact has important implications for how each of the markets in the economy functions.

If firm A lowers its price below that of its rival, firm B, it does not instantly gain all of B's customers. Customers may not know that firm A has lowered its prices; even if they do, they may not be sure that the product being sold by A, or the service it provides in conjunction with the product, is of the same quality as the product sold by B. Thus, imperfect information leads to imperfect competition.

In the labor market, a firm must spend considerable resources trying to screen various applicants to find out which are best suited for the firm. Even then, it will not be perfectly successful. Some of the workers it hires will turn out to be unsuitable. Thus, in many jobs, hiring and training workers is extremely costly. Firms often find that by paying higher wages, they can get a larger and better-quality applicant pool from which to choose workers, and the workers they hire are less likely to quit.

Because of imperfect information, it may be difficult for firms to monitor the activities of their workers. Owners of firms face similar problems in getting the firm's managers to act in the interests of the owners. The owners would like the managers simply to maximize profits or the market value of the firm. People who own shares of a firm's stock are the firm's owners, but the shareholders do not themselves make the decisions concerning what the firm does. They must rely on those who manage the firm, and the managers may not do what is in the interests of the shareholders. Managers may use their position to enhance their lifestyle rather than the profits of the firm; they may use corporate jets not so much to improve productivity but perhaps to fly around to vacation spots also owned by the firm.

Finally, information problems have a major effect on how capital markets work. To take one example, consider a firm that wishes to borrow money. Normally, you might think that if, at the going interest rate, some potential borrower cannot obtain all the funds she wants, all she needs to do is offer to pay a higher interest rate. Lenders would prefer to receive the higher interest rate, and it would seem that no one is precluded from the market. But this does not seem to work, and for a simple reason. Lenders worry that if they charge a higher interest rate, their expected returns will actually decrease because the chance of default will increase. At higher interest rates, safer investors find that it does not pay to borrow. A disproportionate number of those willing to borrow at high rates are highflyers—people who are undertaking high-risk projects that, if successful, will yield high returns, more than enough to cover the interest charge. But if the projects fail, they simply go bankrupt, and the lender is left holding the bag.

Thus, there may be an optimal interest rate, r^*, at which the bank's expected return is maximized. Increasing the interest rate charged above r^* may actually lead to lower expected returns, as the best borrowers with the least risky projects decide not to apply for loans and those who do borrow undertake riskier projects. Lenders will not be willing to lend at a higher interest rate, because they know that their expected returns will actually be lower if they do so. In this situation, economists say there is *credit rationing*. Some borrowers are rationed in the amount of credit they can obtain.

TECHNOLOGICAL CHANGE

The basic competitive model proceeds under the assumption that every firm has a given technology, a given way of converting inputs into outputs. There is a given array of products that are produced. In fact, the development of new products and less expensive ways of producing old products is an essential part of modern industrial economies; the fact that modern market economies do these things so well is often cited as one of their greatest virtues.

Government's interest in promoting technological progress often conflicts with its interest in promoting competition. If a firm is willing to spend its funds to do research and develop new products, it must be able to get a return from any inventions that are the fruit of that research. Governments therefore grant patents, giving

As the inventor of many devices that changed life for common people in the twentieth century, Thomas Edison embodied technological change.

an inventor the exclusive right to an invention for a set period (usually twenty years). The losses from the reduction in competition for this limited period are thought to be outweighed by the gains from the spur to innovation that the patent provides.

Even with a good patent system, there may be insufficient spur to innovation. Firms seldom capture all the benefits that accrue from their inventive activity. Other firms see what they have done, learn from it, and use it as a basis for producing still better products. Customers benefit. Innovation in the computer industry has made faster and faster computers available at lower and lower prices. And in the long run, workers benefit as well, as the improved technology comes to be reflected in higher wages.

IMPLICATIONS FOR MACROECONOMICS

The three extensions of the basic competitive model we have discussed—imperfect competition, imperfect information, and technological change—play an important role in macroeconomics. With imperfect competition, the assumption that prices can adjust freely and quickly to ensure that all markets balance may not be appropriate, and we will see in Part Three that sluggish price and wage adjustment plays a key role in explaining why economies experience periods of high unemployment. Imperfect information on the part of borrowers and leaders helps account for financial market instability and financial crises, and technological change is critical for explaining the tremendous growth in living standards that industrial economies have enjoyed.

Demand

We have already discussed the role of prices in the basic competitive model. In the basic competitive model, prices in the market will measure scarcity. To better understand how prices are determined—what factors affect them and how changes in these factors alter both prices and the quantities of different goods that get produced and consumed—economists use the concepts of *demand* and *supply*.

Economists use the concept of **demand** to describe the quantity of a good or service that a household or firm chooses to buy at a given price. It is important to understand that economists are concerned not just with what people desire but with what they choose to buy given the spending limits imposed by their budget constraints and given the prices of various goods. In analyzing demand, the first question they ask is how the quantity of a good purchased by an individual changes as the price changes, when everything else is kept constant.

THE INDIVIDUAL DEMAND CURVE

Think about what happens as the price of candy bars changes. At a price of $5.00, you might never buy one. At $3.00, you might buy one as a special treat. At $1.25, you might buy a few, and if the price declined to $0.50, you might buy a lot. The table in Figure 2.2 summarizes the weekly demand of one individual, Roger, for candy bars at these

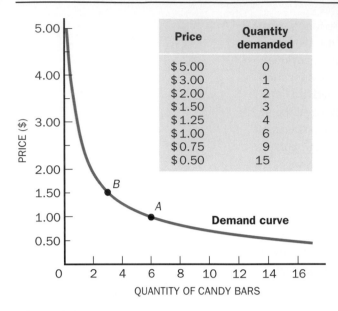

Price	Quantity demanded
$5.00	0
$3.00	1
$2.00	2
$1.50	3
$1.25	4
$1.00	6
$0.75	9
$0.50	15

Figure 2.2

AN INDIVIDUAL'S DEMAND CURVE

This demand curve shows the quantity of candy bars that Roger consumes at each price. Notice that quantity demanded increases as the price falls, and the demand curve slopes down.

different prices. We can see that the lower the price, the larger the quantity demanded. We can also draw a graph that shows the quantity Roger demands at each price. The quantity demanded is measured along the horizontal axis, and the price is measured along the vertical axis. The graph in Figure 2.2 plots the points.

A smooth curve can be drawn to connect the points. This curve is called the **demand curve.** The demand curve gives the quantity demanded at each price. Thus, if we want to know how many candy bars a week Roger will demand at a price of $1.00, we simply look along the vertical axis at the price $1.00, find the corresponding point *A* along the demand curve, and then read down the horizontal axis. At a price of $1.00, Roger buys 6 candy bars each week. Alternatively, if we want to know at what price he will buy just 3 candy bars, we look along the horizontal axis at the quantity 3, find the corresponding point *B* along the demand curve, and then read across to the vertical axis. Roger will buy 3 candy bars at a price of $1.50.

As the price of candy bars increases, the quantity demanded decreases. This can be seen from the numbers in the table in Figure 2.2 and in the shape of the demand curve, which slopes downward from left to right. This relationship is typical of demand curves and makes common sense: the cheaper a good is (the lower down we look on the vertical axis), the more of it a person will buy (the farther right on the horizontal axis); the more expensive, the less a person will buy.

DEMAND CURVE

The demand curve gives the quantity of the good demanded at each price.

THE MARKET DEMAND CURVE

Suppose there was a simple economy made up of two people, Roger and Jane. Figure 2.3 illustrates how to add up the demand curves of these two individuals to obtain a demand curve for the market as a whole. We "add" the demand curves horizontally by taking, at each price, the quantities demanded by Roger and by Jane and adding the two together. Thus, in the figure, at the price of $0.75, Roger demands 9 candy bars and Jane demands 11, so that the total market demand is 20 candy bars. The same principles apply no matter how many people there are in the economy. The **market demand curve** gives the total quantity of the good that will be demanded at each price. The table in Figure 2.4 summarizes the information for our example of candy bars; it gives the total quantity of candy bars demanded by everybody in the economy at various prices. If we had a table like the one in Figure 2.2 for each person in the economy, we would construct Figure 2.4 by adding up, at each price, the total quantity of candy bars purchased. Figure 2.4 tells us, for instance, that at a price of $3.00 per

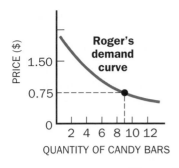 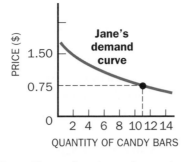 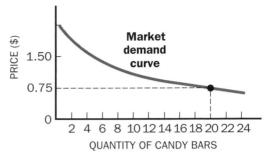

Figure 2.3

DERIVING THE MARKET DEMAND CURVE

The market demand curve is constructed by adding up, at each price, the total of the quantities consumed by each individual. The curve here shows what market demand would be if there were only two consumers. Actual market demand, as depicted in Figure 2.4, is much larger because there are many consumers.

candy bar, the total market demand for candy bars is 1 million candy bars, and that lowering the price to $2.00 increases market demand to 3 million candy bars.

Figure 2.4 also depicts the same information in a graph. As in Figure 2.2, price lies along the vertical axis, but now the horizontal axis measures the quantity demanded by everyone in the economy. Joining the points in the figure together, we get the market demand curve. If we want to know what the total demand for candy bars will be when the price is $1.50 per candy bar, we look on the vertical axis at the price $1.50, find the corresponding point *A* along the demand curve, and read down to the horizontal axis; at that price, total demand is 4 million candy bars. If we want to know what the price of candy bars will be when the demand equals 20 million, we find 20 million along the horizontal axis, look up to find the corresponding point *B* along the market demand curve, and read across to the vertical axis; the price at which 20 million candy bars are demanded is $0.75.

Notice that just as when the price of candy bars increases, the individual's demand decreases, so too when the price of candy bars increases, market demand decreases. At successively higher prices, more and more individuals exit the market. Thus, the market demand curve also slopes downward from left to right. This general rule holds both because each individual's demand curve is downward sloping and because as the price is increased, some individuals will decide to stop buying altogether. In Figure 2.2, for example, Roger *exits the market*—consumes a quantity of zero—at the price of $5.00, at which his demand curve hits the vertical axis.

Price	Quantity demanded (millions)
$5.00	0
$3.00	1
$2.00	3
$1.50	4
$1.25	8
$1.00	13
$0.75	20
$0.50	30

Figure 2.4

THE MARKET DEMAND CURVE

The market demand curve shows the quantity of the good demanded by all consumers in the market at each price. The market demand curve is downward sloping, for two reasons: At a higher price, each consumer buys less, and at high-enough prices, some consumers decide not to buy at all—they exit the market.

SHIFTS IN DEMAND CURVES

When the price of a good increases, the demand for that good decreases—when everything else is held constant. But in the real world, everything is not held constant. Any changes other than the price of the good in question shift the (whole) demand curve—that is, changes the amount that will be demanded at each price. How the

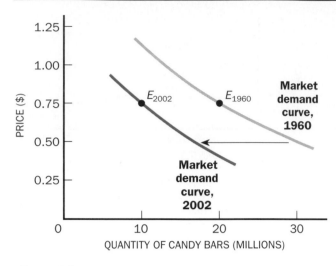

Figure 2.5

SHIFTS IN THE DEMAND CURVE

A leftward shift in the demand curve means that a lesser amount will be demanded at every given market price.

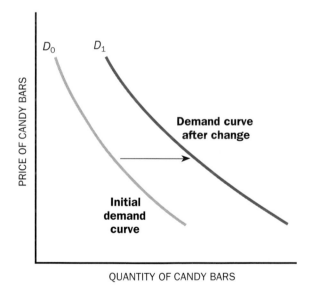

Figure 2.6

A RIGHTWARD SHIFT IN THE DEMAND CURVE

If, at each price, there is an increase in the quantity demanded, then the demand curve will have shifted to the right, as depicted. An increase in income, an increase in the price of a substitute, or a decrease in the price of a complement can cause a rightward shift in the demand curve.

demand curve for candy has shifted as Americans have become more weight conscious provides a good example. Figure 2.5 shows hypothetical demand curves for candy bars in 1960 and in 2002. We can see from the figure, for instance, that the demand for candy bars at a price of $0.75 has decreased from 20 million candy bars (point E_{1960}, the original equilibrium) to 10 million (point E_{2002}), as people have reduced their desire for candy.

Sources of Shifts in Demand Curves Two of the factors that shift the demand curve—changes in income and changes in the price of other goods—are specifically economic factors. As an individual's income increases, she normally purchases more of any good. Thus, rising incomes shift the demand curve to the right, as illutrated in Figure 2.6. At each price, she consumes more of the good.

Changes in the price of other goods, particularly closely related goods, will also shift the demand curve for a good. For example, when the price of margarine increases, some individuals will substitute butter. Two goods are *substitutes* if an increase in the price of one *increases* the demand for the other. Butter and margarine are thus substitutes. When people choose between butter and margarine, one important factor is the relative price, that is, the ratio of the price of butter to the price of margarine. An increase in the price of butter and a decrease in the price of margarine increase the relative price of butter. Thus, both induce individuals to substitute margarine for butter.

Candy bars and granola bars can also be considered substitutes, as the two goods satisfy a similar need. Thus, an increase in the price of granola bars makes candy bars relatively more attractive, and hence leads to a rightward shift in the demand curve for candy bars. (At each price, the demand for candy bars is greater.)

Sometimes, however, an increase in a price of other goods has just the opposite effect. Consider an individual who takes sugar in his coffee. In deciding how much coffee to demand, he is concerned with the price of a cup of coffee *with* sugar. If sugar becomes more expensive, he will demand less coffee. For this person, sugar and coffee are *complements;* an increase in the price of one *decreases* the demand for the other. A price increase for sugar shifts the demand curve of coffee to the left: at each price, the demand for coffee is less. Similarly, a *decrease* in the price of sugar shifts the demand curve for coffee to the right.

Noneconomic factors can also shift market demand curves. The major ones are changes in tastes and in the composition of the population. The candy example shown earlier was a change in taste. Other taste changes over the past decade in the United States include a shift from hard liquor to wine and from fatty meats to low-cholesterol foods. The recent popularity of low-carb diets has shifted the demand curve for beef to the right. Each of these taste changes has shifted the whole demand curve of the goods in question.

Population changes that shift demand curves are often related to age. Young families with babies purchase disposable diapers. The demand for new houses and apartments is closely related to the number of new households, which in turn depends on the number of individuals of marriageable age. The U.S. population has been growing older, on average, both because life expectancies are increasing and because birthrates fell somewhat after the baby boom that followed World War II. So there has been a shift in demand away from diapers and new houses.

Sometimes demand curves shift as the result of new information. The shifts in demand for alcohol and meat—and even more directly for cigarettes—are related to improved consumer information about health risks.

Changes in the availability of credit also can shift demand curves—for goods such as cars and houses that people typically buy with the help of loans. When banks, for example, reduce the money available for consumer loans, the demand curves for cars and houses shift.

Finally, what people think will happen in the future can shift demand curves. If people think they may become unemployed, they will reduce their spending. In this case, economists say that their demand curve depends on expectations.

SOURCES OF SHIFTS IN MARKET DEMAND CURVES

A change in income
A change in the price of a substitute
A change in the price of a complement
A change in the composition of the population
A change in tastes
A change in information
A change in the availability of credit
A change in expectations

GASOLINE PRICES AND THE DEMAND FOR SUVS

When demand for two products is intertwined, conditions affecting the price of one will affect the demand for the other. Changes in gasoline prices in the United States, for example, have affected the types of cars that Americans buy.

Gasoline prices soared in the 1970s, once when the Organization of Petroleum Exporting Countries (OPEC) shut off the flow of oil to the United States in 1973 and again when the overthrow of the shah of Iran in 1979 led to a disruption in oil

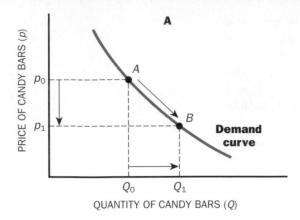

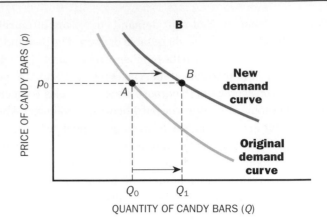

Figure 2.7

MOVEMENT ALONG THE DEMAND CURVE VERSUS SHIFT IN THE DEMAND CURVE

Panel A shows an increase in quantity demanded caused by a lower price—a movement along a given demand curve. Panel B illustrates an increase in quantity demanded caused by a shift in the entire demand curve, so that a greater quantity is demanded at every market price. Panel C shows a combination of a shift in the demand curve (the movement from point A to B) and a movement along the demand curve (the movement from B to C).

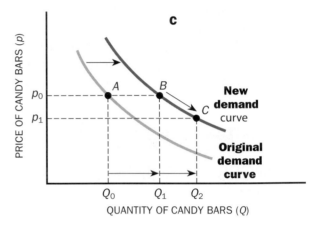

supplies. The price of gasoline at the pump rose from $0.34 a gallon in 1971 to $1.35 a gallon by 1981. In response to the price increases, Americans had to cut back on demand. One way Americans reduced their demand for gasoline was by replacing their old cars with smaller, more fuel-efficient cars.

Analysts classify car sales according to size, and usually, the smaller the car, the better the gas mileage. Just after the first rise in gas prices, about 2.5 million large cars, 2.8 million compacts, and 2.3 subcompact cars were bought each year. By 1985, the proportions had shifted dramatically. About 1.5 million large cars were sold that year, representing a significant decrease from the mid-1970s. The number of subcompacts sold was relatively unchanged at 2.2 million, but the number of compacts sold soared to 3.7 million.

The demand curve for any good (like cars) assumes that the price of complementary goods (like gasoline) is fixed. The rise in gasoline prices caused the demand for small cars to increase (the demand curve shifted to the right) and the demand for large cars to fall (the demand curve shifted to the left).

By the late 1990s, even though the price of gasoline was much higher than it had been in the 1970s, the prices of other goods had also risen significantly. The price of gasoline *relative* to the prices of other goods was about the same as it had been *before* the big gasoline price increases of the 1970s. As a consequence, the demand for large cars increased. This time, the change in demand was reflected in booming sales of sports utility vehicles, or SUVs. Registrations of light-duty trucks (which include SUVs, minivans, and pickups) jumped from less than 20 percent of all vehicles in the 1970s to 46 percent in 1996.

Gas prices again rose in 2003 and 2004. This development led many economists to forecast that consumers would soon be switching away from the large SUVs that had become so popular in the 1990s and back to smaller, more fuel-efficient autos.

SHIFTS IN A DEMAND CURVE VERSUS MOVEMENTS ALONG A DEMAND CURVE

The distinction between changes that result from a *shift* in the demand curve and changes that result from a *movement along* the demand curve is an important one in economics. A movement along a demand curve is simply the change in the quantity demanded as the price changes. Figure 2.7A illustrates a movement along the demand curve from point A to point B; *given a demand curve*, at lower prices, more is consumed. Figure 2.7B illustrates a shift in the demand curve to the right; *at a given price*, more is consumed. Quantity again increases from Q_0 to Q_1, but now the price stays the same.

In practice, both effects are often present. Thus, in panel C of Figure 2.7, the movement from point A to point C—where the quantity demanded has been increased from Q_0 to Q_2—consists of two parts: a change in quantity demanded resulting from a shift in the demand curve (the increase in quantity from Q_0 to Q_1), and a movement along the demand curve due to a change in the price (the increase in quantity from Q_1 to Q_2).

Supply

Economists use the concept of **supply** to describe the quantity of a good or service that a household or firm would like to sell at a particular price. Supply in economics refers to such seemingly disparate choices as the number of candy bars a firm wants to sell and the number of hours a worker is willing to work. As with demand, the first question economists ask is how the quantity supplied changes when price changes, when everything else is kept the same.

Figure 2.8 shows the number of candy bars that the Melt-in-the-Mouth Chocolate Company would like to sell, or supply to the

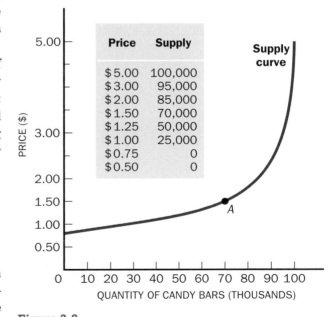

Price	Supply
$5.00	100,000
$3.00	95,000
$2.00	85,000
$1.50	70,000
$1.25	50,000
$1.00	25,000
$0.75	0
$0.50	0

Figure 2.8

ONE FIRM'S SUPPLY CURVE

The supply curve shows the quantity of a good a firm is willing to produce at each price. Normally a firm is willing to produce more as the price increases, which is why the supply curve slopes upward.

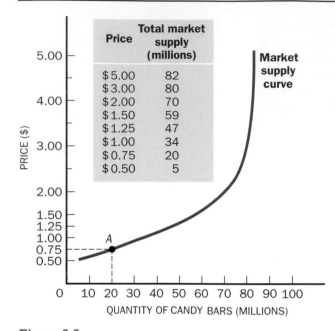

Price	Total market supply (millions)
$5.00	82
$3.00	80
$2.00	70
$1.50	59
$1.25	47
$1.00	34
$0.75	20
$0.50	5

Figure 2.9

THE MARKET SUPPLY CURVE

The market supply curve shows the quantity of a good that all firms in the market are willing to supply at each price. The market supply curve is normally upward sloping, both because each firm is willing to supply more of the good at a higher price and because higher prices entice new firms to produce.

market, at each price. As the price rises, so does the quantity supplied. Below $1.00, the firm finds it unprofitable to produce. At $2.00, it would like to sell 85,000 candy bars. At $5.00, it would like to sell 100,000.

Figure 2.8 also depicts these points in a graph. The curve drawn by connecting the points is called the **supply curve.** It shows the quantity that Melt-in-the-Mouth will supply at each price, holding all other factors constant. As with the demand curve, we put the price on the vertical axis and the quantity supplied on the horizontal axis. Thus, we can read point A on the curve as indicating that at a price of $1.50, the firm would like to supply 70,000 candy bars.

In direct contrast to the demand curve, the typical supply curve slopes upward from left to right; at higher prices, firms will supply more. This is because higher prices yield suppliers higher profits—giving them an incentive to produce more.

SUPPLY CURVE

The supply curve gives the quantity of the good supplied at each price.

MARKET SUPPLY

The *market supply* of a good is simply the total quantity that all the firms in the economy are willing to supply at a given price. Similarly, the market supply of labor is simply the total quantity of labor that all the households in the economy are willing to supply at a given wage. Figure 2.9 tells us, for instance, that at a price of $2.00, firms will supply 70 million candy bars, while at a price of $0.50, they will supply only 5 million.

Figure 2.9 also shows the same information graphically. The curve joining the points in the figure is the **market supply curve.** The market supply curve gives the total quantity of a good that firms are willing to produce at each price. Thus, we read point A on the market supply curve as showing that at a price of $0.75, the firms in the economy would like to sell 20 million candy bars.

As the price of candy bars increases, the quantity supplied increases, other things being equal. The market supply curve slopes upward from left to right for two reasons: at higher prices, each firm in the market is willing to produce more; and at higher prices, more firms are willing to enter the market to produce the good.

The market supply curve is calculated from the supply curves of the different firms in the same way that the market demand curve is calculated from the demand

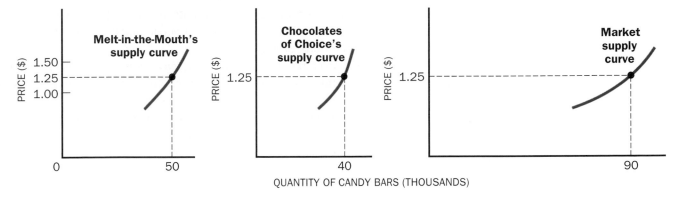

QUANTITY OF CANDY BARS (THOUSANDS)

Figure 2.10

DERIVING THE MARKET SUPPLY CURVE

The market supply curve is constructed by adding up the quantity that each of the firms in the economy is willing to supply at each price. The figure here shows what market supply would be if there were only two producers. Actual market supply, as depicted in Figure 2.9, is much larger because there are many producers.

curves of the different households: at each price, we add horizontally the quantities that each of the firms is willing to produce.

Figure 2.10 shows how this is done in a market with only two producers. At a price of $1.25, Melt-in-the-Mouth Chocolate produces 50,000 candy bars, while the Chocolates of Choice Company produces 40,000. So the market supply is 90,000 bars. The same principle applies to markets with many firms.

SHIFTS IN SUPPLY CURVES

Just as demand curves can shift, supply curves too can shift, so that the quantity supplied at each price increases or decreases. Suppose a drought hits the breadbasket states of mid-America. Figure 2.11 illustrates the situation. The supply curve for wheat shifts to the left, which means that at each price of wheat, the quantity firms are willing to supply is smaller.

Sources of Shifts in Supply Curves There are several sources of shifts in market supply curves, just as in the case of the market demand curves already discussed. One is changing prices of the inputs used to produce a good. Figure 2.12 shows that as corn becomes less expensive, the supply curve for cornflakes shifts to the right. Producing cornflakes costs less, so at every price, firms are willing to supply a greater quantity. That is why the quantity supplied along the curve S_1 is greater than the quantity supplied, at the same price, along the curve S_0.

Another source of shifts is changes in technology. The technological improvements in the computer industry over the past two decades have led to a rightward shift in the market supply

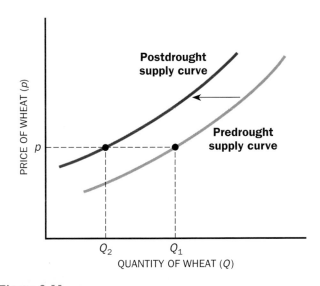

Figure 2.11

SHIFTING THE SUPPLY CURVE TO THE LEFT

A drought or other disaster (among other possible factors) will cause the supply curve to shift to the left, so that at each price, a smaller quantity is supplied.

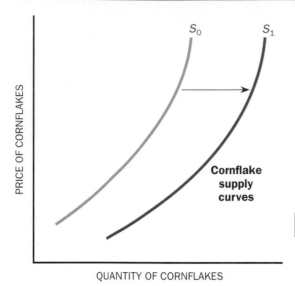

Figure 2.12

SHIFTING THE SUPPLY CURVE TO THE RIGHT

An improvement in technology or a reduction in input prices (among other possible factors) will cause the supply curve to shift to the right, so that at each price, a larger quantity is supplied.

curve. Yet another source of shifts is nature. The supply curve for agricultural goods may shift to the right or left depending on weather conditions, insect infestations, or animal diseases.

Reduction in the availability of credit may curtail firms' ability to borrow to obtain inputs needed for production, and this too will induce a leftward shift in the supply curve. Finally, changed expectations can also lead to a shift in the supply curve. If firms believe that a new technology for making cars will become available in two years, they will discourage investment today, leading to a temporary leftward shift in the supply curve.

SOURCES OF SHIFTS IN MARKET SUPPLY CURVES

A change in the prices of inputs
A change in technology
A change in the natural environment
A change in the availability of credit
A change in expectations

SHIFTS IN A SUPPLY CURVE VERSUS MOVEMENTS ALONG A SUPPLY CURVE

Distinguishing between a movement *along* a curve and a *shift* in the curve itself is just as important for supply curves as it is for demand curves. In Figure 2.13A, the price of candy bars has gone up, with a corresponding increase in quantity supplied. Thus, there has been a movement along the supply curve.

By contrast, in Figure 2.13B, the supply curve has shifted to the right, perhaps because a new production technique has made it cheaper to produce candy bars. Now, even though the price does not change, the quantity supplied increases. The quantity supplied in the market can increase either because the price of the good has increased, so that for a *given supply curve,* the quantity produced is higher; or because the supply curve has shifted, so that at a *given price,* the quantity supplied has increased.

Law of Supply and Demand

This chapter began with the assertion that supply and demand work together to determine the market price in competitive markets. Figure 2.14 puts a market supply curve and a market demand curve on the same graph to show how this happens. The price actually paid and received in the market will be determined by

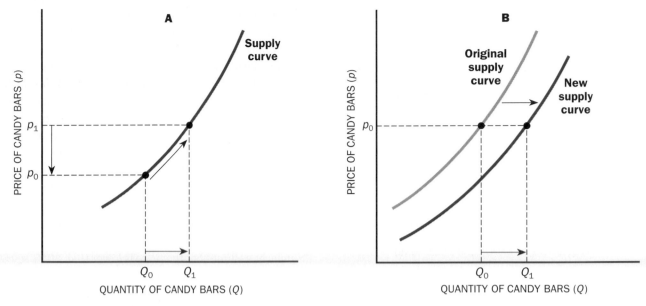

Figure 2.13

MOVEMENT ALONG THE
SUPPLY CURVE VERSUS SHIFT
IN THE SUPPLY CURVE

Panel A shows an increase in quantity supplied caused by a higher price—a movement along a given supply curve. Panel B illustrates an increase in quantity supplied caused by a shift in the entire supply curve, so that a greater quantity is supplied at every market price.

the intersection of the two curves. This point is labeled E_0, for equilibrium, and the corresponding price ($0.75) and quantity (20 million) are called, respectively, the **equilibrium price** and the **equilibrium quantity.**

Since the term **equilibrium** will recur throughout the book, it is important to understand the concept clearly. Equilibrium describes a situation in which there are no forces (reasons) for change. No one has an incentive to change the result— the price or quantity consumed or produced, in the case of supply and demand.

Physicists also speak of equilibrium in describing a weight hanging from a spring. Two forces are working on the weight. Gravity is pulling it down; the spring is pulling it up. When the weight is at rest, it is in equilibrium, with the two forces just offsetting each other. If one pulls the weight down a little bit, the force of the spring will be greater than the force of gravity, and the weight will spring up. In the absence of any further intrusions, the weight will bob back and forth and eventually reach its equilibrium position.

An economic equilibrium is established in the same way. At the equilibrium price, consumers get precisely the quantity of the good they are willing to buy at that price, and producers sell precisely the quantity they are willing to sell at that price. The market clears. To emphasize this condition, economists sometimes refer to the equilibrium price as the **market clearing price.** In equilibrium, neither producers nor consumers have any incentive to change.

But consider the price of $1.00 in Figure 2.14. There is no equilibrium quantity here. First find $1.00 on the vertical axis. Now look across to find point A on the

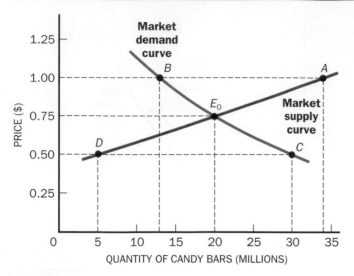

Figure 2.14

SUPPLY AND DEMAND EQUILIBRIUM

Equilibrium occurs at the intersection of the demand and supply curves, at point E_0. At any price above E_0, the quantity supplied will exceed the quantity demanded, the market will be out of equilibrium, and there will be excess supply. At any price below E_0, the quantity demanded will exceed the quantity supplied, the market will be out of equilibrium, and there will be excess demand.

supply curve, and read down to the horizontal axis; point A tells you that at a price of $1.00, firms want to supply 34 million candy bars. Now look at point B on the demand curve. Point B shows that at a price of $1.00 consumers want to buy only 13 million candy bars. Like the weight bobbing on a spring, however, this market will work its way back to equilibrium in the following way. At a price of $1.00, there is *excess supply*. As producers discover that they cannot sell as much as they would like at this price, some of them will lower their prices slightly, hoping to take business from other producers. When one producer lowers prices, her competitors will have to respond, for fear that they will end up unable to sell their goods. As prices come down, consumers will also buy more, and so on until the market reaches the equilibrium price and quantity.

Similarly, assume that the price is lower than $0.75, say $0.50. At the lower price, there is *excess demand:* individuals want to buy 30 million candy bars (point C), while firms only want to produce 5 million (point D). Consumers unable to purchase all they want will offer to pay a bit more; other consumers, afraid of having to do without, will match these higher bids or raise them. As prices start to increase, suppliers will also have a greater incentive to produce more. Again the market will tend toward the equilibrium point.

To repeat for emphasis: At equilibrium, no purchaser and no supplier has an incentive to change the price or quantity. In competitive market economies, actual prices tend to be the equilibrium prices, at which demand equals supply.

This is called the **law of supply and demand.** Note: This law does not mean that at every moment of time the price is precisely at the intersection of the demand and supply curves. As in the example of the weight and the spring, the market may bounce around a little bit when it is in the process of adjusting. What the law of supply and demand does say is that when a market is out of equilibrium, there are predictable forces for change.

USING DEMAND AND SUPPLY CURVES

The concepts of demand and supply curves—and market equilibrium as the intersection of demand and supply curves—constitute the economist's basic model of demand and supply. This model has proved to be extremely useful. It helps explain why the price of some commodity is high, and that of some other commodity is low. It also helps *predict* the consequences of certain changes. Its predictions can then be tested against what actually happens. One of the reasons that the model is so useful is that it gives reasonably accurate predictions.

Figure 2.15 repeats the demand and supply curve for candy bars. Assume now, however, that sugar becomes more expensive. As a result, at each price, the amount of candy firms are willing to supply is reduced. The supply curve shifts to the left, as in panel A. There will be a new equilibrium, at a higher price and a lower quantity of candy consumed.

Alternatively, assume that Americans become more health conscious, and as a result, at each price fewer candy bars are consumed: the demand curve shifts to the left, as shown in panel B. Again, there will be a new equilibrium, at a lower price and a lower quantity of candy consumed.

This illustrates how changes in observed prices can be related either to shifts in the demand curve or to shifts in the supply curve. To take a different example, when Iraq's invasion of Kuwait interrupted the supply of oil from the Middle East in 1990, that was a shift in the supply curve. The model predicted the result: an increase in the price of oil. This increase was the natural process of the law of supply and demand.

CONSENSUS ON THE DETERMINATION OF PRICES

The law of supply and demand plays such a prominent role in economics that there is a joke about teaching a parrot to be an economist simply by training it to say "supply and demand." That prices are determined by the law of supply and demand is one of the most long-standing and widely accepted ideas of economists. *In competitive markets, prices are determined by the law of supply and demand. Shifts in the demand and supply curves lead to changes in the equilibrium price. Similar principles apply to the labor and capital markets. The price for labor is the wage, and the price for capital is the interest rate.*

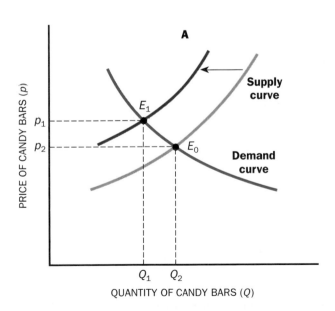

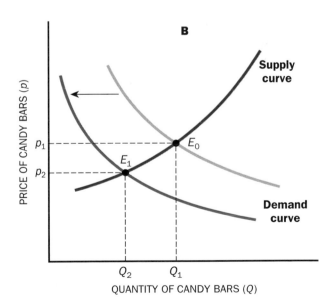

Figure 2.15

USING SUPPLY AND DEMAND CURVES TO PREDICT PRICE CHANGES

Initially the market for candy bars is in equilibrium at E_0. An increase in the cost of sugar shifts the supply curve to the left, as shown in panel A. At the new equilibrium, E_1, the price is higher and the quantity consumed is lower. A shift in taste away from candy results in a leftward shift in the demand curve as shown in panel B. At the new equilibrium, E_1, the price and the quantity consumed are lower.

Thinking Like an Economist
THE STRUCTURE OF ECONOMIC MODELS

Every economic model, including the model of how supply and demand determine the equilibrium price and quantity in a market, is constructed of three kinds of relationships: identities, behavioral relationships, and equilibrium relationships. Recognizing these component parts will help in understanding not only how economists think but also the source of their disagreements.

The market demand is equal to the sum of individual demands. This is an identity. An identity is a statement that is true simply because of the definition of the terms. In other words, market demand is *defined* to be the sum of the demands of all individuals. Similarly, it is an identity that market supply is equal to the sum of the supplies of all firms; the terms are defined in that way.

The demand curve represents a relationship between the price and the quantity demanded. Normally, as prices rise, the quantity of a good demanded decreases. This is a description of how individuals behave, and is called a behavioral relationship. The supply curve for each firm is also a behavioral relationship.

Economists may disagree over behavioral relationships. They may agree about the direction of the relationship but disagree about the strength of the connection. For any given product, does a change in price lead to a large change in the quantity supplied or a small one? But they may even disagree over the direction of the effect. As later chapters will discuss, in some special cases a higher price may actually lead to a *lower* quantity supplied.

Finally, an equilibrium relationship exists when there are no forces for change. In the supply and demand model, the equilibrium occurs when the quantity demanded is equal to the quantity supplied. An equilibrium relationship is not the same as an identity. It is possible for the economy to be out of equilibrium, at least for a time. Of course, being out of equilibrium implies that there are forces for change pushing toward equilibrium. But an identity must always hold true at all times, as a matter of definition.

Even when economists agree about what an equilibrium would look like, they often differ on whether the forces pushing the markets toward equilibrium are strong or weak, and thus on whether the economy is typically close to equilibrium or may stray rather far from it.

Shortages and Surpluses

The law of supply and demand works so well in a developed modern economy, most of the time, that everyone can take it for granted. If you are willing to pay the "market price"—the prevailing price of the good, determined by the intersection of demand and supply—you can obtain almost any good or service. Similarly, if a seller of a good or service is willing to charge no more than the market price, he can always sell what he wants to.

When the price is set so that demand equals supply—so that any individual can get as much as she wants at that price, and any supplier can sell the amount he wants at that price—economists say that the market clears. But when the market does not clear, there are shortages or surpluses. To an economist, a *shortage* means that people would like to buy something, but they simply cannot find it for sale at the going price. A *surplus* means that sellers would like to sell their product, but they cannot sell as much of it as they would like at the going price. The problem is that the "going price" is not the market equilibrium price.

At various times and for various goods, markets have not cleared. There have been shortages of apartments in New York; farm surpluses have plagued both western Europe and the United States; in 1973, there was a shortage of gasoline, with cars waiting in long lines outside of gasoline stations. Unemployment is a type of surplus, when people who want to work find that they cannot sell their labor services at the going wage.

In some markets, like the stock market, the adjustment of prices to shifts in the demand and supply curves tends to be very rapid. In other cases, such as in the housing market, the adjustments tend to be sluggish. When price adjustments are sluggish, shortages or surpluses may appear as prices adjust. Houses tend not to sell quickly, for instance, during periods of decreased demand, which translates only slowly into lower housing prices.

When the market is not adjusting quickly toward equilibrium, economists say that prices are sticky. Even in these cases, the analysis of market equilibrium is useful. It indicates the direction of the changes—if the equilibrium price exceeds the current price, prices will tend to rise. Moreover, the rate at which prices fall or rise is often related to the gap, at the going price, between the quantity demanded and the quantity supplied.

RENT CONTROL IN NEW YORK CITY

New York City adopted rent control on a "temporary" basis during World War II. More than half a century later, it is still in effect. The journalist William Tucker collected stories of well-to-do New Yorkers who benefited from this situation. The minority leader in the state senate, for example, paid $1,800 a month for a *ten-room* apartment overlooking Central Park. Newcomers were paying $1,500 for a one-bedroom apartment in midtown Manhattan. A housing court judge who heard

Many apartments in New York City are still subject to rent control.

rent-control cases paid $93 a month for a two-bedroom apartment in a building where studio apartments (with no separate bedroom) were renting for $1,200.

Of course, people who have been able to pay far below market value for decades tend to favor rent control. But since rent control is effectively a price ceiling, economists, looking to the law of supply and demand, would expect it to lead to problems and indeed it has.

Rent control creates a housing shortage while, at the same time, it discourages the construction of new rental housing. In cities with rent control such as New York, vacancy rates for rental units are quite low—usually around 2 to 3 percent. In contrast, the vacancy rate normally averages around 7 percent in cities such as Chicago, San Diego, and Philadelphia that do not have rent control. When many people are struggling to obtain one of the few available apartments, poor people tend to lose out. Some studies have indicated that rent control in Californian cities such as Santa Monica and Berkeley led to increased gentrification as highly educated professionals hold on to rent-controlled apartments, forcing working-class families (and students in the case of Berkeley) to look for housing in surrounding communities.

It is difficult for newcomers to find rental housing in cities with rent control such as New York and San Francisco. The available apartments are fewer, and they tend to be very expensive. For example, a 1997 survey of rents found that the median rent for an advertised apartment in New York City was about two and half times the median rent for all apartments in the city ($1,350 per month for advertised apartments versus $545 per month for all apartments). In contrast, in Philadelphia, a city that does not have rent control, the median rent for advertised apartments was only $2 more per month than the median for all apartments ($500 per month versus $498 per month). There were many more inexpensive and reasonably priced apartments available in Philadelphia than there were in New York City. The lack of affordable housing due to rent control forces individuals to share apartments or locate farther away from the city where they work, contributing to commuter congestion.

Attempting to provide moderate and low-cost housing is a worthy public goal. But the example of New York and other rent-controlled cities shows that even when the goal is worthy, the law of supply and demand does not simply fade away.[5]

---

[5]William Tucker, "We All Pay for Others' Great Apartment Deals," *Newsday,* May 24, 1986; Tucker, "Moscow on the Hudson," *The American Spectator,* July 1986, pp. 19–21; Tucker, "How Rent Control Drives Out Affordable Housing," *Cato Policy Analysis* No. 274, May 21, 1997.

Review and Practice

SUMMARY

1. The basic competitive model consists of rational, self-interested individuals and profit-maximizing firms, interacting in competitive markets.

2. The profit motive and private property provide incentives for rational individuals and firms to work hard and efficiently.

3. Society often faces choices between efficiency, which requires incentives that enable people or firms to receive different benefits depending on their performance, and equality, which entails people receiving more or less equal benefits.

4. The price system in a market economy is one way of allocating goods and services. Other methods include rationing by queue, by lottery, and by coupon.

5. An opportunity set illustrates what choices are possible. Budget constraints and time constraints define individuals' opportunity sets. Both show the trade-offs of how much of one thing a person must give up to get more of another.

6. A production possibilities curve defines a firm or society's opportunity set, representing the possible combinations of goods that the firm or society can produce.

7. The opportunity cost is the cost of using any resource. It is measured by looking at the next-best use to which that resource could be put.

8. A sunk cost is a past expenditure that cannot be recovered, no matter what choice is made in the present. Thus, rational decision makers ignore them.

9. Most economic decisions concentrate on choices at the margin, where the marginal (or extra) cost of a course of action is compared with its extra benefits.

10. The market demand curve gives the total quantity of a good demanded by all individuals in an economy at each price. As the price rises, demand falls, both because each person demands less of the good and because some people exit the market.

11. The market supply curve gives the total quantity of a good that all firms in the economy are willing to produce at each price. As the price rises, supply rises, both because each firm supplies more of the good and because some additional firms enter the market.

12. The law of supply and demand says that in competitive markets, the equilibrium price is that price at which quantity demanded equals quantity supplied. It is represented on a graph by the intersection of the demand and supply curves.

13. A demand curve shows *only* the relationship between quantity demanded and price. Changes in tastes, in demographic factors, in income, in the prices of other goods, in information, in the availability of credit, or in expectations are reflected in a shift of the entire demand curve.

14. A supply curve shows *only* the relationship between quantity supplied and price. Changes in factors such as technology, the prices of inputs, the natural environment, expectations, or the availability of credit are reflected in a shift of the entire supply curve.

KEY TERMS

basic competitive model
opportunity set
budget constraints
time constraints
production possibilities curve
diminishing returns
relative price
opportunity cost
sunk costs
marginal costs
marginal benefits
perfect competition
Pareto efficient
price system
private property
property rights
imperfect information
demand
demand curve
market demand curve
supply
supply curve
market supply curve
equilibrium price
equilibrium quantity
equilibrium
market clearing price
law of supply and demand

REVIEW QUESTIONS

1. What are the elements of the basic competitive model?
2. Why might government policy to make the distribution of income more equitable lead to less efficiency?
3. What are some of the opportunity costs of going to college? What are some of the opportunity costs a state should consider when deciding whether to widen a highway?
4. Give two examples of a sunk cost, and explain why they should be irrelevant to current decisions.
5. How is marginal analysis relevant in the decision about which car to purchase? After deciding the kind of car to purchase, how is marginal analysis relevant?
6. Why does an individual's demand curve normally slope down? Why does a market demand curve normally slope down?
7. Why does a firm's supply curve normally slope up? Why does a market supply curve normally slope up?
8. What is the significance of the point where supply and demand curves intersect?
9. What factors could shift the demand curve to the right?
10. What factors could shift the supply curve to the left?

PROBLEMS

1. Imagine that many businesses are located beside a river, into which they discharge industrial waste. There is a city downstream, which uses the river as a water supply and for recreation. If property rights to the river are ill-defined, what problems may occur?
2. In some states, hunting licenses are allocated by lottery; if you want a license, you send in your name to enter the lottery. If the system is meant to ensure that those who most want to hunt get a chance to do so, what are its flaws? How would the situation improve if people who won licenses were allowed to sell them to others?
3. Kathy, a college student, has $20 a week to spend; she spends it either on junk food at $2.50 a snack, or on gasoline at $2 per gallon. What is the trade-off between junk food and gasoline? How does the trade-off between junk food and gasoline change if
   (a) a kind relative sends her an additional $10 per week;
   (b) the price of a junk food snack falls to $2;
   (c) the price of gasoline rises to $2.50 per gallon.
4. Why is the opportunity cost of going to medical school likely to be greater than that of going to college? Why is the opportunity cost of a woman with a college education having a child greater than the opportunity cost of a woman with a high school education having a child?
5. Imagine a company lunchroom that sells pizza by the slice. Using the following data, plot the points and graph the demand and supply curves. What is the equilibrium price and quantity? Find a price at which excess demand would exist and a price at which excess supply would exist, and plot them on your diagram.

Price per slice	Demand (Number of slices)	Supply (Number of slices)
$1	420	0
$2	210	100
$3	140	140
$4	105	160
$5	84	170

6. Suppose a severe drought hit the sugarcane crop. Predict how this would affect the equilibrium price and quantity in the markets for sugar and honey. Draw supply and demand diagrams to illustrate your answers.
7. Americans' tastes have shifted away from beef and toward chicken. Predict how this change affects the equilibrium price and quantity in the markets for beef, chicken, and hamburger stands. Draw supply and demand diagrams to illustrate your answer.
8. In 2001, Europeans were concerned about "mad cow" disease, and the dangers of eating contaminated meat. What would this concern do to the *demand curve* for beef? To the demand curves for chicken and fish? To the equilibrium price of beef, chicken, and fish in the short run? What will happen to the price of beef in the long run?

   Mad cow disease is spread by feeding cows food that contains parts from infected animals. Presumably this is cheaper than a diet that relies exclusively on grain. What is the consequence for the *supply curve* of beef of restricting feed to grain? What are the consequences for the price of beef in the long run (a) if the new restrictions fail to restore confidence in beef and (b) if the new restrictions succeed in restoring confidence so that the demand curve returns to its original position?

   At about the same time, there was an outbreak of hoof-and-mouth disease, and to stop its spread large numbers of cattle were killed. What does this do to the supply curve of beef? To the equilibrium price of beef?

Appendix: Reading Graphs

Whether the old saying that a picture is worth a thousand words under- or overestimates the value of a picture, economists find graphs extremely useful.

For instance, look at Figure 2.16; it depicts the budget constraint showing the various combinations of CDs and DVDs that an individual, Michelle, can buy. More generally, a graph shows the relationship between two variables: here, the number of CDs and the number of DVDs that can be purchased. The budget constraint gives the maximum number of DVDs that she can purchase, given the number of CDs that she has bought.

In a graph, one variable (here, DVDs) is put on the horizontal axis and the other variable on the vertical axis. We read a point such as E by looking across to the vertical axis and seeing that it corresponds to 6 CDs, and by looking down to the horizontal axis and seeing that it corresponds to 3 DVDs. Similarly, we read point A by looking across to the vertical axis and seeing that it corresponds to 8 CDs, and by looking down to the horizontal axis and seeing that it corresponds to 2 DVDs.

In the figure, each of the points from the table has been plotted, and then a curve has been drawn through those points. The "curve" turns out to be a straight line in this case, but we still use the more general term. The advantage of the curve over the individual points is that with it, we can read off from the graph points on the budget constraint that are not in the table.

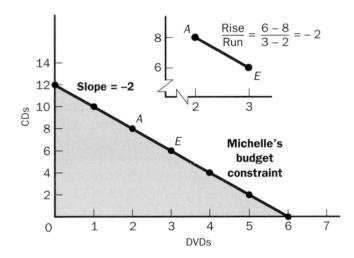

Figure 2.16

READING A GRAPH: THE BUDGET CONSTRAINT

Graphs can be used to show the relationship between two variables. This one shows the relationship between the variable on the vertical axis (the number of CDs) and the variable on the horizontal axis (the number of DVDs). The slope of the curve—here the budget constraint—gives the change in the number of CDs Michelle can purchase if she buys another DVD. The slope of the budget constraint is negative. A small portion of the graph has been blown up to illustrate how to calculate the curve's slope. (The jagged sections of the axes near the blown-up graph's origin indicate that the distance from the origin to the first value on each axis is not drawn to scale.)

Sometimes, of course, not every point on the graph is economically meaningful. You cannot buy half a DVD or half a CD. For the most part, we ignore these considerations when drawing our graphs; we simply pretend that any point on the budget constraint is actually possible.

SLOPE

In any diagram, the amount by which the value along the vertical axis increases from a change in a unit along the horizontal axis is called the *slope,* just like the slope of a mountain. Slope is sometimes described as "rise over run," meaning that the slope of a line can be calculated by dividing the change on the vertical axis (the "rise") by the change on the horizontal axis (the "run").

Look at Figure 2.16. As we move from *E* to *A,* increasing the number of CDs by 2, the number of DVDs purchased falls from 3 to 2. For every two additional CDs bought, the feasible number of DVDs that can be purchased falls by 1. So the slope of the line is

$$\frac{\text{rise}}{\text{run}} = \frac{6-8}{3-2} = \frac{-2}{1} = -2.$$

When, as in Figure 2.16, the variable on the vertical axis falls when the variable on the horizontal axis increases, the curve, or line, is said to be *negatively sloped.* A budget constraint is always negatively sloped. But when we describe the slope of a budget constraint, we frequently omit the term "negative." We say the slope is 2, knowing that since we are describing the slope of a budget constraint, we should more formally say that the slope is negative 2. Alternatively, we sometimes say that the slope has an absolute value of 2.

Figure 2.17 shows the case of a curve that is *positively sloped.* The variable along the vertical axis, income, increases as schooling increases, giving the line its upward tilt from left to right.

In later discussions, we will encounter two special cases. A line that is very steep has a very large slope; that is, the increase in the vertical axis for every unit increase in the horizontal axis is very large. The extreme case is a perfectly vertical line, and we say then that the slope is infinite (Figure 2.18, panel A). At the other extreme is a flat, horizontal line; since there is no increase in the vertical axis no matter how large the change along the horizontal, we say that the slope of such a curve is zero (panel B).

Figures 2.16 and 2.17 both show straight lines. Everywhere along the straight line, the slope is the same. This is not true in Figure 2.19, which repeats the production possibilities curve shown originally in Figure 2.1. Panel B of the figure blows up the area around point *E.* From the figure, you can see that if the output of butter increases by 1 ton, the output of guns decreases by 1 million guns. Thus, the slope is

$$\frac{\text{rise}}{\text{run}} = \frac{69-70}{71-70} = -1.$$

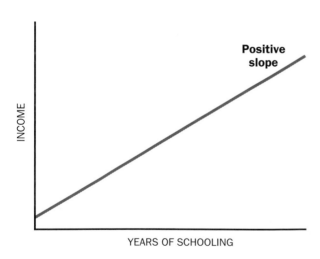

Figure 2.17

POSITIVELY SLOPED CURVE

Incomes increase with the number of years of schooling.

Now look at point *A*, where the economy is producing more butter. The area around *A* has been blown up in panel C. Here, we see that when we increase butter by 1 more unit, the reduction in guns is gre ater than before. The slope at *A* (again, millions of fewer guns produced per extra ton of butter) is

$$\frac{\text{rise}}{\text{run}} = \frac{38-40}{91-90} = -2.$$

With curves such as the production possibilities curve, the slope differs as we move along the curve.

INTERPRETING CURVES

Look at Figure 2.20. Which of the two curves has a steeper slope? The one on the left appears to have a slope that has a larger absolute value. But look carefully at the axes. Notice that in panel A, the vertical axis is stretched relative to panel B. The same distance that represents 20 CDs in panel B represents only 12 CDs in panel A.

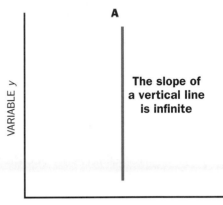

Figure 2.18

LIMITING CASES

In panel A, the slope of a vertical line is infinite. In panel B, the slope of a horizontal line is zero.

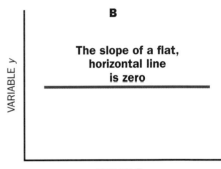

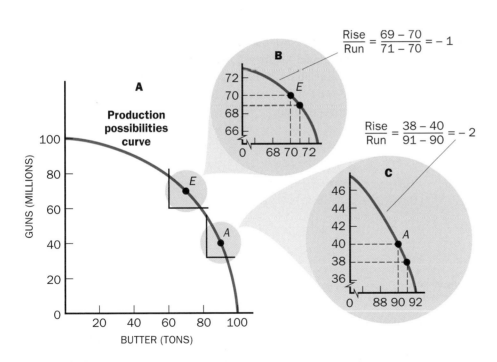

Figure 2.19

THE GUNS AND BUTTER TRADE-OFF

Panel A shows a trade-off between military spending ("guns") and civilian spending ("butter"), where society chooses point *E*. Panel B is an enlargement of the area around *E* that focuses on the slope there, which also measures the marginal trade-offs society faces near that point. Similarly, panel C is an enlargement of the area around *A* and shows the marginal trade-offs society faces near that point.

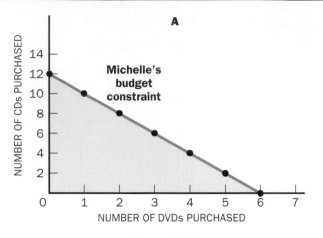

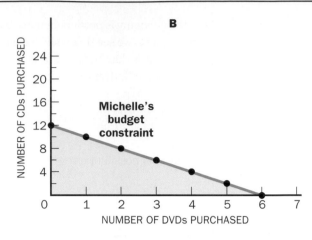

Figure 2.20

SCALING AND SLOPE

Which of these two lines has the steeper slope? The units along the vertical axis have changed. The two curves have exactly the same slope.

In fact, both panels represent the same budget constraint. They have exactly the same slope.

This kind of cautionary tale is also important in looking at graphs of data. Compare, for instance, panels A and B of Figure 2.21. Both graphs show the level of passenger car production from 1980 to 1990. Which one exhibits more variability? Which looks more stable? Panel B appears to show that car production does not change much over time. But again, a closer look reveals that the axis has been stretched in panel A. The two curves are based on exactly the same data, and there is really no difference between them.

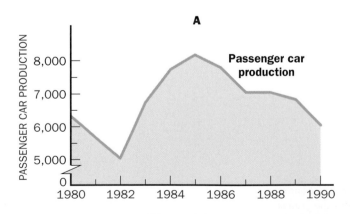

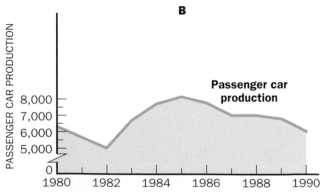

Figure 2.21

SCALING AND GRAPHS OF DATA

Which of these two curves shows greater variability in the output of cars over time? The two curves plot the same data. The vertical scale has again been changed.

SOURCE: Ward's Automotive Reports (1991).

Learning Goals

In this chapter, you will learn

1 How households behave in the product, labor, and capital markets

2 What economists mean by elasticity

3 What present discounted value is

4 How the firm decides how much to produce and how much labor and capital to hire

5 How the product, labor, and capital markets are related in general equilibrium

Chapter 3

HOUSEHOLDS AND FIRMS IN THE MACROECONOMY

In the basic competitive model introduced in Chapter 2, rational households interact with profit-maximizing firms in competitive markets. The supply and demand curves introduced in Chapter 2 give us a framework for analyzing this interaction. In this chapter, we explore the determinants of demand and supply in the product market, the labor market, and the capital market. We will first look at households. Households choose which goods to buy and how much to spend, they decide how much labor to supply, and they decide how much to save. We will then look at firms and their decisions about how much to produce and how much labor and capital to hire. This discussion will provide an understanding of what lies behind the basic demand and supply curves that were introduced in Chapter 2. After considering the decisions of households and firms, we will look at market equilibrium—how firms and households interact in all three markets—and at the implications of these interactions for the economy as a whole.

Households in the Basic Competitive Model

Among the most important economic decisions of households are those about consumption, working, and saving. Each of these decisions is discussed in turn.

THE HOUSEHOLD'S CONSUMPTION DECISION

As we saw in Chapter 2, individuals face a budget constraint. They have a certain amount of money to spend; they can consume more of one good only by consuming less of another. The trade-off is given by relative prices. If the price

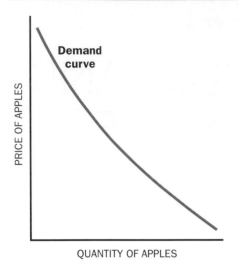

Figure 3.1

DOWNWARD-SLOPING DEMAND CURVE

As the price of any good (here, apples) rises, the quantity demanded of the good decreases.

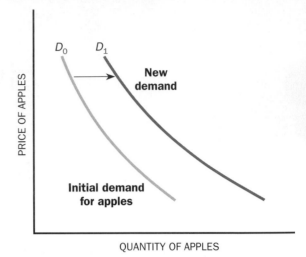

Figure 3.2

SHIFTS IN THE DEMAND CURVE

Changes in income, tastes, or the prices of other goods may lead to a shift in the demand curve for a good.

of apples is twice that of oranges, by giving up one apple, an individual can get two oranges.

Chapter 2 suggested that normally, demand curves are downward sloping, as shown in Figure 3.1; that is, as the price rises, people consume less of a good. There are two reasons for this. First, as the price of apples increases, apples become less attractive relative to oranges and other goods. To get one more apple, Alfred must give up more oranges, so Alfred substitutes oranges (and other fruits) for apples. The reduction in demand resulting from the change in the relative price—to get one more apple, Alfred must give up more oranges—is called the **substitution effect.**

Second, if Alfred spends all or even part of his income on apples, he is worse off when the price of apples increases. He simply cannot buy what he bought before. He is, in this sense, poorer, just as he would be if his income had been reduced. If we define real income as what an individual's income will buy (rather than simply the money received), Alfred's real income has been reduced. When this happens, he spends less on almost every good.[1] The reduction in Alfred's demand for apples resulting from the reduction in real income is called the **income effect.** Both the income and substitution effects lead Alfred to demand fewer apples when their price increases. This is why the demand curve for apples is depicted as downward sloping: at higher prices, fewer apples are demanded.

Chapter 2 identified a number of factors, such as income, tastes, and demographics, that affected the market demand curve. Most importantly, demand in one market is affected by prices determined in other markets. The price of oranges will have an effect on the demand for apples, for instance. On a broader level, the intertwining of

---

[1]There are some exceptions. A good for which demand decreases as income increases is said to be inferior, while goods for which demand increases as income increases are said to be normal. Examples of inferior goods might include cheap cuts of meat, bus travel, and used clothing.

markets is a central feature of macroeconomic analysis; for instance, an increase in wages (as a result of a shift in the demand or supply curves of labor) increases the income that workers have to spend, and thus affects the demand curve for each and every good. Figure 3.2 shows that an increase in income, or a change in tastes or the prices of other goods, may lead to a shift in the demand curve for a good.

SUBSTITUTION AND INCOME EFFECTS

Substitution effect: The reduction in demand resulting from the change in the relative price: the individual substitutes less expensive products for more expensive ones.
Income effect: The reduction in demand resulting from the reduction in real income that occurs when the price of any good rises.

Quantifying the Effects of Price Changes The substitution and income effects explain why demand curves typically are downward sloping. When the demand curve is steep, a given change in price has a relatively small effect on the quantity that is demanded; when the demand curve is flat, a given change in price has a relatively large effect on the quantity demanded. Figure 3.3A illustrates that a given shift in the supply curve has a large effect on price and a small effect on quantity if the demand curve

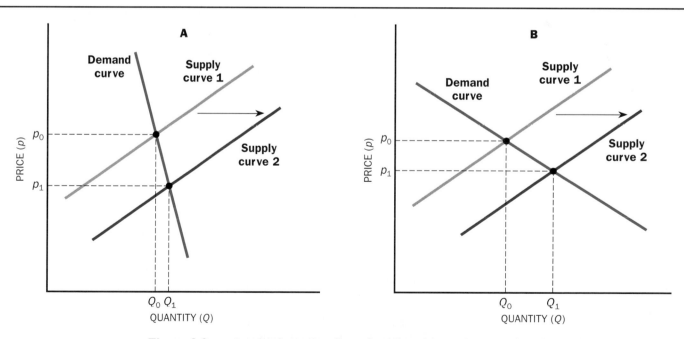

Figure 3.3

DIFFERENT EFFECTS ON PRICE OF A SHIFT IN THE SUPPLY CURVE

Panel A shows the effect of a shift in the supply curve when the demand curve is relatively steep. Panel B shows the effect when the demand curve is relatively flat. The change in the equilibrium price is greater when the demand curve is relatively steep (panel A).

Thinking Like an Economist

INCENTIVES, INCOME EFFECTS, AND SUBSTITUTION EFFECTS

Economists focus on incentives because they want to understand how choices are made. By using the concepts of income and substitution effects, economists are able to analyze the way that prices affect incentives, and therefore choices. The best way to understand income effects and substitution effects—and to begin thinking like an economist—is to use them, as the following example illustrates.

During the winter of 2001, the state of California was hit with an energy shortage. Under laws that partially deregulated the electrical market, the state's major electrical utilities were required to buy electricity on the open market and sell to consumers at prices that were capped. As the cost of wholesale electricity rose sharply, the price the utilities had to pay for electricity soared above what they were allowed to charge their customers. Demand outstripped supply.

When demand exceeds supply, two solutions are possible—increase supply or reduce demand. In a deregulated market system, the price of electricity would have risen, and the higher prices would have provided consumers with the incentive to conserve. A higher price for electricity reduces demand through two channels. As electricity prices rise relative to the prices of other goods purchased by households,

each household has an incentive to economize on electricity. This is the substitution effect. But there is an income effect as well. Because electricity is more expensive, the household's real income is reduced—it has to spend more to obtain the same set of goods (including electricity) that it was consuming. With a reduced real income, the household cuts back its spending on all types of goods, including electricity.

Because higher energy costs may have a disproportionate impact on low-income families, politicians are often reluctant to let energy prices rise. The solution, however, is not to cap prices—keeping prices low simply reduces the incentives of all households to economize on a scarce resource. Instead, suppose the added energy costs for each household average $200. The income effect can be eliminated, while still allowing the substitution effect to do its job in reducing demand, by giving each household a refund of $200. On average, household's real income no longer falls—the impact of higher electricity prices is offset by the refund of $200. But the substitution effect still operates. In spending its income, a household faces a higher relative price of electricity. It therefore still has an incentive to conserve on its use of electricity.

---

is relatively steep. Figure 3.3B illustrates that the same shift in the supply curve has a small effect on price and a large effect on quantity when the demand curve is relatively flat. Economists measure the sensitivity of demand to price changes by the **price elasticity of demand** (for short, the *price elasticity* or the *elasticity of demand*). The price elasticity of demand is defined as the percentage change in the quantity demanded divided by the percentage change in the price. In mathematical terms,

$$\text{elasticity of demand} = \frac{\text{percentage change in quantity demanded}}{\text{percentage change in price}}.$$

If the quantity demanded changes by 8 percent in response to a 2 percent change in price, then the elasticity of demand is 4.

(Price elasticities of demand are really *negative* numbers; that is, when the price increases, the quantity demanded falls. But the convention is to simply refer to the elasticity as an absolute value with the understanding that it is negative.)

It is easiest to calculate the elasticity of demand when the price changes by just 1 percent. Then the elasticity of demand is simply the percentage change in the quantity demanded. For example, if a 1 percent increase in the price of a BMW auto leads to a 3 percent decrease in the quantity demanded, the price elasticity of demand for BMWs is 3. If demand for gasoline falls by 0.5 percent when the price of gasoline increases by 1 percent, then the price elasticity for gas is 0.5.

When price elasticity is less than one, we say that demand is *inelastic;* when price elasticity is greater than one, we say that demand is *elastic.* Demand for necessities, like food, is typically inelastic; demand for luxuries, like expensive cars, is typically elastic. There are two extreme cases. A flat demand curve is perfectly horizontal. We say that such a demand curve is perfectly elastic, or has **infinite elasticity,** since even a slight increase in price results in demand dropping to zero. In contrast, a demand curve that is perfectly vertical is perfectly inelastic, or has **zero elasticity,** since no matter what the change in price, the quantity demanded remains the same.

The Determinants of the Elasticity of Demand One important determinant of the elasticity of demand is the availability of substitutes. The demand for a luxury car may be quite elastic because there are other luxury car brands available. If Lexus increases its prices, its demand may fall significantly as consumers buy cars manufactured by BMW or Mercedes-Benz instead. If you own a car that runs on gasoline, your demand for gas may be quite inelastic as there are no alternative fuels that you can use.

A second factor that determines elasticity of demand is the length of time it takes to make an adjustment. Because it is always easier to find substitutes and to make other adjustments when more time is available to you, elasticity of demand is normally larger in the *long run*—in the period in which all adjustments can be made—than in the *short run,* when at least some adjustments cannot be made. The sharp increase in energy prices during the 1970s provides a good example. In the short run, consumers were stuck with their old gas-guzzling cars, inefficient home furnaces, and poorly insulated houses. In the long run, consumers bought smaller, more fuel-efficient cars, replaced old furnaces with more fuel-efficient models, adjusted to lower average temperatures in their homes, and installed better insulation. The long-run demand curve for energy was therefore much more elastic than the short-run demand curve.

THE HOUSEHOLD'S SAVING DECISION

The same kind of analysis applies to Alfred's decision about how much to save. We can think of this as a decision about how much to consume now and how much to consume in the future. If Alfred reduces his consumption (with a fixed income), he has money left over, which he saves. Suppose he puts this money in a bank (or invests it in some other way) and receives a *return* on his savings. This return is called *interest.* If he puts $1,000 in the bank at the beginning of the year, and the interest rate is 3 percent per year, he will receive $1,030 at the end of the year. The $30 is the payment of interest, while the $1,000 is the repayment of the *principal,* the original amount invested.

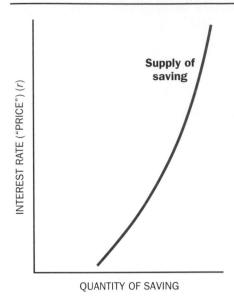

Figure 3.4

THE SUPPLY CURVE FOR SAVING

The supply of saving rises slightly with increases in the interest rate. The substitution effect slightly exceeds the income effect.

To an economist, the interest rate is a price. Economists talk about the relative price of two goods as the amount of one good you have to give up to get one more unit of the other. If the interest rate is 3 percent, then for every dollar of reduced consumption today, you can get $1.03 in the future (one year). Thus, $1.03 is the *relative* price of consumption today versus consumption in the future. If the interest rate rises to 5 percent, consumption today becomes more expensive relative to consumption in the future.

What is the effect on saving of an increase in the interest rate? If Alfred saves, he will have more to consume in the future when the interest rate rises. He is better off. Earlier, we learned that when people's income goes up, they normally consume more of all goods. Likewise, when Alfred is better off, he consumes more now *and* more in the future. This is the income effect of higher interest rates. Alfred consumes more now, which implies that he saves less.

On the other hand, an increase in the interest rate means that future consumption has become less expensive. For each dollar of consumption Alfred gives up today, he gets more consumption in the future; the trade-off has changed. This is the substitution effect, and the substitution effect of higher interest rates leads Alfred to consume less today and more in the future. Thus, an increase in the interest rate has an income effect leading to lower saving and a substitution effect leading to more saving. The net effect is ambiguous, though most studies indicate that on average, the substitution effect slightly outweighs the income effect; saving increases slightly as the interest rate increases. Figure 3.4 shows the supply of saving as a steeply upward-sloping curve.

Expectations A decision about whether to consume today or to consume five years from now is just like the decision about whether to consume apples or oranges. Alfred looks at his preferences and his opportunity set, and especially the trade-offs. But there is an important difference. In making his decisions about the future, Alfred must form expectations. How much he wants to set aside for the future may depend on what he expects his future income, or the prices of his favorite goods, will be.

The Time Value of Money A second important difference between choosing between apples and oranges today and between apples today and apples in the future arises because we express prices in terms of dollars. Because interest rates are normally positive, a dollar today is worth more than a dollar in the future. If the interest rate is 3 percent and you have $1.00 today, you can put it in a bank and receive $1.03 at the end of the year. In short, $1.00 becomes, in this example, $1.03 next year.

Economists call this the *time value of money*. The concept of **present discounted value** tells us precisely how to measure the time value of money. The present discounted value of $100 a year from now is what you would pay today for $100 a year from now. Suppose the interest rate is 10 percent. If you put $90.91 in the bank today, at the end of the year you will receive $9.09 interest, which together with the original amount will total $100. Thus, $90.91 is the present discounted value of $100 a year from now, if the interest rate is 10 percent.

There is a simple formula for calculating the present discounted value of any amount to be received a year from now: just divide the amount by 1 plus the annual rate of interest (denoted by r).

To check this formula, consider the present discounted value of $100. According to the formula, it is $\$100/(1 + r)$. In other words, take the present discounted value, $\$100/(1 + r)$, and put it in the bank. At the end of the year you will have

$$\frac{\$100}{1+r} \times (1+r) = \$100,$$

confirming our conclusion that $\$100/(1 + r)$ today is the same as $100 one year from now.

If the interest rate increases, the present discounted value of $100 a year from now will decrease. If the interest rate should rise to 20 percent, for example, the present discounted value of $100 a year from now becomes $83.33 ($\$100/1.2$).

Understanding present discounted value is important, especially if you win a lottery. We have all heard about the $10 million jackpot lottery winners. What many people do not realize is that the winner does not get $10 million in cash on the spot. Rather, she typically gets a measly $500,000 a year for twenty years. While this is no reason to turn down the prize, its present discounted value is worth much less than

International Perspective

COMPARING REACTIONS TO THE OIL PRICE SHOCK OF 2000

When gasoline prices soared in the fall of 2000, in response to an increase in oil prices, people in Europe took to the streets. Truckers blocked roads and entrances to refineries. There was a massive political outcry. One might have thought that given Americans' greater dependence on oil (Americans use far more gasoline per capita than Europeans) and given that the *percentage* increase in prices in Europe was far smaller (since taxes there constitute a far larger fraction of the total price), the outcry would be louder in the United States. But the difference in reaction brings home an important point: the consequences of the massive price increase depend not only on the level of consumption but also on consumers' ability to absorb the price increase. Europeans already had cut their use of oil down to low levels, because prices they pay for gasoline are so high, and thus may find further cuts in consumption more difficult. Hence, the cost to consumers of a further increase in price may be far greater than when individuals can easily find ways to conserve on the use of oil.

For instance, Americans can easily conserve on gasoline by switching from high-consuming sports utility vehicles, many of which get as few as 15 miles to the gallon, to efficient diesel cars, which can get 50 miles to the gallon or more. Americans can conserve on fuel oil by keeping the temperature in their homes at 68 degrees rather than 72 degrees. But what are Europeans to do, when they already drive small, fuel-efficient cars and already keep their homes at colder temperatures?

These ideas can be related to demand curves. The elasticity of demand is the percentage reduction in the demand resulting from a 1 percent increase in the price. When the price is very low, the demand curve is very elastic; that is, the elasticity of demand is high because there are many ways of conserving on oil. When the price is very high, the demand curve is very inelastic; that is, the elasticity of demand is very low because all of the obvious ways of conserving on oil have already been employed.

$10 million in cash today. Often, the prize winner can choose between $500,000 a year for twenty years or a single cash payment. If the cash payment is $7 million, which should the winner choose?

To make this choice, we need to calculate the present discounted value of the $500,000 each year and compare it to receiving the single payment of $7 million. In calculating the present discounted value of the whole jackpot, we add up the present discounted value of $500,000 next year, plus the present discounted value of $500,000 in two years, plus the present discounted value of $500,000 in three years, and so on. If we assume a 5 percent interest rate, the grand total comes to $6,231,105.17, far less than $10 million in cash today. The winner would be better off taking the $7 million. If the interest rate had been only 3 percent, the present discounted value of $500,000 a year for twenty years would be $7,438,737.43—the winner would have been better off taking the $500,000 per year. (To learn how to do this calculation, see the appendix to this chapter.)

The concept of present discounted value is important because so many decisions in economics are oriented to the future. Whether the decision is made by a person buying a house or saving money for retirement, or by a company building a factory or making an investment, the decision maker must be able to value money that will be received one, two, five, or ten years in the future.

PRESENT DISCOUNTED VALUE

Present discounted value of $1.00 next year $= \dfrac{\$1.00}{1 + \text{interest rate}}$.

Equivalently, denoting the interest rate by r, the right-hand side of the equation becomes $\dfrac{\$1.00}{1 + r}$.

THE COST OF AN AUTO LOAN

The concept of present discounted value plays a key role when intelligent decisions involving time must be made. Take the case of Sarah, who is considering leasing a car. The lease requires her to make a down payment of $2,500 and pay $300 a month for thirty-six months. At the end of thirty-six months, she can buy the car for a final payment of $5,000. Alternatively, she can buy the car today for $15,000. Which is the better deal?

To answer this question, we need to compare the present discounted value of the payments under the lease agreement. Since they occur at different times in the future, we cannot simply add them up. The $5,000 paid in three years is not worth as much as $5,000 today. To calculate the present discounted value, we need to know the interest rate. Suppose Sarah can earn 10 percent per year on her savings if she

PRESENT VALUE CALCULATIONS

The Internet provides several sites that you can use to make present discounted value calculations. If you want to know the present value of a future payment, the calculator at www.unb.ca/web/transpo/mynet/npv.htm allows you to specify the amount, the future date, and the interest rate. It then gives you the present discounted value of the future amount.

The Web site http://learningforlife.fsu.edu/course/fp101/search_frameset.htm provides a convenient table that lets you determine how much you need to discount future dollar amounts. For example, if the interest rate is 5 percent, the table shows that a dollar in 10 years' time is worth 61 cents today and a dollar in 15 years is worth 48 cents today.

does not use the funds to purchase the car today. This is approximately a monthly interest rate of 0.83 percent (10 percent divided by 12), so the first $300 payment in one month has a present discounted value of $300/(1 + 0.0083) = $297.52. The $300 payment in two months is worth $300/(1 + 0.0083)^2 = $295.06, while the final $5,000 payment at the end of three years is worth $3,756.57 ($5,000/(1 + 0.1)^3). When we add up the present discounted value of all the payments under the lease plan, we find they total $15,506 in current dollars. Since Sarah can purchase the car today for $15,000, she saves $506 by buying rather than leasing.

This comparison depends on the interest rate. If the interest rate rises to 15 per cent, the present discounted value of the lease payments falls to $14,351; now it makes sense to take out the lease. A good way to test your understanding of present discounted value is to see if you can explain why the present discounted value of the lease falls as the interest rate rises. When is it better to try to postpone payments, when the interest rate is high or low?

Calculating present discounted values can be complicated when many payments over several periods are involved, as in our car lease example. Spreadsheet programs have built-in functions that enable you to do these calculations quickly. (To obtain the present discounted value of the lease using Excel, for example, simply enter = 2500–pv(10%/12,36,300,5000).)

Inflation and the Real Rate of Interest The interest rate, as we have seen, is a price. It tells how many dollars we can get at a future time if we give up one dollar today. But except for misers like Scrooge or Silas Marner who store money for its own sake, dollars are of value only because of the goods that can be bought with them. Owing to inflation—the increase in prices over time—dollars in the future buy fewer goods than dollars today. In deciding whether to borrow or whether to lend, individuals want to know how much *consumption* they will get tomorrow if they give up a dollar's worth of consumption today. The answer is given by the **real rate of interest.** This is distinguished from the **nominal rate of interest,** the rate one sees posted at a bank or reported in the newspaper, which simply describes the number of dollars one gets next year in exchange for a dollar today.

If the market rate of interest is 6 percent and inflation is 2 percent, part of the 6 percent nominal interest rate represents compensation for the falling value of the dollar. How much? Two percent, since that is the rate at which the value of the dollar is declining. By lending (or saving) a dollar today, you can increase the amount of goods that you get in one year's time by 4 percent.

Consider an individual who decides to deposit $1,000 in a savings account. At the end of the year, at a 6 percent interest rate, she will have $1,060. But suppose meanwhile prices have risen 2 percent. A good that cost $1,000 in the beginning of the year now costs $1,020. In terms of "purchasing power," she has only $40 extra to spend ($1,060 − $1,020)—4 percent more than she had at the beginning of the year. This is her real return. In an inflationary economy, a borrower is in a similar situation. He knows that if he borrows money, the dollars he gives back to repay the loan will be worth less than the dollars he receives today. Thus, what is relevant for individuals to know when deciding either how much to lend (save) or how much to borrow is the *real* interest rate. The real interest rate is what should appear on the vertical axis in Figure 3.4.

The general relationship between the real rate of interest, the market or nominal rate of interest, and inflation is given by

$$\text{real rate of interest} = \text{nominal rate of interest} - \text{inflation.}$$

Elasticity of Supply Earlier, we introduced the concept of demand elasticity to quantify how responsive demand was to price changes. Economists have a similar concept for supply. A steep supply curve, like the supply of saving curve shown in Figure 3.4, means that a large change in price (in this case, the interest rate is the relevant price) generates only a small change in supply. As in our discussion above of demand elasticity, the **price elasticity of supply** is defined as the percentage change in quantity supplied divided by the percentage change in price (or the percentage change in quantity supplied corresponding to a price change of 1 percent):

$$\text{elasticity of supply} = \frac{\text{percentage change in quantity supplied}}{\text{percentage change in price}}.$$

Because the substitute and income effects on saving work to offset each other, the elasticity of supply of savings is low—an increase in the interest rate has only a small effect on the supply of saving. As in the case of demand, if a 1 percent increase in price results in a more than 1 percent increase in supply, we say the supply curve is *elastic;* if a 1 percent increase in price results in less than a 1 percent increase in supply, we say the supply curve is *inelastic.* The supply of saving is inelastic. In the extreme case of a vertical supply curve—where the amount supplied does not depend at all on price—the curve is said to be perfectly inelastic, or to have *zero elasticity.* In the extreme case of a horizontal supply curve, the curve is said to be perfectly elastic, or to have *infinite elasticity.* To simplify our subsequent analysis, we will often assume that the supply of saving has zero elasticity and draw the saving supply curve as a vertical curve.

THE HOUSEHOLD'S LABOR SUPPLY DECISION

We have looked at two of the household's important decisions—how much to consume of different goods and how much to save. A third important decision is how much to work. We can use the same basic reasoning that we employed to analyze the demand for apples and the supply of savings to discuss how much Alfred decides to work. In some jobs, Alfred may have no choice about how many hours he works. If he wants to work for Grinding, Grinders, and Grinders, he may have to put in a sixty-hour week, while if he wants to work for Gnarly Laid-Back Surf Shop, his workweek may be only thirty hours. But the number of hours he wants to work will affect which job he chooses, and economists believe that by and large, employers respond to the preferences of workers. If workers want, on average, shorter workweeks, then over time workweeks will get shorter. In fact, the workweek is considerably shorter today than it was at the beginning of the century.

The question is, What determines how much Alfred would like to work? Again, we need to look at Alfred's opportunity set. If he works less, his income will be lower; he will not be able to consume as much as he otherwise could. In making his decision, he looks at the trade-off: the benefit of the extra leisure time and the cost of the reduced amount of goods he can buy. This trade-off is given by the wage he can earn. The wage is the price of labor, but it is Alfred's **real wage**—the nominal or dollar wage adjusted for the average prices of the goods Alfred buys—that is important. The real wage tells us how much extra consumption Alfred could have if he works an hour more.

What happens when the real wage increases? Again, there is an income effect. Alfred is better off and so would like to consume more of every good. We can view leisure as one of the goods that Alfred will want more of as he becomes better off— that is, as the real wage rises, Alfred will wish to consume more leisure. To do this, he wants to work less. On the other hand, the higher real wage has changed the trade-off. For every hour of leisure he gives up, he now gets, for example, $20 of extra consumption rather than $15. Consumption has become cheaper in terms of leisure. The substitution effect causes him to want to work more. Again, the net effect is ambiguous. For some individuals, the income effect may dominate, and they would reduce their labor supply as the real wage rises. For others, the substitution effect dominates, and they would increase their labor supply as the real wage rises. When we look at the aggregate labor force, however, most studies show that the income and substitution effects are balanced almost precisely. Thus, the aggregate labor supply curve for the economy appears to be fairly steep, as depicted in Figure 3.5. In terms of elasticity, the labor supply curve is inelastic. To simplify our analysis, we will often assume the supply of labor has zero elasticity and draw the labor supply curve as a vertical curve.

To gain leisure time, people must give up working hours and the associated consumption.

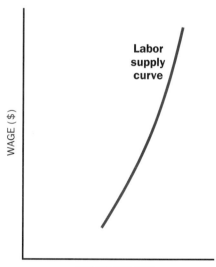

Figure 3.5

THE LABOR SUPPLY CURVE

The supply of labor increases with the wage, but only slightly. The income and substitution effects are almost balanced.

HOUSEHOLD DECISIONS AND INCOME AND SUBSTITUTION EFFECTS

In the product market: A rise in the relative price of a good reduces demand for the good through both income and substitution effects. Because the good costs more, the household is worse off. This income effect causes a fall in the household's demand for all normal goods. Because the good whose price has risen costs more relative to other goods, the substitution effect also causes the household to reduce its demand for the good.

In the capital market: A rise in the real interest rate has opposing income and substitution effects on saving. If the household saves, a higher interest rate means it will have more wealth in the future; the household is better off. This income effect causes the household to increase its consumption of goods today, reducing current saving. An increase in the real interest rate means that future consumption is less expensive. The substitution effect causes the household to increase future consumption by increasing current saving.

In the labor market: A rise in the real wage has opposing income and substitution effects. Since workers are better off when the real wage rises, they will increase their demand for all normal goods, including leisure. So the income effect acts to reduce the supply of labor. The opportunity cost of consuming leisure is higher when the real wage rises, and this causes a substitution away from the now more expensive leisure and toward supplying more labor. Thus, the substitution effect of a rise in the real wage acts to increase labor supply.

Firms in the Basic Competitive Model

Competitive firms maximize their profits.[2] Profits are just revenues minus costs. Revenues are the price of the good the firm produces times the quantity of the good sold. The firm in the basic competitive model believes that it has no effect on price—it takes the market price as given. For instance, any wheat farmer believes that the price of wheat will be unaffected by the amount of wheat he sells. The firm just needs to decide how much to produce.

THE FIRM'S SUPPLY DECISION

In deciding how much to produce, the firm in the competitive model compares the extra revenue it receives from producing one more unit of output—the price—with the extra cost of producing that unit of output, which is called the **marginal cost.** A firm typically has fixed or overhead costs, like rent or the salaries of management, that do not change as production varies. Producing an extra unit of output does not change these costs, so they do not affect marginal costs. However, other costs do increase as output expands—more labor must be hired, and more raw materials

---

[2]Alternatively, we can describe firms as maximizing their market value. To do that, they must maximize their profits. They might be willing to give up some profits today if they think that by doing so, profits in the future will increase enough to compensate.

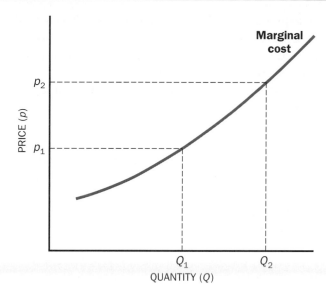

Figure 3.6

THE FIRM'S SUPPLY OF OUTPUT

The supply curve shows the quantity of a good a firm is willing to produce at each price. Normally, a firm is willing to produce more as the price increases, which is why the supply curve slopes upward.

and parts must be bought. Not only do these costs increase as output increases, but they often increase faster than output, at least beyond a certain point. To expand production in the short run, a firm may have to pay wages at overtime rates or utilize its machines for two or three shifts. This is expensive. Thus, marginal cost increases as output rises.

If the price exceeds marginal cost, then the firm can increase its profit by producing one more unit. The additional revenue it receives from selling this additional output—called its **marginal revenue**—exceeds the additional costs from producing it, the marginal cost. As long as marginal revenue is greater than marginal cost, it pays the firm to produce more. If marginal revenue is less than marginal cost, the firm would be better off if it reduced its production. Reducing output by one unit, in this case, lowers the firm's costs more than it reduces its revenues, so profits rise. Profits are maximized when marginal revenue and marginal cost are equal.

In a competitive market, the firm is a price taker. It can sell as much as it would like to at market price. This means that the marginal revenue the firm receives from selling an additional unit is just equal to the market price. So we can restate the condition for profit maximization by saying that a firm in a competitive market will maximize profits when price and marginal cost are equal. Figure 3.6 depicts the firm's marginal cost curve; marginal cost increases as the firm's output increases. If the market price is p_1, the firm will produce output equal to Q_1. At that output level, marginal cost is equal to the market price p_1. If the firm produced an extra unit of output, its profits would fall since the marginal cost of producing that extra unit exceeds the price at which the firm is able to sell it. If the price rises to p_2, the

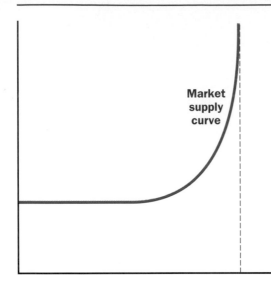

Figure 3.7

THE MARKET SUPPLY CURVE

The figure illustrates a typical shape, with a horizontal portion at price p_0 and an upward-sloping portion beyond that. There is some total capacity of the industry: it simply cannot produce at output beyond Q_C^M.

firm would produce a higher level of output, Q_2. Of course, the firm's total revenue needs to cover all its costs if it is to remain in business. The firm in the competitive model produces the level of output at which price equals marginal costs only if at that price, total revenue equals or exceeds total costs (ignoring sunk costs). If it does not, the firm will supply zero output.

The Market Supply Curve The collection of firms making the same product is called an *industry*. The industry or market supply curve, as we saw in Chapter 2, is found simply by adding up the supply curves of each of the firms in the industry. Figure 3.7 shows the typical upward-sloping shape of a market supply curve. In the figure, the industry cannot produce at an output beyond Q_C^M; this point is referred to as the total *capacity* of the industry. Below this capacity output level, industry supply increases as the price rises.

The Effect of Wage Increases on the Market Supply The amount the industry is willing to supply depends not just on the price it receives. Supply also depends on the marginal costs borne by each firm in the industry. These marginal costs will depend on what the firm must pay for labor and other inputs. Implicitly, we have assumed in the analysis so far that the prices of labor and other inputs are fixed.

An increase in wages (or the price of any other input) shifts the firm's marginal cost curve upward. As a result, the output level ensuring that marginal cost is equal to price is reduced. At each price, the firm produces less. As a result, the supply curve of the industry shifts up.

THE FIRM'S SUPPLY DECISION

Competitive firms produce at the output at which price equals marginal costs, provided that total revenue exceeds total costs. Otherwise, the firm shuts down.

THE FIRM'S DEMAND FOR LABOR AND CAPITAL

The firm's production decision is intimately tied to its demand for labor. At each level of wages and prices, we can calculate the amount firms are willing to supply. But we can also calculate their demand for labor. As wages increase at a given price level, firms' demand for labor will decrease, for two reasons. First, the upward shift in the marginal cost curve means that firms will wish to produce less. With lower levels of production, they will demand less labor. But in addition, if wages increase, labor becomes more expensive relative to other inputs. Firms will thus substitute, where possible, other inputs for labor. In some cases, this may be easy; for instance, some industries can use more machines, or more expensive machines, which require fewer workers to run them. In other cases, it is more difficult.

We can immediately extend this analysis to the industry, and then to the whole economy: as wages increase (at fixed prices), the total amount of labor demanded by all firms together—the market demand for labor—decreases.

Figure 3.8 shows a firm's demand curve for labor, which is downward sloping. It is drawn under the assumption of a given price of output. If the price of output increases, firms will want to produce more; and at the higher level of output, they will want more labor. The demand curve for labor will shift to the right, as depicted in the figure.

Exactly the same kind of analysis applies to the demand for the capital.[3] As the interest rate—the price of using capital—increases, firms' demand for capital decreases; each firm produces less and each firm substitutes other inputs, such as labor, for capital, which has become more expensive.

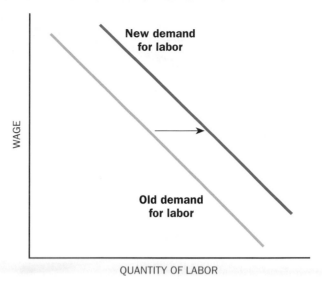

Figure 3.8

THE FIRM'S DEMAND CURVE FOR LABOR

As wages increase, the amount of labor demanded by firms decreases. The demand curve for labor shifts to the right when the price of the good produced by the firm increases.

General Equilibrium

In the previous chapter, we focused on the product market and saw that supply and demand come into balance at an equilibrium price and quantity. In equilibrium, the quantity of goods demanded by consumers equals the quantity supplied by firms. We have seen that capital and labor markets achieve equilibrium in a similar way. In the capital market, saving and investment come into balance at an equilibrium interest rate and quantity; in equilibrium, the amount of saving supplied by households equals the amount of investment demanded by firms. In the labor market, labor supply and demand come into balance at an equilibrium wage and quantity; in equilibrium, the supply of labor by households equals the demand for labor by firms. When all three markets are in equilibrium, the basic economic questions from Chapter 1—What and how much gets produced? By whom? How? For whom?—are resolved through the interactions of households and firms in the marketplace. When all of the economy's central markets have achieved equilibrium in this way, economists say that the economy is in *general equilibrium*.

The basic issues of macroeconomics involve understanding how the central markets of the economy—the product, labor, and capital markets—are interrelated, and how the economy's overall levels of employment, output, and interest rates are determined. When the economy is in general equilibrium, *all* markets, including the labor

---

[3]Recall the discussion of Chapter 1, which pointed out that the term *capital* is used in two different ways: it refers to capital goods—plant and equipment—and to the funds used to purchase these capital goods. Here, we are referring to the latter, to the supply of "funds" made available to firms by households and to the demand for funds by firms to finance their investment.

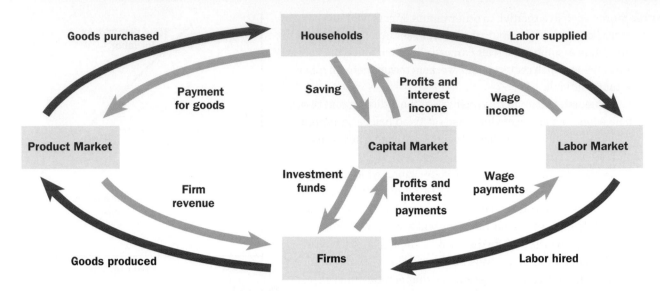

Figure 3.9

A SIMPLE CIRCULAR FLOW DIAGRAM

The simple circular flow diagram can be analyzed from any starting point. For example, funds flow from households to firms in the form of purchases of goods and services and saving. Funds flow from firms to households in the form of payments for the labor of workers, interest, and profits paid to owners.

market, are in equilibrium (often described by saying that all markets clear). In this situation, we describe the economy as being at full employment, since workers are able to supply the amount of labor they desire. Because all markets are interrelated, what goes on in one market may have repercussions throughout the economy. We will analyze a full-employment economy in Part Two.

GENERAL EQUILIBRIUM

The general equilibrium of the economy occurs when all markets clear. The demand for labor equals the supply; the demand for each good equals its supply; and the demand for capital equals the supply.

CIRCULAR FLOWS

The relationships among the various parts of the economy are sometimes illustrated by means of a **circular flow** diagram. Households buy goods and services from firms. Households supply labor and capital to firms. The income individuals receive, whether in the form of wages or the return on their savings, is spent to buy the goods that firms produce.

Figure 3.9 depicts this circular flow for a simplified economy in which there is no government and no foreign trade. Firms hire labor from households and sell goods to households. They also borrow in the capital market to undertake investment projects. The income that firms receive from selling their products goes to pay their workers and to pay interest on the funds they have borrowed. What is left over is paid out to households as profits. Households receive wage, profit, and interest income. They use this income to purchase goods and services from firms. What is left over is their saving, which is lent to firms in the capital market.

A circular flow can be analyzed from any starting point, but let's start in the product market, moving from left to right. Consumers (households) pay money to firms to buy their goods and services, and this money then flows back through the firms to households through the labor market in the form of wages or through the capital market in the form of interest income and profit income. Not only is the circular flow diagram useful in keeping track of how funds move through the economy, but it also enables us to focus on certain balance conditions that must always be satisfied. Thus, the income of households (the flow of funds from firms) must equal the expenditures of households (the flow of funds to firms).

The various balance conditions that make up the diagram are basically identities. *Identities,* as pointed out in Chapter 1, are statements that are always true; they follow from basic definitions of the concepts involved. The interconnections and balance conditions in the diagram are the same as those that arise in the basic competitive model, as discussed earlier in the chapter. But even if the economy is not competitive, the interrelationships and balance conditions of the circular flow diagram are still true. The diagram reminds us that whether the economy is competitive or not, if one element of a balance changes, some other element *must* change. In later chapters we will expand the circular flow diagram to include the government. This will add a new balance condition: the flow of funds into the government from taxes and government borrowing must equal the flow of funds out of the government in the form of spending.

Review and Practice

SUMMARY

1. An increase in the price of a good reduces a person's demand for that good both because of the income effect (the higher price makes the individual worse off, and because she is worse off, she reduces her consumption) and because of the substitution effect (the good is now more expensive *relative* to other goods, so she substitutes other goods).

2. The response of the quantity demanded to changes in price is measured by the price elasticity of demand. If the quantity demanded decreases by more than 1 percent when the price increases by 1 percent, demand is elastic; if the quantity demanded decreases by less than 1 percent when the price increases by 1 percent, demand is inelastic.

3. An increase in the real interest rate has an ambiguous effect on saving and current consumption. The income effect leads to more current consumption (reduced saving), but the substitution effect leads to less current consumption (increased saving). The net effect is probably positive but small, making the saving supply relatively inelastic.

4. A dollar today is worth more than a dollar in the future. That future value in terms of today's dollar is its present discounted value.

5. An increase in the real wage has an ambiguous effect on labor supply. Because individuals are better off, the income effect leads to more leisure (less work). But the substitution effect—the increased consumption made possible by working an additional hour—leads to more work. In practice, the two effects probably just offset each other, making labor supply very inelastic.

6. The typical firm produces at the output at which price equals marginal cost, so long as total revenue equals or exceeds total costs. The typical shape of the market supply curve is relatively horizontal (elastic supply) when output is very low but close to vertical (inelastic supply) as capacity is reached.

7. General equilibrium analysis stresses that all markets are interrelated. Equilibrium occurs when demand equals supply for every good and service and every input; at that point, the product, labor, and capital markets clear.

8. The circular flow diagram shows the flow of funds among the various parts of the economy.

KEY TERMS

substitution effect
income effect
price elasticity of demand
infinite elasticity
zero elasticity
present discounted value
real rate of interest
nominal rate of interest
price elasticity of supply
real wage
marginal cost
marginal revenue
circular flow

REVIEW QUESTIONS

1. Use the concepts of income and substitution effects to explain
   (a) Why the demand curves for goods are normally downward sloping
   (b) Why saving supply may be inelastic
   (c) Why labor supply may be inelastic
2. What are some of the important factors individuals take into account in deciding how much to save?
3. How is the level of output of a firm determined? What is the effect of an increase in wages on the market supply curve?
4. Why may what happens in one market have effects on other markets?
5. What is the circular flow diagram, and what do we learn from it?

PROBLEMS

1. Assume Alfred has $10,000, which he can either consume today or save and consume next year. If the interest rate is 10 percent, how much can he consume next year if he consumes nothing now? Suppose the interest rate falls to 5 percent. Now how much can he consume

next year if he consumes nothing today? Use this example to discuss the income and substitution effects of the decrease in the interest rate.

2. Assume now that Alfred has no income this year, but next year will come into an inheritance of $11,000. The bank is willing to lend money to Alfred at a 10 percent interest rate. How much can he borrow and spend today? How does your answer change if the interest rate charged by the bank falls to 5 percent? Use this example to discuss the income and substitution effects of the decrease in the interest rate; why do both effects work in the same direction?

3. Sam is a senior in high school who is currently not working. He reads in the newspaper that the minimum wage has been increased. How might this news affect his labor supply decision? What is the substitution effect on Sam of the wage increase? What is the income effect on Sam of the wage increase?

4. If Maria is a high school student who is already working part-time, how would her labor supply decision be affected by an increase in the minimum wage? What is the substitution effect on Maria of the wage increase? What is the income effect on Maria of the wage increase?

5. What is the impact on a firm's demand for labor of an increase in the minimum wage?

Appendix: Calculating Present Discounted Value

In the text, we described how to calculate the present discounted value (PDV) of a dollar received a year from now. The present discounted value of a dollar received two years from now can be calculated in a similar way. But how much *today* is equivalent to, say, $100 two years from now? If I were given $PDV today, and I put it in the bank, at the end of the year, I would have PDV(1 + r)$. If I left it in the bank for another year, in the second year I would earn interest on the total amount in the bank at the end of the first year, $r \times$ PDV$(1 + r)$. Therefore, at the end of the two-year period I would have

$$\begin{aligned} \text{PDV}(1+r) + [r \times \text{PDV}(1+r)] \\ = \text{PDV}(1+r)(1+r) \\ = \text{PDV}(1+r)^2. \end{aligned}$$

Thus, the $PDV of $100 in two years is 100/(1+r)^2$. If I put 100/(1+r)^2$ in the bank today, I would have $[\$100/(1+r)]^2 \times (1+r)^2 = \$100$ in two years. In performing these calculations, we have taken account of the interest on the interest. This is called *compound interest*. (By contrast, *simple interest* does not take into account the interest you earn on interest you have previously earned.)

If the rate of interest is 10 percent and is compounded annually, $100 today is worth $110 a year from now and $121 (*not* $120) in two years' time. Thus, the present discounted value today of $121 two years from now is $100. Table 3.1 shows how to calculate the present discounted value of $100 received next year, two years from now, and three years from now.

Table 3.1

PRESENT DISCOUNTED VALUE OF $100

Year received	Present discounted value
Next year	$\frac{1}{1+r} \times 100 = \frac{100}{1+r}$
Two years from now	$\frac{1}{1+r} \times \frac{100}{1+r} = \frac{100}{(1+r)^2}$
Three years from now	$\frac{1}{1+r} \times \frac{100}{(1+r)^2} = \frac{100}{(1+r)^3}$

We can now see how to calculate the value of an investment project that will yield a return over several years. We look at what the returns will be each year, adjust them to their present discounted values, and then add these values up.

Table 3.2

CALCULATING PRESENT DISCOUNTED VALUE OF A THREE-YEAR PROJECT

Year	Return	Discount factor ($r = 0.10$)	Present discounted value ($r = 0.10$)
1	10,000	$\frac{1}{1.10}$	$ 9,091
2	15,000	$\frac{1}{(1.10)^2} = \frac{1}{1.21}$	$12,397
3	50,000	$\frac{1}{(1.10)^3} = \frac{1}{1.331}$	$37,566
Total	$75,000	—	$59,054

Table 3.2 shows how this is done for a project that yields $10,000 next year and $15,000 the year after, and that you plan to sell in the third year for $50,000. The second column of the table shows the return in each year. The third column shows the discount factor—what we multiply the return by to obtain the present discounted value of that year's return. The calculations assume an interest rate of 10 percent. The fourth column multiplies the return by the discount factor to obtain the present discounted value of that year's return. In the bottom row of the table, the present discounted values of each year's return have been added up to obtain the total present discounted value of the project. Notice that it is much smaller than the number we obtain simply by adding up the returns, which is the "undiscounted" yield of the project.

Learning Goals

In this chapter, you will learn

1 What gross domestic product (GDP) is

2 The three ways we can measure GDP

3 The difference between nominal and real GDP

4 How the unemployment rate is measured

5 The four types of unemployment

6 What the natural rate of unemployment is

7 What Okun's Law tells us

Chapter 4

MEASURING OUTPUT AND UNEMPLOYMENT

Every month, when the United States Bureau of Labor Statistics releases its latest figures on the unemployment rate, newspapers and the radio and TV news give them significant coverage. The same is true when new data on economic growth become available. Measures of unemployment and of growth in the economy are yardsticks that are used to gauge economic performance. Such yardsticks help analysts judge how successful economies have been in achieving such policy goals as low unemployment and strong growth. In addition to being frequent topics in the news, many of the most common economic yardsticks—the gross domestic product, the unemployment rate, and the consumer price index—figure prominently in political debates and presidential election campaigns.

In this chapter, we discuss what economists mean by the gross domestic product, what it measures, and how the government goes about actually measuring it. Then, we turn to the unemployment rate and examine how it is measured. Without an understanding of these common yardsticks, we cannot assess their strengths and weaknesses as measures of economic performance. It is especially important to understand the weaknesses of our measures so that we do not make errors in assessing economic conditions. The issues that arise in measuring inflation, another key indicator of economic performance, are discussed in the following chapter.

Measuring Output and Growth

To gauge the economy's success in raising living standards, we need to start by understanding how we measure the total output of the economy. We will learn later in this chapter that the aggregate income of the economy is equal to the aggregate output of goods and services that the economy has produced. Measuring output is our starting point for assessing the economy's performance.

GROSS DOMESTIC PRODUCT

The output of the economy consists of millions of different goods and services. We could report how much of each good or service the economy produced. This would yield a list that might include 1,362,478 hammers, 473,562,382 potatoes, 256,346 heart operations, and so forth. Such a list might be useful for some purposes, but it would not provide us with the information we want. If the following year the number of hammers produced goes up by 5 percent, the potato crop yield goes down by 2 percent, and the number of heart operations performed rises by 7 percent, has the economy's total output gone up or down? And by how much?

We need a single number that summarizes the output of the economy. But how do we add up hammers, potatoes, heart operations, and the millions of other products produced in the economy? We do this by totaling the *money value* of all the *final* goods and services produced. By money value, we mean the dollar value of output. By final goods and services, we mean those goods and services sold for final usage and not those used to make other products. Since the money value of hammer production and the money value of heart operations are in the same units (dollars), we can add them together. The money value of final output is called the **gross domestic product,** or **GDP.** It is the standard measure of the value of the output in an economy. It sums up the total money value of the final goods and services produced within a nation's borders during a given time period, usually a year. It makes no difference whether the production takes place in the private or public sector, or whether the goods and services are purchased by households, the government, or the foreign sector.[1]

GROSS DOMESTIC PRODUCT

The total money value of all final goods and services produced for the marketplace within a nation's borders during a given period of time (usually a year).

Table 4.1 illustrates the calculation of GDP for a simple economy that produces just two goods, personal computers (PCs) and compact discs (CDs). The table shows the number of PCs and CDs produced in two different years, and the average prices at which they were sold. GDP in year 1 is found by multiplying the quantities of each good sold in year 1 by its price in year 1. This gives the money value of PC and CD production. Adding the resulting money values together gives us GDP for this economy. Using the data in the table, we calculate GDP to be $2,550 million in year 1 and $2,985 million in year 2. GDP grew by 17 percent—100($2,985–$2,550)/$2,550—from year 1 to year 2.

---

[1] We use prices not only because they are a convenient way of making comparisons but also because they reflect how consumers value different goods. If the price of an orange is twice that of an apple, it means an orange is worth twice as much (at the margin) as an apple.

Table 4.1

CALCULATING GDP

		Prices and Quantities		
Year	Price of PCs	Quantity of PCs	Price of CDs	Quantity of CDs
1	$1,800.00	1.0 million	$15.00	50.0 million
2	$1,850.00	1.2 million	$17.00	45.0 million
GDP in year 1	= value of PCs + value of CDs = $1,800 × 1.0 million + $15 × 50.0 million = $2,550 million.			
GDP in year 2	= value of PCs + value of CDs = $1,850 × 1.2 million + $17 × 45.0 million = $2,985 million.			

Nominal vs. Real GDP There is one problem with using money as a measure of the economy's output. The value of a dollar changes over time. Candy bars, books, movie tickets, hammers, and heart operations all cost more today than they did ten years ago. We do not want to be misled into believing the economy is producing more when, in fact, prices may simply have risen. In our example from Table 4.1, for instance, one of the reasons why GDP was higher in year 2 than in year 1 was that the prices of the two goods were higher. Even if output had remained unchanged in year 2 at 1.0 million PCs and 50.0 million CDs, GDP would have risen to $2,700 million simply because prices rose.

To keep the comparisons of different years straight, economists adjust GDP for changes in the average level of prices. Unadjusted GDP is known as **nominal GDP;** that is what we calculated in Table 4.1. The term **real GDP** is used for the GDP numbers that have been adjusted for changes in the general level of prices. Real GDP gives a truer year-to-year measure of how much the economy actually produces. One way to think of real GDP is to ask, What would GDP be if all prices had remained unchanged? That is, from the example in Table 4.1, we could ask what GDP would have been in year 2 if prices had remained unchanged from year 1. Table 4.2 gives us the answer. Real GDP in year 2 using year 1 prices is $2,835 million. Since we are using the same prices to make this comparison, the measure of real GDP changes only if the quantities of the goods produced change. In this example, real GDP ($2,835 million) is less than nominal GDP ($2,985 million from Table 4.1), and this tells us that part of the increase in nominal GDP that we found in Table 4.1 reflected price increases. When we use year 1 prices to calculate real GDP in subsequent years, year 1 is called the *base year*.

When economists talk about adjusting nominal GDP for price changes to obtain a measure of real GDP, they say they "deflate" nominal GDP using a measure of the average level of prices called a *price index*. The price index for GDP is called the **GDP**

Table 4.2

NOMINAL AND REAL GDP

Real GDP (using year 1 as the base year): 　　real GDP in year 1　　= \$2,550 million 　　real GDP in year 2　　= \$1,800 × 1.2 million + \$15 × 45.0 million 　　　　　　　　　　　　= \$2,835 million.
Price index (GDP deflator) using year 1 as base year: 　　GDP deflator, year 1　= 100 　　GDP deflator, year 2　= 100 × (year 2 nominal GDP)/(year 2 real GDP) 　　　　　　　　　　　　= 100 × (2,985/2,835) 　　　　　　　　　　　　= 105.3.
Deflating nominal GDP: 　　　　　　　　　　real GDP in year 2　　= nominal GDP/price index 　　　　　　　　　　　　　　　　　　　　= \$2,985/1.053 = \$2,835 billion.

deflator. As we have already seen, nominal GDP reflects changes in prices and quantities, while real GDP is a measure of how much quantities have changed. Real GDP can be defined by the equation

$$\text{real GDP} = \frac{\text{nominal GDP}}{\text{price index}}.$$

If nominal GDP has risen by 3 percent in the past year but prices have also risen by 3 percent, then real GDP would be unchanged. Since we have calculated nominal GDP and real GDP for the economy of Tables 4.1 and 4.2, we can determine that the price index must equal 1.053 (see Table 4.2). This is normally reported as 105.3 (so in the base year the price index is equal to 100), indicating that for this example, prices rose by 5.3 percent from year 1 to year 2.

This approach encounters a problem when *relative* prices change dramatically. If the price of computers falls rapidly as the output of computers increases—as has happened over the past two decades—then real output, using an earlier base year such as 1987, may be distorted. The large increases in computer production are valued at the high prices that existed earlier. Doing so places a high value on computer output, and GDP will look as if it is increasing very rapidly. When the base year used to calculate real GDP is changed—as it is periodically—the growth of the economy will appear to diminish suddenly; in the *new* base year, computer prices are lower, so each computer "counts" for less in GDP. Of course, the growth of the economy did not really diminish; it was only that our previous yardstick distorted the picture.

To address this problem, the Bureau of Economic Analysis (BEA), the agency in the Department of Commerce responsible for the GDP numbers, changed its approach in January 1996. It now provides a measure called the chain-weighted real GDP, which is designed to avoid some of the problems that arise when the prices of certain goods, such as computers, change greatly from the base year.

MEASURING GDP: THE VALUE OF OUTPUT

The general accounting system we use to measure GDP is called the National Income and Product Accounts (NIPA) and is produced by the Bureau of Economic Analysis. In the national income accounts, there are three approaches to measuring GDP (whether real or nominal), each of which yields the same result. Two concentrate on output data. The third—relying on the fact that the value of output becomes income to someone—uses income figures to obtain a measure of output.

The Final Goods Approach On the face of it, measuring GDP is a straightforward task; we gather together the dollar value of all goods and services sold in a country and then add them up. Unfortunately, matters are not this simple, because it is first necessary to distinguish between final goods and intermediate goods. Final goods—such as automobiles, books, bread, and shoes—are sold for final use by consumers, firms, the government, or foreigners. Intermediate goods are used to produce outputs—like coal used to make steel or silica used to make silicon computer chips. A good such as a blank CD can be either a final good or an intermediate good, depending on how it is used. The **final goods approach** used to measure GDP adds up the total dollar value of goods and services produced, categorized by their ultimate users.

The reason why it is so important to distinguish between final and intermediate goods is that the value of the final goods *includes* the value of the intermediate goods that went into making the final goods. When Ford sells a truck for $25,000, that figure may include $250 worth of Uniroyal tires. It would be double counting to list both the value of the truck and the value of the tires on the truck in GDP. Likewise for steel, plastic, and other components that go into making the truck. In fact, cases in which some intermediate goods are used to produce other intermediate goods could lead to even triple or quadruple counting.

One way of calculating the value of the final goods produced in the economy is to consider where those goods go. There are four possibilities. Some of the final goods are consumed by individuals—we call this aggregate *consumption* (and we include all consumption goods, regardless of where they are produced—we will see later how we correct for goods produced in other countries). Some are used by firms to build buildings and make machines—this is called aggregate *investment* (again, we include all investment goods that firms purchase, regardless of where they are

Internet Connection

THE BUREAU OF ECONOMIC ANALYSIS

The home page of the Bureau of Economic Analysis can be found at www.bea.gov. You can find the latest GDP data at this site.

produced). Some are *government purchases.* And some of the goods, called *exports,* go to other countries. If we did not import any goods (that is, buy goods produced in other countries), then GDP would simply consist of goods that went for private consumption, private investment, government purchases, or exports. But not all such goods are produced in this country. For instance, many consumer electronics and automobiles that individuals purchase are produced in other countries. To calculate GDP using the final goods approach, we therefore need a final step of subtracting the amount imported. Thus,

$$GDP = C + I + G + X - M,$$

where C is consumption, I is investment, G is government purchases, X is exports, and M is imports. The difference between exports and imports is referred to as *net exports.* This equation is an *identity;* that is, it is always true (by definition) that the GDP equals consumption plus investment plus government purchases plus net exports.

But what, you might ask, about goods produced during a given year that are still unsold at its end? The value of these goods should be counted in GDP—after all, they were produced during the year—but how can they be counted in final sales if the firms that produced them have not sold them by December 31? An example will help illustrate how this problem is solved in the National Income and Product Accounts. Suppose Dell Computer produces a new laptop on December 1, 2004, but the laptop has not been sold by the end of the year. Instead, it remains in the firm's inventory. This is treated by NIPA as a final sale to the firm itself—it is as if Dell purchased the laptop for its own use. The increase in firms' inventories is counted as part of final sales to firms and included in investment. If Dell sells the laptop to a consumer in January 2005, the sale adds to consumption but it *reduces* inventory holdings. Thus, when we add together consumption purchases and inventory investment, the two transactions cancel each other out—the laptop is correctly counted in 2004 GDP and not in 2005 GDP.

The final goods approach to calculating GDP in the United States can be illustrated using the figures for 2003. According to the Bureau of Economic Analysis,[2] the values for the components of GDP were as follows:

Category	Billions of $
Consumption	7,609.8
+ Investment	1,596.6
+ Government purchases	2,041.4
+ Exports	1,019.8
– Imports	1,523.0
= GDP	10,744.6

By adding these components together, we find that the value of all final goods and services produced within the borders of the United States during 2003 was $10,744.6 billion.

[2]www.bea.gov.

Wrap-Up

GDP equals consumption plus investment plus government purchases plus exports minus imports.

Case in Point

IS SOFTWARE A FINAL GOOD OR AN INTERMEDIATE GOOD?

Measuring output might seem straightforward when the economy produces cars and wheat and houses, but what happens when it produces ideas? The new technologies and the new economy they have created have forced the economists and statisticians at the Bureau of Economic Analysis to revise the National Income and Product Accounts. Such updates and revisions are nothing new; the bureau is always trying to improve its estimates of economic activity. However, the new economy has created some unique problems. One of the major changes in the *1999 Comprehensive Revision of the National Income and Product Accounts* dealt with how software is treated in GDP. Thinking about the correct way to measure the price and quantity of software highlights the differences between final and intermediate goods.

Prior to the new revisions, business and government expenditures on software were treated inconsistently. Software that was bundled in a product—a suite of office software programs such as a word processor and spreadsheet that was installed on a computer, for instance—was treated as a final good and included as an investment. After all, the computer is an investment good, and the value of the software installed on it represents part of its value. If a business purchased the software separately to install on a computer, however, it was treated as an intermediate good. The same was true of software a business produced itself. The costs a business incurred in producing software for its own use was treated as a business expense similar to that for any other intermediate good.

Under the new rules, all software expenditures are treated as investment spending. This is appropriate because software, like other investment goods, produces a flow of services that lasts more than one year. In fact, the Bureau of Economic Activity estimates that the average life of software is between three and five years. The effects of these new rules will be to raise GDP by the amount of software businesses and government agencies purchase and by the amount of software they produce for their own use. These expenditures were not counted as part of GDP when they were viewed as intermediate goods. By treating them as a final good, GDP is increased by the amount spent on them.

How much difference does this make? The revisions boosted GDP during the late 1990s by more than $100 billion per year. This is a large number, but it represents a change in GDP of only around 1 percent.

The Value-Added Approach A second way to calculate the value of GDP is to study the intermediate goods directly. The production of most items occurs in several stages. Consider the automobile. At one stage in its production, iron ore, coal, and limestone are mined. At a second stage, these raw materials are shipped to a steel mill. A third stage involves a steel company combining these ingredients to make steel. Finally, the steel and other inputs such as rubber and plastics are combined by the auto firm to make a car. The difference in value between what the automaker pays for intermediate goods and what it receives for the finished cars is called the firm's **value added.**

value added = firm's revenue − costs of intermediate goods.

GDP can be measured by calculating the value added at each stage of production.

GDP = sum of value added of all firms.

The Income Approach The third method used to calculate GDP involves measuring the income generated by selling products, rather than the value of the products themselves. This is known as the **income approach.** Firms have four claims on their revenue. They must pay for labor they have hired, pay interest on any funds they have borrowed, pay for any intermediate goods they have purchased, and pay indirect taxes such as sales taxes to the government. Anything left over represents the firm's income. Some income must be set aside to replace equipment worn out during the production process (called *depreciation,* which we will discuss later), and the rest is the firm's profit.

revenue = wages + interest payments + cost of intermediate
inputs + indirect taxes + depreciation + profits.

But we already know that the firm's value added is its revenue minus the cost of intermediate goods. Therefore,

value added = wages + interest payments +
indirect taxes + depreciation + profits.

And since GDP is equal to the sum of the value added of all firms, it must also equal the sum of the value of all wage payments, interest payments, indirect taxes, depreciation, and profits for all firms:[3]

GDP = wages + interest payments +
indirect taxes + depreciation + profits.

People receive income from wages, from capital, and from profits of the firms they own (or own shares in). And when firms spend to replace old equipment, that

---

[3]This ignores a few small adjustments such as net income payments from the rest of the world and net subsidies to government enterprises.

spending represents income for those who produce the new equipment. Thus, the right side of this identity is the total income of all individuals and the government revenue from indirect taxes. This is an extremely important result, one economists use frequently, so it is worth highlighting: *aggregate output equals aggregate income.*

Differences Between Individual Incomes and National Income

The notion of income used to calculate GDP differs slightly from the way individuals commonly think about income, and it is important to be aware of the distinction.

First, people are likely to include in their view of income any capital gains they earn on assets. *Capital gains* are increases in the value of assets and accordingly do not represent current production (output) in any way. The national income accounts used to calculate GDP do not include capital gains.

Second, profits that are retained by a firm are included in national income, but individuals may not perceive these retained profits as part of their own income. Again, this is because the GDP accounts measure the value of production, and profits are part of the value of production, whether these profits are actually distributed to the owners of the firm (its shareholders) or are retained by the firm.

Comparison of the Final Goods and Income Approach As Table 4.3 shows, the value of GDP is the same whether it is calculated in terms of final goods output or in terms of income. It is no accident that the two approaches to measuring GDP lead to identical results; it is a consequence of the circular flow of the economy. Every dollar of revenue each firm receives after paying for its intermediate inputs is paid out in the form of wages, profits, interest, rents, or indirect taxes. Income flows back to firms when households purchase consumption goods or when household saving is borrowed by firms to purchase investment goods, such as plant and equipment, or by the government to spend in excess of its tax revenues.

Table 4.3

TWO APPROACHES TO U.S. GDP, 2003

Final Goods	Billions of $	Income	Billions of $
Consumption	7,609.8	Employee compensation	6,179.1
Investment	1,596.6	Profits, rents, interest, etc.	2,448.0
Government expenditures	2,041.4	Indirect taxes	783.5
Net exports	−503.2	Depreciation	1,334.0
Total	**10,744.6**	**Total**	**10,744.6**

SOURCE: www.bea.doc.gov/bea/dn1.htm.

POTENTIAL GDP

Real GDP is a measure of how much the economy actually produces. But sometimes workers may not be fully employed, and some plants and equipment may be operating at less than normal capacity. At other times, the economy may produce more than would normally be sustainable. Firms may put on extra shifts, increase overtime, and delay maintenance in order to temporarily increase output. Another important macroeconomic measure of real output, **potential GDP,** indicates what the economy would produce if labor were fully employed at normal levels of overtime and if plants and machines were used at their normal rates. Real GDP will fall below potential GDP when the economy has above-normal levels of unemployed resources.

In some circumstances, real GDP can exceed potential GDP by a considerable amount. Even when the economy is operating at its normal potential, some unused capacity remains. By fully utilizing this capacity, the economy's real GDP can temporarily exceed its potential. Individuals may be willing to temporarily put in extra overtime; other workers may take a second job when the labor market is particularly strong. Such steps enable real GDP to be greater than would occur at more normal levels of utilization and work hours. One common example of actual production greatly exceeding the economy's normal potential is when a country mobilizes for war. Figure 4.1 shows how real GDP and potential GDP have increased over the past forty years. Output does not grow smoothly; the jagged progression in the figure shows the effects of short-term fluctuations around an upward trend. Sometimes these fluctuations

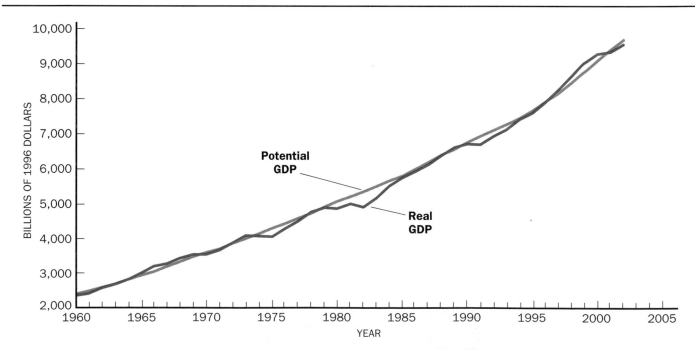

Figure 4.1

POTENTIAL AND REAL GDP

Potential GDP measures how much the economy would produce if it used all its resources at normal levels of overtime and capacity utilization. Real GDP shows what the economy actually produces. Notice that both have been growing over time.

SOURCES: Bureau of Economic Analysis and Congressional Budget Office.

WHAT GETS MEASURED IN THE GDP?

In the United States, illegal activity is not counted as part of GDP. If we are trying to get a measure of market economic activity, excluding occupations like the drug trade means that GDP misses one type of output. For the United States, this omission is unlikely to have a major impact on the usefulness of GDP statistics. But if illegal activity is a major source of income in a given country, then failing to count that income as part of GDP may give a misleading picture of its economy.

Colombia provides a case in point. Colombia is a major exporter of illegal drugs. Drugs are grown, processed, and transported. Each of these steps represents economic activity, yet the incomes generated directly by the trade in illegal drugs have been excluded from its GDP.

The Colombian government has begun to add income earned from illegal drug crops to GDP. It is estimated that treating drug crops like legal crops in this calculation may add as much as 1 percent to Colombia's GDP. The drug trade involves much more than just growing the crops—processing and transporting them are also huge businesses. But as of now, those aspects are omitted from Colombia's GDP. Including them would increase the drug trade's impact on the figures.

While adding even part of the value of drug-related income will raise Colombia's reported GDP, the new figure does not mean the country's income is any higher—it simply means that more of it is being counted in the official statistics. The change does highlight an important point, however. Often the exact definition of a statistic changes over time, or the methods used to collect the data change. Variables that have the same name in two different countries may not measure quite the same thing. We must keep these possible variations in mind when making international comparisons of GDP, especially

For sound economic reasons, Colombia includes the illegal coca leaf crop in its calculation of GDP.

when comparing economies that are quite different. If a particular type of economic activity—say, bread making—is done through markets in one economy and at home in another, bread consumption as measured in GDP will be higher in the former.

Robert Summers and Alan Heston carried out one of the best attempts to construct consistent international data on GDP. Their data, known as the Penn World Table, are available on the Web at http://pwt.econ.upenn.edu/.

---

represent only a slowdown in real growth; sometimes output actually falls. The dips in real GDP from 1971 to 1973, from 1980 to 1981, from 1990 to 1991, and in 2001 represent periods when U.S. economic output actually declined. A strong upward fluctuation is called a **boom,** and a downward one is called a **recession.** A severe recession is called a **depression.** The last depression, called the Great Depression because of its length and depth, began in 1929. The economy did not fully recover until World War II. While there is no technical definition of a boom, a recession is generally said to have occurred when real GDP falls for at least two consecutive quarters. (For statistical purposes, a year is divided into quarters, each three months long.)

Low utilization of capacity, like the unemployment of workers, represents a waste of scarce economic resources. In recessions the economy operates well below its potential. Unemployment is high and a large fraction of machines remain idle or underutilized.

Because the difference between the actual level of GDP the economy produces and its potential level of GDP is an important measure of fluctuations, economists have a special name for it. The percentage difference between GDP and potential GDP is called the **output gap.** When the economy is in a recession, actual GDP is less than potential and the output gap is negative. If actual GDP is greater than potential, the output gap is positive. The output gap will play an prominent role in Part Three when we examine economic fluctuations in more detail.

ALTERNATIVE APPROACHES TO MEASURING GDP

Measuring the value of output:
    consumption + investment + government purchases + net exports
    sum of value added in each stage of production
Measuring income:
    employee compensation + profits, interest, rents + indirect taxes + depreciation
Output = income

PROBLEMS IN MEASURING OUTPUT

The U.S. economy is constantly changing—new industries emerge, old industries decline, new technologies lead to new products and different methods of production. Does the way our economy is being fundamentally altered by new technologies mean that economists will need to rethink how we measure the economy's output? Three problems cause particular difficulties for measuring output.

Measuring Quality Changes With many products, such as computers, improvements in quality occur every year. GDP statisticians try to make adjustments for these changes in quality. But in some sectors, such as the financial and health sectors and the computer industry, the adjustments may be inadequate. Because these sectors are expanding rapidly, the magnitude of the real growth of GDP may be understated.

Measuring Service Output Defining and measuring output in the service sector of the economy are increasingly complex and difficult tasks. Because the service sector is a growing share of the economy, the conventional GDP measure may understate the real growth of the economy.

Measuring Nonmarket Goods Nonmarket goods and services, such as housework done by family members, also present problems. The statistics underestimate the true level of production in the economy, because they ignore such activity. While GDP is designed primarily to measure only market economic activity, there are two important exceptions to this restriction. GDP does include a measure of the value of owner-occupied housing, and it includes the value of homegrown food consumed by farm families. In general, though, nonmarket activity is not included, because without prices a value cannot be assigned to the output.

Conclusions GDP provides our best estimate of the level of production for markets. But changes in the nature of production, from growth in the underground economy to new technological innovations, can affect the ability of GDP to provide an accurate picture of the economy's performance.

MEASURING THE STANDARD OF LIVING

GDP tells us something about the overall level of economic activity in a nation, the goods and services produced for the market. But it is only a partial measure of a society's overall well-being. Literacy rates (the percentage of the population that can read or write), infant mortality rates (the fraction of infants that die), and life expectancy are other social indicators that are often employed in attempts to gauge a nation's standard of living. Real GDP does not take into account these other important components. But at the same time, there is a strong connection between high levels of real GDP per capita and high levels of literacy, high levels of health, and high environmental quality. People in countries that are rich as measured by real GDP per capita are able to enjoy better health, longer life expectancy, higher levels of education, cleaner water, and cleaner air than can people in poor countries.

A GREEN GDP

The national income accounts do not take note of the depletion of the stock of natural resources or the deterioration in the quality of the environment that producing GDP may cause. Harvesting a hardwood forest may increase a country's GDP, but it decreases the country's assets. The output is not sustainable—a fact that a "green GDP" would recognize by subtracting the decrease in the natural resource base from conventional GDP. Such a measure would better indicate whether an economic activity is adding to the nation's wealth or subtracting from it by using up natural resources. A measure of living standards, unlike a measure of goods and service produced for the marketplace, should include changes in the quality of the environment, as well as changes in such factors as levels of health and of crime.

Constructing a means of calculating a green GDP is difficult. Compare the problem of measuring the value of auto production with the problem of measuring the value of the decline in the California sea otter population. In the former case, we can collect statistics on the number of cars produced, and we can use the prices we observe in the marketplace to assign a value to that production. In contrast, while

Green GDP takes account of exhausted natural resources, such as this clear-cut section of forest near Willamette National Forest in Oregon.

we may be able to measure the drop in the otter population, how do we value this decline? There is no market price that we can use. And unless we can value the change in the otter population, the change in old-growth forests, the change in air quality, and the production of cars in a common measure (say dollars), we cannot add them up to obtain an overall measure of a green GDP. So developing an environmental measure of the economy's production is inherently problematic.

Unemployment

Discussions of unemployment frequently take center stage during presidential elections. In the 1992 campaign, two slogans that struck a responsive cord were "Jobs, Jobs, Jobs" and "It's the economy, stupid!" During the 2000 campaign, Vice President Al Gore emphasized the economy's strong performance over the previous eight years. In the 2004 election, candidates focused on the "jobless recovery." The unemployment rate is the most common measure of the economy's performance in creating jobs.

Though the central economic goal over the long run is to increase living standards, unemployment becomes a source of immediate concern when the economy goes into a downturn. Unemployment represents an underutilization of resources. People who are willing and able to work at current market wages are not being productively employed. To the unemployed individuals and their families, unemployment represents economic hardship. People unemployed for a long time will be unable to meet current expenses—utilities, rent, and so on—and will have to move to less-expensive housing and otherwise reduce their standard of living.

Unemployment not only costs individuals their paychecks, it can deal a powerful blow to their self-respect, and their families may be forced to choose between poverty and the bitter taste of government or private charity. Many families break up under the strain.

Unemployment presents each age group of workers with different problems. For the young, having a job is necessary to develop job skills. Persistent unemployment for them not only wastes valuable human resources today but also reduces the future productivity of the labor force. Young people who remain unemployed for an extended period are especially prone to becoming alienated from society and turning to antisocial activities such as crime and drug abuse.

For the middle-aged or elderly worker, losing a job poses different problems. Despite federal and state prohibitions against age discrimination, employers are often hesitant to hire older applicants. If older workers are unemployed for long periods of time, they may lose some of their skills. And the job that the unemployed older worker does succeed in getting often entails lower wages and less status than previous jobs and may make less than full use of his or her skills. Such changes burden the dislocated workers and their families with much stress.

Unemployment is very costly to communities as well. If people in a town are thrown out of work—say, because a big employer closes down or decides to move—their neighbors are also likely to suffer, since there is less income circulating to buy everything from cars and houses to gasoline and groceries. As higher unemployment results in fewer people paying local taxes, the quality of schools, libraries, parks, and police can be threatened.

Unemployment also may reinforce racial divisions in a society. The rate of unemployment for African Americans is generally more than twice that for whites. By 2000, with overall unemployment at its lowest level in thirty years, all groups were benefiting from the strong labor market—unemployment for African Americans was lower than at any time since 1969. As the economy entered a recession in 2001, unemployment rates for all groups rose. By the end of 2002, the unemployment rate for African Americans peaked at 11.4 percent, while white unemployment was only 5.2 percent. The economy was starting to recover by 2002, but unemployment had declined only modestly by the end of 2003. By December 2004, though, the unemployment rate for whites had fallen to 4.6 percent, while the rate for African Americans was still over 10 percent.

UNEMPLOYMENT STATISTICS

In the United States, unemployment data are collected by the Department of Labor, which surveys a representative mix of households every month. The survey takers ask each household whether a member of the household is currently employed, and if not, whether that member is currently seeking employment. The *labor force* is the total number of people employed or actively seeking employment. The **unemployment rate** is the ratio of the number seeking employment to the total

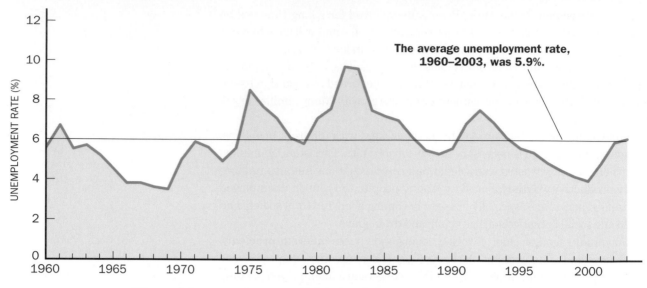

Figure 4.2

OVERALL U.S.
UNEMPLOYMENT RATE

Unemployment in the United States rises during recessions and falls during booms. Between 1960 and 2003, it averaged 5.9 percent. It reached a low of 3.5 percent during 1969 and a high of 9.7 percent in 1982.

SOURCE: *Economic Report of the President* (2004).

labor force. If there are 127 million workers employed and 6 million say they are looking for a job but cannot find one, then the total labor force is 133 million, and the

$$\text{unemployment rate} = \frac{\text{number unemployed}}{\text{labor force}}$$

$$= \frac{\text{number unemployed}}{\text{number employed} + \text{number unemployed}}$$

$$= \frac{6 \text{ million}}{127 \text{ million} + 6 \text{ million}} = 4.5 \text{ percent.}$$

The unemployment rate does not include individuals who are not working but who also are not actively seeking a job. Such individuals are not counted as part of the labor force.

Figure 4.2 plots the unemployment rate for the United States since 1960. The figure illustrates two facts. First, unemployment is persistent; it has averaged just under 6 percent since 1960, and the lowest it has been during this period was 3.5 percent (in 1969). Second, the level of unemployment can fluctuate dramatically. By the end of the 1990s, unemployment in the United States had fallen to levels not seen in thirty years, but as recently as 1983, the unemployment rate was nearly 10 percent. Fluctuations in unemployment were even more pronounced in earlier periods. In the worst days of the Great Depression of the 1930s, more than one-fourth of

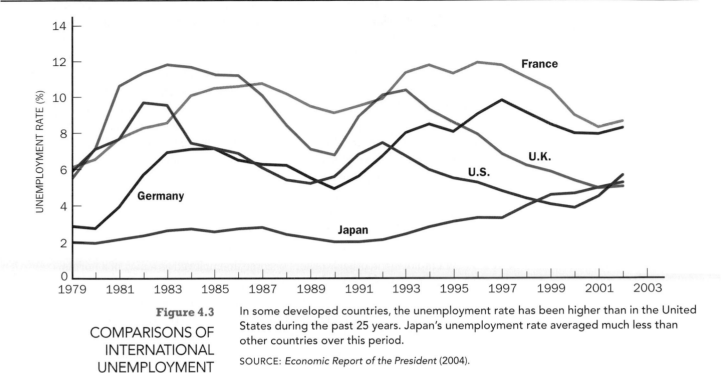

Figure 4.3

COMPARISONS OF
INTERNATIONAL
UNEMPLOYMENT

In some developed countries, the unemployment rate has been higher than in the United States during the past 25 years. Japan's unemployment rate averaged much less than other countries over this period.

SOURCE: *Economic Report of the President* (2004).

the U.S. labor force was unemployed. The unemployment rate among those who worked in manufacturing was even higher—at one point, one out of three workers in manufacturing had lost their jobs.

In recent years, unemployment in other countries often was worse than in the United States (Figure 4.3). In the 1960s, U.S. unemployment rates exceeded those in other major industrialized economies; but European unemployment rates rose dramatically during the 1980s and generally now exceed the rate in the United States. Japan historically has had very low levels of unemployment, but in 1999 the unemployment rate in Japan surpassed that of the United States for the first time. Unemployment in many developing countries is more than 20 percent.

One problem with the unemployment measure is that many individuals are *discouraged* from even looking for a job, especially in a prolonged downturn. Because they are not actively seeking employment, the statistics will not count them as unemployed and thus underestimate the number who would choose to work if a job were available. The fraction of the working-age population that is employed or seeking employment is called the **labor force participation rate.** Because of the effect of discouraged workers, the labor force participation rate tends to decline in recessions and rise in booms.

FORMS OF UNEMPLOYMENT

Even when output is equal to potential, unemployment is not zero. To understand why, we must distinguish between different kinds of unemployment. Economists define four: seasonal, frictional, structural, and cyclical.

Right before Christmas, there is a huge demand for retail salespeople to work in department stores and shopping malls across the nation. In many parts of the country, construction slows down in the winter because the weather makes outdoor work impossible. Conversely, tourism often increases in the summer, as does the number of jobs that cater to tourists. The supply of labor also increases in the summer, as high school and college students enter the labor force on a temporary basis. Unemployment that varies predictably with the seasons is called **seasonal unemployment.** Since these movements in employment and unemployment reflect normal seasonal patterns, the unemployment rate reported on the news is adjusted according to the average amount of seasonal unemployment. These adjustments are called *seasonal adjustments.* If on average the unadjusted unemployment rate is 0.4 percent higher in the summer than at other times during the year, the seasonal-adjusted unemployment rate for July will be the measured unemployment rate minus 0.4 percent.

While workers in construction, agriculture, and tourism regularly face seasonal unemployment, other workers become unemployed as a part of a normal transition from one job to another. For example, new college graduates may spend a month or more looking for a job before finding one. During that month, they are counted as unemployed. This kind of unemployment is referred to as **frictional unemployment.** If people could move from one job to another instantaneously, there would be no frictional unemployment. In a dynamic economy such as in the United States, with some industries growing and others declining, there will always be movements from one job to another, and hence there will always be some frictional unemployment. Not all frictional unemployment represents wasted resources—searching for a new job can be a valuable use of time.

Most individual bouts of unemployment are short-lived; the average person who loses a job is out of work for only about three months. However, about 10 percent of the jobless are unemployed for more than six months. This kind of long-term unemployment often results from structural factors in the economy and is called **structural unemployment.** Substantial structural unemployment is quite often found in the same market as firms with job openings, because the unemployed lack the skills required for the newly created jobs. For example, there may be vacancies for computer programmers while construction workers are unemployed. Similarly, there may be job shortages in parts of the economy that are expanding rapidly (as in the Sunbelt and Silicon Valley during the 1990s) and unemployment in areas that are suffering decline (as in Michigan when the demand for U.S. cars fell).

Seasonal, frictional, and structural unemployment occur even when the economy is operating at its potential level of output. The sum of seasonal, frictional, and structural unemployment is called the **natural rate of unemployment**.

There is a fourth type of unemployment, however, that is associated with economic fluctuations. Unemployment that increases when the economy slows down and decreases when the economy goes into a boom is called **cyclical unemployment** and is one of the fundamental concerns of macroeconomics. Government policymakers are particularly interested in reducing both the frequency and the magnitude of this kind of unemployment, by reducing the frequency and magnitudes of recessions that give rise to it. Government also seeks to reduce its impact by providing unemployment compensation to those temporarily thrown out of work.

FORMS OF UNEMPLOYMENT

Seasonal
Frictional
Structural
Cyclical

OUTPUT GAPS AND THE NATURAL RATE OF UNEMPLOYMENT

Earlier, we defined the output gap as the percentage gap between GDP and potential GDP. When the output gap is zero, real GDP is equal to potential GDP and the economy is at full employment. *Full employment* means not that the total unemployment rate will be zero—there will still be seasonal, frictional, and structural unemployment—but that there is no cyclical unemployment. The unemployment rate that occurs when the output gap is equal to zero is the natural rate of unemployment. When the output gap is equal to zero, the actual unemployment rate equals the natural rate of unemployment. When the output gap is positive, the actual unemployment rate will be below the natural rate of unemployment; when the output gap is negative, it exceeds the natural rate of unemployment.

The natural rate of unemployment can change over time because of such factors as changes in the age composition of the labor force. For example, young workers typically experience higher unemployment rates than do older workers; thus, when the baby boom generation first began entering the labor force in the 1960s, the unemployment rate associated with a zero output gap rose. In the 1970s and 1980s, most economists thought the natural rate of unemployment was around 6 percent. Because workers in their forties and fifties tend to experience lower unemployment rates, the natural rate of unemployment fell as the baby boomers aged. Today, many economists put the natural rate at around 5 to 5.5 percent.

The connection between fluctuations in the unemployment rate and fluctuations in the economy's production is illustrated in Figure 4.4. The horizontal axis plots the output gap. On the vertical axis is the unemployment rate. The downward-sloping relationship between the output gap and the unemployment rate stands out clearly. Arthur Okun, who served as chairman of the Council of Economic Advisors under President Lyndon Johnson, showed that as the economy pulls out of a recession, output increases by a greater percentage than the rise in employment. And as the economy goes into a recession, output decreases by a greater percentage than the reduction in employment. This result is called **Okun's Law.** Current estimates of the relationship between the output gap and employment predict that a 1 percent increase in the unemployment rate will correspond to about a 2 percentage point reduction in the output gap.

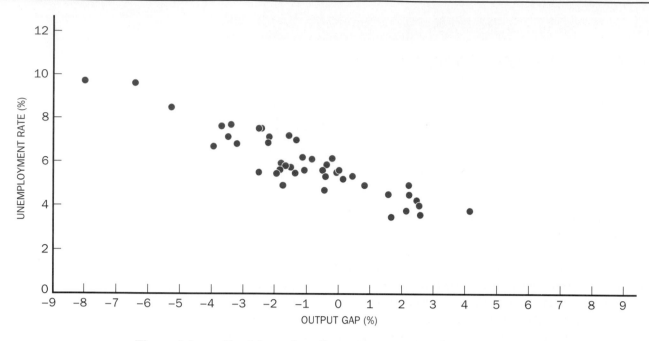

Figure 4.4

OKUN'S LAW, 1959–2002

Okun's Law relates fluctuations in output relative to potential (the output gap) and fluctuations in the unemployment rate. For every 1 percentage point change in the unemployment rate, the output gap changes approximately 2 percentage points.

Figure 4.4 shows that when the output gap is zero, so that real GDP equals potential GDP, the unemployment rate in the United States is usually around 5.5 percent. If real GDP falls below potential GDP and the output gap becomes negative, then unemployment rises above 5.5 percent. This makes sense—when the output gap is zero, the unemployment rate should be equal to the natural rate of unemployment, which, as we have already noted, is usually estimated to be about 5.5 percent.

Okun's Law provides an easy way to link fluctuations in unemployment with fluctuations in the output gap. It can also help us estimate the cost of a recession. In the boom year of 1999, the number of unemployed Americans fell below 6 million. By 2002, just over 8 million American workers were seeking work but unable to find it. From the standpoint of the economy, the loss from an increase in unemployment during a recession is the output that could have been produced if those workers had remained employed. This lost output represents the *opportunity cost* of the higher unemployment, and we can use Okun's Law to roughly calculate it. Unemployment reached 5.8 percent in 2002. Using an estimate of 5.5 percent for the natural rate, we find that cyclical unemployment was 5.8 minus 5.5 percent, or 0.3 percent. According to Okun's Law, that would be associated with a $2 \times 0.3 = 0.6$ percent negative output gap. With real GDP in 2002 equal to roughly $10 trillion, a 0.6 percent output gap means the economy was producing 0.6 percent of $10 trillion, or $60 billion ($60,000,000,000), less per year than its potential. This is the opportunity cost of the rise in unemployment during the recession, an amount equal to just under $200 per person in the United States.

Flows and Stocks

GDP is a measure of output *per year.* Rate measurements such as these are called **flows.** When a financial reporter says, "The quarterly GDP statistic, just released, shows that GDP was $10 trillion per year," she does not mean that $10 trillion of goods and services were produced during the quarter. Rather, the production during the quarter was $2.5 trillion; and if that rate were sustained for a whole year, the total value of goods and services produced would be four times as much: $10 trillion.

Flow statistics need to be contrasted with **stock** statistics, which measure an item at a single point in time. The unemployment rate is a stock—the number of workers unemployed in a particular month as a fraction of the total labor force in that month. Another important figure is the capital stock—the total value of all the buildings and machines that underlie the economy's productive potential. The amount in your bank account is a third example of a stock statistic.

The relationship between stocks and flows is simple. The stock of capital at the end of 2000, for example, consists of the stock of capital at the end of 1999 plus or minus the flows into or out of the stock during 2000. Investment is the flow into the stock of capital. Depreciation is the flow out of the capital stock.

Review and Practice

SUMMARY

1. Gross domestic product (GDP) is the typical way of measuring the value of national output. Real GDP adjusts GDP for changes in the price level.

2. GDP can be calculated in three ways: the final goods approach, which adds the value of all final goods produced in the economy in a given year; the value-added approach, which adds the difference between firms' revenues and costs of intermediate goods; and the income approach, which adds together all income received by those in the economy. All three methods give the same answer.

3. Aggregate output in the economy is equal to aggregate income.

4. Economists distinguish between flows—such as output per year—and stocks—such as the total value of buildings and machines in an economy at a given time (the capital stock).

5. Unemployment imposes costs both on individuals and on society as a whole, which loses what the unemployed workers could have contributed and must supply what is needed to support them in other ways.

6. Seasonal unemployment occurs regularly in sectors such as tourism, construction, and agriculture. Frictional unemployment results when people are in transition between one job and another or when they first enter the labor market to search for work. Structural unemployment occurs when the economy changes, as the new jobs being created have requirements different from the old jobs being lost. Cyclical unemployment increases or decreases as the level of actual real output fluctuates around potential GDP.

7. Seasonal, frictional, and structural unemployment account for the positive unemployment rate even when the economy operates at potential GDP.

8. The natural rate of unemployment is the sum of seasonal, structural, and frictional unemployment.

9. Okun's Law is a relationship between the cyclical unemployment rate and real GDP relative to potential GDP (the output gap).

KEY TERMS

gross domestic product (GDP)
nominal GDP
real GDP
GDP deflator
final goods approach
value added
income approach
potential GDP
boom
recession
depression
output gap
unemployment rate
labor force participation rate
seasonal unemployment
frictional unemployment
structural unemployment
natural rate of unemployment
cyclical unemployment
Okun's Law
flow
stock

REVIEW QUESTIONS

1. What is the difference between nominal GDP, real GDP, and potential GDP?
2. What are the differences among the final goods approach to measuring GDP, the value-added approach, and the income approach?
3. What is the GDP deflator?
4. What are some problems that arise in measuring output?
5. What are the differences between seasonal, frictional, structural, and cyclical unemployment?
6. When there is a reduction in the number of hours worked in the economy, is this normally shared equally by all workers? Are workers in some groups more affected by increased unemployment than those in other groups?
7. What is the natural rate of unemployment?
8. What is Okun's Law?

PROBLEMS

Use the following data for Questions 1–3, and round your answers to the nearest tenth. Assume the economy of Slugian produces two products, lectures and coffee. Output and prices of these two goods for 2002 and 2003 are given in the table:

	Quantities	Prices
2002: Lectures	1,400 lectures	$75 per lecture
2002: Coffee	35,000 cups	$1.55 per cup
2003: Lectures	1,450 lectures	$76 per lecture
2003: Coffee	40,000 cups	$1.45 per cup

1. What was nominal GDP in 2002 for this economy? What was it in 2003? What was the percentage rate of change in nominal GDP between 2002 and 2003?
2. Using 2002 prices as your base year, what was real GDP in 2002? What was real GDP in 2003? What was the percentage rate of change in real GDP between 2002 and 2003?
3. What was the percentage rate of increase in prices in this economy between 2002 and 2003 as measured by the GDP price deflator?
4. Given the following information about the U.S. economy, how much did real GDP grow between 1980 and 1990? Between 1990 and 2000?

	1980	1985	1990	1995	2000
Nominal GDP (trillions)	$2.80	$4.21	$5.80	$7.40	$9.96
GDP deflator (1996=100)	57	73.7	86.5	98.1	106.9

5. Go to the Web site of the National Income Accounts at the Bureau of Economic Analysis (www.bea.doc.gov/bea/dn1.htm). What is the latest figure on the economy's nominal GDP? On real GDP? What was the growth rate of real GDP during the most recently available quarter?
6. Go to the Web site of the Bureau of Labor Statistics (www.bls.gov/) and find the latest data on the unemployment rate. What was the unemployment rate for the most recently available month? How has the unemployment rate changed over the past year?
7. For each of the cases listed, state whether the person is in the labor force or not. If the person is in the labor force, is he or she employed or unemployed? Give your reasons in each case.
   (a) John recently retired from IBM and is looking for a part-time job to supplement his retirement income.
   (b) Christina works 10 hours each week at Starbucks; she would like to find a full-time job.
   (c) Ben recently quit his job at the campus bookstore to have more time to surf.
   (d) Michelle just graduated from college; she has been sending out her resumé but has yet to land a job.
8. Are you currently in the labor force? If so, are you employed or are you unemployed? Explain.
9. If the output gap is a negative 2 percent, what does Okun's Law tell us will be the level of cyclical unemployment?
10. Firms typically do not fire workers quickly as the economy goes into a recession—at least not as quickly as their output is reduced. How might you expect output per worker and output per hour to move over the business cycle?
11. Suppose the Farsighted Forecasting Group, an organization of private economists, predicts that the output gap will fall by 4 percent over the next year. According to Okun's Law, by how much is the unemployment rate likely to rise?

Learning Goals

In this chapter, you will learn

1. The costs of inflation

2. How the consumer price index is measured

3. The recent history of inflation in the United States

Chapter 5

THE COST OF LIVING AND INFLATION

I n the 1920s, the years of silent pictures, a movie ticket cost a nickel. By the late 1940s, in the heyday of the Hollywood studios, the price was up to $0.50. In the 1960s, the price of a movie was $2.00, and now it is more than $8.00. This steady rise is no anomaly. Most other goods have undergone similar price increases over time. This increase in the general level of prices is called *inflation*. While unemployment tends to be concentrated in certain groups within the population, everyone is affected by inflation. Thus, it is not surprising that when inflation becomes high, it almost always rises to the top of the political agenda.

Ensuring that inflation remains low and stable is one of the key goals of macroeconomic policy. In this chapter, you will learn about the costs of inflation and why it is desirable to make sure that inflation remains low. You will also learn about the price index that is used to measure the cost of living. Finally, the chapter ends with a review of American's experience with inflation.

The Costs of Inflation

It is not inflation if the price of only one good goes up. It *is* inflation if the prices of *most* goods go up. The **inflation rate** is the rate at which the *general level* of prices increases. When inflation is positive—that is, the average price level is rising—a dollar buys less and less over time. Or, to put it another way, it takes more and more dollars to purchase the same bundle of goods and service. While the costs of unemployment are apparent—it causes not only a loss in output but also the misery of those who cannot secure gainful work—the costs of inflation are more subtle.

People sense there is something wrong with the economy when there is high inflation. Workers worry that paychecks will not keep pace with price hikes, a failure that will erode their standard of living. Investors worry that the dollars they receive in the future will be worth less than the dollars they invested, leaving them with less than enough to live comfortably in their old age.

When inflation is anticipated, many of its economic costs disappear. Workers who know that prices will be rising by 5 percent this year, for example, may negotiate wages that rise fast enough to offset inflation. Firms may be willing to agree to these larger wage increases since they anticipate being able to raise the prices of the goods they produce. Lenders know that the dollars they will be repaid will be worth less than the dollars they lent, so they take this loss in value into account when setting the interest rate they charge or when deciding whether to make a loan.

But even when inflation is not fully anticipated, workers and investors can immunize themselves against its effects by having wages and returns *indexed* to inflation. For instance, when wages are perfectly indexed, a 1 percent increase in the price level results in a 1 percent increase in wages, preserving the workers' purchasing power. In recent years, both Social Security payments and tax rates have been indexed. Many countries, including the United Kingdom, Canada, and New Zealand, sell indexed government bonds so that savers can put aside money knowing that the returns will not be affected by inflation.

WHO SUFFERS FROM INFLATION?

Although indexing softens the effects of inflation, its protection is far from complete. So who suffers from inflation today? Many people may suffer a little because indexing does not fully protect them, but some are more vulnerable than others. Among the groups most imperfectly protected are lenders, taxpayers, and holders of currency.

Lenders Since most loans are not fully indexed, increases in inflation mean that the dollars that lenders receive back from borrowers are worth less than those they lent out. Many people put a large part of their retirement savings into bonds or other fixed-income securities. These people will suffer if an inflationary bout reduces the purchasing power of their savings. The extent to which they will suffer depends in large measure on whether the price changes were anticipated, as interest rates can adjust to completely compensate lenders for any inflation that was anticipated.

Taxpayers Our tax system is only partially indexed, and inflation frequently hurts investors badly through the tax system. All returns to investment are taxed, including those that do nothing more than offset inflation. Consequently, real after-tax returns are often negative when inflation is high. Consider a rate of inflation of 10 percent and an asset that yields 12 percent before tax. If the individual has to pay a 33 percent tax on the return, the after-tax yield to the investor is only 9 percent—not even enough to compensate for inflation. The after-tax real return in this example is –1 percent.

Holders of Currency Inflation also makes it expensive for people to hold currency because as prices rise, the currency loses its value. Since currency facilitates a variety of transactions, inflation interferes with the efficiency of the economy by discouraging its holding. By taking away the real value of money, inflation acts as a tax on those who hold money. Economists refer to this distortionary effect as an *inflation tax.*

This distortion is not as important in modern economies, where individuals frequently put their money into interest-paying checking accounts instead of keeping their cash. As the rate of inflation increases, the interest rate paid on checking accounts normally increases as well. Even in Argentina in the 1970s, when prices were rising at 800 percent *a month,* bank accounts yielded more than this. Still, poorer individuals who do not have checking accounts—and therefore must hold much of what little wealth they have in the form of currency—are adversely affected. According to the Federal Reserve's 2001 Survey of Consumer Finances, almost 10 percent of American families do not have a checking, savings, or money market account. These families tend to have low incomes and little wealth.

THE ECONOMY

There are two costs of inflation to the economy as a whole. The first has to do with relative prices. Because price increases are never perfectly coordinated, increases in the rate of inflation lead to greater variability in relative prices. If the shoe industry makes price adjustments only every three months, then in the third month, right before its price increase, shoes may be relatively cheap; conversely, right after the price increase, shoes may be relatively expensive. On the other hand, the prices of groceries might change continually throughout the three-month period. Therefore, the ratio of the price of groceries to the price of shoes will change continually. An average inflation rate of only 2 or 3 percent per year does not cause much of a problem. But when the average rate is 10 percent per month, inflation causes real distortions in how society allocates its resources. When inflation gets very high, individuals and firms tend to allocate considerable time and resources to avoiding its costs and to taking advantage of the discrepancies in prices charged by different sellers. Rather than carrying money, which quickly erodes in value, people rush to deposit their money in interest-bearing bank accounts.

The second economy-wide cost of inflation arises from the risk and uncertainty that it generates. If indexing were perfect, the uncertainty about the rate of inflation would be unimportant. But as indexing is not perfect, the resulting uncertainty makes it difficult to plan. People saving for their retirement cannot know how much to put aside if they do not know what a dollar will be worth in the future when they retire. Business firms borrowing money are uncertain about the price they will receive for the goods they produce. Firms are also hurt when they build wage increases into multiyear contracts to reflect *anticipated* inflation. If for any reason a firm finds that the prices it can charge have increased less rapidly than anticipated in the contract, the employer suffers.

Because of these economy-wide costs, countries that experience periods of very high inflation also tend to experience slower real economic growth.

The Costs of Deflation

Our focus has been on the costs of inflation—rising prices—since that has been the experience of the United States and most other countries over the past fifty years. But inflation in many countries declined significantly during the 1980s, and falling prices—**deflation**—has in some places become the concern. Japan, for instance, recently experienced several years of falling prices.

Many of the costs associated with inflation also make deflation costly. Variability in relative prices and increased uncertainty can arise when average prices are falling, just as they can when average prices are rising. And while inflation can hurt lenders, deflation can hurt borrowers. When prices are falling, the dollars a borrower must pay back are worth more than the dollars that were borrowed. In the United States, the 1870s and the 1930s were periods of declining prices. Borrowers, particularly farm families, were hard hit as the wages they earned or the prices they received for their crops fell. Many were forced to leave their farms. These periods have had a lasting impact on America's cultural history. L. Frank Baum's *The Wizard of Oz,* for example, has been interpreted as an allegory on the dangers of the gold standard and in favor of raising the money supply by coining silver. (In Chapter 10, we will learn why a rise in the money supply—as occurred with the discoveries of gold in South Africa in the 1880s—can lead to rising prices.) John Steinbeck's *The Grapes of Wrath* chronicles the hardships faced by Oklahoma farmers who were displaced during the 1930s.

Periods of deflation also have been associated with financial and banking crises. If firms that have taken loans are unable to repay them because of falling prices, they may be forced into bankruptcy. But their failure will prevent them from repaying the banks that have lent money, which therefore may become bankrupt in turn.

The hyperinflation in Germany in the early 1920s was so severe that paper deutsche marks were more valuable as stove fuel than as actual money.

Wrap-Up

REAL COSTS OF INFLATION

Variability in relative prices

Resources devoted to mitigating the costs of inflation and taking advantage of price discrepancies

Increased uncertainty

Case in Point

HYPERINFLATION IN GERMANY IN THE 1920s

Following World War I, the victorious Allied nations required Germany to make substantial "reparations." But the sheer size of the reparations, combined with the wartime devastation of German industry, made payment nearly impossible. In *The*

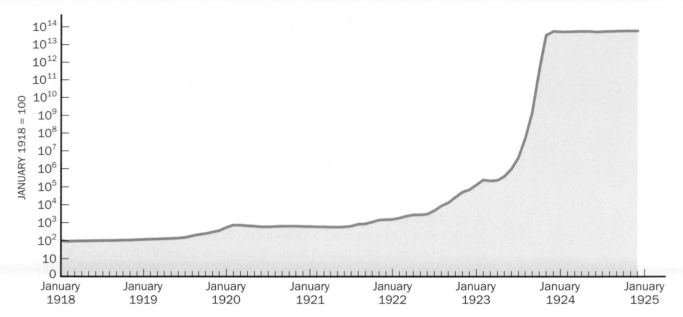

Figure 5.1

HYPERINFLATION: GERMANY'S PRICE LEVEL (LOG SCALE)

Inflation in Germany during the 1920s reached levels that may seem unbelievably high. At the end of 1923, prices were 36 billion times higher than they had been two years earlier.

SOURCE: Thomas Sargent, "The Ends of Four Big Inflations," in R. Hall, ed., *Inflation, Causes and Effects* (Chicago: University of Chicago Press, 1982).

Economic Consequences of the Peace, John Maynard Keynes, then an economic adviser to the British government, warned that the reparations were too large. To pay for some of Germany's financial obligations, the German government started printing money.

The resulting increase in both the amount of circulating currency and the price level can be seen in Figure 5.1. From December 1921 to December 1923, the average price level increased by a factor of 36 billion.[1] People made desperate attempts to spend their currency as soon as they received it, since the value of currency was declining so rapidly. One story Keynes often told was that Germans would buy two beers at once, even though one was likely to get warm, for fear that otherwise, when it came time to buy the second beer, its price would have risen.

At an annual inflation rate of 100 percent, money loses half its value every year. If you save $100 today, in five years it will have a buying power equal to only $3. It is possible for nominal interest rates to adjust even to very high inflation rates; but when those high inflation rates fluctuate in unanticipated ways, the effects can be disastrous.

Periods of hyperinflation create a massive redistribution of wealth. If an individual is smart or lucky enough to hold assets in a form such as foreign funds or land, then the hyperinflation will do little to reduce that person's real wealth. Those who cannot avail themselves of these "inflation-proof" assets will see their wealth fall.

---

[1]Thomas Sargent, "The Ends of Four Big Inflations," in R. Hall, ed., *Inflation, Causes and Effects* (Chicago: University of Chicago Press, 1982), pp. 74–75.

Measuring Inflation

If the prices of all goods and services rose by the same proportion, say, 5 percent, over a year, then measuring inflation would be easy: the rate of inflation that year would be 5 percent. Difficulties arise because the prices of different goods rise at different rates, and the prices of some goods even decline. For example, since the years 1982–1984, which the United States uses as a base reference period, the price of apparel rose by 24 percent, the price of medical care by 186 percent, and the price of housing by 80 percent, yet the price of personal computers fell by 77 percent between 1998 and 2003. To determine the change in the overall price level, economists calculate the *average* percentage increase in prices. But since some goods loom much larger in the typical consumer's budget than others, this calculation must reflect the relative purchases of different goods. A change in the price of housing is much more important than a change in the price of pencils. If the price of pencils goes down by 5 percent but the price of housing goes up 5 percent, the overall measure of the price level should go up.

Economists have a straightforward way of reflecting the differing importance of different goods. They ask, What would it cost consumers to purchase the same bundle of goods this year that they bought last year? If, for example, it cost $22,000 in the year 2005 to buy what it cost consumers $20,000 to purchase in 2004, we say that prices, *on average,* rose by 10 percent. Such results are frequently expressed in the form of a *price index,* which, for ease of comparison, measures the price level in any given year relative to a common base year.

The price index for the base year is, by definition, set equal to 100. The price index for any other year is calculated by taking the ratio of the price level in that year to the price level in the base year and multiplying it by 100. For example, if 2004 is our base year and we want to know the price index for 2005, we first calculate the ratio of the cost of a certain bundle of goods in 2005 ($22,000) to the cost of the same bundle of goods in 2004 ($20,000), which is 1.1. The price index in 2005 is therefore $1.1 \times 100 = 110$. The index 110, using 2004 as a base, indicates that prices are 10 percent higher, on average, in 2005 than in 2004.

There are several different price indexes, each using a different bundle of goods. To track the movement of prices that are important to American households, the government collects price data on the bundle of goods that represent how the average household spends its income. This index is called the **consumer price index, or CPI.** To determine the bundle, the government, through the Bureau of Labor Statistics (BLS) of the Department of Commerce, conducts a Consumer Expenditure Survey. The information from the survey is then used to determine the importance of more than 2,000 different expenditure categories. Weights are assigned to the expenditure categories to reflect the importance of each in household spending. For example, new cars receive a weight of 4.6 out of 100, while men's footwear receives a weight of 0.241. Currently, the CPI is based on an expenditure survey conducted over the period 1993–1995. This survey involved more than 30,000 households who provided information on their buying habits. In the past, a new expenditure survey was conducted once a decade or so. However, the BLS now plans to update the bundle every two years. The BLS provides answers to many questions about the CPI at www.bls.gov/cpi/cpifaq.htm.

To see how a price index like the CPI is constructed, we can calculate one for Bob, who spends all his income on rent, Big Macs, and CDs. Let's suppose his total expenditures during 2003 were $1,500 each month, of which $1,000 went for rent, $200 for 100 Big Macs (which cost $2 each), and $300 for 15 CDs (which cost $20 each). In 2004, his rent increases to $1,200 and Big Macs go up in price to $2.25, while the price of a CD falls to $18. What has happened to Bob's price index? We want to know how much it costs, in year 2004, to buy the same basket of goods Bob purchased in 2003. In 2003, these goods cost $1,500. In 2004, they cost $1,695: $1,200 for rent, $225 for 100 Big Macs, and $270 for 15 CDs. Bob's cost of living has increased. Setting the value of the index equal to 100 in the base year of 2003, Bob's price index in 2004 will equal $100 \times 1{,}695/1{,}500 = 113$.

The inflation rate is the percentage change in the price index. So if we look at Bob's price index, it rose from 100 to 113 between 2003 and 2004, an increase of 13 percent. Inflation as measured by his price index was 13 percent in 2004. Now let's look at the actual CPI for the United States. The CPI in 2003 was 184.0; that is, the general level of consumer prices was 84.0 percent higher than it had been in the base years of 1982–1984. In 2004, the index rose to 187.6. The inflation rate in 2004 was the percentage change in the CPI from 2003 to 2004, or $100 \times (187.6 - 184.0)/184.0 = 1.96$ percent.

Summarizing the movements of masses of prices into a single index provides an easy way to look at price trends over time. The advantages of an index are that once an index number is calculated for a given year, we can compare it with any other year. For example, the CPI for 1973 was 44.4, and for 2002 it was 179.9. Between those years, the index rose by 135.5, so the increase was

$$100 \times 135.5/44.4 = 305 \text{ percent.}$$

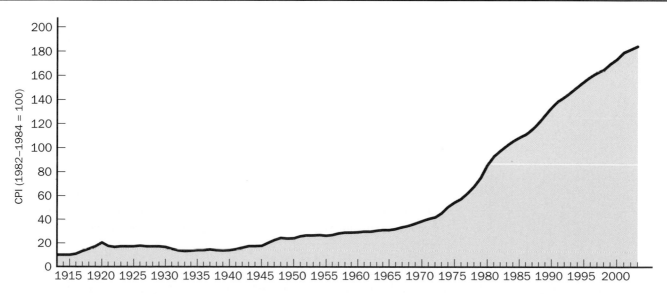

Figure 5.2

THE CONSUMER PRICE INDEX
FOR 1913 TO 2003

Consumer prices have risen significantly since the early years of the twentieth century, with most of the increases occurring since 1970.

SOURCE: Bureau of Labor Statistics.

On average, prices rose 305 percent from 1973 to 2002. Figure 5.2 shows the CPI since 1913.

Case in Point

THE PRICE INDEX MAKES A DIFFERENCE

Price indexes increasingly have come to play an important role in recent economic debates. The Social Security benefits of the elderly rise with the cost of living index (the CPI),[2] and tax brackets and tax exemptions also change with the index. If the index overstates the increases in the cost of living, the real benefits (purchasing power) of the elderly increase, and real inflation-adjusted tax revenues fall. Both distortions increase the budget deficits of the government—the first by increasing its outlays, the second by reducing its receipts.

By early 1994, it had become apparent that the price index the federal government used for adjusting both benefits and tax brackets was seriously flawed—overstating the rate of inflation by between 0.5 and 1.5 percent a year. The government made several changes to partly correct the errors in the index.

The upward bias stems from three problems. The first is the "fixed basket problem." The CPI is calculated by comparing how much it costs to purchase a particular market basket of goods that represents an average consumer's expenditure pattern. But expenditure patterns change steadily over time, while the market basket is revised only infrequently. For instance, in February 1998, the market basket was revised; it is now based on spending patterns in 1993–1995; previously it was based on 1982–1984 expenditure patterns. As people buy more of the goods that have become relatively less expensive (such as computers) and less of the goods that have become relatively more expensive, the index increasingly overweights goods whose prices have risen the most.

---

[2]When a worker retires, his or her initial Social Security benefits are determined by a formula that is indexed to the general level of wages. However, once a worker begins to receive benefits, future benefit levels are indexed to the CPI.

The second major problem is "quality adjustment." New products, which both offer new functions and better perform the existing functions of older products, constantly enter the market. To compare the prices of the new products with the old, some quality adjustment must be made. If the price goes up by 10 percent but the new product lasts longer and works better, then in a real sense the price increase is less than 10 percent and may even represent a price reduction. Sometimes, the quality adjustments are easy; one machine can do what two machines did before. But usually the comparisons are difficult. If we measure the quality of computers by calculations per second, memory, and disk storage, the rate of decrease in computer prices is phenomenal. But even this does not fully reflect their improvements in quality. We can do things with the computer now that were unimaginable twenty-five years ago at any price. And how do we determine the relative value of a new drug that cures a previously incurable disease? The Bureau of Labor Statistics tries to make adjustments for quality. But the consensus is that these adjustments are imperfect and result in an overestimate in the inflation rate of anywhere between a few tenths of a percentage point to more than 1 percent.

The third problem is technical, having to do with the way the data are collected and the details of the calculations.

Many economists believe that the recent revisions will not fully eliminate the CPI bias. They argue that as a result, Social Security and taxes should be indexed to the CPI rate of inflation minus 1 or 0.5 percent.

ALTERNATIVE MEASURES OF INFLATION

The CPI provides one measure of inflation, based on what the average consumer buys. Other price indexes can be calculated using different market baskets. One different measure of prices is the **producer price index,** which measures the average level of prices of goods sold by producers. This index is useful because it gives us an idea of what will happen to consumer prices in the near future. Usually, if producers are receiving higher prices from their sales to wholesalers, eventually retailers will have to charge higher prices. These will be reflected in a higher CPI.

Internet Connection

THE INFLATION CALCULATOR

The Bureau of Labor Statistics has a handy inflation calculator that allows you to find out how much it costs today to purchase goods that cost $100 in some earlier year. For example, it takes $731 today to purchase goods you could have bought for $100 in 1949. Try it out at www.bls.gov/cpi/home.htm.

Learning Goals

In this chapter, you will learn

1 How full employment is achieved in market economies

2 The factors that determine real wages, output, and the real interest rate at full employment

3 The role that the capital market plays in maintaining full employment

Chapter 6

THE FULL-EMPLOYMENT MODEL

Every year, about 1.7 million Americans enter the labor force. Creating jobs for these workers is critically important for the health of the economy and for the general welfare of society. With so many new workers each year, it may seem amazing that market economies like that of the United States are able to create employment opportunities for almost all who seek them. Between 1955 and 2000, for example, the American labor force grew by 117 percent, almost 76 million workers—and incredibly, the number of jobs also grew by 117 percent. This remarkable ability of the economy to generate millions of new jobs is the result of competitive markets. No government official can calculate where to place the millions of new workers who are expected to enter the labor force over the next decade. But past experience makes us confident that somehow, somewhere, the economy will create jobs for them. The economic theories we explore in this and the next four chapters help explain the ability of market economies to create jobs.

Though the economy does generate jobs, the process does not always occur smoothly—in some years, job growth slows and unemployment rises; in other years, when the economy is expanding, the opposite happens. But over the long run, jobs are created to employ those who want to work.

To understand how this happens, we focus on the *aggregate* behavior of the economy—on movements in such macroeconomic variables as total output, interest rates, and average wages—when resources are fully used. We will also focus on a period of time that is long enough so that all wages and prices have had time to adjust to shifts in supply and demand. Many wages and prices do not respond rapidly to such changes, a factor that will play an important role when we turn to economic fluctuations in Part Three. Eventually, however, wages and prices do adjust to bring supply and demand into balance. By using a time horizon that is long enough for these adjustments to occur, we will gain insights into many important macroeconomic phenomena. For example, the framework we develop in this

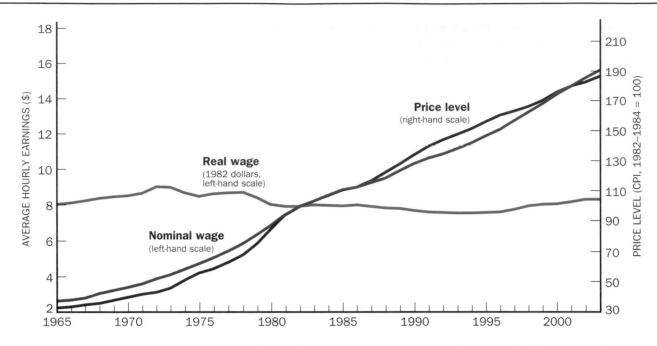

Figure 6.1

NOMINAL WAGES, THE PRICE LEVEL, AND REAL WAGES

The solid blue line shows that average nominal wages in the United States have risen significantly since 1965. The red line shows that the price level also has risen over this period. With average nominal wages and the price level rising at roughly the same rate, average real wages (shown by the green line) in 2003 were only slightly higher than they had been in 1965.

SOURCE: *Economic Report of the President* (2004), Table B-47.

REAL WAGES

The real wage is the nominal or dollar wage adjusted for prices.

Workers care about the real wage that they receive because it measures the purchasing power of their wages.

Firms care about the real wage because it measures the cost of labor.

Figure 6.2 shows the aggregate labor market, with the real wage (w/P) on the vertical axis, the quantity of labor (L) on the horizontal axis, and the aggregate demand and supply curves for labor. With a given set of equipment and technology, the aggregate demand for labor depends on the wages firms must pay, the prices firms receive for the goods and services they produce, and the prices they have to pay for nonlabor inputs such as raw materials and equipment. With the prices of goods and inputs held constant, the aggregate labor demand curve traces out the quantity of labor demanded by firms at different wages. At lower wages, the quantity of labor demand is greater. There are two reasons for this. First, as wages fall, labor becomes relatively less expensive compared with the price of the goods that firms produce. Because profits are greater, firms have an incentive to expand production and hire more workers. Second, as wages fall relative to the cost of machines, it pays firms to substitute workers for machines. Thus, the demand curve for labor slopes down, as shown in the figure.

The two reasons for the negative slope of the aggregate labor demand curve stress the importance of wages relative to the costs of other inputs and the price of the output being produced. If wages fall *and all other prices in the economy also fall in proportion,* the demand for labor will not change. That is why we show the demand for labor as a function of the real wage, w/P.

The figure also shows an aggregate labor supply curve. To simplify matters, the labor supply curve is drawn as a vertical line—we assume that the labor supply is perfectly inelastic. That is, either individuals are in the labor force, working a full (forty-hour) workweek, or they are not. In principle, workers might enter and exit the labor force as real wages go up or down, or they might reduce or increase the hours they work in response to such changes. When real wages rise, two factors are at work. First, higher wages mean the returns for working are greater. Thus workers should want to work more hours—the opportunity cost of leisure is now higher, and the substitution effect works to induce individuals to work more as real wages rise. But higher wages mean that workers have higher incomes, which lead them to want to increase their consumption—including their consumption of leisure. So there is an income effect acting to reduce labor supply as real wages rise. The income and substitution effects act in opposite directions.[2] In Figure 6.2, we assume they offset one another, so that as real wages change, labor supply remains constant.

Basic supply and demand analysis implies that market equilibrium should occur at the intersection of the demand and supply curves, point E. The reason for this is straightforward. If the real wage happens to be above the equilibrium real wage w_1/P—say, at w_2/P—the demand for labor will be L_2, much less than the supply, L_1. There will be an excess supply of workers. Those in the labor force without jobs will offer to work for less than the going wage, bidding down the average wages of those already working. The process of competition will lead to lower wages, until eventually demand again equals supply at point E. Likewise, if the real wage is lower than w_1/P—say, at w_3/P—firms in the economy will demand more labor than is supplied. Competing with one another for scarce labor services, they will bid the wage up to w_1/P.

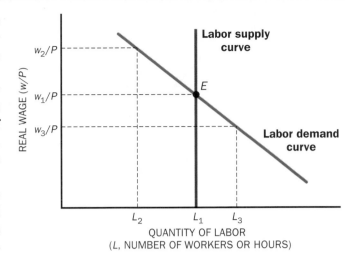

Figure 6.2

EQUILIBRIUM IN THE LABOR MARKET

Equilibrium in the labor market is at the intersection of the labor demand and labor supply curves. If the real wage is above w_1/P, where demand equals supply, there will be unemployment, putting pressure on wages to fall as workers compete to offer their services. Below w_1/P there will be excess demand for labor, which will put pressure on wages to rise.

SHIFTS IN THE DEMAND AND SUPPLY OF LABOR

The full-employment model makes clear predictions about the consequences of shifts in the demand and supply of labor. First, let's consider shifts in the supply curve of labor. These can occur because young people reaching working age

---

[2]To review the definitions of income and substitution effects, see Chapter 3.

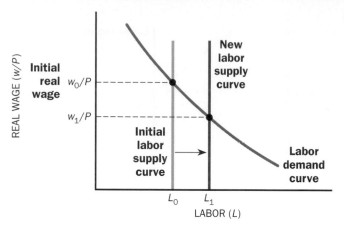

Figure 6.3

EFFECTS OF A SHIFT IN THE SUPPLY OF LABOR

A shift of the supply curve to the right leads to a fall in real wages.

outnumber old people retiring, because of new immigrants, or because of social changes such as the entry of more women into the labor force. For example, the U.S. labor force expanded rapidly in the 1970s as the baby boomers entered the labor force and more and more women worked outside the home. The consequences of such a large shift in the labor supply curve are depicted in Figure 6.3. The supply curve of labor (shown here as vertical) shifts to the right. At each real wage, there are more individuals in the labor force. The equilibrium real wage falls. This fall in the price of labor indicates to firms that labor is less scarce than it was before and they therefore should economize less in its use. Firms respond to the lower real wage by creating more jobs, and employment rises to absorb the increase in labor supply.

Now let's look at the effects of a shift in the demand curve for labor. First, consider the case of a decrease in investment, which leads to a reduction in the quantity of machines and equipment available for use by workers. This in turn reduces the productivity of workers, thereby shifting the demand curve for labor to the left, as depicted in panel A of Figure 6.4. For a given real wage, firms want to hire fewer workers than before. The equilibrium real wage falls.

Panel B depicts the effects of technological progress on the demand for labor. As technological change increases the productivity of workers, each hour of labor input produces more output. From the perspective of the firm, higher labor productivity lowers its effective cost of labor, as it now is able to produce more output per hour of labor hired. At each wage, the demand for labor will rise, shifting the demand for labor curve to the right. The equilibrium real wage rises.

These examples suggest that increases in investment and improvements in technology lead to an increase in the demand for labor (a rightward shift in the labor demand curve). Although this is generally true, the demand for some types of labor, especially unskilled labor, may actually decline with investment in new equipment and technology. At the same time, the demand for skilled workers may increase. In this case, the labor market is really made up of two markets, one containing skilled and the other unskilled workers. An increase in investment or technology may increase the demand for skilled workers, as in panel B, but decrease the demand for unskilled workers, as in panel A. Here, a focus only on the aggregate labor market is not sufficient to understand an interesting macroeconomic phenomenon—the increase in wage inequality based on skill levels that has occurred in the United States in recent years.

LABOR MARKET EQUILIBRIUM

Real wages adjust to equate labor demand with labor supply.

An increase in labor supply at each real wage (a rightward shift in the labor supply curve) lowers the equilibrium real wage, enabling firms to create additional jobs.

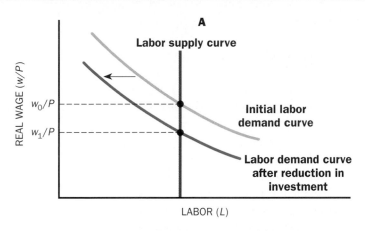

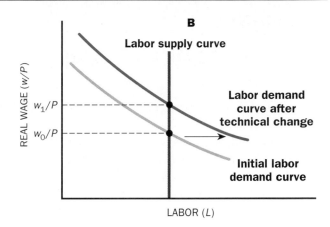

Figure 6.4

EFFECTS OF CHANGES IN INVESTMENT AND TECHNOLOGY

New investment or technological change shifts the demand curve for labor. Panel A shows the effects of a reduction in investment. Workers have fewer machines and equipment to work with, and the demand curve for labor shifts to the left, lowering real wages. Panel B shows an improvement in technology. The demand curve shifts to the right, as workers' marginal productivity increases, leading to higher real wages.

Technological change or new investment increases the demand for labor (shifts the labor demand curve to the right) at each real wage and increases the equilibrium real wage. Increases in labor productivity increase aggregate labor demand and cause the equilibrium real wage to rise.

MASS MIGRATION IN THE NINETEENTH CENTURY

The nineteenth century provides a case study in how labor markets adjust to changes in labor supply. Between 1820 and 1920, 60 million emigrants left Europe for the New World (Argentina, Brazil, Canada, and the United States) and Australia, and about 36 million entered the United States. This mass movement of people had a major impact on wages in both North America and Europe, just as our theory predicts.

Land was scarce and labor was abundant in Europe in 1850. As a consequence, wages were low. In North America, by contrast, land was abundant and labor was scarce. Consequently, wages were high.[3] In 1850, the average real wage in Europe was about half what it was in the New World. Real wages in Ireland, for instance, were 42 percent of the American level. This wage differential provided a powerful

---

[3]To help follow the discussion, you might find it useful to draw two supply and demand diagrams, one to represent the European labor market in 1850 and one to represent the North American labor market. Since our focus here is on labor supply and migration, draw the labor demand curves to be the same in both markets. For Europe, the labor supply curve is to the right of where it is for North America. The equilibrium real wage for this time period is therefore higher in North America.

inducement for workers to migrate from Europe to areas offering higher living standards.

The mass migrations of the late nineteenth century shifted the North American labor supply curve to the right and the European labor supply curve to the left. Our theory predicts that wages adjust to balance the quantity of labor demanded and the quantity of labor supplied. Real wages needed to fall in the United States and rise in Europe in response to these shifts in labor supply.

Did this adjustment of wages occur? Irish real wages doubled between 1855 and 1913, with most of the increase occurring between 1860 and 1895. Average American wages also were rising during this period as a result of rapid accumulation of capital and growth in the wages of skilled workers. But average wages in Ireland rose faster, closing the gap between what workers earned in Ireland and what workers earned in the United States. Just as the theory predicted, real wages adjusted in response to shifts in labor supply to bring the quantity demanded and the quantity supplied into balance in the labor market.[4]

The Product Market

Just as the real wage adjusts to ensure that the demand for labor equals the supply, so too—in our full-employment model—adjustments will occur in the product and

---

[4]For a discussion of the impact of mass migration during the late nineteenth century and of other aspects of the globalization that occurred during this period, see K. H. O'Rourke and J. G. Williamson, *Globalization and History* (Cambridge, Mass.: MIT Press, 1999).

capital markets to ensure that the demand for goods equals the economy's output when it is at full employment.

POTENTIAL GDP

At any point in time, the economy has a given capital stock (a set of machines, equipment, and buildings) that, together with labor and materials, produces output. If more workers are hired, output increases. The relationship between employment and output with a fixed amount of capital is called the **short-run aggregate production function,** depicted in panel A of Figure 6.5. The figure illustrates that as more workers are hired, output goes up, but at a diminishing rate. There are *diminishing returns to labor.* With a fixed amount of capital, the amount of equipment and machinery available for each worker falls as the number of workers employed goes up. For example, the first workers hired may each have their own desktop computers, but as new workers are hired and the amount of capital remains fixed, workers must share computers. As a consequence, output increases as the additional workers are hired, but it does so at a diminishing rate. Diminishing returns to labor also occur because the most productive workers are likely to be hired first; as employment rises, workers with less training and fewer skills will be hired.

In the long run, when the labor market is in equilibrium, we achieve a condition called full employment. Panel B of Figure 6.5 shows the labor market, with the equilibrium real wage at the level that makes the demand for labor equal to the fixed supply. With this fixed supply of labor at full employment, the level of output can be found using the short-run aggregate production function in panel A. The equilibrium level of output when the economy is at full employment is referred to as its **potential GDP** or the **full-employment level of output.** If the supply of labor is not fixed but instead depends on the real wage, so that the supply curve of labor has a positive slope, full employment occurs when labor demand and labor supply are equal. Given the equilibrium level of employment at full employment, potential GDP is found from the short-run aggregate production function.

Potential GDP will be affected if the economy's stock of plant and equipment changes, if technology changes, or if there are changes in the equilibrium that defines full employment. Increases in the stock of plant and equipment would increase the amount of output that can be produced at each level of employment. As a consequence, the short-run aggregate production function would shift upward, increasing potential GDP. Similarly, new technological innovations would shift the short-run aggregate production function upward and increase potential GDP. Increases in labor supply would raise the equilibrium level at full employment and, for a given level of plant and equipment and technology, raise potential GDP.

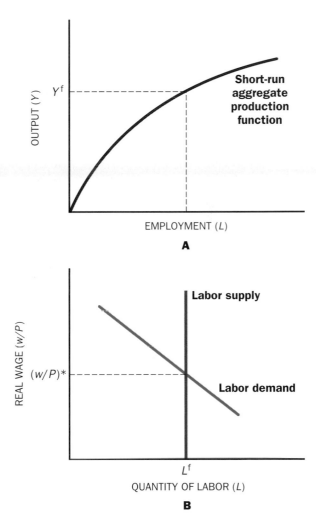

Figure 6.5

EQUILIBRIUM IN THE LABOR MARKET AND THE DETERMINATION OF POTENTIAL GDP

Panel A shows the short-run aggregate production function; in the short run, with given technology and a given set of plant and equipment, output increases as more labor is employed, but with diminishing returns. Panel B shows the labor market with a fixed supply of labor L^f. The equilibrium real wage is w/P^*. At full employment, potential GDP is Y^f.

DEMAND AND EQUILIBRIUM OUTPUT

For the product market to be in equilibrium, the supply of goods and services produced by firms in the economy must balance with the demand for the economy's goods and services. Firms will not continue to produce at the full-employment level if their products go unsold. If the economy is to maintain full employment, the total level of demand in the economy must adjust to balance output at full employment. The economy's financial sector—what we called the *capital market* in Chapter 1—plays a critical role in achieving this balance. By examining that role, we can see more clearly how the interrelation of markets helps ensure macroeconomic equilibrium.

A useful starting point in understanding how demand adjusts to equal full-employment output is to recall our earlier discussion of the circular flow of income. Figure 6.6 shows the circular flow of income for a closed economy, as introduced in Chapter 3. Notice that we have also ignored the government sector for the moment.

The circular flow diagram illustrates the flow of goods and income that links households, business, and financial sectors. In the diagram, the purple lines indicate flows of real resources and goods and services; the green lines represent the

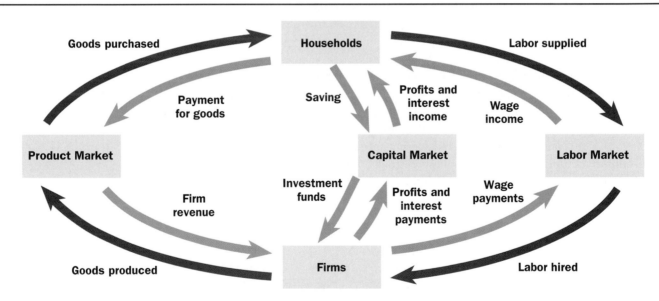

Figure 6.6

THE CIRCULAR FLOW
OF INCOME

The circular flow of income provides a summary picture of how the flows of commodities and payments link the household and firm sectors of the economy. Households provide resources, such as labor, to firms and receive income payments in return. They use this income to purchase goods and services in the product market. The revenue that firms obtain from selling in the product market enables them to make the income payments to households for the labor and other resources that they have used. Saving from the household sector flows into the capital market, where it is available to firms that wish to borrow for investment projects.

payments for those commodities. Households supply resources (labor, capital, land) to firms and in return receive payments for those resources. We have already learned in Chapter 4 that these income payments will equal the value of total production. This means that the household sector receives enough income to purchase all the goods and services that firms have produced.

Of course, households do not choose to spend all their income on goods and services; they save part of it. In our circular flow diagram, this action is shown by the flow of saving to the financial capital market. Thus, household saving is a *leakage* out of the spending stream.

While households in the aggregate do not spend all their income, other sectors of the economy spend more than the incomes they receive. Firms, for example, may wish to invest in buildings, new plant, and equipment. To do so, they need to borrow funds in the capital market. Investment spending is an *injection* into the spending stream.

The total level of spending will balance with the level of output at full employment if the leakages out of the spending stream in the form of saving are balanced by injections into the spending stream in the form of investments. We portray this algebraically by noting that in a closed economy with no government sector, the total demand for what is produced is equal to consumption spending (C) by households plus investment spending (I) by firms. In equilibrium at full employment, consumption and investment spending must add up to full-employment output (Y^f), or $C + I = Y^f$. Subtracting C from both sides of this equation tells us that demand will balance output at full employment if $I = Y^f - C$. But $Y^f - C$ is saving at full employment. So demand will balance output at full employment if investment equals full-employment saving.

But what ensures that this condition is satisfied? To answer this question, we must look at the role of the capital market.

Wrap-Up

PRODUCT MARKET EQUILIBRIUM

When the economy is at full employment, output is equal to potential GDP. This is the output that can be produced by the available labor force with the given set of plant and equipment at normal levels of work hours and capacity utilization.

Increases in the labor supply (rightward shifts in the labor supply curve), increases in the stock of plant and equipment as a result of new investment, and technological change all increase potential GDP.

Total spending will equal potential GDP if leakages at full employment equal injections. In a closed economy with no government sector, leakages are equal to saving and injections are equal to investment.

The Capital Market

When households save, they make funds available to borrowers. Whenever firms undertake investment, they need to borrow.[5] The financial capital market is the market in which the supply of funds is allocated to those who wish to borrow. For this reason, it is also called the **loanable funds market.** In a closed economy with no government sector, equilibrium in the capital market requires that savings (the supply of funds) equal investment (the demand for funds). Our analysis of each builds on the basic competitive model of Part One.

HOUSEHOLD SAVING

The most important determinants of household saving are income and interest rates. Each year, families have to decide how much of their income to spend on current consumption and how much to save for future consumption, for retirement, for emergencies, to pay for their children's college education, or to buy a new car or new home. On average, families with higher incomes spend more *and* save more. Of course, before families can decide how much to consume and how much to save, they must pay any taxes that they owe. What is relevant for consumption and saving decisions is how much income a household has after paying taxes; this is called its **disposable income.** When the government increases taxes, disposable income is reduced. Households will typically reduce both their consumption spending and their saving when disposable income falls.

Because we are ignoring the government sector in this chapter (we add the government in Chapter 7), we also ignore taxes; disposable income therefore will equal total income. In this chapter, we also assume that the stock of plant and equipment, as well as the labor supply, is given. With wages and prices adjusting to ensure that the labor market always clears, aggregate output is fixed at potential GDP, the full-employment level of output. Recalling from Chapter 4 that aggregate income is equal to aggregate output, we can also say that total income is equal to potential GDP.

With income fixed at its full-employment level, the level of saving will depend on the return that households can earn on their savings. When households save, they set aside current income so that they will have more to spend in the future. What matters as they decide how much to save is the interest rate their savings can earn, *corrected for changes in the prices of what they buy.* The interest rate corrected for changes in prices is called the **real rate of interest.** The formula for the real rate of interest is simple: the real interest rate is equal to the market interest rate *minus* the rate of inflation. If the market interest rate is 5 percent and inflation is 2 percent, the real return on your savings is 3 percent.

The real interest rate is the correct measure of the return on savings because it takes into account changes in prices. The evidence, at least for the United States, suggests that household saving is relatively insensitive to change in the real inter-

---

[5]For the sake of simplicity, we have so far assumed that households are the only source of saving. Firms may also save so that they can finance their investment spending from their own cash reserves. This does not change our analysis, since we can think of the firm as borrowing the funds from itself.

est rate (perhaps rising slightly with it). For the sake of simplicity, then, we will often assume saving is completely inelastic—that is, it does not change at all as the real interest rate varies. In this case, changes in the real rate of interest do not lead to any change in saving. This results in a vertical saving function, as shown in Figure 6.7.

The assumption that saving does not respond to changes in the real interest rate might seem to be inconsistent with one of our key economic concepts—that incentives matter. Because a rise in the real rate of interest provides a greater incentive to save, it should lead to an increase in household saving. However, an offsetting income effect works in the opposite direction. If the adults in a household are saving for the college expenses of their children or for their own retirement, a higher real rate of interest means that they need to save less each year to reach their goal in the future. For example, suppose you want to have $15,000 saved up in ten years. If the real rate of interest is 2 percent, you must save $1,370 annually; if the real rate of interest rises to 10 percent, the amount needed each year drops to $941.25. You can reduce your current level of saving and still achieve your goal of $15,000. The income effect of a rise in the real rate of interest works to reduce saving, while the substitution effect of a rise in the real interest rate, the direct incentive effect of the higher return, acts to increase saving. The two effects pull in opposite directions, and the evidence suggests that the result is essentially a draw. That is why household saving is not very sensitive to the real interest rate and why we will often assume it is completely inelastic.

INVESTMENT

Economists use the word *investment* in two different ways. Households think of the stocks and bonds they buy as investments—**financial investments.** These financial investments provide the funds for firms to buy capital goods—machines and buildings. The purchases of new machines and buildings represent firms' investment, referred to as **capital goods investment** or simply as *investment. In macroeconomics, when we refer to* investment, *it is to physical investment in capital goods, not financial investment.*

Firms invest to increase their capacity to produce goods and services. They expect returns from the sales of this additional production to cover the costs of the additional workers and raw materials required, as well as the cost of the funds that financed the investment, leaving the firm with a profit.

There are two key determinants of investment: firms' expectations concerning future sales and profits, which for now we will assume to be fixed, and the real rate of interest. Many firms borrow to finance their investment. The cost of these funds—what they have to pay back to the financial sector for using the borrowed funds—is the interest rate. Since the firm pays back a debt with dollars whose purchasing power depends on inflation, the relevant cost is the real rate of interest.

The higher the real rate of interest, the fewer the investment projects that will be profitable—that is, the fewer the projects that will yield a return sufficient to compensate the firm for the risks undertaken after interest on the borrowed funds is paid back. Even if the firm is flush with cash, the interest rate matters. The real interest rate then becomes the opportunity cost of the firm's money—that is, what

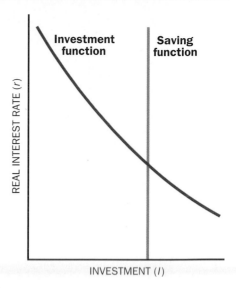

Figure 6.7

THE SAVING FUNCTION AND THE INVESTMENT FUNCTION

If saving is unresponsive to the real interest rates, then the saving function will be vertical. The investment function slopes downward to the right, tracing out the levels of real investment at different real interest rates. As the interest rate falls, investment increases.

the firm could have obtained if, instead of making an investment, it had simply decided to lend the funds to some other firm.

The **investment function** gives the level of (real) investment at each value of the real rate of interest. The investment function slopes downward to the right; investment increases as the real interest rate decreases. This is depicted in Figure 6.7, which shows the real interest rate on the vertical axis and the level of real investment on the horizontal axis.

SAVING VERSUS INVESTMENT

What we often call investing (putting money into a mutual fund, purchasing shares in the stock market) is actually *saving*—setting aside part of our income rather than spending it. These funds are then made available through the financial system to individuals and firms who wish to purchase capital goods such as plant and equipment or build new office buildings, shopping malls, or homes.

Investment refers to such additions to the physical stock of capital in the economy. As the real interest rate rises, the cost of borrowing funds for these investment projects rises. As a result, fewer projects will look profitable, fewer households will buy a new car, and fewer homes will be constructed.

Saving may rise as households reduce consumption to take advantage of higher rates of return on their savings. However, the evidence suggests this effect is small, so we will often assume that saving is inelastic.

EQUILIBRIUM IN THE CAPITAL MARKET

The equilibrium real interest rate is the rate at which saving and investment balance, as depicted in Figure 6.8. Panel A shows saving increasing as the real interest rate rises, while panels B and C illustrate the case of an inelastic saving curve. The impact of an increased demand for investment at each real interest rate is shown in panels A and B. In panel A, both the equilibrium real rate of interest and the equilibrium levels of saving and investment increase. Because the rise in the interest rate induces households to save more, in the new equilibrium the quantity of investment is able to rise. In panel B, only the equilibrium real interest rate changes as a result of the shift in investment demand. Because saving is inelastic in panel B, the change in the interest rate leaves saving unaffected. As a consequence, the quantity of investment must also be unchanged (since saving and investment are equal in equilibrium). Despite the rightward shift in the investment function, the real interest rate increases enough to keep investment unchanged.

Panel C illustrates the effects of a shift in the saving curve. A rightward shift in the saving curve, perhaps caused by households wishing to set aside more for retirement, results in a fall in the equilibrium real rate of interest and a rise in equilibrium investment.

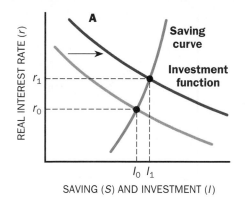
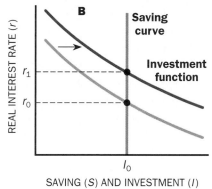
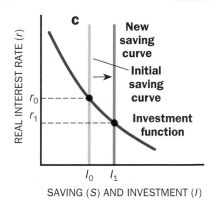

Figure 6.8

EQUILIBRIUM IN THE
CAPITAL MARKET AT
FULL EMPLOYMENT

Equilibrium requires that the demand for funds (investment) equal the supply (saving). The level of desired investment decreases as the real interest rate increases.

In panel A, saving increases slightly with increases in the real interest rate. In panels B and C, saving is not interest sensitive, so the saving curve is a vertical line. The equilibrium level of investment is simply equal to the full-employment level of saving.

A shift in the investment function is depicted in panels A and B. In panel A, equilibrium investment is increased from I_0 to I_1, while in panel B, with inelastic saving, the only effect is to increase the equilibrium real interest rate from r_0 to r_1, leaving investment (and saving) unchanged.

Panel C shows a rightward shift in the saving curve. The level of saving increases at each real interest rate. In the new equilibrium in the capital market, the real interest rate has fallen from r_0 to r_1 and investment has increased from I_0 to I_1.

When the real interest rate adjusts to balance demand and supply in the capital market, saving will equal investment. We can express this same result by saying that when the capital market is in equilibrium, leakages from the spending stream equal injections. This was the condition needed to ensure that the product market was in equilibrium. Therefore, the capital market plays a critical role in ensuring product market equilibrium.

CAPITAL MARKET EQUILIBRIUM

In long-run equilibrium, full employment saving equals investment.

Increases in investment at each real interest rate (shifts to the right in the investment function) lead to a higher equilibrium real interest rate. Equilibrium investment will be unchanged if the saving curve is vertical; equilibrium investment will rise if the saving curve has a positive slope.

Increases in saving at each real interest rate (shifts to the right of the saving curve) lead to a lower equilibrium real interest rate and higher levels of investment.

Capital market equilibrium ensures that leakages equal injections at full-employment output (potential GDP). When saving is equal to investment at full-employment output, aggregate demand equals the economy's full-employment level of output.

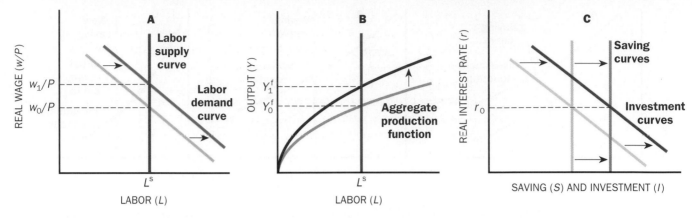

Figure 6.9

EFFECTS OF INTRODUCING
PERSONAL COMPUTERS
INTO THE ECONOMY

Panel A depicts the labor market. The labor supply curve is drawn as a vertical line at L^s. Personal computers increase the marginal product of workers, resulting in a rightward shift of the labor demand curve and an increase in the equilibrium real wage from w_0/P to w_1/P. Panel B depicts the aggregate production function; it shifts up because of the introduction of computers and the increased productivity of workers. Potential GDP increases from Y_0^f to Y_1^f. Panel C depicts the capital market. Investment increases as firms purchase personal computers, and saving increases as a result of increased income. Both the investment and saving curves shift to the right. There may be no net effect on the real interest rate (r_0) as shown here. The actual effect on the interest rate depends on the relative shifts of the saving and investment curves.

The General Equilibrium Model

We can now describe the general, long-run equilibrium of the economy. General equilibrium is a situation in which all the economy's markets are in balance—the labor, product, and capital markets all clear. General equilibrium in the full-employment model occurs when employment and the real wage have adjusted to ensure that the labor market is in equilibrium at full employment, output is equal to potential GDP, and the real interest rate is at the level ensuring that full-employment saving is equal to investment.

Start with the labor market. The real wage adjusts to ensure that the demand for labor equals the supply of labor. This adjustment determines both the equilibrium real wage and the level of employment that constitutes full employment. In the product market, the short-run aggregate production function then determines the level of output produced by firms when the economy is at full employment. This output level is potential GDP—the output that the labor supply, working with the available stock of plant and equipment, can produce when the economy is at full employment. Finally, the capital market balances leakages and injections in the circular flow of income. The real interest rate adjusts to ensure that at the full-employment level of income, saving is equal to investment. This equality also ensures that aggregate demand will equal aggregate supply at the full-employment level of output. The product market clears.

USING THE GENERAL EQUILIBRIUM MODEL

The general equilibrium model is useful because it enables us to understand the effects of various changes in the economy—from the market in which these changes originate to all the other markets in the economy.

Consider the effects on the economy of the introduction of personal computers. By making workers more productive, personal computers increase the marginal product of workers. This change increases the quantity of labor demanded at each real wage, causing a shift in the labor demand curve to the right. The equilibrium real wage rises, as shown in Figure 6.9, panel A.

The change in technology yields greater worker productivity. This change is represented by an upward shift of the short-run production function as shown in panel B. The improvement in productivity yields an increase in full-employment output. Product market equilibrium can be maintained only if aggregate demand also rises so that firms are able to sell the new higher level of output they are producing. As we have seen, this change in demand will occur if the real interest rate adjusts to maintain saving equal to investment in the capital market. Investment at each level of the real interest rate may rise as firms take advantage of the profit opportunities opened up by the new computer technology. At the same time, the increase in full-employment income leads to increases in both consumption and saving at each interest rate. The increases in investment and saving at each interest rate are represented by a rightward shift in both the investment and the saving curves (panel C). In equilibrium, the real interest rate may either rise, fall, or stay the same (as illustrated in panel C), depending on the relative magnitudes of the shifts. Whatever the impact on the real interest rate, we can conclude that equilibrium investment will rise.

We have focused here on the current effects of these changes, but there are important future effects as well. A higher level of investment today will lead to more plant and equipment tomorrow. The economy's future capacity will increase, and this expansion will contribute to future economic growth, a topic we will examine in Chapter 9. Thus, links exist not only between all markets today but also between today's and future markets.

The basic full-employment model also can be used to examine the impact on the labor, product, and capital markets of the rise in labor force participation rates among women. The *labor force participation rate* is the fraction of a group that is in the labor force (either employed or seeking work). In 1970, the female labor force participation rate was 43 percent, compared to 80 percent for men. By 1999, the female rate had risen to 60 percent. The change has pumped almost 20 million additional workers into the U.S. economy.

The effects of this change are shown in Figure 6.10. The increased supply of workers shifts the labor supply curve to the right. As panel A shows, the equilibrium real wage falls, while equilibrium employment rises. Because the level of employment now associated with equilibrium in the labor market has increased, potential GDP rises; this is shown in panel B. With higher incomes, households will increase both their consumption spending and their saving at each level of the real rate of interest. This impact on the capital market is shown in panel C as a rightward shift in the saving curve. While equilibrium saving and investment rise, the equilibrium real interest rate falls.

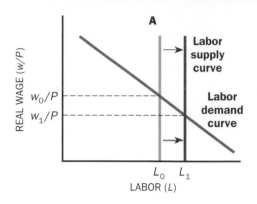 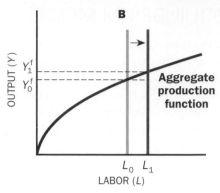 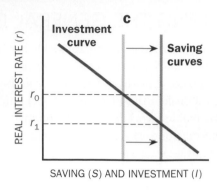

A

REAL WAGE (w/P)

Labor
supply
curve

w_0/P

w_1/P

Labor
demand
curve

L_0 L_1
LABOR (L)

B

OUTPUT (Y)

Y_1^f
Y_0^f

Aggregate
production
function

L_0 L_1
LABOR (L)

C

REAL INTEREST RATE (r)

Investment
curve

Saving
curves

r_0

r_1

SAVING (S) AND INVESTMENT (I)

Figure 6.10

EFFECTS OF AN INCREASE IN
THE SUPPLY OF LABOR

Panel A depicts the labor market. As more women enter the labor force, the labor supply curve shifts to the right, from L_0 to L_1. This results in a decrease in the equilibrium real wage from w_0/P to w_1/P and an increase in employment. Panel B depicts the aggregate production function; with employment higher, potential GDP rises from Y_0^f to Y_1^f. Panel C depicts the capital market. Saving increases as a result of increased income; the saving curve shifts to the right. The real interest rate falls, and in the new equilibrium, both saving and investment have increased.

We have used the full-employment model to analyze the impacts of two important changes in the economy: those associated with the introduction of a new technology (personal computers) and those associated with a change in the labor force. To focus on the effects each would have, we studied each change in isolation, assuming that nothing else was changing. In fact, both effects have been at work for more than thirty years. Both have combined to expand employment and raise potential GDP. Since the introduction of new technologies tends to raise real wages, while the expansion in the labor supply tends to lower real wages, their combined effect on real wages could be to increase them, decrease them, or leave them unchanged.

Computer technology has increased the productivity of a wide range of workers.

Review and Practice

SUMMARY

1. Macroeconomic equilibrium focuses on equilibrium levels of aggregates: employment, output, saving, and investment.
2. The real wage equates the demand for labor with the supply of labor. Increases in labor supply at each real wage are reflected in lower real wages, which induce firms to create additional jobs to match the increases in supply.
3. The full-employment level of output is that level of output which the economy can produce with its given stock of plant and equipment, when labor is fully employed. It will increase with increases in the labor supply or as a result of new technologies.
4. The real interest rate (which takes into account inflation) equates investment and saving. The desired level of investment decreases with increases in the real rate of interest. Household saving depends on income and the real interest rate. When the economy is at full employment, the interest rate is the main variable of concern in determining saving. Saving increases slightly with increases in the real interest rate.
5. A decrease in saving leads to a higher real interest rate and lower investment. A decrease in investment at each real interest rate leads to an unchanged or lower level of investment, depending on the elasticity of saving.
6. An increase in saving leads to a lower real increase rate and to increased investment. An increase in investment at each real interest rate leads to unchanged or higher investment, depending on the elasticity of saving.
7. When saving and investment are equal, the demand for goods and services will equal the level of output at full employment. The capital market balances leakages and injections in the circular flow of income.
8. All the markets in the economy are interlinked. Changes in one market have effects in all other markets.

KEY TERMS

full employment
short-run aggregate production function
potential GDP
full-employment level of output
loanable funds market
disposable income
real rate of interest
financial investments
capital goods investment
investment function

REVIEW QUESTIONS

1. How do competitive markets with flexible wages and prices ensure that labor is always fully employed? What induces firms to create just the right number of additional jobs to match an increase in the number of workers?
2. Describe the effects of changes in labor supply on equilibrium real wages and potential GDP (full-employment level of output).
3. What determines the economy's productive capacity or aggregate supply or potential GDP? How does aggregate supply increase when labor supply increases?
4. What is investment? Why does investment decrease when the real interest rate increases? What role do expectations play in investment?
5. What determines the level of saving? Explain why, if taxes are fixed, disposable income in a full-employment economy is fixed. Explain why saving may not be very sensitive to the real interest rate.
6. How are leakages and injections balanced? Why will demand and supply in the product market be equal if leakages and injections are equal?

PROBLEMS

1. In the text, we assumed that the labor supply did not depend on the real wage. Assume that at higher real wages, more individuals wish to work. Trace through how each of the steps in the analysis has to be changed. Show the equilibrium in the labor market. What happens to real wages, employment, GDP, and saving if the labor supply function shifts to the right?

Learning Goals

In this chapter, you will learn

1 The composition of government expenditures and revenues in the United States

2 How government deficits and surpluses affect the capital market

3 How the government affects the economy's full-employment equilibrium

4 The consequences of fiscal deficits and surpluses for output, investment, and future generations

5 The recent experiences with deficits and surpluses in the United States

Chapter 7

GOVERNMENT FINANCE AT FULL EMPLOYMENT

News stories are filled with debates over government spending and tax policies. In the United States, the federal government spends more than $2 trillion each year on everything from national defense to Social Security to national parks to health and education. State and local governments spend another $1.5 trillion on schools and a variety of services, including police, fire, and health. To pay for these expenditures, governments levy taxes and, when taxes are not sufficient to cover expenditures, they borrow.

During the 1980s and through most of the 1990s, the U.S. government consistently spent more than it raised in tax revenues. To cover this deficit, the government had to borrow in the capital market, just as a firm or household would. The ballooning budget deficit emerged as a major national issue; by the 1992 presidential election, public opinion polls were persistently ranking the huge deficits among the central problems facing the country. By 1998, deficits had apparently been vanquished and the U.S. federal government was collecting more in taxes than it was spending. Debates during the 2000 presidential campaign focused on what to do with these excess tax revenues. Should they be used to finance additional government spending? Or should taxes be cut? In early 2001, Congress took up the debate and eventually approved a large tax cut. Quickly, however, the situation again changed: the war on terrorism led to unanticipated increases in spending while the tax cut and an economic slowdown reduced the government's revenues. By 2002, the federal government was once again spending more than it raised in tax revenues, and a major issue during the 2004 presidential campaign was how to deal with these deficits.

In this chapter, we begin by briefly discussing the major components of the federal government's expenditures and revenues. Then we extend the full-employment model developed in Chapter 6 to include the government sector. By adding the

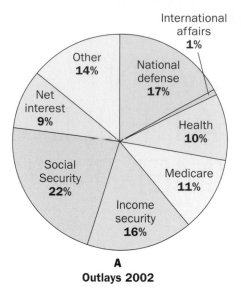

A
Outlays 2002

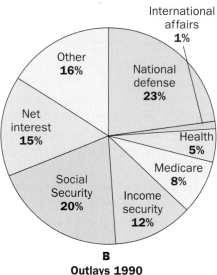

B
Outlays 1990

Figure 7.1

THE COMPOSITION OF
FEDERAL GOVERNMENT
SPENDING

The composition of the federal budget changed between 1990 and 2002: Medicare, income security, and social security programs grew, while net interest and defense spending fell as a percent of the total budget.

SOURCE: *Economic Report of the President* (2004).

government to our full-employment model, we will learn how government decisions about taxes and spending affect the full-employment economy. The chapter concludes with a discussion of some of the major budgetary issues facing the U.S. federal government.

The Composition of Spending and Taxes

The federal government spends more than $2 trillion per year. This total can be divided into two basic categories: **discretionary spending** and **nondiscretionary spending.** Discretionary expenditures—which include spending on the military, government operations, and most education and training programs—are decided on an annual basis. Each year, Congress and the president have the *discretion* to change their levels. Nondiscretionary spending has two components. First, the government must make interest payments on the national debt. Second, the government in various programs has established **entitlements**—certain benefits, such as Social Security, Medicare, and food stamps, to which individuals who meet criteria specified by law are *entitled.*

Panel A of Figure 7.1 shows the composition of federal spending in 2002, by major categories. Health, Medicare, Social Security, income security, and net interest are largely nondiscretionary expenditures, and in 2002 they constituted almost 70 percent of all spending. Panel B shows the same categories in 1990. By comparing the two panels, we see how the composition of government spending changed during this period. Defense spending shrank as a proportion of total spending, while the proportion of spending represented by health, Medicare, Social Security, and income security rose. Increases in health costs were particularly dramatic, doubling from 5 percent of the budget in 1990 to 10 percent in 2002. Net interest payments fell as a proportion of total spending, reflecting the low level of interest rates in 2002 and the decline in the debt caused by the surpluses between 1998 to 2001.

The sources of the government's revenue during this period changed only slightly. As shown in Figure 7.2, individual income tax payments represented just under half of the federal government's receipts in 1990 and 2002.

Extending the Basic Full-Employment Model

Although the basic full-employment model ignored the role of the government, in reality, the government plays a central role in all economies. Major macroeconomic policy issues often center around the impact of government spending and taxation decisions. To address these important policy issues, we need to extend the basic full-employment model.

Adding the Government

Introducing government into the analysis affects both the product market and the capital market. In the product market, the government has an impact on the economy in two ways. First, the government's purchases of goods and services produced by firms affect demand in the product market. Second, taxes subtract from demand in the product market because they reduce disposable income, lowering consumption spending.[1] In the capital market, governments affect the economy if they need to borrow to cover deficits when spending exceeds tax revenues or if they repay government debt when tax revenues exceed spending.

Figure 7.3 shows the circular flow of income when the government sector is added to our model. Households pay taxes to the government sector. These payments, just like household saving, represent a leakage from the spending stream. The government sector's purchases of goods and services represent an injection into the spending stream similar to investment spending. If tax revenues fall short of government expenditures, the government has a **fiscal deficit,** and it will need to borrow in the capital market to cover the difference. If the government runs a **fiscal surplus,** so that its tax revenues exceed its expenditures, then the government, like the household sector, will be a net saver and will represent a source of saving for the economy.

The government *deficit* represents the additional borrowing in a given year, while the accumulated amount the government owes—its *debt*—reflects all the borrowing it has done in the past. When the government runs a surplus, as it did from 1998 to 2001, it takes in more in revenue than it is spending. That surplus is used to repay the government's debt.

THE GOVERNMENT AND THE CAPITAL MARKET

Focusing on the capital market makes clear the effects of the government on the economy's full employment. In Chapter 6, we examined a simplified economy, one with no government and no trade with other countries (i.e., a *closed* economy). There, we saw that at the equilibrium real interest rate, saving was equal to investment. Now let's see how equilibrium in the capital market and the real interest rate are affected when we bring government into the picture. If government expenditures (G) exceed tax revenues (T), then the government must borrow to obtain the funds necessary to finance its expenditures. This means the government will compete with private borrowers for the saving of the private sector. Less saving is available for private investment.

---

[1]Governments also can affect the economy as producers of goods. In the U.S. economy, the government is not a major producer of goods and services and so we will neglect that aspect of the government in our analysis. However, government production is very important in some areas of the economy, education being a prime example.

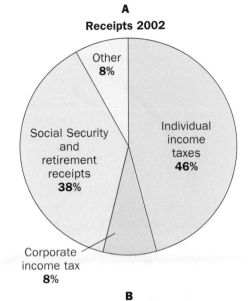

A
Receipts 2002

Other 8%
Social Security and retirement receipts 38%
Individual income taxes 46%
Corporate income tax 8%

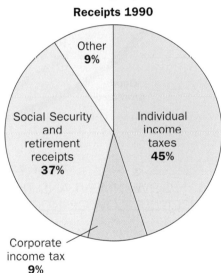

B
Receipts 1990

Other 9%
Social Security and retirement receipts 37%
Individual income taxes 45%
Corporate income tax 9%

Figure 7.2

THE COMPOSITION OF FEDERAL GOVERNMENT REVENUE

The importance of different sources of federal revenue remained relatively constant between 1990 and 2002.

SOURCE: *Economic Report of the President* (2004).

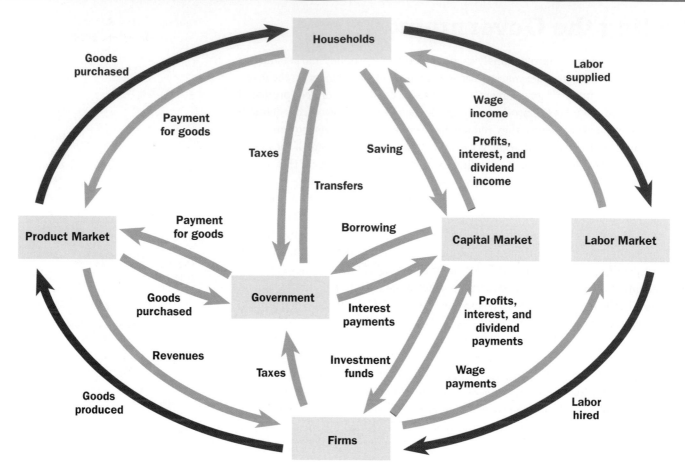

Figure 7.3

GOVERNMENT AND THE
CIRCULAR FLOW OF INCOME

The government purchases goods and services in the product market and receives tax revenues from households and firms. It also makes transfer payments, such as Social Security benefits, to households. Government purchases represent an injection into the spending flow, while taxes (the amount after transfers) represent a leakage. If government expenditures exceed revenues, the government will need to borrow in the capital market. If government revenues exceed expenditures, the government surplus adds to the supply of funds in the capital market. When the capital market is in equilibrium, leakages will again balance injections, and demand and supply in the product market will be equal.

When the government runs a deficit, private saving (S_p) takes on two purposes—to finance private investment (I) and to finance the government's deficit $(G - T)$. Equilibrium in the capital market occurs when private saving is equal to investment plus the deficit, or

$$S_p = I + (G - T).$$

Alternatively, we can think of the deficit as *negative public government saving* (S_g):

$$G - T = -S_g.$$

From this perspective, the first equation can be rewritten as

$$S_p = I - S_g,$$

or

$$S_p + S_g = I.$$

The left side is called **national saving,** the combined saving of the private (households and businesses) and public (government) sectors. When the capital market in a closed economy is in equilibrium, *national saving equals investment.*

The effect in the capital market of a government deficit is illustrated in Figure 7.4. The investment schedule is downward sloping. Saving is assumed to be unresponsive to the interest rate. The initial level of national saving is S_0. The capital market is in equilibrium when the real rate of interest is r_0. Now suppose the government increases expenditures without increasing taxes so that it needs to borrow an amount equal to its deficit, $G - T$, the excess of spending over revenue. The increase in the government deficit reduces national saving, so the saving schedule is now shifted to the left, to S_1. It is shifted to the left by the amount the government has borrowed. Equilibrium in the capital market now occurs at a higher real interest rate (r_1). The higher real interest rate reduces private investment spending. As a consequence, government borrowing is **crowding out** an equal amount of private investment. That is, a rise in government spending is simply displacing private investment spending.

When the government has a budget surplus, the opposite effects occur. With a surplus, public saving is positive. A cut in government expenditures without a corresponding reduction in taxes increases the surplus and shifts the national saving schedule to the right. As a result, the equilibrium real interest rate falls and private investment rises.

Our analysis tells us that *when all else is held constant,* an increase in the government deficit will raise the equilibrium real rate of interest at full employment. Other factors—shifts in the investment function or in private saving—can also affect the equilibrium real rate of interest (as we learned in Chapter 6). Thus, as we assess the impact of the government on real interest rates, the full-employment model predicts that an increase in the deficit will increase the equilibrium real rate of interest *relative to what it would have been without the deficit increase.* To understand the actual evolution of the economy's real interest rate, we need to take these other factors into account. For example, in the late 1990s, an investment boom associated with new information technologies created such a strong demand for capital that it offset the effects on the real interest rate of the federal budget deficit reduction that occurred at the same time. In the first years of the current century, investment collapsed after the bubble in technology stocks burst in 2000 and the recession of 2001 began. This decrease in the demand for capital worked to offset the impact of the big increase in the budget deficit.

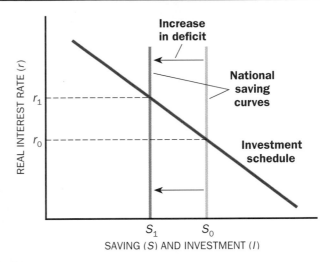

Figure 7.4

EFFECTS OF INCREASED GOVERNMENT DEFICIT ON THE CAPITAL MARKET

An increased government deficit (reduced public saving) reduces national saving. With a leftward shift in the saving curve, the equilibrium level of real interest rates is higher and the equilibrium level of investment is lower.

Everyone has to pay taxes!

The Effects of Changes in Taxes While we have focused on changes in expenditures, the same analysis enables us to understand how the economy would be affected by a tax cut not balanced by a cut in government expenditures. A tax cut increases households' disposable income. To make the example concrete, suppose taxes are reduced by $100 billion. As a result, disposable income rises by the full $100 billion that households no longer need to pay to the government as taxes. They will use this additional disposable income to increase their current consumption spending and to increase their saving.[2] For example, aggregate consumption might rise by $90 billion and saving by $10 billion. If this is the case, private saving will rise by $10 billion, but national saving will fall because the government's deficit rises by $100 billion. Therefore, national saving falls by $90 billion. The leftward shift in the savings curve leads to a higher equilibrium real interest rate and a lower level of investment.

Balanced Budget Changes in Expenditures and Taxes The previous examples considered cases in which expenditures or taxes were changed, leading to changes in public saving. But what happens if the government changes *both* expenditures and taxes by the same amount so that public saving remains unchanged? Suppose initially that the government has a balanced budget: that is,

---

[2]This does not mean every household will use some of the tax cut to increase their saving. Many households might decide to spend the entire amount. Others might decide to save it all. But when we add up all the households in the economy, both aggregate consumption and aggregate saving will have increased.

revenues match expenditures. In 1998, for example, both U.S. federal government receipts and expenditures were roughly $1.7 trillion. Now suppose that the government increases its expenditures, say, by $100 billion. To pay for these expenditures, suppose the government increases taxes by an equal amount. We would describe this as a *balanced budget change in taxes and expenditures*. Since both expenditures and revenues increase by the same amount, the government's overall budget remains in balance. What will be the effect on the macroeconomy of such a balanced budget increase in spending?

Since taxes have risen by $100 billion, the private sector's disposable income—income after paying taxes—has been reduced by $100 billion. When disposable income falls, households typically adjust by reducing both their consumption and their saving. For example, to pay the additional $100 billion in taxes, total consumption might fall by $90 billion and saving by $10 billion. The reduction in consumption and saving totals $100 billion, the amount that households needed to pay the higher taxes.

The reduction in disposable income from the tax increase reduces private saving. Since public saving is unchanged (remember, expenditures and taxes were increased by the same amount), national saving falls. In the capital market, the national saving curve shifts to the left. With an unchanged investment schedule, the equilibrium real interest rate rises and the equilibrium investment level falls. This is an important conclusion. Equal changes in government revenues and expenditures—balanced budget changes in taxes and expenditures—affect investment and the real interest rate. A balanced budget *increase* in taxes and expenditures will *reduce* consumption and investment and *raise* the real interest rate. A balanced budget *decrease* in taxes and expenditures will *increase* consumption and investment and *lower* the real interest rate.

A balanced budget change in expenditures and taxes shifts how output is allocated to private uses (consumption and investment) and public uses (government purchases). Think of total output as a pie to be divided among various uses. A balanced budget change does not alter the total size of the pie; under our assumption that the economy remains at full employment, output remains at its full-employment level. Its effect is simply to change how the pie is divided. If government expenditures and taxes increase, private-sector spending on consumption and investment shrinks—it is crowded out—to make room for increased public-sector spending. Crowding out occurs even if the government increases taxes enough to fully pay for the increased expenditures, as individuals adjust to higher taxes in part by reducing private saving.

In this example, the total pie—full-employment output—was treated as fixed. It is important to understand why this is the case. In Chapter 6 we learned that full-employment output depends on the economy's capital stock, its technology, and the level of employment that occurs when demand and supply balance in the labor market. None of these factors is likely to be affected directly by changes in general government expenditures or taxes. Thus full-employment output, potential GDP, will remain unchanged. However, government expenditures can have an impact on *future* income levels and growth. For example, increased government purchases that lower private-sector investment will reduce the amount of capital that the economy has in the future, thereby lowering full-employment income in the future. When we discuss economic growth and productivity in Chapter 9, we will consider some types of government expenditures and taxes that might affect the discovery of new technologies, the productivity of capital, and the demand for labor by firms. When we deal with these policies, we will need to investigate their impact on potential GDP.

LEAKAGES AND INJECTIONS

We have focused our discussion of government deficits on the capital market. Recall, however, that when the capital market is in equilibrium, balancing national saving and investment, the leakages and injections in the circular flow of income will also be balanced. This result holds just as it did in Chapter 6 when we ignored the government sector. Leakages from the spending flow now consist of household saving and taxes, while injections into the spending flow consist of investment and government expenditures. As they adjust to ensure that national saving equals investment, real interest rates also ensure that leakages equal injections at full-employment output. The total demand for the goods and services produced by firms will balance the total output that is produced at full employment.

Adding Government Incorporating the government into our model gives us three sources of aggregate demand—consumption, investment, and government purchases:

$$\text{demand} = C + I + G.$$

For the economy to be at equilibrium at full employment, demand must equal full-employment income. When the capital market is in equilibrium, desired investment equals national saving (the sum of private saving and government saving). Private saving at full employment is equal to full-employment income Y^f minus consumption and taxes. Government saving is equal to taxes minus expenditures. We can express capital market equilibrium as

$$I = S_N = S_p + S_g = (Y^f - C - T) + (T - G).$$

Rearranging this expression implies that

$$C + I + G = Y^f,$$

which is to say that demand from consumption spending, investment, and government spending equals full-employment income. Thus, aggregate demand equals full-employment output and the product market is in equilibrium at full employment when the capital market is in equilibrium.

International Perspective

DEFICITS IN OTHER COUNTRIES

When the United States ran a huge budget deficit during the 1980s, it was not alone. Most other major economies also witnessed the same problems of deficits and growing government debt. The figure shows estimates from the International Monetary Fund (IMF) of the "structural" budget deficit as a percentage of potential GDP for the United States, Japan, and other major industrialized economies (Canada, France, Germany, Italy, and the United Kingdom). The structural deficit is that part of the government's deficit that is left after it is corrected for the type of business cycle factors we will be studying in Part Three. It corresponds to an estimate of the budget *if the economy were at full employment.* As the figure shows, only Japan among the major industrialized economies experienced a budget surplus during the 1980s.

During the 1990s, the budget situation improved in the United States and the other industrialized economies, again with the exception of Japan. The 1990s, when most industrialized economies enjoyed strong economic growth, are sometimes described as "the lost decade" in Japan, as growth stagnated after the rapid economic expansion of the previous thirty years.

According to the IMF's estimates, the United States had achieved a balanced budget by 1998, and ran surpluses in 1999 and 2000. However, that budget situation changed dramatically after 2001 as a result of tax cuts that reduced government revenue and spending increases that were necessitated by the war on terrorism. But unlike in the 1980s, the other industrialized economies did not show a similar budget picture. In fact, for 2004, the deficit as a percent of potential GDP in the industrialized economies fell to under 2 percent, even as it rose to exceed 4 percent in the United States.

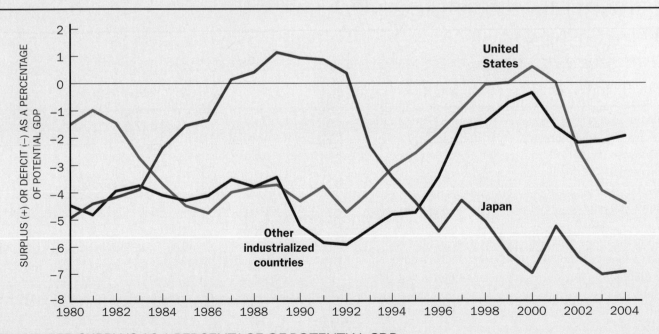

STRUCTURED SURPLUS AS A PERCENTAGE OF POTENTIAL GDP

SOURCE: IMF, *World Economic Outlook* (2004).

GOVERNMENT DEFICITS AND SURPLUSES

Government expenditures and taxes affect the capital market.

Increases in taxes reduce disposable income, and thereby decrease private saving. The equilibrium real interest rate is higher and private investment is lower.

When the government spends more than it receives in revenue, it must borrow to finance its deficit. A deficit reduces public saving, leading to higher real interest rates and lower private investment.

The lower the level of private investment, the smaller the increase in the capital stock. With a smaller capital stock, potential GDP in the future is lower.

A surplus has the opposite effect. When the government spends less than it receives in revenue, public saving and thus national saving rise. This increase leads to lower real interest rates and higher private investment. Higher private

Thinking Like an Economist

DISTRIBUTION, DEFICITS, AND INTERGENERATIONAL TRANSFERS

If you borrow money to buy a car, you can enjoy the car now without paying for it in full. Instead, you can spread the payments out over a relatively long time period. The same is true of governments that borrow. Instead of raising enough in taxes right now to pay for all its expenditures, a government can borrow and use future taxes to repay its debt. But this approach raises the issue of distribution. Let's suppose the government borrows $20 billion today, uses the money to reduce the current level of taxes, and then plans to raise taxes in fifty years to repay the money that it has borrowed. In fifty years, most of the taxpayers who benefited from the tax reduction will have died, and many of those whose higher taxes will repay the debt are not even alive now, when the money is being borrowed. Does this mean that government borrowing results in a transfer of wealth between generations, from future taxpayers to today's?

Some economists argue that the answer is no. They point out that those future taxpayers are the children of today's taxpayers. Rather than spend the tax cut, today's taxpayers can save it, and simply pass it on to their children in the form of a larger inheritance. The children would then have the extra wealth they need to pay the higher taxes they will face. They therefore will not have to reduce their own consumption spending to pay for the tax cut enjoyed by their parents.

Most economists, however, do not believe that private savings increases in this way when taxes are cut. They observe that when people find their disposable incomes higher as a result of a tax cut, they increase their consumption spending. They may save some of the tax cut, but private saving does not increase enough to offset the government's dissaving (deficit). As a consequence, national saving falls. In the capital market, the fall in national saving increases the full-employment equilibrium real interest rate. Investment falls. Lower investment means less capital (plant and equipment) is built, and future generations inherit a smaller stock of capital. The distribution of wealth between generations is affected: current taxpayers have been able to consume more, while future generations will have less capital and therefore lower incomes.

investment increases the capital stock, thereby increasing potential GDP in the future.

Evaluating Government Deficits and Surpluses

We have seen that government deficits and surpluses have significant impacts. Deficits reduce national saving, increase the real interest rate, and reduce investment, and surpluses have the opposite effect. But while our analysis tells us what the consequences of deficits and surpluses are, it does not tell us whether governments should or should not run deficits.

Economists have traditionally argued that government borrowing, just like individual borrowing, may or may not make sense, depending on the purpose for which the funds have been borrowed. It makes sense to borrow to buy a house that you will live in for many years or a car that you will drive for several years. Borrowing is a way to spread the payments for the house or the car over time, so that you can pay for the purchase as you use it. It also makes sense to borrow for an educational degree that will lead to a higher-paying job in the future. But paying this year for a vacation from two years ago makes no economic sense.

Countries are in a similar position. Borrowing to finance a road or a school that will be used for many years may be quite appropriate; borrowing to pay for this year's government salaries or current operating costs poses real problems. Governments in many countries—sometimes the dictators or corrupt regimes of the past—have taken on more debt than they can comfortably pay off, forcing them to raise taxes sharply and reduce citizens' living standards. Others have simply failed to repay what they owe, thereby jeopardizing their ability to borrow in the future.

Financing government expenditures by borrowing rather than by raising taxes—deficit financing—results in higher levels of private consumption in the short run, since individuals' taxes are lower. Thus, borrowing to finance government expenditures can serve to shift the burden onto future generations. For example, the U.S. government financed some of its World War II expenditures by borrowing rather than raising taxes by the full amount necessary to cover the war effort. This debt was discharged, in part, by taxes paid by workers long after the war ended. Thus, some of the cost of the war was borne by the generation who entered the labor force *after* the war. Since these later generations benefited from the Allied victory in World War II, an argument can be made in this case that sharing the burden across generations made sense. If governments borrow for spending that benefits only the current generation, however, forcing future generations to share the cost is less defensible.

There is another way that government borrowing shifts the burden of expenditures onto future generations. When the economy is at full employment, more consumption implies less saving. To maintain the economy at full employment, the real interest rate must rise to balance saving and investment—and a higher equilibrium interest rate reduces investment. As we will see in Chapter 9, lower investment in the present can reduce economic growth in the future, leading to lower incomes and consumption.

Reducing the deficit or actually running a surplus has the opposite effect. It allows the real interest rate to fall, stimulating private investment and thereby promoting economic growth and better living standards in the future.

Wrap-Up

CONSEQUENCES OF GOVERNMENT DEFICITS

If the government runs deficits,

Some of the burden of current expenditures is shifted to future generations directly.

Government deficits also reduce national saving, raise the real interest rate, and lower the level of private investment, thereby making future generations worse off.

If the government runs surpluses,

Some of the burden of future expenditures is shifted to the current generation.

Also, repaying government debt increases national saving, lowers the real interest rate, and increases private investment, thereby making future generations better off.

Government Deficits and Surpluses: Our Recent Experiences

In 1981, federal taxes were cut in the United States, but expenditures on defense and social programs (medical, income security, and Social Security) increased. Figure 7.5 shows the resulting increase in the federal deficit. In twelve years, from 1981 to 1992, the deficit more than quadrupled from $60 billion per year to $280 billion per year. The economy grew over the period shown in the figure, as did the price level, so a better measure of the size of the deficit is obtained by expressing the nominal deficit as a percentage of nominal GDP. Even after making this adjustment, we see that the increase in the deficit was dramatic, as panel B shows. The United States experienced the first major peacetime deficits in its history.

During President Bill Clinton's first term, a number of measures were adopted to raise taxes and limit the growth in federal spending. These succeeded in reducing the deficit. Beginning in 1998, the federal government actually started to run a surplus, with tax revenues exceeding government expenditures. The surpluses were short-lived, however. The federal budget swung back into deficit in 2002 as a result of three factors: the economy entered a recession in 2001, and thus the taxes

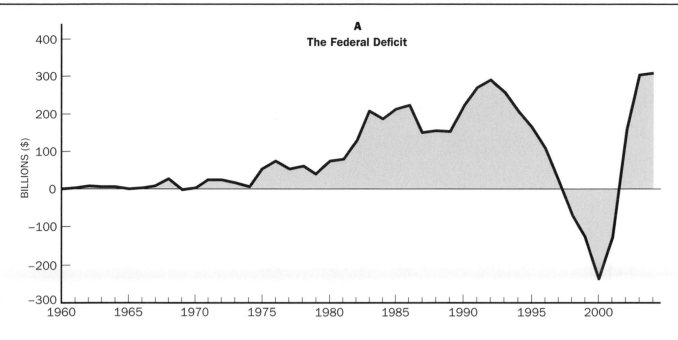

A
The Federal Deficit

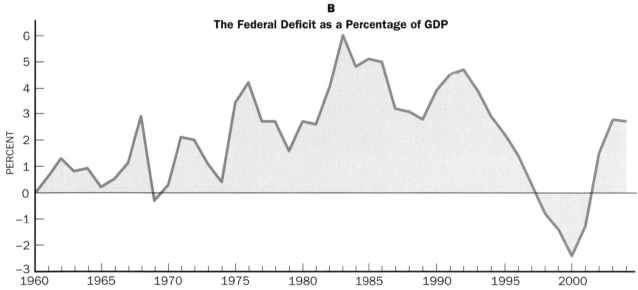

B
The Federal Deficit as a Percentage of GDP

Figure 7.5

THE FEDERAL DEFICIT

Federal borrowing increased dramatically between 1975 and the early 1990s, fell sharply in the late 1990s, and rose steeply again after 2000. Panel A shows the nominal deficit; panel B shows the deficit as a percentage of nominal GDP.

SOURCE: *Economic Report of the President* (2004).

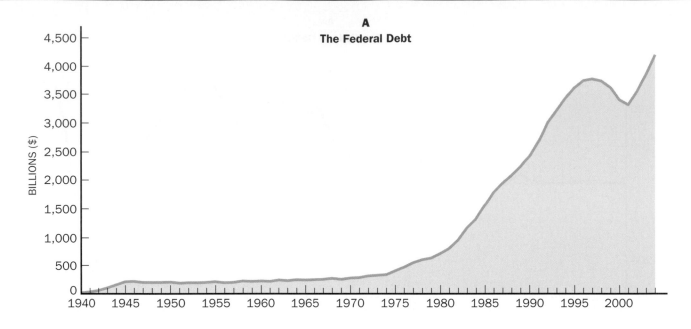

A
The Federal Debt

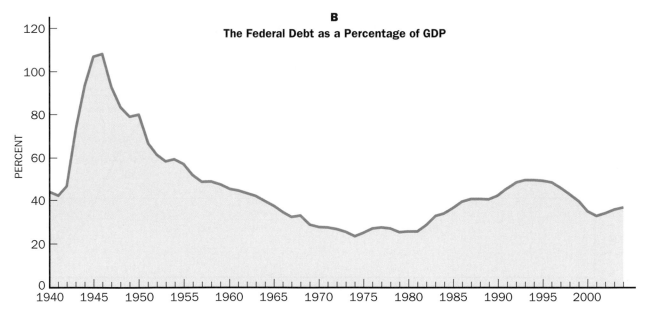

B
The Federal Debt as a Percentage of GDP

Figure 7.6

THE FEDERAL DEBT

The federal debt fell after World War II and rose rapidly after 1982 (panel A). Expressing the debt relative to GDP, panel B shows that the debt reached a peak relative to the size of the economy immediately after World War II, rose between 1982 and 1996, and declined from 1996 until 2000.

SOURCE: *Economic Report of the President* (2004).

collected fell; Congress passed a large tax cut in 2001 (followed by another in 2003); and the war on terrorism led to a rise in federal government spending.

Panel A of Figure 7.6 shows the U.S. federal debt, the accumulated effect of past deficits. The deficits of the 1980s and 1990s pushed the federal debt to record peacetime levels. Debt was reduced during 1998 to 2001 as the government enjoyed budget surpluses. Panel B shows the debt as a percentage of GDP to adjust for the inflation and real economic growth that has occurred over the sixty-odd years shown. As the graph reveals, the debt today is smaller relative to the size of the economy than it was immediately following World War II.

Factors Affecting the Federal Budget

Figure 7.7 shows federal outlays and receipts as a percentage of GDP since 1960, together with projections for 2004 through 2010. Projecting what will happen to the deficit even a few years into the future is often difficult. In 1996, for example, the Congressional Budget Office (CBO) was predicting that the federal government would run a deficit of $259 billion in 2001. In fact, the government enjoyed a surplus in 2001 of $127 billion. In January 2001, the CBO projected a surplus of $397 billion

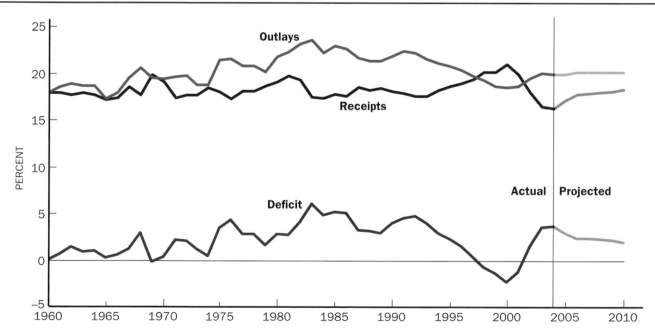

Figure 7.7

FEDERAL OUTLAYS AND
REVENUE AS A PERCENTAGE
OF GDP

The gap between federal outlays and revenues as a percentage of GDP reached a peak of 6 percent in 1983. In 2000, the surplus of revenues over outlays was 2.4 percent of GDP.

SOURCE: Congressional Budget Office.

for 2004. As of 2005, it was clear that the government, instead of running a surplus in 2004, saw the deficit soar above $400 billion.

One reason budget projections often turn out wrong is that in making its calculations the CBO, by law, must assume there will be no changes in tax or expenditure programs. Yet these programs do change, partly in response to the CBO's figures. In the 1990s, the large projected deficits led Congress to change taxes and curb growth in expenditures; in 2000, with the CBO projecting future surpluses, Congress cut taxes to reduce future revenues. Another reason for the projections' inaccuracy is that unforeseen events can alter the government's fiscal position. For example, the recession that started in 2001, further tax cuts, the terrorist attacks of September 11, 2001, and the rise in spending for homeland security all contributed to turning the projected surpluses into actual deficits.

RISK FACTORS FOR THE FEDERAL BUDGET

Three broad factors are likely to play important roles in determining the future budget outlook for the federal government.

Defense Spending From 1983 to 1988, defense spending averaged 6 percent of GDP. The end of the cold war was followed by reductions in defense spending. By 2002, this category had fallen to slightly over 3 percent of GDP. The war on terrorism has led to a rise in defense spending, and it is uncertain how these expenditures will trend in the future.

Higher Social Spending on the Elderly As the elderly population in the United States has grown, not only in absolute number, but also as a proportion of the population, federal expenditures on programs such as Social Security and Medicare (providing health care to the aged) have increased dramatically. These programs are projected to continue to grow, with significant implications for the federal budget. A central question is how much of the government's revenues needs to be set aside to help pay for future Social Security and Medicare benefits.

Increasing Health Expenditures Through Medicare and Medicaid, its program that provides health care to the poor, the government has assumed an increasing share of total health care expenditures, which have soared in recent years. The addition of a prescription drug benefit to Medicare and the rapid increase in drug prices will significantly affect the government's need for revenue in the future. New but expensive medical technologies and the aging of the population are also contributing to the swift escalation of medical costs.

Review and Practice

SUMMARY

1. When the government runs a deficit or a surplus, the capital market is affected. If there is a deficit, the government must borrow in the capital market to finance the deficit.
2. In the full-employment model, an increase in government expenditures matched by an increase in taxes reduces disposable income. This drop, in turn, reduces both consumption and saving at full-employment output. Saving decreases, the equilibrium real interest rate rises, and the equilibrium level of investment falls.
3. Changes in government revenues and expenditures do not affect full-employment output or employment, but they do alter how output is divided between consumption, investment, and government purchases.
4. During the past twenty-five years, the budget of the U.S. federal government has swung from large deficits in the 1980s and early 1990s to surpluses from 1998 to 2001, and then back to large deficits.
5. Government borrowing can be an economic burden for future generations in several ways. First, future generations may bear the responsibility of paying off the debt; there is a transfer of wealth from one generation to another. Second, government borrowing can raise real interest rates and crowd out private investment, thereby reducing future output and wages.
6. Future expenditures by the government on homeland security, Social Security, and Medicare are likely to increase in the future.

KEY TERMS

discretionary spending
nondiscretionary spending
entitlements
fiscal deficit
fiscal surplus
national saving
crowding out

REVIEW QUESTIONS

1. What is the relationship between deficit spending and the government's debt?
2. What are the consequences of an increased deficit for private investment and the real rate of interest?
3. How do government deficits and surpluses affect different generations?
4. Name three factors that contributed to the elimination of deficits at the end of the 1990s.
5. Name three factors that contributed to the return of deficits after 2001.

PROBLEMS

1. Suppose households save 5 percent of their disposable income. If the government increases expenditures and taxes by $100 billion, by how much will saving decline? By how much will consumption decline? What happens to investment? (Assume a closed economy.)
2. Redo Question 1 but assume that households save 10 percent of their disposable income. What happens to consumption and investment? Why does investment decline more with a higher saving rate?
3. The primary deficit is defined as the difference between tax revenues and government expenditures, *excluding interest payments;* it represents what the deficit would have been, had the government not inherited any debt. Discuss why the concept of a primary deficit may or may not be useful or relevant.
4. "The resources that were spent fighting World War II were spent during the period 1940–1945. Hence, the generations that were alive and paying taxes during that period are the generations that bore the burden of the cost of the war, regardless of how it was financed." Discuss.
5. Why does the way the government uses a surplus make a difference for investment spending? Consider the following scenarios:

(a) Assume the government reduces income taxes. What is the total impact on national saving, taking into account the reduction in the surplus and the change in private saving? What is the impact on investment? (Hint: How does your answer depend on the sensitivity of saving to the interest rate?)

(b) Assume the government increases expenditures. What is the total impact on national saving, taking into account the reduction in the surplus and the change in private saving? What is the impact on investment? (Hint: How does your answer depend on the type of expenditures the government increases?)

Learning Goals

In this chapter, you will learn

1. The role of the capital market in an open economy

2. How the net exports and international capital flows are related

3. What exchange rates are, how they are determined, and how they affect the trade balance

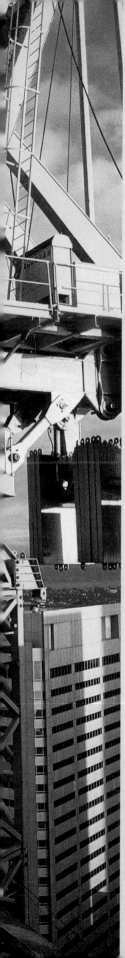

Chapter 8

THE OPEN ECONOMY AT FULL EMPLOYMENT

Modern economies are open economies—actively engaged in international trade and linked to international financial markets. The increasing globalization of the world's economies, and what it means for individual countries and their citizens, has occasioned often strident political debate. Because it is part of the global economy, the United States is affected by, and in turn affects, international economic developments. A financial crisis abroad can have an impact on the value of the dollar and on U.S. exports and imports. U.S. budget deficits influence interest rates and net exports.

The United States and other countries are linked by exchanges both of goods and services and of financial assets. In 2003, the United States sold more than $1 trillion worth of goods and services to the rest of the world. Exports as a percentage of total GDP equaled almost 10 percent; in 1970, they totaled only 5 percent. Americans purchased more than $1.4 trillion in products from other countries in 2003. But these exchanges of goods and services aren't the only international trades that take place. Trade also occurs in financial capital—a British firm borrows money in the U.S. capital market, and interest is paid to Japanese investors who own U.S. government bonds, as well as to U.S. investors who hold Korean government debt. Financial linkages have also grown tremendously over recent decades. It is estimated that foreign-owned assets in the United States grew from $142 billion in 1990 to more than $500 billion in 1999. These flows of financial funds from one country to another play a major role in unifying the global economy. The international exchange of goods and capital has important implications for the macroeconomy.

In this chapter, we extend the full-employment model developed in Chapter 6 to include the foreign sector. By extending the model, we will be able to explore how the international flows of savings affect the domestic capital market and the relationship between national saving and investment. We will also examine how the international financial linkages between countries are related to the balance between exports and imports. Finally, we will discuss how the value of the dollar relative to other currencies is determined in foreign exchange markets, and how the dollar's value affects U.S. exports and imports.

The Open Economy

Globalization and the increasing integration of the world economy are topics encountered in the news all the time. Whether at our local auto dealer, computer store, or grocery store, we find goods produced in many other countries. Financial markets, too, are global in nature. News reports of financial crises in other countries can affect the U.S. stock market. To understand the macroeconomic implications of being part of a world economy, we need to extend our full-employment model to incorporate international trade and finance. In doing so, we turn from the analysis of a closed economy and focus on an open economy. An **open economy** is one whose households and firms trade with other countries and borrow from and lend to other countries. The basic lessons learned from the study of the closed economy continue to guide our analysis of the open economy.

International trade affects the product market because net exports represent a demand for what the economy produces. More importantly, an open economy has access to international sources of funds for financing domestic investment or for financing government deficits. National saving is the domestic source of funds. If the demand for funds for investment exceeds domestic national saving, firms and governments in an open economy can borrow abroad. To understand the role that international trade and international flows of financial capital play, we again start our analysis with the capital market.

THE CAPITAL MARKET IN THE OPEN ECONOMY

Because households and firms in an open economy can borrow or lend abroad, foreign borrowing and lending must be accounted for when we look at equilibrium in the capital market. The moneys coming into the United States—to be deposited in U.S. banks, to buy U.S. government bonds, or to be lent directly to Americans for any reason—are called **capital inflows.** U.S. dollars going to other countries for similar purposes are called **capital outflows.** In the closed economy, as we saw in Chapter 6, equilibrium occurs when national saving and investment are equal. In the open economy, investment can be financed *either* from domestic sources of saving *or* by borrowing abroad, essentially making use of foreign sources of saving, thus:

$$\text{national saving } (S_\text{N}) + \text{borrowing from abroad } (NCF) = \text{investment } (I).$$

We have denoted net borrowing from abroad by *NCF,* which stands for **net capital inflows** (the inflows minus the outflows). If net capital inflows are positive, then the domestic economy is borrowing more from foreigners than it is lending to foreigners. In 2002, for example, national saving in the United States totaled $1.54 trillion (of which private saving was $1.57 trillion and government saving was –$30 billion), while private investment was $1.93 trillion. The difference between investment and national saving was $390 billion, which was financed by a net capital inflow. Because this investment was financed by borrowing from abroad, it represents the amount that foreigners have invested in the United States, and so it is also called *net foreign investment.*

When the capital market in an open economy is in equilibrium, *national saving plus net capital inflows equals private investment.* National saving plus capital flows from abroad can be thought of as the "sources" of funds, and investment can be thought of as the "use" of these funds.

The reaction in the capital market is different if the country is a **small open economy** rather than a **large open economy.** A small open economy is one that is too small to affect the rest of the world with shifts in its domestic saving or investment; it can borrow or lend internationally at the world rate of interest. A large open economy can also borrow and lend in the international capital market. However, domestic shifts in saving or investment in such an economy are substantial enough to affect that market's equilibrium world rate of interest.

The Capital Market in the Small Open Economy Capital market equilibrium requires that national saving plus net capital inflows equal private investment. The implications this has for the economy will depend on the relationship of the supply of funds from both domestic and foreign sources to the real interest rate. A small open economy like Switzerland faces a perfectly elastic supply curve of funds at the world real interest rate. If borrowers in Switzerland were to pay a slightly higher interest rate than that paid in other countries, those with financial capital to lend would divert their funds to Switzerland. If Switzerland were to pay slightly less than the interest rate available in other countries (adjusted for risk), it would not obtain financial capital. Those who have financial investments in Switzerland can take their funds and invest them abroad to earn higher interest rates. These flows of international financial capital play an important role in the global economy. For a small country, the interest rate is determined by the international capital market. Effectively, such a country takes the interest rate as fixed. This is shown in Figure 8.1, where the interest rate is fixed at r^*. A fixed interest rate, in turn, means that the level of investment is fixed, at I^* in Figure 8.1. Any shortfall between the level of domestic national saving and the level of domestic investment is funded by borrowing from abroad. In Figure 8.1, if the level of national saving is given by S_0, the amount of funds borrowed from abroad is B_0. A reduction in the amount of domestic saving increases the amount of foreign borrowing (B_1) but leaves investment unaffected.

This result contrasts with our earlier result for a closed economy, one in which there is no foreign borrowing or lending. There, we noted that lower national saving (a shift to the left in the saving curve) results in less investment. The effect of an increase in government expenditures

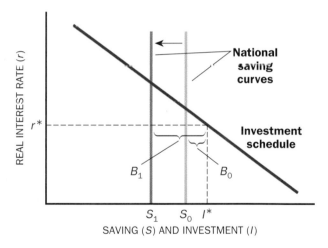

Figure 8.1

SUPPLY OF SAVING IN A SMALL OPEN ECONOMY

In a small open economy, the real interest rate, r^*, is determined by the international capital market. That in turn determines the level of investment, I^*. In the figure, saving is assumed to be fixed, unaffected by the interest rate. If domestic national saving equals S_0, the shortfall, B_0, is made up by borrowing from abroad. A reduction in national saving to S_1, caused, for example, by an increase in the government's deficit, leads to increased international borrowing, B_1, but leaves investment unchanged.

matched by an equal increase in taxes likewise differs in the two economies. In a closed economy, increased taxes reduce national saving, and hence reduce investment (see Figure 7.4 on p. 159). In a small open economy, investment is unchanged. The fall in domestic national saving is fully offset by increased borrowing from abroad (resulting in a net capital *inflow*).

We showed in Chapter 7 that in a closed economy, an increase in government expenditures not matched by an increase in taxes reduces investment and raises the real interest rate. Again, the situation is different in a small open economy. An increase in the government's deficit in a small open economy reduces national saving, but this reduction just leads to an increase in net capital inflows. Domestic investment is left unchanged.

Though investment is unaffected, the increased borrowing from abroad has consequences for the future. Foreigners who have lent funds must be repaid. Income used to repay foreign borrowing is not available for raising domestic standards of living. Access to foreign funds alleviates the need for investment to fall when national saving falls, but the effects of borrowing from abroad on future standards of living are much the same as the effects of a lower level of investment. These effects will be discussed more fully in Chapter 17.

Wrap-Up

THE CAPITAL MARKET IN A SMALL OPEN ECONOMY

In a *closed economy,* changes in the level of national saving affect the real interest rate and investment. An increase in the government's deficit reduces national saving, thereby resulting in a higher real interest rate and lower investment.

In a *small open economy,* the real interest rate is determined by international capital markets. Changes in the level of national saving do not affect the real interest rate or investment. An increase in the government's deficit does not raise the real interest rate; instead, it increases net capital inflows (borrowing from abroad).

The Capital Market in a Large Open Economy: The U.S. Case The United States is a large open economy. Trade is important; in 2002, exports totaled about 10 percent of GDP. Capital flows are also important—the United States has been a net borrower from abroad every year since 1981. But the United States is such a large part of the world economy that changes in its saving function—unlike those in a small country such as Switzerland—affect the international interest rate, with global ramifications. The U.S. economy represents about one-quarter of world output and one-fifth of world saving. A decrease in the level of U.S. saving (implying less national saving at each real interest rate) raises world real interest rates and leads to less investment in the United States. When the world real interest rate rises, investment falls in other open economies as well. Because the full impact is spread throughout the world, the effect on U.S. investment is far less than it would be if the United States were a closed economy.

The discussion so far has also assumed that the world's capital markets are fully integrated. However, this is far from the truth. Individuals know more about what is going on in their own country than about what is going on abroad. American investors require slightly higher returns on foreign investments to compensate for this increased risk. In recent years, as the flow of information has increased, the magnitude of this risk premium—the extra return they must earn for taking the risk of investing abroad—has decreased. But because financial capital still does not flow perfectly freely, interest rates are not equal in all countries, and a decrease in U.S. saving is not fully made up by an increased flow of capital from abroad.

While capital from abroad does not fully offset changes in U.S. saving, foreign saving has been an important source of funds for the United States. In 2002, for example, foreign capital flows were equal to 20 percent of U.S. private investment spending. An increase in U.S. interest rates relative to rates in other countries makes it more attractive for foreigners to lend to American firms and the U.S. government. Conversely, a decrease in U.S. interest rates relative to rates in other countries makes such lending less attractive for foreigners. Thus, the total supply of saving available to finance U.S. investment—the sum of national saving plus net capital inflows—increases as the U.S. interest rate rises. Even if national saving is unresponsive to changes in interest rates (as we have often assumed in drawing a vertical national saving curve), the total supply of funds will increase with the U.S. interest rate. This means that we should draw the saving curve as having a positive slope when we take into account both domestic and foreign sources of saving.

What are the implications of a positively sloped saving curve? Suppose the U.S. investment function shifts to the right. Many economists have argued that this type of shift occurred in the 1990s as firms increased investment at each interest rate to take advantage of new technologies. In a closed economy, such a shift would raise the real interest rate, and investment would be constrained by the availability of domestic saving. But in today's integrated world economy, an investment boom in the United States can be financed by capital inflows. An increase in U.S. investment at each real interest rate raises world interest rates, but the resulting capital inflow increases the supply of saving and results in more investment than would occur when investment must be financed solely from domestic sources.

Wrap-Up

A LARGE OPEN ECONOMY: THE UNITED STATES

The United States is a large open economy. Reductions in the U.S. national saving rate are reflected in increases in the real interest rate internationally (and therefore in the United States also), and reduced levels of investment. But the effects on investment in the United States are smaller than would be the case if the economy were closed, because an increase in U.S. interest rates will attract foreign saving (a capital inflow).

The Basic Trade Identity

The capital market balances saving and investment. In doing so it balances leakages and injections from the spending stream, ensuring that aggregate spending equals potential GDP at full employment. In Chapter 7, we showed that this equation remains valid when the government is added to the basic full-employment model. The same continues to hold true for an open economy. Reexamining the connection between capital market equilibrium and aggregate spending in an open economy, we find an important relationship between net capital flows and the balance between exports and imports.

When the capital market is in equilibrium, investment equals private saving (S_p) plus government saving (S_g) plus net capital inflows:

$$S_p + S_g + NCF = I.$$

Private saving is income minus consumption and taxes: $S_p = Y - C - T$. Government saving is $T - G$, where G represents government purchases. Thus capital market equilibrium implies

$$(Y - C - T) + (T - G) + NCF = Y - C - G + NCF = I.$$

When an economy engages in international trade, there are four sources of aggregate demand: consumption, investment, government purchases, and net exports (NX). Net exports are equal to exports minus imports. In an economy in equilibrium, these four sources of demand must add up to the total output being produced:

$$Y = C + I + G + NX.$$

If we substitute this into the previous equation to eliminate Y, we find that

$$I + NX + NCF = I.$$

Subtracting investment (I) from both sides gives us our key result:

$$NX + NCF = 0.$$

That is, net exports (NX) plus net capital inflows (NCF) equal zero. If net capital flows are positive, net exports must be negative (imports exceed exports). When net exports are negative, we say the country has a **trade deficit.** If net capital flows are negative, net exports must be positive and the country has a **trade surplus.**

The United States has a large net capital inflow and net exports are negative. The large net capital inflow into the United States and the large U.S. trade deficit are not separate phenomena. A country like Japan that lends more aboard than it borrows has a negative net capital inflow and its net exports are positive.

To understand better the relationship between foreign borrowing and the trade deficit, let's trace what happens when an American buys a German car. It appears to be a simple matter: the buyer pays American dollars to a car dealer. The car dealer buys the car—in dollars—from an importer. The importer buys the car from the German manufacturer, who wants to be paid in euros. For the importer, this is no problem. He goes to a bank, perhaps in Germany, and exchanges his dollars for euros. But the bank will not hold on to those dollars. It will sell them, either to someone wanting dollars to purchase U.S. goods or to someone wanting to invest in a dollar-denominated asset.

Every dollar an American spends to buy a foreign import eventually comes back, either to buy American exports or to buy an investment in the United States. We can express this relationship by a simple equation:

$$\text{imports } (IM) \text{ into the United States} = \text{exports } (E) + NCF.$$

Subtracting exports from both sides, we obtain the **basic trade identity:**

$$\text{trade deficit} = IM - E = -NX = NCF.$$

This is just what we obtained earlier by considering the equilibrium in the capital market. The sum of net exports and net capital flows is equal to zero.

Thus, a trade deficit and a net inflow of foreign capital are two ways of describing the same thing. This can be reframed yet again: the only way American consumers and businesses can import more from abroad than they export is if foreigners are willing to make up the difference by lending to or investing in the United States.

In a world of multilateral trade, the accounts between any particular country and the United States do not have to balance. Assume that Japan and Europe are in trade balance and the United States and Europe are in trade balance. Assume also that Japanese investors like to put their money into Europe and Europeans like to invest in the United States. Europe will have a zero net capital inflow, with its positive capital inflow from Japan offset by its negative outflow to the United States. Under these circumstances, the U.S. trade deficit with Japan is offset by a capital inflow from Europe. But what must be true for any country is that *total* imports minus *total* exports (the trade balance) equals *total* net capital inflows.

The basic trade identity can describe a capital outflow as well as a capital inflow. In the 1950s, the United States had a substantial trade surplus, as the

Internet Connection

U.S. TRADE DATA

You can find the latest data on U.S. foreign trade, from information on the overall trade balance to the specifics of our trade with individual countries, at www.ita.doc.gov/td/tic/.

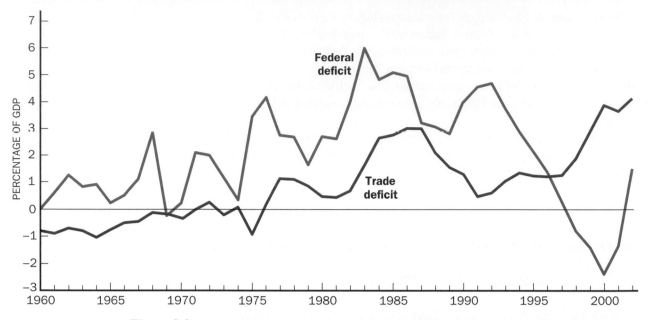

Figure 8.2

THE U.S. FISCAL DEFICIT AND TRADE DEFICIT

Increases in government deficits in the 1980s were accompanied by increases in foreign borrowing. During the late 1990s, the fiscal deficit fell but investment boomed. Beginning in 2001, the government's deficit again increased—and with it, the trade deficit.

SOURCE: *Economic Report of the President* (2004).

country exported more than it imported. Europe and Japan did not receive enough dollars from selling exports to the United States to buy the imports they desired, and they borrowed the difference from American households and firms. There was a net capital outflow from the United States that gradually accumulated. Japan now exports more than it imports, with the difference equal to its capital outflow.

The basic trade identity implies that if U.S. public saving and investment are unchanged and private saving falls, then the U.S. interest rate will rise to attract additional capital inflows, and foreigners will end up holding more American assets. But the identity does not specify which assets they will hold. They may buy government bonds or they may buy stocks or bonds of U.S. companies. In 2003, for instance, foreign investors purchased almost 60 percent of the new debt issued by the U.S. Treasury.

Case in Point

THE TRADE DEFICIT

At the same time that the fiscal budget deficit in the United States was exploding in the 1980s, so too was the trade deficit. From about $20 million a year from 1977 to

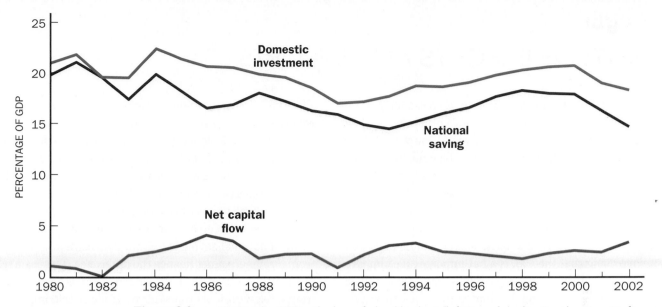

Figure 8.3

NATIONAL SAVING, DOMESTIC INVESTMENT, AND NET CAPITAL FLOWS

During the 1980s, the large federal budget deficits reduced national saving. To finance the high level of private investment, the United States had a large capital inflow. In the late 1990s, the budget deficit was eliminated, and government became a net saver. However, private saving declined and investment rose; investment continued to exceed national saving. At the end of the period shown, the federal government was again running a large deficit, reducing national saving. Since capital inflow is equal to the trade deficit, the United States continues to run a trade deficit.

SOURCE: *Economic Report of the President* (2004).

1982, it soared (in nominal terms) to $142 billion in 1987. It then fell to $20 billion in 1991 before ballooning again, reaching $609 billion (5 percent of GDP) in 2004.

Figure 8.2 shows the trade and federal budget deficits. The two have often moved together. This is no accident; we have already noted that for an open economy, an increase in the government's deficit results in increased foreign borrowing if domestic saving remains constant. But it is important to note that while the trade and fiscal deficits often move together, they are by no means in lockstep. During the late 1990s, for example, the U.S. fiscal deficit fell dramatically while the trade deficit widened significantly. The reason is straightforward—net capital flows reflect the difference between national saving and investment. Looking at Figure 8.2, we can see that the fiscal deficit was reduced in the 1990s. Yet the trade deficit has continued to grow. The reason is that the other two factors at work—private saving and investment—moved to offset the reduction in the fiscal deficit. Figure 8.3 shows domestic investment, national saving, and net foreign borrowing (capital flow) as a percentage of the GDP. By the late 1990s, the U.S. economy was experiencing a record-setting economic boom, increasing the attractiveness of this country as a place to invest. And even though the U.S. private saving rate fell to record lows in the late 1990s, the rise in government saving increased total national saving. Still, the increase in national saving was less than the increase in investment. The net effect was a rise in foreign borrowing (and a larger trade deficit).

e-Insight
HIGH-TECH EXPORTS AND IMPORTS

The United States has emerged as the international leader in many aspects of the new information and computer technologies. Silicon Valley in northern California, home to such firms as Intel, Apple, Sun Microsystems, and Google, has become synonymous with the information-based economy. We thus might naturally expect the United States to be a major exporter of computer-related products. The figure shows the amount, in millions of dollars, of computer-related products exported from and imported to the United States in 2003. It is not surprising that the U.S. is a net importer (i.e., imports exceed exports) of audio and video equipment. Asian companies such as Sony have long dominated this market. But the United States also imports more computer equipment than it exports.

The figure illustrates two important aspects of trade. First, for many categories of products, the United States is both an exporter *and* an importer. For example, the United States produces cars for export, and it imports cars from Asia and Europe.

The United States produces semiconductors for export as well as importing semiconductors.

Second, trade reflects both microeconomic and macroeconomic factors. That the United States leads the world in computing technologies does not necessarily imply that it will be a net exporter of computers. We learned in this chapter that the overall balance between exports and imports reflects the balance between a country's national saving and investment. If national saving is less than investment, borrowing from foreigners must finance the difference. The basic trade identity tells us that when the United States is a net borrower from foreigners, it also must have a trade deficit: imports will exceed exports. The overall U.S. trade deficit grew from $163.1 billion in 1998 to $496.3 billion in 2003. Mirroring this deterioration of the overall trade balance, U.S. imports of computers rose from $7.3 billion in 1998 to $19.7 billion in 2003, as net exports of computers went from a surplus of $1.8 billion in 1998 to a deficit of $11.7 billion in 2003.

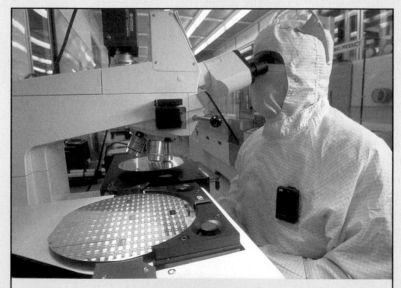

Many foreign-made computers are powered by American-made computer chips, such as those being manufactured here.

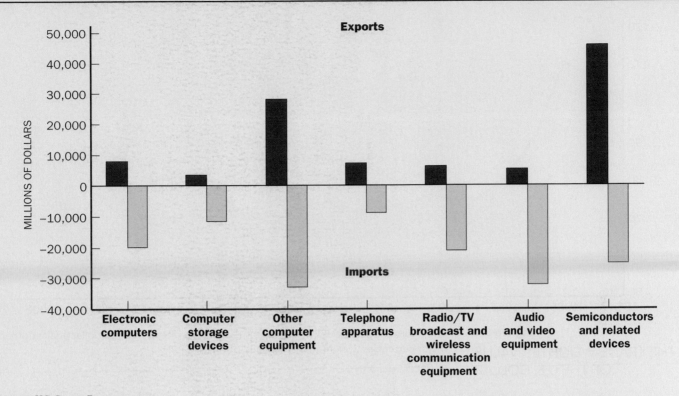

Exports

Imports

SOURCE: U.S. Census Bureau.

EXCHANGE RATES

If a country borrows more (or less) from abroad, what ensures that net exports adjust? The answer is the **exchange rate.** The exchange rate tells how much of one currency can be bought with a given amount of another currency. For instance, in 2004, one dollar could be exchanged for approximately 108 Japanese yen. Exchange rates may change rapidly. In August 1998, a dollar could buy 144 yen. But in January 1999, it could buy only 113 yen. This represents a 21 percent fall in the value of the dollar relative to the yen in just five months. When the dollar becomes less valuable relative to another currency, we say the dollar has **depreciated.** When the dollar becomes more valuable relative to other currencies, we say the dollar has **appreciated.** When the dollar-yen exchange rate fell from 144 to 113 in 1998, the dollar depreciated relative to the yen and the yen appreciated relative to the dollar. Since the United States trades with many countries, it is often useful to measure the value of the dollar relative to an average of other currencies. A standard measure of the value of the dollar is the *trade-weighted exchange rate:* an average of the exchange rates between the dollar and the currencies of our trading partners that reflects the amount of trade the United States does with the other

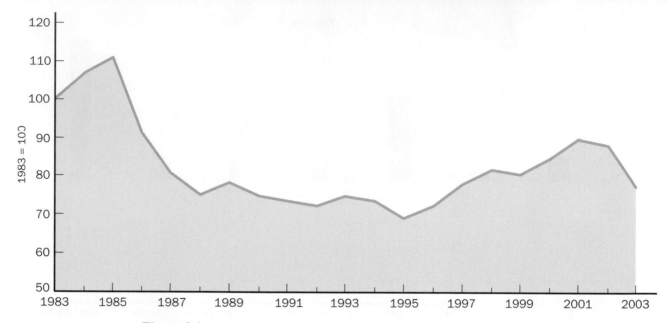

Figure 8.4

THE TRADE-WEIGHTED VALUE
OF THE U.S. DOLLAR

The figure shows an index of the average exchange rate of the U.S. dollar against other major currencies, weighted by the value of trade.

SOURCE: Federal Reserve Board.

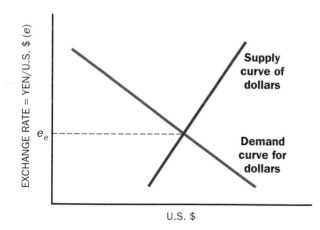

Figure 8.5

EQUILIBRIUM IN THE MARKET
FOR DOLLARS

The exchange rate is the relative price of two currencies. The equilibrium exchange rate, e_e, occurs at the intersection of the supply and demand curves for dollars.

countries. So, for example, the U.S. dollar–Canadian dollar exchange rate is given more weight in the measure than is the U.S. dollar–New Zealand dollar exchange rate because the United States engages in much more trade with Canada. Figure 8.4 shows the trade-weighted value of the U.S. dollar.

Thus, the exchange rate is a price—the relative price of two currencies. Like any price, the exchange rate is determined by the laws of supply and demand. For the sake of simplicity, let's continue to focus on the exchange rate between the dollar and the yen (ignoring the fact that in the world trading system, all exchange rates are interlinked). Figure 8.5 depicts the market for dollars in terms of the exchange rate with the yen. The exchange rate in yen per dollar is on the vertical axis, and the quantity of U.S. dollars is on the horizontal axis. The supply curve for dollars represents the quantity of dollars supplied by U.S. residents to purchase Japanese goods and to make investments in Japan. At higher exchange rates—when the dollar buys more yen—Americans will supply larger quantities of dollars. A Japanese good that costs 1,000 yen costs $10 when the exchange rate is 100 but only $6.67 when the exchange rate rises to 150. Americans will therefore wish to buy more Japanese goods as the exchange rate rises, and the supply curve of dollars thus slopes upward to the right. The demand curve for dollars represents the dollars demanded by the Japanese to purchase American products and to make investments in the United States. At higher exchange rates—when it takes more yen to buy one dollar—the Japanese demand lower quantities of dollars, resulting in a demand curve that slopes downward to the right. The equilibrium exchange rate, e_e, lies at the intersection of the supply and demand curves for dollars.

Now we can see how the exchange rate connects the flow of capital and goods between countries. We continue with the case of the United States and Japan. Suppose the United States wants to borrow more from Japan. Higher U.S. interest rates will attract more Japanese investment to the United States. Japanese demand for dollars increases at each exchange rate, shifting the demand curve for dollars

Thinking Like an Economist
NET EXPORTS AND THE EXCHANGE RATE

Incentives matter, and that is why the balance between exports and imports is affected by the exchange rate. Consumers have choices—for most goods, they can buy a brand produced in the United States, or they can buy a brand produced abroad. Similarly, firms may purchase the inputs they need for production from domestic suppliers or from foreign suppliers. In making choices, consumers and firms alike will respond to the incentives provided by prices. If domestically produced goods rise in price relative to foreign-produced goods, the demand for the domestic goods will fall and the demand for the foreign-produced goods will rise. The exchange rate affects these decisions by affecting the relative prices of domestic and foreign-produced goods.

If the dollar depreciates, it takes more dollars to buy each unit of foreign currency. For example, in 2001, it cost 90 cents to buy one euro. Thus, any good or service with a price of 100 euros would cost $90 to buy. By 2003, the dollar had fallen in value relative to the euro, so that it cost $1.13 to buy a euro. The same 100 euro good now cost an American buyer $113, not $90. Because the dollar's depreciation makes the European-produced good more expensive, our imports from Europe will tend to fall. From the perspective of a European, however, American goods have become less expensive. A U.S. good that sells for $100 cost 111 euros in 2001 (1 euro could buy $0.90, so it took 111 euros to buy the $100

U.S. good), but by 2003, that same $100 good cost only 88.5 euros.

What is important in determining the relative price of foreign and domestic goods is the *real* exchange rate: the exchange rate adjusted for changes in the general level of prices in different countries. Suppose in our previous example that the general price level in the United States had risen by 25 percent between 2001 and 2003 so that instead of still costing $100, the U.S. good had risen in price to $125 in 2003. Then, to Europeans, the fall in the value of the dollar by 25 percent (from $0.90 to $1.13 per euro) would just offset the rise in the dollar price from $100 to $125: the good would still cost 111 euros. Similarly, from the perspective of the American consumer, the good that cost 100 euros in 2001 costs $113 in 2003, a 25 percent rise. Thus, its price has not changed relative to the general level of U.S. prices—the real exchange rate would be unchanged.

In fact, however, prices in the United States rose by only 4 percent between 2001 and 2003. Thus, the 25 percent depreciation of the dollar more than offset that rise and represented a large real depreciation in value. This will create incentives for American consumers and firms to purchase fewer foreign goods and services. Conversely, it will boost U.S. exports by creating incentives for foreign consumers and firms to purchase American products.

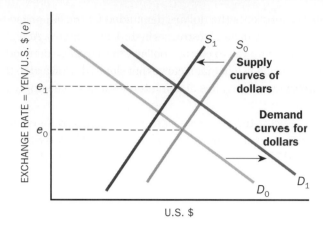

Figure 8.6

EXCHANGE RATE EFFECTS OF INCREASED FOREIGN BORROWING

The equilibrium exchange rate is e_0 before the increase in U.S. borrowing from Japan. Higher interest rates in the United States attract Japanese investment, shifting the demand curve for U.S. dollars to the right. At the same time, more Americans decide to invest in their own country rather than abroad, shifting the dollar supply curve to the left. The equilibrium exchange rate rises from e_0 to e_1. At the higher exchange rate, the dollar buys more yen, so U.S. imports of Japanese products increase. Conversely, U.S. goods are now more expensive for the Japanese, so U.S. exports decrease.

to the right, as depicted in Figure 8.6. The higher U.S. interest rates also will make Japanese investments relatively less attractive to American investors, who will therefore increase their investments at home. Americans will be willing to supply fewer dollars at each exchange rate, shifting the supply curve for dollars to the left. These shifts in the supply and demand curves for dollars cause the exchange rate to rise from e_0 to e_1—the dollar appreciates and the yen depreciates.[1] Since the dollar can now buy more Japanese products, U.S. imports increase (i.e., Japanese exports increase). Since the yen can now buy fewer U.S. products, U.S. exports fall. Changes in the exchange rate thus ensure that the trade deficit moves in tandem with foreign borrowing.

Is the Trade Deficit a Problem?

So far, our discussion has shown the relationship between the trade deficit and the international capital flows that reflect differences between national saving and investment. But we have not said anything about whether a trade deficit is good or bad. Certainly much of the popular discussion about the United States' huge trade deficit suggests that it is a major problem.

---

[1]Later, in Chapter 17, we will see that matters are somewhat more complicated. Investors have to take into account expectations concerning future changes in the exchange rates as well.

Trade deficits mean the country is borrowing from abroad. As is true of borrowing from any other source, such borrowing can be sensible or not depending on its reason.

In its first century, this country borrowed heavily from abroad. By contrast, for most of the twentieth century, the United States lent more money to foreign countries and investors than it borrowed. This pattern is typical. In the early stages of economic development, countries borrow to build up their economies, and they repay the loans with a portion of their economic gains. More mature economies typically lend capital.

The enormous U.S. trade deficits in the 1980s reversed this pattern. When the government borrows year after year, the cumulative budget deficits lead to a high level of government debt. Similarly, when the country borrows from abroad year after year, the cumulative trade deficits (cumulative capital inflows) lead to a high level of debt to foreigners.

The effects of the trade deficits of the 1980s were to convert the United States from the world's largest creditor nation at the beginning of the decade to the world's largest debtor nation by its end. Figure 8.7 shows the net international position of the United States—the value of all American-owned assets abroad plus what others owe Americans minus the value of all assets within the United States owned by foreigners and what Americans owe foreigners. In the mid-1980s, the United States became a net debtor nation. As a result, the U.S. economy will have to pay interest, dividends, and profits to foreign investors each year, spending more dollars abroad for these payments than it is receiving.

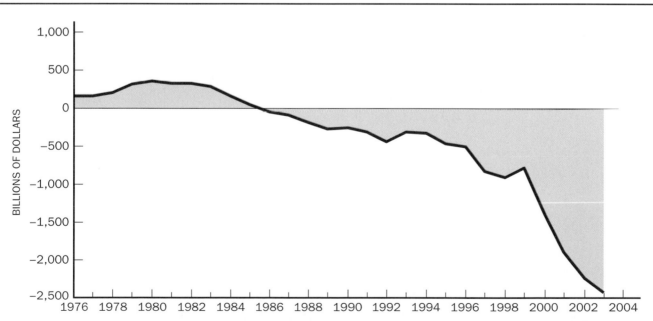

Figure 8.7

THE UNITED STATES BECOMES
A DEBTOR NATION

The United States was a large creditor nation in the beginning of the 1980s; that is, American-held foreign assets exceeded foreign-held U.S. assets. By 1992, it had become a large debtor nation: foreign-held U.S. assets exceeded American-held foreign assets.

SOURCE: *Survey of Current Business* (BEA, Department of Commerce).

But is this good or bad? Suppose you borrow a large sum from a bank. In the future, unless you used the borrowed funds to make an investment that yielded a return at least equal to the interest you had to pay the bank, you would be unable to consume as much as you would otherwise, for the simple reason that you must pay the bank interest as well as principal. The same applies to foreign borrowing. During the 1980s, the large trade deficits were caused by the large fiscal budget deficits that reduced national saving. Because the foreign borrowing was not being used to finance investment spending that would boost future income, the concern was that the large trade deficits represented a future burden on the economy. In contrast, the trade deficit in the late 1990s was a reflection of strong investment spending. But at the beginning of the twenty-first century, with the U.S. government again running a huge budget deficit, the concern again arose that the large trade deficit resulting from these budget deficits represents a future burden.

Review and Practice

SUMMARY

1. In an open economy, investment can be financed from domestic national saving or borrowing from abroad.
2. In a small open economy, changes in national saving will not affect the international real interest rate or the level of domestic investment. Changes in national saving will affect the level of net capital inflows.
3. In a large open economy such as the United States', a fall in national saving will raise the real interest rate. This rise attracts net capital inflows and moderates the decline in domestic investment.
4. The basic trade identity states that net exports plus net capital inflows equal zero. A trade deficit must equal net capital inflows; a trade surplus must equal capital outflows.
5. Changes in the exchange rate ensure that net exports move in tandem with net capital flows.

KEY TERMS

open economy
capital inflows
capital outflows
net capital inflows
small open economy
large open economy
trade deficit
trade surplus
basic trade identity
exchange rate
depreciation
appreciation

REVIEW QUESTIONS

1. What are the consequences of an increased government deficit for private investment in an open economy and in a closed economy?
2. What is the relationship between the trade deficit and an inflow of foreign capital?
3. What is the relationship between the trade deficit and the fiscal deficit?
4. What is the saving-investment identity for an open economy?
5. What is the exchange rate? How is it determined? What role do adjustments in the exchange rate play in ensuring that capital inflows equal the trade deficit?

PROBLEMS

1. Suppose a certain country has private saving of 6 percent of GDP, capital inflow of 1 percent of GDP, and a balanced budget. What is its level of investment? If the budget deficit is 1.5 percent of GDP, how does your answer change?
2. Why does it make a difference if a country borrows abroad to finance the expansion of its railroads or to finance increased Social Security benefits for the elderly?
3. U.S. foreign indebtedness is greater than that of Mexico, Brazil, and Argentina combined. Does this necessarily mean that the United States has a larger debt problem than those countries? Why or why not? Can you think of a situation in which an individual with debts of larger value may actually have less of a debt problem than someone with less debt?
4. If Congress were to pass a law prohibiting foreign investors from buying U.S. Treasury bills, would this prevent government borrowing from leading to capital inflows? Discuss.
5. Japan had large trade surpluses during the 1980s. Would this cause Japan to be a borrower or to be a lender in international capital markets?
6. If a nation borrowed $50 billion from abroad one year and its imports were worth $800 billion, what would be the value of its exports? How does the answer change if, instead of borrowing, the nation lent $100 billion abroad?
7. If U.S. investments increase and world interest rates rise, what is the effect on private investment in other countries? What is the effect on U.S. national saving?

Learning Goals

In this chapter, you will learn

1 The role of labor productivity in raising living standards

2 The factors that lead to productivity growth

3 The sources of economic growth

4 The role of technological change and new ideas

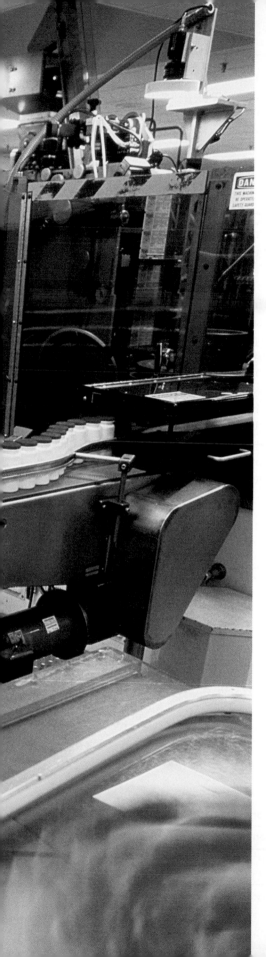

Chapter 9

GROWTH AND PRODUCTIVITY

The changes that took place in the U.S. standard of living during the twentieth century are hard to comprehend. In 1900, the average American's level of consumption was little higher than the average citizen's in Mexico or the Philippines today. Life expectancy was low, in part because diseases such as smallpox, diphtheria, typhoid fever, and whooping cough were still common. People were fifteen times more likely to catch measles in 1900 than they are today. The abundance of land meant that relatively few Americans were starving, but luxuries were scarce. People worked as long as they could, and when they could no longer work, they became the responsibility of their children; there was no easy retirement. Most of the goods that people consume today—from DVDs to cellular phones to frozen pizzas—could not even be conceived of in 1900.

During the nineteenth century, the living standards in England and a few other European countries were perhaps slightly higher than that of the United States. In Asia, Africa, and Latin America, where the vast majority of people lived then as they do now, standards of living were much lower. Famines, which parts of Africa still suffer from today, were common in even Europe's poorer areas, such as Ireland. More than a tenth of the Irish population died during the potato famine of 1845–1848, and more than another tenth migrated to the United States.

The tremendous improvements in our standards of living are the fruits of economic growth—our ability to produce more of the things that provide for our material well-being. To analyze the factors that account for economic growth, we can use the insights provided by the full-employment model that we have used in the previous three chapters. The full-employment model provides what we can think of as a snapshot of the economy. We assumed the economy's capital stock—its plant and equipment—was fixed, and we assumed the labor force was fixed. Now we will look at the economy through a sequence of snapshots in order to obtain a movie that captures the changes occurring over time. At each point, the full-employment model shows how real wages and the real interest rate adjust to ensure that the economy produces at potential GDP. Over time, new investment leads to more machines and buildings, population growth and immigration lead to increases in the labor force, and innovation and research and development generate technological changes that alter what the economy produces and how it is produced.

Rising Standards of Living

Table 9.1 compares the United States in 1900 and 2000. Such a comparison reveals an enormous boost in living standards, demonstrated not just in higher incomes and life expectancy but also in higher levels of education, improved medical services, and a cleaner environment. If we are interested in the economy's ability to provide material goods and services to its residents, then we should focus on **income per capita** and how it has grown. Income per capita is total income divided by the population. Over the twentieth century, the population of the United States grew from 76 million to 281 million, but real GDP grew even more, raising incomes per capita by more than 400 percent—from $6,701 to $34,935, in real terms.

Figure 9.1 shows that during the 1960s, real income per capita grew rapidly. That growth slowed during the 1970s and 1980s, but beginning in the last half of the 1990s, its pace increased. The growth rate of income per capita (Y/N) is equal to the growth rate of output (Y) minus the growth rate of the population (N).

We can write income per capita as the product of output per hour and hours per person:

$$Y/N = (Y/H) \times (H/N).$$

Table 9.1

THE UNITED STATES IN 1900 AND 2000

	1900	2000
Population	76 million	281 million
Life expectancy	47 years	77 years
GDP (in 2000 dollars)	$510 billion	$9,817 billion
GDP per capita (in 2000 dollars)	$6,701	$34,935
Average hours worked each week in manufacturing	59	42
Average hourly wage in manufacturing (2000 dollars)	$5.33	$14.37
Number of telephones	1.3 million	>200 million
% of those age 5–19 enrolled in school	51 percent	92 percent

SOURCES: *Economic Report of the President* (2004); *Statistical Abstract of the United States* (2003).

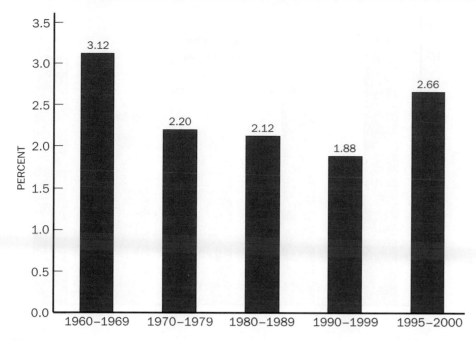

Figure 9.1

PER CAPITA OUTPUT GROWTH

The growth rate of total output per capita declined over the 1970s, 1980s, and the early 1990s. It rose again in the late 1990s.

SOURCE: *Economic Report of the President* (2004).

Output per hour (Y/H) is what we identified in Chapter 4 as *labor productivity*. Hours per person (H/N) reflects both the average number of hours people work and the **labor force participation rate.** The labor force participation rate is the fraction of the population that is actually in the labor force. For income per capita to rise, either labor productivity must rise or the number of hours worked must grow faster than the population.

In many countries, rapid growth in income per capita follows increases in labor force participation. For example, a customary restriction on women's engaging in work outside the home may be loosened. Thus the United States did experience growth in labor force participation, particularly during the 1970s and 1980s, as women entered the labor force in ever greater numbers. The only other way to increase hours per person is to raise the average hours worked—that is, individuals must work longer and sacrifice leisure. For developed economies such as the United States', the key to improving living standards lies in the other element in the equation: growth in labor productivity.

The roles of labor productivity and of hours worked in accounting for economic growth in the United States are shown in Figure 9.2, which expresses the growth rate of total output as the sum of the two factors:

$$\text{growth rate of output} = \text{growth rate of output per hour} + \\ \text{growth rate of hours worked.}$$

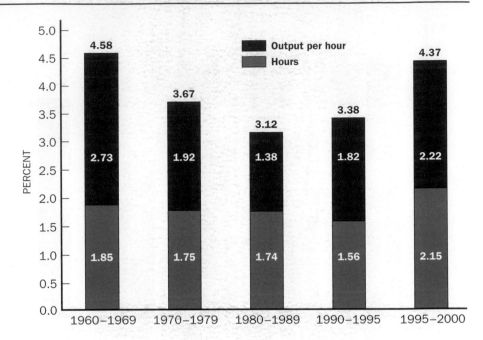

Figure 9.2

OUTPUT GROWTH—HOURS AND PRODUCTIVITY

The growth rate of total output is equal to the growth rate in the number of hours worked plus the growth rate of labor productivity. Total growth slowed during the 1970s through the first half of the 1990s, a decline accounted for by the decline in the growth rate of productivity. Productivity growth increased during the second half of the 1990s.

SOURCE: *Economic Report of the President* (2004).

Two important points stand out from Figure 9.2. First, overall growth declined after the 1960s but then picked up again in the late 1990s. Second, the decline during the 1970s and 1980s was attributable to a decline in productivity growth. This fall—the "productivity slowdown," as it was called—began in 1973, and was not just an American phenomenon: all the industrial economies grew more slowly after 1973.

GROWTH IN PER CAPITA INCOME

The growth rate of per capita income is the sum of the growth rate of labor productivity and the growth rate of hours worked per person.

The number of hours worked per person depends on the labor force participation rate and the average number of hours that each worker works.

Labor productivity is the amount of output produced on average per hour worked.

The growth rate of output is the sum of the growth rate of labor productivity and the growth rate of total hours worked.

Growth in labor productivity is the key to rising standards of living.

Explaining Productivity

For almost a century, the United States has been at the center of the technological advances that have changed the world. The telegraph, telephone, laser, transistor, airplane, assembly line, jet engine, atomic reactor, memory chips . . . the list of U.S. technological achievements goes on and on. Beyond these pathbreaking developments are countless smaller improvements: better as well as new products, and less-expensive ways of making old products. The country has reaped a huge reward from these productivity-enhancing changes—it is through these productivity increases that rising standards of living are possible.

Though a rise in the average rate of productivity growth from about 2 percent to 3 percent may seem inconsequential, it in fact matters enormously because the differences compound over time. Consider this simple calculation. Two countries start out equally wealthy, but one grows at 2 percent a year while the other grows at 3 percent. The difference in productivity would be barely perceptible for a few years. But after thirty years, the slower-growing country would be only three-fourths as wealthy as the faster-growing one.

One way to grasp the importance of even small differences in growth rates is to compare how long it takes for income to double. To do this, we can make use of the *rule of seventy*—dividing the growth rate into 70 will tell us the approximate number of years needed for income to double. For example, if an economy grows at 5 percent per year, income will double in 14 years (70/5 = 14).

Average annual growth rate	Number of years for income to double
1 percent	70
2 percent	35
3 percent	23
4 percent	18
5 percent	14
6 percent	12
7 percent	10
8 percent	9

The difference between growing at 3 percent per year instead of 2 percent may sound small, but as the table shows, over time it is substantial.

Lower growth in productivity means that, on average, people will have less of everything—smaller houses, poorer health care, less travel, and fewer government services than otherwise. When output growth is sustained through increases in the number of hours worked rather than through productivity gains—when families raise their income only by having both spouses working, for instance—reduction in leisure also leads to increased strain. In this case, to focus on the income increases alone would exaggerate the rise in living standards.

The critical role played by productivity growth in improving living standards accounts for the attention that has been given to the speedup in productivity growth since the mid-1990s. Many commentators argue that the tremendous advances in computer and information technologies in recent years will contribute to higher productivity growth and rising standards of living.

To understand these fluctuations in productivity, we need to understand what causes increases in output per hour in the first place. There are four key factors: saving and investment, education and the quality of the labor force, the reallocation of resources from low- to high-productivity sectors of the economy, and technological change. The following sections discuss each factor in turn.

THE CAPITAL STOCK AND THE ROLE OF SAVING AND INVESTMENT

Workers today are much more productive than they were one hundred or even twenty years ago. One important reason is that they have more and better machines to work with. An American textile worker can produce far more than a textile worker in India, partly because of the differences in their equipment: in India, handlooms similar to those used in America two hundred years ago are often still employed.

The amount of capital per worker increases when investment exceeds the amount of capital that depreciates. **Depreciation** is the amount of capital that wears out or becomes obsolete. Higher levels of investment relative to GDP increase the capital stock and result in more capital per worker, a process that economists call **capital deepening.** As capital per worker increases, the amount of output that each worker can produce increases. In Chapter 6, we introduced the concept of the aggregate production function: the relationship between employment and output, when the amount of capital is fixed. When we focus on economic growth, we need to take into account the increases in the capital stock that come about through investment. The effect of having more capital per worker is shown in Figure 9.3. As each worker has more capital to work with, output per worker (labor productivity) rises. But because of diminishing returns, the effects on labor productivity become smaller as the economy accumulates more and more capital.

Capital deepening can increase labor productivity and standards of living, as economies get more capital by investing in plant and equipment. In Chapters 6 to 8, we discussed the relationship between investment and saving. In a closed economy, national saving equals investment, as illustrated in Figure 9.4. In the figure, we assume saving does not depend on the real interest rate. A rise in saving (a shift in the saving curve to the right) leads to lower real interest rates, and lower real interest rates lead to higher investment. In a closed economy, the way to increase investment and obtain a faster-growing stock of capital is to increase national saving. One reason many people are concerned about the low rate of private saving in the United States and the large federal government deficits is that America's low national saving rate may in the future decrease the capital available per worker.

In an open economy, matters are more complicated. Domestic national saving need not equal investment, because a country can finance investment by borrowing from abroad. But even though the U.S. economy is open, U.S. saving and investment tend to move together. A reduction in national saving does lead to greater foreign borrowing—but not enough more to prevent some reduction in investment.

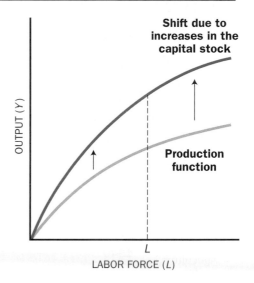

Figure 9.3

INCREASES IN CAPITAL AND THE PRODUCTION FUNCTION

The short-run aggregate production function relates employment to output for a given stock of capital and for a given level of technology. With more capital, workers will be more productive; thus at each level of employment, output will be higher. The effect of an increase in the economy's capital stock is shown by the shift in the production function.

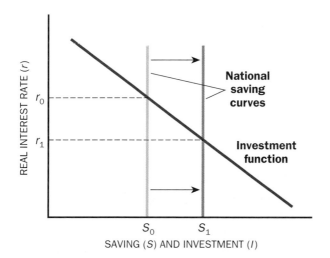

Figure 9.4

SAVING AND INVESTMENT

Higher saving rates lead to lower real interest rates and higher investment.

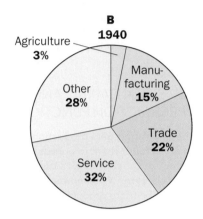

A
1900

Other 21%
Agriculture 39%
Service 8%
Trade 10%
Manu-facturing 22%

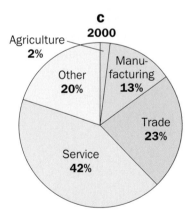

B
1940

Agriculture 3%
Manu-facturing 15%
Other 28%
Trade 22%
Service 32%

C
2000

Agriculture 2%
Manu-facturing 13%
Other 20%
Trade 23%
Service 42%

Figure 9.5

SECTORAL SHIFTS

Employment in the U.S. economy shifted from agriculture to manufacturing in the first half of the twentieth century, and from manufacturing to services in the second half.

SOURCES: *Historical Statistics of the United States* (1975), *Economic Report of the President* (2004).

THE QUALITY OF THE LABOR FORCE

As important as saving and investment rates are in explaining the growth rate of labor productivity, capital deepening is not the whole story. Even more important today is a second major source of productivity growth: a higher-quality labor force. Running a modern industrial economy requires a well-educated workforce. In addition, an economy on the cutting edge of technological change needs trained scientists and engineers to discover and shape innovations.

Spending money on education and training improves workers' skills and productivity. These expenditures are investments—just like investments in machines and buildings. And just as expenditures on plant and equipment result in physical capital, we say that expenditures on education and training result in **human capital.** Human capital is the stock of accumulated skills and experience that makes workers productive. Increases in human capital increase the amount of output that workers can produce and thus shift the aggregate production function up, just as increases in physical capital do.

The United States has a highly educated workforce. Even as the number of educated workers has increased, the returns to investing in education have grown. In 2000, the median full-time worker with at least a bachelor's degree earned about 90 percent more per week than one with only a high school diploma—up from 36 percent in 1979. Though some of this difference may be attributed to the likelihood that those who graduated from college are more able (and hence would have earned high incomes whether or not they had attended college), the returns to education appear significant even after factors such as family background and high school performance are taken into account. Just a year of college has been estimated to increase earnings by a minimum of 5 to 10 percent.

THE REALLOCATION OF RESOURCES FROM LOW- TO HIGH-PRODUCTIVITY SECTORS

During the past century, the United States has evolved from an agricultural economy to an industrial economy to a service economy. Figure 9.5 shows this dramatic structural change. The service sector, broadly defined, includes not only traditional services such as those provided by barbers and waiters but also the more sophisticated services provided by doctors and lawyers, educators, and computer programmers, among others. The medical sector alone has grown to the point that it accounted for about 15 percent of GDP in 2000.

The movement out of agriculture and into industry explains some of the productivity increase in the early part of the twentieth century. Though the level of productivity in agriculture was increasing rapidly, it remained lower than that in industry. Thus, as workers shifted out of low-productivity jobs in agriculture into high-productivity jobs in manufacturing, average productivity in the economy increased. With almost all labor now out of agriculture—and with agricultural productivity increased to the point that incomes in that sector are comparable to those in the rest of the economy—this kind of shift can no longer be a source of overall productivity growth. But other opportunities remain. Productivity in the telecommunications industry, other high-tech sectors, and export sectors is substantially higher than that in other parts of the economy. Telecommunications deregulation in the 1990s facilitated the movement of resources into that sector. Rapid innovation in computer technology is affecting all sectors of the economy. Increasing globalization will open up new opportunities for export growth. These changes are contributing to the overall increase in productivity that the United States has experienced since the mid-1990s.

TECHNOLOGICAL CHANGE AND THE ROLE OF IDEAS

While capital—both physical and human—is important for explaining the huge changes in living standards over the past two hundred years, just having more machines or better-educated workers cannot account for the truly amazing differences between the economy in 1900 and the economy today. We are not producing more of the same goods the economy produced in 1900; we are producing goods that the people of 1900 never dreamed of. Instead of using more machines to produce more horse-drawn carriages, we produce cars and airplanes. Instead of producing more horseshoes, we produce tires and jogging shoes. Key to the whole growth process, then, is technological progress—thinking up new ways to do old things and new ways to do entirely new things. This means that *ideas* are central to explaining economic growth. Indeed, economists estimate that as much as two-thirds of all increases in productivity prior to 1973 were due to technological progress.

Investment increases the economy's stock of physical capital, and education leads to increases in human capital, but what leads to technological progress? To understand the economics of technological progress, we need to start by considering how ideas are different from such goods as a laptop computer or a piece of chocolate cake. These goods are *rivalrous;* if I eat that piece of chocolate cake, you can't. But ideas are different. If both you and your roommate are taking economics, both of you can use an idea like the law of supply and demand. If your roommate does her homework first, the idea is still available to you when you get around to studying. When Tim Berners-Lee, Robert Cailliau, and their colleagues at the European particle physics center (CERN) in Geneva, Switzerland, invented the World Wide Web and hypertext markup language, or HTML, in 1990, programmers from around the world could use their ideas. If you use HTML to construct a Web page, the idea is still also available to others—it is a *nonrivalrous* good. This is a key property of ideas; they cannot be used up.

One of the major differences between the economy today and in 1900 is the routine nature of the change brought about by new ideas. This technological progress is accomplished through the activities of thousands of entrepreneurs and innovators, particularly in the computer industry, and thousands of scientists and engineers engaged in large-scale research projects in the business, government, and university sectors. Much of modern research is centered in huge laboratories, employing large numbers of people. While the government runs some of these—such as the Brookhaven, Argonne, and Lawrence laboratories that carry out research in basic physics—many are private, as was Bell Laboratories, where the transistor and

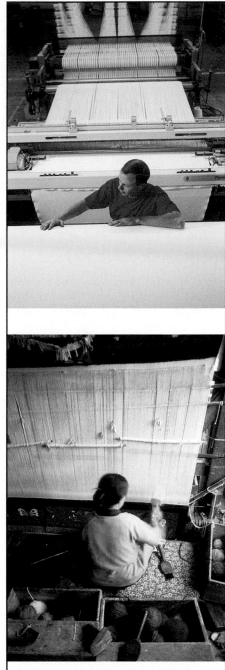

Modern textile manufacturing bears little resemblance to the traditional hand loom, which is still used in underdeveloped areas such as Darjeeling, India.

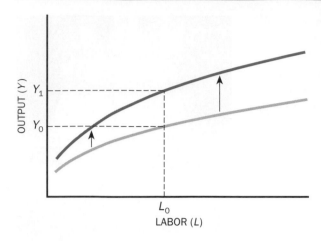

Figure 9.6

TECHNOLOGICAL CHANGE

Improvements in knowledge and technology shift up the production function; at each level of physical and human capital per worker, higher levels of output per worker can be achieved.

the laser were developed. Indeed, most major firms spend about 3 percent of their gross revenues on research and development (R & D).

We have become so accustomed to the current level of technological progress that it is hard to believe how different the view of reputable economists was in the early 1800s. Real wages of workers were little higher than they had been more than four centuries earlier, when the bubonic plague killed a large part of the population of Europe and thereby created a scarcity of labor that raised real wages. After half a millennium of slow progress at best, Thomas Malthus, one of the greatest economists of that time, saw population expanding more rapidly than the capacity of the economy to support it. His prediction of an inevitable decline in living standards earned economics the nickname of "the dismal science." Today, many continue to predict that the world economy will be unable to grow faster than the population and that living standards must necessarily decline. Such calculations have been proved wrong over and over again, as technological advances have rendered their premises false. The role of technological change in the economy's aggregate production is depicted in Figure 9.6. Improved technology enables the economy to achieve more output per worker at each level of physical and human capital per worker.

The Production of Ideas Knowing that ideas are important for economic growth tells us little about how they are produced. Can we use some of the basic ideas of economics to understand the production of ideas?

To start, think about the incentives that face a potential inventor. Those incentives will be greatest if the inventor can charge a fee to anyone who uses her new idea. She must be able to prevent its employment by those unwilling to pay. But some ideas are hard to maintain control over. Once Henry Ford came up with the idea of the modern assembly line, he might have kept it secret for a while by barring visitors to his factory, but certainly anyone who saw his new method of manufacture could take the idea and set up a new factory. Most software companies keep their source code secret in order to exclude its use by those who have not paid a licensing fee. The incentive to produce new ideas will be increased if inventors are able to profit from such licenses. To that end, inventors must be granted **property rights** to their ideas, as those ideas are given form in a specific process, machine, article of manufacture, composition of matter, or design. Property rights give their holder legal authority to determine how a resource is used, including the right to charge others for its use. If property rights are insecure, if a firm planning on engaging in research is uncertain about whether it will be allowed to capture the benefits of any new ideas it produces, then fewer resources will be invested into research and the production of new ideas.

Society has another consideration, however. Producing a new idea may be very costly, but it need be produced only once. Your laptop embodies thousands of new ideas, but these ideas did not have to be reproduced each time a new laptop was made. The screen, memory chips, and case did have to be produced for each laptop; they are examples of rivalrous goods—the memory chips in your laptop cannot be in your roommate's laptop. But the design of the laptop is a nonrivalrous good, and its marginal cost is therefore zero. So from society's perspective, the idea should be freely available to everyone. After all, it costs nothing to let others use it.

There is a tension, then, between providing incentives for the production of new ideas and ensuring that they can be widely used. Inventors need secure property rights that enable them to benefit from their ideas; they need to be able to exclude users who do not pay. Yet once an idea is invented, its zero marginal cost of production suggests that it should be freely available.

The digitization of music has brought the issue of intellectual property rights into sharp focus. Many music lovers think nothing of downloading and sharing music files at no cost, and companies such as Napster developed software to make this sharing possible. But the music actually "belongs" to the copyright holder, who has a right to demand payment for its use. Representatives of the music industry have repeatedly brought companies and individuals to court over the downloading and sharing of music files. Record labels cite declining sales of CDs as evidence that music piracy will reduce their financial incentives to find and market new artists. Now, major companies such as Apple and Sony run online music stores that allow individuals to download songs for a fee.

Society addresses the tension between making intellectual property widely available and protecting the property rights of inventors through copyright and patent laws. Once issued, a patent gives an inventor the exclusive rights to his invention. Because others can use it only with his permission, the inventor can impose a licensing fee to capture some of the benefits of his idea. But in the United States, patents are valid only for a fixed period (usually twenty years), and after they expire their ideas are freely available. Copyrights on written work generally now last for the life of the author plus seventy years. In this way, society both increases the incentive to produce new ideas and ensures that they eventually become available to everyone.

Expenditures on R & D Innovations and technological process do not simply happen. They require deliberate investment in research and development. Pharmaceutical manufacturers devote millions of dollars and thousands of scientists to the search for new drugs; companies such as Intel and AMD fund projects to develop the next generation of computer chips; and the thousands of firms that produce consumer goods ranging from household cleaners to garden hoses are constantly seeking improvements in their products as a way to increase their profits.

Industry accounts for about 65 percent of U.S. R & D expenditures, with the remainder provided by the government, universities, and nonprofit organizations. In 2002, just under 30 percent of R & D spending was by the government. Historically, roughly half of the federal spending on R & D has been for defense, which now accounts for about 15 percent of total U.S. R & D expenditures. This percentage has fallen steadily; it was more than 30 percent in 1970.

Some analysts put the private returns on R & D expenditures at more than 25 percent; and since many of the returns accrue to firms other than those undertaking the research, social returns are estimated to be even higher. Such rewards may make the relatively low level of investment in research somewhat surprising. High risk and limitations on the ability to borrow to finance R & D provide part of the explanation for this seeming underinvestment.

FACTORS CONTRIBUTING TO PRODUCTIVITY GROWTH

Saving and investment (capital accumulation)
Improved quality of the labor force
Reallocation of labor from low-productivity to high-productivity sectors
Technological progress

Total Factor Productivity: Measuring the Sources of Growth

In an advanced economy like that of the United States, reallocation of resources from low- to high-productivity sectors is not viewed as a major source of further growth. Investment in physical and human capital and technological change are therefore the three sources of growth in productivity. But how important is each? To assess the relative contribution of each, economists use **total factor productivity analysis,** a methodology that helps them determine the change in total output that can be "attributed" to increases in the stock of capital (both human and physical) and increases in the supply of labor. Any output growth that cannot be attributed to capital or labor is attributed to technological change.

Similarly, that part of economic growth that cannot be explained by increases in capital or labor is called the increase in **total factor productivity (TFP).** The increase in TFP reflects the increasing efficiency with which an economy's resources are used. Efficiency can increase because new production methods make it possible to produce more goods and services with the same inputs of labor and capital as before, or because innovations result in new, higher-valued goods and services being produced. The introduction of the assembly line by Henry Ford is an example of a change that enabled more cars to be produced with the same inputs. The past few decades—which have witnessed the development of personal computers, VCRs, DVDs, cell phones, new pharmaceuticals, and more—are replete with examples of innovations that change the nature of the goods and services the economy produces.

Figure 9.7 shows the sources of increases in productivity for three different periods—1959–1973, 1973–1995, and 1995–2000. We can draw several conclusions from the chart. First, the overall rate of growth was much higher before 1973 than it was during the period from 1973 to 1995. Second, between 1973 and 1995, almost all of the growth in output can be explained by increases in the inputs of capital and labor, while before 1973 and after 1995, there was a large

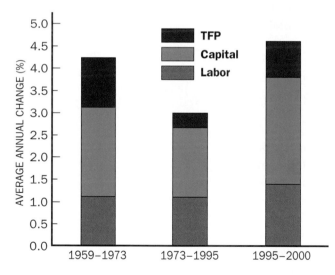

Figure 9.7

GROWTH ACCOUNTING

More than half the decline in growth between 1973 and 1990 is left unexplained after changes in the growth rates of capital and labor are accounted for. The second half of the 1990s saw an increase in TFP growth, returning it to levels similar to those seen in the 1959–1973 period. Increases in capital also account for the faster growth experiences during the second half of the 1990s.

SOURCE: D. W. Jorgensen, M. S. Ho, and K. J. Stiroh, "Projecting Productivity Growth: Lessons from the U.S. Growth Resurgence," *Federal Reserve Bank of Atlanta Economic Review* 87, no. 3 (2002): 1–13.

residual (i.e., TFP). The decrease in TFP appears responsible for most of the growth slowdown in the 1970s and 1980s. Third, the decline in productivity after 1973 was caused, in part, by a decline in the contribution of capital; but since 1995, increases in capital have, together with increases in TFP, accounted for the increase in the growth rate of output. The rapid growth at the end of the 1990s represented a return to the high growth rates of the 1950s and 1960s after two intervening decades of slow productivity growth.

These results pose major problems for those involved in long-term forecasting. Was the rapid growth in the 1959–1973 period an aberration? Or were the 1970s and 1980s atypical, with the late 1990s representing a return to the higher growth rates of earlier decades as fundamentally new technologies, such as computers, came into wider use? Throughout most of human history, technological change and economic growth have been rare. From this longer perspective, the aberration has been the past 250 years of economic growth.

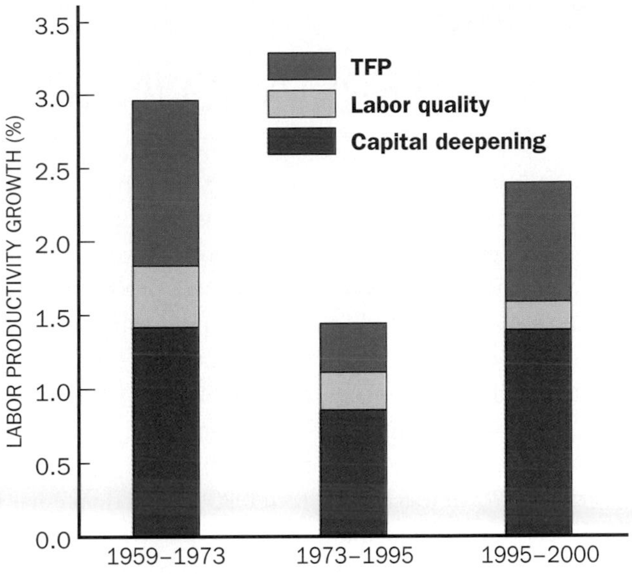

Figure 9.8

SOURCES OF LABOR PRODUCTIVITY GROWTH

Growth in labor productivity is due to capital deepening, increases in labor quality, and increases in total factor productivity. During the late 1990s, labor productivity growth increased because of the contributions of capital deepening and TFP.

SOURCE: D. W. Jorgensen, M. S. Ho, and K. J. Stiroh, "Projecting Productivity Growth: Lessons from the U.S. Growth Resurgence," *Federal Reserve Bank of Atlanta Economic Review* 87, no. 3 (2002): 1–13.

Case in Point

CALCULATING TOTAL FACTOR PRODUCTIVITY IN THE 1990s

Between 1995 and 2000, private domestic output in the United States grew by 20 percent, or 4.6 percent per year. Dale Jorgensen, Mun Ho, and Kevin Stiroh[1] in 2002 estimated that average labor productivity grew by 2.36 percent per year over this period—each hour of labor input produces more output than previously. The accounting used earlier to explain the contribution of various factors to economic growth also can be used to explain the sources of this growth in labor productivity.

One of the reasons why labor might become more productive is capital deepening. According to Jorgensen, Ho, and Stiroh, capital deepening accounted for 1.4 percentage points, or about 60 percent, of the 2.36 percent growth rate of labor productivity. Figure 9.8 shows that labor productivity growth increased during the second half of the 1990s, and part of this increased growth can be explained by capital deepening. But this source of labor productivity growth is still less today than it was in the 1959–1973 period.

A second source of labor productivity growth is increases in the *quality* of labor. Labor quality can increase through education or through shifts in the composition of the labor force. For instance, in the early 1970s, the baby boom generation entered the workforce and changed its composition—now more workers were younger and relatively inexperienced. Such a shift acts to reduce labor productivity. In the 1990s, as these baby boomers gained more work experience and training, the overall quality of the labor force increased, a change that contributed to rising labor

[1]D. W. Jorgensen, M. S. Ho, and K. J. Stiroh, "Projecting Productivity Growth: Lessons from the U.S. Growth Resurgence," *Federal Reserve Bank of Atlanta Economic Review* 87, no. 3 (2002): 1–13.

COMPUTERS AND INCREASED PRODUCTIVITY GROWTH

If the recent increases in productivity growth are due to new information and computer technologies, then we might expect that all the major industrialized economies would be benefiting from them. Panel A shows average labor productivity growth for the seven advanced economies known since 1976 as the "Group of Seven," or the G-7 (the G-7 became the G-8 with the addition of the Russian Federation in 1998). As the chart shows, only the United States has seen labor productivity increase in recent years. For all the other members of the group, productivity growth was higher from 1980 to 1995 than it has been since. Yet the new information and computer technologies are available to all these countries; so why hasn't growth increased in all of them? Should we conclude that the new technologies are not the source of America's increased productivity growth?

Perhaps the acceleration in U.S. productivity growth has not been matched in these other industrialized economies

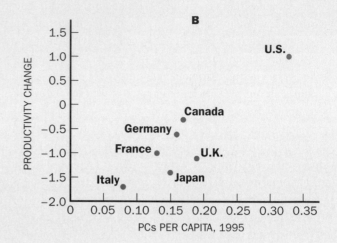

PCs AND PRODUCTIVITY GROWTH

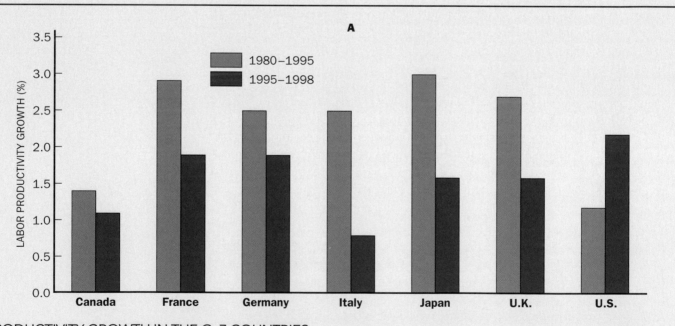

PRODUCTIVITY GROWTH IN THE G–7 COUNTRIES

Physicians can now make virtual house calls using time-saving technology such as videoconferencing.

because the United States has been more successful in adopting new technologies throughout the economy and has done so more quickly. For example, the Organization for Economic Cooperation and Development (OECD) estimated that in 1995 the number of personal computers (PCs) per capita was almost twice as high in the United States as in Canada and 75 percent higher than in the United Kingdom. As shown in Panel B, the change in productivity growth between the 1980–1995 and 1995–1998 periods does appear to be associated with the adoption of computers. The United States, with the most PCs per capita in 1995, experienced the biggest increase in growth, while Italy, with the fewest PCs per capita in 1995, had the largest growth slowdown. While this association between PCs and productivity growth cannot prove whether the adoption of computers has helped *cause* America's growth speedup, it is suggestive.

SOURCE: Casey Cornwell and Bharat Trehan, "Information Technology and Productivity," *Economic Letter*, No. 2000-34, Federal Reserve Bank of San Francisco, November 10, 2000.

productivity. In the second half of the 1990s, however, increases in labor quality accounted for less than 10 percent of the total growth in labor productivity.

The final source of labor productivity growth is increases in TFP. As the figure shows, TFP has increased significantly over the levels experienced between 1973 and 1995.

Fundamentals of Growth

GROWTH IN THE ECONOMY'S LABOR FORCE

The economy's potential output will increase with growth in the labor force. However, rising standards of living depend on increaasing the growth rate of *per capita* output. Growth in the *quality* of the labor force through investments in human capital that increase the skills of the work force will lead to higher incomes per capita.

GROWTH IN THE ECONOMY'S CAPITAL STOCK

Economic growth occurs when workers have more capital goods to work with. The success of many of the newly industrialized economies of Asia is due in large part to thier high rates of saving, which allowed them to invest and accumulate capital goods rapidly.

TECHNOLOGICAL CHANGE

Perhaps the most important sources of economic growth and rising standards of living are the productivity increases that arise from innovation and technological change.

Are There Limits to Economic Growth?

In the early 1800s, the famous British economist Thomas Malthus envisioned a future in which the ever-increasing labor force would push wages down to the subsistence level, or even lower. Any technological progress that occurred would, in his view, raise wages only temporarily. As the labor supply increased, wages would eventually fall back to the subsistence level.

Over the past century, there has been a decrease in the rate of population growth in developed countries, a phenomenon perhaps as remarkable as the increase in the rate of technological progress. We might have expected improved medicine and health conditions to cause a population explosion, but the spread of birth control and family planning has had the opposite effect, at least in the more-developed countries. Today family size has decreased to the point that in many countries population growth (apart from migration) has almost halted. Those who worry about the limits to growth today believe that *exhaustible* natural resources—such as oil, natural gas, phosphorus, or potassium—may pose a limit to economic growth as they are used up in the ordinary course of production.

Most economists do not share this fear, believing that markets do provide incentives for wise use of most resources—that as any good becomes more scarce and its price rises, the search for substitutes will be stimulated. Thus, the rise in the price of oil led to smaller, more efficient cars, cooler but better-insulated houses, and a search for alternative sources of energy such as geothermal resources and synthetic fuels, all of which resulted in a decline in the consumption of oil.

Still, there is one area in which the price system does not work well—the area of externalities. Without government intervention, for example, producers have no incentive to worry about air and water pollution. And in our globally connected world, what one country does results in externalities for others. Cutting down the rain forest in Brazil, for instance, may have worldwide climatic consequences. The less-developed countries feel that they can ill afford the costs of pollution control, when they can barely pay the price of any industrialization. Most economists do not believe that we face an either/or choice. We do not have to abandon growth to preserve our

Thinking Like an Economist

TRADE-OFFS AND THE COSTS OF ECONOMIC GROWTH

Faith in the virtues of economic progress is widespread. Few openly embrace the alternative of economic stagnation and lower standards of living. Yet not everyone benefits from changes in technology, and there may be environmental and other costs associated with growth.

In the early 1800s, English workmen destroyed labor-saving machinery rather than see it take over their jobs. They were referred to as *Luddites,* after their leader, Neil Ludd (whose role may have been largely mythical). Concerns about workers thrown out of their jobs as a result of some innovations are no less real today.

What needs to be kept in mind, and has already been stressed earlier in this book, is that technological progress *creates* jobs as it destroys them. Of course, it can be hard to retrain workers in declining industries to gain the skills necessary for new jobs, so middle-aged or older workers who lose jobs may have real difficulty in getting another one that is as good.

Not surprisingly, technical progress frequently meets with resistance. Although there is growing acceptance that such resistance is futile—change will eventually come—and that the benefits of economic progress exceed the costs, many also recognize the role of government in assisting individuals who are displaced by technological change in their transition to alternative employment. Such assistance can be thought of as a form of insurance. Most workers face the possibility that their jobs will be made technologically obsolete. Knowing that if they are thrown out of work for this reason they will be at least partially protected helps create a sense of security, something most workers value highly.

An important cost of economic growth can be its toll on the environment. As we noted in Chapter 4, a green GDP measure might give a different picture of growth as it would include the economic costs to the environment of producing more goods and services. Accounting for all the costs, as well as the benefits, of growth would provide a clearer picture of the trade-offs that growth can involve.

environment. Nevertheless, a sensitivity to the quality of our environment may affect how we go about growing. This sensitivity is building a new consensus in favor of **sustainable development**—that is, growth not based on the exploitation of natural resources and the environment in a way that cannot be sustained. In many cases, policies can be devised to improve economic efficiency, and thus promote economic growth, at the same time that they decrease adverse environmental effects. These include elimination of energy subsidies and certain agricultural subsidies that encourage farmers to use excessive amounts of fertilizers and pesticides.

Review and Practice

SUMMARY

1. The United States experienced a marked slowdown in the rate of productivity growth in the early 1970s, compared with the preceding two decades. Since the late 1990s there has been a remarkable increase in productivity growth. Even seemingly small changes in the rate of increase in productivity will have powerful effects on the standard of living over a generation or two.

2. There are four major sources of productivity growth: increases in the accumulation of capital goods (investment); qualitative improvements in the labor force; greater efficiency in allocating resources; and technological change. Since 1973 almost all of the increase in productivity can be attributed to increases in capital, improvements in human capital, and expenditures on research and development. In recent years, the relative role of human capital has increased and the role of physical capital has decreased.

3. Increases in human capital—improved education—are a major source of productivity increases. There are large returns to investments in education.

4. The twentieth century was marked by shifts in the U.S. economy from an agricultural base to an industrial base and then to a service base.

5. Improvements in technology, partly as a result of expenditures on research and development (R & D), are a major source of increases in productivity. Government supports R & D through both direct spending and tax incentives, though direct support for R & D that is not defense-related has actually declined during the past quarter century.

6. There has long been concern that certain natural resources (like oil) will run out someday, causing economic growth to halt. However, most economists would argue that the price of resources will increase as they become more scarce, and this rise will encourage both greater conservation and a search for substitutes.

7. Sustainable development requires growth strategies that use resources and the environment in ways that do not jeopardize future potential growth.

KEY TERMS

income per capita
labor force participation rate
depreciation
capital deepening
human capital
property rights
total factor productivity analysis
total factor productivity (TFP)
sustainable development

REVIEW QUESTIONS

1. True or false: "Since growth-oriented policies might have an effect of only a percent or two per year, they are not worth worrying much about." Explain.

2. What are the four possible sources of productivity growth?

3. What is the link between changes in the capital stock (investment) and the rate of growth of productivity in the short run? What is the link between changes in the capital stock and the *level* of productivity (output per worker) in the long run? What is meant by capital deepening?

4. What policies might the government use to increase investment in R & D?

5. What is total factor productivity and how is it measured?

6. Are there limits to economic growth? What was Malthus's view? Is growth limited by exhaustible resources?

PROBLEMS

1. Explain how the following factors would increase or decrease the average productivity of labor:
   (a) Successful reforms of the educational system
   (b) The entry of new workers into the economy
   (c) Earlier retirement
   (d) Increased investment

2. Explain why a rapid influx of workers might result in a lower output per worker (a reduction in productivity). Would the effect on productivity depend on the skill level of the new workers?
3. Explain, using supply and demand diagrams, how a technological change such as computerization could lead to lower wages for unskilled workers and higher wages for skilled workers.
4. Using the model of Chapter 8, discuss the effect on the level of investment for an open economy of (a) an increased government deficit; (b) an increase in government expenditure, financed by taxes on households that reduce their disposable income; (c) an investment tax credit. How will such policies affect future living standards of those living in the country?
5. Calculate the growth rate in the number of hours worked per capita, total output, and output per capita from the following information:

Growth rate in number of hours worked = 1.5 percent

Growth rate of the population   = 1.2 percent

Growth rate of productivity   = 2.3 percent

What happens to the growth rates of total output and per capita output if the growth rate of productivity rises to 3.3 percent? What happens to the growth rates of total output and per capita output if the growth rate of the population rises to 2.0 percent?
6. The table below gives growth rates for the United States for various time periods. Using these data, calculate the growth rate of average hours worked per capita for each period.

	1970–1979	1980–1989	1990–1999	2000–2002
Output	3.67%	3.12%	3.38%	2.27%
Output per capita	1.12%	1.31%	2.05%	2.26%
Productivity	1.92%	1.38%	1.82%	3.43%
Total hours	1.75%	1.74%	1.56%	−1.17%

7. Assume investments in human capital yield a return of 15 percent, private investments yield a total return of 10 percent, and public investments in research yield a return of 25 percent. Assume the deficit is $100 billion per year, and the government wishes to eliminate it. What will be the impact on economic growth of a deficit reduction package that consists of reducing Medicare expenditures by $50 billion, education expenditures by $40 billion, and research expenditures by $10 billion?

Learning Goals

In this chapter, you will learn

1 How the general level of prices is related to the money supply

2 The factors that determine the money supply in a modern economy

3 The role of the Federal Reserve, and the tools it can use to affect the supply of money

Chapter 10

MONEY, THE PRICE LEVEL, AND THE FEDERAL RESERVE

Our discussion of the full-employment model in Chapter 6 left out some crucial dimensions of the macroeconomy: most importantly, the role of money and the determination of the average level of prices and inflation. Most people find the topic of money fascinating, especially when they learn how banks "create" money. In modern economies, banks are active participants in the capital market *and* are key to understanding how the supply of money is determined. In this chapter, we concentrate on the role of banks and the government in the economy's financial market and on their role in affecting the price level and inflation.

While you might care about how much money you have because it provides a measure of how much you may be able to spend, macroeconomists focus on the supply of money in the economy because of its connection with the price level and inflation. Over the past fifty years, the general level of prices has risen significantly, as Figure 10.1 shows. The index of consumer prices has risen by more than 1500 percent since 1913. In other words, something that cost $1 in 1913 would cost more than $16 today. A rising price level—inflation—is associated with growth in the supply of money. As Figure 10.2 shows, the inflation rate has varied greatly since the early twentieth century. Unpredictable swings in inflation can be costly to the economy. The variability of relative prices associated with volatile inflation, the increased uncertainty about future prices that makes planning more difficult, and the capricious shifts in wealth between borrowers and lenders are some of the costs of inflation that were discussed in Chapter 5.

Our first task in this chapter is to explain how the general level of prices is determined in the full-employment model. Answering this question will lead us to a discussion of the role of money, how the money supply is determined, and how government policy can affect the money supply.

No discussion of prices and money is complete without an understanding of the role played by the Federal Reserve. In the United States, monetary policy is

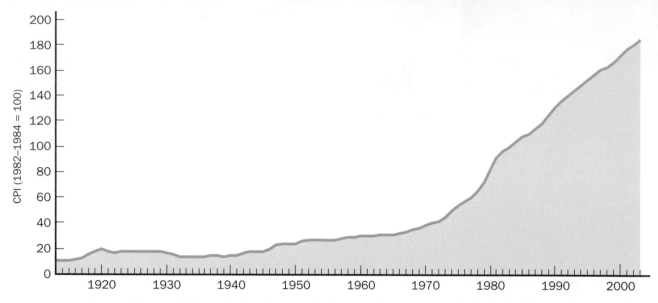

Figure 10.1

THE CONSUMER PRICE INDEX

During the past ninety years, the consumer price index has increased enormously. Most of the rise has occurred since 1973.

SOURCE: Bureau of Labor Statistics.

conducted by the Federal Reserve System. In this chapter, you will learn about the Federal Reserve and the policy tools it can use to affect the money supply.

Prices and Inflation

The discussion of the long-run, full employment model in Chapter 6 was conducted entirely in *real* terms; real output, real employment, real saving and investment, real wages, and the real rate of interest. *We were able to explain the factors that determine the economy's full-employment output level (potential GDP) without any mention of the aggregate price level.* We could do so because the economy's real equilibrium at full employment is independent of the level of prices. That is, regardless of whether the average level of prices is high or low, potential GDP is the same. This implication is represented in Figure 10.3, which has real output on the horizontal axis and the price level on the vertical axis. Potential GDP is denoted by Y^f. Since Y^f is determined by labor demand and labor supply (both of which depend on *real* wages) and the economy's aggregate production function (which depends on the state of technology and the capital stock), it will be the same at all price levels. Because full-employment output is independent of the price level, we have drawn a vertical line in Figure 10.3 at Y^f.

The price level simply tells us how many dollars (or euros in France or Germany, yen in Japan, pesos in Mexico) it takes to buy a basket of goods and services. We measure the price level by using price indexes (see Chapter 5), most commonly either the GDP deflator or the consumer price index (CPI). The GDP deflator reflects

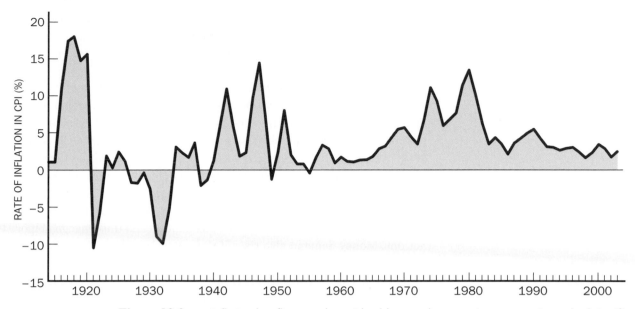

Figure 10.2

THE RATE OF INFLATION

Inflation has fluctuated considerably over the past ninety years. It reached significant levels during World War I, World War II, and the Korean War, and was negative (i.e., prices fell) during most of the period between the two world wars. The period from the late 1960s until the early 1980s is sometimes described as the Great Inflation, because it represented an extended period of high inflation not associated with wartime.

SOURCE: Bureau of Labor Statistics.

the prices of all the goods and services that the economy produces as part of GDP. The CPI measures the prices of things purchased by households. In 2004, the CPI was equal to 189. This means that in 2004 it took $1.89 to purchase what could have been bought for $1.00 in the index base year (an average of prices in 1982–1984).

Because the price level tells us how much it costs to purchase goods and services, it is a measure of the value of money. If the price level rises, each dollar will buy fewer goods and services: the value of money falls. If the price level falls, each dollar will buy more goods and services: the value of money rises.

The value of money, like the value of other commodities, is determined by the interaction of demand and supply. To understand what determines the price level, we will need to examine the factors that affect the demand for and supply of money.

MONEY DEMAND

Money is a financial asset, just like stocks and bonds. But money differs from those other assets because we use it to carry out our day-to-day transactions. If you want to buy a cup of coffee, you cannot present the sales clerk with a share of Microsoft Corporation and expect change. In the United States, you have to present cash. Or you can pay with a credit card—but to pay for those credit purchases, you need to write a check at the end of the month. Cash and balances in checking accounts are the primary forms of money that we use. The more transactions we engage in, or the higher the average value of these transactions, the more of those forms of money

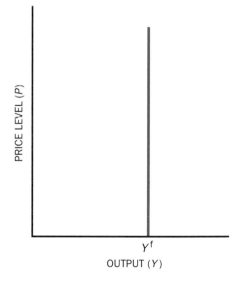

Figure 10.3

POTENTIAL GDP AND THE AGGREGATE PRICE LEVEL

The economy's potential GDP does not depend on the price level; this is represented by drawing a vertical line at potential GDP.

we need to hold. Money we do not need for transactions is better used to purchase financial assets that earn interest. Increases in the dollar value of transactions increase the demand for money; decreases in the dollar value of transactions decrease the demand for money.

A useful simplifying assumption is that the amount of money individuals hold is proportional to the dollar value, or nominal value, of their income. The same will be true when we aggregate the economy; the overall demand for money will be proportional to aggregate nominal income, which we measure by GDP. As we learned in Chapter 4, we can express GDP as PY, the price level (P) times the real GDP (Y). If nominal income in the economy rises, people hold, on average, more money. Nominal income can rise because of an increase either in real incomes or in the price level. If their real incomes rise, people will typically hold more money on average, since they are likely to increase consumption and thus engage in more transactions. Money demand also rises if the general level of prices rise, even if real income remains constant, because each transaction will involve more dollars. When every cup of coffee costs, say, $3 rather than $2.50, it takes $30 rather than $25 to fill up a tank of gasoline, and the bill for a trip to the grocery store is $60 rather than $50, individuals, on average, will need to hold more money to carry out their transactions.

Velocity The relationship between the aggregate demand for money and aggregate nominal income can be represented by the **quantity equation of exchange,** which defines the amount of money that individuals wish to hold as proportional to nominal GDP. We can write this equation as

$$MV = PY,$$

where M is the quantity of money demanded and PY is the nominal GDP. The final term in the equation is the factor of proportionality or **velocity,** V. Suppose, for example, that each individual in the economy held enough money to pay for one month's worth of spending. In this case, velocity for each individual would equal 12—annual expenditures would be twelve times the average level of money held. If an individual's annual income was $60,000, on average he would want to hold $5,000. If velocity were 26, so that on average individuals held an amount of money equal to only two weeks' worth of expenditures, someone with an annual income of $60,000 would hold $2,308. When we add up all the individuals in the economy, velocity enables us to predict the aggregate demand for money when the aggregate income is known. For example, suppose GDP is $11.2 trillion per year and velocity is 26. Then the demand for money will be $11.2 trillion divided by 26, or $43 billion. Velocity, therefore, is a measure of how many times a given dollar gets spent over the course of a year. The higher the value of velocity, the more times a dollar is spent—the faster it speeds from one transaction to another.

Velocity will depend on the methods available in the economy for carrying out transactions. If many purchases are made with money, V is larger than if money is rarely used in making transactions. If innovations in the financial industry reduce the average amount of money that individuals need to hold, velocity rises.

Since we are interested in the demand for money, we can rearrange the quantity equation to express it as

$$\text{money demand} = PY/V.$$

Money demand changes in proportion to changes in nominal income. An increase in velocity reduces the demand for money at each level of nominal income.[1]

MONEY SUPPLY

The supply of money is affected by government policies. In particular, governments influence the amount of money in circulation through *monetary policy*. In the United States, monetary policy is conducted by the Federal Reserve, commonly called "the Fed." How the Fed conducts policy and how monetary policy affects the economy will be discussed later in this volume (in Chapters 13, 14, and 15). For now, we will simply assume the government determines the supply of money. Our focus will be on understanding the consequences for the economy if the government changes that supply.

THE PRICE LEVEL

We now have the information we need to explain how the price level is determined when the economy is at full employment. The supply of money is set by the government. The demand for money depends on the dollar value of transactions in the economy. The supply of money and the demand for money must be equal when the economy is in equilibrium. If the supply of money increases, so that at the initial value of GDP the supply of money is greater than the demand for money, GDP must rise to restore the balance between money demand and money supply.

GDP can adjust through changes in either the price level or real GDP (or both). In a full-employment equilibrium, however, real GDP is determined by the level of employment consistent with equilibrium in the labor market and with the aggregate production function that determines how much the economy produces when employment is at that level. At full employment, GDP is equal to PY^{f}, where Y^{f} is full-employment real GDP. We can then write the requirement that the demand for money equal the supply of money as

$$\text{money demand} = PY^{\text{f}}/V = M = \text{money supply}.$$

For a given level of velocity, it is the price level P that adjusts to ensure that the demand for money is equal to the supply of money.

---

[1]The inverse of velocity, $1/V$, also has its own name—the Cambridge constant—after the formulation of money demand used by economists (including John Maynard Keynes) at Cambridge University in the early twentieth century, and it is usually denoted by k. We can then write the demand for money as kPY. The Cambridge constant is equal to the fraction of nominal income held as money.

What happens if the supply of money increases? At the initial price level P, individuals are now holding more money than they want to. The easiest way to reduce the amount of money you are holding is to spend it. From the perspective of firms, increased spending by consumers provides a signal to increase prices. Faced with higher prices, workers demand high nominal wages. As prices rise, individuals must hold more money to carry out the same transactions. Equilibrium between demand and supply for money is restored when prices have risen enough that the increase in the quantity of money demanded equals the increase in the money supply. Nominal wages will have risen by the same proportionate amount to maintain the real wage at the level that clears the labor market and maintains full employment. *An increase in the money supply leads to an increase in the general level of prices and nominal wages.*

In the labor market, as noted, the increase in the price level will be matched by an increase in the nominal wage, so that the *real* wage remains at its original level. At this real wage, the demand for labor continues to equal the supply of labor. Thus the effect on the labor market of an increase in the price level is simply a proportionate increase in the nominal wage. There are no real effects—the equilibrium real wage and the equilibrium level of employment are unaffected.

In the capital market, real saving and investment both depend on the real interest rate, which is not affected by the increase in the price level. Accordingly, the equilibrium real interest rate remains unchanged. Only the *nominal* levels of saving and investment change in proportion to the change in the price level.

We can say something more about how much the price level will increase if the money supply rises. We have assumed the demand for money is proportional to GDP. If the money supply rises by 10 percent, GDP must rise by 10 percent to ensure that the money demand increases by the same amount as the money supply. With full-employment output unaffected, this means that the price level must also rise by 10 percent. The aggregate price level will move in proportion to changes in the money supply.

Most economists agree that in a full-employment economy, a onetime change in the money supply affects the price level but little else in the long run. In particular, it does not affect the quantity of goods and services produced or the number of workers employed. An imaginary example may help us understand the point. Suppose that instantaneously, the entire supply of money in the economy was increased by a multiple of ten. In effect, we have tacked a zero onto the money supply. Stores,

Internet Connection

HOW MUCH CASH DO WE HOLD?

The Web site at the Federal Reserve Bank of Atlanta provides some facts and figures on America's money. For instance, did you know that in 1920, we had just over $50 in cash per person, while by 2000 this figure rose to over $2,000? Check out the site at www.frbatlanta.org/publica/brochure/fundfac/html/home.html.

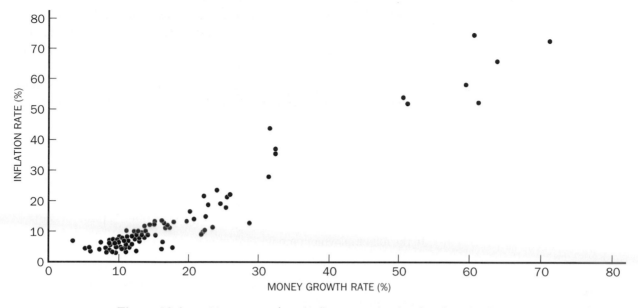

Figure 10.4

MONEY GROWTH AND INFLATION

Money growth and inflation are closely related, as this figure shows. Each dot represents the 1960–1990 average annual inflation rate and rate of money growth for a single country. In all, 110 countries are shown.

SOURCE: George T. McCandless Jr. and Warren E. Weber, "Some Monetary Facts," *Federal Reserve Bank of Minneapolis Quarterly Review* 19, no. 3 (Summer 1995): 2–11.

acting perfectly efficiently, and knowing that the money supply has multiplied by ten, would increase their prices tenfold. Thus, the actual amount of goods and services produced and consumed would be the same. There would be no real effects: the only difference would be the numbers on the bills, bank statements, and price tags.

The lesson is more general. A change in the supply of money accompanied by a proportionate change in the price level has no real effects on the economy. When changing the money supply has no real effect, we say that money is *neutral*. If the economy is at full employment and wages and prices are perfectly flexible, prices will change proportionally to any change in the money supply. Thus, the **neutrality of money** is a basic implication of the full-employment model.

Suppose that instead of thinking about onetime changes in the level of the money supply, we think about what would happen if the money supply grows at 10 percent per year. Then, the price level and nominal wages also would rise at 10 percent per year; the rate of inflation would be 10 percent per year, equal to the rate of growth of the money supply. Rapid money growth would be accompanied by high rates of inflation; low money growth would be accompanied by low rates of inflation. Figure 10.4 provides some evidence on this implication of the full-employment model. It shows average annual money supply growth rates and inflation rates for 110 countries for the period 1960–1990. Just as the full-employment model predicts, there is close to a one-for-one relationship between the growth rate of the money supply and the rate of inflation. Rapid money growth and high inflation go together; slow money growth and low inflation go together.

While the neutrality of money is a basic property of our full-employment model with flexible wages and prices, it is important to keep in mind the limitations of the model. If price increases themselves really had no real consequences, then inflation would not be a matter of much concern. But as we learned in Chapter 5, it *is* a concern. Later chapters will explore the more complicated effects of changes in the money supply and prices when the economy is not at full employment and wages and prices are not perfectly flexible.

MONEY AND THE PRICE LEVEL

In the full-employment model, employment, the real wage, real output, and the real rate of interest are independent of the price level.

Changes in the nominal supply of money produce proportional changes in the price level, nominal wages, and the nominal value of output.

Money is neutral when changing the money supply has no real effect.

The Financial System in Modern Economies

We have now learned that the level of prices is related to the supply of money. But we have not discussed the role of banks, the financial sector, and government policy in determining the supply of money. We will begin by explaining the role that financial institutions play and how banks create money. We focus on banks because they are key players in financial markets generally and help provide an important link between government policy and the money supply.

The capital market is the market where the supply of funds is allocated to those who wish to borrow. In everyday language, we often refer to this as the country's financial market or financial system. Broadly speaking, a country's *financial system* includes all institutions involved in moving savings from households and firms whose income exceeds their expenditures and transferring it to other households and firms that would like to spend more than their current income allows.

The financial system in the United States not only makes it possible for consumers to buy cars, televisions, and homes even when they do not have the cash to do so, but it also enables firms to invest in factories and new machines. Sometimes money goes directly from, say, a household engaged in saving to a firm that needs some additional cash. For example, when Ben buys a bond from General Motors that promises to pay a fixed amount in 90 or 180 days (or in five or fifteen years), he is lending money directly to the company.

But most funds flow through *financial intermediaries*—firms that stand between the savers, who have extra funds, and the borrowers, who need them. The most important of these are banks, but there are many other financial intermediaries, including life insurance companies, credit unions, and savings and loan associations. All are engaged in looking over potential borrowers, ascertaining who among them are good risks, and monitoring their investments and loans. The intermediaries take "deposits" from consumers and put the funds into many different investments, thereby reducing risk. One investment might turn sour, but it is unlikely that many will. Diversifying provides the intermediary with a kind of safety it could not obtain if it put all its eggs in one basket. Financial institutions differ in who the depositors are, where the funds are invested, and who owns the institution. Table 10.1 provides a glossary of the major types of financial intermediaries.

Financial intermediaries have a key function in our financial system. After all, few firms have the resources to undertake investments in new buildings, factories, or equipment without borrowing. And in recent years, venture capitalists have played a critical role in providing the funding that enables high-tech firms to get started. In

---

Table 10.1

A GLOSSARY OF FINANCIAL INTERMEDIARIES

A variety of financial intermediaries take funds from the public and lend them to borrowers or otherwise invest them. Of the many legal differences between these institutions, the principal ones relate to the kinds of loans or investments made. The following list is ranked roughly by the asset size of each intermediary.

Commercial banks	Banks chartered by either the federal government (national banks) or a state (state banks) to receive deposits and make loans.	**Mutual funds**	Financial intermediaries that take funds from a group of investors and invest them. Major examples include stock mutual funds, which invest the funds in stocks; bond mutual funds, which invest in bonds; and money market mutual funds, which invest in liquid assets such as Treasury bills and certificates of deposit. Many mutual funds allow account holders to write checks against the fund.
Life insurance companies	Companies that collect premiums from policyholders out of which insurance payments are made.		
Savings and loan associations (S&Ls, or "thrifts")	Institutions originally chartered to receive deposits for the purpose of making loans to finance home mortgages; in the early 1980s, they were given more latitude in the kinds of loans they could make.	**Institutional money market mutual funds**	Money market mutual fund accounts held by institutions.
Credit unions	Cooperative (not-for-profit) institutions, usually organized at a place of work or by a union, that take deposits from members and make loans to members.	**CMA accounts (cash management accounts)**	Accounts at a brokerage firm (the name was trademarked by Merrill Lynch, the first to establish such accounts) that enable people to place stocks, bonds, and other assets into a single account, against which they can write checks.

return, venture capitalists often receive a share in the ownership of the new firm. For the sake of simplicity, our discussion in the rest of this chapter will focus on one very important group of financial intermediaries: commercial banks.

Traditionally, banks have been the primary avenue for businesses to raise capital. When the banking system collapses, as it did in the Great Depression in the United States, firms cannot obtain funds to make their investments, consumers lose their deposits, and the entire economy suffers. For this reason, governments have developed banking regulations intended to ensure greater financial stability. During the 1930s, hundreds of U.S. banks closed, leaving thousands destitute. Today, banks are more tightly regulated, and deposits are insured by the federal government so that individuals' losses will be limited even if their bank goes bankrupt. Problems can still occur, however. In the early 1980s, changes in government regulations allowed savings and loan associations (S&Ls), which traditionally had invested in home mortgages, to branch into much riskier areas, particularly commercial real estate. Almost immediately thereafter the commercial real estate market collapsed, bankrupting many S&Ls. Depositors were protected by federal deposit insurance, but the cost to the U.S. government reached around $150 billion.

In addition, the actions of commercial banks affect the supply of money, which in turn influences the overall level of prices in the economy. Because of their central role, banks are critical to how monetary policies affect the economy.

While our focus will be on banks, it is important to recognize that to varying degrees, other financial intermediaries perform the same functions. For instance, in accepting deposits and making loans, savings and loan associations today are almost indistinguishable from banks.

Case in Point

WHEN ATLANTA PRINTED MONEY

In the nineteenth and early twentieth centuries, in the rural South and West, cash for everyday transactions was often in short supply. Workers could not shop for food or clothing, bills were not paid, and the local economy lurched sideways or backward.

It was common in such cases for towns, private companies, and sometimes states to print their own currency, known politely as "scrip" and less politely as "soap wrappers," "shinplasters," "doololly," and many less-printable names. The idea was that issuing scrip could keep the local economy going until official currency became available again, at which point people could cash in their scrip.

The last major issue of scrip in the United States came during the Great Depression. In the early 1930s, banks were crashing right and left, and bank runs were a daily occurrence. Remember, these were the days before deposits were insured. When President Franklin Roosevelt took office in March 1933, one of his first major actions was to declare a "bank holiday." He closed all the banks for the week of March 6–12 to give everyone time to relax and get their bearings.

But these were also the days before checking accounts had become widespread; workers were paid weekly, in cash. If firms could not get to the bank, they could not pay their workers. How could the local economy react to these sorts of financial disturbances?

Each area adapted in its own way. Let's consider Atlanta.[2] The city printed about $2.5 million in scrip, in eight different issues, during the first half of the 1930s. One of the first payments was to schoolteachers, and the city made sure that Rich's, a prominent local department store, would take the scrip at full face value. Many other stores, however, would count the scrip only at 75 percent or less of face value. Note that by taking scrip, which it would later turn in to the city for cash, stores were effectively lending money to Atlanta, which had issued the scrip.

Such stories of scrip may sound antiquated today (though in its 1992 financial crisis, California paid its workers with something akin to scrip). But they emphasize the fact that without something to serve as a medium of exchange and a measure and (short-term) store of value, an economy simply cannot function. Today the Federal Reserve acts to ensure that currency is available. But in the 1930s, issuing scrip was one step a city could take on its own to cushion the ravages of the Great Depression.

Creating Money in Modern Economies

Banks have long played a key role in the financial sector. Indeed, today's money supply is created not by a mint or a printing press but largely by the banking sector. The money supply consists not only of the cash we carry but also the deposits in our checking accounts. The total level of deposits in the banking system is an important part of what we mean by the money supply. Whenever you make a deposit to or a withdrawal from your checking account, you are potentially affecting the overall quantity of money.

When you put $100 into the bank, the bank does not simply put it in a slot marked with your name and keep it there until you are ready to take it out. Banks know that not all their thousands of depositors will withdraw their money on any given day. Some people will withdraw their money in a week, some in two weeks, some not for a year or more. In the meantime, the bank can lend out the money deposited and charge interest on the loans it makes. The more money the bank can persuade people to deposit, the more it can lend out and the more money it will earn. To attract depositors, the bank pays interest on some of its deposits, effectively passing on (after taking its cut) the interest earned on its loans.

MONEY IS WHAT MONEY DOES

What do bank deposits and loans have to do with the total amount of money in the economy? When we talk about money, we often mean much more than just currency. In speaking of how much money someone makes, we are really referring to

[2]See William Roberds, "Lenders of the Next-to-Last Resort: Scrip Issue in Georgia During the Great Depression," *Economic Review of the Federal Reserve Bank of Atlanta,* September–October 1990, pp. 16–30.

her income. Or we say someone has a lot of money, but what we really mean is that he is wealthy, not that he has piles of currency stashed away.

Economists define *money* by the functions it serves, and three functions are critical.

Money as a Unit of Account Money serves as a means of measuring the relative values of different goods and services. This is its **unit of account** function. If a laptop computer costs $1,800 and a desktop computer costs $900, then a laptop is worth twice as much as a desktop. People wishing to trade laptops for desktops will trade at the rate of one laptop for two desktops. Money provides a simple and convenient measure of relative market values.

Imagine how difficult it would be for firms to track their profitability without money. Their accounting ledgers would record how many items were sold or purchased, but firms would not know whether these transactions had left them better or worse off. Firms need to know the relative value of what they sell and what they purchase, and money provides that unit of account.

Money as a Medium of Exchange Money's primary function is to facilitate trade—the exchange of goods and services. This is called its **medium of exchange** function. Trade that involves the direct exchange of goods without the use of money is called *barter*. For example, barter occurs when a mechanic fixes a plumber's bad speedometer cable in exchange for the repair of a leaky sink. Nations sometimes sign treaties phrased in barter terms; a certain amount of oil might be traded for a certain amount of machinery or weapons.

Barter works best in simple economies, and it also requires a *double coincidence of wants.* That is, one individual must have what the other wants, and vice versa. If Helen has compact discs (CDs) and wants DVDs, and Joshua has DVDs and wants CDs, bartering will make them both better off. However, if Joshua doesn't want CDs, then Helen's bartering for his DVDs will require that one or both of them search for people with other goods in hopes of putting together a multilateral exchange. Money provides a way to make multilateral exchanges much simpler. Helen sells her CDs for money, which she can use to buy Joshua's DVDs. Money is essential for the billions of exchanges that take place in a modern economy.

Money can be thought of as a social convention. People accept money in payment for what they sell because they know that others will accept it for what they themselves want to buy. Any easily transportable and storable good can, in principle, be used as a medium of exchange, and different cultures have chosen widely different goods to use as money. South Sea Islanders once used cowry shells. In World War II prisoner of war camps and in many prisons today, cigarettes are a medium of exchange.

All developed countries today use paper and metal coins produced by the government as currency. However, most business transactions require not currency but checks drawn on banks, credit cards whose balances are paid with checks, or funds wired from one bank to another. Since the promise of a transfer from a checking account is accepted as payment at most places, economists view checking account balances as money. Most people keep much more money in their checking accounts than they do in their wallets, so economists' measure of the money supply is much larger than the amount of currency in circulation.

Money as a Store of Value People will exchange what they have for money only if they believe that they can later exchange money for things they need. For money to serve as a medium of exchange, it must hold its value. Economists call this third function of money the **store of value** function. Governments once feared that paper money by itself would not hold its value unless it was backed by a commodity such as gold. People had confidence in paper money because they knew they could exchange it at banks for a precious metal.

Today, however, all major economies have *fiat money*—money that has value only because the government says it has value and because people are willing to accept it in exchange for goods. Dollar bills carry the message "This note is legal tender for all debts, public and private." The term *legal tender* means that if you owe $100, you have fully discharged that debt if you pay with a hundred dollar bill (or a hundred one-dollar bills).

We are now ready for the economic definition of **money.** Money is anything that is generally accepted as a unit of account, a medium of exchange, and a store of value. Money is, in other words, what it does.

MEASURING THE MONEY SUPPLY

What should be included in the money supply? A variety of things fulfill some of the functions of money. For example, in a casino, gambling chips are a medium of exchange, and they may even be accepted by nearby stores and restaurants. But no establishment except the casino is obligated to take chips; they are neither a generally accepted medium of exchange nor a unit of account.

Economists' measure of money begins with the currency people carry around. Economists then expand the measure to include other items that serve money's three functions. Checking accounts, or **demand deposits** (so called because you can get your money back on demand), are part of the money supply, as are some other forms of bank accounts. But what are the limits? It is helpful to imagine items on a continuum: at one pole are those that everyone would agree should be called money, at the other are those that should never be considered part of the money supply, and in between are what works as money in many circumstances.

Economists have developed several measures of the money supply to take account of this variety. The narrowest, called **M1,** is the total of currency, traveler's checks, and checking accounts. More simply, M1 is currency plus items that can be treated like currency throughout the banking system. In late 2003, M1 totaled $1.3 trillion.

A broader measure, **M2,** includes everything that is in M1, plus some items that are *almost* perfect substitutes for M1. Savings deposits of $100,000 or less (i.e., up to the limit covered by federal insurance) are included. So are certificates of deposit (deposits put in the bank for fixed periods of time, between six months and five years), money market funds held by individuals, and eurodollars, or U.S. dollars deposited in European banks. In late 2003, M2 totaled $6 trillion.

The common characteristic of assets in M2 is that they can be converted easily into M1. Economists describe as *liquid* an asset that is easily converted into M1 without losing value. You cannot just tell a store that the money needed to purchase a shirt is in your savings account. But if you have funds in a savings account, it is not

A

M1 (Billions, US$)

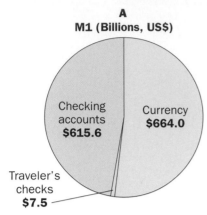

Checking accounts **$615.6**

Currency **$664.0**

Traveler's checks **$7.5**

B

M2 (Billions, US$)

M1 **$1,287.1**

Saving deposits/ money market accounts **$3,144.9**

Money market mutual funds (gen) **$806.8**

Small saving deposits **$805.8**

C

M3 (Billions, US$)

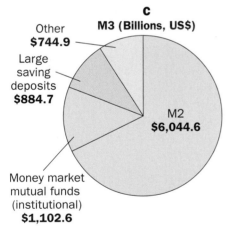

Other **$744.9**

Large saving deposits **$884.7**

M2 **$6,044.6**

Money market mutual funds (institutional) **$1,102.6**

Figure 10.5

THE MEASURES OF MONEY IN 2003

The money supply can be measured in many ways, including M1, M2, and M3.

SOURCE: *Economic Report of the President* (2003), Tables B-69, B-70.

---

hard to change these funds into either currency or a checking account, so that you can pay for the shirt with cash or a check. A car is a much less liquid asset; if you want to convert your car into cash quickly, you may have to sell it for much less than you might get if you had more time.

A third measure of the money supply, **M3,** includes everything that is in M2 (and thus in M1) plus large-denomination savings accounts (more than $100,000) and institutional money market mutual funds. M3 is nearly as liquid as M2. In late 2003, M3 totaled $8.7 trillion.

Table 10.2 provides a glossary of the financial assets used in the various definitions of money, and Figure 10.5 shows the relative magnitude of M1, M2, and M3.

MONEY AND CREDIT

One of the key properties of money, as noted, is that it is the medium of exchange. However, many transactions today are completed without any of the elements of the money supply presented in M1, M2, or M3. They involve credit, not money. In selling a suit of clothes or a piece of furniture or a car, stores often do not receive money. Rather, they receive a promise from you to pay money in the future. Credit is clearly tied to money; what you owe the store is measured in dollars. You want something today, and you will have the money for it tomorrow. The store wants you to buy today and is willing to wait until tomorrow or next week for the money. There is a mutually advantageous trade. But because the exchange is not *simultaneous,* the store must rely on your promise.

Promises, the saying goes, are made to be broken. But if they are broken too often, stores will not be able to trust buyers, and credit exchanges will not occur. There is therefore an incentive for the development of institutions, such as banks, that can ascertain who is most likely to keep economic promises and can help ensure that such promises are kept once they have been made.

When banks are involved, the store does not need to believe the word of the shopper. Rather, the shopper must convince the bank that he will in fact pay. Consider a car purchase. Suppose the bank agrees to give Todd a loan, and he then buys the car. If he later breaks his promise and does not pay back the loan, the car dealer is protected. It is the bank that tries to force Todd to keep his commitment. Ultimately, the bank may repossess the car and sell it to recover the money it lent to Todd.

Modern economies have relied increasingly on credit as a basis of transactions. Banks have a long tradition of extending *lines of credit* to firms—that is, agreeing to lend money to a business automatically (up to some limit) as it is needed. As Visa and MasterCard and the variety of other national credit cards came into widespread use in the 1970s and 1980s, lines of credit also were extended to millions of consumers, who now can purchase goods even when they lack the currency or checking account balances to cover the price. Today, many can also get credit based on the equity in their homes (the difference between the value of the house and what they owe on their mortgage, which is the loan taken out to buy the house). This type of credit is called a *home equity loan.* When house prices increased rapidly in the 1980s and again in the 1990s, millions of home owners gained access to a ready source of credit.

Table 10.2

GLOSSARY OF FINANCIAL TERMS

One of the problems in defining money is the wide variety of assets that are not directly used as a medium of exchange but can be readily converted into something that *could* be so used. Should they be included in the money supply? There is no right or wrong answer. Below are definitions of eight terms, some of which have been introduced already. Each of these assets serves, in progressively less satisfactory ways, the function of money.

Currency	One, five, ten, twenty, and hundred dollar bills; pennies, nickels dimes, quarters, and half dollars.	**Certificates of deposit**	Money deposited in the bank for a fixed period of time (usually six months to five years), with a penalty for early withdrawal.
Traveler's checks	Checks issued by a bank or a firm such as American Express that you can convert into currency upon demand and are widely accepted.	**Money market accounts**	Another category of interest-bearing bank checking accounts, often paying higher interest rates but with restrictions on the number of checks that can be written.
Demand deposits, or checking accounts	Deposits that you can withdraw upon demand (that is, convert into currency upon demand), by writing a check.	**Money market mutual funds**	Mutual funds that invest in Treasury bills, certificates of deposit, and similar safe securities. You can usually write checks against such accounts.
Savings deposits	Deposits that technically you can withdraw only upon notice; in practice, banks allow withdrawal upon a demand (without notice).	**Eurodollars**	U.S. dollar bank accounts in banks outside the United States (mainly in Europe).

These innovations make it easier for people to obtain credit. But they also have changed how economists think about the role of money in the economy—blurring definitions that once seemed quite clear.

Case in Point

"BOGGS BILLS" AND THE MEANING OF MONEY

J. S. G. Boggs is an artist who explores the social meaning of money. He starts by drawing one side of a banknote, completely accurate except for some crucial details. The bill might say "In God We Rust" instead of "In God We Trust."

With the Boggs bill in hand, the artist sees if someone will accept it at face value in payment for actual goods or services. For example, he might offer a restaurant a $20 Boggs bill in exchange for a meal. If the restaurant accepts the bill and provides any change, Boggs notes the details of the transaction on the bill before turning it over. Boggs then sells the receipt and the change. An art dealer might purchase the receipt and change and then track down the restaurant and try to buy the Boggs bill. The dealer then resells the bill, the receipt, and the change. One such "transaction" sold for $420,000! The British Museum, the Museum of Modern Art, and the Smithsonian are among the museums holding Boggs transaction pieces in their permanent collections.

Boggs bills illustrate the social nature of fiat money—anything can serve as money if others are willing to accept it as money. As Boggs puts it, "Nobody knows what a dollar is, what the word means, what holds the thing up, what it stands in for. And that's also what my work is about. Look at these things, I try to say. They're beautiful. But what the hell are they? What do they do? How do they do it?"

The Secret Service has taken a dim view of Boggs's efforts and has taken him to court. In its 1998 ruling against the artist, the U.S. Court of Appeals for the District of Columbia stated, "Art is supposed to imitate life, but when the subject matter is money, if it imitates life too closely it becomes counterfeiting."

THE MONEY SUPPLY AND THE BANK'S BALANCE SHEET

The banking system's role in the economy is critical because demand deposits are an important component of the money stock, representing almost 50 percent of M1. An understanding of what determines the money stock in a modern economy begins

Thinking Like an Economist

EXCHANGE, MONEY, AND THE INTERNET

Imagine how difficult it would be to organize exchange without money. As individuals, we probably think about the value of money in terms of the wealth it represents. The cash we carry in our pockets has no intrinsic value—we cannot eat it, for instance—but it does represent value, because it can be exchanged for things that are of direct utility to us: food, clothing, housing, and the thousands of goods and services we consume.

An economist naturally thinks of the benefits that are gained from voluntary exchange, and so thinks of the social benefits that money provides by reducing the costs of exchanging goods and services. The music store employee does not have to accept compact discs (CDs) for wages and then find a landlord who is willing to rent an apartment for CDs. Instead, wages are paid in money, and the landlord is happy to take money for rent, knowing that she can use the money to purchase the goods and services she wants. Thus, the role of money in helping to carry out transactions cheaply and efficiently is the most important service it provides.

The classic problem faced by barter systems—the need to find someone who has what you want and wants what you have—may be reduced by the ability of the Internet to match sellers and buyers. A number of companies have set up Web sites that arrange barter transactions. Yet even with the information-processing capabilities of the Internet, these barter Web sites still rely on a form of money. Barter Systems, Inc. (www.bartersys.com) is typical. A seller receives "trade dollars," which then can be used to make purchases from other sellers. U.S. dollars are not used, but trade dollars serve just like a local currency to avoid the requirement of double coincidence of wants that makes barter inefficient.

Table 10.3

AMERICABANK BALANCE SHEET

Assets		Liabilities	
Loans outstanding	$28 million	Deposits	$30 million
Government bonds	$ 2 million		
Reserves	$ 3 million	Net worth	$ 3 million
Total	$33 million	Total	$33 million

with a look at the assets and liabilities of a typical bank. One convenient way to look at the assets and liabilities of a bank (or a firm or individual, for that matter) is to organize them in what is known as a *balance sheet*. A balance sheet simply lists all the assets of the bank in one column and the liabilities in a second column.

The assets of the bank are what the bank owns, including what is owed to it by others. Since the loans that the bank has made represent funds that the borrowers owe the bank, loans are listed as assets on the bank's balance sheet. Liabilities are what the bank owes to others. We can think of the bank's depositors as having lent money to the bank. That is why deposits are treated by the bank as liabilities.

Table 10.3 shows the balance sheet of a typical bank that we will call AmericaBank. Its assets are divided into three categories: loans outstanding, government bonds, and reserves. Reserves are the deposits the bank has not used to make loans or buy government bonds. The cash a bank keeps in its vault to meet daily business needs is one part of its reserves. Another part is kept in an account elsewhere. In the United States, the Federal Reserve acts as a bank for banks, and private banks that are members of the Federal Reserve System can have accounts with the Fed. The bank's riskiest assets are its loans outstanding. These consist of loans to business firms, real estate loans (mortgages), car loans, house-remodeling loans, and so on. Government bonds are more secure than loans to households or firms, and banks typically concentrate their holdings in Treasury bills (or T-bills)—short-term bonds maturing in thirty, sixty, or ninety days after their date of issue.[3] Most secure are the reserves that are held on deposit at the local Federal Reserve bank and the cash in the vault.

The amount of money that people need to set aside for emergencies depends (in part) on how easily they can borrow. The same is true for banks. If they can borrow easily from other banks to meet any shortfall, they need to keep very little in their reserves. In the United States, the Federal Reserve banks act as the banker's bank, lending money to other banks. (Banks do not, however, have an automatic right to borrow; the Fed must concur with the request. Many central banks use this discretionary power to steer private banks' behavior.) But unlike individuals, banks are

---

[3]Long-term bonds are volatile in price, because their price changes with changes in interest rates. By instead holding short-term government bonds, the banks avoid risk, since price changes are much less likely over relatively short periods of time.

Table 10.4

REQUIRED RESERVES

Bank deposits and type	Minimum reserve required (percentage of deposits)
Checking accounts at banks with more than $46.5 million in deposits	10
Checking accounts at banks with less than $46.5 million in deposits	3
All other deposits	0

SOURCE: *Federal Reserve Bulletin* (1999).

required to hold reserves, at levels imposed by the Fed. Today, the amount of reserves they hold is dictated more by regulations than by the banks' own perceptions of what is prudent. After all, holding T-bills is just as safe as holding reserves with the Fed—and yields higher returns. And the level of reserves required by the Fed is designed primarily with an eye not to maximizing their profit but to controlling the money supply and thereby the level of economic activity. Table 10.4 shows the current reserve requirements. This system of banking, in which banks hold a fraction of the amount on deposit in reserves, is called a **fractional reserve system.**

The liability side of AmericaBank's balance sheet consists of two items: deposits and net worth. Deposits include checking accounts, which are technically known as *demand deposits,* and a variety of forms of savings accounts, which are technically known as *time deposits.* The bank's net worth is simply the difference between the value of its assets and the value of its liabilities. In other words, if the bank's assets were sold and its depositors paid off, what remained would equal the net worth of the bank. By including net worth in the column for liabilities, we ensure that the numbers on both sides of the balance sheet always balance when we add up each column.

HOW BANKS CREATE MONEY

As we have seen, the currency manufactured by the Treasury is a relatively small part of the money supply. The rest of the money is created by banks. To understand this process, let us consider all 9,500 U.S. banks as one huge superbank. Now suppose that a multibillionaire deposits $1 billion in currency into her account with this superbank.

The bank knows it must keep enough funds to satisfy the reserve requirement set by the Fed. Currently, the Fed requires that reserves be 10 percent of demand deposits, so its reserve-to-deposit ratio must be 1 to 10. The bank also has a long line of loan applicants. When the bank makes a loan, it does not actually give the borrower currency. It credits him with funds in his checking account. It does this by

e-Insight
ELECTRONIC CASH

A TV ad shows a thirsty older gentleman who finds himself short of change for a soda trying to steal coins out of a fountain, while a young girl points her cellular phone at the same machine and retrieves a drink. The message? Cash is for old folks.

Cold, hard cash is becoming a rarity in the United States. Americans increasingly rely on credit cards and ATM cards for all but the smallest transactions. Credit card purchases are often an easy, if expensive, method of taking out a consumer loan. But even consumers who pay off their balances every month enjoy the convenience of using cards instead of cash. They get complete records of their purchases every month, they do not have to write checks for recurring bills, and they can collect such benefits as air miles for their purchases. Such consumers choose automatic credit card payment for their phone bills, magazine subscriptions, and even their medical and dental bills. Cash is reserved for occasional purchases of small items at convenience stores. Soon even these "microtransactions" that still require cash may be taken over by electronic payment options.

Electronic cash cards are plastic "smart cards" that resemble the phone cards now widely used for long-distance calls. They contain microchips that enable users to transfer money from bank accounts to the cards at special ATMs or phones. The cards can then be used to make purchases at participating merchants. The purchases take place almost instantly, because, unlike credit card and ATM transactions, they do not require authorization over a phone line or verification of a password. Merchants are eager for this technology, as authorization charges and password verification are expensive (an expense that explains the minimum purchase requirements for credit card or ATM card transactions in some stores). In a world of e-cash, consumers will never need

Money cards are now used to buy a wide variety of goods at all sorts of retail stores.

to worry about minimum purchase requirements or about having the right change for a bus or a vending machine. The microchip in their e-cash card will communicate with the microchip at a store or vending machine, and once the chips determine that there are no security issues, the transaction is complete.

For further discussion of the future of cash, see Kevin P. Sheehan, "Electronic Cash," *FDIC Banking Review* 11, no. 2 (1998): 1–8.

placing an entry into its books on both the left- and right-hand side of the balance sheet; there is a loan on the asset side and a deposit on the liabilities side. With the initial deposit of currency of $1 billion by the billionaire, the bank can make $9 billion worth of loans. If it lends $9 billion, its liabilities will have gone up by $10 billion (the $1 billion in currency originally deposited by the billionaire plus the $9 billion in new deposits that result from the new loans). On the asset side, the bank takes the $1 billion in currency to the Fed and is credited with the amount, so it now has $1 billion in reserves. Because its reserves have increased by $1 billion and its deposits by $10 billion, it has satisfied the 10 percent reserve requirement. The bank also has $9 billion in loans, so its assets have gone up by $10 billion, the $1 billion in reserves and the $9 billion in loans.

This relationship between the change in reserves and the final change in deposits is called the **money multiplier.** We can reach the same conclusion by a slower route, as shown in Table 10.5.

Money Multipliers with Many Banks The money multiplier works just as well when more than one bank is involved. Assume our billionaire deposits $1 billion in currency with BankNational, which then, after setting aside 10 percent to meet its reserve requirement, lends $900 million to Desktop Publishing. Desktop Publishing then orders equipment from ComputerAmerica, which banks with BankUSA. When Desktop Publishing writes a check for $900 million to ComputerAmerica, $900 million is transferred from BankNational to BankUSA. Once that $900 million has been transferred, BankUSA will find that it can lend more than it could previously. Out of the $900 million increase in deposits, it must set aside 10 percent, or $90 million, to satisfy the reserve requirement, but it can then lend out the rest, or $0.9 \times \$900 = \$810$ million. Suppose it lends the $810 million to the NewTelephone Company, which uses the money to buy a machine from Equipment Manufacturing. If Equipment Manufacturing promptly deposits its payment into its bank account at BankIllinois, then BankIllinois will find that its deposits have increased by $810 million; it therefore can lend $0.9 \times \$810 = \$729$ million after meeting the 10 percent reserve requirement. In this example, total deposits have increased by $1 billion plus $900 million $810 million plus $729 million, or $3.439 billion. But this is not the end of the process. As each bank receives a deposit, it will increase its lending. The process will continue until the new equilibrium is identical to the one described earlier in the superbank example, with a $10 billion increase in deposits. The banking system as a whole will have expanded the money supply by a multiple of the initial deposit, equal to 1/(reserve requirement).

In this example, there were no "leakages" outside the banking system. That is, no one decided to hold currency rather than put the money back into a bank, and sellers put all that they received into their bank after being paid. With leakages, the increase in deposits and thus the increase in the money supply will be smaller. In the real world these leakages are large. After all, currency held by the public amounts to almost 50 percent of M1. The ratio of M1 to currency plus reserves held by the banking system is under 3, and even for M2 the ratio is less than 10. Nevertheless, the increase in bank reserves will lead to an increase in the money supply by some multiple.

When there are many banks, individual banks may not even be aware of the role they play in this process of expanding the money supply. All they see is that their deposits have increased and therefore they are able to make more loans.

The creation of multiple deposits may seem somewhat like a magician's trick of pulling rabbits out of a hat; it appears to make something out of nothing. But it is, in

Table 10.5

SUPERBANK BALANCE SHEET

Before-deposit equilibrium

Assets		Liabilities	
Loans outstanding	$ 91 billion	Deposits	$100 billion
Government bonds	2 billion		
Reserves	10 billion	Net worth	3 billion
Total	103 billion	Total	103 billion

First round
(Add $1 billion deposits, $0.9 billion loans)

Assets		Liabilities	
Loans outstanding	$91.9 billion	Deposits	$101 billion
Government bonds	2 billion		
Reserves	10.1 billion	Net worth	3 billion
Total	104 billion	Total	104 billion

Second round
(Add $0.9 billion deposits, $0.81 billion loans to previous round[a])

Assets		Liabilities	
Loans outstanding	$92.71 billion	Deposits	$101.9 billion
Government bonds	2 billion		
Reserves	10.19 billion	Net worth	3 billion
Total	104.9 billion	Total	104.9 billion

Third round
(Add $0.81 billion deposits, $0.73 billion loans to previous round[a])

Assets		Liabilities	
Loans outstanding	$ 93.44 billion	Deposits	$102.71 billion
Government bonds	2 billion		
Reserves	10.27 billion	Net worth	3 billion
Total	105.71 billion	Total	105.71 billion

After-deposit equilibrium
(Add $10 billion new deposits, $9 billion new loans to original equilibrium)

Assets		Liabilities	
Loans outstanding	$100 billion	Deposits	$110 billion
Government bonds	2 billion		
Reserves	11 billion	Net worth	3 billion
Total	113 billion	Total	113 billion

[a]In each subsequent round, new deposits equal new loans of the previous round; new loans equal 0.9 × new deposits.

fact, a process with a physical trail. Deposits are created by making entries in records; today, electronic impulses create these records in computer files. The rules of deposit creation, which specify when certain entries can be made in these files—in particular, the fractional reserve requirements—also give rise to the system's ability to expand deposits by a multiple of the original deposit increase.

The money multiplier provides the link between the quantity of reserves in the banking system and the quantity of money. However, we have not yet explained where reserves come from. What determines the quantity of reserves, and therefore the money supply? To answer this question, we need to look more closely at the behavior of banks and the behavior of the Federal Reserve.

Wrap-Up

MONEY MULTIPLIER

An increase in reserves leads to an increase in total deposits by a multiple of the original increase.

If the reserve requirement is r percent, the maximum increase in deposits will be $1/r$ times any increase in reserves.

The Federal Reserve

We have already learned that the Federal Reserve serves as a bank for banks and that it sets the reserve requirement that determines the money multiplier. But the Fed's role in the economy extends much further. Federal Reserve decisions affect the level of reserves in the banking system, the money supply, and the rate of inflation. Learning about the tools the Fed can use and how they affect the supply of money is important for understanding the behavior of money and prices.

Our focus remains on the economy at full employment. As we will see in Part Three, when the economy experiences fluctuations that lead to cyclical unemployment, the Federal Reserve plays an important stabilizing role. Like most central banks in the major industrial economies, the Fed has, in recent years, used its policy tools to influence the level of market interest rates rather than attempting to control the supply of money. Chapter 14 discusses how that influence is wielded.

The Federal Reserve is the **central bank** of the United States. A *central bank* is the government bank that oversees and monitors the rest of the banking system, serves as a bank for banks, and is responsible for the conduct of monetary policy. In Canada, the Bank of Canada is the central bank; in the United Kingdom it is the Bank of England; in the twelve-member European Economic and Monetary Union, it is the European Central Bank; and in Mexico, it is Banco de Mexico. A nation's central bank often functions largely to regulate commercial banks. The Fed's most important role, in contrast, arises from its responsibility for the conduct of monetary policy and the influence it has on the level of nominal interest rates and the supply of money.

The Federal Reserve was created by an act of Congress in 1913. In other countries, the central bank is a purely governmental institution, similar to the U.S. Treasury or the Environmental Protection Agency. When Congress set up the United States' central bank, however, it established a unique hybrid with both public and private aspects. The Federal Reserve is overseen by a seven-member Board of Governors in Washington, D.C. Governors are appointed to fourteen-year terms (although the average length of service is about seven years) by the president, subject to confirmation by the Senate. The president appoints one of the governors to serve as chair (also subject to Senate confirmation); the chair serves for four years and can be reappointed. From 1987 to 2005, the chair was Alan Greenspan, who was originally appointed by President Ronald Reagan and was reappointed by Presidents George H. W. Bush, Bill Clinton, and George W. Bush. Because the Fed chair plays a critical role in setting U.S. monetary policy, the chair is often described as the second most powerful person in the United States.

In addition to the Federal Reserve Board, the 1913 Federal Reserve Act established twelve regional Federal Reserve banks; their location is shown in Figure 10.6. These banks are officially "owned" by the private commercial banks that are members of the Federal Reserve System (about 3,700 member banks in total). The directors of each regional Federal Reserve bank are appointed by the member banks and by the governors of the Federal Reserve Board. These directors, in turn, choose the presidents of the regional Federal Reserve banks.

The Federal Reserve Board of Governors in Washington, D.C., and the regional Federal Reserve banks collectively form the *Federal Reserve System*. The structure

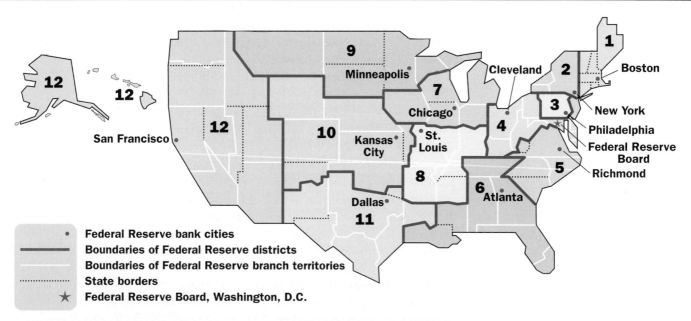

Federal Reserve bank cities
Boundaries of Federal Reserve districts
Boundaries of Federal Reserve branch territories
State borders
Federal Reserve Board, Washington, D.C.

Figure 10.6   The nation is divided into twelve Federal Reserve districts.

FEDERAL RESERVE DISTRICTS

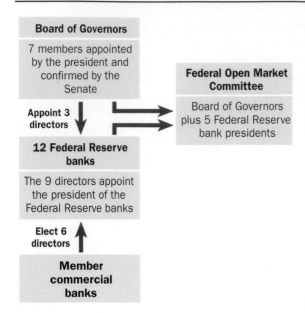

Board of Governors

7 members appointed by the president and confirmed by the Senate

Appoint 3 directors

12 Federal Reserve banks

The 9 directors appoint the president of the Federal Reserve banks

Elect 6 directors

Member commercial banks

Federal Open Market Committee

Board of Governors plus 5 Federal Reserve bank presidents

Figure 10.7

THE STRUCTURE OF THE FEDERAL RESERVE

The Federal Reserve operates at both a national level and a district level. The president appoints the Board of Governors; the district level includes some directors appointed nationally and some from within the district; and the Federal Open Market Committee includes the governors, appointed by the president, and representatives from the district banks.

of the Federal Reserve System is depicted in Figure 10.7. The **Federal Open Market Committee,** or **FOMC,** is responsible for making monetary policy. The name of the FOMC comes from the way the committee operates. The Fed engages in **open market operations**—so called because (as discussed in more detail below) they involve the Fed's entering the capital market directly, much as a private individual or firm would, to buy or sell government bonds. Once the FOMC has set its policy targets, its operations are carried out by the Federal Reserve Bank of New York because that bank is closest to the huge capital markets in New York City.

The FOMC has twelve voting members. These include the governors appointed by the president and some of the regional bank presidents, who are appointed, in part, by private member banks. The seven governors of the Federal Reserve are all voting members of the FOMC, as is the president of the Federal Reserve Bank of New York. The remaining four votes rotate among the other eleven presidents of the regional Federal Reserve banks.

HOW THE FED AFFECTS THE MONEY SUPPLY

Earlier, we said that the money supply depends on the level of bank reserves in the economy. Thus, by controlling the level of reserves, the Fed can affect the money supply. It uses three different policy tools: open market operations, the discount rate, and reserve requirements. Because open market operations are by far the most important of these tools, we will begin by describing what they are and how they affect the level of bank reserves.

Open Market Operations   The Fed alters the stock of bank reserves through the use of open market operations during which it buys or sells financial assets, normally government securities. Imagine that the Fed buys $1 million of government bonds from a government bond dealer. The dealer deposits the Fed's $1 million check in its bank, AmericaBank, which credits the dealer's account for $1 million. (These transactions are in fact all electronic.) AmericaBank presents the check to the Fed, which credits the bank's reserve account with $1 million. AmericaBank now has the bond dealer's $1 million of new deposits on its books, matched by $1 million in new reserves; accordingly, it can lend out an additional $900,000, holding the remaining $100,000 to meet its 10 percent reserve requirement. As we saw earlier, the money multiplier then goes to work, and the total expansion of the money supply will be equal to a multiple of the initial $1 million in deposits. And credit—the amount of outstanding loans—will also increase by a multiple of the initial increase in deposits.

The purchase of the same bonds by a private citizen, Jane White, has quite a different effect. In this case, the dealer's deposit account goes up by $1 million but Jane's account goes down by $1 million. As a consequence, the dealer's bank gains $1 million in funds but Jane's bank loses $1 million in funds. The total funds available in the banking system as a whole remain unchanged. The money multiplier goes to work only when "outside" funds, in particular those from the Federal Reserve, are used for the bonds.

The process works in reverse when the Federal Reserve sells some of the government securities it holds. If the Fed sells $1 million to a bond dealer, the dealer pays with a check drawn against its account at its bank, NationalBank. The Fed presents the check for payment to NationalBank and deducts $1 million from NationalBank's reserve account. The total amount of reserves in the banking system has been reduced by $1 million. This change in reserves then has a multiplied impact in reducing the money supply and bank credit.

The **Open Market Desk** at the New York Federal Reserve Bank conducts the Fed's open market operations. But you might be wondering where the Fed gets the money to purchase government securities in the first place, especially since purchases (or sales) on a given day might amount to more than $1 billion rather than the $1 million of our example. When the Fed credited AmericaBank's reserve account for $1 million to settle the check it had used to purchase bonds, the Fed simply made an electronic entry in its bookkeeping system. In effect, it created the $1 million in reserves out of thin air! And when it sold government bonds and deducted $1 million from NationalBank's account, the reserves were simply gone.

Discount Rate Changes The Federal Reserve has another tool it can use to affect the level of reserves. Banks can obtain reserves by borrowing them from the Federal Reserve, which lends at an interest rate called the **discount rate.** By altering it, the Fed can influence how much banks borrow. When the Fed increases the discount rate, banks find borrowing reserves more expensive; they therefore borrow less and the total level of reserves in the banking system falls. If the Fed lowers the discount rate, banks will borrow more and the total level of reserves will rise. The discount rate is the only interest rate directly set by the Fed; all others are set in the market, by the forces of supply and demand.

Internet Connection

THE FEDERAL RESERVE BANKS AND INTERNATIONAL CENTRAL BANKS

Each of the regional Federal Reserve banks maintains a Web site that contains a variety of useful information related to monetary policy and general economic conditions. The Web site of the Board of Governors of the Federal Reserve System provides links to all the regional banks at www.federalreserve.gov.

The Bank for International Settlements in Basel, Switzerland, lists links to ninety-six central banks in countries around the world, from Albania to Zimbabwe. These can be found at www.bis.org/cbanks.htm.

Reserve Requirements Finally, the Fed establishes how much banks must hold as reserves. The reserve requirements are its third tool. If the Fed increases reserve requirements, banks must set aside a larger fraction of their deposits as reserves and thus can lend out less. A rise in the reserve requirement reduces the money multiplier and reduces the impact that a change in the level of reserves has on the money supply. A reduction in the reserve requirement increases the money multiplier and increases the effects of a dollar change in reserves on the money supply.

Wrap-Up

INSTRUMENTS OF MONETARY POLICY

1. Reserve requirements—the required ratio of reserves to deposits. The Fed can change the amount banks must hold as reserves. Increasing the reserve ratio forces banks to hold a larger fraction of deposits as reserves.
2. Discount rate—the rate that the Fed charges member banks on borrowed reserves. An increase in the discount rate raises the opportunity cost of borrowing from the Fed. As a result, banks reduce their borrowing and total reserve supply falls.
3. Open market operations—purchases and sales of Treasury bills by the Fed. When the Fed buys government bonds from the public, the stock of reserves is increased. When the Fed sells government bonds to the public, the stock of reserves falls.

Selecting the Appropriate Tool Of its three tools, the Federal Reserve uses open market operations most frequently. The effects of changes in the discount rate and in reserve requirements are inexact compared with the fine-tuning that open market operations make possible. Thus, the former are used infrequently, primarily to announce major shifts in monetary policy. Such changes can be quite effective in signaling the advent of tighter conditions (that is, higher interest rates and reduced credit availability) or looser conditions (that is, the reverse). Banks foreseeing a tightening of credit may cut back on their lending and firms may postpone their planned investment.

The Stability of the U.S. Banking System

The fractional reserve system explains how banks create money. It also explains how, without the Fed, banks can get into trouble. Well-managed banks, even before the establishment of the Fed and its reserve requirements, kept reserves equal to some average expectation of day-to-day needs. A bank could soon face disaster if one day's needs exceeded its reserves.

If (for good reasons or bad) many depositors lose confidence in a bank at the same time, they will attempt to withdraw their funds all at once. The bank simply will not have the money available, since most of it will have gone out in loans that cannot be called in instantaneously. This situation is called a *bank run*. Bank runs were as common in nineteenth-century America as they were in the old western movies, which often depicted customers in a small town lining up at the bank while it paid out what reserves it had on a first-come, first-served basis until nothing was left. Such a run could quickly drive even a healthy bank out of business. If a rumor spread that a bank was in trouble and a few savers ran to the bank to clean out their accounts, then other investors would feel they were foolish not to rush to the bank themselves and withdraw their deposits. One vicious rumor could result in a healthy bank shutting down, and the panic could set off a run on other banks, thus destabilizing the banking system and the whole economy.

REDUCING THE THREAT OF BANK RUNS

Bank runs and panics have periodically afflicted the American banking system. In fact, one reason the Fed was set up in 1913 was to make them less likely. The last major panic occurred in the midst of the Great Depression in 1933. Since then, the modern banking system has evolved a variety of safeguards that have ended the threat of bank runs for most banks. There are four levels of protection.

First, the Fed acts as a "lender of last resort." If a bank faces a run, it can turn to the Fed to borrow funds to tide it over. The certainty that the bank can meet its obligations means, of course, that there is no need for anyone to run to the bank. The Fed lends money when a bank faces a liquidity problem: that is, it has a temporary shortage of funds, but its assets still exceed its liabilities. It is, in other words, solvent. The objective of the next two measures is to reduce the likelihood that banks face problems of illiquidity or insolvency.

Second, the Fed sets reserve requirements. Even bank executives who might like to live recklessly, getting along on minimal reserves, are unable to do so.

The third level of protection is provided by the owners of the bank. Most banks are started by investors who put up a certain amount of money in exchange for a share of ownership. The net worth of the firm—the difference between the bank's assets and its liabilities—is this initial investment, augmented or decreased over time by the bank's profits or losses. If the bank makes bad investment decisions, then these shareholders can be forced to bear the cost. This cushion provided by shareholders not only protects depositors but also encourages the bank to be more prudent in its loans. If the bank makes bad loans, the owners risk their entire investment. But if the owners' net worth in the bank is too small, the owners may see themselves in a "Heads I win, tails you lose" situation. If risky investments turn out well, the extra profits accrue to the bank; if they turn out badly and the bank goes bankrupt, the owners lose little because they have little at stake. To protect against this danger, the government requires banks to maintain certain ratios of net worth to deposits. These are called *capital requirements*. Capital requirements protect against insolvency; they ensure that if the bank invests badly and many of its loans default, the bank will still be able to pay back depositors. (By contrast, reserves and the ability to borrow from the Fed protect against illiquidity; they ensure that if depositors want cash, they can get it.) On occasion a bank will make so many bad loans that its net worth shrinks to the point at which it can no longer satisfy the capital requirements.

As a fourth and final backstop, the government introduced the Federal Deposit Insurance Corporation (FDIC) in 1933. Since then, federal banks and savings and loans have had to purchase insurance, which guarantees that depositors can get all their money back, up to $100,000 per account. Because deposits are secured by the federal government, depositors fearing the collapse of a bank have no need to rush to withdraw their money. The deposit insurance thus not only protects depositors but also enormously increases the stability of the banking system. Simply because it exists, the threat against which it insures is much less likely to occur. It is as if life insurance somehow prolonged life.

Deposit insurance has an offsetting disadvantage, however: depositors no longer have any incentive to monitor banks, to make sure that banks are investing their funds safely. Regardless of what the bank does, their funds are protected. Thus— to the extent that capital requirements fail to provide banks with appropriate incentives to make good loans—bank regulators must assume the full responsibility of ensuring the safety and soundness of banks.

Review and Practice

SUMMARY

1. In the long run, the full-employment model implies that money is neutral. Changes in the quantity of money affect the price level and the level of nominal wages but leave real output, real wages, and employment unaffected.

2. Money is anything that is generally accepted in a given society as a unit of account, a medium of exchange, and a store of value.

3. The Federal Reserve is the central bank of the United States. Its policy actions affect the level of reserves and the money supply.

4. There are many ways of measuring the money supply. The most common measures in the United States are M1, M2, and M3. All include currency and demand deposits (checking accounts); M2 and M3 also include assets that are close substitutes for currency and checking accounts.

5. Financial intermediaries, which include banks, savings and loan institutions, mutual funds, insurance companies, and others, all form the link between savers who have extra funds and borrowers who desire extra funds.

6. Government is involved with the banking industry for two reasons. First, by regulating the activities banks can undertake and by providing deposit insurance, government tries to protect depositors and ensure the stability of the financial system. Second, by influencing the willingness of banks to make loans, government attempts to influence the level of investment and overall economic activity.

7. By making loans, banks can create an increase in the supply of money that is a multiple of any initial increase in the bank's deposits. If every bank lends all the money it can and every dollar lent is spent to buy goods purchased from other firms that deposit the checks in their accounts, the money multiplier is 1 divided by the reserve requirement imposed by the Fed. In practice, the multiplier is considerably smaller.

8. The Federal Reserve can affect the level of reserves by changing the reserve requirement, by changing the discount rate, or by conducting open market operations.

9. The chief tool of the Fed is open market operations, which affect the supply of reserves.

10. The reserve requirement, capital requirements, the Fed's status as lender of last resort, and deposit insurance have made bank runs rare.

KEY TERMS

quantity equation of exchange
velocity
neutrality of money
unit of account
medium of exchange
store of value
money
demand deposits
M1
M2
M3
fractional reserve system
money multiplier
central bank
Federal Open Market Committee (FOMC)
open market operations
Open Market Desk
discount rate

REVIEW QUESTIONS

1. What is meant by "the neutrality of money"?
2. What is the name of the committee that sets monetary policy for the United States? Who are the members of this committee?
3. What are the three characteristics that define "money"?
4. What are the differences between M1, M2, and M3?
5. What are the three instruments of the Federal Reserve?
6. Why do reserves fall if the Fed engages in an open market sale? Why do they rise if the Fed engages in an open market purchase?
7. Why do borrowed reserves fall if the Fed raises the discount rate?

PROBLEMS

1. Identify which of money's three traits each of the following assets shares, and which trait each does not share:
   (a) A house
   (b) A day pass for an amusement park
   (c) Russian rubles held by a resident of Dallas, Texas
   (d) A painting
   (e) Gold

2. Why will only the price level and money wages be affected by a change in the money supply in the full-employment economy? How is the rate of inflation related to the rate of growth of the money supply?

3. Down Home Savings has the following assets and liabilities: $6 million in government bonds and reserves; $40 million in deposits; $36 million in outstanding loans. Draw up a balance sheet for the bank. What is its net worth?

4. While gardening in his backyard, Bob finds a mason jar containing $100,000 in currency. After he deposits the money in his bank, where the reserve requirement is 5 percent, by how much will the money supply eventually increase? Suppose Bob decides to keep $5,000 of his find as cash and deposits only $95,000 in his bank. By how much will the money supply increase?

5. Why is it that the money supply changes when the Fed sells government bonds to a bank but the money supply does not change if a large corporation sells government bonds to a bank?

6. In 1999, there was broad concern about the Y2K computer problem. Banks and the Fed predicted that many people would want to hold additional cash in case there were financial problems on January 1, 2000. Use the money multiplier analysis to predict what would happen to deposits and the money supply if people increased their holding of cash and the Fed kept total reserves fixed.

Part 3

MACROECONOMIC FLUCTUATIONS

Learning Goals

In this chapter, you will learn

1. The terms economists use to describe economic fluctuations

2. Why economies experience fluctuations in production and employment

3. The four key concepts that help economists analyze short-run fluctuations in output and employment

Chapter 11

INTRODUCTION TO MACROECONOMIC FLUCTUATIONS

Modern economies are dynamic economies—new products are constantly being introduced, old ones disappear, consumer demand shifts from one good to another, technological innovations lead to job losses in some sectors and the creation of new jobs in others. Most of the time, these developments have effects that are primarily microeconomic in nature (felt in individual industries, for example). But sometimes, major disruptions affect the entire economy. Thus, large swings in oil prices, increases or decreases in government spending or taxes, shifts in consumers' attitudes that cause households to alter overall spending and saving levels, or modifications in Federal Reserve policy can lead to macroeconomic changes reflected in overall levels of production, employment, and inflation. By understanding the impact these factors have on the economy, we will better understand why unemployment in the United States reached nearly 11 percent in November and December of 1982 and why it fell to 3.9 percent in April 2000, why real GDP actually declined in 2001, and why inflation was over 10 percent in 1979 and only 3 percent in 2004.

To make sense of these sorts of fluctuations in the economy, we need to shift our focus from the long-run perspective adopted in Part Two, which allowed all wages and prices time enough to adjust and ensure that markets cleared, to a short-run perspective, in which adjustments in wages and prices may be incomplete. While the theory of long-run macroeconomics offers important insights into the effects of fiscal deficits on interest rates and exchange rates, the impact of changes in the supply of labor on the economy, the sources of economic growth, and the use of monetary policy to control inflation, it does not explain the fluctuations in real economic activity and employment that also characterize market economies.

Over the long run, the economy has managed to create jobs to keep pace with the increasing number of workers. But we also learned in Chapter 4 that in a dynamic market economy, the unemployment rate is never zero. Some firms and industries are shrinking—jobs are being lost—at the same time that new jobs are being created. Workers voluntarily quit jobs to relocate or look for better positions. In the United States, analysts estimate that 8 to 10 percent of workers—more than 10 million people—change jobs each year. Unemployment also varies seasonally. We call these normal patterns in unemployment structural, frictional, and seasonal unemployment. But at times the unemployment rate becomes much higher than usual, as the economy experiences periods of slow job growth and rising unemployment. Labor markets seem not to clear—the demand for labor is less than the supply. At other times, unemployment drops to unusually low levels, plant and equipment operate at high rates of utilization, and the economy booms. We call the fluctuations of the unemployment rate around its normal level *cyclical unemployment*. These fluctuations in the economy are the primary focus of Part Three.

The key to understanding cyclical unemployment is the recognition of two important "facts" about modern economies. First, prices and wages do not always adjust quickly. As a result, the demand for labor and the supply of labor will not always balance—the economy can depart from full employment. Second, wages and prices eventually do adjust in response to demand and supply, bringing markets—including the labor market—back into balance. Given enough time, wages will normally adjust to restore full employment, returning the economy to the long-run equilibrium we studied in Part Two.

In this and the next four chapters, we will examine how the economy behaves when prices and wages have not adjusted to balance demand and supply in the labor market. This study will enable us to understand what causes cyclical unemployment, why the economy experiences fluctuations, and how monetary and fiscal policy affect inflation and cyclical unemployment.

Economic Fluctuations

All industrialized market economies experience fluctuations in the general level of economic activity. Panel A of Figure 11.1 shows the fluctuations in U.S. GDP over the past forty years. A smooth trend line has been drawn through the data, tracing out a hypothetical path the economy would have taken had it grown uniformly throughout this forty-year period. This trend line provides an estimate of the path of potential output—what the economy would produce if full employment were always maintained. The economy is sometimes above the trend line and sometimes below. The shaded bars in the figure mark out economic **recessions,** or periods during which output declines significantly. Over the time period shown, there were seven recessions; the most recent was in 2001. Panel B shows the percentage by which the economy has been above or below the trend line. As discussed in Chapter 4, the percentage deviation between actual and potential GDP is called the **output gap;** when the output gap is negative, the economy experiences higher than normal unemployment as firms scale back production and workers lose jobs. When output rises above potential and the output gap is positive, unemployment drops to low levels as employment rises and the economy's capital stock is utilized intensively. The close (negative) relationship between the unemployment rate and the output gap is illustrated in the figure.

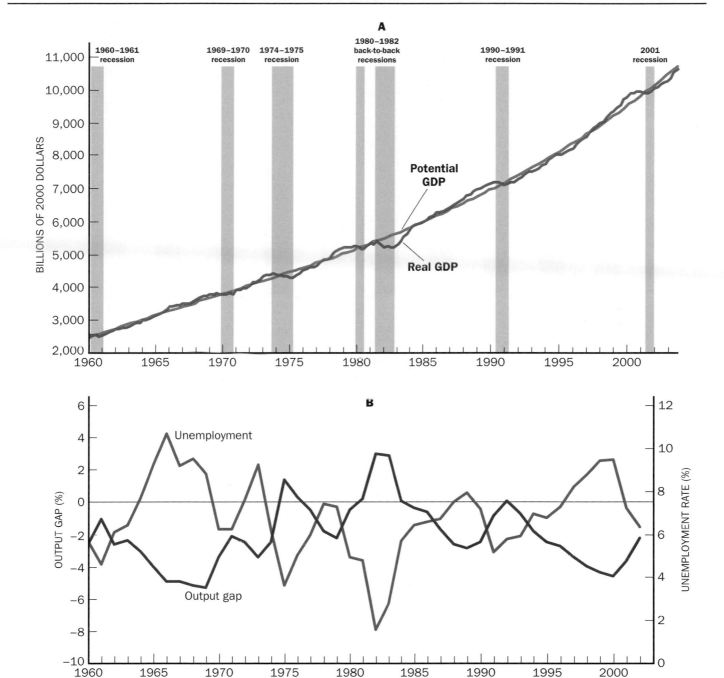

Figure 11.1

ECONOMIC FLUCTUATIONS: OUTPUT AND EMPLOYMENT

Panel A shows how real GDP from 1960 to 2003 has moved above and below potential GDP. Panel B compares the percentage deviations of GDP from potential (the output gap) with the unemployment rate. When the output gap is positive, unemployment tends to be low, and when the output gap is negative, unemployment tends to be high. The relation between the output gap and unemployment, as we learned in Chapter 4, is called Okun's Law.

SOURCES: *Economic Report of the President* (2004) and Congressional Budget Office, *The Budget and Economic Outlook* (January 2004).

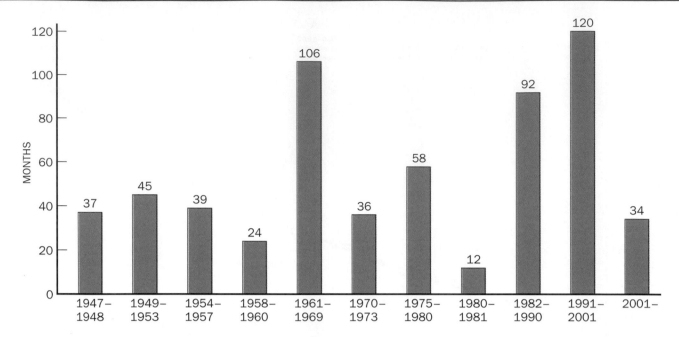

Figure 11.2

THE DURATION OF ECONOMIC EXPANSIONS

Over the past fifty-seven years, the duration of economic expansions has varied greatly. The average complete expansion has lasted 57 months; the shortest was 12 months, and the longest completed expansion was 120 months.

SOURCE: NBER Business Cycle Reference Dates (www.nber.org/cycles.html).

Since 1960, the unemployment rate has averaged just a little below 6 percent of the civilian labor force. But during recessions, it rises much higher. In 1982 and 1983, for example, the unemployment rate exceeded 9 percent for more than eighteen months. Perhaps the difference between 6 percent unemployment and 9 percent sounds small, but with a U.S. labor force numbering above 110 million at the time of the 1982 recession, those 3 percentage points translated into more than 3 million additional workers unemployed.

Economic **expansions** are periods in which output grows. Economists apply the terms **peaks** and **troughs,** respectively, to the points when the economy moves from an expansion to a recession and from a recession to a new period of economic expansion. A high point in output is a peak; a low point, a trough. These fluctuations in economic activity are called **business cycles,** which themselves differ in both length and severity. Since World War II, the length of time between recessions has varied significantly, as Figure 11.2 shows. The average duration of expansions since World War II has been 57 months; the shortest was 12 months, and the longest was 120 months (1991–2001).

Figure 11.3 provides a close-up of changes in real GDP since 1980. The four recessions that occurred during this twenty-five-year period can be seen clearly. The troughs were in 1980, 1982, 1991, and 2001, and the peaks were in 1981, 1990, and 2001. The expansion that peaked in 1981 was unusually short and weak, making the whole period from 1980 to 1982—a time associated with Federal Reserve Chairman Paul Volcker's actions to reduce inflation—one of weak economy growth. Since 1982, however, the United States has experienced more than 275 months of expansion, broken only by two brief recessions lasting only 8 months each: one in 1990–91 and the other in 2001.

Cyclical unemployment reflects unused labor resources. Periods of high unemployment also lead to idle factories and underutilized plant and equipment. There is a cost to the economy if its labor and capital resources are not fully employed. The output that could have been produced with these resources is the opportunity cost of cyclical unemployment.

Because of the potentially high costs, and the individual hardships, caused by high levels of cyclical unemployment, most governments attempt to manage macroeconomic policies to reduce its occurrence. In the United States, the Full Employment Act of 1946 and the Full Employment and Balanced Growth Act of 1978 (often called the Humphrey-Hawkins Act) reflect the commitment of the federal government to bear the responsibility for maintaining full employment. As noted in Chapter 1, the Humphrey-Hawkins Act mandates that the federal government "promote full employment and production, increased real income, balanced growth, a balanced Federal budget, adequate productivity growth, proper attention to national priorities, achievement of an improved trade balance, . . . and reasonable price stability." How governments try to achieve these goals and how successful their efforts have been are among the topics we will discuss in the next few chapters.

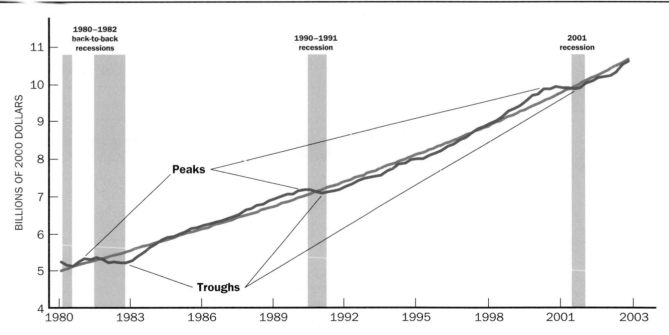

Figure 11.3

PEAKS AND TROUGHS
SINCE 1980

There have been four economic recessions since 1980. After reaching a peak in January 1980, the economy entered a recession that lasted until July 1980, when the trough was reached. The next peak was in July 1981, making this the shortest expansion in U.S. history. The trough of the 1981–1982 recession came in November 1982. The economy then entered a long expansion, whose peak occurred in July 1990. The longest expansion on record lasted from the trough in July 1990 to the peak in March 2001. The recession of 2001 ended in November 2001.

SOURCE: NBER Business Cycle Reference Dates (www.nber.org/cycles.html).

DATING BUSINESS CYCLE PEAKS AND TROUGHS

Almost all the data that economists use to study the economy are produced by the government. In the United States, the Department of Commerce and the Bureau of Labor Statistics within the Department of Labor collect much of the data economists use, such as the statistics on unemployment and GDP. The widely accepted dates for the peaks and troughs of business cycles, however, are determined by the members of the Business Cycle Dating Committee of the National Bureau of Economic Research (NBER), a private, nonprofit research organization. The NBER publishes business cycle dates going back to 1854; the entire list is available at the NBER's Web site (www.nber.org/cycles.html). The NBER defines a recession as "a recurring period of decline in total output, income, employment, and trade, usually lasting from six months to a year, and marked by widespread contractions in many sectors of the economy." In popular usage, the economy is usually considered to be in a recession if real GDP declines for two consecutive quarters.

ECONOMIC FLUCTUATIONS

Recessions: periods of significant decline in real GDP.

Expansions: periods of growth in real GDP.

Output gap: the deviation (a percentage) of observed real GDP from potential real GDP.

ESTIMATING THE OUTPUT COSTS OF A RECESSION

Recessions are periods when workers suffer from higher than normal levels of unemployment. By using the output gap and Okun's Law, economists have developed a way to estimate the opportunity cost of idle workers who are willing and able to work at the going wage. For example, Figure 11.1 shows that the output gap reached –8 percent during the 1982 recession. Since potential GDP in 1982 was approximately $5.2 trillion (in 2000 dollars), the cost of the recession in 1982 was about $420 billion (8 percent of $5.2 trillion) in lost income. The gap fell to only –3.2 percent in the recession of 1991; by then potential GDP had risen to $7.1 trillion, so a 3.2 percent shortfall represented a loss of $218 billion in 1991. These figures agree with most observers' view that the recession of 1982 was much more severe. Yet even a relatively mild recession is serious; to provide some perspective, in 1991 the total real value of expenditures by the federal government for all nondefense programs was only $183 billion.

Thinking Like an Economist

EMPLOYMENT FLUCTUATIONS AND TRADE-OFFS

We measure the cost of cyclical unemployment by the output that could have been produced if full employment had been maintained. This represents the *opportunity cost* to society of *cyclical* unemployment. Not all unemployment represents an opportunity cost, either to the individual worker or to society. A worker who voluntarily quits a job to look for another is classified as unemployed, but she must believe that the value of seeking a new job, one that either pays better or has other advantages over her old job, exceeds the temporary loss in wages. Time spent in job search can thus represent a productive use of time.

To measure the cost of employment fluctuations, we need to take into account the trade-offs that individuals face. For some, the value of time spent in leisure and other nonmarket activities (taking care of children, for example) is greater than the real wage that could be earned from working.

In Chapter 4 we learned that according to Okun's Law, the unemployment rate rises above the natural rate of unemployment level (the unemployment rate at full employment) by 1 percentage point for every 2 percentage points that the output gap shrinks. Using Okun's Law, we can translate an 8 percent output gap such as the United States experienced in the 1982 recession into an added 4 percentage points of unemployment. Since most estimates at the time placed the natural rate of unemployment at around 6 percent, the figure provided via Okun's Law (about 10 percent unemployment) is consistent with the actual 9.7 percent unemployment rate in 1982.

As a lingering result of the recession in 2001, the unemployment rate averaged 6.0 percent in 2002. Most estimates of the natural rate of unemployment for 2002 put it in the range of 5 to 5.5 percent. We can use this information, together with Okun's Law, to estimate the output cost of 2002's cyclical unemployment. For the purposes of this example, we will set the natural rate of unemployment at 5 percent.

Step 1: Cyclical unemployment is the difference between the actual unemployment rate (6 percent) and the rate estimated to correspond to full employment (5 percent), or 1 percent.

Step 2: Okun's Law tells us that the percentage gap between actual output and full-employment output is about twice the level of cyclical unemployment. So the lost output was roughly $2 \times 1 = 2$ percent of real GDP.

Step 3: In 2002, real GDP was $10 trillion. Thus $200 billion (2 percent of $10 trillion) is the value of the output lost as a result of cyclical unemployment that year.

Why Economies Experience Fluctuations

It is difficult to reconcile the economic fluctuations we observe, and the associated changes in unemployment, with the full-employment model. According to the full-employment model, the real wage—the nominal rate adjusted for the price level—always adjusts to ensure that the labor market clears: that is, labor demand and labor supply are equal. If, for whatever reason, the demand for labor were to fall, the real wage should simply decline to maintain full employment. In the real world, this rarely seems to happen. In the Great Depression of the 1930s, for example, when unemployment rose dramatically, real wages in the manufacturing sector for those who remained employed actually rose.[1] More recently, from 2000 to 2002, unemployment rose from 4 percent to 5.8 percent, yet real hourly earnings rose by 2.6 percent. Figure 11.4 shows little connection over the past forty years between the large fluctuations in the unemployment rate that the United States has experienced and movements in the real wage.

When the real wage fails to adjust in the face of a decline in the demand for labor, the labor market no longer clears: labor demand is less than labor supply. People are willing to work at the going wage, but the work is not there. Because firms demand fewer workers, they stop hiring and even lay off existing employees. As a result, unemployment rises.

Figure 11.5 illustrates what happens if there is a shift in the demand curve for labor with no corresponding fall in the real wage. The labor market is stuck in disequilibrium: demand does not equal supply. At the real wage w_0/P, the amount of labor that workers would like to supply remains L_0. But as the demand for labor shifts, the number of workers hired at w_0/P falls from L_0 to L_1. The difference,

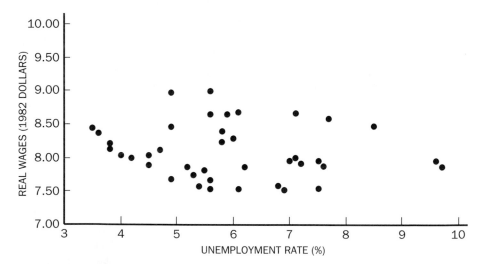

Figure 11.4

REAL WAGES AND UNEMPLOYMENT, 1964–2003

When real wages and unemployment are plotted on a graph, no pattern emerges. Apparently large changes in unemployment may be accompanied by relatively small changes in real wages.

SOURCE: *Economic Report of the President* (2004), Tables B-42, B-47.

---

[1]Nominal wages did fall during the Great Depression, but prices fell even more; consequently, the real wage rose.

$L_1 - L_0$, is the level of cyclical unemployment. People are willing to work *at the going real wage,* but the work is not there. The same argument holds even if there is a slight adjustment of the real wage that is too small to align demand and supply. *It is the failure of the real wage to adjust when the labor demand curve shifts to the left that leads to increases in unemployment.* But why don't real wages adjust quickly? By definition, the real wage is the nominal wage relative to the prices of goods and services; the failure of the real wage to adjust can therefore be traced to a lack of change in both nominal wages and many prices.

NOMINAL VERSUS REAL WAGES

When we discuss the labor market, it is important to keep in mind the distinction between the real wage and the money, or *nominal,* wage. The nominal wage is the wage expressed in dollars. The real wage is a measure of purchasing power, and what happens to the real wage as the nominal wage changes depends on how prices are changing. In 2003, the average hourly nominal wage in the private sector was $15.38. In 1982, it was $7.86. To compare these two wages, though, we need to take into account the marked overall rise in prices between 1982 and 2003. When expressed in terms of 1982 prices, the real wage in 2003 was equal to $8.29. Thus, while nominal wages almost doubled between 1982 and 2003, real wages increased by only 5 percent. Economists focus on real wages because individuals care about the purchasing power of their income, and firms care about the real costs of labor.

THE SLOW ADJUSTMENT OF NOMINAL WAGES

There are several reasons why nominal wages adjust slowly; we will briefly mention three.

Wage Contracts Some wages may be set by union contracts that typically last for a fixed period—three years is common. If the contract is signed just before an economic downturn, more than two years may pass before any wage adjustment can occur. Average union wages adjust slowly to changes in unemployment, since different contracts expire in different months and different years. Similar rigidities may persist even in the absence of any formal labor contract, because the relations between employers and employees are governed by a host of understandings developed over time. These implicit understandings are referred to as an **implicit labor**

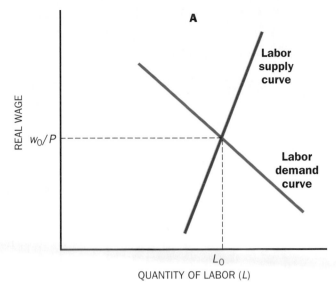

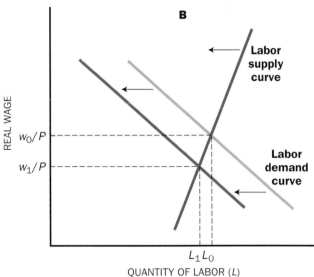

Figure 11.5

CHANGES IN THE DEMAND FOR LABOR AND REAL WAGES

Panel A shows the labor market in equilibrium at full employment. The real wage is equal to w_0/P and employment is equal to L_0. In panel B, the labor demand curve has shifted to the left. Traditional theory predicts that when such a shift occurs, the real wage will fall to w_1/P. Full employment is maintained, although the level of employment in equilibrium declines to L_1. If the labor supply curve had been completely inelastic (vertical), the real wage would have fallen with no change in employment.

Henry Ford made headlines in 1914 when he doubled the standard wage for auto workers in an effort to promote productivity.

contract. Although most workers are not covered by formal contracts, wages or salaries are commonly adjusted only once a year, again contributing to the sluggish movement of nominal wages.

Efficiency Wages Firms want to pay the **efficiency wage:** that is, the wage that minimizes their total labor costs. *If paying higher wages leads to greater worker productivity, firms may find that their profits increase when they pay a real wage higher than the one at which the labor market would clear.* When Henry Ford opened his automobile plant in 1914, he paid his workers $5 per day—a rate more than double the going wage. The high wage ensured that Ford's employees worked hard, for they knew they would have trouble finding another job that paid as well if they were fired. Henry Ford knew that his new technique of production—the assembly line—when combined with motivated workers, would increase his profits. The high wage also reduced turnover of the workforce, because few workers wanted to quit a high-paying Ford job; and lower turnover saved Ford the cost of training a fresh, inexperienced worker each time someone with experience left. By boosting productivity and lowering turnover costs, the high wage paid off for Ford.

Productivity can depend on the wage for several reasons. One has already been mentioned: above-average wages create an incentive for workers to work hard and remain with the firm. Moreover, a firm that cuts its wages when demand falls may so sharply reduce worker morale and labor productivity that its costs of production actually increase. In addition, when a firm cuts wages, workers are more likely to quit to look for another job—and as the firm's **labor turnover rate** rises, it incurs increased costs of hiring and training new workers. Compounding the damage, those most likely to leave in response to a wage cut are a firm's best, most experienced workers, whose departure will significantly hurt overall productivity.

Risk and Uncertainty Cutting wages may be a risky strategy for a firm that wants to reduce its labor force. Whether the wage cut succeeds in encouraging workers to quit will depend on what other firms do—are they also cutting wages? The firm may reduce its uncertainty by simply laying off the workers it doesn't need.

To summarize, when sluggish nominal wages prevent the real wage from adjusting to maintain labor market equilibrium, shifts in labor demand will result in fluctuations in cyclical unemployment, as we illustrated in Figure 11.5. Such shifts in labor demand can occur fairly rapidly, mainly because of changes in output. Wages fail to fall enough to restore equilibrium (the balance between labor demand and labor supply) when labor demand shifts downward, resulting in a rise in cyclical unemployment.

THE SLOW ADJUSTMENT OF PRICES

In the short run, variation in the demand for goods and services has the most effect on changes in output and, therefore, on the demand for labor. If a firm experiences a decrease in demand, it can respond by either lowering its price or reducing the quantity it produces. If a firm experiences an increase in demand, it can respond by either raising its price or boosting production, since even in economic booms,

Thinking Like an Economist

INFORMATION AND MEASURING THE BUSINESS CYCLE

Designing macroeconomic policy requires accurate information about the economy. Economists' conclusions about the severity of business cycles and whether the economy has become more stable are affected by the quality of their information.

Though some recessions are more severe than others, most economists have accepted the view that recessions since World War II have been, on average, milder than the recessions experienced by the United States earlier in the century. Christina Romer of the University of California, Berkeley, disagrees. She notes that the macroeconomic data now available to economists are vastly better than the data used in the early decades of the twentieth century to gauge macroeconomic performance. She has argued that in large part the apparent decline in the severity of business cycles simply reflects improvements in our ability to measure fluctuations in the economy. However, most economists believe that better data do not explain the whole story. Economists do assess the economy more accurately today than was possible before World War II, but changes in the economy and improvements in economic policymaking also have helped make business cycles less severe.

Even though the quality of economic data has improved, accurately judging the behavior of the economy remains difficult. Policy must be based on some measures, such as potential GDP, that must be estimated rather than observed directly. During the 1970s, the growth of potential GDP slowed, but this slowdown was not apparent to analysts at the time. By overestimating potential GDP, the Federal Reserve, along with most other analysts, made errors in evaluating the level of the output gap and cyclical unemployment. These errors led to policy decisions that, in hindsight and with better data, now look to have been misguided.

---

firms normally have some spare capacity. *In the short run, firms typically adjust production rather than prices in response to changes in demand.* Economists have identified two key reasons for this tendency.[2]

The Role of Costs The first explanation emphasizes the implications of sluggish wage adjustment. Labor costs are, for most businesses, the major component of their costs of production. In competitive markets, prices move in tandem with marginal costs and changes in wages translate into changes in the marginal costs of production. Some firms, at least in the short run, use a simple rule of thumb in pricing their goods—they set price as a given markup over costs (e.g., 120 percent of costs). In this case, prices adjust slowly to changes in demand because wages (and therefore costs) adjust slowly.

Risk and Uncertainty Risk and imperfect information can significantly slow price adjustments just as they did wage adjustments. In perfectly competitive markets, firms simply take prices as given; with imperfect competition, firms have some

---

[2]In some cases, these explanations seem to explain too much—they suggest that in some situations, prices and wages will not adjust at all to, say, small changes in demand or costs. But the economy consists of many firms in different circumstances. Some may not be able to respond at all, while others may respond fully. The *average* for the economy demonstrates a slow response.

control over the price of the goods they produce. But firms face a great deal of uncertainty about the consequences of price changes. The effect of a lower price on a firm's sales depends on how other firms in the industry as well as its customers respond. If rivals lower their prices, the firm may fail to gain market share, and the price decline may simply put its profits into a nosedive. If rivals have no reaction, the firm may gain a competitive advantage. The behavior of customers is also unpredictable. If they think this is just the first of several price cuts, they may decide to wait until prices get still lower before they buy. Thus, a decrease in prices might even result in lower sales.

Often much greater uncertainty is associated with changing prices than with changing output and employment. When a firm cuts back on production, provided that the cuts are not too drastic, it risks only depleting its inventories below normal levels should sales be stronger than expected. If that happens, it can simply increase production. Thus its added risk is small, as long as production costs do not change much over time.

Since firms like to avoid risks, they try to avoid making large changes in prices (and wages, as discussed earlier). They would rather accept somewhat larger changes in the amount produced and in employment. As a result, prices are sticky.

Wrap-Up

CYCLICAL UNEMPLOYMENT

Cyclical unemployment is typically generated by shifts in the aggregate demand curve for labor when real wages fail to adjust. These shifts often arise from changes in aggregate output.

Real wages can fail to adjust because nominal wages and many prices are sticky.

Understanding Macroeconomic Fluctuations: Key Concepts

We have argued that the full-employment model of Part Two cannot explain cyclical unemployment. To understand economic fluctuations and how government policies can affect the economy, economists have developed a basic model that differs from the long-run, full-employment model in several critical respects. Fortunately for ease of understanding, the two models also share many features.

Four key ideas are fundamental to helping us understand economic fluctuations. A brief discussion of each will give an overview of the model of fluctuations, before each is developed in more detail in the remainder of this chapter and in the chapters that follow.

The first two fundamental ideas reflect behavior we observe around us—the slow adjustment of wages and prices. When wages (and prices) have had enough time to adjust, supply and demand will balance in all markets, including the labor market. Once this has happened, the level of employment, potential output, the real rate of interest, and the price level are determined as the full-employment model of Part Two explained. Because it takes time for wages and prices to adjust fully, we often refer to the full-employment model as describing the economy in the **long run**—a length of time sufficient to allow wages and prices to adjust to equilibrate supply and demand.

When wages or prices adjust sluggishly, the basic price mechanism that leads to equilibrium can't function effectively. The **short run** is that period during which wages or prices have failed to keep demand and supply in balance. In the short run, the level of employment can diverge from the full-employment level, and wages and prices will not respond quickly enough to move the economy back to full employment. But as noted above, once wages and prices have had enough time to adjust, the economy does return to full employment and the model of Part Two holds sway.

The third and fourth of our fundamental ideas entail simplifying assumptions about how individuals, firms, and economic policymakers behave. They will play an important role in clarifying the implications of the slow adjustment of wages and prices for short-run economic fluctuations.

STICKY WAGES

Our first key concept is one we have already discussed: the fundamental explanation for cyclical unemployment is that wages do not adjust quickly enough when either the demand or the supply for labor shifts. *At least for a while, and sometimes for extended periods of time,* the demand for labor at market wages can differ from the supply of labor. Because this is such a crucial assumption in macroeconomics, some of the reasons for the slow adjustment of wages have already been discussed in this chapter.

Fundamentals of Fluctuations 1

STICKY WAGES

In the short run, shifts in labor supply or demand often result in labor surpluses (high unemployment) or shortages (very low unemployment) because nominal wages tend to adjust slowly.

STICKY PRICES

Like nominal wages, many prices are also sticky. And just as shifts in labor demand lead to fluctuations in unemployment when wages fail to adjust, so shifts in product demand will lead to fluctuations in production. When demand for a firm's product falls, the firm might respond by lowering its price or by reducing production. Our analysis of economic fluctuations is based on a fundamental insight:

e-Insight
CYCLICAL AND STRUCTURAL PRODUCTIVITY

Productivity growth is the key to economic growth and rising standards of living, and the information technologies we associate with the "new economy" have contributed significantly to the rapid growth in productivity that the United States has enjoyed since the mid-1990s. When productivity increased sharply in 1996, few commentators thought the numbers heralded a new period of sustained rapid growth. By 2000, most were convinced that the economy's average, or *structural,* rate of productivity growth had risen.

One reason it can take several years to discover shifts in structural productivity growth is that the business cycle itself influences productivity. When the economy goes through recessions and booms, GDP and employment fluctuate. Measures of productivity such as output per hour—real GDP divided by the total number of hours worked—will be affected as GDP and employment change over the business cycle. It therefore can be difficult to determine whether productivity is changing because of a new structural growth rate or simply because of short-run business cycle fluctuations.

The best way to understand how the business cycle affects productivity is to visualize what happens in a small firm as the economy enters a recession. Let's call this firm YourPlace.com, a business offering specialized Internet consulting and troubleshooting services to other businesses. YourPlace.com employs 20 people: the owner, an accountant, a sales manager, 16 computer service technicians who actually visit the clients' sites and provide the consulting services, and a person who manages and coordinates their schedules. Suppose that initially YourPlace.com has 96 clients, with each service technician responsible for 6 clients. When the economy starts to go into a recession, YourPlace.com finds that the demand for its business services falls. Some of its clients may go bankrupt, while others may seek to lower their costs by scaling back their contracts with firms like YourPlace.com. Suppose YourPlace.com loses 12 clients; in response, it lays off 2 technicians. Even though business has fallen, it still needs the scheduler to handle its remaining 14 technicians, and it still needs its sales manager and its accountant. While YourPlace.com's business has dropped by 12.5 percent (from 96 to 84 clients), so that it is producing 12.5 percent less, its workforce fell by only 10 percent (from 20 to 18 employees). In other words, labor productivity goes down. (For the sake of simplicity, we are

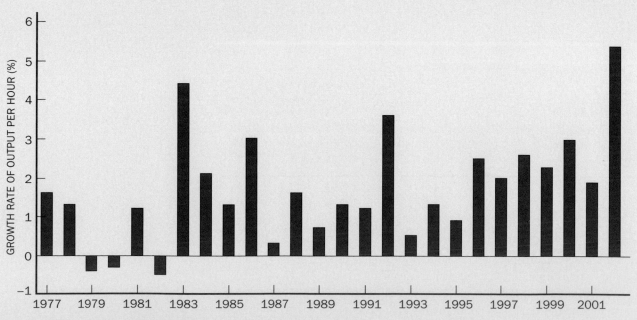

SOURCE: *Economic Report of the President* (2004).

assuming that the firm's output is proportional to the number of clients it has.)

When the economy comes out of the recession, the firm can hire new technical staff as it adds new clients. It doesn't need to add a new accountant or sales manager or scheduler. As a result, its output will increase more (in percentage terms) than its employment, and its labor productivity rises.

Labor productivity falls as the economy goes into a recession; it rises when the economy comes out of a recession. The bar graph, which shows jumps in labor productivity in 1983 and 1992 following the ends of recessions, illustrates this pattern very clearly. Such cyclical fluctuations in productivity can easily mask changes in structural productivity for a time—as happened in the United States in the 1990s. When productivity first increased, the economy was recovering from the 1990–1991 recession. In 1992, productivity grew by 3.7 percent, well above estimates for structural productivity growth. This rise was the normal cyclical effect of an economy coming out of recession.

Usually, once a recovery is well under way, productivity growth tends to settle in at the economy's structural rate. And that is what seemed to be occurring after the initial spurt in productivity growth in 1992; as the chart shows, productivity growth slowed significantly in 1993. But the increase in productivity growth that began in 1996 did not fit the expected pattern. By 1999, it was clear that the sustained rise in productivity growth represented a change in structural productivity growth rather than a temporary rise caused by cyclical factors. While debate still rages over the precise source of this increase, most economists attribute it to new information technologies.

At the beginning of 2001, the U.S. economy again entered a recession. Though productivity growth slowed, it remained much higher than in previous recessions. The recession ended in late 2001, and 2002 saw the expected postrecession jump in labor productivity. Because of the higher structural productivity growth rate *and* the cyclical contribution to productivity growth, labor productivity in 2002 grew at its fastest rate in at least fifty years.

in the short run, firms adjust production and employment in response to changes in demand. They initially adjust production, not prices. This is the second key concept in understanding fluctuations.

When demand at retail stores rises in December because it is the holiday season, stores could respond by raising prices and keeping sales relatively constant. Instead, they generally keep prices constant and satisfy the greater demand with increased sales. In some markets, prices do respond quickly to shifts in demand; competitive markets such as those for agricultural products or for commodities like oil are usually characterized by rapid price adjustments. In many markets, both price and production adjust. If an automobile company sees demand fall, it may offer rebates or other price reductions to spur demand, but it will also scale back production, perhaps closing an assembly line and laying off workers. Most markets, particularly those characterized by imperfect competition, undergo adjustments in production as demand shifts.

Fundamentals of Fluctuations 2

STICKY PRICES

In the short run, shifts in demand lead firms to adjust production and employment. This occurs because the prices of many goods and services tend to adjust slowly.

INFLATION ADJUSTMENT

The first two fundamental ideas for understanding economic fluctuations—that wages and prices do not adjust rapidly—set the stage for the model that is developed over the next two chapters. They imply that changes in demand will cause fluctuations in employment and production. But in macroeconomics, we are also interested in the factors that determine inflation, and our other two fundamental ideas will serve to link fluctuations in unemployment and inflation.

The adjustment of inflation turns out to be one of the keys to understanding how economies return eventually to full employment. While many prices are slow to adjust, they do not remain constant; the rate of inflation is the rate at which the aggregate price level is changing.

To understand the behavior of inflation, it is important to avoid two common confusions. The first potential problem involves a failure to distinguish between the *price level* and the *rate of inflation*. The price level is an index number that measures overall prices relative to a base year (the construction of price indexes is discussed in Chapter 5). In 2004, the consumer price index (CPI) was equal to 188.9. The base year for the CPI is an average of 1982–1984 prices. Because the CPI is by definition equal to 100 in the base period, the index shows that by 2004 the prices of the goods and services in its basket had risen 88.9 percent since that period. The *price level* in 2004 is higher than it was in 1982–1984.

The inflation rate tells us how fast the price level is rising. In 2004, the CPI inflation rate was 2.7 percent. In other words, the price level in 2004 was 2.7 percent higher than it had been in 2003. The higher the inflation rate, the faster the rise in the price level. A negative inflation rate (deflation) would indicate that prices were falling.

A higher price level does not mean that inflation is higher. For example, the price level was much higher in 2004 than it was in 1982, but the inflation rate was lower. Inflation in 1982 was 6.2 percent; in 2004, it was only 2.7 percent, and thus prices were rising more slowly.

The second potential confusion arises if *sticky* is not distinguished from *constant*. In calling wages and prices "sticky," economists mean that they fail to adjust rapidly in the face of shifts in supply and demand, not that they are constant—that is, that they never change. Both wages and prices do adjust over time. The rate at which the general level of prices changes, the inflation rate, will be one of the key macroeconomic variables in our model of short-run fluctuations.

What Causes Inflation to Adjust? The law of supply and demand tells us that whenever supply and demand are out of balance in a market, pressures will be brought to bear on the price in that market to adjust. The same applies for the aggregate economy. The balance between labor demand and supply, as reflected in cyclical unemployment, is an important factor influencing how wages change. As unemployment falls—that is, as labor markets become *tight*—firms must boost the wages they pay to attract new workers and retain their existing workforce. In unionized sectors, a tight labor market increases the bargaining power of unions, enabling them to negotiate larger wage increases. Wages therefore rise more rapidly in tight labor markets. Conversely, wages will rise more slowly when cyclical unemployment rises. For most firms, labor costs are their primary costs of production. If wage hikes outpace increases in workers' productivity, firms' labor costs rise. As labor costs go up, firms will raise their prices; when labor costs fall—as occurs, for instance, if labor productivity increases faster than wages rise—firms will cut their prices. This means that for a given rate of increase in labor productivity, prices will rise more rapidly—that is, inflation will be higher—when wages rise more rapidly; when wages rise slowly, so will prices, and inflation will be lower. Thus, cyclical unemployment affects wages, which in turn affect inflation.

This connection between cyclical unemployment and inflation points to a trade-off in the economy. When the economy experiences a business cycle expansion and enjoys lower unemployment, inflation is likely to start to rise. To lower inflation typically requires a period of high cyclical unemployment. Thus, if inflation is too high, the cost of lowering it will be temporarily high unemployment. Of course, cyclical unemployment isn't the only factor affecting inflation, but it is among the most important. The short-run trade-off between cyclical unemployment and inflation can present policymakers with hard choices.

Fundamentals of Fluctuations 3

SHORT-RUN INFLATION–UNEMPLOYMENT TRADE-OFF

In the short run, policymakers face a trade-off between unemployment and inflation. This trade-off occurs because attempts to reduce unemployment cause nominal wages to increase faster than labor productivity, raising firms' labor costs. Higher costs, in turn, lead to more rapidly rising prices (i.e., inflation increases). Attempts to reduce inflation require periods of high cyclical unemployment to reduce the rate of wage increases.

INFLATION, MONETARY POLICY, AND SPENDING

We have just set out three of the key concepts we will use as we explore how the economy behaves in the short run. These will help us begin to understand economic fluctuations, but they also open up new questions. For example, if firms respond to shifts in demand by adjusting production and employment, what explains the level of demand and its shifts? And is spending, like cyclical unemployment, also related to that other important macro variable, inflation?

The answer to this last question is yes. As inflation starts to rise, governments are likely to undertake policies designed to bring it back down. Maintaining stable, low rates of inflation is a primary goal of most countries, and central banks—the

Federal Reserve in the United States, for example, or the European Central Bank for the members of the Economic and Monetary Union—are the government institutions responsible for achieving this goal through their use of monetary policy. To keep inflation under control, central banks in developed and many developing economies seek to reduce aggregate spending when inflation rises and to boost spending when inflation falls. They follow such policies as a consequence of our third fundamental idea, that reducing inflation in the short run requires a rise in cyclical unemployment. Thus, when inflation rises, central banks act to reduce aggregate spending in accord with our second key concept, that firms react to a fall in demand by reducing production. When production falls, cyclical unemployment rises, and consequently the initial rise in inflation is moderated. Since central banks wish to keep inflation stable, they will also act to counter a decline in inflation by increasing aggregate spending and production. As the boost to production reduces cyclical unemployment, inflation begins to rise.

This relationship between inflation and aggregate spending depends critically on how monetary policy is conducted. The behavior of the economy, as it experiences disturbances, will depend on what policies the government institutes in response, just as it does on how firms and households respond to changing economic conditions. If we want to understand how the economy operates—how it adjusts, say, when world oil prices jump or there is a financial crisis in Asia—we will need to take into account the government's actions.

To understand short-run fluctuations in the economy, we particularly need to grasp the role of the Federal Reserve and its decisions regarding monetary policy. In Chapter 7, the basic tools of the Fed were explained. We also learned, however (see Chapter 6), that the real interest rate—that is, the nominal interest rate adjusted for inflation—has the most influence on households' saving decisions and firms' investment decisions. *In the long run,* at full employment, the real interest rate balances national saving and investment. *In the short run,* when the economy can fluctuate around full employment, the Fed is able to affect the real interest rate by influencing the nominal interest rate.

Like many other central banks, the Fed reacts to changes in inflation. If inflation increases, the Fed uses its policy tools to reduce aggregate spending. If inflation declines, the Fed uses its policy tools to increase aggregate spending. These responses help keep inflation low and stable. The Fed's concern with inflation has been most apparent during the past twenty-five years; during earlier periods, particularly the 1960s and 1970s, it was criticized for not taking strong enough action when inflation rose. In Chapter 13, we will see how an economy's short-run fluctuations in inflation and output depend on how central banks behave.

The type of monetary policy reaction to changes in inflation that we will incorporate into our model of economic fluctuations occurs most explicitly in countries whose central banks follow a policy of trying to keep inflation equal to a target value—so-called inflation-targeting policy regimes. But in fact a wide range of monetary policy behavior, and not just inflation targeting, is consistent with a link between inflation and spending. This link between inflation, monetary policy, and aggregate spending is our fourth key concept. It will be the focus of Chapter 13.

INFLATION, MONETARY POLICY, AND SPENDING

In the short run, central banks act to reduce aggregate spending when inflation increases and to increase aggregate spending when inflation falls. This relationship depends critically on the way in which the central bank reacts to inflation and how much importance it places on controlling inflation. Because this relationship depends on monetary policy, it can differ in different countries and at different times.

Case in Point

INFLATION TARGETING

During the 1990s, many central banks adopted policies that economists call *inflation targeting*. Under inflation targeting, the central bank strives to achieve a low and stable rate of inflation. In some countries, such as the United Kingdom, New Zealand, Canada, and Sweden, the government or the central bank formally announces a target for the inflation rate. In the United Kingdom, for example, the Bank of England's inflation target is 2 percent. We will learn more about inflation targeting in later chapters, but it is useful to discuss inflation-targeting policies here because they illustrate our four key concepts.

The basics of an inflation-targeting policy are simple. The central bank wants to keep the inflation rate equal to a targeted value. If inflation rises above the target, the central bank implements policies to reduce aggregate spending (key concept 4). Because wages and prices are sticky, this spending reduction causes firms to cut back production, leading to a rise in unemployment (key concepts 1 and 2). Higher cyclical unemployment moderates inflation (key concept 3) and helps bring the inflation rate back to the target. The process works in reverse when inflation falls below the central bank's target.

Wrap-Up

FUNDAMENTALS OF SHORT-RUN FLUCTUATIONS IN OUTPUT, EMPLOYMENT, AND INFLATION

1. *Sticky wages:* Wages do not adjust rapidly to shifts in labor supply and labor demand. As a result, the labor market may not always be in equilibrium.

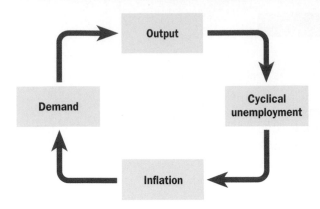

Figure 11.6

AGGREGATE DEMAND AND INFLATION

The four fundamental keys to understanding short-run fluctuations serve to link together demand, output, cyclical unemployment, and inflation. The next three chapters examine these links.

2. *Sticky prices:* When the labor market does not clear, shifts in the demand for goods and services in the product market lead firms to adjust production rather than simply change prices (see Chapter 12).

3. *Short-run inflation–unemployment trade-off:* A fall in cyclical unemployment leads to an increase in inflation—increases in cyclical unemployment reduce inflation. This relationship implies that policymakers face a trade-off in the short run between lower unemployment and higher inflation (see Chapters 13 and 15).

4. *Inflation, monetary policy, and spending:* As inflation rises, monetary policy works to reduce aggregate spending. When inflation falls, monetary policy acts to boost aggregate spending. This relationship between monetary policy, inflation, and aggregate spending can vary over time as the central bank's policy goals change (see Chapters 13 and 14).

LINKING THE FOUR KEY CONCEPTS

The four key concepts work together to explain how output and inflation are determined when the economy is not at full employment. Figure 11.6 shows how. We can start at any one of the boxes and use the key concepts to travel around the circle. For example, let's suppose something causes demand to drop. It might be a financial crisis in Asia or Latin America that reduces sales of U.S. goods in those countries. The drop in demand causes U.S. firms to scale back production—output falls. With production now at lower levels, firms do not need as many workers, so layoffs occur and cyclical unemployment rises. Wages fail to adjust quickly enough to keep the economy at full employment. High cyclical unemployment leads to slower wage growth, and inflation declines. In the face of a decline in inflation, the Fed acts to boost some types of spending, helping to offset some of the initial drop in demand that started the process.

Over the next few chapters, we will examine each of these links in detail, learning about how they operate and how they help us understand the causes of economic fluctuations.

Review and Practice

SUMMARY

1. Economies experience recessions and booms in which output fluctuates around its full-employment level. Recessions are periods in which real GDP declines; in booms, real GDP increases. The fluctuations in output are called business cycles.
2. If wages and prices do not adjust quickly enough to ensure that markets are always in equilibrium, so that demand and supply are balanced, the economy may experience fluctuations in cyclical unemployment.
3. To explain cyclical unemployment, we need to explain why the aggregate labor market does not clear. If real wages do not adjust when the demand curve for labor shifts to the left, then the quantity of labor supplied will exceed the quantity demanded at the prevailing wage and there will be cyclical unemployment.
4. Wages may be slow to adjust because of union contracts and implicit contracts that lead to infrequent wage changes. Firms minimize total labor costs by paying the efficiency wage. Cutting wages may raise costs by lowering productivity, as the best workers are most likely to leave, or by leading to higher labor turnover costs.
5. In the short run, firms adjust production in response to fluctuations in demand. Thus, aggregate demand plays a critical role in determining the short-run equilibrium level of output.
6. Our model of fluctuations will be built around four key components: (1) wages are sticky, (2) prices are sticky, (3) there is a trade-off between inflation and cyclical unemployment in the short run, and (4) inflation and aggregate spending are linked by monetary policy.

long run
short run

REVIEW QUESTIONS

1. If the labor market always clears, is there any unemployment? Any cyclical unemployment? What does it mean for the labor market "not to clear"? What gives rise to cyclical unemployment?
2. If the labor market always clears, what factors can cause fluctuations in the level of employment?
3. What inferences can you draw from the following two facts, assuming that both hold simultaneously?
   (a) The labor supply curve is relatively inelastic.
   (b) Large variations in employment coexist with relatively small variations in real wages.
4. What might shift the aggregate demand curve for labor?
5. What are the four key concepts that help explain economic fluctuations?
6. If cyclical unemployment increases, what would you expect to happen to inflation? If cyclical unemployment falls, what would be the effect on inflation?
7. If inflation falls, why will aggregate expenditures rise? If inflation rises, why will aggregate expenditures fall?
8. What are some explanations for sticky wages?
9. Give three reasons why productivity may depend on the level of wages paid.
10. How does an efficiency wage differ from a wage that clears the labor market?

KEY TERMS

recessions
output gap
expansions
peaks
troughs
business cycles
implicit labor contract
efficiency wage
labor turnover rate

PROBLEMS

1. In the 1970s, a large number of new workers entered the U.S. economy from two main sources. The baby boom generation grew to adulthood and the proportion of women working outside the home increased substantially. If wages adjust, what effect will these factors have on the equilibrium level of wages and quantity of labor? If wages do not adjust, how does your answer change? In which case will unemployment exist? Draw a diagram to explain your answer. What is the effect of the increased

labor supply on the product market? Illustrate your answer diagrammatically.

2. Soon after Iraq invaded Kuwait in August 1990, many firms feared that a recession would occur. Anticipating a lack of demand for their goods, they began cutting back on production. If wages adjust, what will happen to the equilibrium level of wages and employment? If wages do not adjust, how does your answer change? In which case will unemployment exist?

3. For the most part, macroeconomics focuses on aggregate employment, ignoring distinctions among different categories of workers, but it sometimes considers broad categories, such as skilled and unskilled workers. Assume, for the sake of simplicity, that there are just these two categories, and that in general they cannot be substituted for each other.

   (a) Draw demand and supply curves for skilled and unskilled workers, marking the initial equilibrium in each market.

   (b) Assume now there is a technological change that increases the demand for skilled labor at each wage, while it shifts the demand curve for unskilled labor to the left. If wages do not adjust, can there be job vacancies of one type of labor at the same time there is unemployment of another type?

4. Would you be more likely or less likely to observe implicit contracts in industries in which most workers hold their jobs for only a short time? What about industries in which most workers hold jobs a long time? Explain.

5. Go to the National Bureau of Economic Research's Web site (www.nber.org/cycles.html) and find the Business Cycle Reference Data for all peaks and troughs since 1854. What has been the average length of recessions since 1854? Since 1945? What has been the average length of expansions since 1854? Since 1945?

6. In the Case in Point on page 250, the cost of cyclical unemployment was estimated for 2002 by assuming that the unemployment rate associated with full employment was 5 percent. Suppose changes in the age structure of the workforce meant that full employment in 2002 was actually associated with an unemployment rate of 4.5 percent rather than the 5 percent figure used earlier. Recalculate the output costs of the recession. Explain why they are higher.

Learning Goals

In this chapter, you will learn

1 How equilibrium GDP is determined in the short run

2 What happens to GDP when the level of aggregate expenditures changes

3 The components of aggregate expenditures

4 How the real interest rate affects aggregate expenditures

Chapter 12

AGGREGATE EXPENDITURES AND INCOME

In Chapter 11, we learned that recessions and booms can result from shifts in the demand for the goods and services that the economy produces. When demand falls, firms scale back production and need fewer workers—current employees are laid off and few new ones are hired. Wages and prices fail to adjust quickly enough to ensure that the economy remains at full employment, and the unemployment rate rises. When demand increases, firms expand production and the economy expands—employment increases and the unemployment rate falls.

The task of this chapter is explaining the relationship between equilibrium output and **aggregate expenditures,** the name economists give to the overall demand for what the economy produces. Aggregate expenditures are the total spending by households, firms, government, and the foreign sector on the goods and services produced. There is a feedback relationship between spending and income—changes in spending affect the equilibrium level of production and income, and changes in income influence spending. Understanding the connection between aggregate expenditures and income is important. Shifts in aggregate expenditures, increased pessimism among households that results in a drop in consumption spending, and the introduction of new technologies that lead to increased investment spending by firms are important causes of economic fluctuations. We will also discuss the major factors that affect the three components of private expenditures: consumption, investment, and net exports.

Income–Expenditure Analysis

Aggregate expenditure has four components: consumption, investment, government purchases, and net exports.[1] We can think of aggregate expenditures as the

---

[1]Since our objective is to explain *real* GDP and employment, our focus continues to be on *real* consumption, *real* investment, *real* government purchases, and *real* net exports.

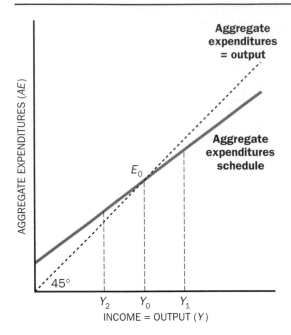

Figure 12.1

THE AGGREGATE EXPENDITURES SCHEDULE AND INCOME–EXPENDITURE ANALYSIS

The aggregate expenditures schedule gives the sum of consumption, investment, government purchases, and net exports at each level of national income. Aggregate expenditures increase with income. Equilibrium occurs at the intersection of the aggregate expenditures schedule and the 45-degree line, where aggregate expenditures equal income (at point E_0). At outputs greater than Y_0, such as Y_1, aggregate expenditures are less than output (remember, income equals output). Some goods that are being produced are not being sold; there are unintended accumulations of inventory. The reverse is true for outputs less than Y_0, such as Y_2.

total expenditures in the four parts of the economy: households spending on consumption, firms on investment goods, the government on public goods, and foreigner buyers on net exports. We have already seen in Chapter 4 that total income (output) is equal to the sum of consumption, investment, government purchases, and net exports. Income depends on spending, but spending also depends on income. When their income rises, for example, households will increase their consumption spending. This spending then becomes income for the producers of the goods and services purchased. Understanding the implications of this feedback loop is critical to understanding why the economy experiences fluctuations in production and employment.

The key to solving for the equilibrium level of output and the equilibrium level of aggregate demand is the **aggregate expenditures schedule.** The aggregate expenditures schedule traces out the relationship between aggregate expenditures and national income—the aggregate income of everyone in the economy. It is depicted in Figure 12.1, where the vertical axis measures aggregate expenditures and the horizontal axis measures national income.

The aggregate expenditures schedule has three critical properties. First, it is upward sloping—as national income goes up, so do aggregate expenditures. Changes in other variables (such as interest rates, tax rates, and exchange rates) cause the aggregate expenditures schedule to shift up or down, and they may even alter its slope. Later in this chapter, we will examine why expenditures increase with income and how the aggregate expenditures schedule is shifted by changes in other variables.

Second, as income increases by $1 billion, aggregate expenditures increase by less than $1 billion—consumers save some of their additional income. If a household's income increases by $1,000, its consumption might rise by $900 and its saving by $100. The same logic applies to other components of aggregate expenditures; they will rise less than the increase in income. Figure 12.1 also shows a line through the origin at a 45-degree angle. The slope of this line is one. All along this line, a change in the horizontal axis (income) is matched by an equal change in the vertical axis (aggregate expenditures). By contrast, the aggregate expenditures schedule is flatter than the 45-degree line, since aggregate expenditures increase less than dollar-for-dollar with increased income.

Third, at very low levels of national income, aggregate expenditures will exceed income. Households, for example, will use up their savings to maintain consumption if aggregate income falls to dramatically lower levels.

The facts that (1) the aggregate expenditures schedule slopes up, (2) the aggregate expenditures schedule is flatter than the 45-degree line through the origin, and (3) aggregate expenditures are greater than income at very low income levels imply that the aggregate expenditures schedule intersects the 45-degree line, as seen in Figure 12.1.

This brings us to our central questions: What determines the (short-run) equilibrium level of aggregate expenditures? Where on the schedule in Figure 12.1 will the economy find itself? To answer these questions, we need to add two more concepts to our analysis.

THE NATIONAL INCOME–OUTPUT IDENTITY

National income is equal to national output (as explained in Chapter 4). Their equality reflects the fact that when a good or service is purchased, the money that is paid must eventually wind up as someone's income—as wages, in the pockets of the workers in the firm that produced the good (or of the workers who produced the intermediate goods that were used in the production of the final good); as interest payments, in the pockets of those who lent the firm money; or as profits, in the pockets of the owners of the firm.[2] If Y is used to represent national income, this identity can be written as

$$\text{GDP} = \text{national income} = Y.$$

The equation allows us to interpret the horizontal axis in Figure 12.1 in two different ways. We can say that the aggregate expenditures schedule gives the level of expenditures at each level of national income. We also can say that it gives the level of expenditures at each level of national output.

EQUILIBRIUM OUTPUT

Normally, firms will produce only what they believe they can sell. As a result, the total output produced by all firms will equal the total demand for output. In equilibrium, aggregate expenditures, which we will denote by AE, must equal aggregate output (GDP). Since aggregate output also equals national income (Y), we have the simple equation

$$AE = \text{GDP} = Y.$$

In Figure 12.1, the 45-degree line through the origin is labeled "Aggregate expenditures = output." All points on the 45-degree line have the property that aggregate expenditures, measured on the vertical axis, equal aggregate output, measured on the horizontal axis. Only points on this 45-degree line satisfy the equilibrium requirement that aggregate expenditures equal output.

Equilibrium lies at the point on the aggregate expenditures schedule that also satisfies the "Aggregate expenditures = output" condition. That point is at E_0 in the figure, where the aggregate expenditures schedule intersects the 45-degree line. The corresponding equilibrium value of aggregate output, for given inflation and interest rates, is denoted Y_0.

The analysis that determines equilibrium output by relating income (output) to aggregate expenditures is called **income–expenditure analysis.** We can take two approaches to demonstrating that Y_0 is the equilibrium. The first way is to note that it is the only point that satisfies the two conditions for equilibrium. In equilibrium, everything produced must be purchased. Thus, aggregate expenditures must be equal to output, as represented by the 45-degree line. In equilibrium, the level of

---

[2]For the sake of simplicity, we will assume that the residents of the country neither receive money (net) from abroad nor make payments (net) abroad.

aggregate expenditures also must be what households, firms, government, and the foreign sector want to spend in total at that level of national income (output), as represented by the aggregate expenditures schedule. Only point E_0 is consistent with both conditions.

The second way is to consider what happens at a level of income, Y_1, in excess of Y_0. At that point, the aggregate expenditures schedule lies below the 45-degree line. What households, firms, government, and the foreign sector would like to spend at that level of national income, as reflected in the aggregate expenditures schedule, is less than national income (output). More goods are being produced than individuals want to buy. Some of the goods, like strawberries, cannot be stored. They simply spoil. The goods that can be stored go into inventories. Since firms find they cannot sell all the goods they produced, the income level Y_1 is not the equilibrium level of output. Firms will respond by cutting back production until national income falls to Y_0. At Y_2, in contrast, the aggregate expenditures schedule lies above the 45-degree line. Households, firms, government, and the foreign sector are spending more than national income. They are purchasing more than what is being produced. This is possible (temporarily) because firms can sell out of inventories. When firms find they are selling more than they are currently producing, they respond by increasing production. Aggregate output rises until equilibrium is restored at Y_0.

SHIFTS IN THE AGGREGATE EXPENDITURES SCHEDULE

The aggregate expenditures schedule can shift through a variety of changes in the economy that lead households, firms, the government, and the foreign sector to decide, at each level of income, to spend more or less. Panel A of Figure 12.2 shows what happens if the level of aggregate expenditures increases at each level of national income by the amount S. The new aggregate expenditures schedule is denoted AE_1. Equilibrium output increases from Y_0 to Y_1. The increase in equilibrium output *is greater than the amount S;* the size of the increase depends on the slope of the aggregate expenditures schedule.

To understand why, think about an economy that is initially in equilibrium at the output level Y_0 in panel A. At this level of income, the amount that households, firms, the government, and the foreign sector wish to purchase (given by the AE_0 schedule) is exactly equal to Y_0, the amount of output that firms are producing. Now, planned spending increases at each level of income, represented by the shift of the aggregate expenditures schedule to AE_1. If firms continued to produce at Y_0, demand would exceed output; inventories would decline and this would signal to firms that they should increase production.

As output rises, households find that their incomes have risen. This boost leads them to increase their spending. Consequently, aggregate expenditures end up increasing by more than the initial amount S that the aggregate expenditures schedule shifted up. If the aggregate expenditures schedule is steep, a rise in income increases spending significantly, and the final increase in equilibrium output will be large. If the schedule is flatter, rising income has a smaller impact on spending, and the final increase in equilibrium output will be smaller. In panel B of Figure 12.2, the aggregate expenditures schedule shifts up by the same amount as it did in panel A, but the aggregate expenditures schedule is flatter and, as a result, equilibrium output rises by less.

MATHEMATICAL FORMULATION

We can describe the equilibrium by using simple algebra. The aggregate expenditures equation can be written

$$AE = A + bY,$$

where A is the vertical intercept of the aggregate expenditures schedule (the value of AE when $Y = 0$), and b is the slope of the aggregate expenditures schedule (an increase in Y of \$1 increases AE by \$$b$). The fact that the slope is positive but less than 45 degrees implies that b is between 0 and 1. Equilibrium requires that aggregate expenditures equal income, which, under our simplifying assumptions, equals Y:

$$AE = Y.$$

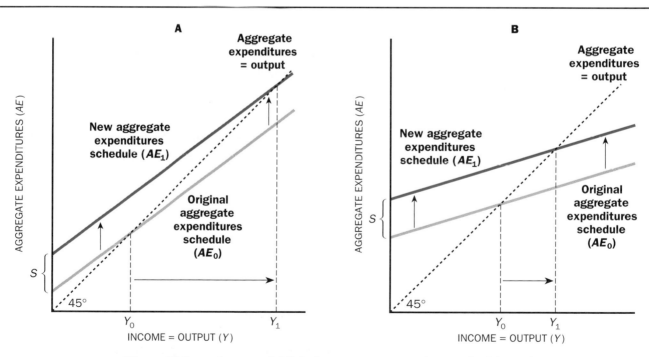

Figure 12.2

EFFECT OF A SHIFT IN THE AGGREGATE EXPENDITURES SCHEDULE

An upward shift in the aggregate expenditures schedule results in an increase in the equilibrium level of output. The magnitude of this increase in equilibrium output is greater than the magnitude of the upward shift; that is, $Y_1 - Y_0$ exceeds S, the magnitude of the shift.

The flatter the aggregate expenditures schedule, the smaller the magnitude of the increase in output resulting from a given upward shift in the schedule.

Substituting the second equation into the first equation yields

$$Y = A + bY,$$

which can be solved for Y:

$$Y = A/(1 - b).$$

This equation tells us that if A changes by \$1, Y will change by $1/(1 - b)$. For example, if $b = .9$, a \$1 increase in A increases Y by \$10. The factor $1/(1 - b)$ is called the **multiplier.** It tells us how much total aggregate expenditures and output increase when the aggregate expenditures schedule shifts by \$1.

Wrap-Up

INCOME–EXPENDITURE ANALYSIS

1. Equilibrium output is the point where the aggregate expenditures schedule equals output (income).
2. Increases in the aggregate expenditures schedule result in increases in equilibrium output. Decreases in the aggregate expenditures schedule result in decreases in equilibrium output.
3. The changes in equilibrium output are larger than the initial shift in the aggregate expenditures schedule. How much larger they are depends on the slope of the aggregate expenditures schedule. The steeper the slope, the greater the change.

As you will learn in the next few chapters, changes in aggregate expenditures will also influence interest rates, net exports, and inflation in ways that will act to reduce the ultimate effect of shifts in the aggregate expenditures schedule on equilibrium output. When we have incorporated these additional adjustments into our analysis, the change in equilibrium output per dollar change in the AE schedule is closer to 1.5 to 2 in the short run; it is close to 0 in the longer run as wages and prices have time to completely adjust.

A Look Forward

We have just learned two of the central principles of macroeconomics: (1) shifts in the aggregate expenditures schedule determine changes in the equilibrium output of the economy, and (2) the magnitude of these changes is greater than the magnitude of the shift up or down in the aggregate expenditures schedule. We also have learned that the magnitude of the change in output increases with the slope of the aggregate expenditures schedule. The remainder of this chapter explores two critical questions. First, why does the aggregate expenditures schedule have a positive slope and what determines that slope? And second, what factors lead to shifts in the aggregate expenditures schedule?

To address these questions, we will take a brief look at each of the four components of aggregate spending: (1) consumption: purchases by households of goods and services, such as food, television sets, and clothes; (2) investment: purchases of capital goods, machinery, and buildings by firms to help them produce goods and services; (3) government purchases, both of goods and services bought for current use (government consumption) and of goods and services such as buildings and roads bought for the future benefits they produce (public investment); and (4) net exports. We say *net exports,* because to determine the total purchases of goods and services produced domestically (and therefore included in GDP), we must subtract from the value of goods sold abroad (exports) the value of the goods and services purchased by U.S. households, businesses, and the government that were produced abroad (imports).

Consumption

Consumption is by far the largest component of aggregate expenditures. In the United States, consumer expenditures represent about two-thirds of total expenditures. Three factors are of primary importance in determining consumption. These are disposable income, expectations about future income, and wealth.

DISPOSABLE INCOME

Figure 12.3 shows real consumption and real GDP in the United States since 1960. The figure, in addition to illustrating that consumption is a large fraction of GDP, also reveals that the two tend to move together. That should not be surprising. Though GDP represents the economy's total output, national output is also equal to national income—and income is the most important determinant of consumption. On average, families with higher incomes spend more.

The measure of income most pertinent to household consumption is **disposable income,** the income of households after taxes are paid. Figure 12.4 plots aggregate real consumption against aggregate real disposable income for the United States from 1960 to 2002; the close relationship is quite obvious. As disposable income goes up, consumption rises; as disposable income falls, consumption falls.

The Marginal Propensity to Consume The amount by which consumption changes as income changes is called the **marginal propensity to consume,** or **MPC.** For example, if a household's disposable income rises by $2,000 per year and its consumption spending rises by $1,600 per year, the marginal propensity to consume is found by taking the change in consumption and dividing it by the change in income, or 1,600/2,000 = .8. Another household might increase its spending by $1,900 if its income rose by $2,000; the MPC of this second household would be .95. Since

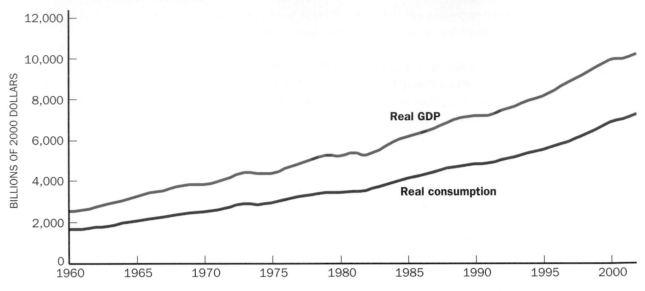

Figure 12.3

CONSUMPTION AND GDP

Real consumption spending is the largest component of aggregate expenditures. It moves closely with total real income in the economy.

SOURCE: *Economic Report of the President* (2004).

our concern is with the aggregate behavior of the economy, we are most interested in the change in aggregate consumption as aggregate income changes. The *aggregate MPC* can be thought of as an average, over the millions of households in the economy, of all the individual marginal propensities to consume. The aggregate MPC is equal to the slope of the aggregate consumption function.

The aggregate MPC conveys important information. Since consumption is a large fraction of total aggregate expenditures, the upward slope of the aggregate expenditures schedule shown in Figure 12.1 is closely related to the MPC. As aggregate income rises, disposable income rises, and households increase their consumption spending. If the MPC is high, indicating that changes in disposable income cause large changes in consumption, then the aggregate expenditures schedule will be steep. If households save a large fraction of any increase in income, then the MPC will be small and the aggregate expenditures schedule will be flatter.

The Marginal Propensity to Save Individuals must either spend or save each dollar of disposable income. The definition "disposable income = consumption plus saving" tells us that if consumption rises by 90 cents when disposable income rises by a dollar, saving must rise by 10 cents. The higher level of saving stemming from an extra dollar of income is called the **marginal propensity to save (MPS).** Since the extra dollar is either spent or saved, the marginal propensity to consume and the marginal propensity to save must always sum to one:

marginal propensity to consume + marginal propensity to save = 1.

This relationship holds both for the individual households in the economy and for the aggregate economy. Thus if the MPS is large, the MPC must be small.

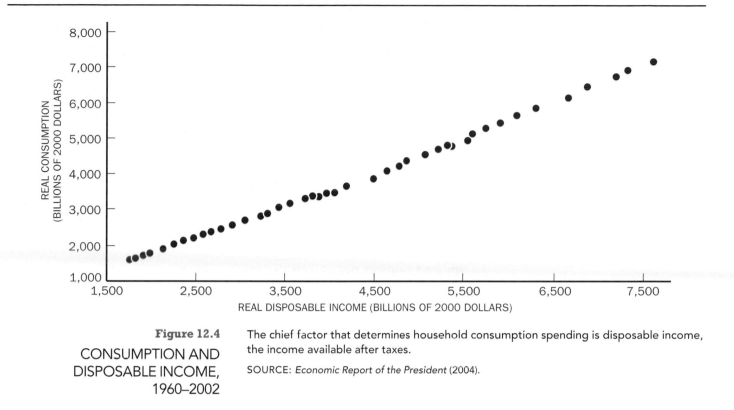

Figure 12.4

CONSUMPTION AND
DISPOSABLE INCOME,
1960–2002

The chief factor that determines household consumption spending is disposable income, the income available after taxes.

SOURCE: *Economic Report of the President* (2004).

In that case, the aggregate expenditures schedule will be flatter than if the MPS is small.

Taxes and the Aggregate Expenditures Schedule Consumption spending by households depends on their disposable income. For a given level of total income, an increase in taxes reduces disposable income and leads to a fall in consumption. Tax increases therefore shift the aggregate expenditures schedule down. Tax decreases shift it up.

Taxes have a second effect on the aggregate expenditures schedule. The government's tax revenues typically go up when income rises and fall when income declines. Personal income taxes, for instance, are related to income. Individuals with higher incomes generally pay more in taxes. As total national income rises, tax revenues rise. This statement implies that disposable income will increase by less than the increase in total income. The same process works in reverse if income falls. As total income declines, so do taxes. Since people pay less in taxes, disposable income declines less than total income. For example, if the average tax rate on the last dollar of income earned (the marginal tax rate) is 30 percent, then a $1 fall in income reduces taxes by $0.30; disposable income falls by only $0.70.

What does this imply for the slope of the aggregate expenditures schedule? Because changes in total income lead to smaller changes in disposable income when taxes vary with income, the changes in consumption spending also will be smaller. Assume the marginal propensity to consume out of disposable income is .9 and the marginal tax rate is 30 percent. Of a $1 increase in total income, $0.30 must be paid in taxes, so disposable income rises by only $0.70. With a marginal propensity to consume of .9, consumption rises by .9 times the $0.70 increase in disposable income, or by $0.63. A rise in total income leads to a smaller rise in spending. The aggregate expenditures schedule is therefore flatter if marginal tax rates are high. As we have already learned, a flatter schedule means the multiplier will be smaller.

Taxes that increase with income are an example of an **automatic stabilizer.** Automatic stabilizers are factors that, like taxes, act to reduce the fall in aggregate expenditures as income declines or reduce the rise in aggregate expenditures as income rises. By reducing the multiplier, automatic stabilizers make the economy more stable. A shift down in the aggregate expenditures schedule results in a smaller drop in total output. A shift up results in a smaller rise in output. These effects occur automatically because tax revenues change automatically as income changes. Automatic stabilizers will be discussed more fully in Chapter 15.

The Marginal Propensity to Consume, Taxes, and the Multiplier

As Figure 12.4 suggests, consumption is closely related to disposable income. Suppose the relationship between the two is

$$C = a + MPC \times Y_d,$$

where MPC is the marginal propensity to consume, a is an intercept term (equal to the value of consumption if disposable income were zero), and Y_d is disposable income. If the other components of aggregate expenditures (in a closed economy, investment and government purchases) are equal to a fixed amount denoted by E, then total aggregate expenditures will be

$$AE = C + I + G = a + MPC \times Y_d + E.$$

Disposable income is equal to total income minus taxes. While taxes are of various types (for example, income taxes, payroll taxes such as Social Security and Medicare taxes, sales taxes, and property taxes), many are related to income. Just as the taxes that an individual pays usually increase as her income rises, so total taxes paid by households increase as total incomes in the economy rise. For the sake of simplicity, we will assume that taxes are equal to a constant fraction, t, of income. In this case,

$$Y_d = (1 - t)Y.$$

Hence, in equilibrium, with aggregate expenditures equaling income,

$$Y = AE = a + MPC(1 - t)Y + E.$$

If we now solve this equation for Y, we obtain

$$Y = (a + E)/[1 - (1 - t)MPC].$$

As a numerical example, let $a = \$2$ trillion, $E = \$3$ trillion, $MPC = .8$, and $t = .25$. Substituting these into the expression for equilibrium output yields $Y = \$12.5$ trillion. If any of the components of E changes by \$1, equilibrium output changes by $1/(1 - (1 - t)MPC)$. For example, suppose E increases to \$4 trillion. Equilibrium output rises to \$15 trillion. The multiplier is equal to the change in output (\$15 trillion − \$12.5 trillion = \$2.5 trillion) per dollar change in E (\$1 trillion), or 2.5. This can also be found directly as $1/(1 - (1 - t)MPC) = 1/[1 - (1 - .25) \times .8] = 2.5$. By contrast, the multiplier without taxes would be $1/(1 - MPC) = 5$, or twice as large. The reason that the multiplier is larger without taxes is simple. Without taxes, every dollar of extra income translates into 80 cents of extra spending. With taxes, when income goes up by a dollar, disposable income rises by 75 cents and consumption increases by only $.8 \times .75$ cents = 60 cents.

EXPECTATIONS OF FUTURE INCOME

Current disposable income is a key determinant of consumption, but households' decisions about how much to consume are also influenced by their expectations about future income. If households expect that their income will fall in the future, they are likely to reduce their current consumption so that they can save more. By saving more today, they will be better able to preserve their standard of living when their income declines later. Thus, a projected or expected tax increase that will reduce future disposable income may reduce consumption spending even before it goes into effect. Conversely, if households expect that their future income will rise, they are likely to increase their consumption spending immediately. A projected or expected tax decrease can lead to a rise in consumption before households actually see their disposable income go up.

The dependence of current spending on expectations about future income has another very important implication. Households are likely to increase spending more when their current income rises if they expect the income increase to be permanent—that is, if they expect both their current and future income to be higher. Similarly, a tax cut viewed as temporary is likely to lead to a smaller increase in consumption than a tax cut that is viewed as permanent. Another way to express this implication is to say that the marginal propensity to consume out of permanent changes in income will be larger than the marginal propensity to consume out of temporary or transitory changes in income.

If consumption changes when expected future income changes, even when current income is still the same, then shifts in expectations will cause the aggregate expenditure schedule to shift. When households become more optimistic about their future income, aggregate consumption will increase at each level of current disposable income. The result is an increase in aggregate expenditures at each level of national income, shifting the aggregate expenditure schedule upward.

WEALTH

A third factor that is important for determining consumption is household wealth. Wealthier households will consume more (at each level of current income). Just as changes in individuals' wealth will affect their consumption choices, so changes in aggregate wealth will affect aggregate consumption.

For example, the stock market boom of the late 1990s caused many people to feel wealthier. As a result, they increased their consumption spending at each level of current income. These increases had the effect of shifting the aggregate expenditures schedule upward. When the stock market crashed in 2000, the same individuals experienced a drop in their wealth and reduced consumption spending; the aggregate expenditures schedule therefore shifted downward.

CONSUMPTION AND THE AGGREGATE EXPENDITURES SCHEDULE

Three key determinants of consumption are
1. Disposable income: the marginal propensity to consume and the tax rate, by affecting how much consumption changes when total income changes, affect the slope of the aggregate expenditures schedule and the multiplier.
2. Expectations about future disposable income: changes in expectations about future income shift the aggregate expenditures schedule.
3. Wealth: changes in household wealth shift the aggregate expenditures schedule.

Investment

Variation in investment spending is probably the principal cause of shifts in the aggregate expenditures schedule. The volatility of investment is shown in Figure 12.5. Since 1960, investment has averaged about 13 percent of GDP, but it has ranged from a low of 10 percent to a high of 17 percent.

Investment spending comprises three broad categories. The first is firms' purchases of new capital goods (everything from new factories and buildings to machinery to the cash registers, computers, and desks used by firms). These make up the **plant and equipment** component of total investment. Firms also invest in **inventories,** storing their output in anticipation of sales or storing the raw materials they will need to produce more goods. The third investment category consists of households' purchases of new homes, or **residential investment.**

The purchases of previously owned capital goods or houses do not count in investment spending because they are not purchases of current production. Recall from Chapter 4 that GDP is defined as total final goods and services *produced* in the current year. We exclude from investment any purchases of capital goods or houses that were built in earlier years. If one person buys a home built ten years ago, he might view it as an investment. But for the seller it is a "disinvestment," so the transaction represents no new investment in the economy but simply a change in who owns an existing asset.

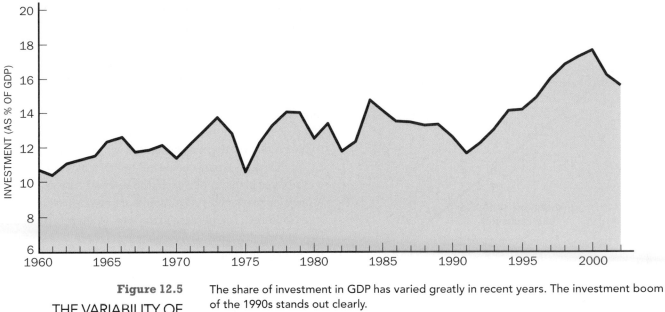

Figure 12.5

THE VARIABILITY OF
INVESTMENT

The share of investment in GDP has varied greatly in recent years. The investment boom of the 1990s stands out clearly.

SOURCES: *Economic Report of the President* (2004), Table B-2.

INVESTMENT AND THE REAL INTEREST RATE

To undertake investment in new plants or equipment, firms must believe that the expected future returns will be large enough to compensate them for the risks of the investment. Moreover, firms are aware that a dollar in the future is worth less than a dollar today; if they had the dollar today, they could put it in a bank and get back the dollar *with interest* a year later. *As the interest rate rises, future dollars are worth less relative to today's dollars.* As a result, there will be fewer investment projects with future returns large enough to offset the forgone interest. To put the relationship between investment and interest another way, think of a firm as having to borrow money for the investment project. As higher interest rates increase the cost of undertaking the project, fewer projects will have an expected return high enough to yield a profit after those higher interest costs are paid. Thus, higher interest rates lead to lower levels of investment.

The relationship between interest rates and investment is the investment function introduced in Chapter 6. It is depicted as the downward-sloping curve in Figure 12.6. Of course, what matters for investment spending is the *real interest rate,* or the cost of funds after taking into account the effect of inflation. If the *nominal* interest rate increases but expected inflation increases by the same amount, firms' investment will be unaffected. (The real interest rate is the nominal interest rate minus the expected rate of inflation.) When there is inflation, the dollars that the firm uses in the future to pay back the funds borrowed today for investment will be worth less than those borrowed dollars. If inflation is 5 percent, then each year, the value of goods and services that a dollar can purchase drops by 5 percent. If the interest rate is 8 percent, the real cost of the loan is only 3 percent (the 8 percent nominal interest rate minus the 5 percent rate of inflation).

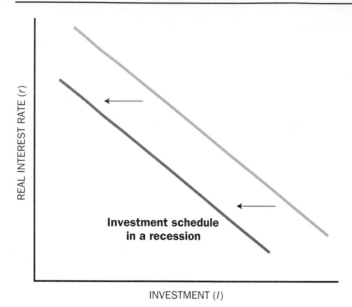

Figure 12.6

THE INVESTMENT SCHEDULE

At higher real interest rates, firms are willing to invest less. As the economy enters a recession, expectations of profits decrease, the ability to share risks decreases, and the availability of financing decreases. These changes lead to a shift in the investment schedule to the left.

While we have focused our discussion on investment spending by firms, the same principles are at work when individuals decide to make investment purchases—for example, buying a new car. If someone plans to take out a car loan, the interest rate on the loan is an important factor that will influence whether or not she buys a car and, if she does, what type of car she buys and how much she ends up spending on it. An increase in the interest rate on car loans will increase the cost of buying a car, and in response to the greater cost, some consumers will purchase less-expensive cars, while others may decide not to buy a new car at all. Even if a car buyer plans to pay cash, the interest rate is still relevant. Money earmarked for a car could instead be saved at the going rate of interest. An increase in the level of interest rates increases the opportunity cost (the forgone interest income) of spending the money on a car.

Investment Variability   Investment decisions must be based on expectations about future returns. Predicting the future is always difficult. There may be *technological risks*—the firm may introduce a new technology that could prove unreliable. In most cases, there are *market risks*. Will there be a market for a new product? At what price will it sell? What will labor costs be in the future? What about the prices of energy and other inputs? Firms must base investment decisions on educated guesses, recognizing that much often remains uncertain.

The risks associated with investment spending are the primary reason that investment is so volatile. Expectations about the future may oscillate sharply. When sales are up today, firms may expect future sales to be high and perhaps even to continue to increase. In response, they will want to add more plant and equipment for the future—that is, they will want to invest more. If sales dip, firms may decide to scale back or even cancel their plans for new capital goods, and thus investment will fall. Changes in current output therefore will shift the investment schedule. For instance, when the economy goes into a recession, the investment schedule typically shifts to the left, as depicted in Figure 12.6. Expectations of future profits decrease, risks appear larger, and the ability and willingness to bear risks are reduced.

INVENTORY INVESTMENT

One of the most volatile components of investment is inventories—the materials that are held in storage awaiting either use in production or sale to customers. Inventories are typically very large. Usually, about $1.50 worth of goods and services is held in inventory for every $1 of goods sold each month.

Inventory investment is equal to the *change* in the stock of goods in inventory. Firms hold inventories of intermediate goods used as inputs in production; doing so facilitates production by ensuring that parts are available when they are needed. Similarly, stores hold inventories so that customers can obtain the goods they want without waiting; otherwise, they may seek those goods elsewhere. Finally, because gearing up a production facility and then closing it down as sales fluctuate can be costly, firms find it profitable to produce at a relatively constant rate, adding to inventories when sales weaken and selling out of inventories when sales strengthen.

Inventory investment is the most volatile component of aggregate expenditures. One reason for this variability may again be the impact of the availability of credit on naturally risk-averse firms. When the economy enters a recession, firms often find that their net worth is decreased. This can make it harder for them to obtain credit to finance their inventory investment. They may also become less willing to make any kind of investment, in inventories or otherwise. Indeed, when possible, they would like to disinvest, or convert their assets back into cash. By far, the easiest method of disinvestment is to sell off inventories.

As the economy goes into a recession or simply slows down, inventories often build up involuntarily. Retail stores, for instance, base their orders on expected sales; if the sales fail to materialize, the store holds the unsold merchandise as "inventories." This unintended accumulation of inventory can rapidly affect production, as stores respond by reducing their factory orders. Lower orders, in turn, lead quickly to cutbacks in production. The cutbacks in production as firms try to restore their inventories to a normal size relative to sales are referred to as *inventory corrections.* Cyclical variability induced by inventories is called *inventory cycles.*

Wrap-Up

DETERMINANTS OF INVESTMENT

1. Investment spending will depend negatively on the real interest rate.
2. Shifts in the investment schedule can be caused by changing assessments of risk or changes in expectations about future returns.
3. Fluctuations in current economic conditions can affect current investment by altering firms' expectations about future sales.

MACROECONOMIC IMPLICATIONS OF INVESTMENT

Three important macroeconomic implications can be drawn from this discussion of investment spending. First, we have identified another reason for the positive slope of the aggregate expenditures schedule: as current output rises, firms will increase investment spending, while if current output falls, they will scale back their investment plans. Because both consumption and investment expenditures will rise as income increases, the slope of the *AE* schedule is positive.

Second, investment depends on the real interest rate: at each level of income, a rise in the real interest rate will lower investment. A higher real interest rate lowers total aggregate expenditures, shifting the *AE* schedule down. Conversely, a reduction in the real interest rate will shift the *AE* schedule up.

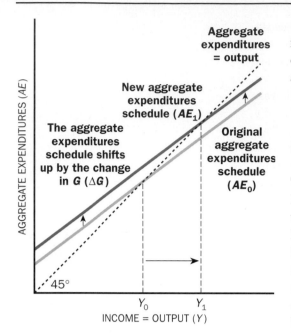

Figure 12.7

THE EFFECT OF AN INCREASE IN GOVERNMENT PURCHASES

Government purchases (*G*) are one of the components of aggregate expenditures. An increase in government purchases shifts the aggregate expenditures schedule up by the amount of the increase. Because of the multiplier effect, the increase in equilibrium output, $Y_1 - Y_0$, is greater than the increase in government purchases, ΔG.

Third, changing perceptions of risk or of future economic conditions affect investment expenditures. Their influence helps account for the volatility of investment, and they can be added to our list of factors that shift the aggregate expenditures schedule.

Government Purchases

The third component of aggregate expenditures is government purchases. In later chapters, when we discuss fiscal policy in the United States, we will usually focus on the expenditure and tax policies of the federal government. However, this category consists of the purchases of goods and services by *all* levels of government—federal, state, and local. In fact, of the total government purchases of roughly $2 trillion (about 18 percent of GDP), only about one-third—under $700 billion—are made by the federal government. Its total *expenditures* of about $3 trillion exceed those by state and local governments, but a large fraction of federal expenditures are for programs such as Social Security that do not directly purchase goods and services. The largest component of federal government purchases is defense, equal to roughly two-thirds of the total.

At this point in our analysis, it is useful to assume that total government purchases do not vary with income but instead are simply fixed—say, at $2 trillion. Earlier, we learned that taxes vary with income, so government revenue will rise and fall as income fluctuates. But because the government can borrow (run a deficit) when tax revenues are less than expenditures, and repay its debt when tax revenues exceed expenditures, government spending does not need to move in lockstep with tax revenues. In later chapters we will study in greater detail the role of fiscal policy, government expenditures, and tax policies. For now, though, we will assume that government purchases are fixed (in real terms).

Government purchases (*G*) are one component of aggregate expenditures. An increase in *G* will raise aggregate expenditures at each level of total income. This rise shifts the *AE* schedule up by the amount of the increase in *G,* as Figure 12.7 shows. Equilibrium again occurs at the intersection of the aggregate expenditures schedule and the 45-degree line. The total increase in equilibrium output depends on the size of the change in *G* and on the multiplier.

Net Exports

The analysis so far has ignored the important role of international trade. Such an omission is appropriate for a closed economy, an economy that neither imports nor exports, but not for an open economy, one actively engaged in international trade. Today, the United States and other industrialized economies are very much open economies.

The effect of exports and imports on aggregate expenditures is straightforward. Recall that what we are concerned with here is total purchases of *domestically* produced output. Consequently, exports of U.S.-produced goods to other countries represent another component of aggregate expenditures, just like consumption, investment, and government expenditures. However, some of what households, firms, and the government purchase are goods made abroad. To calculate the total demand for domestically produced goods, we must subtract the value of imports from the total. The net effect of international trade on aggregate expenditures is measured then by exports minus imports, or *net exports*. Exports minus imports are also sometimes referred to as the **balance of trade.**

Figure 12.8 shows net exports as a percentage of GDP for the United States. Since the mid-1970s, U.S. imports have exceeded U.S. exports, making net exports negative. Chapter 8, from the long-run perspective of the full-employment model, discussed how net exports were affected by the U.S. investment boom in the late 1990s and the large increases in the federal budget deficit in recent years. Our focus in the current chapter is on the short run, so just as we did when discussing the other components of aggregate expenditures, we need to ask whether net exports depend on income (and if so, how), and we need to ask what factors might shift net exports at each level of income.

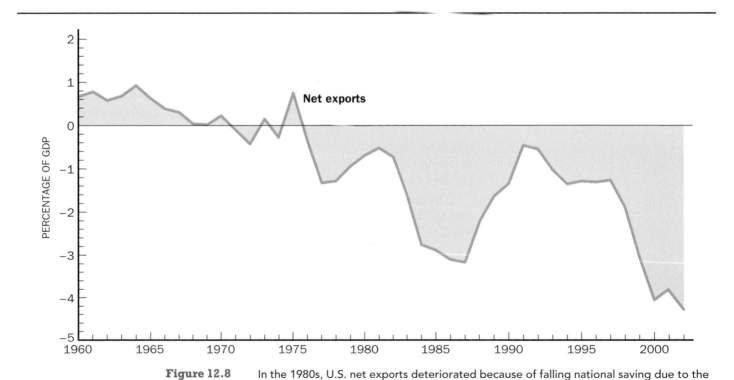

Figure 12.8

NET EXPORTS AS A
PERCENTAGE OF GDP

In the 1980s, U.S. net exports deteriorated because of falling national saving due to the federal budget deficit (see Chapters 7 and 8). During the past several years, strong growth in U.S. incomes, recessions in many countries we trade with, and a burgeoning federal budget deficit have caused net exports to fall dramatically.

SOURCE: *Economic Report of the President* (2004).

EXPORTS

What foreign consumers buy from the United States depends on their income, not income in the United States. Exports may also depend on other factors, such as the marketing efforts of American firms and the prices of American goods relative to foreign goods. To simplify, we will assume that income in other countries does not depend on what happens in the United States. Exports, like government purchases, will not vary with U.S. income.

Exports do depend on the relative cost of goods produced in different countries. If the price of a Toyota 4Runner built in Japan rises relative to the cost of an American-manufactured Ford Explorer, consumers in other countries will buy more Ford Explorers and fewer Toyota 4Runners, so U.S. exports will rise.

The relative price of goods produced abroad and goods produced domestically is affected by the exchange rate, as explained in Chapter 8. If the dollar falls in value, U.S. goods become less expensive. As a result, consumers and firms in the rest of the world will tend to increase their purchases of U.S.-produced goods and U.S. exports will rise. Changes in the exchange rate affect exports at each level of income. A rise in the value of the dollar makes U.S.-produced goods more expensive on world markets and reduces U.S. exports; a fall in the value of the dollar has the opposite effect and increases U.S. exports.

IMPORTS

When their incomes rise, households buy not only more American-made consumer goods but also more goods from abroad. We can draw an **import function** in much the same way as the consumption function that we used to illustrate the relationship between disposable income and consumption. The import function shows the levels of imports corresponding to different levels of income. For the sake of simplicity, we assume that imports are bought by consumers and that disposable income determines the level of imports. The import function, depicted in Figure 12.9, shows imports rising as disposable income rises.

The **marginal propensity to import** gives the amount of each extra dollar of income that is spent on imports. If the marginal propensity to import is .1, then imports rise by $100 if income rises by $1,000 ($100 is .1 × $1,000). The marginal propensity to import is given by the slope of the import function.

As incomes increase, imports rise while exports remain unchanged. Thus net exports fall as income rises. This fact helps explain the decline in U.S. net exports in the latter half of the 1990s (see Figure 12.8). At a time when the U.S. economy was booming and many other countries were in recession, our imports rose significantly, reducing net exports.

Imports also depend on the relative cost of goods produced abroad and domestically, which in turn is affected by the exchange rate. If the dollar rises in value, foreign goods become less expensive. Households tend to increase their purchases of goods produced abroad, and imports rise. One reason for the big drop in U.S. net exports in the mid-1980s was a significant rise in the dollar's value. As foreign goods became less expensive, imports rose. Changes in the exchange rate affect imports at each level of income. A rise in the value of the dollar shifts the import function up; a fall in the value of the dollar shifts the import function down.

Changes in the exchange rate affect imports for the same reason that they affect exports. If the dollar rises in value, U.S. goods become relatively more expensive. Foreigners buy fewer American goods and our exports will fall. Since this exchange rate alteration makes foreign goods relatively cheaper, our imports rise, so net exports fall. Conversely, a fall in the value of the dollar will stimulate exports and reduce imports, leading to an increase in net exports.

MACROECONOMIC IMPLICATIONS

Net exports affect the aggregate expenditures schedule in two ways. First, net exports alter its slope. As incomes rise, imports also rise, thereby reducing the net increase in expenditures on domestically produced goods and services. Aggregate expenditures rise with income because consumption and investment increase, but the slope of the AE schedule will be flatter in an open economy. If the marginal propensity to import is small, then the slope of the AE schedule is reduced only slightly; if the marginal propensity to import is large, as it might be in a very open economy, then the slope will be reduced significantly.

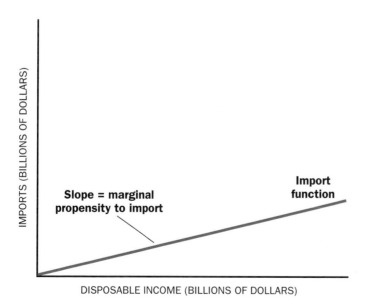

Figure 12.9

THE IMPORT FUNCTION

Imports (M) increase steadily as disposable income (Y_d) rises. The slope of the import function is equal to the marginal propensity to import.

Second, factors such as exchange rates and income developments in other countries can affect net exports and lead to shifts in the *AE* schedule. A recession in Europe will reduce U.S. exports and shift the aggregate expenditures schedule for the United States down. In the absence of any other change, equilibrium output in the United States will fall. In the late 1990s, the financial crises and subsequent recessions in many Asian economies raised the concern that the resulting fall in U.S. exports would lead to a recession here. The drop in exports shifted the *AE* schedule for the United States down. Fortunately, not everything else remained unchanged, and the United States continued to enjoy an economic boom. This bit of recent history illustrates an important point. We often use our theoretical models to illustrate what would happen if one factor changed, when all other things were held constant, because doing so enables us to understand clearly the distinct effects of changes in each factor. In the real world, however, many of the things we assumed to be constant are also changing, and we need to use our models to analyze simultaneous changes in many factors.

PUTTING INTERNATIONAL TRADE INTO THE EQUATION

When we add exports (X) and imports (M), aggregate expenditures are given by

$$AE = C + I + G + X - M.$$

Imports are related to disposable income by the import function,

$$M = MPI \times Y_\mathrm{d},$$

where MPI is the marginal propensity to import. Exports are assumed to be fixed. Hence, aggregate expenditures are

$$AE = a + MPC \times (1 - t) \times Y + I + G + X - MPI \times (1 - t) \times Y.$$

Since aggregate expenditures equal income, in equilibrium,

$$Y = (a + I + G + X)/[1 - (1 - t)(MPC - MPI)],$$

so the multiplier is

$$1/[1 - (1 - t)(MPC - MPI)].$$

If $t = .25$, $MPC = .8$, and $MPI = .1$, the multiplier is

$$1/[1 - .75(.8 - .1)] = 2.1,$$

smaller than it was in the absence of trade (2.5).

Calculating Equilibrium Output

At this point, it may be helpful to work through two simple examples, one illustrating the calculation of equilibrium GDP in a closed economy and the other showing the same calculation for an open economy. Suppose we have the following information on a closed economy. Each row in Table 12.1 gives the level of income (Y) in the first column and the levels of taxes (T), consumption (C), investment (I), and government purchases (G) at that level of income. I and G are assumed to be constant, regardless of the level of income, but both taxes and consumption rise with income. The final column calculates aggregate expenditures; it is simply equal to $C + I + G$ for our closed economy.

Equilibrium output occurs at the point where Y is equal to $C + I + G$. Using the information in Table 12.1, we can add up C, I, and G. If we do this, we find that equilibrium output is 7,000. At this output level, consumption is 4,600, investment is 1,200, and government purchases are 1,200; therefore, $AE = C + I + G = 4,600 + 1,200 + 1,200 = 7,000 = Y$.

Suppose G increases to 1,600. Recalculating aggregate expenditures $(C + I + G)$ at each income level, we can find that the new equilibrium level of output will be 8,000. The increase of G by 400 increases Y by 1,000, so the multiplier is 2.5.

We also know that when taxes depend on income, the multiplier is equal to $1/[1 - (1 - t)MPC]$, where t is the marginal tax rate. Using the information in the table, we can see that as income rises by 1,000, say from 7,000 to 8,000, taxes increase by 250, one-fourth as much. So $t = .25$. As total income increases by 1,000, disposable income increases by 750. Consumption then rises by 600. In the same example, as

Table 12.1

EQUILIBRIUM OUTPUT IN A CLOSED ECONOMY

Y	T	C	I	G	AE
1,000	200	1,000	1,200	1,200	3,400
2,000	450	1,600	1,200	1,200	4,000
3,000	700	2,200	1,200	1,200	4,600
4,000	950	2,800	1,200	1,200	5,200
5,000	1,200	3,400	1,200	1,200	5,800
6,000	1,450	4,000	1,200	1,200	6,400
7,000	**1,700**	**4,600**	**1,200**	**1,200**	**7,000**
8,000	1,950	5,200	1,200	1,200	7,600
9,000	2,200	5,800	1,200	1,200	8,200
10,000	2,450	6,400	1,200	1,200	8,800
11,000	2,700	7,000	1,200	1,200	9,400
12,000	2,950	7,600	1,200	1,200	10,000
13,000	3,200	8,200	1,200	1,200	10,600

Y goes from 7,000 to 8,000, disposable income goes from 5,300 (7,000 − 1,700) to 6,050 (8,000 − 1,950). Consumption rises from 4,600 to 5,200, an increase of 600. The MPC is the increase in C per dollar increase in disposable income, or 600/750 = .8. Using these values, we can calculate the multiplier to be $1/(1 − (1 − .25) \times .8) = 1/(1 − .75 \times 8) = 1/(1 − .6) = 1/.4 = 2.5$, the same value we found directly by finding the new equilibrium after an increase in G.

How would things change if we were dealing with an open economy? In an open economy, aggregate expenditures consist of $C + I + G + X − M$, where X denotes exports and M denotes imports. Suppose we have the information in Table 12.2. Exports do not depend on the level of GDP; in our example, they are equal to 500. Imports rise with income, and the example assumes a marginal propensity to import of .1. Just as in the closed economy, equilibrium occurs when $Y = AE$. In this example, as in the previous one, the equilibrium level of GDP is 7,000. For this economy, net exports are positive at the equilibrium level of GDP. A comparison between the AE column in the two tables reveals that as income rises, aggregate expenditures increase faster in the closed economy than in the open economy. In the latter, a positive marginal propensity to import means that imports rise as income rises, reducing net exports.

Given a marginal propensity to import of .1, a marginal propensity to consume of .8, and a marginal tax rate of .25, the formula for the multiplier tells us that a $1 increase in G will increase equilibrium income by $1/[1 − .75(.8 − .1)] = 2.1$. If G increases by 400, then equilibrium income will increase by 840, from 7,000 to 7,840. Recall that in the closed economy described in Table 12.1, the multiplier was 2.5. Again, the marginal propensity to import explains why it is smaller in the open economy.

Table 12.2

EQUILIBRIUM OUTPUT IN AN OPEN ECONOMY

Y	T	C	I	G	X	M	AE
1,000	200	1,000	1,200	1,100	900	200	4,000
2,000	450	1,600	1,200	1,100	900	300	4,500
3,000	700	2,200	1,200	1,100	900	400	5,000
4,000	950	2,800	1,200	1,100	900	500	5,500
5,000	1,200	3,400	1,200	1,100	900	600	6,000
6,000	1,450	4,000	1,200	1,100	900	700	6,500
7,000	**1,700**	**4,600**	**1,200**	**1,100**	**900**	**800**	**7,000**
8,000	1,950	5,200	1,200	1,100	900	900	7,500
9,000	2,200	5,800	1,200	1,100	900	1,000	8,000
10,000	2,450	6,400	1,200	1,100	900	1,100	8,500
11,000	2,700	7,000	1,200	1,100	900	1,200	9,000
12,000	2,950	7,600	1,200	1,100	900	1,300	9,500
13,000	3,200	8,200	1,200	1,100	900	1,400	10,000

AGGREGATE EXPENDITURES AND OUTPUT

Aggregate expenditures and output are equal where the aggregate expenditures schedule crosses the 45-degree line.

Shifts in the aggregate expenditure schedule have a multiplied impact on the level of equilibrium output. This multiplier depends on the marginal propensity to consume, the marginal tax rate, and the marginal propensity to import.

Factors that can shift the aggregate expenditures schedule up and increase equilibrium output include
- increases in wealth or expectations of higher future disposable income
- a reduction in the perceived risks of investment
- a fall in the value of the dollar
- a fall in the real rate of interest.

Aggregate Expenditures and the Real Interest Rate

Our discussion has highlighted a number of factors in addition to national income that can alter aggregate expenditures at each level of national income: expectations about future income, wealth, the exchange rate, and one of the most important, the real rate of interest. The impact of the interest rate on aggregate expenditures provides monetary policy a key means of affecting economic activity. Changes in the real interest rate influence investment spending and household purchases of new homes and durables like autos. Chapters 17 and 18 will discuss how interest rates also affect the exchange rate and therefore net exports. This connection offers another channel through which monetary policy can attempt to control aggregate expenditures.

Each of the aggregate expenditures schedules used in this chapter was drawn for a given real rate of interest. A change in the real rate of interest shifts the *AE* schedule. A decrease in the real rate, for instance, raises investment spending as credit becomes more readily available and firms find it less costly to borrow to undertake new projects. Such a decrease would therefore shift the *AE* schedule up, increasing the equilibrium level of GDP. An increase in the real interest rate has the opposite effect, shifting the *AE* schedule down and reducing equilibrium GDP.

For an open economy, interest rate changes can also affect net exports by causing the exchange rate to change. This link between interest rates and aggregate

INCENTIVES AND THE REAL AFTER-TAX RATE OF INTEREST

In other chapters we have emphasized that real values determine incentives. Thus, decisions to save and invest respond to real interest rates. So far, deriving the real interest rate from the nominal interest rate has been straightforward: subtract the rate of inflation from the nominal interest rate. But for the sake of simplicity we have ignored another important factor, the effect of taxation. In the absence of taxes on interest income, a nominal interest rate of 2 percent and 0 percent inflation yields the same real return as a nominal interest rate of 6 percent and 4 percent inflation. If nominal interest income is taxed, then the relationship between the nominal interest rate, inflation, and the real interest rate becomes more complicated.

Suppose nominal interest income is taxed at a 25 percent rate. If inflation is 0 percent and the nominal interest rate is 2 percent, the *after-tax* nominal return would be the 2 percent return minus the taxes ($.25 \times 2$ percent = 0.5 percent), leaving an after-tax nominal return of 1.5 percent. With 0 percent inflation, this is also the real return.

Now consider the situation when inflation rises to 4 percent. If the nominal interest rate were to rise to 6 percent, the after-tax return would be 6 percent minus taxes ($.25 \times 6$ percent = 1.5 percent), leaving a nominal after-tax return of 4.5 percent. Since inflation was 4 percent, the *real after-tax* return is only 0.5 percent! Even though the nominal interest rate rose by the same amount as inflation, the real after-tax return fell.

To maintain the same 1.5 percent real after-tax return that was obtained with 0 percent inflation, the nominal interest rate would need to rise to 7.33 percent when inflation increases to 4 percent. With a nominal return of 7.33 percent, the nominal after-tax return would be 5.5 percent, and the real after-tax return would be 1.5 percent. The nominal interest rate must more than match increases in inflation in order to maintain the same real return. In this example, if inflation increases 4 percent, the nominal interest rate must rise 5.33 percent.

The relationship would be different if countries designed their tax systems to tax real returns rather than nominal returns. In the case of 4 percent inflation, a nominal interest rate of 6 percent would yield a real before-tax return of 2 percent and an after-tax return of 1.5 percent, the same after-tax return as was earned with 0 percent inflation and a 2 percent nominal interest rate.

expenditures will be explained in Chapter 17; here we can note that it serves to reinforce the negative effect on aggregate expenditures of a rise in the real rate. Thus the basic effects of interest rates on the *AE* schedule in a closed economy will also be observed when we are studying the determination of GDP in an open economy.

THE REAL INTEREST RATE AND EQUILIBRIUM OUTPUT

A fall in the real rate of interest increases investment spending and household purchases of durables and new homes. These increases shift the aggregate expenditures schedule up, raising equilibrium output.

Review and Practice

SUMMARY

1. Income-expenditure analysis shows how the equilibrium level of output in the economy is determined when firms produce to meet demand.

2. Equilibrium output is determined by the intersection of the 45-degree line and the aggregate expenditures schedule. The aggregate expenditures schedule shows the level of expenditures at each level of national income, while the 45-degree line represents the points where aggregate expenditures equal output.

3. Shifts in the aggregate expenditures schedule give rise to changes in equilibrium output. The magnitude of the increase in output resulting from an upward shift in the schedule depends on the slope of the schedule. Much of macroeconomic analysis focuses on what determines the slope of the schedule, what causes shifts in the schedule, and how government policies affect the schedule.

4. Aggregate expenditures are the sum of consumption, investment, government purchases, and net exports.

5. Consumption increases as disposable income increases. The amount by which consumption increases when disposable income increases by a dollar is called the marginal propensity to consume.

6. The multiplier tells us how much total aggregate expenditures and output increase when the aggregate expenditures schedule shifts up by $1. The multiplier is larger if the marginal propensity to consume is large.

7. If tax revenues rise with income, the aggregate expenditures schedule is flattened and the multiplier is reduced. Taxes act as an automatic stabilizer. Increases in government purchases shift the schedule up.

8. Imports increase with income. The relationship between imports and income is called the import function; its slope is the marginal propensity to import. Exports are determined by factors in other countries. Trade reduces the multiplier, because as income increases, some of it goes to purchase foreign rather than domestic goods.

9. Both imports and exports depend on the exchange rate. A fall in the value of the dollar increases exports and reduces imports; this increase in net exports shifts the aggregate expenditures schedule up.

10. Changes in the real interest rate affect investment, the exchange rate, and net exports. A rise in the real interest rate reduces investment and net exports, leading to a downward shift in the aggregate expenditures schedule. Consequently, the level of output consistent with equilibrium falls as the real interest rate rises.

KEY TERMS

aggregate expenditures

aggregate expenditures schedule

income–expenditure analysis

multiplier

disposable income

marginal propensity to consume (MPC)

marginal propensity to save (MPS)

automatic stabilizer

plant and equipment investment

inventory investment

residential investment

balance of trade

import function

marginal propensity to import

REVIEW QUESTIONS

1. What is the aggregate expenditures schedule? What are the components of aggregate expenditures?

2. If output is determined by aggregate expenditures, explain how the equilibrium level of output is determined. Why are points on the aggregate expenditures schedule above the 45-degree line not sustainable? Why are points on the aggregate expenditures schedule below the 45-degree line not sustainable?

3. What factors might cause shifts in the aggregate expenditures schedule? List at least four.

4. How is the multiplier affected by the marginal propensity to consume? By the marginal tax rate? By the marginal propensity to import?

5. Why does an increase in the real rate of interest lower equilibrium output?

PROBLEMS

1. In the economy of Consumerland, national income and consumption are related in this way:

National income	$1,500	$1,600	$1,700	$1,800	$1,900
Consumption	$1,325	$1,420	$1,515	$1,610	$1,705

   Calculate national saving at each level of national income. What is the marginal propensity to consume in Consumerland? What is the marginal propensity to save? If national income rose to $2,000, what do you predict consumption and saving would be?

2. To the economy of Consumerland, add the fact that investment will be $180 at every level of output. Graph the consumption function and the aggregate expenditures schedule for this simple economy (no government or net exports). What determines the slope of the aggregate expenditures schedule? What is the equilibrium output?

3. Calculate the effect of a one-dollar increase in investment on output for each of the following economies:
   (a) A simple consumption and investment economy where the MPC is .9

   (b) An economy with government but no foreign trade, where the MPC is .9 and the tax rate is .3
   (c) An economy with an MPC of .9, a tax rate of .3, and a marginal propensity to import of .1

4. If, at each level of disposable income, saving increases, what does this imply about what has happened to the consumption function? What will be the consequences for the equilibrium level of output?

5. If the government made it easier for people to borrow money, perhaps by enacting programs to help them get loans, would you expect consumption spending to become more sensitive or less sensitive to current income? Why? How is the marginal propensity to consume affected? How is the multiplier affected?

6. Suppose the consumption function is given by $C = a + bY_d$ where a and b are constants (b is the marginal propensity to consume), and Y_d is disposable income, equal to $Y - T$. Taxes vary with income and are equal to $t_0 + tY$ where t_0 and t are constants (t is the marginal tax rate).
   (a) What is the effect on consumption of a $1 change in total income?
   (b) What is the effect on saving of a $1 change in total income?

Learning Goals

In this chapter, you will learn

1 What a monetary policy rule is, and how it depends on inflation

2 What the aggregate demand–inflation (ADI) curve is, what determines its slope, and what causes it to shift

3 How the ADI curve can be used to understand important macroeconomic events

4 How output and inflation respond to aggregate demand shocks and aggregate supply shocks

Chapter 13

AGGREGATE DEMAND AND INFLATION

Every six weeks, the members of the Federal Open Market Committee (FOMC), the policymaking committee of the Federal Reserve, gather in Washington, D.C. They come from across the nation to discuss the state of the economy and to make decisions that can determine the outlook for U.S. inflation and unemployment over the next several years. Stock markets can rise or fall in anticipation of FOMC decisions. On April 14, 2000, when the government released the latest figures suggesting a rise in inflation, the Dow Jones Industrial Average fell 616 points, its largest one-day point loss ever, in response to investors' fears that the FOMC would raise interest rates. Nine months later, on January 3, 2001, the Dow jumped 300 points and the NASDAQ went up 325 points when the FOMC cut interest rates. Investors know that if the economy booms and inflation rises, the Fed will increase interest rates; if the economy slows and inflation falls, the Fed will lower interest rates. These decisions by the FOMC affect the cost of credit for major corporations as well as for small family businesses. They affect the cost of car loans, student loans, and home mortgages. The importance of the FOMC for everyone in the economy has spawned a distinct industry of "Fed watchers" who try to predict what the FOMC will do. Since 1986, the chair of the Federal Reserve has been Alan Greenspan, and Fed watchers closely follow every speech and statement made by Chairman Greenspan for clues about future policy actions.

The Fed's actions have an important influence on GDP and inflation. In Chapter 12, we learned that the economy's level of output (GDP) is determined in the short run by the level of aggregate demand. One factor that affects aggregate demand is the real rate of interest. We now need to bring inflation back into the picture so that we can understand the linkages among inflation, the real interest rate, and aggregate demand. Monetary policy plays a critical role in this story. This should not be surprising, for Chapter 10 has already noted that when the economy is at full employment, the average inflation rate is determined by monetary policy. In the

United States, monetary policy is the responsibility of the Federal Reserve, our central bank.

Keeping inflation low and stable is a primary responsibility of any central bank, and, particularly during the past twenty-five years, many countries have undertaken central bank reforms that specify low inflation as the major or even sole objective of monetary policy. To maintain control over inflation, the Fed needs to keep its eye on the level of aggregate demand relative to the economy's full-employment output. If aggregate demand rises relative to the economy's full-employment output, inflation will rise: firms can boost prices and low unemployment will lead to wage increases in excess of productivity gains that push up firms' costs. If demand falls relative to potential output, inflation will eventually moderate. To keep inflation stable, the Fed acts to reduce demand when it starts to rise and to increase demand when it falls.

In the previous two chapters, we focused on the first two of the four key concepts for understanding short-run economic fluctuations—wages and prices do not adjust fast enough to keep the economy always at full employment. As a result, unemployment and output fluctuate around the full-employment level, and equilibrium occurs when output equals aggregate expenditures. In this chapter, we bring into our analysis the third and fourth key concepts—there is a short-run trade-off between inflation and unemployment, and increases in inflation reduce aggregate spending. By the end of the chapter, you will have a simple framework for understanding many important macroeconomic debates.

The Real Interest Rate and the Capital Market

Any news report on the Fed and monetary policy is sure to involve a discussion of interest rates. The reason is simple: central bank policies influence the level of aggregate demand by affecting the cost and availability of credit. In Chapter 12, we examined the four components of aggregate expenditures—consumption, investment, government purchases, and net exports—and their determinants, and we learned that the real interest rate is one of the main factors influencing aggregate expenditures. To simplify the analysis in this and the next two chapters, we will concentrate on the case of a closed economy. This focus enables us to ignore net exports. Despite the growing importance of international trade, the vast bulk of goods and services purchased in the United States are produced in the United States, so even an initially circumscribed analysis can provide important insights into macroeconomics. In Chapter 18 we will discuss how the lessons learned from a study of a closed economy need to be modified when we deal with an open economy.

In a closed economy, a higher real interest rate lowers aggregate expenditures by two primary mechanisms: (1) it reduces the profitability of investment, leading businesses to scale back investment projects, and (2) it affects consumer loans and mortgages, causing households to cut back on purchases of new homes and of consumer durables such as autos.

When we discuss interest rates and monetary policy, it is natural to start with the capital market. We have already seen, in Chapter 6, how the real rate of interest balances saving and investment when the economy is at full employment. When the economy is not at full employment, saving and investment must still balance to ensure that the capital market is in equilibrium. Figure 13.1 shows capital market equilibria for two different levels of output. When the economy is producing at full employment, as we assumed in Part Two, the saving and investment schedules are given by S^f and I^f. (For the sake of simplicity, we have assumed saving does not vary with the real interest rate—that is why it is drawn as a vertical line.) The equilibrium real rate of interest is r_0. If the economy's output is at less than its full-employment level, household income will be lower, and households will save less at each value of the real interest rate. This outcome is shown by the saving schedule S_1, to the left of S^f. The saving schedule shifts left because the marginal propensity to consume is less than one—a one-dollar decline in income reduces consumption by less than a dollar, which means that saving is also reduced. If there is no change in the investment schedule, the capital market will again be in equilibrium at an income level below full employment when the real interest rate rises to r_1.

However, investment will not remain the same if GDP drops. When output falls and the economy enters a recession, the investment schedule will also be affected. Declines in production lead to higher unemployment of labor *and* lower utilization of plant and equipment. The drop reduces the need for new investment, and firms are less likely to invest when the business outlook is bleak. The leftward shift in the investment schedule is depicted by the investment schedule I_1 in Figure 13.1. In this case, the equilibrium real interest rate is r_2. Depending on the relative shifts of the saving and investment schedules, the new equilibrium real interest rate may be greater or less than r_0.

When the economy is at full employment, equilibrium in the capital market determines the full-employment real interest rate. But what determines output and the real interest rate at less than full employment? To answer this question, we turn now to the connection among inflation, spending, and monetary policy.

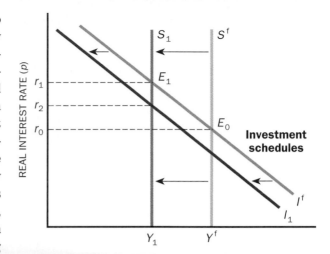

Figure 13.1

CAPITAL MARKET EQUILIBRIUM AT DIFFERENT INCOME AND INTEREST RATES

A fall in income from Y^f to Y_1 will shift the savings line to the left, from S^f to S_1. If the investment schedule remains unchanged, capital market equilibrium will occur at a higher real interest rate, r_1, and lower level of real income. A decline in output, however, is likely to shift the investment schedule to the left as firms roduce planned investment spending at each value of the real rate of interest. If the new investment schedule is I_1, the equilibrium real rate of interest is r_2. Depending on the magnitudes of the shifts, the final equilibrium real interest rate could be higher or lower than r_0.

The Aggregate Demand–Inflation Curve

In Chapter 11, we listed the effect of inflation on aggregate expenditures as the fourth of the key concepts for understanding short-run fluctuations of the economy. Now this relationship must be explored in more detail. Because monetary policy plays an important role in determining how changes in inflation affect aggregate expenditures, we need to focus on Fed policy.

THE FED'S POLICY RULE

The Fed is concerned about inflation, and it knows that as unemployment falls, inflation tends to rise (our third key concept). As inflation rises, the Fed acts to reduce aggregate demand in order to slow the economy down and lessen any upward pressure on inflation. The Fed can affect aggregate demand by influencing the real interest rate. An increase in the real interest rate will reduce investment spending, for example. As inflation falls, the Fed acts to lower the real interest rate to boost aggregate expenditures. These changes in aggregate demand move the economy's equilibrium level of output.

The Fed's systematic reaction to the economy is called a **monetary policy rule.** It describes how the Fed moves the interest rate in response to economic conditions. Initially, we will assume a very simple policy rule: the Fed raises interest rates when inflation increases and lowers interest rates when inflation falls. In 2004, for example, the Fed was concerned that inflation was rising, so it raised interest rates. In actuality, the Fed doesn't react only to inflation—a financial crisis might cause the Fed to lower interest rates even though inflation is unchanged, the Fed might be concerned that economic growth is slowing, and so on. For instance, on January 3, 2001, when the FOMC cut its interest rate target, it explained that "these actions were taken in light of further weakening of sales and production, and in the context of lower consumer confidence, tight conditions in some segments of financial markets, and high energy prices sapping household and business purchasing power. Moreover, inflation pressures remain contained."

When the Fed responds to factors other than inflation, the policy rule linking the interest rate to inflation changes. *A given policy rule reflects the adjustment of interest rates to inflation; a change in the policy rule occurs when, at a given level of inflation, the Fed sets a different interest rate than before.* Because the monetary policy rule describes how a central bank behaves, it can change over time. In the United States, as noted in Chapter 11, the Fed has taken much stronger action against inflation during the past twenty years than it did in the 1960s and 1970s.

There is one more point to keep in mind. Aggregate expenditures depend on the real interest rate (i.e., the nominal interest rate adjusted for inflation). To influence it, the Fed must move the nominal interest rate in the same direction as inflation, but by more. Thus, if inflation rises by 1 percentage point—say, from 3 to 4 percent—the Fed must raise the nominal interest by *more* than 1 percentage point to increase the real interest rate and aggregate spending. Only then can it affect the real rate of interest and aggregate spending. To simplify our analysis here, we will postpone discussing the details of how the Fed affects the nominal interest rate until Chapter 14.

Inflation and Aggregate Expenditures Our discussion of the Fed's policy rule leads to the following conclusion: there is a negative relationship between inflation and aggregate expenditures.

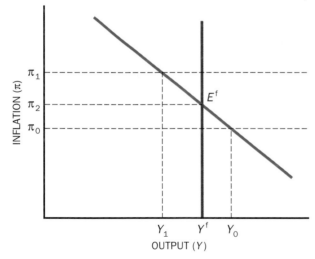

Figure 13.2

EQUILIBRIUM OUTPUT AND THE ADI CURVE

For each rate of inflation, the ADI curve shows the economy's equilibrium level of output. If inflation is π_0, the equilibrium output level is Y_0; at Y_0, aggregate expenditures equal output. At a higher inflation rate such as π_1, the real interest rate is higher, aggregate expenditures are lower, and the equilibrium level of output is only Y_1. The vertical line at Y^f denotes full-employment output.

Because equilibrium GDP is determined by aggregate expenditures in the short run, we can also say that there is a negative relationship between inflation and the short-run equilibrium level of GDP, given the central bank's policy rule. This relationship between inflation and GDP is called the **aggregate demand–inflation (ADI) curve** and is shown in Figure 13.2. Output (GDP) is on the horizontal axis, and inflation is on the vertical axis. The ADI curve in Figure 13.2 shows equilibrium output at each rate of inflation. If the inflation rate is π_0, equilibrium output will equal Y_0. At a higher inflation rate such as π_1, equilibrium output will be lower, equal to Y_1.

What Determines the Slope of the ADI Curve? When we use a demand and supply framework to analyze how price and quantity are determined, both the positions and the slopes of the demand and supply curves are important. Similarly, the adjustment of inflation and output to economic disturbances will depend on whether the ADI curve is relatively flat or relatively steep. Changes in inflation lead to changes in equilibrium output that are large when the ADI curve is relatively flat but small when the ADI curve is relatively steep. Understanding the factors that determine the slope of the ADI curve will be important for understanding the behavior of the economy in the short run.

The slope of the ADI curve in the closed economy has two main determinants. The first important factor is how the central bank adjusts interest rates as inflation changes—that is, the monetary policy rule. When the central bank responds more aggressively, a change in inflation will result in a larger change in the real rate of interest. A given change in inflation then leads to a larger fall in aggregate expenditures, making the ADI curve relatively flat. In contrast, a weaker reaction by the central bank will lead to a smaller rise in the real interest rate and a smaller decline in aggregate expenditures. As a result, the ADI curve will be relatively steep.

The second factor that affects the slope of the ADI curve is the impact of the real interest rate on the decisions by households and firms about how much to spend on consumption and investment. For example, if investment spending is very sensitive to the real interest rate, then the ADI curve will be quite flat—that is, a given change in the real interest rate caused by inflation will lead to a large change in aggregate expenditures. If investment and household spending do not respond much to changes in the real interest rate, then the ADI curve will be steep.

Figure 13.3 illustrates two different ADI curves. In an economy where the central bank responds aggressively to changes in inflation, or investment spending is very sensitive to changes in the real interest rate, or both, the ADI curve would be relatively flat, such as the curve labeled ADI_0. In an economy where the central bank responds weakly to changes in inflation, or investment spending is not very sensitive to changes in the real interest rate, or both, the ADI curve would be relatively steep, such as the curve labeled ADI_1.

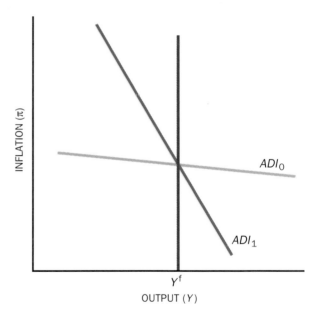

Figure 13.3

THE ADI SLOPE

If monetary policy responds aggressively to changes in inflation, or investment is sensitive to real interest rates, or both, the ADI curve will be flat, as illustrated by the curve ADI_0. If monetary policy does not respond strongly to changes in inflation, or investment is insensitive to real interest rates, or both, the ADI curve will be steep, as illustrated by the curve ADI_1. The vertical line at Y^f denotes full-employment output. Both ADI curves are drawn to be consistent with achieving full-employment output at the same rate of inflation.

Finally, although we have emphasized the role of the central bank's policy rule in producing the negative slope of the ADI curve, other factors are also at work. When the rise in prices outpaces the growth in money, the real value of money held by households and businesses is reduced. This reduction in real wealth may cause consumption and investment spending to decline. When prices rise more rapidly than nominal wages, real wages fall and this may cause consumption and spending to decline. In an open economy, more rapidly rising prices will, for a given exchange rate, increase the prices of domestically produced goods relative to foreign-produced goods. As a result, demand will shift away from domestic goods and toward foreign goods, reducing the overall demand for domestic output. These factors, like the monetary policy response we have emphasized, contribute to the negative relationship between inflation and GDP that is captured by the ADI curve.

To summarize, the negative relationship between inflation and short-run equilibrium GDP represented by the ADI curve is based on the following set of linkages:

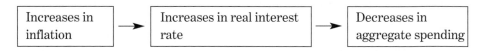

| Increases in inflation | → | Increases in real interest rate | → | Decreases in aggregate spending |

THE AGGREGATE DEMAND–INFLATION (ADI) CURVE

The ADI curve shows, for each value of inflation, the economy's short-run equilibrium level of output. Higher rates of inflation are associated with higher real interest rates, lower aggregate expenditures, and lower equilibrium output.

The central bank's monetary policy rule—the way monetary policy reacts to inflation—and the sensitivity of aggregate spending to the real interest are important in determining the negative slope of the ADI curve.

WHAT CAN SHIFT THE ADI CURVE?

Just as it is important to understand why the ADI curve has a negative slope, so too we need to understand the factors that can cause the curve to shift. For a given monetary policy rule, an ADI curve shows the equilibrium level of GDP for each rate of inflation. Movements in aggregate demand and GDP caused by changes in inflation translate into movements along a given ADI curve. Changes in any other factor that, for a given inflation rate, affect aggregate demand will *shift* the curve. Two of the most important examples of factors that can cause such a shift are fiscal policy and changes in the central bank's policy rule.

Fiscal Policy A change in government purchases or taxes alters the level of aggregate expenditures, and therefore output, for a given rate of inflation. An increase in government purchases, for example, raises aggregate expenditures at each level of the inflation rate; for every value of inflation, total expenditures (and therefore equilibrium GDP) are higher. This effect of a rise in government purchases is shown in Figure 13.4. The increase causes a rightward shift in the ADI curve. If the initial level of inflation was π_0, the initial level of output was Y_0. After the increase in government purchases, equilibrium output increases from Y_0 to Y_1. At the inflation rate π_0, output is now Y_1.[1]

Changes in taxes also shift the ADI curve. An increase in taxes reduces disposable income and leads to a fall in consumption. At each rate of inflation, aggregate spending will be lower. The ADI curve will shift to the left.

Changes in the Monetary Policy Rule The position of the ADI curve also depends on monetary policy. We have already learned how the slope of the ADI curve is affected by the policy rule that describes how the central bank adjusts the real interest rate in response to changes in inflation and how aggregate spending reacts to changes in the real interest rate. The slope has this automatic reaction to changes in inflation built into it. But we can also investigate what would happen if, at each rate of inflation, the central bank changed interest rates—that is, if the policy rule were to shift. For example, suppose the Fed decides to cut interest rates for a given rate of inflation. The Fed did just this in 1998 when it was concerned that the financial crisis in Asia would harm the United States. How will such an interest rate cut affect the ADI curve?

To answer this question, we need to work out the effects of the policy change on the real interest rate and then determine the impact on aggregate expenditures. That will tell us whether equilibrium GDP has increased or decreased. Since we are holding the rate of inflation constant, an increase in GDP will cause the ADI curve to shift to the right; a decrease in GDP will cause a shift to the left.

The Fed's decision to cut interest rates at a given rate of inflation first lowers the real rate of interest. We know that this reduction, in turn, will boost aggregate expenditures by lowering the cost of credit to households and firms. The rise in aggregate expenditures leads to an increase in equilibrium GDP. Hence, we can conclude that the ADI curve shifts to the right when, at each rate of inflation, the Fed cuts nominal interest rates.

We could run through the same steps to determine that the reverse happens to the ADI curve when the Fed raises interest rates at each rate of inflation. Since monetary policy ensures that each rate of inflation now leads to a higher real interest rate, aggregate expenditures will be lower. The fall in aggregate expenditures at each value of inflation lowers equilibrium GDP, shifting the ADI curve to the left.

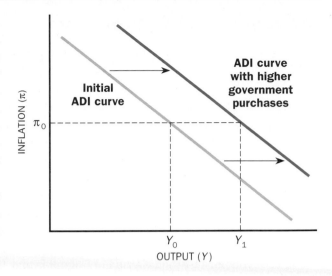

Figure 13.4

THE EFFECT OF GOVERNMENT PURCHASES ON AGGREGATE EXPENDITURES AND THE ADI CURVE

An increase in government purchases raises aggregate expenditures at each value of the rate. This increase in aggregate expenditures increases equilibrium output. At the initial inflation rate π_0, this change represents an increase in output from Y_0 to Y_1. The rise in government purchases causes the ADI curve to shift to the right, as shown.

---

[1]The size of the increase in output is determined by the magnitude of the initial increase in spending and the multiplier, as explained in Chapter 12.

HOW DO OTHER CENTRAL BANKS REACT TO INFLATION?

The reaction of the central bank to inflation is a critical factor in determining the slope of the ADI curve. One implication of the bank's role is that ADI curves in different countries may have different slopes, because central banks do not all react to inflation in the same way. Countries whose central bank responds aggressively to inflation, pushing up interest rates at its slightest hint and cutting interest rates whenever it falls below target, will have flatter ADI curves than will countries with central banks that fail to react to changes in inflation.

Three economists—Rich Clarida of Columbia and Jordi Galí and Mark Gertler of New York University—have estimated how various central banks respond to inflation. For the Federal Reserve, the German Bundesbank (prior to the formation of the European Economic and Monetary Union), and the Bank of Japan, they find strong evidence consistent with the type of policy rule we have used to represent monetary policy. When inflation increases, these central banks raise nominal interest rates by more than that increase. If inflation rises by 1 percentage point, the nominal interest rate must rise by more than 1 percentage point to ensure that the real interest rate rises. When inflation falls, these central banks reduce the nominal interest rates by more so that the real interest rate falls.

Yet despite their similar responses to inflation, Clarida, Galí, and Gertler also found some differences among these central banks. Of the three, the Bank of Japan was judged to respond the most strongly to changes in inflation, while the Bundesbank showed the weakest reaction. From what we have learned about the factors that affect the slope of the ADI curve, these differences in policy rules among Germany, Japan, and the United States mean that the slopes of each country's ADI curve will differ. Japan's response to inflation, because it is stronger, should produce a flatter ADI curve than Germany's. However, we also learned that the policy rule is not the only factor that affects the ADI slope, so we would also need to know how sensitive spending in each country is to changes in the real interest rate before we could make a final prediction about how their ADI slopes might differ.

Monetary policy rules can change over time. In the 1960s and 1970s, most central banks did not react as aggressively to inflation as they do today. Because inflation reached undesirable levels in the 1970s, central banks today focus on ensuring that inflation remains low and stable.

SOURCE: R. Clarida, J. Galí, and M. Gertler, "Monetary Policy Rules in Practice: Some International Evidence," *European Economic Review* 42, no. 6 (1998): 1033–1068.

OTHER FACTORS THAT CAN SHIFT THE ADI CURVE

While fiscal policy and monetary policy are key factors that can shift the ADI curve, similar effects occur if investment or consumption behavior changes at each value of the inflation rate. For example, the stock market boom of the 1990s boosted consumption spending for given levels of income and inflation. This type of wealth effect on consumption spending increases total aggregate expenditures and the equilibrium level of output. Greater optimism about the future can encourage consumption and investment spending, also increasing aggregate expenditures. For a given level of the inflation rate, equilibrium output would be higher, an outcome represented by a rightward shift of the ADI curve.

If households and firms become more pessimistic about the future and scale back their spending, or if wealth falls because of a stock market collapse, for example, aggregate expenditures would fall at each level of the inflation rate. The result is a leftward shift in the ADI curve.

FACTORS THAT SHIFT THE AGGREGATE DEMAND–INFLATION (ADI) CURVE

Factors that increase aggregate expenditures at each rate of inflation (and shift the ADI curve to the right) include

increases in government purchases,

decreases in taxes,

an increase in wealth,

an increase in business or household optimism, and

a cut in interest rates at each rate of inflation.

Factors that decrease aggregate expenditures at each rate of inflation (and shift the ADI curve to the left) include

decreases in government purchases,

increases in taxes,

a decrease in wealth,

an increase in business or household pessimism, and

an increase in interest rates at each rate of inflation.

Factors That Have Shifted the ADI Curve Over the past forty years, the ADI curve in the United States has been shifted by fiscal and monetary policy actions, as well as by changes in spending behavior by households and firms. Among the major factors affecting the ADI curve were

- The increase in government purchases associated with the Vietnam War in the 1960s
- The increase in interest rates that resulted from the major shift in Fed policy in 1979, which was designed to bring inflation down from the high levels reached in the 1970s
- The drop in consumption as households became more pessimistic at the time Iraq invaded Kuwait in 1990
- The increase in consumer spending due to the wealth effects of the stock market boom of the late 1990s
- The increase in investment spending associated with the introduction of new information technologies in the 1990s

For each of these examples, be sure that you can explain whether the ADI curve shifted to the left or to the right and why it did so.

Using the ADI Curve

We have now learned about one of the key components of the theory of economic fluctuations, the ADI curve. In the short run, firms adjust production in response to changes in demand at each level of inflation. That means that *the economy's short-run equilibrium GDP will be determined by the level of aggregate demand.* In Figure 13.2, the economy's equilibrium level of GDP will be Y_0 if the inflation rate is equal to π_0. If inflation is higher, say, at π_1, equilibrium output will be lower, at Y_1.

Figure 13.2 includes a vertical line at the economy's full-employment level of output, denoted as Y^f. As we know from Chapter 6, full-employment output, or potential GDP, is determined by the level of employment that occurs when labor demand and labor supply are balanced and by the economy's stock of capital and its current level of technology. Because full-employment output (and thus potential GDP) does not depend on the rate of inflation, we have drawn a vertical line at Y^f. If the inflation rate were equal to π_2, the economy's equilibrium would be at point E^f in the figure, and the economy would be at full employment.

In the short run, as already observed, wages and prices do not respond quickly enough to keep the labor market always in equilibrium at full employment. Employment and output fluctuate around their full-employment levels. In some markets—the stock market, or the market for gold and other commodities such as wheat or oil—prices move rapidly to adjust to shifts in demand and supply curves. But for most goods and services, whether sold by producers, wholesalers, or retailers, wages and prices change with considerable sluggishness. For now, we will assume that the inflation rate adjusts slowly in our short-run analysis of the product market and equilibrium output. This assumption is consistent with most empirical evidence, which suggests that output adjusts more rapidly than inflation when economic disturbances occur.

OUTPUT EFFECTS OF A SHIFT IN THE ADI CURVE

Consider what happens in the short run if the aggregate demand–inflation curve shifts to the left, as depicted in Figure 13.5 by the move from ADI_0 to ADI_1. A leftward shift in the ADI curve like that shown in the figure occurred in 1990 when American households became more pessimistic about the future and scaled back their consumption spending. Similarly, when Japan's financial sector collapsed in the early 1990s, households and firms reduced their spending, shifting the ADI curve for Japan to the left.

Suppose the economy starts out with an inflation rate equal to π_0. We have drawn a horizontal line at this initial inflation rate and labeled it IA_0 (for *inflation adjustment* line). The **inflation adjustment line** shows the current rate of inflation. We will use it to keep track of how the inflation rate adjusts when the economy fluctuates around full-employment output.

When the ADI curve shifts to ADI_1, the new equilibrium is at point E_1, where ADI_1 crosses the IA_0 line. At the inflation rate π_0, output falls from Y^f to Y_1, as firms will produce only the quantity they can sell. One result of the reduced output will be a decrease in the demand for labor. Because wages do not adjust quickly, this decrease leads to a fall in employment and a rise in cyclical unemployment. The economy enters a recession.

But the story does not end there. At point E_1, output is below potential, and there is cyclical unemployment. Because of the decline in production and the increase in unemployment, workers will likely have to settle for smaller wage increases, and firms will be less able to pass along cost increases by increasing their prices. As a result, inflation declines. This impact of cyclical unemployment on inflation was set out in Chapter 11 as the third of our four key concepts: increases in cyclical unemployment lead to declines in inflation, while decreases in cyclical unemployment lead to increases in inflation. Its implication for our analysis is that the economy will not remain at point E_1; instead, over time, inflation will start to come down.

Imagine that we return to Figure 13.5 after a few months. Inflation will have fallen from π_0 to some lower level. As long as output remains below the full-employment level, inflation will continue to decline. If the aggregate demand–inflation curve remains in its new position (ADI_1), the economy will move down along the aggregate demand curve as inflation falls. Along the ADI curve, aggregate spending rises as inflation falls, increasing the equilibrium level of output and moving the economy back toward full employment. The process of adjustment continues until eventually the inflation adjustment line has shifted down to IA_1, with GDP equal again to output at the full-employment level. Once the gap between GDP and potential GDP

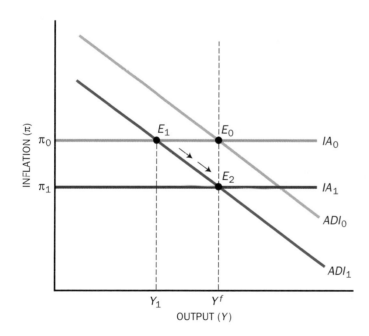

Figure 13.5

A RECESSION CAUSED BY A SHIFT IN AGGREGATE DEMAND

The full-employment level of output is given by the vertical line at Y^f. The initial inflation rate is π_0 and the aggregate demand inflation curve is ADI_0. The equilibrium is at E_0, with output equal to Y^f. If the ADI curve shifts to the left (to ADI_1), equilibrium GDP will fall below the full-employment level of output; the new short-run equilibrium level of GDP is Y_1. Eventually, if output remains below Y^f, inflation will decline and the economy will move down the ADI curve until full employment is restored at E_2 at an inflation rate of π_1.

is eliminated and the economy is back at full employment, there is no further downward pressure on inflation. Eventually the economy reaches a new long-run equilibrium at full employment at the point E_2, with an inflation rate of π_1.

THE VOLCKER DISINFLATION

In 1979 and 1980, there was widespread agreement that something should be done to halt inflation. At the time, inflation was at a postwar high and appeared to be moving even higher. The economy was at a point such as E_0 in Figure 13.5—it was at full employment (the unemployment rate was 5.8 percent in 1979, about equal to estimates of full employment at the time), but the inflation rate was very high (over 8 percent in 1979 as measured by the GDP price deflator).

Paul Volcker, then the chair of the Federal Reserve Board, pushed through a sharp increase in interest rates in order to choke off inflation. This action represented a major shift in the monetary policy rule. As a result of the higher real interest rates, firms cut back their investments, and households cut back their purchases of items such as new cars and homes. Interestingly, at the same time that the Fed was taking actions to restrict aggregate spending, fiscal policy was stimulating the economy. President Reagan cut taxes without cutting government expenditures by an

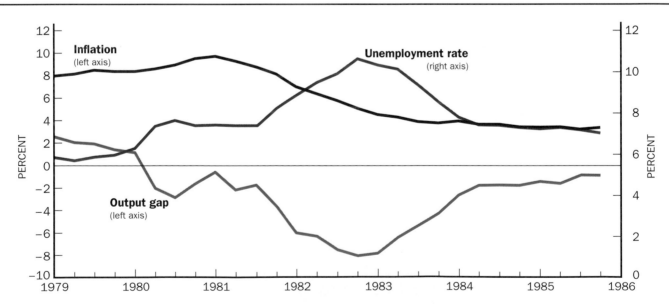

Figure 13.6

THE OUTPUT GAP, UNEMPLOYMENT RATE, AND INFLATION RATE IN THE 1980s

In the late 1970s and early 1980s, the Federal Reserve Board, worried about runaway inflation, acted to restrict credit and thus consumption and investment. The decrease in aggregate demand raised unemployment and lowered output below potential. The effects more than offset the expansionary effects of the 1981 tax cut. Inflation gradually declined, and by 1985, the economy was back at full employment, with a lower rate of inflation.

SOURCES: Unemployment, *Economic Report of the President* (2001), Table B-35; inflation, *Economic Report of the President* (2001), Table B-64; output gap, Federal Reserve Board.

offsetting amount. But the contractionary impact of monetary policy more than offset the expansionary effect of lower taxes, and the ADI curve shifted to the left, as shown in Figure 13.5.

Figure 13.6 shows the results of this shift in monetary policy. Output declined below potential GDP and the unemployment rate briefly hit a post–World War II high of 11 percent. However, the recession did succeed in curbing inflation, which dropped from around 9 percent in 1980 to just 3.2 percent in 1983.[2] As the economy moved to its new equilibrium at point E_2 in Figure 13.5, unemployment fell; by 1985, the economy was essentially back at full employment.

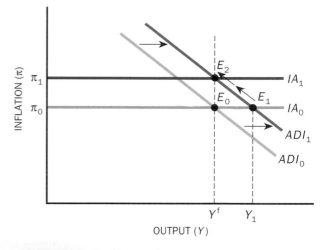

An Expansionary Shift in the ADI Curve

Figure 13.7 illustrates a different scenario, one in which the ADI curve has shifted to the right. This type of shift is caused by a positive shock to spending; perhaps firms have become more optimistic about the future and have increased investment spending on plant and equipment. Or perhaps the government has increased its purchases or cut taxes. In response to the growth in demand, firms expand production. They hire more workers, average weekly hours rise as workers work more, and unemployment falls. Firms utilize their plant and equipment more intensively, perhaps adding extra shifts or delaying maintenance in order to keep production lines running at top speed. These adjustments enable output to rise above levels associated with normal conditions. Output rises above Y^f, moving the economy to E_1; the new equilibrium level of output is now Y_1.

Just like a recession caused by a drop in spending, the boom caused by increased spending does not last forever. To attract and retain workers, firms are willing to increase wages more rapidly, and they can push up prices with less fear of losing markets. As inflation rises, the Fed boosts interest rates. As it does so, the economy's equilibrium level of output will tend to fall back toward the full-employment level. The economy moves up the ADI curve from point E_1 toward point E_2 in Figure 13.7. Eventually, output will return to Y^f at point E_2 with a higher rate of inflation.

Figure 13.7

A BOOM CAUSED BY A SHIFT IN AGGREGATE DEMAND

If the aggregate demand curve shifts to the right (from ADI_0 to ADI_1), firms will increase production. Output and employment rise, and the new short-run equilibrium level of output is Y_1. Eventually, wages and prices will start rising more rapidly and the economy will move up the aggregate demand–inflation curve toward the full-employment equilibrium at point E_2, where output has returned to Y^f but inflation is now higher at π_1.

Case in Point

THE KENNEDY TAX CUT

In 1963, the unemployment rate in the United States seemed to be stuck at an unacceptably high level, 5.5 percent. Ten years earlier it had been 2.8 percent. President

---

[2]The peak rate of inflation was even higher if measured by the consumer price index (CPI), reaching 13 percent in 1980.

John F. Kennedy's economic advisers believed that a cut in the individual income tax would cause households to consume more. This increased consumption would lead to a rightward shift in the ADI curve. An increase in aggregate expenditures, Kennedy's advisers believed, would result in increased output and a lower unemployment rate, not higher inflation. They argued that inflation would not rise, because the economy had excess capacity—productive workers and machines were lying idle. As a result, the shift in the ADI curve would be translated into increases in output, as shown in Figure 13.7.

Increases in output, as we have learned, imply increases in employment. The predictions of the economic advisers turned out to be correct. After taxes were cut in 1964, unemployment fell to 4.4 percent in 1965 and stayed under 4 percent for the rest of the 1960s. In addition, real GDP grew at the remarkable rate of 5.5 percent from 1964 to 1966, while inflation initially remained at low levels. Figure 13.8 shows these developments. Output was below potential in 1962 and 1963, but the output gap was shrinking and the unemployment rate was falling. The tax cut boosted the economy and pushed output above potential by 1965.

According to our model, wages and prices start to rise more rapidly when the economy is operating above potential. This is just what happened. Throughout the late 1960s, inflation rose. Eventually, the economy fell back toward potential GDP, just as the analysis illustrated in Figure 13.7 predicts. By the end of 1970, unemployment was back above 5.5 percent. Inflation, which had averaged 1.3 percent in 1963, averaged 5.7 percent in 1970.

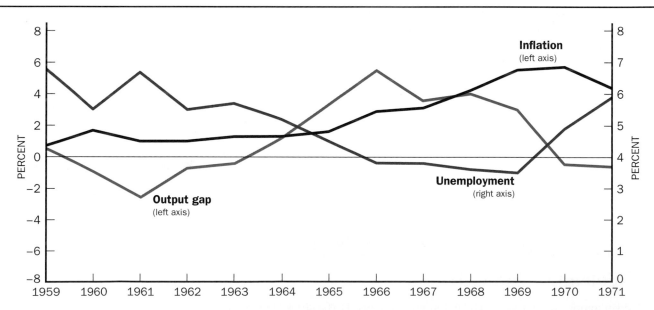

Figure 13.8

THE OUTPUT GAP, UNEMPLOYMENT RATE, AND INFLATION RATE IN THE 1960s

The increase in aggregate demand during the 1960s lowered unemployment. As the economy continued to expand above full-employment GDP, the rate of inflation increased. By the end of the decade, the economy was back at full employment but with a higher rate of inflation.

SOURCES: *Economic Report of the President* (2004) and Congressional Budget Office.

Thinking Like an Economist

TOUGH TRADE-OFFS

The Volcker policy to control inflation in late 1979 provides a graphic illustration of the trade-offs policymakers are often forced to make. Inflation had risen to unacceptable levels in the United States, but the only way the Federal Reserve could bring it down was to create a recession. It had to make a trade-off. The Federal Reserve could continue to let inflation remain at high levels, accepting the concomitant distortions. Or it could act to lower inflation, knowing that the cost would be an increase in cyclical unemployment, with all the attendant hardships for the unemployed.

In weighing the costs of higher cyclical unemployment against the benefits of lower inflation, we must remember an important implication of our model of fluctuations. The rise in cyclical unemployment would be temporary. Eventually, the economy would return to full employment. That may not be much comfort to the workers who lost their jobs during the recessions in 1980 and 1982, but it was an important fact for policymakers to keep in mind. In assessing trade-offs, we need to know whether the consequences of an action are likely to be permanent or only temporary. If the Federal Reserve policymakers had believed that its disinflation policies would lead to permanently higher unemployment, they might have made a different choice.

In April 1980, the federal funds rate peaked above 17.5 percent (for comparison, during the first half of 2004, the federal funds rate stood at 1 percent). Just two years earlier, in 1978, it had been only 6.89 percent. Of course, what matters for spending decisions is the real interest rate, so we need to adjust the federal funds rate for inflation. During 1978, inflation averaged almost 9 percent, while in 1980 it was more than 12 percent. Between 1978 and 1980, the real federal funds rate

swung from a negative 2.11 percent (6.89 percent minus 9 percent inflation) to a positive 5.5 percent (17.5 percent minus 12 percent inflation). This rise in the real interest rate reduced aggregate expenditures, as we learned it would in Chapter 12.

The Federal Reserve's policy actions in 1979 and 1980 eventually did succeed in bringing inflation down. But cyclical unemployment rose significantly during the period of disinflation. From an average of 6 percent of the labor force in 1978–1979, the unemployment rate averaged 8.5 percent over 1980–1983.

In Chapters 15 and 20, we will learn more about the short-run trade-off between inflation and unemployment.

In pursuit of lower inflation policymakers have sometimes accepted the closing of factories and the resulting higher cyclical unemployment.

MACROECONOMIC POLICY AND SHIFTS IN THE ADI CURVE

Our examples have illustrated the effects on aggregate demand and output in the short run. For each example, we assumed the economy started out at full employment. Tracing through the effects of a single disturbance on output and employment in the short run can be useful. More commonly, however, we want to use our macroeconomic model not to focus on such effects but to analyze how policy might help maintain the economy at full employment. In Figure 13.5, the initial leftward shift in the ADI curve pushed the economy into a recession, with output at E_1, below the economy's full-employment output at point E_0. If the aggregate demand curve remains at ADI_1, inflation will eventually fall and the economy will reach full employment at point E_2 with an inflation rate of π_2. If inflation adjusts slowly, it may take a long time for full employment to be restored. An expansionary fiscal or monetary policy that shifts the aggregate demand curve to the right would push the short-run equilibrium output level closer to full employment. If the ADI curve is shifted all the way to ADI_0, full employment is restored at the original rate of inflation, π_0.

Shifts in the Inflation Adjustment Curve

So far, we have concentrated on the impact of shifts in the ADI curve on the economy. Such a focus is natural in that aggregate expenditures determine output (and employment) in the short run, and inflation typically adjusts relatively slowly. But economies also experience disturbances that directly affect inflation. Two of the most important are changes in energy prices and shifts in potential GDP.

CHANGES IN ENERGY PRICES

For a given level of cyclical unemployment, inflation can be affected by shocks that alter firms' costs of production. For example, during the 1970s, oil prices increased dramatically. Oil prices also rose substantially in 2004, because of both greater demand for oil as the economies of China and the United States grew and fears of disruptions in supply as the fighting in Iraq continued. By raising the price of energy, an increase in oil prices pushes up the costs of production. In response, firms will raise prices, leading in turn to a jump in the inflation rate.

We can analyze the consequences of an inflation shock such as an oil price increase using the ADI curve and inflation adjustment line. To do so, suppose the economy is initially at full employment with an inflation rate equal to π_0. This condition is shown as point E_0 in Figure 13.9. The inflation shock causes inflation to increase to π_1, as shown by the upward shift in the inflation adjustment curve to IA_1. The new equilibrium is at E_1. Economic disturbances that shift the inflation adjustment curve—inflation shocks—are often also called **supply shocks.**

The economy will not remain at point E_1, however. Over time, inflation will decline because the economy is operating below potential GDP. As inflation falls, the IA curve shifts back down. Eventually, the equilibrium returns to point E_0, with the inflation rate and output back at their initial values.

Supply shocks present policymakers with difficult choices. To prevent output from declining and unemployment from rising, the central

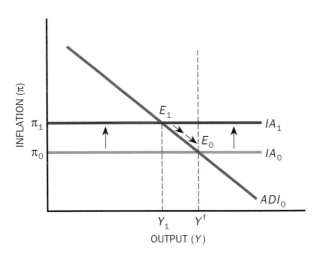

Figure 13.9

THE IMPACT OF AN INFLATION SHOCK

An increase in the cost of production at each level of output increases the inflation rate, shifting the inflation adjustment curve up, from IA_0 to IA_1. The short-run equilibrium is at the point of intersection between the inflation adjustment and ADI curves. The upward shift in the inflation adjustment curve moves the economy to E_1, where output has fallen to Y_1. If there are no further inflation shocks, inflation declines because output is below its full-employment level. Eventually, full employment and an inflation rate of π_0 are restored.

bank could cut interest rates at each rate of inflation (changing its policy rule). Such cuts would shift the ADI curve to the right. The central bank's effort to keep output equal to potential GDP will prevent unemployment from rising, but at the cost of leaving inflation at the higher level, π_1. Alternatively, if the central bank wants to prevent any rise in inflation, it must pursue a tighter policy and higher interest rates (changing its policy rule, this time toward a higher interest rate at each rate of inflation). When the ADI curve is shifted to the left, inflation can be maintained at π_0, but at the cost of a deeper recession and a larger increase in cyclical unemployment.

Case in Point

OIL PRICE SHOCKS OF THE 1970s

The Arab-Israeli War in 1973 led the Organization of Petroleum Exporting Countries (OPEC) to restrict oil exports to Western industrialized economies and to raise the price of oil sharply. The fuel and utilities component of the consumer price index jumped more than 16 percent in 1973. Overall inflation as measured by the GDP deflator rose from 4.14 percent in 1972 to 5.23 percent in 1973 to 8.58 percent in 1974 as the impact of higher oil prices raised the prices of goods and services throughout the economy.

The hike in inflation resulting from the oil price increases shifted the inflation adjustment curve up, as illustrated in Figure 13.9. Our model of fluctuations predicts a decline in output after such an inflation shock, and that is just what happened. Unemployment, which had averaged 4.9 percent in 1973, rose to 8.5 percent by 1975 as the economy entered a recession. Figure 13.10 shows the path of the output gap, unemployment rate, and inflation rate from 1972 until 1977. The high level of cyclical unemployment during the recession put downward pressure on inflation. As inflation declined during 1976 falling to 5.7 percent from 9.0 percent in 1975, output recovered and unemployment began to decline; it eventually reached 5.8 percent in 1979, a level close to most estimates of full employment.

A SHIFT IN POTENTIAL GDP

Changes in the economy's potential GDP can shift the inflation adjustment curve. Potential GDP might shift because of productivity changes or because of labor market changes that increase the level of employment associated with full employment, leading to higher output at full employment. Many of the recent discussions about the new economy and the impact of information technologies in boosting productivity can be thought of as arguing that potential GDP has risen.

Consider what happens if there is a productivity increase that boosts full-employment GDP. In Figure 13.11, the initial equilibrium is at E_0. Potential GDP shifts from the old level of potential output (Y_0^f) to the new, higher value (Y_1^f). If there is

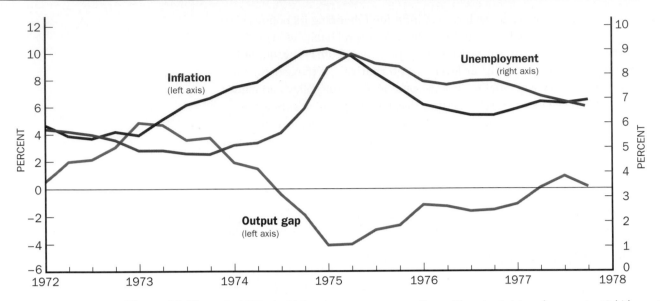

Figure 13.10

THE 1973 OIL PRICE SHOCK

In 1972, the U.S. economy was expanding, with output rising above potential (the output gap was positive) and unemployment declining. In 1973, OPEC sharply raised the price of oil. This inflation shock pushed up U.S. inflation and sent the economy into a recession. The output gap fell and unemployment rose. After peaking in 1975, inflation started to decline. As Figure 13.9 would suggest, falling inflation was associated with a rise in output and fall in unemployment as output returned to potential. A second oil price shock hit the economy in 1979.

SOURCES: *Economic Report of the President* (2003) and Congressional Budget Office, *The Budget and Economic Outlook*, January 2004.

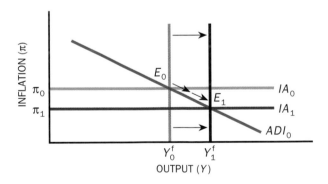

Figure 13.11

THE IMPACT OF AN INCREASE IN POTENTIAL GDP

If potential GDP increases from Y_0^f to Y_1^f, initially equilibrium remains at the point where the inflation adjustment line at the current inflation rate π_0 intersects with the ADI curve (E_0). Eventually, the economy achieves its new, higher level of potential GDP at the inflation rate π_1.

no change in the ADI curve, equilibrium output remains at point E_0 at the initial inflation rate π_0.

The economy will not remain at E_0, however. At an output equal to the old level of potential GDP, Y_0^f, firms now have excess capacity—the increase in productivity means they could produce more than before with the same resources. The change places downward pressure on inflation. As inflation declines, the real interest rate also falls, leading to an increase in aggregate expenditures and equilibrium output (i.e., to a movement along the ADI curve). Eventually the economy will reach point E_1, with output now at the new, higher level of potential GDP and inflation lower than initially.

In Figure 13.11, the ADI curve was held fixed. But if potential output rises, there may be a direct impact on the ADI curve as well. Higher potential output means that total incomes in the economy are higher. Households' desire to increase their consumption spending when they expect their real incomes to rise can lead to a rightward shift in the ADI curve. As a consequence, the economy may move to a higher level of output with very little change in inflation.

THE 1990s

Now that we have a complete model for understanding how the economy adjusts, we can use it to analyze the U.S. economy at the end of the 1990s. Figure 13.12 shows the unemployment rate, the output gap, and the inflation rate since 1990. The recession of 1990–1991 shows up clearly in the path of the unemployment rate, which rose from 5.6 percent of the labor force in 1990 to 7.5 percent in 1992. This recession was caused by demand factors that shifted the ADI curve to the left. Both consumption and investment spending dropped, as people became more pessimistic about the future at the time of the Gulf War.

Our model predicts that a drop in aggregate expenditures will lead to an increase in unemployment and a decline in inflation. Output will eventually return to potential (see Figure 13.5), so unemployment should return to its full-employment level, but inflation will remain lower. In the late 1980s and early 1990s, estimates of the unemployment rate at full employment were in the 5.5 to 6 percent range. As Figure 13.12 shows, by 1996 the unemployment rate had returned to its prerecession level, and inflation remained at a level lower than its prerecession value.

From 1996 to the end of the 1990s, the economy continued to expand, and both unemployment *and* inflation continued to fall. Economic output displayed strong

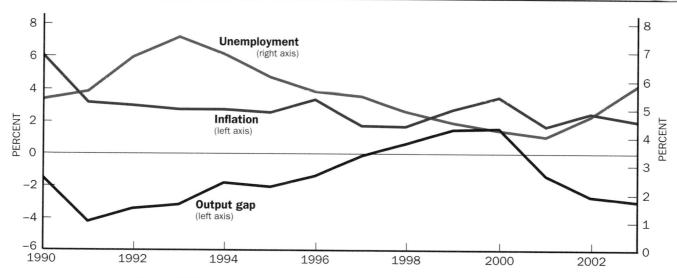

Figure 13.12

THE BOOM OF THE 1990s

The U.S. economy began the 1990s recovering from the recession of 1990–1991. Steady growth throughout the decade brought the output gap back to zero and led to a significant reduction in unemployment. Inflation remained stable. In 2001, the economy experienced a recession—GDP fell and unemployment rose.

SOURCES: *Economic Report of the President* (2003) and Congressional Budget Office, *The Budget and Economic Outlook*, 2004.

PRODUCTIVITY GROWTH AND THE PUNCH BOWL

To prevent inflation from rising, the Fed must not let the economy overheat—if output rises above potential, the tight labor market will lead wages to rise in excess of productivity growth. As firms face increasing labor costs, they will boost their prices, and inflation will rise. Sometimes it seems that just when the good times of low unemployment arrive, the Fed starts raising interest rates to slow things down. An old adage about monetary policy is that the job of the Fed is to take the punch bowl away just when the party really gets going. Increases in productivity growth brought on by new technologies will enable the Fed to leave the punch bowl out a bit longer during booms.

The Fed's actions have to do with the relationship between wage increases, productivity, and inflation. As long as wages do not increase faster than productivity, firms' costs of production will not rise. The reason is simple—firms may have to pay more to their workers, but their workers are producing more. The labor costs of producing each unit of output—unit labor costs—do not increase when wages rise at the same rate as productivity. The faster productivity grows, the faster wages can rise without fueling price increases.

Sometimes the Fed is criticized for raising interest rates whenever wages start to rise. It is not wage increases themselves that concern the Fed, however, but inflation. As long as wage increases are in line with increases in productivity, they do not increase firms' costs or contribute to inflation. So the Fed looks at unit labor costs to determine if wage increases are inflationary or not. As the chart illustrates, during the early 1980s, wage increases far outstripped increases in productivity, causing unit labor costs to rise rapidly. The opposite occurred during the 1990s. While wages started rising faster in the late 1990s, so did productivity.

The years 1999 and 2000 illustrate some of the difficulties facing the Fed as it makes its policy decisions. Wage growth had increased. If the observed increases in productivity growth heralded the arrival of a "new economy" in which such growth would remain strong, then wages could rise much faster than previously without arousing concerns that they would ignite a new bout of inflation. If the increased productivity growth turned out to be only temporary, then the faster wage growth would start to push up unit labor costs and prices. Information and computer technologies are transforming the economy, and if these changes lead

growth and the growth rate of productivity increased. These developments were consistent with a supply shock that lowered the unemployment rate at full employment and shifted the inflation adjustment curve down, as illustrated in Figure 13.11. As our model predicts, this resulted in lower unemployment and lower inflation. The prime candidate for such a favorable supply shock is the new computer and information technologies that have transformed so many parts of the American economy.

As the 1990s ended, the Fed was concerned that the booming economy would eventually lead to higher inflation. To guard against this, the Fed raised interest rates several times in 1999 and 2000. These interest rate hikes were designed to slow the economy by reducing demand, and signs that the economy's strong growth was weakening appeared by the end of 2000. The year 2000 also saw the collapse to sustained increases in productivity growth, workers' real wages will rise faster than was usual during the previous quarter century. But when wages outpace productivity, even workers in the new economy will discover that the Fed will have to put away the punch bowl to keep inflation under control.

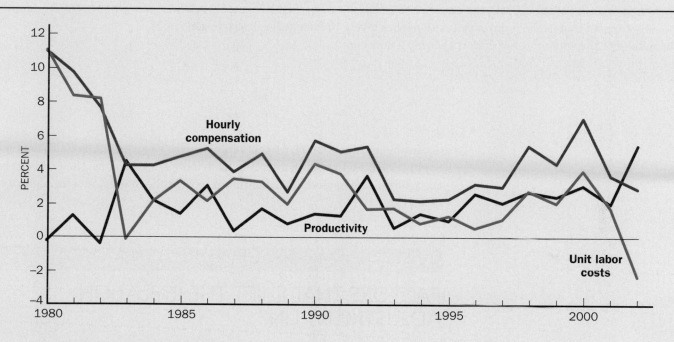

LABOR COMPENSATION, PRODUCTIVITY, AND COST

SOURCE: *Economic Report of the President* (2004).

of the stock market and a drop in business investment. By December 2000, economic conditions were weakening much more quickly than had previously been expected. As a consequence, the Fed's concerns shifted; it now needed to focus on preventing the economy from entering a recession. In a dramatic action on January 3, 2001, the FOMC cut its interest rate target by a full half percentage point, from 6.5 percent to 6 percent. The move caught most commentators by surprise, since the decision was made between regularly scheduled committee meetings. The U.S. economy officially entered a recession in March 2001. The Fed cut its interest rate target several times more during 2001, bringing the rate down below 2 percent by the end of the year. Though the recession ended in November 2001, the economy did not recover rapidly. Amid continuing weak growth, the Fed continued to reduce interest rates; at the end of 2003, they were 1 percent. By that time, real output was growing strongly again, but cyclical unemployment had failed to decline significantly.

In the middle of 2004, as economic growth recovered, the Fed's concerns again turned to preventing inflation from increasing. In June, the FOMC raised the interest rate modestly, and continued to raise the interest rate throughout the next year.

Wrap-Up

FACTORS THAT SHIFT THE INFLATION ADJUSTMENT LINE

Costs of production: an increase in firms' costs of production, such as an increase in energy prices, boosts inflation at each level of output. This rise shifts the inflation adjustment line up.

Potential GDP: an increase in potential GDP lowers inflation at each level of output. This reduction shifts the inflation adjustment line down.

Review and Practice

SUMMARY

1. Aggregate demand depends negatively on inflation. As inflation increases, the Fed or other central bank raises interest rates, thereby reducing aggregate expenditures. This negative relationship is called the aggregate demand–inflation or ADI curve.
2. At a given rate of inflation, the economy's equilibrium level of output is given by the ADI curve.
3. The slope of the ADI curve depends on the central bank's behavior. If it increases interest rates sharply when inflation rises, the impact on aggregate demand will be large and the ADI curve will be relatively flat. If the bank responds less strongly to inflation changes, the ADI curve will be steeper.
4. Changes in fiscal policy, private investment, consumption spending, or monetary policy at a given rate of inflation shift the ADI curve.
5. The slope of the ADI curve also depends on the responsiveness of investment to interest rate changes. If increases in the real interest rate have a large impact on investment and spending, the ADI curve will be relatively flat.
6. If GDP is below the full-employment level, inflation will fall, shifting the inflation adjustment line down and increasing equilibrium output. This process continues until full employment is restored.
7. If GDP is above the full-employment level, inflation will rise, shifting the inflation adjustment curve up and decreasing equilibrium output. Eventually full employment is restored.
8. Once inflation has adjusted, the economy will be at full employment. Shifts in the ADI curve affect GDP in the short run, but in the long run such shifts only affect the inflation rate.

KEY TERMS

monetary policy rule
aggregate demand–inflation (ADI) curve
inflation adjustment line
supply shocks

REVIEW QUESTIONS

1. How can the capital market be in equilibrium at different levels of aggregate output? If income is below the full-employment level, can we say whether the interest rate that balances saving and investment will be higher or lower than the equilibrium rate at full employment?
2. If the inflation rate is slow to adjust and is initially above a level at which aggregate expenditures equal potential GDP, what will be the level of output? What will happen if the aggregate demand–inflation (ADI) curve shifts to the left? To the right? If long-run potential GDP decreases? Increases?
3. How does the slope of the ADI curve depend on monetary policy?
4. If investment is not very sensitive to changes in real interest rates, will the ADI curve be relatively flat or relatively steep? Explain why.
5. If current output is below potential GDP, what will happen to the inflation rate? How does inflation adjustment move the economy back to full employment?
6. Use the ADI curve to describe some of the major episodes of the post–World War II period.

PROBLEMS

1. Use the ADI curve to describe how the economy would respond to a productivity shock that increases full-employment output. If there is no impact on the ADI curve, what will happen to output in the short run?
2. Suppose that as a result of the Fed's policy, the relationship between the real rate of interest and the inflation rate is given by the following table (all numbers are annual percentages):

Inflation	0	2	4	6	8	10
Real interest rate	3	4	5	6	7	8

The relationship between aggregate expenditures and the real interest rate is given by the following table (expenditures are in trillions of 2000 dollars):

Real interest rate	3	4	5	6	7	8
Aggregate expenditures	8.3	8	7.7	7.4	7.1	6.8

Plot the ADI curve. If inflation is 4 percent, what is the level of aggregate expenditures? Suppose investment now becomes more sensitive to interest rate changes. How would this affect the ADI curve?

3. Draw an ADI curve. As we move up and to the left on a given ADI curve, the real rate of interest increases. Explain why.

4. Suppose output is initially equal to potential GDP. Now assume the government cuts taxes (and assume government expenditures remain unchanged). How does this affect the ADI curve? What happens in the short run to equilibrium output? To unemployment? Over time, will inflation tend to rise or to fall? Explain how the adjustment of inflation works to return the output gap to zero. What happens to the real interest rate?

5. Suppose output is initially equal to potential GDP. Now assume the Fed shifts its policy rule by raising interest rates at each rate of inflation. How does this affect the ADI curve? What happens in the short run to equilibrium output? To unemployment? Over time, will infla-tion tend to rise or to fall? Explain how the adjustment of inflation works to return the output gap to zero. What happens to the real interest rate?

6. Suppose output is initially equal to potential GDP and inflation is equal to 2 percent. Suppose a new chair of the Federal Reserve is appointed. This new chair believes that average inflation should be reduced to 1 percent. To achieve this new lower rate of inflation, should the Fed shift its policy rule by raising interest rates at each rate of inflation or by lowering interest rates at each rate of inflation? What are the consequences for the output gap in the short run of the policy shift that results? What are the consequences for the output gap in the long run?

7. Go to the Federal Reserve's Web site (www.federal reserve.gov), follow the links to Monetary Policy and the FOMC, and find the press releases ("statements") from the last two FOMC meetings. Has the FOMC raised or lowered interest rates at these meetings? What reasons do the press releases give for these actions? Would you describe these actions as move-ments along a given policy rule (i.e., interest rate changes arising from a concern about inflation) or as shifts in the policy rule (i.e., policy actions in response to factors other than inflation)? If you feel the policy rule has shifted, what factors was the FOMC reacting to?

Learning Goals

In this chapter, you will learn

1 About the federal funds market and the federal funds interest rate

2 How the Federal Reserve uses its policy tools to influence the federal funds rate

3 The reasons that central banks today focus on interest rates rather than on the money supply

Chapter 14

THE FEDERAL RESERVE AND INTEREST RATES

In the previous chapter, we assigned a key role to the Federal Reserve's response to inflation in the model of short-run fluctuations. The downward slope of the aggregate demand–inflation curve reflected the Fed's policy reaction as inflation varied. What we did not discuss, though, was exactly how the Federal Reserve is able to move interest rates. Chapter 10 did examine the three basic tools of the Federal Reserve—open market operations, the discount rate, and reserve requirements—but there the focus was on how these are used to influence bank reserves and the money supply. The objective in this chapter is to explain how the Fed uses its tools to implement monetary policy by influencing market interest rates.

The Federal Funds Market

At meetings of its policymaking committee, the Federal Open Market Committee (FOMC), the Fed establishes a target interest rate. The FOMC focuses on the **federal funds rate;** and to understand what this key interest rate is and how the Fed is able to affect the economy, we need to understand the workings of a very important financial market, the **federal funds market.**

We usually think of banks lending to consumers wishing to buy cars or homes, or to firms seeking to build factories or stores or to finance their inventories. But banks also lend to each other. Often, a bank's need is very short-term; AmericaBank might borrow from NationalBank and repay the loan just one day later. Banks borrow and lend funds overnight in the federal funds market, and the interest rate on these loans is the federal funds rate. Before examining this market in detail, we will first look at the details of what the Fed does every business day to influence the level of reserves and the federal funds rate.

A DAY AT THE TRADING DESK

The Fed is able to affect the federal funds rate by controlling the supply of bank reserves in the federal funds market, and it does so by using **open market operations.** As we saw in Chapter 10, by entering the market directly to buy or sell government securities, the Fed is able to increase or decrease the supply of bank reserves. More specifically, these open market operations are conducted by the Trading Desk located at the Federal Reserve Bank of New York. In a typical workday, Trading Desk personnel gather information about reserve market conditions, evaluate this information to assess the level of reserves required to keep the funds rate at the target value set by the FOMC, and engage in actual open market operations to affect the supply of reserves.

Around 7 A.M. every morning, the staff at the Trading Desk begins the process of collecting information about financial developments. Information about factors that may affect reserves arrives from other Federal Reserve banks and is used to develop projections of reserve levels.

As the financial markets open in the United States, staff members talk with the primary dealers on government security markets and with the managers of reserve positions for the largest banks. These conversations provide the Trading Desk with information about the likely demand and supply conditions in the federal funds market. If the demand for reserves, at the current funds rate, exceeds the current supply, the funds rate will rise unless the Trading Desk increases the supply. If the supply of reserves at the current funds rate exceeds demand, the funds rate will fall unless the Trading Desk acts to reduce supply.

Reserve conditions can also be affected by the net cash flow of the U.S. Treasury, which has cash accounts with the Federal Reserve. If tax payments exceed government expenditures on a particular day, there will be a net flow of funds into the Treasury accounts at the Fed and a corresponding fall in funds held by the banking sector. This decline in total reserves in the banking sector pushes up the funds rate unless offsetting open market operations are undertaken. Treasury balances with the Fed are fairly stable from year to year, but they can fluctuate greatly from day to day. Once all this information is collected, the Trading Desk decides on its program for open market operations. A conference call then takes place between the Trading Desk, Federal Reserve Board staff in Washington, D.C., and one of the four presidents of a regional Federal Reserve bank (other than New York) currently serving as a voting member of the FOMC. This call, which lasts about fifteen minutes, reviews the plans formulated by the Trading Desk and the information about financial conditions on which it is based. Afterward, a member of the Federal Reserve Board staff prepares a brief summary report that is distributed to all the governors and reserve bank presidents.

The next step in the process is the actual execution of open market operations, which takes place at between 9:20 A.M. and 9:40 A.M. (EST) each day; a die is used to randomly choose the exact minute. The Trading Desk informs dealers of the details of the operation. Is it buying or selling? How much? Does the sale or purchase involve a repurchase (or resale) at a later date? (If the Trading Desk forecasts a change in reserve conditions that is expected to be temporary, it uses what are known as **repurchases** or **RPs,** transactions that involve, for example, a combined

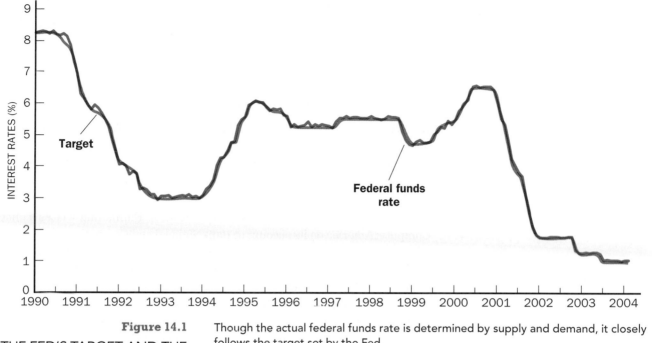

Figure 14.1

THE FED'S TARGET AND THE
FUNDS RATE

Though the actual federal funds rate is determined by supply and demand, it closely follows the target set by the Fed.

SOURCE: Federal Reserve Board.

sale of a government security and an agreement to repurchase it at a future date—perhaps the next day.)

The last major activity of the day is a 3:15 P.M. telephone meeting with representatives of the government security market dealer firms. The interchange of information helps keep the Trading Desk informed of the dealers' perceptions of developments in the financial markets.[1]

The Fed's Target for the Funds Rate The activities of the Trading Desk are designed to affect the level of the federal funds rate, which plays a critical role in the economy precisely because it is the rate that the Federal Reserve can most directly control. At each FOMC meeting, the members of the committee must decide whether the federal funds rate should remain unchanged, be raised, or be lowered. Though the FOMC decides on its *target* for the funds rate, the rate itself is determined by the interplay of demand and supply in the market for federal funds. Thus the federal funds rate can diverge from the Fed's target—but by influencing supply in the federal funds market every day through its open market operations, the Fed can keep these divergences very small, as Figure 14.1 shows.

To grasp what the Fed does and how it affects the economy, we must examine the factors that determine demand and supply in the federal funds market. We can

[1]For an excellent and detailed discussion of how monetary policy is conducted in the United States, see Ann-Marie Meulendyke, *U.S. Monetary Policy and Financial Markets* (New York: Federal Reserve Bank of New York, 1998).

then understand how the Fed is able to influence the market to make sure the equilibrium level of the federal funds rate is kept close to the target established by the FOMC.

THE DEMAND FOR RESERVES

Banks hold reserves for two reasons. First, they must satisfy the legal reserve requirement imposed by the Fed. Second, even if reserve requirements were zero (as they are in some countries), banks need to hold some reserves to meet their daily transaction needs. Deposits and withdrawals cannot be predicted perfectly each day, so a bank must make sure it has enough cash on hand in case withdrawals happen to exceed deposits. Similarly, when Desktop Publishing writes a check to ComputerAmerica on its account at BankNational and ComputerAmerica deposits that check into its account with BankUSA, BankNational must have enough reserves to transfer to BankUSA to cover the check. Of course, BankNational will receive funds as it collects on checks it has received in deposits that are from accounts in other banks, but the daily balance of payments and receipts is unpredictable. BankNational needs to ensure that it has access to reserves to make certain it can always settle its account. The reserves a bank holds over and above its required reserves are called **excess reserves.** Because reserves do not earn interest, banks try to keep excess reserves to a minimum. In 2000, for example, required reserves totaled $40 billion, while excess reserves were only just over $1 billion.

What happens if a bank discovers that it does not have enough reserves to meet its needs? It has two options. It can try to borrow reserves from the Fed. If the Fed agrees to lend reserves to the bank, the interest rate on the loan is called the **discount rate.** Unlike interest rates on other types of loans, the discount rate is not determined by conditions of demand and supply; the Fed simply sets it. In some countries, the discount rate is linked directly to market-determined rates of interest. If the discount rate is increased, banks find it more expensive to borrow from the Fed.

The second option a bank has is to borrow reserves from another bank. Just as some banks find themselves short of reserves, other banks may find they have larger reserve holdings than they need. Since the Fed does not pay interest to banks on reserve account balances, and vault cash similarly earns the bank no interest, a bank with more reserves than it needs will want to lend them out in the federal funds market. In this way, it can earn the federal funds interest rate on its extra reserves. The federal funds rate adjusts to balance supply and demand in the federal funds market.

The quantity of federal funds demanded will fall if the federal funds rate increases. A higher federal funds rate makes it more costly to borrow reserves from other banks. Each bank has an incentive to take extra care to ensure that it does not run short of reserves. Figure 14.2 shows the demand for federal funds as a downward-sloping function of the funds rate.

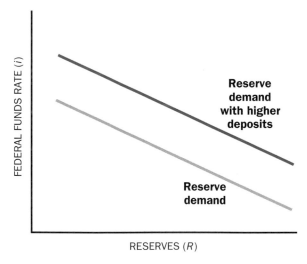

Figure 14.2

THE DEMAND FOR RESERVES IN THE FEDERAL FUNDS MARKET

When the federal funds rate increases, it becomes more expensive to borrow reserves from other banks. Banks will turn to other sources (such as the Fed) or adjust their balance sheets to reduce the likelihood that they will need to borrow in the funds market.

The position of the demand curve for reserves will depend on banks' lending opportunities and on the general volume of transactions. Suppose, for example, that a new technological innovation causes firms to want to invest more money in new equipment. To finance this investment, firms try to borrow more from banks. As the quantity of bank loans demanded increases, interest rates on bank loans will rise. Any bank that was holding excess reserves will have a greater incentive to make additional loans because the interest that can be earned has risen (recall that reserves earn no interest). Other banks may not have an excess of reserves, but to take advantage of the higher returns on loans, they will try to borrow additional reserves in the federal funds market. Consequently, the demand curve for reserves shifts to the right.

Changes in the volume of transactions through the banking system also can shift the reserve demand curve. For example, as real incomes rise, the dollar volume of transactions in the economy will rise. Banks hold reserves because they cannot predict perfectly their daily flow of deposits and withdrawals. As these flows become larger, banks will need to hold additional reserves.

THE SUPPLY OF RESERVES

The supply of reserves arises from two sources. First, some banks have borrowed reserves from the Fed. These reserves are called **borrowed reserves.** As the federal funds rate increases, it becomes more expensive to obtain funds from other banks in the federal funds market, and banks instead borrow more from the Fed. If the discount rate is increased, borrowing from the Fed becomes more expensive and borrowed reserves fall. Such borrowing is not the main source of reserves, however. In 2000, borrowed reserves accounted for only $400 million out of a total stock of reserves equal to about $40 billion. The difference between **total reserves** and borrowed reserves is called **nonborrowed reserves.** The supply of nonborrowed reserves is under the Fed's immediate control, and it is by adjusting the supply of nonborrowed reserves that the Fed affects the funds rate.

OPEN MARKET OPERATIONS

In Chapter 10, we saw that open market operations are the Fed's most important tool for influencing the economy. Whenever the Fed buys government securities from the private sector in an open market purchase, it pays for them by simply creating nonborrowed reserves; whenever it sells government securities to the private sector, the level of nonborrowed reserves held by the banking sector is reduced. If the Fed wishes to increase nonborrowed reserves, it undertakes an open market purchase. If it wants to reduce nonborrowed reserves, it undertakes an open market sale.

Through these open market operations, the Fed can control the *total* supply of reserves. For example, suppose banks increase their borrowing from the Fed so that the level of borrowed reserves rises. The Fed can sell government securities to reduce the supply of nonborrowed reserves if it wants to keep total reserves from

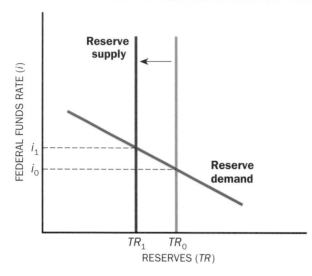

Figure 14.3

THE SUPPLY OF RESERVES AND EQUILIBRIUM IN THE FEDERAL FUNDS MARKET

The total supply of reserves consists of borrowed and nonborrowed reserves. The total reserves supply schedule is drawn as a vertical line. An open market sale decreases the total supply of reserves, shifting the reserve supply curve from TR_0 to TR_1.

The equilibrium federal funds rate is determined at the intersection of reserve demand and reserve supply. If the initial equilibrium funds rate is i_0 and the Fed wishes to increase the funds rate to i_1, it reduces the stock of nonborrowed reserves, shifting the supply schedule to the left until the equilibrium funds rate is i_1.

changing. Because the Fed, if it chooses, can always offset any change in borrowed reserves by adjusting nonborrowed reserves, we can simplify the situation by treating the supply of *total reserves,* the sum of borrowed and nonborrowed reserves, as controlled directly by the Fed. In Figure 14.3, the stock of total reserves set by the Fed is shown as a vertical line, labeled TR_0. An open market sale decreases total reserves, shifting the supply to TR_1.

EQUILIBRIUM IN THE FEDERAL FUNDS MARKET

We can now see how the Fed is able to affect the value of the funds rate through its control of the stock of total reserves. Figure 14.3 depicts the quantity of reserves demanded as depending negatively on the funds rate. Suppose the Fed's target for the federal funds rate is i_0. To achieve this target, the Fed must ensure that the funds market clears at the interest rate i_0, the point where the quantity of reserves supplied and the quantity demanded are equal. For this to occur, the level of total reserves the Fed will need to supply is TR_0. At this level, the supply curve for total reserves intersects the demand curve at the desired interest rate i_0.

Now, assume the Fed decides to increase its target for the funds rate (as it did in mid-2004). If the new target is i_1, the Fed must reduce reserve supply to TR_1. By engaging in open market sales, the Fed can reduce the supply of total reserves from TR_0 to TR_1. The new equilibrium funds rate is i_1, the desired target value. The funds rate is determined by supply and demand in the funds market, but by adjusting the supply of reserves, the Fed is able to keep the funds rate equal to its target.

As conditions change in the economy, the quantity of reserves demanded at each funds rate may shift. If its target for the funds rate is unchanged, the Fed has to adjust total reserves in response to any shifts in the demand curve for reserves. For instance, a change in bank deposits will shift the demand curve for reserves. The consequences of an increase in deposits that increases banks' demand for reserves are depicted in Figure 14.4. Initially, the funds market is in equilibrium with the funds rate at i_0. If the Fed does nothing, a rightward shift in the demand for reserves will push the funds rate up to i_1. To prevent this from happening, and to keep the funds rate at its target value i_0, the Fed must increase the supply of nonborrowed reserves through an open market purchase, thereby shifting the total reserve supply curve to the right. In this way, the Fed can respond to shifts in reserve demand and keep the funds rate equal to its target.

The demand for reserves at each funds rate will also shift if the Fed changes the required reserve ratio. Suppose the Fed increases the reserve ratio. At each level of deposits, banks must now hold a higher level of reserves. The reserve demand curve therefore shifts to the right. If the Fed keeps total reserves constant, the equilibrium funds rate rises. If the Fed wishes to prevent the funds rate from changing, it needs to engage in an open market purchase to increase the total reserve supply.

These shifts in the reserve demand curve illustrate another important consequence of a monetary policy that targets the funds rate. The rightward shift of the reserve demand curve shown in Figure 14.4 led to an equal shift in reserve supply to keep the funds rate from changing. While the funds rate remained constant, the *quantity of reserves* rose, from TR_0 to TR_1. Through the money multiplier process discussed in Chapter 10, this rise in reserves will increase the supply of money.

When monetary policy is implemented through control of the federal funds rate, shifts in the quantity of reserves demand are accommodated automatically. If banks' demand for reserves at each federal funds rate were to increase, the Fed would automatically allow the supply of reserves to rise so that the funds rate would not be affected.

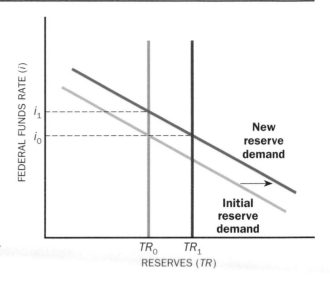

Figure 14.4

THE EFFECT OF AN INCREASE IN THE QUANTITY OF RESERVES DEMANDED

Suppose the demand curve for reserves shifts rightward. If the Fed leaves the stock of nonborrowed reserves unchanged, the funds rate rises to i_1, where reserve demand and reserve supply are again equal. If the Fed wishes to keep the funds rate at i_0, it increases nonborrowed reserves in order to shift the supply schedule to the right by an amount equal to the shift in demand. Total reserves rise from TR_0 to TR_1.

THE FEDERAL FUNDS MARKET

1. The federal funds rate is determined by supply and demand in the federal funds market.
2. The Fed is able to keep the funds rate equal to the target set by the FOMC by using open market operations to control the supply of total reserves.

Monetary Policy Operating Procedures

The actual manner in which a central bank implements monetary policy is often called the monetary authority's **operating procedures.** In the case of the Fed, the federal funds rate is the key interest rate used to implement monetary policy. Its policy goals and assessment of the economy led the FOMC to set a target for the funds rate. The Trading Desk at the Federal Reserve Bank of New York conducts the actual open market operations required to keep the funds rate equal to the target established by the FOMC. Implementing monetary policy in this fashion is often called an *interest rate operating procedure.*

An interest rate procedure is not the only way monetary policy can be implemented, and over the course of the past twenty-five years, the Fed has changed its operating procedures several times. The main alternative to an interest rate procedure is a *money supply operating procedure* that focuses on controlling a quantity—either a reserve quantity such as total reserves or a monetary aggregate such as

M1 (the total of currency, traveler's checks, and checking accounts). Rather than letting reserve supply adjust automatically to achieve an interest rate target, the Fed could decide on a target for the money supply or the quantity of reserves, letting the funds rate adjust automatically to clear the federal funds market.

Under a money supply procedure, just as under an interest rate procedure, monetary policy discussions start with an assessment of the state of the economy and a determination of what changes in policy are needed, if any, to achieve the agreed-on goals. Once the path for the money supply consistent with those goals of policy is determined, open market operations are conducted to supply a level of reserves that leads to the desired level of the money stock.

During the 1970s, many economists argued that the Fed should focus on controlling the money supply. They had two reasons. First, inflation was then the primary policy problem. Our full-employment model shows that the average rate of inflation and the average rate of money growth are related; if the monetary authority controls money growth, it can control inflation. Second, economists at the time saw a tight link between a measure of the money supply such as M1 and total dollar GDP. By controlling M1, the argument went, the Fed could control total aggregate income. In the 1980s, however, the tight link between M1 and nominal GDP appeared to break down, making a money supply operating procedure less useful for implementing monetary policy.

INFLATION, MONEY SUPPLY, AND THE NOMINAL RATE OF INTEREST

Because the link between money and nominal GDP became unstable in many countries, most central banks now implement monetary policy by setting a target interest rate. But such policies can lead to problems when inflation rises, as it did in the late 1960s. The full-employment model tells us that increases in the money supply provide the fuel for inflation. Under an interest rate policy, an initial increase in inflation can lead to automatic increases in the money supply that allow the inflation to continue.

Suppose prices have been stable in the economy—an inflation rate of zero. Then, suppose inflation rises to 5 percent. As prices rise, the dollar value of transactions in the economy increases. A sandwich that costs $5.00 one year will cost 5 percent more annually, or $5.25 after one year, $5.51 after two years, and $8.14 after ten years. People will want to hold, on average, about 5 percent more money each year, both as cash for everyday transactions and in their checking accounts. Thus the demand for money grows.

Because the volume of transactions through the banking system has increased, banks will need to hold more reserves to balance their payment flows. This increase in the demand for reserves at each value of the funds rate shifts the reserve demand curve to the right. If its target for the funds rate is kept unchanged, the Fed will need to increase the supply of reserves over time, allowing the money supply to rise with the increased demand for money. From our money multiplier analysis, we know that by allowing the supply of reserves to increase, the Fed also ensures that the quantity of money increases. *When the monetary authority tries to keep the nominal interest rate constant, the quantity of money automatically increases as prices rise. Inflation causes the money supply to automatically increase, further fueling and sustaining the inflation.*

In the full-employment model, we assumed that government controlled the supply of money directly. Because full-employment output is determined by such factors as labor supply, the capital stock, and the economy's technology, changes in the money supply led to proportional changes in the price level (see Chapter 10). When the central bank adjusts the reserve supply to achieve an interest rate target, the supply of money adjusts in line with prices. To halt the rise in inflation, the central bank must raise its target interest rate to prevent the ongoing expansion of the money supply. When inflation rose to high levels in the 1970s, central banks therefore shifted from interest rate operating procedures to procedures that focused more directly on controlling the money supply.

Review and Practice

SUMMARY

1. The federal funds market is the market in which banks can borrow or lend reserves.
2. The federal funds rate, which is the interest rate on overnight interbank loans, adjusts to balance the supply and demand for reserves.
3. The Federal Reserve can affect the market for reserves by changing the reserve requirement, by changing the discount rate, or by open market operations.
4. Open market operations are the chief tool used by the Fed to affect the market for reserves. By controlling the supply of reserves, they enable the Fed to achieve the target for the federal funds rate set by the FOMC.
5. Under a money supply operating procedure, open market operations can be used to achieve a target for the money supply. Because the speed with which money circulates in the economy (and therefore the optimal money supply) has become less predictable in recent years, most central banks implement policy by setting the nominal interest rate, an interest rate operating procedure.

KEY TERMS

federal funds rate
federal funds market
open market operations
repurchases (RPs)
excess reserves
discount rate
borrowed reserves
total reserves
nonborrowed reserves
operating procedures

REVIEW QUESTIONS

1. Why do nonborrowed reserves fall if the Fed engages in an open market sale? Why do they rise if the Fed engages in an open market purchase?

2. Why do borrowed reserves fall if the Fed raises the discount rate? Why do they rise if the federal funds rate increases?
3. If the FOMC raises its target for the federal funds rate, will the Fed need to increase or to decrease the supply of reserves? Will it need to engage in an open market purchase or a sale to accomplish this?
4. Why does the Fed increase the supply of reserves when prices rise if it is targeting the federal funds rate? What would happen to the funds rate if prices rose and the Fed held the supply of reserves fixed?

PROBLEMS

1. Why does an open market purchase increase the supply of reserves in the banking sector?
2. Using a supply and demand diagram of the federal funds market, show how an increase in reserve requirements would affect the equilibrium federal funds rate.
3. Suppose the economy's income falls, reducing the demand for money. If the Fed keeps its target for the funds rate constant, what happens to reserve demand and the supply of reserves? If instead the Fed keeps the supply of reserves constant, what happens to the funds rate?
4. In 1999, there was broad concern about the Y2K computer problem. Banks, and the Fed, predicted that many people would want to hold additional cash in case software glitches blocked access to their bank accounts on January 1, 2000. Use a money multiplier analysis (see Chapter 10) to predict what happens to deposits and the money supply if people increase their holdings of cash and the Fed attempts to keep the federal funds rate constant. What are the consequences for the money supply of the increased demand for cash?
5. Does money growth cause inflation, or does inflation cause money growth? Discuss. How does your answer depend on the behavior of the Fed?

Learning Goals

In this chapter, you will learn

1 Modern views of the macro-economic trade-offs that policymakers face

2 The roles of automatic stabilizers and discretionary policy

3 The monetary policy rule and what it depends on

4 How monetary and fiscal policies differ in their impacts on the economy

Chapter 15

THE ROLE OF MACROECONOMIC POLICY

Economic policy debates have always been at the core of macroeconomics. After all, macroeconomics began as an attempt to understand the causes of the Great Depression of the 1930s and to formulate government policies that might end it. Discussions in the United States in recent years have been dominated by the debate over job creation after the 2001 recession, the huge federal government deficits and their possible impact on economic growth, and the implications of the trade deficit.

Economies are constantly buffeted by shocks and disturbances—the stock market collapse in 2000; the financial crises in Asia, Europe, and Latin America in the late 1990s; large swings in the federal budget deficit; new technological innovations transforming many sectors of the economy—that have the potential to create recessions or ignite inflation. In the face of these disturbances, policymakers must try to ensure that the economy continues to operate at potential GDP while inflation remains low and stable.

In this chapter, we will examine the role of both monetary and fiscal policy in affecting the economy in the short run. Chapters 11 to 13 have provided a framework for understanding the impact of government on the economy. In those chapters, the analysis treated policy in isolation—explaining how a change in fiscal or monetary policy affected the economy. But macroeconomic policy decisions are not taken in isolation—governments use monetary and fiscal policy to try to stabilize the economy, and this role of macroeconomic policy is the topic of the present chapter.

would be expected to produce). To counteract these forces, President Lyndon Johnson imposed a 10 percent income tax surcharge in 1968; the hope was that this tax increase would cause households to scale back their consumption spending, thereby helping to offset the expansion in demand caused by the increased government spending. Unfortunately, the policy did not have the full effect that its designers had sought—because the tax surcharge was temporary, lasting only one year, most households had little reason to significantly change their behavior.

In the United States, discretionary fiscal policy is usually viewed as very slow to respond. As is discussed in greater detail at the end of this chapter, there are inevitably delays both in recognizing a problem and—more significantly—in drafting and passing legislation to address it. Congress rarely works swiftly. As a result of these lags in implementation, at least for the United States, fiscal policy operates mainly through automatic stabilizers in helping to stabilize the economy. When the economy enters a recession, tax revenues decline automatically as incomes fall. And as incomes and employment levels fall, some government expenditure programs, such as unemployment insurance, automatically increase. These responses help stabilize the disposable income and consumption spending of households.

Using Discretionary Fiscal Policy to Combat a Recession When the economy goes into a recession, the role of fiscal policy is usually hotly debated; despite their practical difficulties as tools to fine-tune the economy, discretionary policy actions are frequently proposed. During 1990 and 1991, the U.S. economy was caught in recession, and "It's the economy, stupid" was one of the most memorable lines from Bill Clinton's successful 1992 campaign against the incumbent president, George H. W. Bush. Clinton argued for a more active fiscal response to help end the recession, although by the time he took office, the economy was already expanding and the recession was clearly over.

In 2001, soon after President George W. Bush took office, the U.S. economy entered a recession, and the president used the emerging signs of an economic slowdown to push a tax cut through Congress. He argued that an expansionary fiscal policy was needed because of the recession. We can use the ADI framework to analyze the impact of a fiscal expansion during a recession.

Internet Connection

THE ECONOMIC REPORT OF THE PRESIDENT

Every February, the president's Council of Economic Advisors issues the *Economic Report of the President*. This report discusses the state of the economy and developments in fiscal policy. As well as providing a wealth of data on the economy, each chapter of the report deals with a current policy debate. The latest report can be found at www.gpo access.gov/eop/index.html.

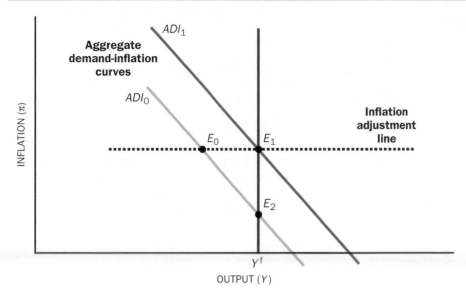

Figure 15.2

USING FISCAL POLICY TO END A RECESSION

The initial short-run equilibrium is at E_0, with the economy in recession. An expansionary fiscal policy—an increase in government purchases or a tax cut—would shift the ADI curve to the right and increase equilibrium output. If the fiscal stimulus can be designed to move the ADI curve to ADI_1, full employment would be restored at E_1. In the absence of any policy actions, full employment would eventually be restored as inflation declined, and the economy would be at E_2. If the adjustment of inflation is slow, the economy would experience a long period of high unemployment as it moves to E_2.

Figure 15.2 shows the economy in a recession at point E_0. Output is below the full-employment level Y^f. The decline in output, with the associated rise in cyclical unemployment, has resulted from a leftward shift in the ADI curve.

An expansionary fiscal policy can end a recession and eliminate the cyclical unemployment. Increasing government purchases or cutting taxes raises aggregate expenditures at each inflation rate, shifting the ADI curve to the right. If the size of the fiscal policy is judged correctly, the ADI curve can be shifted to ADI_1, moving the economy's short-run equilibrium back to full employment.

If no policy action were taken, the economy would eventually return to full employment at E_2. With high cyclical unemployment, inflation will tend to fall, shifting the inflation adjustment line down (not shown in the figure). As inflation declines, the Fed lowers the interest rate to stimulate aggregate expenditures, causing output to begin to increase. This process continues until full employment is restored at a lower rate of inflation at point E_2 in the figure.

THE FULL-EMPLOYMENT DEFICIT

Because tax revenues rise and fall with income, the government's surplus or deficit also varies with income. As the economy expands and tax revenues increase, the

International Perspective
FISCAL TRANSFERS

The role of fiscal policy and automatic stabilizers has been a topic of debate within the twelve European countries that all use the euro as their currency. There, the concern is the lack of automatic fiscal stabilizers that can help mitigate economic fluctuations within the euro zone when the economies of some members are in recession while those of others are booming.

The members of the European Economic and Monetary Union (EMU) that use the euro share a single monetary policy, conducted by the European Central Bank (ECB) in Frankfurt. The ECB bases that policy on overall economic conditions in the union, but what is right for the union might not be the best policy for individual countries within the union. For example, suppose Germany, France, and Italy, the three biggest economies in the union, are experiencing an economic boom, while Portugal is in a recession. The ECB might raise interest rates to dampen the boom in Germany, France, and Italy, but this action would make the Portuguese recession even worse. Because the ECB affects interest rates for the whole union, its policy cannot be tailored to meet the individual needs of each member country.

But how is this different from the situation in the United States, with fifty individual states? The Fed bases its policy on conditions in the entire country. Some states might be in recession and therefore would like the Fed's policy to be more expansionary, while for others, in a booming economy, a tighter policy would be better.

What the United States has, and Europe lacks, is a federal fiscal system that automatically helps stabilize the overall economy. If one state is in a recession, federal tax payments from that state fall and federal transfer payments to the state increase. Such transfers promote demand in that state. The federal system serves to shift income from expanding states to contracting states, helping to dampen demand in

the booming states while helping to offset the recession in the contracting states.

No such fiscal transfers exist among the member countries of the EMU. Though the twelve members have a common monetary policy, their fiscal policies are not unified. If the economy of Germany is booming and Portugal's economy is in a slump, the increased tax payments generated by rising Germany incomes are not used to provide increased fiscal transfers to Portugal.

The headquarters for the European Central Bank

surplus will expand (or the deficit will shrink). When the economy goes into a recession, tax revenues fall, decreasing the surplus (or increasing the deficit). These automatic changes in the surplus or deficit show the effects of taxes' role as an automatic stabilizer. But how can we determine what part of, say, a larger deficit has resulted from a discretionary increase in government purchases rather than from a decline in overall economic activity?

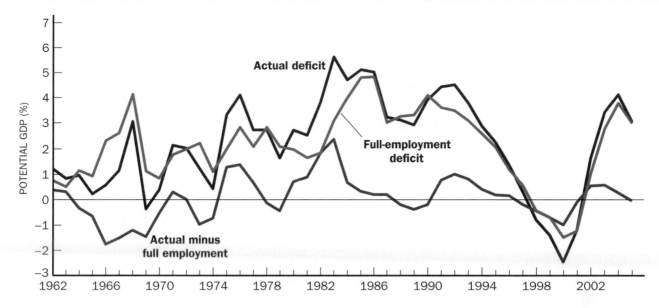

Figure 15.3

ACTUAL AND
FULL-EMPLOYMENT DEFICITS

The government's deficit fluctuates with movements in GDP. The full-employment deficit provides an estimate of what the deficit would be if the economy were at full employment—that is, with the cyclical component of the deficit removed. The figure shows the difference between the actual and full-employment deficits (blue line). When cyclical unemployment is positive, the actual deficit exceeds the full-employment deficit.

SOURCE: Congressional Budget Office.

One way to separate out the effects of automatic stabilizers from these active changes in policy is to focus on the **full-employment deficit**—what the deficit would have been had the economy been operating at full employment. The full-employment deficit adjusts for the stage of the business cycle; it adjusts for the changes in taxes and spending that vary over the business cycles. For instance, in a recession when incomes fall, the actual deficit increases because tax revenues decline with the drop in income. The full-employment deficit corrects for this cyclical effect on taxes by calculating what the deficit would be if the economy had not gone into a recession. It changes, therefore, only when there are discretionary changes in taxes or spending and gives a better measure of the impact of discretionary fiscal policy actions.

If the economy booms and tax revenues swell, the full-employment deficit will be greater than the actual deficit; if the economy goes into a recession and tax revenues fall, the full-employment deficit will be less than the actual deficit. Most economists view the government as fiscally responsible so long as there is no deficit when the economy is at full employment—that is, the full-employment deficit should be zero. Balancing the budget at full employment would allow automatic stabilizers to work during business cycle fluctuations. Figure 15.3 shows the actual U.S. federal deficit and an estimate of the full-employment deficit. In 2003 (the last year shown), cyclical unemployment was almost zero, so the full-employment deficit and the actual deficit were equal.

FISCAL POLICY

Automatic stabilizers increase expenditures and reduce taxes automatically as the economy goes into a recession. They act to reduce the impact of economic shocks on GDP by stabilizing aggregate expenditures.

The full-employment deficit adjusts for the stage of the business cycle and gives a measure of what the deficit (or surplus) would be if the economy were at full employment. It provides a clearer picture of the effects of discretionary fiscal policy actions.

Monetary Policy

Monetary policy affects the level of nominal interest rates, the money supply, and average inflation in the economy. Decisions by the Federal Reserve about interest rates are a major focus of participants in the financial market and of news reports. Speeches by the chair of the Federal Reserve Board—from 1987 until January 2006, Alan Greenspan—are closely examined for hints about possible interest rate changes, and speculation can reach a fever pitch when the Federal Open Market Committee (FOMC) meets to decide on policy.

Some aspects of monetary policy are similar to automatic stabilizers as they work to keep the economy more stable. But like fiscal policy, monetary policy has also been used actively to achieve macroeconomic goals.

We have already mentioned one common behavior of the Fed in our discussion of the aggregate demand–inflation curve. As inflation increases, the Fed, like other central banks in major industrialized economies, raises the nominal interest rate. And the nominal rate is raised enough so that the real interest rate rises. This normal reaction works exactly as does an automatic stabilizer when the economy expands above potential and inflation starts to rise. Raising the interest rate curtails aggregate spending and helps stabilize the economy at its potential. A critical issue in the design of good monetary policy is determining how large such an increase should be. The strength of this response to an increase in inflation significantly affects the slope of the ADI curve.

BEHIND THE ADI CURVE—THE ROLE OF MONETARY POLICY

When the ADI curve was introduced in Chapter 13, we saw that as inflation increases in the short run, the Fed seeks to raise the real rate of interest. This increase lowers aggregate expenditures and equilibrium output. Now it is time to take a closer look at the role of monetary policy in affecting the shape and position of the ADI curve.

Conducting Monetary Policy The FOMC meets approximately every six weeks to decide on monetary policy. The central banks in most industrial economies conduct monetary policy by setting a target for a nominal interest rate; in the case of the United States, the target is the federal funds rate, the rate on overnight bank-to-bank loans. Chapter 14 explained how the Fed uses its control of bank reserves to achieve that target. At the close of each FOMC meeting, a vote is taken on whether to raise, lower, or leave unchanged the interest rate target, and any change is immediately announced in a press release. Occasionally, the FOMC will change its target between meetings, as it did on January 3, 2001, in response to mounting evidence that the economy was slowing down and an interest rate cut was necessary.

Figure 15.4 shows the Fed's target for the funds rate, the actual funds rate, and the prime interest rate—that is, the interest rate charged on loans to banks' best customers. Two facts stand out. First, the Fed is extremely successful in achieving its target, which in the figure is almost indistinguishable from the actual funds rate. Our focus here is not on how this is done—open market operations and their implications for the supply of reserves and of money were discussed in Chapter 14—but on the consequences of changes in interest rates for the economy and on the factors that influence the Fed in setting its target.

The second point illustrated by the figure is that the prime interest rate moves in tandem with the funds rate. The prime rate is always higher, reflecting the greater risk of business loans. But whenever the funds rate is raised or lowered, the prime rate also rises or falls. If an increase in the funds rate increases the real interest

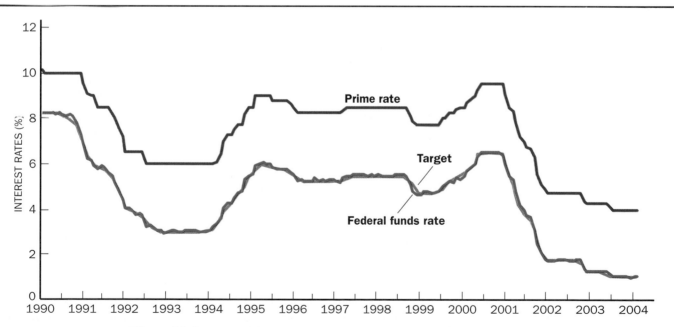

Figure 15.4

THE FED'S TARGET, THE FUNDS RATE, AND THE PRIME RATE

Though the actual funds rate is determined by supply and demand, it closely follows the target set by the Fed. The prime interest rate is the rate that banks charge on loans to their best business customers. It also moves closely with changes in the Fed's target for the funds rate.

SOURCE: Federal Reserve Board.

rate, borrowing will become more costly: the real cost of auto loans, mortgage interest rates, and commercial loans to firms will increase. As credit becomes more costly, households and firms will scale back their spending plans.

Because changes in the funds rate affect the entire range of market interest rates, we simplified the discussion in previous chapters by assuming that the Fed sets the level of nominal interest rates. In Chapter 14, we learned that other approaches to implementing monetary policy are also used. For example, between 1979 and 1985, the Fed often focused more closely on various measures of the money supply than on the funds rate. Since 1985, however, setting a target for the funds rate has been the Fed's main tool of monetary policy. Chapter 14 explained *how* the Fed influences interest rates; what we need to examine now is *why* the Fed decides to raise or lower market interest rates. And to do that, we must examine the goals of monetary policy.

Case in Point

ANNOUNCING THE FED'S DECISIONS

After each FOMC meeting, any policy decisions are conveyed to the Federal Reserve Bank of New York for implementation. In recent years, these directives have specified the average value for the federal funds rate that the FOMC believes is consistent with its policy objectives. The FOMC also issues a press release that summarizes any policy actions taken during the meeting and offers an assessment of economic conditions. For example, the press release of August 10, 2004, begins

> The Federal Open Market Committee decided today to raise its target for the federal funds rate by 25 basis points [i.e., 1/4 of a percentage point] to 1-1/2 percent.

> The Committee believes that, even after this action, the stance of monetary policy remains accommodative and, coupled with robust underlying growth in productivity, is providing ongoing support to economic activity. In recent months, output growth has moderated and the pace of improvement in labor market conditions has slowed. This softness likely owes importantly to the substantial rise in energy prices. The economy nevertheless appears poised to resume a stronger pace of expansion going forward. Inflation has been somewhat elevated this year, though a portion of the rise in prices seems to reflect transitory factors.

The Committee perceives the upside and downside risks to the attainment of both sustainable growth and price stability for the next few quarters are roughly equal. With underlying inflation still expected to be relatively low, the Committee believes that policy accommodation can be removed at a pace that is likely to be measured. Nonetheless, the Committee will respond to changes in economic prospects as needed to fulfill its obligation to maintain price stability.

REAL INTEREST RATES AND NOMINAL INTEREST RATES

To understand the links between the Fed's decisions and real output and inflation, we must start by recalling an important distinction between *real interest rates* and *nominal interest rates*. The nominal, or market, interest rate gives the percentage rate of return on a deposit, loan, or financial asset *without taking into account the effects of inflation*. When prices are rising, the value of a dollar is falling since each dollar will buy fewer and fewer goods and services over time. The dollars a borrower repays are worth less than the dollars that were borrowed. When prices are falling, the value of a dollar is rising since each dollar will buy more and more goods and services over time. The dollars a borrower repays are then worth more than the dollars that were borrowed. The nominal interest rate as a measure of the cost of a loan or the rate of return on a financial asset fails to correct for these changes in the value of money.

New York Stock Exchange traders listen to the results of a recent FOMC meeting.

The real rate of interest is the percentage return on a deposit, loan, or other financial asset *after the effects of inflation are taken into account*. It represents the change in the real purchasing power that the lender receives. If the market rate of interest is 6 percent and inflation is 2 percent, the real interest rate is 4 percent; 2 percentage points of the 6 percent nominal interest rate represent compensation for the falling value of the dollar. The relationship between the real rate of interest, the nominal rate of interest, and inflation[3] is given by

nominal rate of interest = real rate of interest + inflation.

Figure 15.5 shows the nominal federal funds rate, the inflation rate, and the nominal funds rate minus the inflation rate as a measure of the real interest rate. Two points are worth noting. First, the level of nominal and real interest rates can differ significantly. In the 1970s, for instance, the nominal funds rate was high, yet the real rate was negative for most of the decade. In the 1990s, the nominal funds rate was lower than it had been in the 1970s, yet the real rate was higher. Second, the average level of the funds rate moves closely with inflation. Periods of high inflation typically are associated with a high nominal interest rate; periods of low inflation typically are associated with a low nominal rate.

Given the definition of the nominal interest rate, it is easy to understand why nominal interest rates are high when inflation is high. Both borrowers and lenders

---

[3]We are ignoring taxes on interest income here.

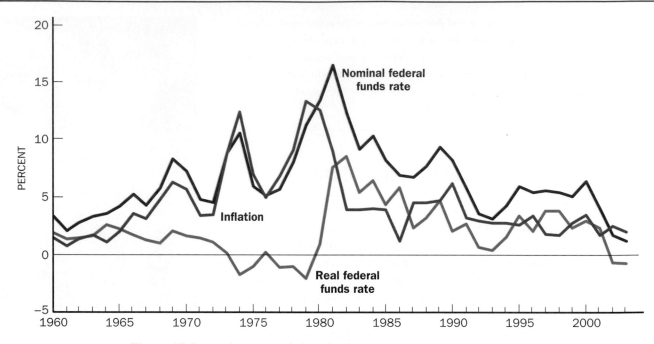

Figure 15.5

NOMINAL AND REAL
FEDERAL FUNDS RATES

The nominal federal funds rate is the market interest rate most directly influenced by Federal Reserve policy. The major channel through which policy has its effects is the real federal funds interest rate (the market rate adjusted for inflation). During the 1970s, the funds rate was high, but so was inflation. Consequently, the real interest rate was low, and at times even negative.

SOURCE: *Economic Report of the President* (2004).

care about the real interest rate, which determines the purchasing power they must give up to borrow or the purchasing power they receive by making the loan. If inflation rises, lenders demand and borrowers are willing to pay a higher market interest rate. And a market interest rate of 10 percent with inflation equal to 6 percent represents the same real interest rate as a market rate of 5 percent with inflation of 1 percent. The interest rates we hear or read about are nominal; they are not adjusted to take into account changes in the value of money. Economic decisions—decisions about how much to consume or save, whether to invest in a new plant, or whether to buy a new home—are based on real interest rates.

THE CENTRAL BANK POLICY RULE

In setting its nominal interest rate target, the Fed attempts to influence the level of aggregate expenditures. When inflation rises, or when it expects inflation to rise, the Fed raises the nominal interest rate. But because the spending plans of households and firms depend on the real interest rate, the Fed must raise the nominal interest rate enough to ensure that the real interest rate rises. When it does so, aggregate expenditures fall, lowering equilibrium output and reducing the upward pressure on prices. Similarly, if the economy is entering a recession and inflation is falling, the Fed will reduce the nominal interest rate to lower the real interest rate, stimulate aggregate expenditures, expand output, and moderate the recession.

We illustrate the connection between inflation and the nominal interest rate the central bank sets in panel A of Figure 15.6. The real interest rate is the nominal rate minus inflation, so the nominal interest rate must rise proportionally more than increases in inflation to ensure that the real interest rate increases.[4] This means that the slope of the line in the figure is greater than 1. If the inflation rate increases from π_0 to π_1, the nominal interest rate is raised from i_0 to i_1. The change in the nominal interest rate, i_1 to i_0, is greater than the change in the rate of inflation, π_1 to π_0.

The relationship between inflation and the interest rate set by the central bank is an example of the type of **monetary policy rule** we introduced in Chapter 13. A policy rule is just a description of how the central bank behaves. We have assumed that the policy rule takes a very simple form: the central bank changes the nominal interest rate in response to changes in inflation. We will discuss later in this chapter how the central bank may respond to other macroeconomic variables. Even our simple rule, though, captures important aspects of actual Fed behavior over the past twenty years. It implies that the real rate of interest increases as inflation rises, as shown in panel B of Figure 15.6. Conversely, a fall in inflation leads to a decline in the real interest rate.

Because the Fed sets a target for the nominal federal funds interest rate, we have discussed monetary policy in terms of its effects on interest rates. The relationships shown in panel B would also arise if the central bank instead targeted the money supply. Such was the case from 1979 until 1984, while Paul Volcker was chair of the Federal Reserve; policy focused on target growth rates for measures of bank reserves and the money supply. As an increase in the inflation rate drives prices up faster, individuals will need more money on hand to carry out transactions. The demand for money, including bank deposits, rises. Banks will need to hold more reserves—at each level of the federal funds rate, the demand for reserves shifts up. If the Fed holds the supply of reserves constant, the funds rate will rise. So the policy rule represented in Figure 15.6 would also hold under a policy focused on controlling money supply.

The policy rule illustrates how the Fed responds to inflation. If the Fed reacts to other factors, the line representing the policy rule will shift. For example, suppose at a given rate of inflation the Fed decides to lower interest rates, as it did in January 2001 to offset rising unemployment. This action would shift the entire policy rule downward; at each rate of inflation, the nominal (and real) interest rate would therefore be lower.

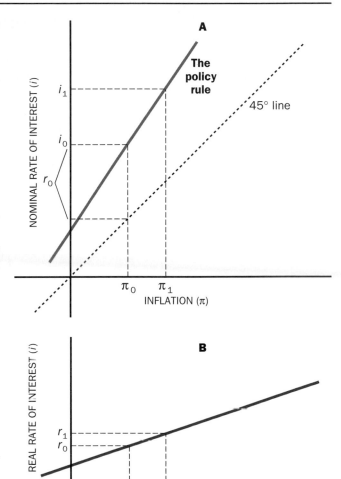

Figure 15.6

INTEREST RATES AND INFLATION: THE FED'S POLICY RULE

To ensure that the real interest rate increases when inflation rises, the Fed must raise the nominal interest rate more than proportionally with an increase in inflation. In panel A, at an inflation rate of π_0, the central bank sets the nominal rate equal to i_0; the real rate of interest is $r_0 = i_0 - \pi_0$. If inflation increases to π_1, the nominal interest rate increases to i_1. This increase is greater than the increase in inflation, so the real rate, shown in panel B, increases as inflation rises.

---

[4]If nominal interest income is taxed, the nominal rate will need to rise proportionally more than inflation to ensure that the real, after-tax interest rate rises.

Do Central Banks Respond Only to Inflation? We have assumed that the central bank adjusts policy when inflation changes. This convenient simplification captures an important aspect of how many major central banks conduct policy today. It helps explain why the Fed did not initially raise interest rates as the unemployment rate fell to very low levels in the late 1990s—as long as inflation seemed stable, the Fed did not alter its policy.

But few central banks (if any!) react *only* to inflation. The goals of monetary policy are low, stable inflation *and* overall economic stability and growth. If the economy enters a recession, central banks normally lower interest rates to help stimulate aggregate expenditures and moderate the rise in unemployment. That the Fed cannot simply look at inflation is illustrated by two recent cases in point.

Thinking Like an Economist

REAL VALUES MATTER FOR INCENTIVES

Economists believe that to understand how individuals and firms behave, we should assume they make rational decisions. In making decisions, individuals and firms respond to incentives. But to affect decisions, a change in incentives has to be a *real* change—it has to reflect an actual alteration in the trade-offs the decision maker faces. A worker will thus be concerned with how much her wages can purchase—the real value of wages, not simply their amount in terms of dollars. If a worker's nominal wage rises by 10 percent but prices also rise by 10 percent, her incentive to supply labor is unaffected. Supplying an extra hour of labor increases her nominal income by more than before, but it yields the same real income as it did before prices and wages rose. The incentive to work is unchanged.

Similarly, households and firms will base decisions about borrowing and investing on the *real* costs of borrowing and the *real* returns to investing, and the riskiness associated with each. In deciding whether to borrow to finance a car, an individual must weigh the consumption of other goods and services that must be given up in order to make that purchase. If the interest rate on the car loan is 12 percent, but he expects prices and his nominal income to be rising at 3 percent each year because of inflation, then the dollars he uses each year to pay the interest on the loan will be worth 3 percent less than the year before. The effective real interest rate on the loan is 9 percent. Now suppose that when he took out the car loan, inflation had been zero rather than 3 percent per year. His incentive to borrow would be unaffected if the interest rate on the loan fell to 9 percent: though he would pay fewer dollars each year, those dollars would be worth more since there is no inflation. The real cost is the same; so if nothing else has changed, the incentives to borrow are also unchanged.

The riskiness of an investment also depends on inflation. Suppose you invest in a bond that will pay you 8 percent interest for the next six years. It may seem to be riskless—after all, you know you will receive 8 percent on your investment. But if inflation turns out to average 2 percent, your real return will only be 6 percent; and if inflation averages 8 percent, your real return will be zero! Because there is always some uncertainty about future inflation, real returns will be uncertain even when the nominal rate of return is fixed.

Economic decisions are based on the real interest rate, not the nominal interest rate. Changes in the real interest rate alter individuals' incentives to act.

THE INTEREST RATE CUT OF JANUARY 3, 2001

The effects of the interest rate hikes engineered by the Fed during 1999 and the first part of 2000 started to make themselves felt by the end of 2000. And when signs of a slowdown in economic activity began to appear, they seemed to indicate that the economy might be headed toward a recession. On January 3, 2001, new figures showed that auto sales by U.S. domestic manufacturers were down almost 8 percent from the level of a year earlier. Chrysler announced that it would be shutting down five of its twelve North American factories for two weeks, putting as many as 30,000 workers on temporary furloughs. The day before, the National Association of Purchasing Management released its index of activity in the manufacturing sector during December—which had fallen to its lowest level since the previous recession, in 1991. Declines in the stock market during the last few months of 2000 had also created concerns that households would become more pessimistic about the economy and scale back their spending.

At the same time, inflation appeared to be relatively stable, averaging just under 3 percent during the last six months of 2000. It actually edged upward in early 2001; during the first six months of 2001, the inflation rate averaged above 4.5 percent. If the Fed were concerned only with inflation, it might have responded by raising interest rates. But faced with growing evidence that the chances of a recession were rising, the FOMC cut its federal funds rate target from 6.5 percent to 6 percent on January 3, 2001. By cutting interest rates, the FOMC hoped to stimulate investment and consumption spending. A central bank that cared only about the rate of inflation would not have taken this action; in fact, as the January 3 case shows, the Federal Reserve is concerned not just with inflation but also with maintaining overall economic stability.

SEPTEMBER 11, 2001

On September 11, 2001, the terrorist attack on the World Trade Center in New York City caused not only a grievous loss of life but a tremendous shock to the U.S. economy's financial sector. The attack led to a one-week closure of the New York Stock Exchange and disrupted the payments system through which transactions between banks are cleared. For example, one side effect of the suspension of air flights within the United States was to slow the process of clearing checks. In periods of great uncertainty, banks and other financial institutions often contract their lending activity, and the demand for safe assets such as money generally increases. The Fed needed to make sure that any rise in money demand was satisfied. Shortly before September 11, deposits at Federal Reserve Banks had averaged under $20 billion. They rose to more than $100 billion on September 12, as the Fed provided additional reserves to the banking system to meet the demand for money.[5] This reaction illustrates how central banks must respond to ensure macroeconomic stability whenever the economy is threatened with disruption, even if inflation remains low and stable.

---

[5]See Christopher J. Neely, "The Federal Reserve Responds to Crises: September 11 Was Not the First," *Review* (Federal Reserve Bank of St. Louis), 86, no. 2 (2004): 27–42.

e-Insight

THE DOT-COM BUBBLE AND MACROECONOMIC STABILITY

Just think if in June 1996 you had invested $20,000 in a little-known and fledgling new company called Yahoo. It would have been a risky decision; Yahoo was offering a free service to users of the Internet—something that most Americans still knew little about. A share of stock in Yahoo was selling for $2.09.

It would have been a great investment decision. As the year 2000 dawned, each share of Yahoo's stock was worth $176.50 and your $20,000 investment would have been worth $1,688,995! This represented a 255 percent annual return. A year later, in January 2001, things would have looked a bit different. You would no longer be a millionaire, since your Yahoo stock had plunged until it was worth only $262,010, a fall of 84 percent. Each of your shares would have been selling for just $27.38.

The experiences of Yahoo were mirrored by hundreds of other dot-com firms that had begun in the 1980s and 1990s as small start-ups and then saw their share prices break all records for growth as investors clamored for their shares when these companies "went public." Thousands of dot-com mil-

lionaires, and quite a few billionaires, were created, and millions of Americans who had never before thought of investing in stocks started speculating in the market. Fluctuations in the New York Stock Exchange or the Nasdaq exchange became part of daily conversations. But just as quickly, it seemed, the high-flying days ended during 2000. Dot-com start-ups started going bankrupt, and the technology-heavy Nasdaq index, after reaching a peak at just over 5,000 in March 2000, had fallen to 2,291.46 by New Year's Day in 2001. By March 2001, it was below 2,000.

The stock market affects macroeconomic conditions and in turn is influenced by economic conditions. Several times during the 1990s, the stock market was feared to be a source of instability in the economy. For example, consumption spending was fueled by soaring stock prices in the mid-1990s, a situation that concerned the Federal Reserve for two reasons. First, increased consumption spending in an economy already experiencing a strong expansion threatened to overheat the

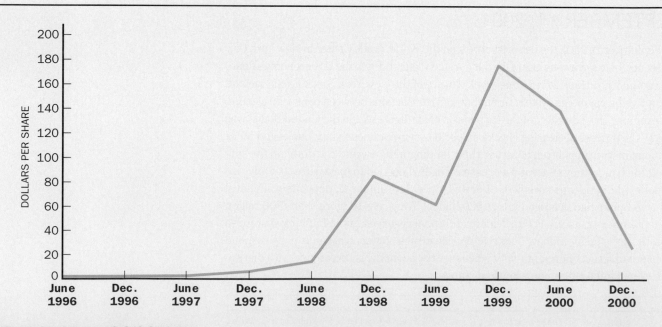

THE PRICE OF YAHOO'S STOCK

economy and lead to a resurgence of inflation. Second, many feared that the stock market boom was based on unrealistic expectations about the value of the new dot-com businesses. Although many of these firms had yet to actually earn profits, investors were bidding their stock prices higher and higher in expectation of future profitability. If expectations were to become less optimistic, the stock market might collapse suddenly, leading to spending cutbacks by households as they saw their wealth fall.

The stock market boom generated by dot-com businesses represented a major source of uncertainty for the Federal Reserve. Was the boom based on realistic expectations of the value of new economy firms? Or was it simply so much "irrational exuberance," as Federal Reserve Chair Greenspan labeled it in a widely quoted speech of December 1996? Did it reflect the fundamental soundness of the new economy, or was it setting the economy up for an inevitable market crash, much as had occurred in 1929? When the market slumped in the fall of 1998, the Fed cut interest rates, and this action helped restore optimism to the market. During the summer of 2000, the market drifted downward as the Fed boosted interest rates to slow the economy and head off a possible increase in inflation. Many economists have argued that the Fed should act to tighten monetary policy whenever a stock market boom seems to be based simply on expectations of continued unrealistic increases in stock prices— a so-called speculative bubble. Yet as so many changes are affecting the economy, and as new firms producing totally new products are constantly emerging, judging whether the stock market was reflecting the fundamental reality of the new economy or simply irrational exuberance is a difficult task.

THE POSITION OF THE POLICY RULE

We can further explore the position of the monetary policy rule by asking what nominal interest rate a central bank would want to target if the economy were at full employment. Two factors will be important: the equilibrium real rate of interest at full employment and the target inflation rate that the central bank would like to achieve.

The Equilibrium Real Interest Rate Recall from Chapter 6 that the full-employment model made an important prediction about the real interest rate: when the economy is at full employment, the real interest rate does not depend on the inflation rate or on monetary policy. Consequently, monetary policy cannot influence what real interest rate will balance savings and investment at full employment.

This implication of the full-employment model has significant consequences for monetary policy and the relationship between the nominal interest rate and inflation. Suppose, for instance, that the equilibrium real interest rate when the economy is at full employment is 3 percent. A central bank that could control the real interest rate directly would want to set it at 3 percent to keep the economy at full employment. But because central banks work indirectly, we must ask, What nominal interest rate will the central bank wish to set when the economy is at full employment?

The answer to this question depends on the average rate of inflation the central bank would like to achieve. Many central banks, such as the Bank of England, aim to keep inflation equal on average to 2 percent.[6] The nominal interest rate, in

---

[6]Central banks set a target for inflation slightly above zero because they want to avoid the possibility of deflation (i.e., falling prices or negative inflation). Moreover, because most common measures of inflation are thought to contain a slight upward bias, price stability would still lead to a small but positive measured rate of inflation.

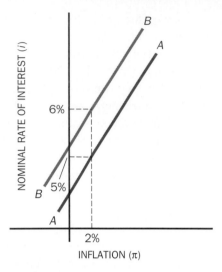

Figure 15.7

THE MONETARY POLICY RULE AND THE EQUILIBRIUM REAL INTEREST RATE AT FULL EMPLOYMENT

The central bank's policy rule needs to be consistent with the economy's equilibrium real interest rate at full employment and the central bank's target inflation rate. If the equilibrium real interest rate at full employment is 3 percent and the central bank's inflation target is 2 percent, then the nominal interest rate must be 5 percent when inflation is equal to its target, as shown by the policy rule line AA.

If the equilibrium real interest rate at full employment rises to 4 percent, the central bank must set the nominal rate equal to 6 percent when inflation is on target. The entire policy line shifts up to BB.

our hypothetical full-employment economy, must then be 5 percent—the full-employment equilibrium real interest rate (3 percent) plus the desired inflation rate (2 percent). Figure 15.7 shows the policy rule for this example (the line labeled AA); when inflation is equal to 2 percent, the policy rule shows that the central bank sets the nominal interest rate equal to 5 percent.

If the equilibrium real rate of interest at full employment changes, the central bank will need to shift its policy rule. For example, in Chapter 6, we learned that an increase in the fiscal deficit would increase the equilibrium real interest rate at full employment. Suppose the full-employment real interest rate rises from 3 percent to 4 percent. Now, when inflation is on target (equal to 2 percent), the central bank must ensure that the nominal interest rate at full employment is 6 percent—the 4 percent real rate plus 2 percent for inflation. The monetary policy rule must shift up, as illustrated by the line labeled BB in Figure 15.7. When the full-employment real interest rate falls—owing to a reduction in the fiscal deficit or a rise in household saving, for example—the central bank must shift its policy line down. Thus, the position of the policy rule will depend on the economy's full-employment equilibrium real interest rate.

These shifts in the policy rule as the full-employment equilibrium real interest rate changes are not automatic; the Fed must make an explicit decision to alter its policy rule. Failure to do so can harm the economy, and some of the policy errors of the past forty years can be attributed to the Fed's not adjusting its policy rule when the full-employment equilibrium real interest rate changed.

The 1960s provide a case in point. As already noted in this chapter, the 1964 tax cut and the expansion in government spending associated with the Vietnam War and the War on Poverty pushed the U.S. economy above potential output by the end of the decade, causing inflation to start to rise. Figure 15.8 illustrates this situation. The initial equilibrium, at full employment, is labeled as E_0. The fiscal expansion shifted the ADI curve to the right, leading to the economy's new, short-run equilibrium at E_1. As we learned in Chapter 13, the inflation adjustment curve shifts up when the output gap is positive. Eventually, full employment is restored at E_2, with a higher rate of inflation.

The fiscal expansion raised the full-employment equilibrium real interest rate. In response, to prevent inflation from rising, the Fed should have shifted its policy rule. At each inflation rate, it should have set a higher interest rate. Doing so would have counteracted the rightward shift in the ADI curve; as a result, full employment would have been restored at E_0, with both output *and* inflation returning to their original levels.

This simple statement of what the Fed should have done ignores an important complication: the equilibrium real rate of interest cannot be directly observed by economists. The Fed must try to estimate the equilibrium real rate, a task that can be difficult. Thus even if the Fed recognizes the need to adjust its policy rule, it may not know by how much. For example, tax cuts and expenditure increases that took place between 2001 and 2004 are projected to lead to huge fiscal deficits over the next several years. These deficits will increase the equilibrium real interest rate. But the effects of the deficits will depend on how the president and Congress eventually adjust taxes and expenditures to deal with the deficit and on when those adjustments are made.

The Inflation Target The position of the monetary policy rule also depends on the central bank's target inflation rate. As we just learned, at full employment the central bank will set the nominal interest rate equal to the equilibrium real interest rate plus the target for the rate of inflation. Suppose the central bank decides to lower its inflation target from 2 percent to 1 percent. And let's assume the full-employment equilibrium real interest rate is 3 percent. Figure 15.9 depicts the initial policy rule, the one for a target inflation rate of 2 percent, as *AA*. When inflation is equal to the target, the nominal interest rate is 5 percent (the 3 percent real interest rate plus 2 percent inflation). When the inflation target is reduced to 1 percent, the nominal interest rate at full employment falls from 5 percent to 4 percent (the 3 percent real interest rate plus the new target inflation rate of 1 percent). The policy rule shifts up to *BB*, as illustrated in the figure. At each rate of inflation, the nominal rate is now set at a higher value.

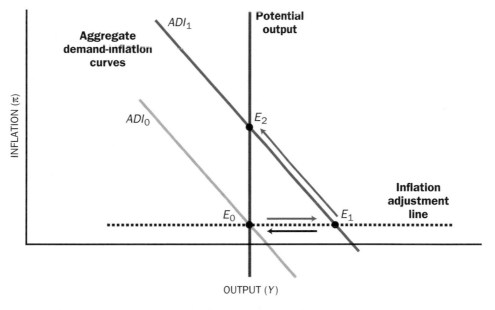

OUTPUT (*Y*)

Figure 15.8

A FISCAL EXPANSION WHEN THE FED'S POLICY RULE DOES NOT ADJUST AND WHEN IT DOES

The figure illustrates the consequences if the Fed fails to adjust its policy rule when the equilibrium real interest rate at full employment changes. A fiscal expansion shifts the aggregate demand–inflation curve from ADI_0 to ADI_1. In the short run, equilibrium output rises and the new equilibrium is at E_1. If the Fed does not adjust its policy rule, the economy eventually returns to full employment at E_2 with higher inflation. The green arrows show the path the economy takes. To prevent the fiscal expansion from leaving inflation higher, the Fed must raise interest rates at a given rate of inflation. This shift in the Fed's policy rule is necessary because a fiscal expansion raises the real interest rate that balances the capital market at full employment. If the Fed's policy rule shifts, then the ADI curve is shifted back to ADI_0, the economy returns to full employment, and inflation returns to its initial level at E_0 along the black arrow.

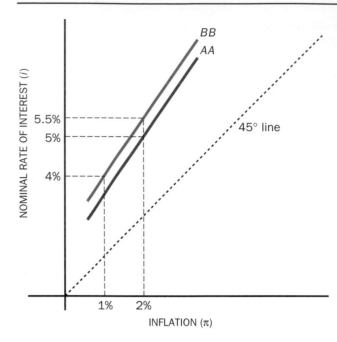

Figure 15.9

THE EFFECT OF A SHIFT IN THE INFLATION TARGET ON THE CENTRAL BANK'S POLICY RULE

The position of the monetary policy rule depends on the central bank's target for inflation. Policy rule *AA* is based on an inflation target of 2 percent and an equilibrium real interest rate of 2 percent at full employment. If the central bank reduces its inflation target to 1 percent, the policy rule shifts up. At a given inflation rate, the central bank will set nominal interest rates higher.

This shift in the policy rule does succeed in lowering inflation. If the economy initially has 2 percent inflation, the central bank increases the nominal interest rate in line with the new policy rule *BB*. As shown in the figure, the nominal rate rises to 5.5 percent. Since inflation is still equal to 2 percent, this represents a rise in the real interest rate from 3 percent to 3.5 percent, which dampens aggregate spending and causes output to decline in the short run. The decline puts downward pressure on inflation. The economy suffers an increase in cyclical unemployment in the short run, but eventually full employment is restored at a lower rate of inflation.

THE SLOPE OF THE POLICY RULE

The slope of the monetary policy rule tells us how much the central bank adjusts interest rates when inflation changes. Suppose the central bank reacts aggressively to inflation, hiking interest rates whenever inflation rises and cutting them sharply whenever it falls. Such behavior would be represented by a policy rule that has a steep slope, indicating that changes in inflation lead to large changes in interest rates. In contrast, the policy rule for a central bank that reacts more moderately to changes in inflation would be relatively flat. Many central banks react more strongly to inflation today than they did in the 1970s. Therefore, we would draw a steeper policy rule to reflect current practices of central banks than we would if we wanted to represent their behavior in the 1970s.

The slope of the policy rule is important because, as we learned in Chapter 13, it helps determine the slope of the ADI curve. If the central bank reacts aggressively to changes in inflation, aggregate expenditures will vary more as inflation changes; the ADI curve will be relatively flat. If the central bank has little response as inflation changes, then aggregate expenditures will be less affected by inflation and the ADI curve will be steeper.

The slope of the ADI curve significantly affects how the economy responds to inflation shocks. As we learned in Chapter 13, a positive inflation shock causes inflation to increase and output to decline in the short run by an amount that depends on how much aggregate expenditures fall. If the ADI curve is steep—either because changes in inflation lead to little change in interest rates or because changes in interest rates induce little change in aggregate spending—the impact of an inflation shock on output will be small. Because the rise in cyclical unemployment is small in this case, the moderating effects of a recession on wage growth and inflation are small, and it may take longer for inflation to return to its initial level. If the ADI curve is flat—either because changes in inflation lead to large changes in interest rates or because changes in interest rates induce large changes in aggregate spending—the impact of an inflation shock on output will be larger. But because cyclical unemployment increases more in the latter case, the downward pressures on wage growth and inflation are larger, and the initial rise in inflation is likely to be reversed more quickly.

This discussion returns us to the trade-offs that were examined earlier in this chapter. By responding strongly to changes in inflation, the central bank can keep inflation more stable but at the cost of larger fluctuations in real output and unemployment. By responding less aggressively to changes in inflation, real output and unemployment can be kept more stable but at the cost of greater instability in inflation.

THE MONETARY POLICY RULE

A monetary policy rule describes how the central bank adjusts its policy in response to economic conditions. Inflation is one of the major factors that central banks respond to.

The position of the policy rule will depend on the central bank's target rate of inflation and the equilibrium real rate of interest at full employment.

The slope of the policy rule affects the slope of the ADI curve. If the central bank reacts aggressively to inflation, the ADI curve will be relatively flat. Inflation shocks will lead to larger movements in output but inflation will be more stable. Weaker policy responses to inflation lead to more stable output but less stability in inflation.

Interactions Between Monetary and Fiscal Policies

So far, we have treated monetary and fiscal policies as if they were entirely distinct. In the United States, fiscal policy is the responsibility of Congress and the president, while monetary policy is the responsibility of the Federal Reserve. This division of labor makes it convenient to discuss them separately. In fact, what is important for the economy is the net impact of both types of policies and the important interactions between them. Consider the earlier discussion of a fiscal stimulus. If the Fed raises interest rates as the stimulus occurs, monetary policy may partially or totally offset the expansionary effect of fiscal policy, pulling in the opposite direction. This happened in the early 1980s, when restrictive monetary policy more than offset expansionary fiscal policy and the economy went into a major recession.

We also have seen how a change in fiscal policy may require the Fed to alter its policy rule. If one of the goals of monetary policy is to maintain a low and stable inflation rate at full employment, then the central bank will need to offset the effects that fiscal policy might otherwise have on inflation.

Both fiscal policy and monetary policy can be used to expand aggregate demand and increase output in the short run. Both types of policies can be used to dampen aggregate demand when inflation threatens to increase. But they do more than just affect aggregate demand. Because these two policies have different implications for investment, they can have different longer-run effects on the economy. A monetary expansion lowers real interest rates, stimulating investment. In contrast, a fiscal expansion reduces national saving and results in a higher real interest rate and lower investment. Using fiscal policy to stimulate the economy, by reducing private investment, may have harmful effects on future potential output.

Fiscal and monetary policies differ as well in their impact on exports and imports. A monetary expansion that lowers interest rates will also tend to cause the currency to depreciate as foreign investors seek higher returns elsewhere.[7] A depreciation decreases imports (by making foreign goods more expensive) and increases exports. In contrast, a fiscal expansion that causes interest rates to rise also causes the currency to appreciate; net exports fall as foreign goods become less expensive.

In recent decades, monetary policy has been the chief tool for macroeconomic stabilization policies, and discretionary fiscal policy has played little role in the United States. The chief reason, as already noted, is the lags inherent in the fiscal policy process—particularly the **inside lag,** or time needed to implement the necessary expenditure or tax changes. First, it takes time to recognize the need to stimulate or restrain aggregate spending. Data are subject to revision, and conflicting developments often can frustrate attempts to determine the true condition of the economy. For example, after the 2001 recession, one survey of households tended to indicate strong employment growth even as a survey of firms showed continued job losses. Then, after some change in the economy is recognized, there is the delay due to the time it takes to design a package of new tax or spending initiatives (whether increases or cuts) and get it approved by Congress. While the delay in recognizing changed economic conditions is the same whatever the approach, the inside lag is much longer for fiscal than for monetary policy. Postwar recessions have lasted less than a year on average. By the time—often longer than a year—a tax bill is approved by Congress, the economy is entering a different phase of the business cycle. A policy that makes sense when it is introduced may easily turn out to be inappropriate when it comes into effect. This unwieldiness limits the effectiveness of discretionary fiscal policy. In contrast, the FOMC meets every six weeks, and, if conditions warrant, committee members can hold telephone conferences more frequently. Hence, monetary policy can act swiftly to deal with new economic developments.

Monetary and fiscal policies also differ in the speed with which a policy action affects the economy. Monetary policy stimulates the economy by lowering interest rates, thereby increasing investment in equipment and housing and increasing net exports. Even after firms see a decrease in the real interest rate, it may take some time before they commit to new investment, and before the capital goods industry starts producing the newly ordered goods. Similarly, though in the long run a lower real interest rate leads to increased demand for housing, it takes a while before plans are drawn up, permits are obtained, and construction starts. Typically, six months or longer must pass before monetary policy's effects on output are realized. By contrast, increased government purchases have a direct and immediate effect on total spending. The time required for the change in policy to affect the economy is called the **outside lag,** and it is normally shorter for fiscal policy.

---

[7]The reason that interest rate changes affect the exchange rate is discussed in Chapter 18.

DIFFERENCES BETWEEN MONETARY AND FISCAL POLICY

Effects on Aggregate Demand

Fiscal policy and monetary policy have different effects on the economy. Expansionary fiscal policy raises the real interest rate and crowds out private investment spending. Expansionary monetary policy lowers the real interest rate and stimulates private investment spending.

Policy Lags

Inside lag: The time required to recognize a need for a change in policy and to implement the policy change. The inside lag is much shorter for monetary policy.
Outside lag: The time required for the change in policy to affect the economy. The outside lag is normally shorter for fiscal policy.

Review and Practice

SUMMARY

1. The actual fiscal deficit increases in a recession as tax revenues decline. This process provides an important automatic stabilizer. To measure discretionary shifts in fiscal policy, economists look at the full-employment budget deficit.

2. The aggregate demand–inflation (ADI) curve depends on the monetary policy rule used by the central bank. The slope of the policy rule affects the slope of the ADI curve, while shifts in the policy rule are reflected in shifts in the ADI curve.

3. If the central bank wants to keep inflation stable, it must adjust its policy rule whenever the equilibrium full-employment real interest rate changes. The policy rule must be shifted up if the full-employment real interest rate increases, leading to a higher nominal interest rate at each inflation rate.

4. The monetary policy rule shifts if the central bank alters its target for inflation. If it reduces its inflation target, the policy rule shifts up, leading to a higher nominal interest rate at each rate of inflation.

5. Both fiscal and monetary policies can affect aggregate demand and output in the short run. They have different effects on the interest rate. A fiscal expansion raises the real interest rate; a monetary expansion lowers the real interest rate. Consequently, investment will be higher in the short run if monetary policy is used to stimulate the economy.

6. The inside lag is shorter for monetary policy than for fiscal policy. The outside lag is shorter for fiscal policy.

KEY TERMS

automatic stabilizer
discretionary action
full-employment deficit
monetary policy rule
inside lag
outside lag

REVIEW QUESTIONS

1. What are automatic stabilizers and how do they affect the economy?

2. What happens to the government surplus when the economy goes into a recession? What happens to the full-employment surplus when the economy goes into a recession?

3. How does the slope of the ADI curve depend on the monetary policy rule?

4. If the central bank wants to keep inflation equal to its target, how must the monetary policy rule shift if the equilibrium full-employment real interest rate falls?

5. How does the monetary policy rule shift if the central bank's target for inflation is reduced? How does this reduction affect the ADI curve?

6. In addition to the effects of monetary policy on aggregate demand that operate through the real interest rate, what other channels are there through which monetary policy may affect aggregate expenditures?

7. Compare the effects of monetary and fiscal policies on the level of investment and the composition of output.

PROBLEMS

1. Why would the economy be more stable or less stable if there were no automatic stabilizers?

2. In recent years, many central banks have placed increased emphasis on controlling inflation. Suppose the central bank of the nation of Economica decides that it will move interest rates sharply whenever inflation differs from its desired target of 1 percent. Previously, policymakers in Economica had adjusted interest rates only slightly in response to inflation.
    (a) How will this switch in policy affect the central bank's monetary policy rule?
    (b) How will it affect the slope of the ADI curve?
    (c) Suppose Economica suffers an inflation shock that increases inflation. Use a graph to illustrate how output and inflation respond under both the old and the new policy rules.

3. Assume that the economy is currently at full employment with an inflation rate of 2 percent. The government embarks on a major new expenditure program that increases aggregate expenditures (assume that full-employment output is unaffected).

   (a) If the central bank's policy rule remains unchanged, what will be the short-run and long-run effects on output and inflation of this change in fiscal policy? What will be the long-run effects on the real interest rate at full employment?

   (b) Suppose the central bank's policy rule adjusts to reflect the change in the full-employment real interest rate. Will this alter the short-run or long-run effects of the fiscal expansion?

4. In late 2000, there were signs the U.S. economy might be heading into a recession. Some argued that the rise in energy prices during 2000 was the cause of the economic slowdown. Others pointed to the decline in the stock market and argued that this decline in wealth would reduce consumption spending. Assume the economy is initially at full employment.

   (a) Using the ADI-IA (inflation adjustment) framework, explain how a rise in energy prices would affect output and inflation in the short run.

   (b) Using the ADI-IA framework, explain how a fall in stock prices would affect output and inflation in the short run.

   (c) Suppose you are chair of the Federal Reserve Board. If your *only* concern is keeping inflation stable, would you raise interest rates or would you lower them if you believe energy prices are the cause of the slowdown? Would you raise interest rates or would you lower them if you believe the stock market decline is the cause of the slowdown?

   (d) Suppose you are chair of the Federal Reserve Board. If your *only* concern is keeping unemployment stable, would you raise interest rates or would you lower them if you believe energy prices are the cause of the slowdown? Would you raise interest rates or would you lower them if you believe the stock market decline is the cause of the slowdown?

5. Suppose a fall in net exports due to a recession among our major trading partners causes a recession in the United States.

   (a) If fiscal policy is used to stimulate the economy and return it to full employment, what happens to the real interest rate, investment, and future output?

   (b) If monetary policy is used to stimulate the economy and return it to full employment, what happens to the real interest rate, investment, and future output?

6. In parliamentary governments, such as the United Kingdom, the prime minister can announce a change in taxation or expenditure and implement that change almost immediately. How might this fact affect the balance between the use of monetary and fiscal policy for short-run stabilization?

Part 4

THE GLOBAL ECONOMY

Learning Goals

In this chapter, you will learn

1 How international trade can benefit all countries

2 The role comparative advantage plays in determining what countries produce and trade

3 Why countries erect barriers to trade and who the winners and losers are when international trade is restricted

4 Why international trade agreements are often controversial

Chapter 16

INTERNATIONAL TRADE AND TRADE POLICY

Exchange was one of the core concepts in economics discussed in Chapter 1. Economists often use the words *trade* and *exchange* interchangeably. When Chip goes to work, he exchanges, or trades, his labor services for income. When Juanita purchases a new cell phone, she exchanges, or trades, income for the product she chooses. The subject of international trade—the exchange of goods and services across national borders—is an extension of the basic principle of exchange. Individuals in our economy are involved in countless voluntary trades. They "trade" their labor services (time and skills) to their employer for dollars. They then trade dollars with a multitude of merchants for goods (such as gasoline and groceries) and services (such as plumbing and hair styling). A firm trades the goods it produces for dollars, and then trades those dollars for labor services.

Why is it that people engage in all these complex sets of economic exchanges with one another? The answer is simple: trading leaves them better off. Just as individuals *within* a country find it advantageous to trade with one another, so too do countries find foreign trade advantageous. And just as it is impossible for any individual to be self-sufficient, it is impossible for a country to be self-reliant without sacrificing its standard of living.

Trade Between Countries

The United States has long been part of an international economic community. Its participation has grown in recent decades—a process often referred to as *globalization*—increasing the interdependence among the United States and its trading partners. How has this development affected the three major markets in the U.S. economy?

INTERDEPENDENCE IN THE PRODUCT MARKET

Foreign-produced goods are commonplace in U.S. markets. In the 1990s, for instance, more than one-fourth of the cars sold in the United States were imported (**imports** are goods produced abroad but bought domestically), along with a third of apparel items, a third of the oil, and virtually all the diamonds. Many of the materials essential for the U.S. economy must also be imported from abroad. At the same time, American farmers export almost two-fifths of the agricultural goods they produce (**exports** are goods produced domestically but sold abroad), including almost three-fourths of the wheat and one-third of the cotton.

Imports have grown in recent decades, not only in dollar terms but also as a percentage of overall production. Exports have grown almost as much. Figure 16.1 shows how exports and imports have increased relative to the nation's total output. As a percentage of GDP, both have more than doubled over the past twenty-five years. Countries with smaller economies are even more dependent on international trade than the United States is. Britain and Canada import one-fourth of their goods, France one-fifth.

INTERDEPENDENCE IN THE LABOR MARKET

International interdependence extends beyond simply the shipping of goods between countries. More than 99 percent of U.S. citizens either came here from another

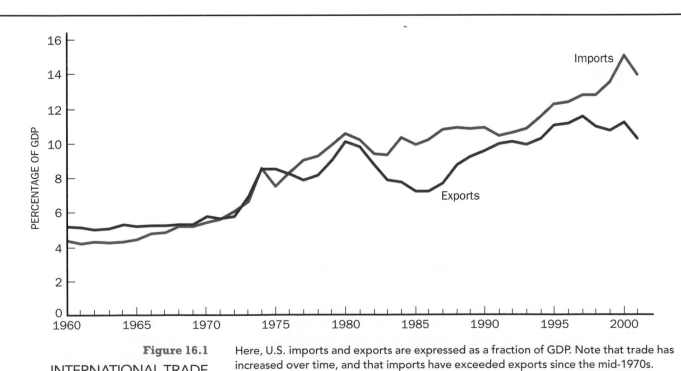

Figure 16.1
INTERNATIONAL TRADE

Here, U.S. imports and exports are expressed as a fraction of GDP. Note that trade has increased over time, and that imports have exceeded exports since the mid-1970s.

SOURCE: *Economic Report of the President* (2004).

country or are descended from people who did. Though the flow of immigrants, relative to the size of the population, has slowed since its peak a century ago, millions still arrive each year.

The nations of Europe have increasingly recognized the benefits that result from this international movement of workers. One of the most important provisions of the treaty establishing the European Union, an agreement initially among most of the countries in western Europe but now extended to include many in eastern Europe, allows for the free flow of workers within the member countries.

INTERDEPENDENCE IN THE CAPITAL MARKET

The United States has become a major borrower from abroad, but the country also invests heavily overseas. In 2002, for example, U.S. private investors owned approximately $180 billion worth of assets (factories, businesses, buildings, loans, etc.) in foreign countries, while foreign investors owned $707 billion worth of assets in the United States. American companies have sought out profitable opportunities abroad, where they can use their special skills and knowledge to earn high returns. They have established branches and built factories in Europe, Japan, Latin America, and elsewhere in the world. Foreign companies have likewise invested in the United States. Major automobile producers such as Toyota and BMW have built factories in the United States to manufacture cars.

MULTILATERAL TRADE

Often, we think of trade as a two-way exchange—the United States sells airplanes to Japan and buys Japanese-produced consumer electronics. Such transactions between two individuals or countries are called **bilateral trade.** But exchange between two parties is often less advantageous than that among several parties, called **multilateral trade.** Such trades are often observed among sports teams. One highly publicized trade in 2004 involved the Boston Red Sox, the Chicago Cubs, the Montreal Expos, and the Minnesota Twins. At its heart were three shortstops— Nomar Garciaparra, a five-time all-star, who went from the Red Sox to the Cubs; Alex Gonzalez, who went from the Cubs to Montreal; and Orlando Cabrera, who went from Montreal to Boston—but other players and a fourth team (the Twins) were also involved. No two teams were willing to make a bilateral trade, but all thought they could benefit from the multilateral deal.

Countries function similarly. China imports oil from Saudi Arabia. Saudi Arabia wants wheat and food for its oil, not just the textiles that China can provide. So Saudi Arabia uses revenue obtained by selling oil to China to buy wheat and food from the United States, and the United States buys textiles from China. This three-way trade, shown in Figure 16.2, offers gains that two-way trade cannot. The scores of nations that are active in the world economy create patterns far more complex than these simple examples.

When trade is multilateral, the trade between any two countries may not balance. In Figure 16.2, Saudi Arabia sends oil to China but gets no goods (only yuan)

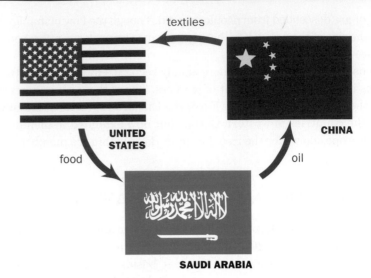

Figure 16.2

MULTILATERAL EXCHANGE

The figure illustrates exchange in international trade. Note that no two of the countries have the ingredients for a mutually beneficial exchange.

in return. No one would fault this trade policy. Yet some members of Congress, newspaper columnists, union leaders, and business executives complain that because the United States imports more from a particular country (often China or Japan) than it exports to that country, the trade balance is "unfair." According to a misguided popular cliché, "Trade is a two-way street." But trade in the world market is a complex network involving hundreds of possible streets. While the overall U.S. trade deficit raises legitimate concerns, there is no reason why U.S. exports and imports with any particular country should be balanced.

Comparative Advantage

We have so far focused on exchanges of existing goods. But clearly, most of what is exchanged must first be produced. Trade enables individuals and countries to concentrate on what they produce best.

Some countries—because they have more highly educated workers, more capital (plant and equipment), or more abundant natural resources—may be more efficient at producing almost all the different goods that their citizens wish to consume. The possession of superior production skills is called having an **absolute advantage.** Why would a country with an absolute advantage wish to trade with countries that are less efficient? And how can such disadvantaged countries successfully engage in trade? The answer to these questions lies in the principle of **comparative advantage,** which states that individuals and countries specialize in those goods in whose production they are *relatively,* not absolutely, most efficient.

Table 16.1

LABOR COST OF PRODUCING COMPUTERS AND WHEAT (WORKER HOURS)

	United States	Japan
Labor required to make a computer	100	120
Labor required to make a ton of wheat	5	8

To see what comparative advantage means, let's say that both the United States and Japan produce two goods, computers and wheat. The amount of labor needed to produce these goods is shown in Table 16.1. (These numbers are all hypothetical.) The United States is more efficient (spends fewer worker hours) at making both products. America can rightfully claim to have the most efficient computer industry in the world, and yet it imports computers from Japan. Why? The *relative* cost of making a computer (in terms of labor used) in Japan, relative to the cost of producing a ton of wheat, is low, compared with that in the United States. That is, in Japan, it takes 15 times as many hours (120/8) to produce a computer as a ton of wheat; in the United States, it takes 20 times as many hours (100/5) to produce a computer as a ton of wheat. While Japan has an absolute *dis*advantage in producing computers, it has a *comparative* advantage.

The principle of comparative advantage applies to individuals as well as countries. The president of a company might type faster than her secretary, but it still pays to have the secretary type her letters, because the president may have a comparative advantage at bringing in new clients, while the secretary has a comparative (though not absolute) advantage in typing.

PRODUCTION POSSIBILITIES CURVES AND COMPARATIVE ADVANTAGE

The easiest way to understand the comparative advantage of different countries is to use the production possibilities curve first introduced in Chapter 2. Figure 16.3 depicts parts of hypothetical production possibilities curves for two countries, China and the United States, producing two commodities, textiles (garments) and airplanes. In both, point *E* represents the current level of production. Let us look at what happens if each country changes its production by 100 airplanes.

China has a comparative advantage in producing textiles. If it reduces its airplane production by 100, its textile production can be increased by 10,000 garments. This trade-off between airplanes and garments is called the *marginal rate of transformation*.

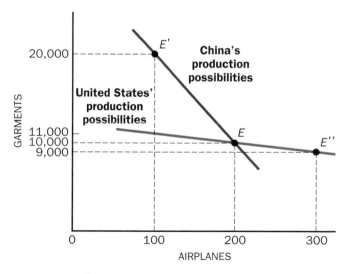

Figure 16.3

EXPLOITING COMPARATIVE ADVANTAGE

The production possibilities schedules for China and the United States, each manufacturing two commodities, textiles and airplanes, illustrate the trade-offs at different levels of production. Point *E* shows the current level of production for each country; *E'* and *E"* illustrate production decisions that better exploit each country's comparative advantage.

By contrast, if the United States reduces its airplane production by 100 airplanes, its textile production can be increased by only 1,000 garments. Conversely, if it increases its airplane production by 100, it will have to reduce its garment production by only 1,000 garments. We can now see why the world is better off if each country exploits its comparative advantage. If China moves from E to E' (decreasing airplane production by 100), 10,000 more garments can be produced. If the United States at the same time increases its airplane production by 100 from E to E'', it will produce only 1,000 fewer garments. In the new situation, the world production of airplanes is unchanged ($100 + 300 = 200 + 200$), but world production of garments has increased by 9,000 (the difference between $20,000 + 9,000$ and $10,000 + 10,000$). So long as the production trade-offs differ—that is, so long as the marginal rates of transformation differ—it pays for China to specialize increasingly in textiles, and the United States to specialize increasingly in airplanes. Notice that the analysis depends on knowledge only about the production trade-offs. We do not need to know how much labor or capital is required in either country to produce either airplanes or garments.

Though it pays countries to increase the production and export of goods in which they have a comparative advantage and to import goods in which they have a comparative disadvantage, doing so may not lead to complete specialization. Thus the United States continues to be a major producer of textiles, in spite of heavy imports from the Far East. Its engagement in this industry does not violate the principle of comparative advantage: not all textiles require the same skill and expertise in manufacturing. While China may have a comparative advantage in inexpensive textiles, the United States may have a comparative advantage in higher-quality textiles. At the same time, the comparative advantage of other countries is so extreme in producing some goods—TVs and VCRs, for example—that it does not pay for the United States to produce them at all.

Comparative Advantage and Specialization To see the benefits of specialization, consider the pencil. A tree of the right kind of wood must be felled; it must be transported to a sawmill, and there cut into pieces that can be further processed into pencil casings. Then the graphite that runs through the pencil's center, the eraser at its tip, and the metal that holds the two together must each be produced by specially trained people. The pencil is a simple tool. But to produce it by oneself would cost a fortune.

Why Specialization Increases Productivity Specialization increases productivity, thereby enhancing the benefits of trade, for three reasons. First, specializing eliminates the time it takes a worker to switch from one production task to another. Second, by repeating the same task, the worker becomes more skilled at it. And third, specialization creates a fertile environment for invention.

Dividing jobs so that each worker can practice and perfect a particular skill (called the *division of labor*) may increase productivity hundreds or thousands of times. Almost anyone who practices activities—cooking, writing, adding a column of numbers, and so on—will be quite a lot better at them than someone who has not practiced. Similarly, a country that specializes in producing sports cars may develop a comparative advantage in their manufacture. With its relatively large scale of production, it can divide tasks into separate assignments for different people; as each becomes better at his own tasks, productivity is increased.

At the same time, the division of labor often leads to invention. As someone learns a particular job extremely well, she might figure out ways of doing it better—including devising a machine to do it. Specialization and invention reinforce each other. A slight initial advantage in the production of some good leads to greater production of that good, thence to more invention, and thence to even greater production and further specialization.

Limits of Specialization The extent of the division of labor, or specialization, is limited by the size of the market. Specialization has greater scope in mass-produced manufactured goods like picture frames than in custom-made items like the artwork that gets framed. That is one reason why the costs of production of mass-produced goods have declined so much. Similarly, there is greater scope for specialization in a big city than in a small town. That is why small stores specializing in a particular food or type of clothing thrive in cities but are rare in smaller towns.

The very nature of specialization limits its benefits. Repetitive jobs can lead to bored and unproductive workers. And single-track specialization inhibits the new insights and ideas that engagement in a variety of work activities can spark.

WHAT DETERMINES COMPARATIVE ADVANTAGE?

Earlier we learned that comparative advantage determines the pattern of trade. But what determines comparative advantage? In the modern world, this turns out to be a complex matter.

Natural Endowments In first laying down the principle of comparative advantage in the early 1800s, the great British economist David Ricardo used the example of Portugal's trade with Britain. In Ricardo's example, Portugal had an absolute advantage in producing both wool and wine. But it had a comparative

THE UNITED STATES' COMPARATIVE ADVANTAGE IN THE INTERNET AGE

The United States holds a comparative advantage in information technology and Internet-based commerce. Large U.S. firms such as Microsoft, Intel, and Sun Microsystems have led the surge in information technology over the past two decades, and Internet-based businesses such as Amazon, Yahoo, and eBay have come to define the so-called new economy. How has the United States established itself as a leader in this field? Let's consider this question from the standpoint of the sources of comparative advantage described in this chapter.

The key to the United States' success in the information revolution has been its ability to innovate. U.S. firms have developed new types of computers and software, as well as new applications of these resources across various industries. This prowess in innovation derives from acquired endowments, superior knowledge, and specialization.

The human skills needed for innovation represent acquired endowments that have led to superior knowledge, some of which was gained as a by-product of America's massive expenditures on defense-related research. Another aspect of acquired endowments that has played a major role is the distinctive set of *institutions* in the United States that are particularly well suited for promoting research. These institutions include a special set of financial institutions (venture capital firms) that are better able to supply capital to new and small enterprises, which have played a pivotal role in the new economy, and strong research universities, which often have close ties to firms that can translate basic research into market applications. More broadly, both American labor and capital seem more able and willing to bear the high risks associated with new innovative enterprises, many of which may fold after a relatively brief existence. Americans' willingness to bear these risks may be connected to the gener-ally high levels of employment that have characterized the U.S. economy for the past two decades.

Partly as a result of these acquired advantages and of superior knowledge, the United States has developed a relative specialization in high-tech industries; it has become, to a large extent, the world's research center.

Intel's strength in computer chip production exemplifies the U.S. comparative advantage in information technology.

advantage in producing wine, and Britain had a comparative advantage in producing wool. In this and other early examples, economists tended to assume that a nation's comparative advantage was determined largely by its *natural endowments*. Countries with soil and climate that are *relatively* better for grapes than for pasture will produce wine; countries with soil and climate that are relatively better for pasture than for grapes will produce sheep (and hence wool).

In the modern economy, natural endowments still count: countries such as China that have an abundance of low-skilled labor relative to other resources have a comparative advantage in producing goods like textiles, which require a lot of handwork. But in today's technological age nations can also act to *acquire* a comparative advantage.

Acquired Endowments   Japan has little in the way of natural resources, yet it is a major player in international trade, in part because it has *acquired endowments*. Japan's case underscores the principle that by saving and accumulating capital and building large factories, a nation can acquire a comparative advantage in goods like steel that need large amounts of capital for their production. And by devoting resources to education, a nation can develop a comparative advantage in those goods that require a skilled labor force. Thus, the resources—human and physical—that a country has managed to acquire for itself can also give rise to comparative advantage.

Superior Knowledge   In the modern economy, comparative advantage may come simply from expertise in using resources productively. Switzerland has a comparative advantage in watches because, over the years, the people of the country have accumulated superior knowledge and expertise in watchmaking. Belgium has a comparative advantage in fine lace; its workers have developed the requisite skills. A quirk of fate might have led Belgium to acquire a comparative advantage in watches and Switzerland in lace.

Specialization   Earlier we saw how comparative advantage leads to specialization. Specialization may also lead to comparative advantage. The Swiss make fine watches, and have a comparative advantage in that market because of years of unique experience. Such superior knowledge, however, does not explain why Britain, Germany, and the United States, which are at roughly the same level of technological expertise in building cars, all trade cars with one another. How can each country have a comparative advantage in making cars? The answer lies in specialization.

Both Britain and Germany may be better off if Britain specializes in producing sports cars and Germany in producing luxury cars, or the converse, because specialization increases productivity. Countries enhance, or simply develop, a comparative advantage by specializing just as individuals do. As a result, similar countries enjoy the advantages of specialization even when they specialize in different variations of products that are fundamentally similar.

Interactions   The different sources of comparative advantage can serve to reinforce each other. Pittsburgh provides a good example of some of these interactions. Its rivers and deposits of bituminous coal (natural endowments) gave it an early comparative advantage as a location for industries such as steel production. George Westinghouse, founder of the corporation that bears his name, came to Pittsburgh because he needed steel for a tool he had designed to get derailed train cars back onto their tracks, and he could take advantage of Pittsburgh's established steel industry. Carnegie Technical Schools, the ancestor of today's Carnegie Mellon University, was created to help supply the area's industries with the engineers they needed. The availability of engineers (acquired endowments) made Pittsburgh an attractive place for other industries to locate.

THE FIVE BASES OF COMPARATIVE ADVANTAGE

Natural endowments, which consist of geographical determinants such as land, natural resources, and climate

Acquired endowments, which are the physical capital and human skills a nation has developed

Superior knowledge, including technological advantages, which may be acquired either as an accident of history or through deliberate policies

Specialization, which may create comparative advantages between countries that are similar in all other respects

Interactions, which reinforce the other sources of comparative advantage

The Perceived Costs of International Interdependence

If the argument that voluntary trade must be mutually beneficial is so compelling, why has there been, from time to time, such strong antitrade sentiment in the United States and many other countries? This antitrade feeling is often labeled **protectionism,** because it calls for "protecting" the economy from the effects of trade. Those who favor protectionism raise a number of concerns. Some of the objections to international trade parallel the objections to trade among individuals noted earlier. Was the trade a fair deal? Was the seller in a stronger bargaining position? Such concerns, for individuals and countries, revolve around how the *surplus* associated with the gains from trade is divided. Weak countries may feel that they are being taken advantage of by stronger countries. Their weaker bargaining position may lead to the stronger countries getting *more* of the gains from trade. But this outcome does not contradict the basic premise: both parties gain from voluntary exchange. All countries—weak as well as strong—are better off as a result of voluntary exchange.

But trade among individuals and trade among countries differ in one important way. Some individuals within a country benefit from trade and some lose. Since the trade as a whole is beneficial to the country, the gains to the winners exceed the losses to the losers. Thus, in principle, those who benefit within the country could more than compensate those who don't. In practice, however, those who lose remain losers and obviously oppose trade, arguing that it results in lost jobs and reduced wages. Such worries have become particularly acute as unskilled workers face competition with low-wage unskilled workers in Asia and Latin America: how can they compete without lowering their income?

These concerns figured prominently in the debate in 1993 over ratification of the **North American Free Trade Agreement (NAFTA),** which allows Mexican and Canadian goods into the United States with no duties at all. Advocates of NAFTA pointed out that (1) more jobs would be created by the new export opportunities than would be lost through competition from Mexican and Canadian firms and (2) the jobs that were created paid higher wages, reflecting the benefits from specialization in areas where the United States had a comparative advantage.

Opponents of free trade are not swayed by these arguments, but instead stress the costs to workers and communities as particular industries shrink in response to foreign imports. The textile worker in North Carolina who loses his job as a result of imports of inexpensive clothing from China cannot instantly convert himself into a computer programmer in California or an aircraft engineer working for Boeing. But the fact is that jobs are being destroyed and created all the time, irrespective of trade. Over the long run, the increased demand for computer programmers and aircraft engineers leads to higher salaries for those workers, thereby strengthening the incentives for young workers to gain the skills needed for these jobs and for others to relocate to areas where new jobs are being created. The declining demand for textile workers lowers salaries for textile workers, reducing the incentives for workers to remain in that industry. The United States is characterized by a high degree of labor mobility, and as jobs are created in one part of the country and disappear in other parts, individuals and families often move to seek new employment opportunities.

On balance the country benefits from these changes, but the benefits are not distributed evenly. The unemployed textile worker sees only the economic hardship she faces and the cost of free trade. For this reason, many economists argue that policies must be implemented to help retrain and relocate workers displaced by trade so that they too can share in the benefits that accrue from international interdependence. To the extent that such assistance increases the number of winners, it should reduce opposition to trade.

While the perceived costs of economic interdependence cannot be ignored—especially when they become the subject of heated political debate—the consensus among the vast majority of economists is that the country as a whole benefits from freer trade. We can summarize this central tenet as follows: *There are gains from voluntary exchange. Whether it occurs between individuals or across national borders, voluntary exchange can benefit all. Trade enables parties to specialize in activities in which they have a comparative advantage.*

Trade Policies

In spite of the gains from trade, countries have imposed a variety of barriers to it. In the remainder of this chapter, we explore some of the common trade barriers and the major initiatives to remove them.

Thinking Like an Economist
EXCHANGE AND THE GLOBALIZATION CONTROVERSY

In recent decades, transportation and communication costs have come down markedly. So too have artificial barriers to the movements of goods and services—trade barriers such as tariffs and quotas. The result is that the economies of the world are now more closely integrated than ever before.

From an economic perspective, this trend toward globalization would seem to offer a great benefit to the world. As we know, one of the core ideas of economics is that *voluntary exchange* is mutually beneficial to the parties involved. Yet globalization has been a subject of great controversy. For instance, some critics see globalization as a one-sided process mainly benefiting rich countries and large multinational firms. Others on the opposite side of the debate see it as the best opportunity to increase the standards of living in poor countries. How do we make sense of this controversy from an economic perspective? A close look at the globalization controversy shows that some of the criticisms are misplaced, while others have merit.

Globalization no doubt has made us more aware of the huge inequalities around the world. Some workers in China, Africa, and India, for instance, earn less than a dollar a day working under conditions that appear inhumane by American standards. But, for the most part, globalization has not caused their misery; it has only brought their plight to global attention. Many of these workers have moved to jobs in seemingly awful factories—some run by multinational firms, others selling their goods to multinational firms—because their previous jobs were even worse or because they had no previous jobs. It may seem cruel for corporations to exploit these workers, especially when working conditions could be improved at moderate expense. But even so, in many cases the workers have benefited from globalization.

Another economic aspect of globalization is that the *distribution* of its benefits may be highly uneven. For example, the owners of factories that make goods for multinational firms typically benefit more than the workers they employ. As a result, even if everyone is better off, inequality increases. Critics attacking the issue from a normative stance—emphasizing social values about fairness—may see increased inequality as the primary concern. In their view, the poor, who in some cases may

Are the jobs of these Chinese workers a cost or benefit of globalization?

benefit the least from globalization, are the very people who deserve to benefit more. But even if we agree with this contention, we have to recognize that it does not refute the basic economic principle about the benefits of voluntary exchange.

A further criticism of globalization maintains that some individuals are actually made worse off. Can this be? The answer is yes, and an example helps illustrate the point. The theory of comparative advantage says that countries should produce the goods that they are relatively good at producing. But when they are protected from foreign competition, firms may produce goods that are not part of the country's comparative advantage. The United States may produce cheap clothes, simply because of the limits put on importing inexpensive foreign-made clothes. Removing the protection may make the production of the inexpensive clothes unprofitable. The factory may have to shut down, and workers will be left unemployed. But in theory, these conditions should not last for long. If markets work well, some new enterprises will be created to take advantage of the country's comparative advantage. Resources are redeployed from where they are less productive to where they are more productive, a shift that increases the country's income. But this process does not happen automatically, or always quickly; in the meanwhile, those who are pushed into unemployment often object to the removal of the protection.

Such problems are especially severe in developing countries, where there is a shortage both of entrepreneurs and of capital to start new enterprises. Workers who lose their jobs can be at particular risk, since they have no unemployment insurance or welfare system to fall back on. In many cases it may be true that the gains of those who benefit from freer trade more than offset the losses of those who suffer. Therefore, in principle, the gainers could compensate the losers so that everyone could be made better off. But in practice, such compensation is seldom paid. Thus, although a country may benefit from globalization, some of its citizens may suffer until the process of redeployment works itself out.

COMMERCIAL POLICY

Countries that have *no* barriers to trade are said to practice **free trade,** but most countries engage in some form of protectionism—that is, in one way or another they restrict the importation of goods. Policies directed at affecting either imports or exports are referred to as **commercial policies.** This and the next section examine the forms that trade barriers take, their economic costs, and their economic and political rationale. The final section explores international attempts to reduce them.

There are five major categories of trade barriers—tariffs, quotas, voluntary export restraints, other *nontariff barriers,* and a set of so-called fair trade laws that, by and large, actually serve to impede trade.

TARIFFS

Tariffs are simply a tax on imports. Since a tariff is a tax that is imposed only on foreign goods, it puts the foreign goods at a disadvantage and discourages imports. A tax on imports makes consumers worse off, as the price they pay is increased. It makes domestic producers of the goods that compete with imports better off, as they can raise their own prices and expand production. Because domestic production is increased and consumption reduced, imports are reduced; the domestic industry has been protected against foreign imports, but at a cost borne by consumers.

QUOTAS

Rather than setting tariffs, many countries impose **quotas**—limits on the amount of foreign goods that can be imported. For instance, in the 1950s, the United States imposed a quota on the amount of oil that could be imported, and until 2005 strict quotas controlled imports of textiles.

Producers often prefer quotas. Because the quantity imported is limited, the domestic price increases above the international price. Quotas enable domestic producers to know precisely the magnitude of the foreign supply. If foreign producers become more efficient or if exchange rates change in their favor, they still cannot sell any more. In that sense, quotas provide domestic producers with greater certainty than do tariffs, insulating them from the worst threats of competition.

Quotas and tariffs both succeed in raising the domestic price above the price at which the good could be obtained abroad. Both thus protect domestic producers. There is, however, one important difference: quotas enable those possessing permits to import to earn a profit by buying goods at the international price abroad and selling at the higher domestic price. The government is, in effect, giving away its tariff revenues. These profits are referred to as **quota rents.**

VOLUNTARY EXPORT RESTRAINTS

In recent years, international agreements have reduced the level of tariffs and restricted the use of quotas. Accordingly, countries have sought to protect themselves from the onslaught of foreign competition by other means. One approach that became popular in the 1980s was the use of *voluntary export restraints* (VERs). Rather than limiting imports of automobiles, for example, the United States persuaded Japan to limit its exports.

There are two interpretations of why Japan might have been willing to go along with this VER. One is that it worried the United States might take a stronger action, such as imposing quotas. From Japan's perspective, VERs are clearly preferable to quotas, because VERs allow the quota rents to accrue to Japanese firms. A second interpretation is that VERs enable Japanese car producers to act collectively in their self-interest to reduce production and raise prices, engaging in a kind of collusion otherwise illegal under American antitrust laws. The VER "imposed" on the Japanese car producers output reductions that they would have chosen themselves if they had been permitted to under law. No wonder, then, that they agreed to go along! The cost to the American consumer of the Japanese VER was enormous. American consumers paid more than $100,000 in higher prices for every American job created.

OTHER NONTARIFF BARRIERS

VERs and quotas are the clearest nontariff barriers, but today they are probably not the most important. A host of regulations have the same effect of imposing barriers to trade. For instance, health-related regulations have been abused in ways that restrict trade. When, in 1996, Russia threatened to halt U.S. exports of chickens on the grounds that its health regulations were not satisfied, U.S. chicken exporters were faced with a nontariff barrier. Various types of regulations have been used to establish nontariff barriers.

During the 1980s, as tariff barriers were being reduced, nontariff barriers increased. A study by the International Monetary Fund concluded that whereas about one-eighth of all U.S. imports were affected by protectionism in 1980, by the middle of the 1990s the figure had risen to one-fourth. It is estimated that trade barriers (including nontariff barriers) may prevent consumers and business from buying as much as $110 billion in imports they would otherwise have purchased. Japan was particularly harmed by these actions. By the early 1990s, about 40 percent of Japan's exports to the United States were limited by some form of U.S. protectionism.

COMPARISON OF QUOTAS AND TARIFFS

Both can be used to restrict imports by the same amount, with the same effect on consumers and domestic producers.

In the case of quotas, the difference between domestic price and international price accrues to the importer, who enjoys a quota rent.

In the case of tariffs, the difference accrues to government as tariff revenues.

VERs (voluntary export restraints) are equivalent to quotas, except that the quota rents are given to foreign producers.

"FAIR TRADE" LAWS

Most people believe competition should be fair. When someone can undersell them, they suspect foul play. The government has imposed a variety of laws to ensure that there is genuine and fair competition domestically. Laws have also been enacted by most countries to ensure "fair competition" in international trade. But most economists believe that in practice these are protectionist measures, reducing competition and restricting imports. To ensure fair competition, economists argue that the same laws that apply domestically should be extended internationally—that is, there should not be two standards of fairness, one applying domestically, one internationally. The two most important "fair trade" laws that represent nontariff barriers are antidumping laws and countervailing duties.

Antidumping Laws Dumping refers to the sale of products overseas at prices that are not only lower than those in the home country but below cost. Normally, consumers greet discounted sales with enthusiasm. If Russia is willing to sell aluminum to the United States at low prices, why should we complain? One possible concern is that by selling below cost, the foreign companies hope to drive American firms out of business. Once they have established a monopoly position, they can raise prices. In such a case, American consumers gain only in the short run. In competitive markets, however, this scenario simply cannot occur, for firms will have no power to raise prices. In almost all of the cases in which dumping has been found, markets are sufficiently competitive that predation is not of concern.

As administered, the antidumping laws are more frequently used as a protectionist tool. If dumping is discovered, a duty (tariff) is levied equal to the difference between the (calculated) cost of production and the price. Critics of the dumping laws worry that other countries will imitate American practices. If so, just as the international community has eliminated tariff barriers, a whole new set of trade barriers will have been erected.

Countervailing Duties A second trade practice widely viewed as unfair is for governments to subsidize domestic firms' production or exports. For example, the government may give certain domestic industries tax breaks or pay a portion of the firms' costs. These subsidies give the companies receiving them an unfair advantage. Trade is determined on the basis not of comparative advantage but of relative subsidy levels.

The usual logic of economics seems to be reversed. If some foreign government wants to subsidize American consumers, who benefit from the lower prices, why should consumers complain? Presumably, they would have a grievance only if the subsidies are part of a policy intended to drive American firms out of business and establish a monopoly position, after which prices would be raised. Most foreign subsidies do not fall into this category.

Opposition to these subsidies arises from the companies who see their businesses hurt. While the gains to consumers outweigh the losses to businesses, the gain to each consumer is small, and consumers are not well organized. Producers, being far better organized, are able and willing to bring their case to Washington. In response, Congress has passed laws allowing the U.S. government to impose **countervailing duties,** that is, taxes that offset any advantage provided by these subsidies.

But even governments that preach against other countries' providing subsidies engage in the practice themselves, most commonly in agriculture. At various times, the U.S. government has subsidized the export and production of wheat, pork, peaches, and a host of other commodities.

Political and Economic Rationale for Protection

Free trade, by allowing each country to concentrate production where it has a comparative advantage, can make all countries better off. Why is protection nevertheless so popular? The basic reason is simple: protection raises prices. While the losses to consumers from higher prices exceed the gains to producers in higher profits, producers are well organized and consumers are not; hence producers' voices are heard more clearly in the political process than are consumers'.

There is an important check on firms' ability to use the political process to advance their special interests: the interests of exporters, who realize that if the United States closes off its markets to imports, other countries will reciprocate. Thus, exporting firms like Boeing have forcefully advocated for an international regime of freer and fairer trade through the kind of international agreements that will be described in the next section.

Before turning to a review of these international agreements, we need to take a closer look at some of the other economic aspects of protection. While free trade may make the country as a whole better off, certain groups may actually become

SURROGATE COUNTRIES AND CANADIAN GOLF CARTS

Question: How, if Canada did not produce golf carts, could the cost of Canadian golf carts be used to accuse Poland of dumping? Answer: The United States sometimes achieves wonders when its markets are at stake.

The standard criterion for judging whether a country is dumping is whether it is selling commodities on the U.S. market at prices below those for which it sells them at home or elsewhere, or at prices below the costs of production. For non-market economies, the Department of Commerce formulated a special criterion: Is the price below what it would have cost to produce the good in a "comparable" (or "surrogate") country?

The Department of Commerce, which is responsible for implementing the law, knows no shame. In a famous case involving Polish golf carts, it decided that the country most like Poland was Canada—at a time when Poland's per capita income was a fraction of Canada's, and when Canada did not make comparable golf carts. Thus, the Commerce Department faced the question: What would it have cost for Canada to produce these golf carts, had it chosen to do so? Not surprisingly, the resulting cost estimate was higher than the price the real golf carts were being sold for in the United States, and Poland was found guilty of dumping.

Similar charges have been made on similar grounds against Russian sales of natural resources. For years, Western countries had preached to the Soviet Union and the other socialist countries the virtues of the market. Beginning in 1989, with the demise of communism, former iron-curtain countries sought to transform their economies into market economies. Under the old regime, these countries had traded mainly with themselves, and generally engaged in barter. In the new era, they sought to enter international markets, like any other market economy.

Though the design and production quality of many of its manufactured goods made them unsuitable for Western markets, Russia had a wealth of natural resources—including uranium and aluminum—that it could produce on a competitive basis. Moreover, with the reduction of defense expenditures—good news from virtually every perspective—Russia's demand for many of these raw materials was greatly reduced.

American producers attempted to discourage Russian exports by filing, or threatening to file, dumping charges. Though Russia was probably not selling these commodities at prices below those prevailing at home or elsewhere, or at prices below the cost of production, the "surrogate" country criterion made the dumping charges a very real threat. Russia agreed to a cutback in aluminum production in 1994, to be matched by cutbacks in other countries.

To the Commerce and State Departments, this may have seemed a reasonable way to avoid trade conflict. But consumers paid dearly, in higher prices for aluminum and products using aluminum.

worse off. Those especially affected include displaced firms and workers, low-wage workers, and those in industries that enjoyed limited competition without free trade.

DISPLACED FIRMS AND WORKERS

China has a comparative advantage in inexpensive textiles while the United States has a comparative advantage in manufacturing complex goods like advanced telephone exchanges. If the United States starts to import textiles from China, U.S. textile manufacturers may be driven out of business, and their workers will have to find work elsewhere. The gains to the export industries more than offset these losses. In principle, the gainers could more than compensate the losers, but such compensation is seldom made: hence, the losers oppose moves to open trade.

Economists shed few tears for businesses that are hurt when trade becomes open. Loss of profits is just one risk that businesses face, and for which they are typically well compensated. New innovations destroy old businesses. But barring the door to new technologies or cheaper foreign products is bad economics—and bad economic policy.

Thinking Like an Economist
DISTRIBUTION AND TRADE LIBERALIZATION

Trade liberalization may make a country as a whole better off, but it does not make everyone in the country better off. The gains to the winners are large enough that, in principle, any losers could be compensated, to everyone's benefit. But in practice, compensation is seldom made. Thus, trade liberalization often entails trade-offs to balance the gains of one group in the economy against the losses of another group. The problem is that often the losers are among the poorest in the country. For example, trade liberalization threatens to force low-paid textile workers in the United States into unemployment. It is little comfort for the textile workers in South Carolina to know that new jobs are being created for aircraft engineers in Seattle or that all American consumers of textile products are now better off. In the United States, however, labor markets work reasonably well, and the laid-off textile worker can eventually get a new job, though often at markedly reduced wages.

While low-wage textile workers in the United States are hurt by trade liberalization, low-wage textile workers in developing economies gain. Trade liberalization increases the demand for the textiles they produce, and thus increases the demand for their labor. Unfortunately, matters can be far bleaker for those in developing countries to whom trade liberalization brings increased competition. In many developing countries, unemployment is 15 percent or more, so the loss of a job is likely to have severe consequences.

In Mexico, since the North American Free Trade Agreement was enacted wages have soared for those who produce goods for American car companies or other firms near the border of Texas. But in the south of Mexico, the poor have become even poorer. Highly subsidized American corn has depressed the already low incomes of Mexican farmers. To be sure, urban workers benefit, since they can buy corn for a lower price than would otherwise have been possible.

When diverse groups are affected so differently, it is not clear whether trade liberalization is a good thing *in the absence of policies to address its distributional effects.* But such assessments are not made by economists; in democracies, they are left to the political processes. Society as a whole does benefit from trade liberalization, and the role of the economist is to point out this potential for gain. Economists also have a role to play in explaining who will be affected, and to what degree.

Often, however, more sympathy is felt for workers affected by trade—though there is no reason why concern should be greater over displacements caused by open trade than by new innovations. When the economy is running at close to full employment, workers who lose their jobs typically do find new positions. But they often go through a transition period of unemployment, and when they do find a new job, chances are good that their wages will be lower (in the United States, in recent years, a worker who finds full-time employment experiences on average a 10 percent wage decline). While these particular laborers are worse off, workers as a whole benefit, because those who get newly created jobs in the export industries are paid far more (on average 13 to 15 percent more) than the average for the economy. Concern about the transitional costs borne by displaced workers has motivated Congress to pass laws to provide special assistance for these workers in finding new jobs and obtaining the requisite training.

BEGGAR-THY-NEIGHBOR POLICIES

Concerns about unemployment have provided the strongest motivation for protectionist policies. The argument is simple: if Americans do not buy foreign goods, they will spend the money at home, thereby creating more jobs for Americans. Deliberate attempts to increase national output and employment by reducing imports are called **beggar-thy-neighbor policies,** because the jobs gained in one country are at the expense of jobs lost in another. Such efforts ignore an important fact: if we do not buy goods from abroad, foreign purchasers will not buy our goods. As a result, U.S. exports to other countries will fall in tandem with our imports from other countries, causing jobs in our export industries to disappear. The benefits of specialization are denied to everyone, and national incomes fall.

The worst instances of beggar-thy-neighbor policies occurred at the onset of the Great Depression. In 1930, the United States passed the Hawley-Smoot Tariff Act, raising tariffs to a level that effectively prohibited many imports. Other countries retaliated. As U.S. imports declined, incomes elsewhere in the world fell and as other countries imposed retaliatory tariffs, they bought fewer goods from the United States. U.S. exports plummeted, contributing to the economic downturn in the United States. The downturn in international trade that was set off by the Hawley-Smoot Tariff Act, charted in Figure 16.4, is often pointed to as a major factor contributing to the depth and severity of the Great Depression.

Wrap-Up

INTERNATIONAL TRADE AND JOBS

Restricting imports as a way of creating jobs tends to be counterproductive.

It is the responsibility of macroeconomic policy, not trade policy, to maintain the economy at full employment.

WAGES IN AFFECTED SECTORS

Beyond these short-run problems of transition and unemployment, long-run problems may face workers in affected sectors. The United States has a comparative advantage in producing goods such as airplanes and high-tech products that require highly skilled workers. As the United States exports more of these goods, its demand for these workers increases, driving up their wages. Similarly, the United States has a comparative disadvantage in producing goods that require much unskilled labor, such as lower-quality textiles. As imports compete against these U.S. industries and their production decreases, the demand for unskilled labor decreases. As a result, the wages of the unskilled workers are driven down.

This loss in income for unskilled workers is often blamed on imports from third world countries like China, where wages are but a fraction of those in the United States. The consensus among economists who have looked closely at the matter is that international trade explains a relatively small part of the decline in wages—perhaps 20 percent. Nonetheless, those who see their livelihood being threatened are among the most ardent advocates of trade restrictions. Again, economists argue that the appropriate response is not to restrict trade but to increase skills. The workers gaining the skills are better off, as their wages rise

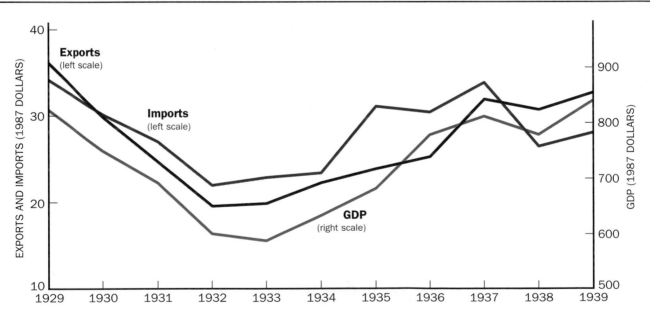

Figure 16.4

THE DECLINE IN INTERNATIONAL TRADE AND THE GREAT DEPRESSION

U.S. exports and imports fell dramatically during the Great Depression. One contributing factor in the decline in trade was the Hawley-Smoot Tariff Act, passed in 1930.

SOURCE: Bureau of Economic Analysis (www.bea.doc.gov).

commensurately with the increase in their productivity. In addition, as more workers become skilled, the supply of workers still unskilled is reduced; and the smaller supply of unskilled workers leads to a rise in their real wages, offsetting the adverse effects of trade.

INCREASED COMPETITION

International trade has other adverse effects in industries in which competition is limited. Limited competition enables firms to enjoy monopoly or oligopoly profits. Workers often receive some of these extra profits: particularly when the industries are unionized, they may earn wages far higher than workers of comparable skill employed elsewhere in the economy. After international trade introduces more competition, monopoly and oligopoly profits get competed away. Firms are forced to pay competitive wages—that is, the lowest wage that they can for workers with a given skill.

From the perspective of the overall economy, this competition that erodes market power and induces greater efficiency and responsiveness to consumers is one of the major virtues of free trade. From the perspective of those who see their higher wages and profits vanishing, it is one of free trade's major vices.

Wrap-Up

EFFECTS OF TRADE ON WAGES

International trade may lower wages of unskilled U.S. labor and those working in industries where competition is limited.

International trade raises wages of skilled U.S. workers.

THE INFANT INDUSTRY ARGUMENT

Job loss and decreased wages and profits from international competition provide much of the political motivation behind protection, but economists have asked if there are any *legitimate* arguments for protection. That is, are there circumstances where protection may be in the *national* interest, and not just in the interests of those being protected? Two arguments have been put forward.

The first is the **infant industry argument.** Costs in new industries are often high, dropping as experience is gained. The infant industry argument is that firms, particularly in less-developed countries, will never be able to get the experience required to produce efficiently unless they are protected from foreign competition.

Economists have traditionally responded to this argument skeptically. If it pays to enter the industry, eventually entrants will earn profits. Thus, the firm should be

TRADE LIBERALIZATION IN INFORMATION TECHNOLOGY AND FINANCIAL SERVICES

In recent years, there have been important trade agreements in information technology (IT) and financial services. This is a distinct change from the past, when trade agreements focused on traded goods, such as cars, steel, and textiles. But the two areas draw markedly different reactions in many developing countries: while IT liberalization has been welcome, there is extensive opposition to liberalization in financial services. Why the difference?

Economic theory says that unilateral liberalization—opening up one's market to the cheaper goods of foreigners—is a good thing. Even if domestic producers are worse off, their losses are more than offset by the gains of consumers. Unfortunately, producers often have a greater voice in the political process, and consumers cannot unite to compensate the producers for their losses. Countries therefore often resist trade liberalization. But IT is different. Most developing countries do not have a large IT sector that would be hurt by liberalization. Instead, both producers and consumers in developing countries are purchasers of IT products, and both gain by having access to IT at lower prices.

Financial service liberalization is quite a different matter. The existing domestic banks in developing countries fear greater competition from foreign banks. The greater efficiency of foreign banks is not their only worry; depositors may feel safer putting their money in a large American or European bank than in a small domestic bank. In addition, many firms in developing countries believe that the foreign banks are more likely to lend to Coca-Cola and IBM than to small domestic firms, and there are some grounds for these concerns. The government, too, may worry that the foreign banks will be less subject to pressure from the government. Sometimes such pressure is part of corruption—members of the government lean on the bank to lend to their friends. But it can also be part of economic policy—the government leans on the bank to increase lending in an economic downturn and to contract lending when the economy is overheated. In developing countries, this "guidance" from the government may be an important tool for macroeconomic stability.

Today, as many countries liberalize their financial markets, they are asking, "How can we gain the advantages of the new competition without suffering the disadvantages?" Until they find effective ways of ensuring a flow of capital to small domestic businesses, banks in developing countries will find powerful allies in resisting financial market liberalization.

willing to initially charge a price below cost to gain the necessary experience, because today's losses will be more than offset by future profits. But more recently, the infant industry argument has found more favor. Firms can operate at a loss only if they can borrow funds. If capital markets do not work well, firms may not be able to borrow even if their eventual prospects are reasonable. Such market failures are a particular danger in less-developed countries.

This may be a legitimate argument. But it points to a need not for protection but for assistance, which can take the form of loans or direct subsidies. Economists argue for direct assistance rather than protection because the assistance is transparent: everyone can see that it is a subsidy to producers. Economists criticize protection because it is a hidden tax on consumers, with the proceeds transferred to producers. The lack of transparency encourages industries to spend resources on persuading government to impose these hidden taxes that benefit themselves.

STRATEGIC TRADE THEORY

Another argument for protection is that it can give a country a strategic trade advantage over rivals by helping to reduce domestic costs. There may be economies of scale: the larger the level of production, the lower the marginal costs. Protection ensures a large domestic sales base, and therefore a low marginal cost. The instances in which **strategic trade theory** might provide a rationale for protection appear to be relatively rare, however. Even then, it tends to be effective only when foreign governments do not retaliate by taking similar actions.

International Cooperation

Recognizing both the temptation of shortsighted trade policies and the potential gains from trade, nations large and small have engaged since World War II in a variety of efforts to reduce trade barriers.

GATT AND THE WTO

The **General Agreement on Tariffs and Trade (GATT),** an organization established after World War II, was replaced in 1995 by the **World Trade Organization (WTO).** GATT was founded on three guiding principles: *reciprocity*—if one country lowered its tariffs, it could expect other countries in GATT to lower theirs; *nondiscrimination*—no member of GATT could offer a special trade deal that favored only one or a few other countries; and *transparency*—import quotas and other nontariff barriers to trade should be converted into tariffs to allow their effective impact to be ascertained.

The lowering of trade barriers has proceeded in a number of stages, called *rounds* (the Kennedy Round, completed in 1967; the Tokyo Round, completed in 1979; the Uruguay Round, completed in 1994; and the Doha Round, currently slated to be completed by the end of 2005). Collectively, the rounds have reduced tariffs on industrial goods markedly, from an average of 40 percent in 1947 to less than 5 percent today.

The Uruguay Round produced agreements to reduce agricultural subsidies and to ensure that intellectual property rights—patents and copyrights—were respected. It also created the WTO to help enforce the trade agreements. Previously, a country that believed it was suffering from an unfair trade practice could bring a case to a GATT panel that would examine the evidence. However, there was little in the way of effective enforcement of subsequent decisions. Under the WTO, a country injured by an unfair trade practice will be authorized to engage in retaliatory actions. For example, Brazil won a major WTO case in 2004 against U.S. cotton subsidies. Though that decision is under appeal, if the United States loses the appeal and then fails to remove its subsidies to cotton farmers, Brazil will be able to retaliate against U.S. exports to Brazil.

The Doha Round began in 2001 and almost collapsed in 2003 when delegates from developing nations walked out in protest over the subsidies that developed nations such as the United States and members of the European Union provide to their farmers.

The European Union has agreed in principle to eliminate export subsidies on farm products; the United States has not yet made a similar commitment.

THE GROWING PROTEST AGAINST THE WTO

In December 1999, the WTO held a meeting in Seattle to launch a new round of trade negotiations. But thousands of protesters—some violent—dominated the stage. What brought on such a vehement reaction? Old-fashioned protectionist sentiment played a role, but there were other important factors.

Some WTO critics believed that the agenda in previous rounds of trade negotiations had been set by the more advanced industrial countries—to further their interests—and that the outcomes reflected their economic power. Not only had they gained the lion's share of the benefits, but they had done so at the expense of some poorer countries. The World Bank estimated that after the round of trade negotiations concluded in 1994, the poorest region in the world, sub-Saharan Africa, was actually worse off. While poorer countries were forced to cut their tariffs against goods produced in the more advanced industrial countries, the more advanced industrial countries continued to protect their agricultural sectors. While financial services had been opened up, industries that relied more heavily on unskilled workers, such as the construction and maritime industries, remained closed.

Environmental and human rights issues were two other prominent areas of intense debate. Environmentalists and human rights advocates wanted to use trade policy to help achieve their objectives. They worried that countries with inadequate protections of the environment or of labor rights would be able to undercut American firms, whose losses would increase pressure within the United States to erode those standards here. The insistence by some on including clauses in trade agreements concerning labor and the environment was met with an equally adamant resistance by others, threatening to stall all efforts at trade liberalization. There was consensus on a few issues—for example, countries should not be allowed to export goods produced by child or prison labor. But beyond that, the debate raged on and it is likely to continue in the foreseeable future.

Thousands of protestors converged in Seattle to protest the WTO Conference held there in December 1999.

Case in Point

THE BANANA WAR

How could a dispute over bananas lead to unemployment among Scottish cashmere workers? The explanation lies in the spillover effect of the banana war between the United States and the European Union (EU). This dispute revolved around the claim by the United States that the EU was following discriminatory trade practices.

Beginning in 1993, the EU imposed a banana import tariff that favored producers in former European colonies in the Caribbean, Africa, and the Pacific over those in Latin America. The United States and five Latin American countries complained to the WTO. The United States claimed that EU banana import tariffs were harming the country. Since the United States does not produce bananas, one might reasonably ask how it could be harmed by the EU's policy on banana imports. While not a producer itself, the United States is home to two food distributors, Chiquita Brands and Dole, that do grow bananas in Central America.

The WTO ruled that the EU regime was in violation of GATT and ordered the EU to change its policies. The EU did, instituting a new banana import regime on January 1, 1999. However, the United States and Latin America banana producers argued that the new policy still effectively discriminated against them, and the dispute was sent to the WTO Dispute Settlement Body. The United States claimed victory in the banana war when, in April 1999, the Dispute Settlement Body accepted the results of the WTO arbitrators, agreeing that the new EU policies harmed the United States. This decision paved the way for the United States to impose sanctions against EU products. The WTO ruled that the United States could impose $191 million in sanctions against the EU, an amount determined by estimating the economic damages to the United States resulting from the EU policies.

To retaliate against Europe, the United States imposed 100 percent tariffs on a range of European products, effectively doubling their prices in the United States. The list of goods hit by the punitive tariffs included Scottish cashmere, Italian cheese, and German coffee makers. The targeted products were chosen to bring maximum political pressures on the EU. The WTO ruling allowed the United States to impose these high tariffs until the EU revised its banana policy to eliminate discrimination against Latin American producers. The EU conceded defeat, and the banana war ended.

REGIONAL TRADING BLOCS

GATT and WTO have made some progress in reducing trade barriers among all countries. But the difficulties of reaching agreements involving so many parties have made progress slow. In the meantime, many countries have formed *regional trade blocs,* agreeing with their more immediate neighbors not only to eliminate trade barriers but also to facilitate the flow of capital and labor. Perhaps the most important of these is the **European Union,** the successor to the *Common Market,* which now embraces most of Europe. The North American Free Trade Agreement creates a free trade zone within North America—that is, an area within which goods and services trade freely, without tariffs or other import restrictions. There are also many smaller free trade zones, such as those between New Zealand and Australia, and among groups of countries in Latin America and in Central America.

While the gains from internationally coordinated reductions in trade barriers are clear, the gains from regional trading blocs are more controversial. Reducing trade barriers within a region encourages trade by members of the trading bloc. Lowering barriers among the countries involved results in **trade creation.** But it also leads to **trade diversion.** Trade is diverted away from countries that are not members of the bloc but might, in fact, have a comparative advantage in a particular commodity. Under these conditions, the global net benefits will be positive if the trade creation exceeds the trade diversion. Typically, when trade blocs are formed, tariffs against outsiders are harmonized. If the external trade barriers are harmonized at the lowest common level (rather than at the average or highest levels) at the same time that internal trade barriers are lowered, the effects of trade creation are more likely to exceed those of trade diversion.

Expanding regional trading blocs to cover investment flows raises particular anxieties, especially when the bloc includes countries with very different standards of living.

TRADE AND TRADE POLICY

During the debates over NAFTA, some argued that Mexico would suck up huge amounts of investment that would otherwise have gone to businesses in the United States. According to this view, American firms would move to Mexico to take advantage of the low-wage labor and the capital that flowed to Mexico would not be available for investment in the United States.

Such arguments failed to take into account that capital markets were already global. Capital flows to good investment opportunities wherever they are. Good opportunities to invest in the United States will attract capital, regardless of how much Americans invest in Mexico. Investment barriers impede this flow of capital to its most productive use, thereby lowering world economic efficiency.

Often trade debates are based on a "zero sum" view of the world, the belief that when one country (here, Mexico) gains, another (the United States) must lose. For example, many people argue that when a country imports, it loses jobs: the gains to foreign workers from their exports are at the expense of domestic firms to which those jobs somehow belonged. The debate over "outsourcing"—the move by U.S. firms to import goods and services that these same firms formerly produced in the United States—is of this sort. Earlier in this chapter we learned what was wrong with this argument. The theory of comparative advantage says that when countries specialize in what they produce best, *both* countries are better off. Workers enjoy higher wages when they move into sectors where their productivity is highest, and consumers benefit from the lower prices. So too with investment. When investment flows to where its return is highest, world output (income) is increased.

But just as not everyone necessarily gains from trade according to comparative advantage, so too not everyone will necessarily gain from the free flow of capital. There will be some investment diversion from other countries to Mexico, as Mexico becomes more attractive to investors throughout the world because of its improved access to the huge American market. Most economists believe that the net effect on investment in the United States will be negligible, and could even be positive. Industries within the United States that see their opportunities expand by selling more to Mexico will increase their investment, more than offsetting the reduced investment from firms that decline in the face of competition from Mexican imports.

In fact, investment flows augment the gains from trade that would occur in their absence because there are important trade-investment links. American companies producing abroad tend to use more parts from America, just as French companies producing abroad tend to use more French parts. Thus, flows of investment often serve as a precursor to exports.

Wrap-Up

AREAS OF INTERNATIONAL COOPERATION

Multilateral trade agreements—WTO
    based on principles of reciprocity, nondiscrimination, and transparency
Regional trade agreements—NAFTA, European Union
    risk of trade diversion rather than trade creation
    may be better able to address complicated issues, such as those involving investment

Review and Practice

SUMMARY

1. The benefits of economic interdependence apply to individuals and firms within a country as well as to countries within the world. No individual and no country is self-sufficient.

2. The principle of comparative advantage asserts that countries should export the goods in which their production costs are *relatively* low.

3. Specialization tends to increase productivity for three reasons: specializing eliminates the time it takes a worker to switch from one production task to another, workers who repeat a task become more skilled at it, and specialization creates a fertile environment for invention.

4. A country's comparative advantage can arise from natural endowments, acquired endowments, superior knowledge, specialization, or interactions of these factors.

5. There is a basic difference between trade among individuals and trade among countries: trade among countries may actually leave some individuals within the country worse off. Though free trade enhances national income, fears about job loss and wage reductions among low-skilled workers have led to demands for protection.

6. Countries protect themselves in a variety of ways besides imposing tariffs. The most important nontariff barriers are quotas, voluntary export restraints, and regulatory barriers. Quotas and voluntary export restraints are now banned by international agreement.

7. While all countries benefit from free trade, some groups within a country may be harmed. In the United States, unskilled workers and those in industries where, without trade, there is limited competition may see their wages fall. Some workers may lose their jobs and may require assistance to find new ones.

8. Laws nominally intended to ensure fair trade—such as antidumping laws and countervailing duties—often are used as protectionist measures.

9. Beggar-thy-neighbor policies, which attempt to protect jobs by limiting imports, tend to be counterproductive.

10. The WTO, which replaced GATT, provides a framework within which trade barriers can be reduced. It is based on reciprocity, nondiscrimination, and transparency.

KEY TERMS

imports
exports
bilateral trade
multilateral trade
absolute advantage
comparative advantage
protectionism
North American Free Trade Agreement (NAFTA)
free trade
commercial policies
tariffs
quotas
quota rents
dumping
countervailing duties
beggar-thy-neighbor policies
infant industry argument
strategic trade theory
General Agreement on Tariffs and Trade (GATT)
World Trade Organization (WTO)
European Union
trade creation
trade diversion

REVIEW QUESTIONS

1. Why are all voluntary trades mutually beneficial?

2. Does a country with an absolute advantage in a product necessarily have a comparative advantage in that product? Can a country with an absolute disadvantage in a product have a comparative advantage in that product? Explain.

3. Why does specialization tend to increase productivity?

4. "A country's comparative advantage is dictated by its natural endowments." Discuss.

5. What are the various ways in which countries seek to protect their industries against foreign imports?

6. How do tariffs and quotas differ?

7. Why are consumers worse off as a result of the imposition of a tariff?

8. What are nontariff barriers to international trade?
9. How is it possible that while there are gains to free trade, some groups are harmed? Which are the groups in the United States that are most adversely affected?
10. What are beggar-thy-neighbor policies? What are their consequences?
11. What is meant by trade diversion versus trade creation?

LABOR COSTS OF PRODUCING CARS AND TV SHOWS (WORKER HOURS):

	European Union	United States
Labor required to make a car	100	80
Labor required to produce a TV show	600	400

PROBLEMS

1. David Ricardo illustrated the principle of comparative advantage in terms of the trade between England and Portugal in wine (port) and wool. Suppose in England it takes 120 laborers to produce a certain quantity of wine, while in Portugal it takes only 80 laborers to produce the same quantity. Similarly, in England it takes 100 laborers to produce a certain quantity of wool, while in Portugal it takes only 90. Draw the opportunity set for each country, assuming each has 72,000 laborers. Assume each country commits half its labor to each product in the absence of trade, and designate that point in your graph. Now describe a new production plan, with trade, that can benefit both countries.

2. If you continue with the example of Problem 1, which country has an absolute advantage in wine? In wool? Which country has a comparative advantage in wine? In wool?

3. For many years, an international agreement called the Multifiber Agreement limited the amount of textiles that the developed economies of North America and Europe could buy from poor countries in Latin America and Asia. Textiles can be produced by relatively unskilled labor with a reasonably small amount of capital. Who benefited from the protectionism of the Multifiber Agreement? Who suffered? The Multifiber Agreement expired on January 1, 2005. Who should benefit from its end? Who will suffer?

4. Both the European Union and the United States produce cars and television shows. Assume the labor costs (in worker hours) required for the production of cars and programs are as follows:

Assume each region has 240,000 worker hours to divide between producing cars and television shows. Initially, assume workers are divided equally between producing cars and television shows.
   (a) What are the initial levels of production of cars and TV shows in each region? What is total production in the two regions?
   (b) Draw the production possibilities curves for the two regions.
   (c) Which region has an absolute advantage in producing cars? Which region has an absolute advantage in producing television shows?
   (d) Which region has a comparative advantage in producing cars? Which region has a comparative advantage in producing television shows?
   (e) Starting with the initial levels of production, demonstrate how comparative advantage can be exploited to raise joint production of cars by 10 while leaving television show output unchanged.

5. In 2002, President George W. Bush imposed tariffs on foreign-produced steel. Who gained from this policy? Who lost? (In 2003, the WTO ruled that the tariffs were illegal.)

6. Many Americans have objected to the importation of textiles and garments from poor countries because the conditions of production in those countries are much worse than those for most American workers. If these imports from poor countries are reduced, who benefits? Who loses?

7. If Mexican workers receive a third of the wages that U.S. workers do, why don't all American firms move down to Mexico?

8. If Mexico becomes a more attractive place to invest, is the United States helped or hurt?

Learning Goals

In this chapter, you will learn

1 What factors determine international exchange rates

2 How fixed exchange rate systems differ from flexible exchange rate systems

3 How a fixed exchange rate system restricts the use of monetary policy

Chapter 17

THE INTERNATIONAL FINANCIAL SYSTEM

After working all year, you have saved enough to buy that new, fuel-efficient Toyota Prius. You have located one at a local car dealer, and the price is $20,000. You give the dealer $20,000 and drive away. But is that the end of the transaction? No. The car was built in Japan, so Toyota needs yen, the Japanese currency, and not U.S. dollars to pay the workers in Japan who manufactured it. The dealer who imported the Prius to the United States therefore will need to convert those dollars into yen to pay Toyota; the dealer needs to sell dollars and buy yen. Similarly, when Boeing sells an airplane to Garuda Indonesia, it needs to convert the Indonesian rupiah into U.S. dollars to pay its workers, suppliers, and owners. The market in which different currencies can be bought and sold is called the *foreign exchange market:* it enables the car dealer to sell dollars and buy yen and Boeing to sell rupiah and buy U.S. dollars.

Every day, U.S. exporters like Boeing receive payments from their sales in foreign countries that they need to convert to dollars, while U.S. importers need foreign currencies to pay their foreign suppliers. Foreign investors wishing to purchase American assets need to buy dollars, while others may be selling American assets in order to switch their investments into a different country. If Toyota decides to expand its production facilities in the United States, it will need to purchase dollars to carry out its investment plans. All these transactions involve one or more currencies and give rise to a huge volume of foreign currency trading—about $1.5 trillion every day.

The international financial system that has developed to carry out these trades, and that enables Americans to invest in Brazilian stocks and Ford to buy Volvo, Japanese investors to buy U.S. Treasury bonds and Toyota to build assembly plants in Tennessee, links together the members of the global economy. Because of these financial links, international factors can play a critical role in the macroeconomy.

Opening a country's financial markets to foreign investors can have many benefits. The most important is that domestic investment is no longer constrained by domestic saving. There are also potential costs, however, a point driven home in 1996 and 1997 when a financial crisis that began in Thailand spread to other countries in Asia and Latin America, and again in 1998 when Russia faced a financial crisis that led to the largest one-day fall in prices on the London stock exchange in a decade. In this chapter, we will focus on the factors that affect foreign currency trading and how international capital flows in foreign exchange markets influence the value of the dollar.

Determining the Exchange Rate

The starting point for understanding the international financial system is the foreign exchange market, in which currencies of different countries are bought or sold. This market has no single location; instead, it involves thousands of currency traders at computer terminals around the globe, buying and selling different currencies. Most trading is heavily concentrated, though, in three major centers: London, New York, and Tokyo. London is the largest, with a daily trading volume of more than $600 billion.

The *exchange rate* is the rate at which one currency can be traded for another. If the dollar–yen exchange rate is 110, then $1 will buy 110 yen. Systems in which exchange rates are determined by the law of supply and demand, without government interference, are called **flexible exchange rate systems.** The United States, Japan, and the European Economic and Monetary Union (EMU) all have flexible exchange rate systems. We have already looked briefly, in Chapter 8, at how exchange rates are determined by supply and demand in the foreign exchange market. Governments often intervene in foreign exchange markets, and later in this chapter we will examine the different forms that this intervention takes. But first we need to understand what determines the exchange rate in a flexible exchange rate system.

Consider a world consisting of only two currencies, the U.S. dollar and the euro used by members of the EMU. Americans and Europeans exchange dollars for euros. There are three reasons why Europeans might want dollars and therefore be willing to supply euros in trade for dollars in the foreign exchange markets: to buy American goods (American exports, or imports into Europe), to make investments in the United States (that is, to buy U.S. stocks, other financial assets, or real assets such as land or factories), or to speculate—that is, if Europeans think that the dollar is going to gain value relative to the euro, speculators might want to buy dollars now and sell them later when they are more valuable. Similarly, there are three reasons why Americans might want euros, and accordingly supply dollars to the foreign exchange market to trade for euros: to buy European goods, to make investments in Europe, or to speculate if they think that the euro is going to become more valuable relative to the dollar. The question is, How many euros will an American get in exchange for a dollar, or, conversely, how many dollars will a European get in exchange for a euro? The exchange rate can be thought of as the *relative price* of dollars and euros. It will tell us how many dollars it takes to purchase one euro and how many euros it will take to purchase one dollar.

The foreign exchange market in Yerevan, Armenia

SUPPLY AND DEMAND IN THE FOREIGN EXCHANGE MARKET

In competitive markets, prices are determined by demand and supply. Similarly, exchange rates are determined by demand and supply in foreign exchange markets. In our example of just two currencies—dollars and euros—it makes no difference whether we look at things from the perspective of the demand for and supply of dollars or from the perspective of the demand for and supply of euros. The European supply of euros on the foreign exchange market is equivalent to the European's demand for dollars. The U.S. supply of dollars is equivalent to Americans' demand for euros.

Panel A of Figure 17.1 shows supply and demand curves in the foreign exchange market. The horizontal axis measures the volume of dollars; the vertical axis measures the exchange rate, the value of the dollars in terms of euros. We express the value of the dollar as the number of euros it takes to buy 1 dollar in the foreign exchange market. Thus, if the exchange rate is 2 euros to the dollar, the dollar is expensive in terms of euros—it takes 2 euros to buy 1 dollar. If the exchange rate is one half a euro to the dollar, the dollar is cheap—it only takes a half a euro to buy 1 dollar (or, equivalently, 1 euro will buy 2 dollars). The higher the exchange rate, the more expensive the dollar is in terms of euros.

The demand for dollars has been drawn as a downward sloping curve. As the exchange rate falls, dollars become cheaper. Just as demand for a good goes up when its price falls, so, as dollars become cheaper, Europeans will want to purchase more of them.

The supply curve of dollars has been drawn in the figure with a positive slope. As the exchange rate rises, Americans will be able to get more euros for every dollar they sell in the foreign exchange market. As they do so, the supply of dollars will increase. The equilibrium exchange rate is the value of dollars in terms of euros that balances the demand for dollars and the supply of dollars. In the figure, e_0 is the equilibrium exchange rate. At a lower exchange rate such as e_1, the demand for dollars exceeds the supply of dollars. Just as in the market for wheat, if demand exceeds supply, the price will rise. In this case, the value of the dollar will rise. At an exchange rate such as e_2, supply exceeds demand and the dollar will fall in value.

Panels B and C illustrate the effects on the exchange rate of a shift in the supply of dollars and the demand for dollars, respectively. In panel B, the supply curve has shifted to the right, increasing the supply of dollars at each exchange rate. Perhaps a change in European tax law has made investing in Europe more attractive to American firms (other factors that might shift the supply curve will be discussed below). At the initial exchange rate e_0, there is now an excess supply of dollars. The dollar will fall in value until the new equilibrium is reached at the exchange rate e_1.

Panel C illustrates another change in the foreign exchange market—this time a shift to the left in the demand curve for dollars, reflecting a smaller demand for dollars at each exchange rate. Such a shift might be caused by a change in U.S. tax law that makes it less attractive for European firms to invest in the United States. At the initial exchange rate e_0, there is now an excess supply of dollars. The value of the dollar falls until the new equilibrium is reached at the exchange rate e_1. At this lower value, the demand for dollars and the supply of dollars are again equal.

Earlier, we noted three reasons why Europeans might wish to sell euros to buy dollars and, conversely, Americans might wish to sell dollars to buy euros. We can now discuss how each of these factors affects demand and supply in the foreign exchange market.

Exports and Imports Consider what happens if a U.S. firm sells a product in Europe. Suppose, for example, Levi Strauss sells jeans in Europe. The company can do three things with the euros it receives for the goods it has sold. First, it could try to convert them into dollars. Second, it could sell the euros to an American firm

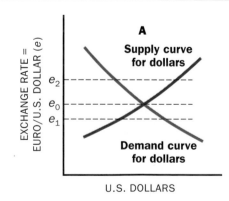
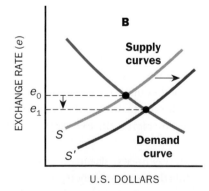
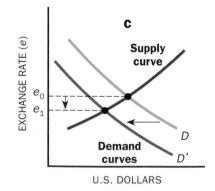

Figure 17.1

THE EXCHANGE RATE

In equilibrium, the exchange rate is determined where the demand for dollars equals the supply, as in panel A. A rightward shift in the supply curve of dollars (panel B) or a leftward shift in the demand curve for dollars (panel C) results in a lower exchange rate; that is, the dollar depreciates.

that wants to use the euros to buy European goods and import those goods back into the United States. Third, it could lend the euros to a European borrower. To simplify the discussion, we will imagine that no one in Europe would lend to anyone in America, and no one in America would lend to anyone in Europe. Foreign borrowing and lending will be considered separately.

A European firm that sells goods in the United States will find itself in a similar position. The firm will receive U.S. dollars, and it could try to convert them into euros or sell them to a European importer who needs them to buy American goods for import back into Europe. In a situation in which some parties (U.S. exporters and European importers) want to trade euros for dollars, while others (U.S. importers and European exporters) wish to trade dollars for euros, mutually beneficial exchanges are clearly possible.

Figure 17.2 illustrates the market for foreign exchange (dollars and euros in our two-currency example). The supply curve for dollars is determined by U.S. importers who want to sell dollars to buy the euros they need and by European exporters who want to sell the dollars they have earned. At a low value of the dollar, such as e_1, U.S. imports (European exports) will be low because dollars buy few euros. From the perspective of Americans, European goods are expensive—it takes many dollars to purchase European goods. At a high value of the dollar, such as e_2, U.S. imports (European exports) will be high because, from the perspective of Americans, European goods are cheap. Thus, the supply curve of dollars in the foreign exchange market slopes up.

The demand curve for dollars is determined by U.S. exporters who want to sell the euros they have earned and buy dollars and by European importers who want to buy dollars to purchase American goods. At a low value of the dollar, such as e_1, U.S. exports (European imports) will be high because a euro buys many dollars. From the perspective of Europeans, American goods are cheap. At a high value of the dollar, such as e_2, U.S. exports (European imports) will be low because, from the perspective of Europeans, American goods are expensive. Thus, the demand curve of dollars in the foreign exchange market slopes down. The value of the dollar at which the demand for dollars equals the supply of dollars is the equilibrium exchange rate—in the figure, this point is e_0—where exports and imports are equal. As we will see, exports and imports need not be equal once we take foreign borrowing and lending into account.

We can use the demand and supply model of the foreign exchange market to analyze how the equilibrium exchange rate is affected when other factors change and shift the demand or supply curves. For example, suppose Americans adopt a "buy American" campaign that reduces the demand for European imports at each value of the exchange rate. We can represent the impact of this campaign by a leftward shift in the supply curve of dollars as U.S. imports (European exports) fall, as illustrated in Figure 17.3. The equilibrium exchange rate rises. When the dollar rises in value relative to other currencies, we say that the dollar **appreciates.** Because the higher value of the dollar makes U.S. goods more expensive for foreigners, U.S. exports fall. In the new equilibrium, both U.S. imports *and* exports have fallen by the same amount, since exports equal imports in equilibrium. A "buy American"

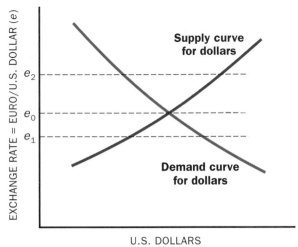

Figure 17.2

THE EQUILIBRIUM EXCHANGE RATE

At the exchange rate e_2, supply exceeds demand. At e_1, demand exceeds supply. At e_0 equilibrium is achieved.

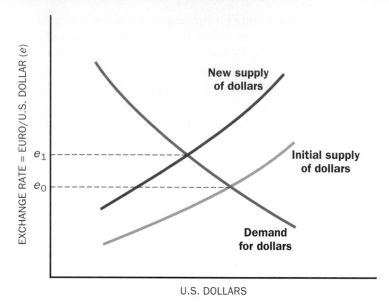

Figure 17.3

THE IMPACT OF A "BUY AMERICAN" CAMPAIGN ON THE EQUILIBRIUM EXCHANGE RATE WITH NO BORROWING OR LENDING

The supply of dollars is determined by the U.S. demand for imported goods and the demand for dollars is determined by the foreign demand for U.S. goods. The figure shows that a "buy American" campaign that causes Americans to import less at any exchange rate shifts the supply of dollars curve to the left and results in a higher exchange rate (a higher value of the dollar). At the higher exchange rate, U.S. exports fall below their initial level.

campaign increases output and employment in industries that produce substitutes for the goods that had been imported, but output and employment decline in U.S. export industries. In contrast, a change that increased the demand by Americans for European goods—perhaps a shift in tastes—would cause the dollar to fall in value; when the dollar falls in value, we say the dollar **depreciates.** Such a shift in tastes would increase American imports from Europe *and* American exports.

Foreign Borrowing and Lending The massive amount of international borrowing and lending now commonplace is the second factor that affects supply and demand in the foreign exchange market and determines the exchange rate. Financial capital markets, the markets in which funds are borrowed and lent, are global. Investors in Japan, Europe, and the United States, constantly seeking to maximize their returns, will shift their funds from Japan or Europe to the United States if returns there are highest. If returns drop in the United States, funds will move to other countries where returns are higher. When investors respond quickly and shift their funds in response to slight differences in expected returns, economists say that capital is **perfectly mobile.**

In today's world, capital is highly but not perfectly mobile. American investors may still feel slightly more comfortable keeping their money invested in the United

States than moving it to Europe or Japan. And this preference becomes even stronger when they contemplate investing in countries threatened by political or economic instability. Many countries have defaulted on their debts; recent examples include Russia, which in 1998 defaulted on some of the debt it owed and called a moratorium on interest payments to foreign creditors, and Argentina, which in 2002 defaulted on payments it owed. The more stable the political and economic environment of the world, the more mobile capital becomes across countries.

When foreign borrowing and lending occurs, it affects the equilibrium exchange rate, which thus is no longer just a matter of balancing imports and exports. The international flows of financial capital will influence demand and supply in the foreign exchange market, as illustrated in Figure 17.4. Consider the case of foreign investors who want to take advantage of the rates of return available in the United States on U.S. stocks, bonds, real estate, or other American assets. To buy U.S. assets, they need dollars, and therefore the demand for dollars increases. On the other hand, Americans who wish to invest in European assets such as shares of a German company or bonds issued by the Japanese government will need to sell dollars to buy foreign currencies, thereby increasing the supply of dollars in the foreign exchange market. How these new motives for supply and demand affect the equilibrium exchange rate depends on the relative amounts that foreigners want to invest in the United States and Americans want to invest abroad.

Because of international borrowing and lending, interest rates in different countries significantly influence exchange rates. If interest rates in Japan rise relative to interest rates available in the United States, investors will want to put their money into Japanese investments. To do so, the investor will first need to buy yen; thus an increase in Japanese interest rates will increase the demand for yen and boost the currency's value. Similarly, if interest rates in the U.S. rise relative to rates in other countries, the demand for dollars will rise and the equilibrium exchange rate will rise to reflect a higher value of the dollar. If U.S. interest rates fall relative to those available in other countries, the demand for dollars will also fall and the dollar will depreciate. An important implication of this discussion is that changes in interest rates in different countries will affect equilibrium exchange rates and the foreign exchange market.

Speculation The third important factor in determining the exchange rate is speculation. The demand for any asset depends on beliefs about what that asset could be sold for in the future; that is, it depends on expectations. If Americans believe that the Japanese yen is going to increase in value relative to the dollar, they may want to buy yen. For instance, consider what happens if the current exchange rate is 200 yen to the dollar and investors believe that the yen is going to appreciate to a value of 100 to the dollar by the end of the month. They believe, in other words, that if they took $1,000 and bought 200,000 yen (each dollar exchanged for 200 yen), at the end of the month they could exchange the yen back into dollars and receive $2,000 (100 yen buying each dollar). By holding yen for a month, they would earn a phenomenal 100 percent return. American investors

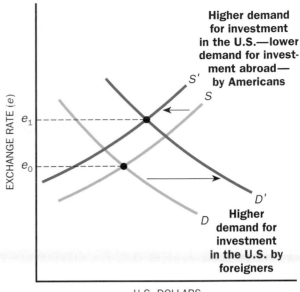

Figure 17.4

INCREASED ATTRACTIVENESS OF INVESTING IN THE UNITED STATES

As some Americans decide not to invest abroad, the supply curve of dollars shifts to the left. As more foreigners wish to invest in the United States, the demand curve shifts to the right. Both shifts serve to increase the equilibrium exchange rate.

with such a belief will want to hold more yen today, and the resulting increase in the demand for yen will cause the equilibrium value of the yen to rise. In this way, expectations about future changes in exchange rates are translated *immediately* into changes in exchange rates *today*.

Seeking currency to benefit from the possible gains from its appreciation is called *foreign exchange speculation.* Once it is added to the picture, exchange rates depend not only on the demand for and supply of exports, imports, and investment today but also on expectations about future changes in those factors.

Thinking Like an Economist

INCENTIVES AND THE REAL EXCHANGE RATE

Whether their concern is real GDP, real consumption, real interest rates, or real exchange rates, economists focus on *real* variables. In the case of real GDP, they look at a measure of production and correct for changes in the general level of prices. In the case of the real interest rate, they find that saving and investment decisions are based on interest rates corrected for changes in price levels. Similarly, when dealing with exchange rates, economists distinguish between the *nominal* exchange rate—how many euros or pesos one dollar can buy—and the **real exchange rate**—the nominal exchange rate adjusted for changes in the relative price levels in different countries. It is this relative price of domestic and foreign goods that affects our incentives to choose between oods produced in different countries and thus affects net exports.

To understand why we need to adjust for relative prices in different countries, consider an Italian bike that sells for 1,430 euros in Italy. An American consumer trying to decide between the Italian bike and an American-made bike that sells for $1,200 needs to know the exchange rate between euros and dollars. Let's suppose it is 1.1 euros to the dollar. Thus $1,300 is required to obtain the 1,430 euros needed to buy the bike. So the consumer needs to compare the features of the U.S.-built bike for $1,200 with the Italian bike for $1,300 to decide which is the better buy. The U.S. bike costs 8 percent less than the Italian bike. To make this price comparison, we needed to know three things—the dollar price of the U.S. bike, the euro price of the Italian bike, and the nominal exchange rate.

Now suppose prices are rising an average of 2 percent per year in the United States and 5 percent in Italy. If nothing else changes, the price of the U.S. bike would rise to $1,224 and the Italian bike to 1,502 euros after a year. If the nominal exchange rate is still 1.1 euros to the dollar, the dollar price of the Italian bike would be $1,365. The U.S. bike now costs about 10 percent less than the Italian bike. Even though the *nominal* exchange rate has not changed, the relative price of the two bikes has changed. The U.S. bike is now relatively cheaper, so consumers are likely to buy more U.S. bikes and fewer Italian bikes. If the euro falls to 1.13 euros to the dollar, then the relative price of the two bikes would remain unchanged.

This example illustrates why we need to adjust for changes in the price levels to determine whether a change in the nominal exchange rate will affect net exports. If the change simply reflects differences in the price levels in different countries, the relative price of domestic and foreign goods will not change, and net exports will not be affected. Such was the case in our example when the nominal exchange rate rose from 1.1 to 1.13 euros to the dollar. In practice, when the nominal exchange rate rises or falls, the real exchange rate usually moves similarly. But when two countries have very different inflation rates, distinguishing between the nominal exchange rate and the real exchange rate can be very important.

Expectations about changes in the exchange rate in fact play a role in all overseas investment. Suppose you have saved up some money for a new car, but you don't plan to buy it until the summer you graduate from college, eighteen months away. A savings account, U.S. government bonds, and the stocks of an American company are among the many options you have for investing the funds until you need them. You also could choose to invest in European assets. If you do, you will first need to sell your dollars for euros. But in eighteen months, you will need dollars for your new car; you will have to sell the European assets you purchased and then convert the euros you receive back into dollars. Thus, in deciding whether to make investments in Europe while you wait to buy your new car, you must form expectations about how much the dollar will be worth in eighteen months when you want to sell euros for dollars. If you think the euro will rise in value (i.e., the dollar will fall in value) over the next year and half, investing in Europe will look more attractive, since you anticipate that each euro will get you more dollars when it is sold. But if you think the euro will fall in value (the dollar will rise in value) over the next eighteen months, then investing in Europe will look less attractive because each euro will get you fewer dollars when you need them.

As this simple example illustrates, expectations that the dollar will fall in value in the future make investing abroad look more attractive. Conversely, expectations that the dollar's value will rise make investing abroad look less attractive. The same is true from the perspective of a foreign investor: investing in the United States looks less attractive if the dollar is expected to fall and more attractive if the dollar is expected to rise in value.

The role played by expectations helps us understand how speculation in foreign exchange markets can introduce a source of instability. Suppose investors suddenly decide the Mexican peso is going to fall in value, perhaps because new reports of corruption have caused worries about Mexico's political stability. Each investor will want to sell pesos before they fall in value; but as all investors attempt to sell, the collapsing demand for pesos pushes its value down immediately. Thus expectations that the peso would depreciate become self-fulfilling. This process is key in international currency crises, a topic we will return to later.

Wrap-Up

WHAT DETERMINES THE EXCHANGE RATE?

The U.S. exchange rate is determined by the supply of and demand for dollars. Foreigners' demand for U.S. dollars and Americans' supply of dollars are determined by
1. Underlying trade factors: the overseas demand for U.S. goods (U.S. exports) and Americans' demand for foreign goods (U.S. imports)
2. Underlying investment factors: the returns to investments in the United States and abroad
3. Speculation based on expectations about future changes in the exchange rate.

Exchange Rate Management

Fluctuations in exchange rate can have important effects on an economy. As a country's currency appreciates, its exports become more expensive for foreign buyers, causing declines in production and employment in export-producing industries. Many developing countries have foreign debts that must be repaid in dollars. Depreciation in their currency will make buying the dollars to repay their debt more expensive, increasing its burden. Because of the link between interest rates and exchange rates, central banks in many countries have attempted to use their influence over interest rates to "manage" the exchange rate. In some cases, they have simply tried to smooth out day-to-day fluctuations in the foreign exchange market. In others, they have tried to permanently move the exchange rate higher or lower. There are two extremes of this continuum. At one pole, countries have flexible exchange rates that move in response to fluctuations in demand and supply; they do not intervene directly in the foreign exchange market. At the other pole, countries fix their exchange rates, announcing a value and then intervening in the foreign exchange market to keep the exchange rate at that level.

Fixed Exchange Rate Systems The United States has had a flexible exchange rate for more than three decades. Before 1971, the world had a **fixed exchange rate system:** that is, exchange rates were pegged at a particular level. Thus the U.S. dollar was pegged to gold, valued at $32 per ounce, while other currencies were fixed in terms of the dollar. Exchange rates changed only as the result of explicit government decisions. Before the euro was introduced as the common currency of the European Economic and Monetary Union, the member countries of the union permanently fixed the exchange rates between their currencies. Often smaller countries will decide to fix their exchange rate relative to an important trading partner. Estonia's exchange rate, for example, is fixed in terms of the euro. From this brief description, three questions follow: How does a country "fix" its exchange rate? What are the consequences of fixed exchange rates for monetary policy? And what are the pros and cons of a fixed exchange rate system?

Fixing the Exchange Rate Let's suppose the government of Mexico has decided to fix the exchange rate between the peso and the dollar at 9 pesos to the dollar; this was approximately the peso-dollar exchange rate in 1998. Figure 17.5 depicts the foreign exchange market for pesos. It is important to note that we have drawn the figure to represent the market for pesos, so the quantity on the horizontal axis is expressed in terms of pesos and the exchange rate is dollars per peso. (Our earlier figures focused instead on the dollar exchange rate; the quantity along the horizontal axis was dollars, and the vertical axis was

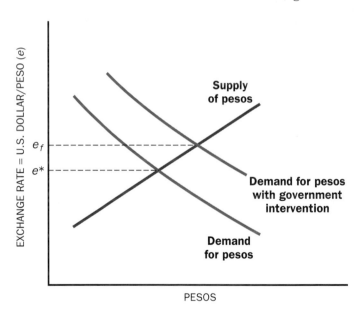

Figure 17.5

GOVERNMENT INTERVENTION IN A FIXED EXCHANGE RATE SYSTEM

If the "fixed" value for the dollar-peso exchange rate under the fixed exchange rate system, e_f, differs from the market equilibrium rate, e^*, then sustaining the fixed exchange rate requires government intervention. When e_f is above e^*, the government enters the foreign exchange market demanding pesos (supplying dollars or other foreign currencies) until the equilibrium exchange rate is equal to the pegged rate e_f.

expressed in terms of the value of the dollar.) As drawn in Figure 17.5, the market equilibrium exchange rate (e^*) is below the pegged rate (e_f). Without some sort of government intervention, the peso will depreciate until the exchange rate reaches e^*. At the pegged rate e_f, the supply of pesos exceeds the demand for pesos. To keep the value of the pesos from falling, the Mexican government would need to shift the demand curve for pesos to the right, as shown in the figure. The government can do this by buying pesos with the dollars, other foreign currencies, or gold that it holds. Thus, to keep the exchange rate equal to the level e_f, the government will need to intervene in the foreign exchange market to offset shifts in the demand or supply of the currency.

Much as speculation can be destabilizing, as discussed earlier, it can also be stabilizing. If the exchange rate should fall to e^*, foreign investors convinced that the government is planning to intervene to bring it back to e_f will seek to buy pesos now, when they are cheap. Later, after the government intervenes, their value will rise and the speculators expect to earn large profits by then selling the pesos and buying dollars. But their actions shift the demand curve for pesos to the right, helping to drive the equilibrium exchange rate back to e_f.

Problems can arise when investors believe that the equilibrium exchange rate and the pegged rate are far apart. Recall that the way the Mexican government attempted to sustain the exchange rate was by selling its holdings of dollars, other currencies, or gold for pesos. But if the government has insufficient resources and investors believe that the government will be unable to, or unwilling to, sustain the exchange rate at e_f, a disaster may follow. Once investors are convinced that the peg will be abandoned and the exchange rate will fall, they expect a capital loss on their peso holdings. Their best bet is to try to unload pesos before the peg is abandoned. The supply curve shifts to the right, widening the gap between the peg and the equilibrium exchange rate. To sustain the peg, the government now has to use up even more of its non-peso holdings. The gap between supply and demand at the original rate e_f becomes enormous. Eventually, the government may be forced to abandon the pegged rate, letting the exchange rate fall and proving the speculators who dumped pesos to have been correct.

When the government announces a new, lower exchange rate under a fixed exchange rate system, it is said to **devalue** the currency.

Monetary Policy Under a Fixed Exchange Rate System One cost of a fixed exchange rate system is the loss of a key tool of macroeconomics policy— monetary policy. To understand why this loss occurs, recall first that monetary policy affects the interest rate and credit conditions, influencing aggregate expenditures and therefore output and inflation. With this in mind, suppose Canada decides to fix the Canadian dollar–U.S. dollar exchange rate. Given a high degree of capital mobility between Canada and the United States, consider what would happen if interest rates in Canada were above those in the United States. Investors would shift funds from the United States into Canada to take advantage of the higher returns. This increased demand for the Canadian dollar would cause it to appreciate. If Canadian interest rates were below those in the United States, the reverse would occur, causing the Canadian dollar to depreciate. Only if Canadian interest rates are equal to interest rates in the United States will the exchange rate between Canadian dollars and U.S. dollars remain constant. Thus, to maintain a fixed exchange rate, the Bank of Canada (Canada's central bank) must ensure that it keeps the Canadian interest rate equal to the U.S. interest rate. If the Bank of Canada tries to reduce interest rates slightly, perhaps in an attempt to stimulate Canadian investment spending if Canada is in a recession, foreign investors will sell Canadian dollars as they take their capital out of the country to earn higher yields in the United States. To prevent the exchange rate from changing, the Bank of Canada would have to push interest rates back up. Similarly, any attempt to raise interest rates would attract a capital inflow that would push the value of the currency up. To keep the exchange rate at its pegged rate, the central bank would have to lower interest rates back down. By the same argument, if the Federal Reserve increases the U.S. interest rate, the Bank of Canada will have to follow suit and raise the Canadian interest rate if it wishes to maintain its fixed exchange rate. *In a small open economy under a fixed exchange rate system with perfect capital mobility, the central bank must keep the interest rate equal to the foreign interest rate. The country cannot run an independent monetary policy.*

This result can help us understand three important recent episodes. First, it helps explain why the European economies decided to adopt a common currency once they integrated their economies and fixed their exchange rates. No individual country in the monetary union can run an independent monetary policy, so the members of the union have given up their own national currencies and delegated monetary policy for the entire union to the European Central Bank.

Second, it helps us understand why in 1992 the United Kingdom dropped out of the European Monetary System, a system of fixed exchange rates that preceded the Economic and Monetary Union. The United Kingdom was in a recession, and many economists argued for interest rate cuts to help expand aggregate expenditures. As long as the United Kingdom wanted to maintain its fixed exchange rate, it could not cut interest rates. Because speculators thought the country might drop out of the European Monetary System and cut interest rates, they expected the pound to depreciate. This expectation shifted the demand curve for pounds to the left; and to offset this downward pressure on the pound exchange rate, the Bank of England had to keep its interest rates higher than those in Germany just when domestic factors called for interest rate cuts. Finally, the system collapsed; the United Kingdom dropped out of the European Monetary System, cut its interest rates, and let the pound depreciate against the other European currencies.

Third, the loss of monetary control under a fixed exchange rate system explains why countries that have experienced high inflation rates often decide to fix their exchange rate as part of a disinflation policy. In fact, while the loss of an independent monetary policy is one of the chief arguments against a fixed exchange rate system, paradoxically it is also one of the chief arguments in favor of this system for countries that have a history of high inflation and bad monetary policy.

Pegging the nominal exchange rate forces a high-inflation country to bring its own inflation rate down. If it does not, its exports will become more and more expensive as its price level rises faster than that of other countries (a real appreciation). As its net exports decline, the demand for its currency, at the fixed exchange rate, falls. To maintain the fixed exchange rate, the central bank must raise interest rates. Doing so reduces aggregate expenditures, reducing output and ultimately inflation.

One of the attractions of the European Monetary System of fixed exchange rates for countries like Italy was that it linked their monetary policy with that of Germany, a low-inflation country. Before the creation of the EMU, Italy's inflation rate was higher than Germany's. Maintaining a fixed nominal exchange rate with Germany forced Italy to bring down inflation by reducing its net exports, thereby reducing aggregate expenditures, output, and eventually inflation.

Reducing Exchange Rate Volatility A major argument for a fixed exchange rate system is that it reduces risks from exchange rate volatility. Many economists have been concerned about the high degree of volatility in exchange rate markets. Exchange rates have fluctuated greatly, both on a day-to-day and on a longer-term basis. The Japanese yen went from 94 yen to the dollar in 1995 to 131 yen in 1998, back to 107 yen in 2000, and then to 110 in 2004. The euro went from 87 cents in early 2002 to $1.25 two years later. The dollar has had single-day declines of more than 1 percent against the German mark (February 18, 1985), and more than 1 percent against the Japanese yen (October 14, 1987). This may not seem like a lot, but a 1 percent decline every business day for a year would result in the exchange rate declining by more than 240 percent within that year. Many of these gyrations, particularly the ones that happen from day to day, cannot be explained by any correspondingly large changes in the economy. They seem explainable only in terms of large shifts in expectations.

As was noted above, dollars or yen are assets. That is why the value of the exchange rate today depends on what investors expect the exchange rate will be next year. Thus, the stability of the exchange rate depends on the stability of the expectations of investors. For instance, when the dollar is lower, foreign investors might expect it to rise again. In that case, as the value of the dollar declines, the expected return to holding dollars increases: investors believe that the dollar is likely to appreciate and that they will benefit from a capital gain when it does. Here expectations help stabilize the market, since foreign investors may help limit any decline in the dollar by buying it as it falls.

But if as the dollar depreciates foreign investors expect further depreciation, then their willingness to invest in America may actually decrease as the dollar falls in value. In that case, an initial decline in the value of the dollar in effect shifts the demand curve for dollars down, leading to further decreases in value.

Whatever their cause and whatever the nature of expectations concerning future movements, huge swings in exchange rates add to the risk of doing business in the world market and thus discourage businesses and countries from pursuing their comparative advantages. If the exchange rate appreciates greatly, exporters suddenly find that the market for their goods has dried up, unless they drastically cut prices; either way, their profits are dramatically reduced. Even American firms that produce only for the American market face great risks as a result of exchange rate fluctuations. Shoe manufacturers may find the American market flooded with cheap Brazilian shoes if the dollar appreciates relative to the Brazilian real; again, they either lose sales or must cut their prices, and in either case, profits fall.

Exporting and importing firms can take steps to mitigate the effects of foreign exchange risks in the short run—say, the next three to six months. Consider an American firm that exports abroad. It has a contract to deliver so many ball bearings to France at so many euros per ball bearing. But it pays its workers in dollars, not euros. If the euro depreciates, when the firm takes the euros it receives

International Perspective
GLOBAL FINANCIAL CRISES

The decade of the 1990s witnessed three global financial crises. The first occurred in 1992, forcing the United Kingdom, Italy, and Sweden to abandon pegged exchange rates and leading several other members of the European Monetary System (EMS) to devalue their currencies. The second occurred in 1994 with the collapse of the Mexican peso. The collapse raised concerns among speculators about the financial health of other Latin American countries, and their currencies also came under pressure. This process by which concerns about one country spread to others is called *contagion*. Because the 1994–1995 crisis was centered in Latin America, the fallout from the Mexican crisis has been called the *tequila effect*.

The third crisis of the 1990s was set off in mid-1997 when speculators began selling the Thai currency, the baht. In June, the Thai government stopped fixing the value of the baht and it immediately devalued. As investors continued to shift into safer currencies, such as the dollar, the Thai economy continued to suffer. Between June 1997 and December 1998, the Thai stock market lost almost half its value—as if the Dow Jones average in the United States had fallen from 11,000 to 5,500. As stock prices and other asset prices fell, banks that had lent money using the inflated asset values as collateral were threatened.

Initially, no one expected what seemed to be an isolated event in Thailand to lead to a global financial crisis. It did, because investors' assessments of the risks of investing in emerging market economies like Thailand's changed. Investors started pulling funds out of Indonesia, Malaysia, and the Philippines. As these countries were forced to let their currencies depreciate, Singapore and Taiwan stopped fixing the value of their currencies out of concern that their exports would otherwise be at a competitive disadvantage. As investments in emerging markets looked increasingly risky, investors wanted out. They started selling holdings in other Southeast Asian economies. The Hong Kong stock market fell 23 percent in just four days in October 1997. Even the U.S. market was hit by fears of a crisis. The Dow Jones industrial average dropped 554 points on October 27, 1997, at that time the largest one-day point loss ever. In Asia, selling pressure spread from Thailand to Indonesia, South Korea, Taiwan, and Malaysia before jumping around the globe to hit Russia and Brazil.

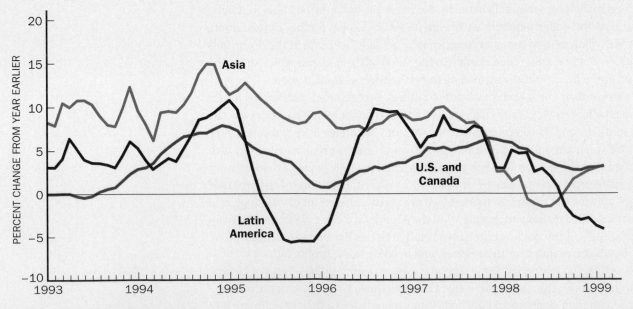

WORLD INDUSTRIAL PRODUCTION

SOURCE: IMF, *World Economic Outlook* (1999).

As speculators withdrew capital, the governments of the affected countries faced difficult choices. One option was to simply let their currencies depreciate. Unfortunately, in many of these countries, domestic banks and firms had borrowed heavily from foreign sources; a devaluation would make it more difficult to repay these loans because it would raise the domestic currency value that must be repaid. Devaluation would therefore threaten the solvency of the banking sector of these countries. The second option was to prevent a devaluation by raising interest rates high enough to halt the capi-

tal outflow. But doing so would severely constrict investment, cut aggregate expenditures, and lead to output declines and increases in unemployment.

The devastating economic consequences of financial crises are clear from the declines in production in Latin America during 1995 and 1996 and the declines in Asia in 1998 and 1999. The chart illustrates the very high rates of economic growth experienced in Asia throughout most of the 1990s. These growth rates started falling in Asia in mid-1997, turning negative in 1998.

and converts them into dollars, its revenues will fall short of the dollars it has already paid to workers. It can insure itself by making a contract (with either a bank or a dealer in the foreign exchange market) for the future delivery or sale of those euros at a price agreed on today. It can thus avoid the risk of a change in the foreign exchange rate. However, firms cannot easily buy or sell foreign exchange for delivery two or three years into the future. Since many investment projects have a planning horizon of years or even decades, investors are exposed to foreign exchange risks against which they cannot insure themselves. But, as noted above, even firms that do not buy or sell in foreign markets are exposed to risks from foreign exchange rate fluctuations: American firms cannot buy insurance against the longer-term risk that the American market will be flooded with cheap imports as a result of an appreciation of the U.S. dollar. These risks are reduced if the exchange rate is fixed.

FLEXIBLE EXCHANGE RATE SYSTEMS

Today, while most governments do not peg the exchange rate at a particular value, they do frequently intervene in the foreign exchange markets, buying and selling in an attempt to reduce day-to-day variability in exchange rates. Rather than let the exchange rate freely *float* as demand and supply vary, as would occur under a flexible exchange rate system, governments take action. Economists sometimes refer to this as a *"dirty float"* system.

Stabilizing the Exchange Rate Given the costs of exchange rate instability, some have demanded that the government should actively try to stabilize the exchange rate. Producers are particularly concerned that the real exchange rate be stabilized, so that if inflation in the United States is higher than in foreign countries, American exporters can still sell their goods abroad. As Figure 17.6 shows, there have been large movements in real exchange rates, just as there have been in nominal exchange rates.

Any government program to stabilize the (real) exchange rate must meet three requirements. First, the government must choose what the exchange rate should be. Second, it must have a mechanism for keeping the real exchange rate at that value.

European Monetary Union, Frankfurt, Germany

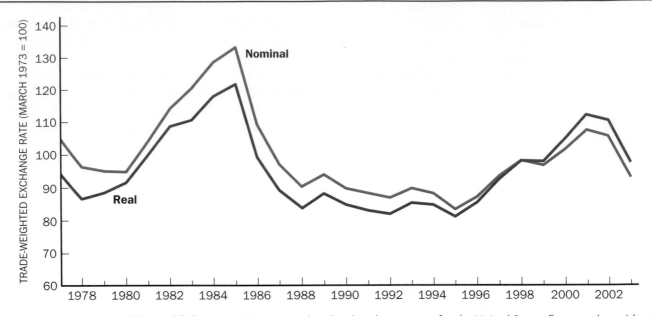

Figure 17.6

VOLATILITY OF NOMINAL AND REAL EXCHANGE RATES

Both the nominal and real exchange rates for the United States fluctuated considerably over the 1980s. The figure shows the trade-weighted value of the dollar relative to other currencies, unadjusted (nominal) and adjusted (real) for price-level changes in the United States and abroad.

SOURCE: *Economic Report of the President* (2004).

For example, if the dollar seems to be climbing too high against the yen, a plan might propose that the Fed sell dollars and buy yen, thereby pushing up the demand for yen and increasing the supply of dollars. Producers in the United States may be delighted by this move; demand for exports will increase, as will demand for goods that compete closely with imports. But producers in Japan will have just the opposite reaction. If the Japanese government, responding to these pressures, were to intervene simultaneously and start selling yen and buying dollars, the two efforts would offset each other. In effect, it would be as if the U.S. government sold dollars in exchange for yen directly to the Japanese government, with private markets unaffected.

This brings up a third requirement of exchange rate stabilization proposals: there must be some degree of cooperation among countries. This is particularly true in the modern world economy, where no single country is dominant. There are several big players—Japan, the Economic and Monetary Union, and the United States—and setting exchange rates requires these governments to work together.

Case in Point

CURRENCY BOARDS AND DOLLARIZATION

Currency crises in Latin America and Asia have increased interest in new forms of monetary reform that could avoid future crises. Two suggestions that have figured prominently in discussions are a **currency board** and **dollarization.**

Under a currency board, the exchange rate between the local currency and, say, the dollar is fixed by law. The central bank holds enough foreign currency to back all the domestic currency and reserves it has issued. This precaution makes a run on the currency unlikely—the central bank always has enough dollars to pay off anyone who shows up wanting to exchange the domestic currency for dollars. Since there is never any fear the country will run out of reserves, investors will have no reason to panic and try to get their funds out before the pegged rate is abandoned.

Argentina operated with a currency board between 1991 and 2001. Because Argentina had a history of high inflation, a currency board was viewed as a means of establishing a credible, low-inflation environment by tying the Argentinean currency to the U.S. dollar. The disadvantages of a currency board are two. First, exchange rate adjustments can help ensure macroeconomic stability when two countries face different economic disturbances. For example, a recession in Argentina might be lessened by an exchange rate depreciation that spurs exports. A currency board, like other fixed exchange rate systems, leaves countries unable to conduct an independent monetary policy. If a country has a history of bad monetary policy, however, such a limitation may be desirable. Second, under a currency board the central bank cannot create reserves in the event of a domestic banking crisis—it can no longer serve as the lender of last resort.

A more extreme solution to exchange rate volatility and currency crises is to simply abandon the domestic currency and use the U.S. dollar, a policy called *dollarization*. Ecuador *dollarized* in 2000; the Ecuadorian currency, the sucre, is no longer used for transactions and all prices are quoted in U.S. dollars. By eliminating the possiblity of exchange rate changes and tying itself to Federal Reserve policy, it is argued, countries can benefit from the effects of reduced risk and lower uncertainty. Like other fixed exchange rate systems, dollarization removes mone-

Ecuadorians read about their country's switch to the U.S. dollar as the official currency in 2000.

tary policy from a country's control—in this case, giving it to the Fed. The potential drawback is that the Fed bases its policy decisions on U.S. economic conditions and would be unlikely to alter monetary policy in response to a domestic economic or financial crisis in a country that had switched to dollars.

At the time it dollarized, Ecuador faced the threat of hyperinflation. By adopting the dollar as its currency, Ecuador has enjoyed low inflation instead. Thanks to high oil prices, real output has grown.

Can Governments Stabilize Exchange Rates? Some economists are skeptical about the ability of government to stabilize the exchange rate even in the short run. If the current exchange rate between the peso and the dollar is 10 pesos to the dollar, and if the market knows that the exchange rate must change in the near future to 12 pesos to the dollar, it will be futile for the Mexican government to try to maintain the current exchange rate in the short run. Mexican investors, believing that there will be a devaluation of the peso, know that the gains from holding assets in dollars will be enormous. By converting their pesos to dollars and holding them for the short period until the peso is devalued, they obtain a large return.

The result will be what is referred to as a *run* on the peso, as those holding assets denominated in pesos seek to sell them now. This run will be too large for the Mexican government to stop by buying pesos and selling dollars, as more private individuals are willing to sell pesos and buy dollars than the Mexican government has resources to cope with. The government may be successful in postponing the fall of the peso for a few days, but in doing so it may pay a huge price. It would have obtained the capital gain on the dollars it held if it had not sold dollars for pesos. Instead, the capital gain is earned by private individuals. If the government spends $1 billion trying to support the peso and the peso goes down 20 percent (as in our example), the cost of the short-run support is more than $200 million.

Critics of government stabilization programs make several points. First, they stress the difficulties in determining the equilibrium exchange rate that is supposed to be stabilized. Is there any reason, they ask, to believe that government bureaucrats are in a better position to make judgments about the equilibrium exchange rate than the thousands of investors who buy and sell foreign exchange every day? If the government makes mistakes, as it is almost bound to do, it can actually contribute to destabilizing the exchange rate rather than to stabilizing it.

Exchange rates often need to change. For example, if one economy grows faster than another or has higher inflation than another, the exchange rate will have to adjust to compensate. How will a scheme for stabilizing exchange rates let them adjust naturally while controlling them at the same time?

Second, critics of government stabilization programs question whether international economic cooperation is achievable. Running domestic economic policy is difficult enough. For example, will a country take steps to raise its exchange rate and thus hurt its exporters to keep a political agreement with foreign countries?

Thus, there are serious questions about whether stabilizing the currency is possible either economically or politically.

Review and Practice

SUMMARY

1. In a flexible exchange rate system, exchange rates are determined in the foreign exchange market by the forces of supply and demand.
2. The demand for and supply of dollars are determined by exports and imports, by foreigners' desire to invest in the United States and Americans' desire to invest abroad, and by speculators who base their demands for various currencies on expectations about changes in future exchange rates.
3. In the absence of foreign borrowing and lending, exports and imports would always need to balance.
4. A rise in interest rates will attract a capital inflow and cause the exchange rate to rise; a fall in interest rates will cause the exchange rate to fall.
5. Under a fixed exchange rate system, the government must intervene in the foreign exchange market to ensure that demand and supply balance at the pegged exchange rate.
6. In a small open economy with perfect capital mobility, under a fixed exchange rate system the domestic interest rate must equal the foreign interest rate. Monetary policy therefore must be used to peg the exchange rate and cannot be used to address other macroeconomic goals.
7. It may not be possible for the government to stabilize exchange rates effectively. It is difficult to determine the equilibrium exchange rate that is supposed to be stabilized, and international coordination may not be achievable.

KEY TERMS

flexible exchange rate systems
appreciation
depreciation
perfectly mobile capital
real exchange rate
fixed exchange rate system
devaluation
currency board
dollarization

REVIEW QUESTIONS

1. Name three factors that cause exchange rates to shift.
2. If the European Central Bank raises interest rates in Europe while the Fed leaves U.S. interest rates unchanged, would you expect the dollar to appreciate or to depreciate?
3. Why are expectations concerning changes in the exchange rate important? How do relative rates of inflation affect those expectations?
4. What are the costs of exchange rate instability? How might the government attempt to reduce instability in exchange rates?
5. What problems result from government attempts to stabilize the exchange rate at a level that is not the equilibrium level?
6. Can a country run an independent monetary policy to achieve domestic economic policy goals if it is committed to maintaining a fixed exchange rate?
7. Under a fixed exchange rate system, when will speculation by foreign investors be stabilizing? When will it be destabilizing?

PROBLEMS

1. Tell whether each of the economic actors in the following list would be suppliers or demanders in the foreign exchange market for U.S. dollars:
   (a) An American tourist in Europe
   (b) A Japanese firm exporting to the United States
   (c) A British investor who wants to buy U.S. stocks
   (d) A Brazilian tourist in the United States
   (e) A German firm importing from the United States
   (f) A U.S. investor who wants to buy real estate in Australia
2. Explain whether each of the following changes would tend to appreciate or to depreciate the U.S. dollar, using supply and demand curves for the foreign exchange market to illustrate your answers:
   (a) Higher interest rates in Japan
   (b) A boycott of American goods by Europeans
   (c) A tight U.S. monetary policy
   (d) An expansionary U.S. fiscal policy

3. Suppose that at the start of 2001, a U.S. investor put $10,000 into a one-year euro investment. If the exchange rate was 1.5 euros per dollar, how much would $10,000 be in euros? Over the course of the year, the euro investment paid 10 percent interest. But when the investor switched back to dollars at the end of the year, the exchange rate was 2 euros per dollar. Did the change in the exchange rate earn the investor more money or less money? How much? How does your analysis change if the exchange rate had fallen to 1 euro per dollar?

4. If the government wanted to reduce the trade deficit by altering the exchange rate, what sort of monetary policy should it employ? Explain.

5. If the government succeeds in raising the exchange rate, who benefits and who is injured?

6. Suppose Americans go on a "buy American" campaign that reduces imports. Use a supply and demand model of the foreign exchange market to show how this campaign would affect the value of the dollar. Does the change in the exchange rate act to increase the reduction in imports or does it partially offset the initial reduction in imports? Explain.

Learning Goals

In this chapter, you will learn

1 How open economy factors affect the ADI curve

2 How foreign events can affect the U.S. economy

3 How monetary and fiscal policies affect the exchange rate and net exports

4 How open economy factors influence the effectiveness of monetary and fiscal policies

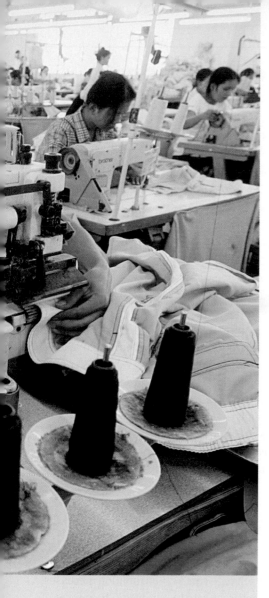

Chapter 18

POLICY IN THE OPEN ECONOMY

The previous chapter focused on the foreign exchange market, and on some of the differences between flexible and fixed exchange rate systems. The world's three major economic blocs—the United States, the European Union, and Japan—all have adopted flexible exchange rate systems. The forces of supply and demand that were discussed in Chapter 17 operate to determine the relative values of the dollar, the euro, and the yen. The purpose of this chapter is to incorporate exports, imports, and international financial capital flows into the model of short-run fluctuations that was developed in Part Three.

When short-run fluctuations associated with business cycles were first discussed, for the sake of simplicity we focused on a closed economy, ignoring the role of international trade and financial linkages. Now it is time to add the international dimension to the model to see if any of the basic conclusions we reached in the earlier chapters need to be altered. Fortunately, the fundamental connections between inflation, interest rates, and output operate in much the same manner as before. But by adding in the linkages that tie together the global economy, we can better understand how U.S. fiscal policy and Federal Reserve decisions affect the value of the dollar and the U.S. trade balance. In addition, these new linkages with monetary policy can affect the economy, and international factors can be a source of economic fluctuations.

The aggregate demand–inflation (ADI) curve and the inflation adjustment (IA) line form the core framework for understanding economic fluctuations. Our main objective in this chapter will be to see how international trade in goods and financial assets affects these two key relationships. We will focus on economies like that of the United States that have a flexible exchange rate determined by the interplay of supply and demand in the foreign exchange market.

The ADI Curve and the Open Economy

In the closed economy, the components of aggregate spending are consumption, investment, and government purchases. In the open economy, net exports must be added to this list. An increase in net exports, just like an increase in government purchases, leads firms to expand production and employment. If foreigners purchase more U.S.–produced goods and services, U.S. exports rise. The firms producing these goods increase production and employment. If U.S. residents switch from buying goods produced in the United States to buying more foreign goods—purchasing Olympus rather than Kodak cameras or Heineken beer rather than Bud—U.S. firms see demand drop, and they respond by cutting back production and employment. The impact of exports and imports on domestic aggregate demand is measured by *net exports*—exports minus imports.

The ADI curve developed in Chapter 13 summarized the relationship between aggregate demand and inflation in a closed economy. Increases in inflation lead to increases in the real interest rate, and these reduce household and business spending on consumption and investment. This connection between inflation and demand continues to hold in an open economy like the U.S. economy—changes in inflation continue to result in interest rate changes through the actions of monetary policy. But these interest rate changes now affect the exchange rate—the value of the dollar relative to other currencies such as the euro, the yen, or the peso—and net exports. To understand how they do so is our next task.

INFLATION, THE INTEREST RATE, AND THE EXCHANGE RATE

How does an increase in inflation affect the exchange rate? When inflation increases, monetary policy responds to cause the real interest rate to increase. The impact of inflation on the real interest rate depends on the central bank's monetary policy rule, as we learned in Chapter 15. International investors constantly seek out the most attractive financial investments around the globe; thus, when interest rates rise in the United States, they sell financial assets in other countries in order to invest here. As they do so, exchange rates are affected.

If interest rates in the United States rise relative to the rates of return available in other countries, international investors, rather than lending funds in the capital markets of Japan or Europe, will lend their funds in U.S. capital markets to take advantage of those higher rates. But borrowers in the U.S. capital market want to borrow dollars, not yen or euros. International investors therefore need to buy dollars in the foreign exchange market if they want to lend those dollars to U.S. borrowers.[1] This increase in the demand for dollars causes the price of dollars to rise, just as a rightward shift in the demand curve for any other good would cause its price to rise.

---

[1] See Chapter 17 for a discussion of the foreign exchange market.

While this discussion has focused on the demand for dollars by foreign investors, the supply of dollars in the foreign exchange market will also be affected. With U.S. interest rates higher, U.S. investors will be less likely to buy foreign securities, thereby reducing the supply of dollars in the foreign exchange market. Again, the result is to raise the value of the dollar as demand increases and supply decreases.

Our discussion took as its starting point a rise in U.S. interest rates. Though the increase leads to an appreciation of the dollar, from the perspective of other countries it causes their currencies to depreciate. For example, if U.S. interest rates rise relative to interest rates in Canada, the Canadian dollar will depreciate, falling in value relative to the U.S. dollar. To take another example: in June 2000, the European Central Bank boosted interest rates. Because higher returns could now be earned on European financial assets, investors sold off some holdings of dollar assets in order to invest in euro assets. But to make those investments, they needed to use their dollars to buy euros. The greater demand for euros pushed up the price of euros in terms of dollars—that is, the exchange rate changed and euros appreciated relative to dollars.

Two points are worth noting. First, the value of the dollar is affected by changes in interest rates in other countries. This point illustrates just one of the ways in which international economic developments can affect the U.S. economy. Second, in our examples of how interest rates affect exchange rates, interest rates in one country change relative to interest rates in other countries—and that change is what causes investors to shift funds in pursuit of higher returns. If the Fed raises the interest rate in the United States and other countries respond by increasing their interest rates, the dollar will not appreciate.

THE EXCHANGE RATE AND AGGREGATE EXPENDITURES

Changes in the value of the dollar affect net exports. As the dollar appreciates, U.S. exports fall and imports rise. As dollars become more expensive, foreign buyers find that U.S. goods cost more in terms of their own currencies. Faced with this increase in cost, they will buy fewer goods produced in the United States. And conversely, foreign goods are now cheaper for Americans to purchase since dollars buy more in terms of other currencies. U.S. imports rise as Americans buy more goods produced abroad.

The fall in exports and rise in imports mean that U.S. *net* exports fall. Thus the total demand for U.S. goods and services (consumption plus private investment plus government purchases plus net exports) falls. As firms producing for the export market see their sales decline, and as consumers shift their spending toward imported goods, total production and employment in the U.S. decline.

As a result, the ADI curve continues to have a negative slope when we take into account that modern economies are open economies. Just as in our earlier analysis, a rise in inflation leads the central bank to boost the real interest rate, and this increase reduces private spending, particularly investment spending. In addition, as the interest rate rises, the dollar appreciates; net exports are therefore reduced. So equilibrium output falls when inflation rises, because investment spending *and* net exports fall. A movement along a given ADI curve now involves changes in both the interest rate and the exchange rate.

Net Exports and Shifts in the ADI Curve Net exports depend on the real exchange rate, but they also can be affected by other factors. For instance, U.S. exports will be affected by the level of income in other countries. If incomes in Mexico rise, Mexicans will buy more goods and services, including more U.S.-produced goods. So U.S. exports to Mexico will rise when incomes in Mexico rise. And similarly, if Mexico suffers a recession, U.S. exports to Mexico will fall.

Shifts in net exports at a given real exchange rate cause the ADI curve to shift, just as shifts in government purchases do. A case in point occurred in the late 1990s. Financial crises in several Asian and Latin American economies led to severe recessions in many of these countries. As incomes fell, households and firms cut back spending. As a consequence, the demand for U.S.-produced goods fell, lowering U.S. exports. At the same time, the financial crises reduced the value of many Asian currencies relative to the dollar. This rise in the value of the dollar also acted to reduce U.S. net exports. At a given rate of inflation, total demand for U.S. goods fell, shifting the ADI curve to the left.

If this shift in net exports had been the only factor affecting the U.S. economy at the time, the impact would have been to push the United States into a recession. But in fact, the 1990s was one of the strongest periods of U.S. growth in the twentieth century. So what happened? Is our model wrong? Two things prevented the Asian financial crisis from creating a recession in the United States. First, domestic consumption and investment spending remained very strong in the United States. The growth in these components of demand served to offset the drop in net exports. The second factor was the Fed's response. As problems in Asia developed during 1995, the Fed cut the federal funds rate. The Fed's target for the funds rate fell from 6 percent in 1995 to 5.25 percent in February 1996. This action is a good example of the type of stabilization policy discussed in Chapter 15. To offset a potential leftward shift in the ADI curve due to a drop in net exports, the Fed cut the interest rate to boost investment spending.

Foreign Interest Rates and Shifts in the ADI Curve Policy actions by foreign governments also have the potential to affect interest rates and exchange rates. If the European Central Bank, for example, decides to raise interest rates in Europe, euro assets become more attractive and the euro appreciates in value relative to the dollar. This appreciation makes European goods more expensive for Americans to buy, and it makes American goods cheaper for Europeans to buy. The appreciating euro increases U.S. net exports as our exports rise and our imports fall. For a given inflation rate in the United States, this increase in demand for U.S. output means the ADI curve has shifted to the right. In the short run, U.S. output rises. The effect of a rise in European interest rates on U.S. output is illustrated in Figure 18.1.

This discussion can be summarized in two points. First, the ADI curve is downward sloping in the open economy, just as it was for the closed economy. There is a new channel from inflation to spending, however, and this affects the slope of the ADI curve—as inflation rises, and the real interest rate rises, the value of the domestic currency

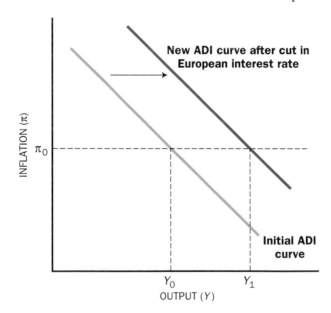

Figure 18.1

THE EFFECTS OF A RISE IN EUROPEAN INTEREST RATES ON U.S. OUTPUT

If European interest rates rise, the dollar will depreciate. This depreciation increases U.S. exports, and the increased demand leads to a rise in U.S. output.

rises and its appreciation reduces net exports. Second, international developments—booms or recessions abroad or changes in foreign interest rates—can have a direct impact on the U.S. economy by shifting the ADI curve.

INTERNATIONAL FACTORS THAT AFFECT THE SLOPE OF THE ADI CURVE

When monetary policy increases interest rates in response to a rise in inflation, the dollar appreciates. An appreciation reduces net exports, one of the components of aggregate spending. A rise in inflation leads to a fall in investment and net exports.

When monetary policy decreases interest rates in response to a fall in inflation, the dollar depreciates. A depreciation increases net exports, one of the components of aggregate spending. A fall in inflation leads to an increase in investment and net exports.

INTERNATIONAL FACTORS THAT SHIFT THE ADI CURVE

Factors that increase aggregate expenditures at each rate of inflation (and shift the ADI curve to the right) include

    economic booms abroad
    a rise in interest rates abroad.

Factors that decrease aggregate expenditures at each rate of inflation (and shift the ADI curve to the left) include

    economic recessions abroad
    a fall in interest rates abroad.

The Exchange Rate and Inflation

Because net exports are one of the components of aggregate spending, fluctuations in net exports can affect the equilibrium level of output. Fluctuations in output around potential output in turn will affect inflation. The impact of output on inflation was summarized in Chapters 11 and 13. But changes in the exchange rate can also influence inflation more directly.

IMPORTED INPUTS

The prices in dollars that American firms must pay for imported goods depend both on the prices charged by the foreign producers of these goods *and* on the value of the dollar. If the dollar falls in value (depreciates), foreign goods cost more, just as

Thinking Like an Economist

INTEREST PARITY AND INCENTIVES

Whenever expected returns on different assets are unequal (after adjusting for any differences in risk), an economist sees a profit opportunity. By selling the lower-yielding assets and buying the higher-yielding one, an investor can increase her total return. Investors have an *incentive* to adjust their portfolios to take advantage of the opportunity offered by the higher-yielding assets. This idea—that investors seek out the highest returns—lies at the heart of what is known as the **interest parity condition,** which states that expected returns will be equal in different countries. Whenever expected returns differ across countries, the attempts by investors to take advantage of these differences by shifting funds from one country to another will cause exchange rates to adjust. In equilibrium, with perfect capital markets, expected returns would have to be equal in different countries.

When expected returns differ in, say, Canada and the United States, investors have an incentive to sell their holdings in the country with the lower return and invest in the country with the higher return. For example, suppose the interest rate is 8 percent in Canada and 5 percent in the United States. Furthermore, suppose investors do not expect any change in the Canadian-U.S. exchange rate. Such conditions create a strong incentive to sell financial assets in the United States and invest in the high-yielding Canadian assets. As investors try to take advantage of the high Canadian interest rates by buying Canadian assets, they first need to buy Canadian dollars. This increased demand for Canadian dollars causes the currency's value to rise—the Canadian dollar appreciates. Its rise may lead investors to worry that it is overvalued and likely heading for a fall, perhaps back to its earlier value. Now, the 8 percent interest rate in Canadian starts to look less attractive. If the Canadian dollar is expected to fall, say by 2 percent, then investing in Canadian financial assets will yield a return of only 6 percent (an 8 percent interest rate minus the 2 percent depreciation). This is still better than the 5 percent return in the United States, but the incentive to shift funds to Canadian is smaller than it was initially. As investors continue to respond to the incentive offered by the higher expected returns in Canada, the Canadian dollar will continue to appreciate. In this example, once investors expect a future 3 percent depreciation of the Canadian dollar, they no longer have any incentive to shift funds out of the United States and into Canada.

When capital markets are perfect, any difference in expected returns is quickly eliminated as investors respond to the incentives offered by these differences, a process economists call *arbitrage.* If you look at the major industrial economies—countries whose financial markets are closely linked—and see interest rates higher in one country than in another, you can therefore conclude that investors must believe that the currency of the country with the higher interest rate is going to depreciate.

---

if the foreign producers had raised their prices. Firms face increased costs for inputs when the value of the dollar falls; and if firms set prices as a markup over costs, prices will rise. As a consequence, inflation rises temporarily. For a given output gap and inflation expectations, changes in the exchange rate can shift the IA line.

CONSUMER PRICE INFLATION AND THE EXCHANGE RATE

The most relevant price index for measuring changes in the cost of living is the consumer price index (CPI), which is an index of the prices of goods and services that households purchase—including those that are foreign-produced. The price of French cheese does not figure in the U.S. GDP price index, since the U.S. does not produce French cheese. But U.S. households buy French cheese, so their price is included in the CPI. Because the CPI includes both domestically produced and foreign-produced goods, it is affected by changes in the exchange rate.

If the dollar appreciates, the dollar prices of foreign goods will fall. Because the CPI includes foreign consumer goods while the GDP price index does not, the CPI will fall relative to the GDP index. When the dollar depreciates, the opposite will occur: the CPI index will rise relative to the GDP index. Fluctuations in the exchange rate are one reason for the differences in reported inflation rates, differences that depend on which price index is used to measure inflation.

Comparing Monetary and Fiscal Policies in the Open Economy

In today's open economy, policymakers designing macroeconomic policies must take into account the effects of the exchange rate. In a closed economy, expansionary monetary policy has a short-run effect on aggregate expenditures through lower interest rates and an increase in available credit, while expansionary fiscal policy eventually crowds out private investment. In the open economy, we have already seen how the effects of changes in exchange rates, and their impact on net exports, come into play when we analyze macroeconomic policy. In an open economy, the relative utility of monetary and fiscal policies changes—monetary policy becomes more effective in the short run while fiscal policy becomes less so.

MONETARY POLICY WITH FLEXIBLE EXCHANGE RATES

When discretionary monetary policy actions are undertaken, their impact on the economy is reinforced by the exchange rate. Suppose the Fed decides to raise interest rates in the United States. And suppose Japan, members of the European Economic and Monetary Union, and other countries do not match the interest rate increase. The higher yields on U.S. bonds make them more attractive to both foreign and U.S. investors. The resulting demand for U.S. dollars leads the dollar to appreciate.

The dollar's appreciation discourages exports and encourages imports. Thus, monetary policy succeeds in dampening aggregate demand both through the interest rate effect on private investment spending—the channel that operates in a closed economy—and through the effect the exchange rate has on net exports. This impact on net exports reinforces the effect on investment, strengthening monetary policy's influence on aggregate expenditures and output.

When monetary policy expands the economy by lowering interest rates, the exchange rate depreciates; this depreciation encourages exports and discourages imports. The improvement in net exports is part of the overall impact of monetary policy in expanding aggregate expenditures. For small economies in which net

---

e-Insight

NEW TECHNOLOGY AND THE INTEGRATION OF WORLD FINANCIAL MARKETS

New information technologies are leading to tremendous reductions in the costs of carrying out transactions—particularly in financial markets. Today, you can search the Web for low-cost brokers and trade in financial stocks and bonds in markets in New York, London, Frankfurt, or Tokyo, right from your home computer.

The increased integration of world financial markets alters the impact that fiscal policy has on the economy. To see how it does so, imagine a world in which shifting investment funds from one country to another is prohibitively expensive. Economists describe such a world as one in which transaction costs are very high. High transaction costs will limit opportunities to take advantage of high returns in other countries. If you consider investing in the United Kingdom, you first need to sell your dollars to buy pounds, the local currency. Buying pounds will involve a transaction fee. Next, you need to buy a U.K. financial asset such as a bond with your pounds, and the purchase will also involve a transaction fee. Finally, when your investment pays interest to you in pounds, you have to convert those pounds back into dollars. Again, you have to pay a transaction fee. As an investor, you need to evaluate the return you can earn from investing in a foreign country by taking into account the interest rate available, any change in the exchange rate you expect, *and* your unavoidable transaction costs.

Even though U.K. interest rates might be higher than interest rates in the United States, the difference may not be enough to compensate for the transaction fees you will have to pay if you try to shift your investments to the United Kingdom. If you do not shift your investments, you do not need to buy pounds. When fees are high, the rise in U.K. interest rates does not increase the demand for pounds, and the value of the pound does not rise.

In this imaginary world, an expansionary fiscal policy in the United Kingdom leads to a rise in U.K. interest rates, but this rise in interest rates does not lead to an appreciation of the pound.

Now consider what happens in today's world with its lower transaction costs. Again, assume there is an expansionary fiscal policy in the United Kingdom. As interest rates start to rise in the United Kingdom, the higher returns attract international investors. These investors buy pounds so that they can shift their investments into U.K. assets. As a result, the value of the pound rises, increasing the price of U.K. exports on world markets and lowering the price of imported goods to U.K. consumers. The United Kingdom's net exports decline. Because net exports are one of the components of aggregate expenditures, the fall in net exports offsets the initial expansionary fiscal policy. As transaction costs fall, world financial markets become more closely integrated, making exchange rates more sensitive to interest rate movements and reducing the impact that fiscal policy can have on the economy.

exports are a large fraction of total spending, these exchange rate effects are the main channel of monetary policy.

Although monetary policy may be more effective in the short run in an open economy, one of our key earlier conclusions continues to hold: as wages and prices eventually adjust, the economy returns to full employment. So even in an open economy, the long-run effect of monetary policy is on inflation, not on output or unemployment.

FISCAL POLICY WITH FLEXIBLE EXCHANGE RATES

Though changes in the exchange rate tend to reinforce the impact of monetary policy, they act to reduce the impact of fiscal policy. The reason again can be traced to the way interest rates move. We have already learned that a fiscal expansion that shifts the ADI curve to the right increases output and eventually inflation. As inflation starts to rise, the central bank will act to raise interest rates. Since central banks react to anticipate future increases in inflation, interest rates are likely to rise even if initially the actual increase in inflation is small. Also, a fiscal expansion raises the equilibrium full-employment real interest rate. As we learned in Chapter 15, a central bank that desires to maintain a stable inflation rate will shift its monetary policy rule when the equilibrium full-employment real interest rate changes. In the case of a fiscal expansion, this shift will lead to higher interest rates.

As interest rates increase, the exchange rate will appreciate, thereby dampening net exports. Any decline in net exports works to offset the original fiscal stimulus to aggregate expenditures. As a consequence, the exchange rate adjustment limits the impact of fiscal policy on expenditures. In the long run, as the economy returns to full employment, an increase in the government's deficit crowds out private investment and net exports, as the full-employment model of Chapter 8 explains.

Exchange rates, unlike wages and prices, adjust very rapidly, but exports and imports often do not adjust as quickly. A change in government expenditures may have an immediate impact on aggregate expenditures, while the offsetting movements in net exports may occur much later.

Wrap-Up

POLICY IN AN OPEN ECONOMY

In an open economy, the force of monetary policy is strengthened because it may affect the real exchange rate and, through the exchange rate, the level of aggregate expenditures. This effect reinforces the impact of monetary policy on aggregate expenditures through interest rates and credit availability.

In an open economy, the force of fiscal policy is dampened because it may affect the real exchange rate and, through the exchange rate, the level of net exports. The change in exchange rates caused by a fiscal expansion reduces net exports, offsetting some of the expansion's impact.

International Perspective
IS A STRONG DOLLAR GOOD FOR THE UNITED STATES?

Politicians and news commentators frequently associate the "strength" of a nation's currency with the underlying health of its economy. And concerns are often expressed when the value of a currency falls. The experience with the euro provides a case in point. The euro came into existence on January 1, 1999, when eleven European countries joined together to form a monetary union. The exchange rate between the euro, its new currency, and the dollar was initially $1.16. That is, it took $1.16 to purchase one euro. Over the next seventeen months, the euro declined in value. By May 2000, an American could buy a euro for only 91 cents. The fall in the euro caused some to worry greatly as they suggested that the weakness of the euro was a sign of the monetary union's failure.

But is a weak currency really bad for an economy? Should the European Central Bank have taken action to prevent the

euro from weakening? Since early 2002, the euro has strengthened against the dollar. Should the Fed have acted to prevent this fall in the dollar's value? To answer these questions, we can focus on the role that exchange rates play in helping to stabilize the macroeconomy and on how different sectors of the economy are affected.

Movements in the exchange rate serve to offset fluctuations in aggregate expenditures. In this way, they help stabilize the economy. For instance, at the end of the 1990s, European economies were in recession. As the euro fell in value, European goods became cheaper on world markets. As a result, Europe's exports increased. The fall in the euro made imported goods more expensive for Europeans to buy, thereby decreasing Europe's imports. The falling euro boosted Europe's net exports, helping to end the recession. If the European

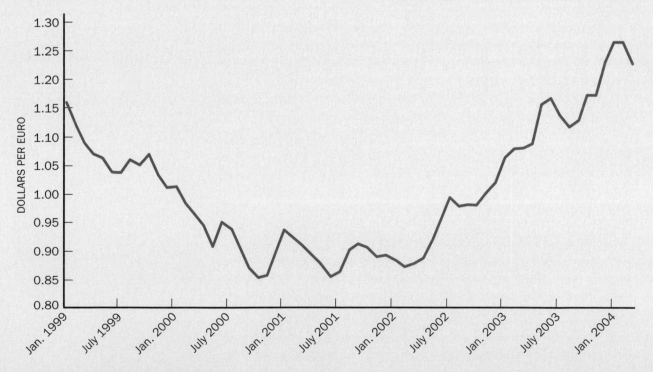

THE EURO–DOLLAR EXCHANGE RATE

SOURCE: Federal Reserve Board, Release G.5, 2004.

Central Bank had increased the interest rate to try to prevent the weakening of the euro, it would have made Europe's recovery from recession more difficult.

A weak currency will boost exports and reduce imports; a strong currency has the opposite effect. The United States has a huge trade deficit. The fall in the value of the dollar over the past few years will help reduce this deficit by making foreign goods more expensive for Americans and making American goods cheaper for foreigners. Thus, if you buy lots of imported goods, you benefit from a strong dollar. But if you are a business that sells abroad, your sales suffer from a strong dollar. If you work for a company that competes against foreign imports, your company is hurt by a strong dollar. Farmers therefore may see world demand for American wheat fall when the dollar appreciates, while consumers enjoy lower prices for imported electronics goods. Exchange rate movements create both winners and losers; so, apart from buttressing macroeconomic stability, a strong dollar has no grounds to be always preferred.

One additional argument is often made in favor of maintaining a strong dollar. Foreign investors have lent the United States huge amounts over the past twenty years. If they think the dollar will fall in value, they may sell their holdings of U.S. financial assets. Because the United States has been able to maintain a high level of investment, despite its low national savings rate, by borrowing from abroad, these foreign sources of funds might dry up if the dollar were to weaken. However, what matters most in attracting foreign investors is not the level of the exchange rate but the rate of return that these investors expect to earn; and those returns depend on U.S. interest rates and the expected rate of dollar depreciation. If foreign investors expect the dollar to fall, then interest rates will have to rise to continue to attract foreign investment to the United States.

Policy Coordination

Net exports provide one of the channels through which economic conditions in one country affect others. Interest rates provide another linkage. Because of these connections, the major industrialized economies of North America, Europe, and Asia meet regularly to discuss global economic conditions and often try to coordinate macroeconomic policies. The summits of the Group of Eight, or G-8, consisting of the United States, Canada, Japan, Germany, France, Italy, the United Kingdom, and Russia provide a forum for discussions of international economic developments. In recent years, these discussions have included such topics as the ongoing Japanese recession and policies to end it, the emerging market economies and the Russian economy, the role of international organizations such as the International Monetary Fund and the World Bank, and the debt burden of developing nations.

The argument that countries may gain from coordinating their macroeconomic policies is best illustrated with an example. Suppose two countries are in recession. Each contemplates using expansionary fiscal policy to try to speed its return to full employment. Each realizes, however, that if it expands fiscal policy while the other country does not, its currency will appreciate. Such appreciation would have a detrimental impact on the net exports of the country undertaking the fiscal expansion and negate some of the effect desired from the policy action. But suppose both countries could agree to undertake fiscal expansions. As their economies expand, interest rates in *both* countries will rise, and thus the exchange rate can remain at its initial level—the fiscal expansions are not offset by a movement in exchange rate.

Review and Practice

SUMMARY

1. In the open economy, net exports are a component of aggregate spending. Both imports and exports depend on the real exchange rate. A lower real exchange rate increases exports and reduces imports.

2. Changes in the real interest rate affect investment, the exchange rate, and net exports. A rise in the real interest rate reduces domestic investment and net exports, leading to a downward shift in aggregate expenditures.

3. The aggregate demand–inflation (ADI) curve in an open economy has a negative slope—the level of output consistent with equilibrium falls as inflation rises. The ADI curve can shift if incomes abroad fluctuate or if foreign interest rates rise or fall relative to the U.S. interest rate.

4. Exchange rate movements can have a temporary but direct effect on U.S. inflation. If the dollar depreciates, the prices of imported inputs rise, and firms may pass this increase through in the form of higher prices.

5. Exchange rate movements can directly affect the consumer price index (CPI) measure of inflation, because the CPI includes the prices of imported goods purchased by households.

6. Monetary policy is more effective in an open economy—changes in interest rates affect private investment, but they also cause reinforcing changes in net exports through the exchange rate channel.

7. Fiscal policy is less effective in an open economy—the change in exchange rate causes net exports to offset the initial fiscal action.

KEY TERM

interest parity condition

REVIEW QUESTIONS

1. What is the relationship between the interest rate and the exchange rate? What is the relationship between the exchange rate and net exports?

2. As we move up and to the left on a given ADI curve, what happens to the value of the domestic currency and net exports?

3. If firms import a lot of raw materials, what impact would a depreciation in the dollar have on the inflation adjustment (IA) curve?

4. How does a fiscal expansion affect the real exchange rate and net exports?

5. How does a monetary policy expansion affect the real exchange rate and net exports?

6. If the United States raises its interest rate and Canada does not, will the Canadian dollar appreciate or will it depreciate? If Canada follows the United States and also raises its interest rate, what will happen to the value of the Canadian dollar?

PROBLEMS

1. Explain how U.S. net exports would be affected by each of the following:
   (a) An economic expansion in western Europe
   (b) Financial crises in Asia and Latin America that cause the U.S. dollar to appreciate
   (c) An interest rate increase by the European Central Bank

2. Using the information in the table below, calculate the real exchange rate between the nations of Nordamer and Sudamer (the nominal exchange rate is the number of Nordamer dollars that can be purchased with one Sudamer dollar):

	Price level in Nordamer	Price level in Sudamer	Nominal exchange rate
Year 1	100	100	1
Year 2	110	100	1.1
Year 3	121	100	1.21
Year 4	133	100	1.33

   (a) Has the Sudamer dollar appreciated or depreciated in nominal terms?
   (b) Has the real exchange rate appreciated or depreciated?
   (c) Have Nordamer goods become less expensive for Sudamers to buy? Explain.

3. Suppose a fall in net exports due to a recession among our major trading partners causes a recession in the United States.
   (a) If fiscal policy is used to stimulate the economy and return it to full employment, what happens to the real interest rate, investment, and future output?
   (b) If monetary policy is used to stimulate the economy and return it to full employment, what happens to the real interest rate, investment, and future output?
4. The United States is a major export market for Canadian goods. Use the ADI and IA framework to illustrate how Canadian output and inflation will be affected if the Fed increases interest rates.
5. Suppose the U.S. economy is in a recession. The government is considering using expansionary fiscal or monetary policy to help get the economy back to full employment. Which type of policy will result in a higher level of net exports?
6. True or false: "A contractionary monetary policy hurts export industries; a fiscal contraction helps export industries." Explain why fiscal and monetary policies might have different effects on industries that produce a lot of goods for export.

Learning Goals

In this chapter, you will learn

1 How developing economies differ from developed economies such as the United States, Japan, and western Europe

2 What the impediments to growth in developing economies are, and what policies these countries can pursue to improve their standards of living

3 What *globalization* is and why some people are skeptical of it

4 How resources were allocated under the old communist system, and how the transition economies have fared since the collapse of communism

Chapter 19

DEVELOPMENT AND TRANSITION

Every year, thousands of Mexicans risk their lives to cross into the United States. The reason is simple: they seek a way out of their poverty. In the United States, a family of four is said to be in poverty—to have insufficient income for a minimal standard of living—if its income is less than $18,811. This income is about equal to that of the *average* family of four in Mexico! The average income per capita in Mexico is one-sixth of that in the United States. The minimum wage in the United States is now more than $5 an hour. In many developing countries, workers receive a mere $1 a day. Figure 19.1 shows the huge differences in income per capita between developed countries such as the United States and Italy and *less-developed countries* such as Ethiopia and Nigeria. These less-developed countries sometimes are referred to as the *third world* and sometimes as *developing countries*. Unfortunately, many of these low-income countries have not been developing—some have even been declining, with income per capita falling. Today, three-fourths of the world's population live in these developing countries.

Another group of countries also differs markedly from the advanced industrial countries. These are the so-called *economies in transition*—in transition from communism to a market economy. Figure 19.2 shows how these countries, the most important of which is Russia, have fared since the ending of communism. In many cases the transitions to market economies have yet to bear fruit, and in some cases the results have been disastrous.

There have been exceptions to this picture: countries such as Hungary and Poland have recently joined the European Union, signaling closer economic integration with western Europe, and China, the most populous country in the world and a half century ago one of the poorest, has grown rapidly. In the past two decades, incomes in China have soared, and the poverty rate has fallen from 80 percent to 5 percent.

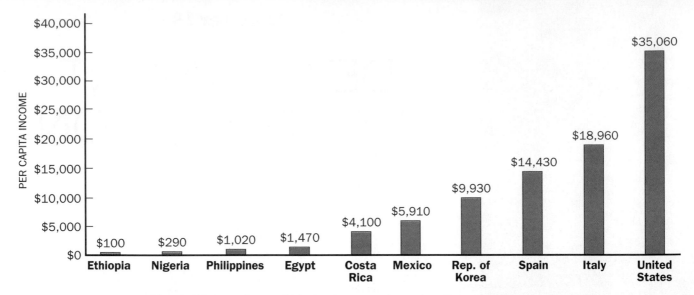

Figure 19.1

DIFFERENCES IN
PER CAPITA INCOME

Some middle-income countries such as Costa Rica have per capita incomes that are up to ten times those of the world's poorest nations, and yet only one-tenth of those of the world's wealthiest nations.

SOURCE: *World Development Indicators 2004*, www.worldbank.org/data/.

This chapter explores the issues of economic development and transition. We will see that many of the challenges faced by developing and transitional economies relate to the process by which the world has become increasingly integrated economically. This process, called *globalization,* has created opportunities for some countries, but it has also been a source of contention and even conflict.

Development

Three-fourths of the world's population live in **less-developed countries,** or **LDCs.** Statistics cannot convey the full measure of what it means to live in an LDC, but they can provide a start. In the United States, life expectancy at birth is about 78 years. In Peru, it is 70 years; in India, 63 years; and in Ethiopia, 42 years. In the United States, 7 infants die for every one thousand live births; in Brazil, 31 die; in Pakistan, 84; and in Ethiopia, 116. The average American completes twelve years of schooling, while the average African gets only five years. India, with a population three and a half times that of the United States, has a GDP roughly one-twentieth that of the United States. This means that per capita income in India is about 1 percent of that in the United States.

The statistics connect with one another in a vicious cycle. Little or no education, malnutrition, and poor health care reduce productivity and thus incomes. With low incomes, people in the LDCs cannot afford better education, more food, or better health care. In many African countries, whose standards of living were already low, population has been growing faster than national income, and thus per capita income

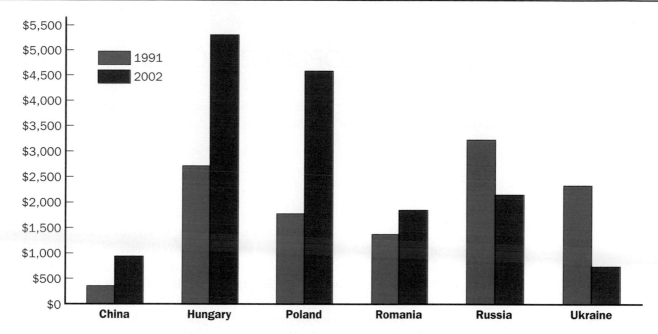

Figure 19.2

INCOME PER CAPITA IN THE
TRANSITION ECONOMIES

The figure shows how some economies that are in transition from communism to a market economy have fared over the past decade. While some countries, such as China, Hungary, and Poland, have made progress, the nations of the former Soviet Union such as Russia and Ukraine have not.

SOURCE: World Bank (http://devdata.worldbank.org/data-query/).

has been falling. Life is getting worse, not better. The AIDS epidemic has ravaged Africa and threatens much of the rest of the developing world, making a bad situation even worse. Some countries, like Zambia, have seen life expectancy fall by ten years in less than a decade. More than one-fourth of the population in southern Africa is infected with HIV.

The United Nations and the World Bank (a bank established by the major industrialized countries after World War II that provides loans to LDCs) group countries into three categories: low-income countries, with GDP per capita of $735 or less in 2002; high-income countries, with GDP per capita above $9,076; and middle-income countries, with GDP per capita in between. The low-income countries are the LDCs. The high-income countries are referred to as **developed countries.** Because their higher level of income is based on their higher level of industrialization, they also are referred to as the **industrialized countries.** In the Western Hemisphere, hardly 200 miles lie between one of the richest countries, the United States, with a per capita income of $35,060 in 2002, and one of the poorest, Haiti, with a per capita income of $440.

The income gap between high-income countries, including the countries of western Europe, the United States, Canada, Japan, Australia, and New Zealand, has narrowed considerably over the past hundred years, but the gap between the high-income countries and the low-income countries has not. However, there are signs that change is possible. Some countries have made notable progress in recent years.

THE WORLD BANK'S DEVELOPMENT GOALS

The World Bank has established goals for reducing poverty, improving education, reducing child mortality, and achieving other indicators of economic development and improved standards of living. They are listed at www.developmentgoals.org.

First, several countries have moved from the circle of LDCs to the ranks of middle-income countries. These are referred to collectively as **newly industrialized countries,** or **NICs** for short. Those with success stories include the "gang of four": South Korea, Taiwan, Singapore, and Hong Kong. In the thirty years after the devastating Korean War, for instance, South Korea moved from being a backward country to a major producer—not just of simple products such as textiles but of automobiles (the Hyundai) and computers, whose production requires a reasonably high level of technological expertise. Even more impressive, Japan has moved from the category of middle-income country to become one of the most prosperous nations in the world. But the success stories are not limited to East Asia: Botswana, while today suffering greatly from AIDS, has managed to have sustained growth of more than 8 percent annually for thirty years, among the most impressive records anywhere in the world. India, which for decades after independence hardly seemed to grow, has experienced sustained growth of more than 5 percent for a decade.

Second, there have been pockets of remarkable progress *within* the LDCs. In the early 1960s, agricultural research centers around the world (funded largely by the Rockefeller Foundation) developed new kinds of seeds, which under proper conditions enormously increase yields per acre. The introduction and dissemination of these new seeds—accompanied by far-reaching improvements in agricultural practices, known as the **green revolution**—led to huge increases in output. India, for example, finally managed to produce enough food to feed its burgeoning population and now sometimes exports wheat to other countries.

Third, even the grim statistics for life expectancy—62 years in Bangladesh and 46 years in sub-Saharan Africa (compared to 78 years in the United States, as noted above)—represent improvements for many countries. But these improvements have a darker side in some countries: a population explosion reminiscent of the Malthusian nightmare. Thomas Malthus envisioned a world in which population growth outpaced increases in the food supply. In Kenya during the early 1980s, for instance, improved health conditions enabled the population to grow at 4.1 percent a year, a remarkable rate at which the population would double every seventeen years, while output increased at only 1.9 percent a year. Increases in output do nothing to improve per capita income when the population grows even faster.

LIFE IN A LESS-DEVELOPED COUNTRY

Just as there are large differences between the LDCs and the industrialized countries, so there are large differences among the LDCs. The largest LDC of all, China, has a communist government. The second-largest, India, functions as the world's largest democracy. Literacy standards in Costa Rica rank with those of the industrialized countries, whereas more than half of the adult population in sub-Saharan Africa is illiterate. One must be careful in generalizing about LDCs. Still, certain observations are true for *most* of them.

Table 19.1 summarizes some of the most important dimensions of living standards, contrasting the United States, a high-income country; Mexico (its nearest neighbor to the south), a middle-income country; and India, a low-income country.

Incomes and life expectancies in most LDCs are low. A large fraction of the population lives in the rural sector and is engaged in agriculture. Lacking modern equipment like tractors, the farmers work on small plots (an acre or two, compared to an average of more than a hundred acres in the United States). In many cases, they lack the resources to buy productivity-increasing inputs such as fertilizer and pesticides; on average they use less than half the fertilizer per acre that farmers in more-developed countries use. In many countries, most farmers are landless, tilling the landlord's land under **sharecropping** arrangements that give the landlord half the output. In several countries with policies of **land reform,** land has been

Table 19.1

STANDARD OF LIVING MEASUREMENTS IN THE UNITED STATES, MEXICO, AND INDIA

Category	United States	Mexico	India
GNP per capita ($)	35,060	5,910	480
Life expectancy (years)	78	72	63
Agriculture as percentage of GDP	2	5	28
Energy consumption per capita (kilograms of oil equivalent)	8,076	1,501	479
Annual average growth of population (%)	1	1.8	1.8
Infant mortality rate (per 1,000 live births)	7	30	70
Maternal mortality rate (per 100,000 live births)	8	48	410
Urban population (% of total)	77	74	28
Television sets (number per 1,000 people)	847	261	69
Personal computers (number per 1,000 people)	458.6	47	2.7

SOURCE: *World Development Report 2004.* Data are for the most recent year available, 2002 in most cases.

redistributed to the peasants. Such land reforms were a precursor to the remarkable growth in Taiwan and Japan. In other countries, such as the Philippines and Peru, the land reforms have been only partially successful.

Over the past fifty years, most LDCs have experienced gradual urbanization. Those who live in the cities have a much higher standard of living, including access to better education and health facilities. The marked differences between the cities and rural areas have led some to refer to these economies as **dual economies.** While there are large income disparities between rural and urban sectors, disparities within the urban sectors are equally large: government workers and those few lucky enough to get jobs in manufacturing earn many times the average wage. These high wages attract migrants from the rural sector, often resulting in high urban unemployment (exceeding 20 percent) in some cities.

One reason for the poverty in LDCs is a lack of resources. These countries have less physical capital per capita and less human capital, with high illiteracy rates and a low average number of years of schooling. The lower levels of physical capital per capita are not the result of low saving rates—in fact, the saving rates of most LDCs are considerably higher than the rate in the United States. Because of their high population growth rates, they have to save a lot just to stand still.

High population growth rates have another effect. They have increased enormously the proportion of the young, who depend on others for their income. And they have made the task of improving educational levels even harder, creating a vicious circle. Typically, less-educated women have larger families, in part because they are less likely to be informed about family planning but also because the opportunity cost of having children is lower—they forgo less income. If educational levels can be improved, this vicious cycle can be turned into a virtuous cycle: more-educated women have smaller families, lowering population growth rates. Between 1980 and 2000, the average population growth rate for countries with 1980 per capita incomes below $1,000 was 3.3 percent per year. For those with 1980 per capita incomes between $1,000 and $3,000, it was 2.6 percent per year; with 1980 incomes over $3,000, only 1.3 percent. These lower rates reduce the proportion of the young and make the task of further improving educational levels easier.

Low educational levels and lack of capital prevent these economies from availing themselves of much of the most advanced technologies. With important exceptions, they specialize in low-skill *labor-intensive* industries (those whose products require much labor relative to the amount of equipment they employ), like textiles.

These problems are compounded by *institutional* failures. The lack of good financial institutions means that what capital is available may not be invested well; the lack of financial markets means that businesses cannot obtain some of the inputs they need; and the lack of good legal systems means that creditors find it difficult to force a recalcitrant borrower to repay, and consequently are willing to lend only at high interest rates that can compensate them for their risk. All these failures inhibit the entry of new firms and the expansion of old firms.

Many LDCs also are marked by high levels of inequality. Their limited incomes are shared even more unequally than are the incomes in the more advanced countries, leading to high levels of poverty. Throughout the developing countries as a whole, the number in poverty, living on less than $2 a day, was 2.8 billion at the end of the twentieth century, and the number in absolute poverty, living on less than $1 a day, was 1.2 billion.

Some of this inequality is simply due to the law of supply and demand. Because unskilled labor is abundant and skilled labor and entrepreneurs are scarce, unskilled wages are low and those who have skills prosper. Indeed, earlier theories suggested that inequality contributed to economic growth. Sir Arthur Lewis, who received the Nobel Prize for his work on development economics, argued that what he called the **surplus of labor** kept wages low and profits high. Workers earning subsistence wages could not save, but capitalists could; thus higher profits contributed to a higher saving rate. In this view, there is a trade-off between growth and equality. Current views are different. Today, many economists believe that growth and equality are in fact complementary, as evidenced by the East Asian miracle.

Wrap-Up

SOURCES OF PROBLEMS IN LESS-DEVELOPED COUNTRIES

A lack of resources, both human and physical, and high population growth, which makes raising educational levels difficult

The lack of financial markets and inadequate legal systems

A high level of income inequality

THE SUCCESS OF EAST ASIA

The most successful efforts at development, anywhere at any time, have been in East Asia in the decades after World War II. Sustained growth over three to four decades has led to eightfold or greater increases in per capita income. There are several ingredients to this success:

- Macroeconomic stability—avoiding for the most part high inflation or high levels of unemployment. As part of this strategy, governments maintained a high level of fiscal responsibility, eschewing the huge budget deficits that characterize many LDCs.
- High saving rates. With saving rates of 25 percent or more, the countries could invest heavily.
- Smart investment of savings. As important as the high level of saving is the fact that the savings were invested well; in other countries with high saving rates (either forced, as in the communist countries, or the result of a natural resource bonanza, as in Venezuela), they were not.
- Heavy investment in education, including the education of women. This investment resulted in a highly skilled labor force that was able to absorb new technologies.
- Heavy investment in technology. What separates developed from less-developed countries is not only a shortage of capital but also a "gap" in knowledge. East Asian countries developed technology policies aimed at

closing this gap, with remarkable success. Some countries, like Singapore, encouraged foreign firms to invest directly, bringing with them access to foreign markets as well as new technology. Other countries, like Korea, focused on licensing new technologies from the more advanced countries.

- Political and social stability, which provides an environment conducive to investment.

So impressive have the outcomes in East Asia been that many refer to them as the *East Asian miracle*. Some economists, however, find nothing miraculous in them—the growth can be explained largely by standard economics of the kind that we have studied in this text (see Chapter 9). High saving rates, high investment in both capital and education, and knowledge are part of the standard recipe. Still, one point argues for a miracle: no other set of countries has been able to achieve similar outcomes.

Underlying these successes were both good policies (such as those that led to macroeconomic stability) and strong institutions (such as newly created financial institutions that allocated the capital well). Three features of East Asia's development strategy deserve special attention: the roles of government, exports, and egalitarian policies.

The Role of Government Perhaps the most distinctive feature of the East Asia model was the balance the countries achieved between the role of the state and the role of the market. Their governments pursued market-oriented policies that encouraged development of the private sector. They sought to augment and "govern" the market, not to replace it.

They also fostered high saving rates—often in excess of 25 percent. In Japan, more than a third of these savings went into accounts at the postal savings banks established by the government. In Singapore, the government established a provident fund, to which all workers were required to contribute 40 percent of their income.

These governments also influenced the allocation of capital in myriad ways. Banks were discouraged from making real estate loans and loans for durable consumer goods. This action helped to increase private saving rates and to discourage real estate speculation, which often serves to destabilize the economy. As a result, more funds were available for investment in growth-oriented activities like purchasing new equipment. In addition, governments established development banks to promote long-term investment in sectors such as shipbuilding, steel mills, and the chemical industry. These interventions have been more controversial, and their success has been mixed. On the positive side, the steel firms in Taiwan and Korea are among the most efficient in the world. With more mixed results, the Japanese and Korean governments took a variety of initiatives to promote certain industries, including the computer chip industry. By the early 1980s, Japan seemed poised to completely dominate that market. During the late 1980s and early 1990s, a series of agreements reached between Japan and the United States lowered tariffs on semiconductors and allowed U.S. manufactures access to the Japanese market. These changes served to level the playing field, enabling American producers such as Intel to draw on America's comparative advantage in chip production and reassert leadership in the industry. The dangers of government intervention are often symbolized by the Japanese government's failed attempt to discourage Honda (originally a manufacturer of motorcycles) from entering the auto market, arguing that there were already too many producers.

Export-Led Growth A second factor that distinguished the countries of East Asia from less successful LDCs was their emphasis on exports. A growth strategy focusing on exports is called **export-led growth.** Firms were given a variety of encouragements to export, including increased access to credit, often at subsidized rates.

Export-led growth enables firms to produce according to their long-term comparative advantage. This is not current comparative advantage, based on current resources and knowledge. It is dynamic comparative advantage, which relies on acquired skills and technology, and on recognition of the importance of learning by doing—that skills and productivity improve with production experience. When an LDC emphasizes exports, demand for the goods it produces is not limited by the low income of its citizens. The world is its market.

Advocates of export-led growth also believe that the competition provided by the export market is an important stimulus to efficiency and modernization. The only way for a firm to succeed in the face of keen international competition is to produce what consumers want, at the quality they want, and at the lowest possible cost. This keen competition forces specialization in areas where low-wage LDCs have a comparative advantage, such as in the production of labor-intensive products.

Finally, export-led growth has facilitated the transfer of advanced technology. Producers exporting to developed countries not only come into contact with efficient producers within those countries but also learn to adopt their standards and production techniques.

Fostering Equality Another distinctive aspect of East Asia's development strategy was its emphasis on equality. Examples of these egalitarian policies include Singapore's home ownership program; the almost universal provision of elementary and secondary education, extended to girls as well as boys; and the land redistribution programs that were the precursor of growth in several of the countries, including Taiwan and Japan. In many of these countries, the governments also tried to curb excessive wage inequality and to discourage conspicuous consumption by the rich. Their experience has shown that high saving rates are possible without either the oppressiveness of Soviet-style governments or vast inequalities. The equality measures have actually promoted economic growth. The land reforms have resulted in increased agricultural production, and the high educational levels have directly increased productivity and facilitated the transfer and adoption of more advanced technology. More education for women is associated with smaller families, and thus with declining rates of population growth.

EAST ASIA'S SUCCESS

Key ingredients to East Asia's success include macroeconomic stability, high saving rates to finance investment, investment in education and in technology, and political and social stability.

Governments pursued market-oriented policies that encouraged saving and investment.

Growth strategies emphasized *export-led growth*.

Income equality was fostered.

ALTERNATIVE DEVELOPMENT STRATEGIES

The development strategies pursued by East Asia stood in marked contrast to those followed in much of the rest of the world, and many economists attribute, at least in part, the differences in performance to differences in strategies. As the developing countries first experienced independence, many came under the sway of socialism and government took a central role in planning development. Having been dominated by foreign governments, they worried that opening themselves up to foreign investment would lead to a new form of domination—domination by large multinational firms. Some countries, trying to reduce their reliance on imports, focused on *import substitution* policies, and a few, like Brazil, had a short period of success following that strategy. But by and large, the countries following these strategies stagnated or grew very slowly.

Even before the end of the cold war seemed to provide convincing proof that the socialist or planning model was badly flawed, its weaknesses as implemented in the developing countries seemed apparent. Governments did not do a good job of planning, often managing and allocating resources inefficiently. "White elephants" such as huge and inefficient steel mills dotted the landscape. Protectionist barriers were erected, nominally to help support domestic industries but all too often to allow friends of the government to enjoy high profits insulated from outside competition. In some cases, the inefficiencies were so extreme that the value of the inputs imported for use in production was greater than the value of the output, had it been sold at international prices. Protection had been granted using the *infant industry argument*—the argument that new industries had to be protected until they could establish themselves sufficiently to meet the competition. But in many of the developing countries, the infants seemed never to grow up: protection became permanent.

In the early 1980s a new development strategy emerged. Recognizing the limits of a state-dominated economy, many countries swung to the other extreme, arguing for a minimal role for government. Governments were urged to privatize and liberalize, to sell off state companies and eliminate government intervention. These policies, together with macroeconomic stability, were often referred to as the *Washington consensus,* since they were advocated by the U.S. Treasury and two international institutions located in Washington, the International Monetary Fund (IMF) and the World Bank. In many cases, these policies proved little better than their predecessors in promoting growth over an extended period of time. Reducing tariff barriers led to losses of jobs, and the developing economies were not able to generate new enterprises. Advocates believed that liberalization would lead resources to move from low-productivity uses to high-productivity uses, as the theory of comparative advantage suggested; in practice, workers frequently moved from low-productivity jobs into unemployment. All too often the policies that were designed for macroeconomic stability included very high interest rates—so high that new investment to create new jobs simply was not forthcoming.

By the mid-1990s, it became increasingly clear that neither of the extremes— the Washington consensus or state-dominated planning—provided much help. The success of the East Asian countries, even after taking into account the setback of the financial crisis of 1997–1998, stood in marked contrast to the experiences of those that had tried one or the other of these recipes for success. The East Asian countries had been more successful not only in producing growth but also in reducing poverty. Markets were seen to be at the center of development, but government had a vital role in catalyzing change and in helping to make the markets work better, to transform the economy and society through education and technology, and to regulate the economy so that it could function better. Greater attention was focused on how to make not only markets but also governments work better.

GLOBALIZATION AND DEVELOPMENT

The six decades since World War II have seen major efforts at reducing trade barriers. However, from the developing countries' perspective, the trade liberalization agenda has been driven primarily by the interests of the advanced industrialized countries, which continue to subsidize agriculture and protect textiles, making it difficult for the less-industrialized countries to sell some of the main goods that represent their comparative advantage.

These concerns are but one part of a broader dissatisfaction with globalization and the international economic institutions that help manage it. **Globalization** is the name given to the closer integration of the countries of the world— especially the increased level of trade and easier movements of capital—brought on by lower costs of transportation and communication. There are three important international economic institutions: the World Trade Organization (WTO), which provides a venue for international trade agreements and resolving trade disputes; the IMF, which was created to help support global financial stability, providing funds to countries in times of crisis, but which has expanded its activities to include giving assistance to developing and transition economies; and the World Bank, which promotes development and the alleviation of poverty in poor and middle-income countries.

A HISTORICAL PERSPECTIVE ON GLOBALIZATION

There has been much discussion of globalization, the closer integration of the economies around the world. The most dramatic aspect of globalization is the growth of trade, of exports and imports. But there are other aspects. Workers migrate from one country to another, multinational firms do business across borders, billions of dollars of capital flow from one country to another, and ideas and knowledge are ceaselessly communicated via the Internet.

It is sometimes forgotten, however, that the world went through a process of globalization once before. In the decades before World War I, trade grew enormously, eventually reaching a percentage comparable to that attained more recently. World War I and the Great Depression led to retrenchment. As the economies of the world plunged into a downturn at the end of the 1920s, they erected trade barriers.

Today, many analysts worry about a possible backlash against globalization—as evidenced by protest marches in Seattle, Washington, Prague, and Genoa. While many of the marchers saw globalization as threatening their own jobs, others took a broader moral stance: they viewed the way globalization had been proceeding as fundamentally unfair, as rich countries ordered the poor to open their markets to them while keeping their own markets protected. After the round of trade negotiations completed in 1994 (called the Uruguay Round, after the place where it was initiated), the poorest region in the world, sub-Saharan Africa, was actually worse off, while the United States and Europe boasted enormous gains.

Economists argue that free trade enables each country to benefit by taking advantage of its comparative advantage. Even the unilateral opening up of a market makes the country as a whole better off. But some individuals may be worse off, and typically they are not compensated. Finding ways to ensure that *all* can benefit from lower trade barriers can convert a conflict into a win-win situation, but few countries have successfully done so.

In poor developing countries, the problems are even more complicated. In these countries, unemployment rates are high, entrepreneurship is limited, and capital is scarce. Bringing down trade barriers can destroy jobs and enterprises quickly, but the country may not be able to make the investments required for it to take advantage of its comparative advantage. Jobs are destroyed faster than they are created, throwing into question the argument that the country as a whole benefits. While moving workers from low-productivity employment to employment of higher productivity as measured by comparative advantage would increase national income, moving workers from low-productivity employment to unemployment would lower national income. To increase incomes, the opening up of trade must be accompanied by other measures to help these poor countries take advantage of their comparative advantage.

Trade Giving less-developed economies access to the U.S. markets is a win-win policy. American consumers win by having a greater variety of goods at lower prices. The LDCs benefit by having a huge market for their goods. The United States has a system of preferential treatment for poor countries called the *general system of preferences,* or GSP. Of course, as always with trade, some U.S. producers and their workers complain about the loss of jobs to these low-cost competitors. As argued in Chapter 16, the total benefits to trade generally outweigh the losses to certain groups. In many cases, however, these potential losers have more influence. Many developing countries find that even as they open up their markets to U.S. products, the United States does not fully reciprocate, especially in areas such as agriculture and textiles—sectors that are of particular importance to developing countries. Though the European Union has not done much better, its members have agreed on a striking initiative, offering to eliminate all trade barriers to the lowest-income countries on all commodities except guns.

While the world as a whole, and the LDCs in particular, has much to gain from globalization—after all, we saw how growth in East Asia was spurred by its exports—unless those in developing countries can be persuaded that the playing field has been made more level, hostility toward globalization may grow.

Outsourcing One source of opposition to globalization in the United States has been the perception that jobs in America are being moved overseas in what has come to be called **outsourcing,** the process by which firms buy goods and services from others rather than producing the goods and services themselves. Outsourcing is not a new phenomenon. For example, car manufacturers have long outsourced the production of many car parts to independent firms. The practice has become controversial because many believe that Americans ranging from phone operators staffing customer help lines to software engineers are losing their jobs as firms move production to other countries or purchase the services from foreign firms. For example, new information technologies have made feasible the electronic transmission of tax returns to India for overnight processing, reducing the demand for American tax preparers.

Although outsourcing generated a great deal of news and debate during the presidential campaign in 2004, two facts are frequently ignored. First, very few U.S. jobs have moved overseas. The U.S. Labor Department reported that in the first quarter of 2004, there were 239,361 mass layoffs (layoffs that involved 50 or more workers); of these workers, only 9,985 lost jobs that were moved to a different location, and in only about half those cases (affecting 4,633 workers) did the job move to a foreign country. Overall, less than 2 percent of the mass layoffs could be described as the result of outsourcing to a foreign country. This practice is not responsible for the major changes in American patterns of employment.

Second, the United States benefits from what could be called *insourcing*—the employment of American workers by foreign firms. Toyota, for example, has established manufacturing facilities in the United States and is a major employer of American workers. Infosys Technologies of Bangalore, India, a company that helps U.S. firms shift jobs to India, opened a major consulting operation in California in

THE COMMUNIST SYSTEM IN THE SOVIET UNION

The government owned the means of production and determined what should be produced and how it should be produced under a system of central planning.

Because wages and prices were set by the government, they could not function to balance supply and demand. Shortages were common and many goods were rationed.

By the 1980s, the failures of Soviet agriculture and Soviet industry's inability to keep up with rapid innovation in the West led first to attempts at economic and political reform and then to the collapse of the Soviet Union.

THE MOVE TOWARD A MARKET ECONOMY

Russia and many of the other new republics quickly moved toward a market economy. They believed that replacing the inefficient central planners with markets and the price system would solve their economic woes. Private property would provide incentives. Free trade would provide competition; a supply of inputs to Russia's factories; a supply of consumer goods to Russia's consumers, who had been deprived of so much for so long; and a ready market for what Russia produced. The cornerstones of its strategy were thus *privatization* and *liberalization*—eliminating the myriad constraints that marked the Soviet system. Replacing the inefficient Soviet system thus was bound to raise living standards. The optimists thought it would happen overnight; the pessimists, that it might take six months or perhaps a year.

What happened in the next decade came as a surprise. For most of the countries, growth in the decade after the beginning of the transition was slower than growth during the decade before the transition. The economy of the former superpower has shrunk to the point where it is comparable with that of the Netherlands or Denmark. Social statistics reflect the deteriorating economic conditions: life spans are shorter, and divorce rates are higher. While 2 percent of the population was in poverty at the beginning of the transition, a decade later the number was estimated to be approaching 40 percent.

There are some exceptions to this bleak picture: Poland has a GDP today that is 50 percent higher than it was a decade ago, and China, another country making the transition from central planning to a market economy, has seen its income quadruple over the past twenty years.

What accounts for these transition successes *and* failures? To be sure, because each country began the transition in different circumstances, some had an advantage over others. Poland and several of the other Eastern European countries had a higher standard of living before becoming communist than did Russia; China had a much lower level of income. The countries of Eastern Europe had easier access to Western markets, and the lure of entry into the European Union helped speed up the reforms required for admission. Some countries, like Uzbekistan, are landlocked, a limitation that poses distinct problems. A few countries have been plagued with ethnic strife or conflicts with their neighbors (such as between Armenia and Azerbaijan). Some countries produced commodities, such as cotton and gold, that had ready markets in the West; others, accustomed to producing such goods as parts for Russian tractors or cars, found themselves with limited markets.

Gradualism Versus Shock Therapy In the beginning of the transition, many countries faced a problem of extremely high inflation. Under communism, prices were controlled at levels that were too low, and goods were thus rationed. When the restrictions were abolished, prices soared. The initial challenge for these countries was to bring this inflation under control. Many adopted a policy that was referred to as *shock therapy*—dramatic reductions in government expenditures and very tight monetary policy. This policy induced deep recessions but did manage to get inflation under control. At that point, two schools of thought developed.

The first argued for a continuation of rapid change. As they said, "You cannot cross a chasm in two jumps." They pushed for quick privatization and liberalization. After privatization, the owners of the assets would have an incentive to manage their assets well. Trade liberalization would ensure that there were competing products available from abroad, encouraging efficiency and ensuring that even if the number of firms in the domestic market was low, their ability to exercise market power would be limited.

The second argued for more gradual change. In the battle of metaphors, they pointed out that "It takes nine months even to have a baby." According to the gradualists, time was needed to establish the *institutional infrastructure* underlying a market economy, institutions without which market economies simply cannot function but that those in the West simply take for granted. Earlier, in the context of development, we noted the importance of legal and financial institutions, and a tax system must also be in place. Russia is a country rich in natural resources. Selling those resources for a pittance, or giving them away, would leave future governments coping with a shortage of revenues unless they could impose taxes on the newly privatized companies. Gradualists also argued that changes were needed not only in the economy but also in the society; change could not be imposed from above, especially in a democracy. For democratic reforms to be durable (sustainable), time was needed to change the mind-set of the people, and there would have to be demonstrated successes. The problems confronting Russia and the other countries were particularly severe because the people had been indoctrinated throughout their lives in the evils of capitalism, and because there was little "rule of law"—or at least the kinds of laws required for a market economy—on which to build.

Well-functioning markets require both competition and private property. But if both could not be obtained simultaneously, which should be stressed more? Some advocates of rapid change, like Andrei Shleifer of Harvard University, took the position that the underlying legal structure mattered little; once private property was introduced, owners would create political pressure to build the necessary institutional infrastructure. They argued that the specific recipients of the state's assets mattered little, since even if the first-round owners were not particularly efficient managers, they would have an incentive either to resell the assets to someone who was an efficient manager or to hire efficient managers.

In the end, the shock therapy approach won out in policy circles, especially in the West. The U.S. Treasury and the IMF pushed for rapid privatization and liberalization. They argued not only for eliminating trade barriers but also for opening up capital markets. Doing so, they asserted, would demonstrate to outside investors that Russia was a business-friendly place in which to invest. To be sure, they said that the institutional infrastructure was important, but they believed that this infrastructure would develop in time.

Not all the countries followed their advice. Poland and Slovenia, once their hyperinflation was contained, took a more gradualist strategy. China charted its own innovative course of development and transition, but it too was based on gradualism. The decade-long decline of Russia and most of the other countries that followed the shock therapy approach laid bare the weaknesses in this strategy, as compared to that followed by China and Poland.

A Comparison of Transition Strategies Consider some of the key differences between transition strategies in Russia and China:

- China placed more emphasis on creating jobs and enterprises than on restructuring enterprises. In China, *local* townships and villages took their savings and created millions of new enterprises. These new businesses represented a new institutional form: they were not really private, but neither were they like the old government-run, state-owned enterprises.
- China put more emphasis on competition than on privatization. In a sense, the new township and village enterprises were publicly owned, but each had to compete against the other; thus the reforms promoted efficiency. Local control and competition helped solve the *governance problem*. The old state enterprises had suffered from a lack of effective oversight. Government bureaucrats in Moscow or Beijing simply could not keep tabs on what was going on in remote provinces. By contrast, those living in the townships and villages could see clearly whether jobs were being created and their incomes were rising, and how they were faring relative to neighbors. This transparency put enormous pressure on managers.
- The gradualist approach built on existing institutions, the communes (townships and village authorities) that previously had been responsible for agriculture. But early on in the reforms, China introduced what it called the *individual responsibility system,* in which land was effectively turned over to the farmers and they reaped the benefit of their own hard work—a standard application of the conventional theory of incentives. The communes then turned their attention from agriculture to industrialization. Because the new enterprises were put in the villages and townships, there was much less social disruption than would have occurred had the industrialization been centered in urban areas. The contrast with Russia could not have been greater. There, the erosion of *social capital*—a sense of "community" and of law and order—had enormous consequences. The entire process of reform was conducted in ways that seemed unfair to the average Russian. While a few oligarchs became billionaires, the government did not pay workers and retirees what was their due. Inflation had wiped out

the value of existing savings. Mafia-like activity made it increasingly difficult for ordinary individuals to conduct business. Overall, according to a World Bank study, corruption in the region was second only to that in Africa.

- Privatization of Russia's major revenue sources at bargain-basement prices not only lent a sense of unfairness to the whole process but also, since an effective tax collection system had not been put into place, left the government continually facing a revenue shortage.

The Future of Transition The debate about the transition continues to rage. Those who led the reform in Russia and its Asian republics claim that things would have been even worse had there not been shock therapy. They are hopeful that success is "just around the corner." The critics of shock therapy say that China, Slovenia, Poland, and Hungary show that alternative approaches were possible, and that Russia would have fared better if *their* advice had been heeded. They worry about a backlash resulting from the failures—a return not to communism but to authoritarianism or nationalism—and periodic attacks on parts of the media have been unsettling. They contend that Russia's huge inequality, together with the devastation of the middle class, does not bode well for Russia's future. Only time will tell.

In many respects, China has been the most successful transition economy. It has an increasing and thriving private sector, which includes high levels of innovation in the new economy, but it faces many challenges. It has moved gradually, in part to preserve the authoritarian political control exercised by the Communist Party, and the process of democratization is just beginning. The process of restructuring the large state-owned enterprises lies largely ahead. While all parts of China have seen growth, the disparity between the richest parts, largely along the coast, and the poorer parts, in the western regions, is increasing.

Meanwhile, many of the countries of eastern Europe that were part of the Soviet Union have become part of the European Union. They are adapting their legal systems and beginning to integrate their economies with Europe's. While their transition may not be easy, for them there is a bright light at the end of the tunnel.

Wrap-Up

TRANSITION STRATEGIES

The two basic strategies the former communist countries have followed are called *gradualism* and *shock therapy*.

The more gradual reform strategy stresses the creation of competition and the development of the institutional infrastructure necessary for markets to function adequately. Countries following this strategy have fared better over the past decade than those adopting shock therapy.

Review and Practice

SUMMARY

1. In less-developed countries, or LDCs, life expectancies are usually shorter, infant mortality is higher, and people are less educated than in developed countries. Also, a larger fraction of the population lives in rural areas, and population growth rates are higher.

2. In recent years, newly industrialized countries (NICs) such as South Korea, Singapore, Hong Kong, and Taiwan have managed to improve their economic status dramatically. Other LDCs, like India, have expanded food production considerably. But the standard of living in some of the poorest LDCs, such as many African nations, has actually been declining, as population growth has outstripped economic growth.

3. Among the factors contributing to underdevelopment are lack of physical capital, lack of education, lack of technology, and lack of developed capital markets. The factors interact: low education levels impede the transfer of advanced technology; low incomes make it difficult to invest heavily in education.

4. The success of the countries of East Asia is based partially on activist government policies. These include helping to develop and use markets rather than replacing them; maintaining macroeconomic stability; promoting high levels of investment (including in public infrastructure) and saving; providing strong support for education, including the education of women; improving capital markets, which facilitate an efficient allocation of scarce capital; promoting exports; fostering equality; and promoting technology. The policies of these countries helped to create a positive investment climate (including for foreign investors) and to reduce population growth.

5. Under communism, the state was responsible for all production: central planners decided what to produce, how it was to be produced, and for whom it was to be produced. While there were some successes, especially in the system's early decades, eventually the lack of incentives, the central planners' lack of information, and the distortions that were rife in the system took their toll.

6. The transition to a market economy has not been easy. In most countries, output fell markedly and poverty increased markedly. A few countries fared well.

7. After more than ten years of transition, it now appears that the countries that rapidly brought inflation down to moderate levels, then took a more gradual approach to broader reforms—with greater emphasis on creating an institutional infrastructure, creating jobs and new enterprises, and creating competition—have done better than those that adopted a more wholesale, shock therapy approach.

KEY TERMS

less-developed countries (LDCs)
developed countries
industrialized countries
newly industrialized countries (NICs)
green revolution
sharecropping
land reform
dual economies
surplus of labor
export-led growth
globalization
outsourcing
central planning

REVIEW QUESTIONS

1. List some important ways in which LDCs differ from more-developed countries. How have different developing countries fared over recent decades?

2. What are the most important factors inhibiting growth in the LDCs? Why is capital shortage *alone* not the most important factor? How do some of the factors interact with each other?

3. How does rapid population growth make it more difficult for a country's standard of living to increase?

4. What are some of the factors that contributed to the East Asian miracle?

5. Why might fostering equality promote economic growth?

6. What are some of the roles that government can play in promoting economic development and growth?
7. How were resources allocated under the former Soviet (communist) system?
8. What were some of the problems with the communist system, and why was the switch to a market economy expected to lead to increased incomes?
9. What were two of the different strategies for moving from communism to a market economy?
10. How have different countries fared in the transition? How do you explain the different performances?

PROBLEMS

1. In the United States, the economy grew by 2.6 percent per year (in real terms) during the 1980s. In India, the economy grew by 5.3 percent during the 1980s. However, population growth in the United States was 0.8 percent annually, while population growth in India was 2.1 percent annually. Which country increased its standard of living faster for the average citizen? By how much?
2. Nominal GNP in Kenya was 9 billion shillings in 1967 and 135 billion shillings in 1987. The price level in Kenya (using 1980 as a base year) rose from 40 in 1967 to 200 in 1987, and the population of Kenya increased from 10 million to 22 million in those twenty years. What was the total percentage change in real GNP per capita in Kenya from 1967 to 1987?
3. True or false: "LDCs do not have much capital because their rates of saving are low. If they saved more or received more foreign aid, they could rapidly expand their economic growth." Discuss.
4. How might each of the following hinder entrepreneurs in LDCs?
   (a) Lack of functioning capital markets
   (b) Pervasive government control of the economy
   (c) Lack of companies that offer business services
   (d) A tradition of substantial foreign control of large enterprises
5. What is the economist's case for having the government be responsible for providing infrastructure?
6. If many LDCs simultaneously attempted to pursue export-led growth, what would be the effect in world markets on the quantities and prices of products sold mainly by LDCs, such as minerals, agricultural goods, and textiles? What effect might these quantities and prices have on the success of such export-led growth policies?
7. Explain how the idea of import substitution conflicts in the short run with the idea of comparative advantage. Need the two ideas conflict in the long run? Why or why not?
8. Why might a family in an LDC face a lower opportunity cost of having more children than a family in a developed country?

Part 5

FURTHER TOPICS IN MACROECONOMICS

Learning Goals

In this chapter, you will learn

1. What the short-run Phillips curve is and why it shifts

2. The three factors that affect inflation

3. The short-run inflation–unemployment trade-off and the role of expectations

Chapter 20

INFLATION AND UNEMPLOYMENT

During the 1970s, the most pressing macroeconomic policy issue facing industrialized economies was inflation. Despite repeated attempts to reduce it, inflation remained stubbornly high throughout the decade. Figure 20.1 shows the inflation rates for the United States, Japan, and western Europe. All display roughly similar patterns. Inflation had remained relatively low during the 1960s, but it jumped to much higher levels in the following decade.

To understand how governments might control inflation, we need to understand what causes inflation. How do we explain why some countries have higher rates of inflation than others? What are the costs of reducing inflation? Why do the United States and most other industrialized economies have lower inflation rates today than they did twenty-five years ago? And why do some countries continue to suffer from high rates of inflation?

We have already learned about the costs of inflation in Chapter 5. Many of these costs are associated with *variability* in inflation rates. Countries that experience high average inflation also experience greater inflation variability than do countries with low average inflation. It is this unpredictibility that can impose large costs on the economy. When inflation turns out to be higher than anticipated, lenders lose as the dollars they receive are worth less than the dollars they lent; borrowers gain since the dollars they repay are worth less than the dollars they borrowed. Conversely, if inflation turns out to be lower than anticipated, borrowers lose and lenders gain. The possibility of these unanticipated gains and losses increases uncertainty and the general level of risk in the economy. We also learned in Chapter 5 that inflation imposes further costs on the economy as individuals devote resources to trying to avoid its costs.

If inflation disrupts the economy, why don't governments simply get rid of it? The answer is that normally, inflation can be reduced only at a cost—only if the unemployment rate is allowed to increase temporarily. This chapter looks at that short-run trade-off. Most economists believe that in the long run, there is no trade-off—the full-employment model shows that once real wages have adjusted, the economy will be at full employment, no matter what the rate of inflation might be.

In Chapter 13 we assumed that inflation rises and falls as the economy moves above or below potential GDP. The adjustment of inflation played a critical role in eventually moving the economy to full employment. In this chapter, we will examine the foundations of inflation adjustment in more detail. Three factors are important for explaining how inflation varies over time. First, while wages do not adjust quickly to keep demand equal to supply, they do respond over time whenever demand does not equal supply. Increases in cyclical unemployment lead to lower inflation; decreases in cyclical unemployment lead to higher inflation. Second, wages and prices depend on workers' and firms' expectations about inflation. For example, if workers expect prices to rise faster, they will demand higher wage increases. An increase in *expected* inflation leads to an increase in *actual* inflation. Third, economies occasionally experience inflation shocks—increases in costs such as the dramatic rise in oil prices of the 1970s. We will see that increases in inflation expectations or inflation shocks that boost actual inflation force policymakers to make difficult trade-offs.

Short-Run Inflation Adjustment

The framework for thinking about how demand and supply pressures influence the rate of change of wages is summarized in a famous relationship called the **Phillips**

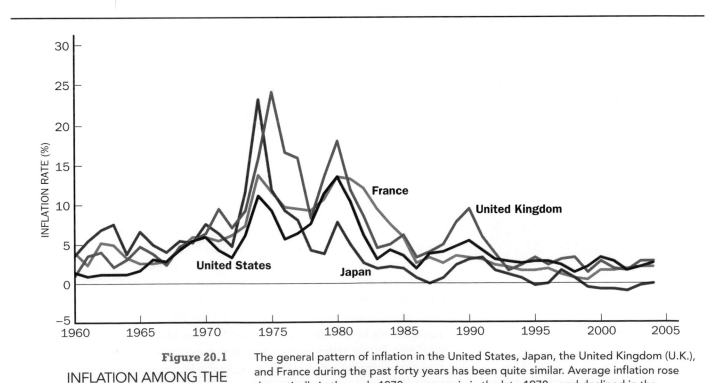

Figure 20.1

INFLATION AMONG THE MAJOR INDUSTRIALIZED ECONOMIES

The general pattern of inflation in the United States, Japan, the United Kingdom (U.K.), and France during the past forty years has been quite similar. Average inflation rose dramatically in the early 1970s, rose again in the late 1970s, and declined in the early 1980s.

SOURCE: International Financial Statistics (2005).

curve. A. W. Phillips was a New Zealander who taught economics in England during the 1950s. He examined data from England on unemployment and the rate of increases in nominal or money wages. He found a negative relationship between the two, and this relationship is known as the *Phillips curve*. At higher unemployment rates, money wages rose more slowly. At lower unemployment rates, money wages rose more quickly. The relationship he found is shown in Figure 20.2.

The logic behind the Phillips curve is straightforward. If unemployment is low, firms have greater difficulty hiring workers. The result is upward pressure on wages, as firms attempt to attract workers by paying more. If unions and firms negotiate over wages, the union will be in a stronger bargaining position, better able to get larger wage increases, if labor markets are "tight." At low unemployment rates, workers are more likely to decide that the time is right to look for another job. Firms that do not keep pace with wage increases elsewhere may discover that their best workers are leaving. If workers believe that finding another job will be easy, they may worry less about being fired. As a consequence, they may not work as hard. To maintain worker productivity, firms will need to raise wages more rapidly. In contrast, if unemployment is high, there will be little upward pressure on real wages. Money wages will increase more slowly or even decrease for some workers.

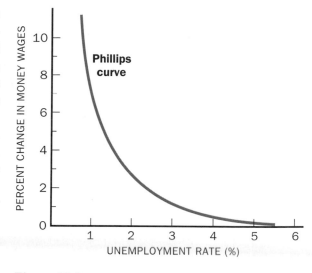

Figure 20.2

THE ORIGINAL PHILLIPS CURVE

The Phillips curve shows that the rate of wage growth rises as the unemployment rate falls. The curve shown here is the one Phillips plotted in 1958 for the British economy.

From Wages to Prices The Phillips curve relates unemployment to the rate at which wages are changing. The bigger the imbalance between labor demand and labor supply, the faster money wages will change.

The link between the rate at which wages are changing and the rate at which prices are changing—the rate of inflation—is direct. Labor costs are, for most businesses, the major component of their costs of production. In competitive markets, prices will move in tandem with marginal costs, and an increase in wages will translate directly into an increase in the marginal costs of production. Some firms, at least in the short run, use a simple rule of thumb in setting prices—they set price as a given markup over costs (e.g., 120 percent of costs). Under that system, changes in the rate at which wages are changing will translate directly into changes in the rate of inflation. Figure 20.3 shows the close historical relationship between the two.

Because they move together, we can replace the rate of nominal wage increase on the vertical axis of the Phillips curve with the rate of inflation. Even though Phillips himself originally studied the behavior of unemployment and wages, it is more common today to see Phillips curves that have the inflation rate on the vertical axis. We will adopt this practice from now on when we use the Phillips curve.

The Phillips Curve and Cyclical Unemployment The relation between inflation and unemployment that Phillips found for the United Kingdom also has been found for other countries. Figure 20.4, which shows inflation and unemployment for the United States during different periods, reveals an important fact. The Phillips curve seems to shift. During periods of relative low inflation, such as 1960 to 1969 and 1984 to 2003, the inflation-unemployment relation is closer to the origin

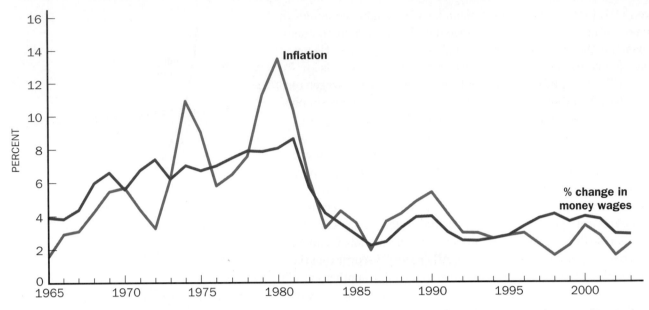

Figure 20.3

THE RATE OF WAGE
INCREASE AND INFLATION
MOVE TOGETHER

The original Phillips curve related the rate of wage increase to the rate of unemployment. Because the rate of increase in money wages moves closely with the overall rate of inflation, we also use the Phillips curve to relate inflation to the rate of cyclical unemployment.

SOURCE: *Economic Report of the President* (2004), Tables B-47, B-64.

than it was during the high inflation period from 1974 to 1983. In other words, the relationship between inflation and unemployment is not stable. Understanding why the Phillips curve shifts is a primary objective of this chapter. To explain these shifts, economists draw on the concept of the natural rate of unemployment and the role of expectations.

The Natural Rate of Unemployment There are reasons why unemployment is always positive. Not every worker is qualified to do every job. When there is unemployment of autoworkers and excess demand for computer programmers, unemployment in Detroit and vacancies in Seattle occur at the same time. In Chapter 4, we referred to this type of unemployment as *structural*. By the same token, there will always be some workers moving between jobs. This latter type of unemployment is referred to as *frictional* unemployment. Structural and frictional unemployment account for positive unemployment even at full employment. The unemployment rate that occurs at full employment, when the economy is producing at potential output, is usually called the **natural rate of unemployment.**

The pressures on wages that lead to increases or decreases in inflation are produced by *cyclical* unemployment—that is, fluctuations in total unemployment around the natural rate. When output is below potential so that cyclical unemployment is positive, total unemployment exceeds the natural rate of unemployment. Labor markets are slack, and wages rise more slowly. When output rises above potential output, then total unemployment falls below the natural rate, labor markets are

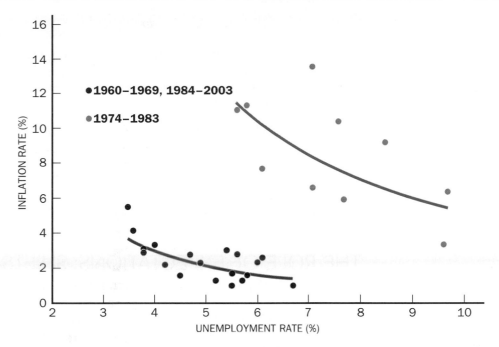

Figure 20.4

THE PHILLIPS CURVE FOR THE
UNITED STATES

The figure depicts the Phillips curve relationship for the United States during different periods. Notice that the Phillips curve has shifted over time.

SOURCE: *Economic Report of the President* (2004).

tight, and wages rise more rapidly. It is the rate of cyclical unemployment, not the total level of unemployment, that best measures the inflationary pressures in the economy.

In Chapter 13, we combined the aggregate demand–inflation (ADI) curve with an inflation adjustment (IA) line. We drew the IA line as a horizontal line at the economy's current rate of inflation. If equilibrium output rose above or fell below full-employment output, we shifted the IA line to reflect the changes in inflation over time. The horizontal IA line provided a starting point for understanding how fluctuations in the economy can cause inflation to rise or fall. Now we can use our knowledge of the Phillips curve to elaborate on the relationship between output and inflation. As output expands and unemployment falls below the natural rate, inflation will rise. The resulting relationship between output and inflation is called the **short-run inflation adjustment (SRIA) curve.** It is shown as the green line in Figure 20.5. In the figure, Y^f is the economy's potential level of output. If actual output rises above potential, say to Y_1, unemployment falls below the natural rate and wages rise more rapidly. Higher wages increase the costs of production for firms, and prices rise more rapidly. Because the inflation rate increases to π_1, the short-run inflation adjustment curve in Figure 20.5 is drawn with a positive slope, rather than as a horizontal line.

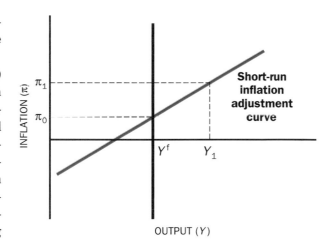

Figure 20.5

THE INFLATION ADJUSTMENT CURVE

Increases in output above potential lead to higher inflation. Y^f is potential output. If the economy expands from Y^f to Y_1, inflation rises from π_0 to π_1. The expansion in output causes unemployment to fall below the natural rate. The result is that wages increase faster, and inflation rises.

INFLATION AND CYCLICAL UNEMPLOYMENT

The *natural rate of unemployment* is the unemployment rate when the economy is at potential GDP and cyclical unemployment is zero.

The *short-run inflation adjustment (SRIA) curve* shows the rate of inflation at each level of output relative to potential GDP, for a given expected rate of inflation.

The SRIA curve has a positive slope. If output increases above potential, inflation increases. If output falls below potential, inflation falls.

THE ROLE OF EXPECTATIONS: SHIFTS IN THE SHORT-RUN INFLATION ADJUSTMENT CURVE

Figure 20.4 illustrated a second characteristic of the relationship between unemployment and inflation—the relationship does not seem to be stable. It has shifted over time. Though the relationship between cyclical unemployment and inflation was stable in the 1960s, that stability disappeared in the 1970s. The U.S. economy experienced high unemployment *and* high inflation. *Stagflation* was the term coined to describe this undesirable situation. High inflation occurred while output was below potential. At other times, output was above potential, yet inflation was low. The SRIA curve is not stable.

There is a simple explanation for this instability: the level of cyclical unemployment is not the only factor that affects wages. For one thing, expectations of inflation also matter. Take the case of a union contract. If workers and firms expect that inflation will be 3 percent per year over the life of the contract, then the nominal wage called for in the contract will rise 3 percent per year even if the negotiated real wage remains constant. Employers are willing to let the nominal wage increase, because they believe they will be able to sell what they produce at higher prices.

If unemployment is low and people are expecting inflation, wages may rise even faster than is necessary simply to offset expected inflation. When unemployment is low and output above potential, workers enjoy better job prospects and are more likely to quit to take better jobs, while firms will find it harder to hire replacements. Wages will rise faster as firms try both to prevent their existing workers from leaving and to attract new workers. If an inflation rate of 3 percent is expected, nominal wages might rise at 5 percent per year (3 percent to compensate for increases in the cost of living and 2 percent because labor markets are tight). If workers and firms expect a much higher rate of inflation, say, 10 percent, then low unemployment may lead money wages to rise at 12 percent per year (10 percent to compensate for the rising cost of living, plus 2 percent because labor markets are tight).

Because expectations of inflation affect actual inflation, the SRIA curve shows the relationship between output (relative to potential) and inflation, *for a given expected rate of inflation.* This is represented diagrammatically in Figure 20.6. A vertical line is drawn at the level of full-employment output Y^f to indicate that Y^f does not depend on the rate of inflation. The position of the SRIA curve depends on the level of expected inflation. Because it includes inflationary expectations, we refer to it as the *expectations-augmented SRIA curve.*

To better understand the role of the natural rate of unemployment, consider how expectations about inflation are affected both by recent experience and by anticipated changes in policy and economic conditions. Take the simple case of **adaptive expectations**[1]—that is, expectations that respond or adapt to recent experience. Assume an economy in which prices have been stable for an extended period of time. Given this historical experience, workers and firms expect zero inflation. The SRIA curve is represented in Figure 20.6 by the curve labeled "Expected inflation = 0." Suppose the government reduces unemployment below the natural rate by expanding output above potential (where actual inflation equals expected inflation). In the short run, the actual inflation rate rises to π_1. With actual inflation now positive, workers and firms will not continue to expect zero inflation. They will come to expect positive inflation. If they now expect inflation to be π_1, the expectations-augmented SRIA curve shifts up, so there will be a higher rate of inflation at each level of output. The new SRIA curve is labeled "Expected inflation = π_1" in Figure 20.6. If the government continues to maintain output above Y^f, inflation will rise to π_2. Now workers and firms will start to expect inflation at the rate π_2, and this higher expected inflation will be incorporated into wage- and price-setting behavior. The expectations-augmented SRIA curve shifts up again as shown in Figure 20.6 by the curve labeled "Expected inflation = π_2." Inflation rises further.

We can now understand why the data on unemployment and inflation for the United States shown in Figure 20.4 seem to shift over time. The 1960–1969 period was one of low average inflation. The data from this period show the negatively sloped relationship between inflation and unemployment that is implied by the SRIA curve. Both inflation and expected inflation were much higher from 1974 to 1983. The SRIA curve in that period shifted up, as can be seen in Figure 20.4. Finally, the period since 1984 has seen much lower inflation and reductions in inflationary expectations. Declines in expected inflation have shifted the SRIA curve again—this time in, toward the origin, as our analysis predicts.

The recognition that the SRIA curve shifts as inflationary expectations change brings us to an important conclusion: *When output remains above potential (the unemployment rate remains below the natural rate of unemployment), the rate of inflation increases; when it remains below potential (the unemployment rate remains above the natural rate), inflation decreases. An economy cannot keep its unemployment rate below the natural rate without facing ever-increasing rates of inflation.* An economy cannot "buy" higher output and lower unemployment by accepting a slightly higher (but stable) inflation rate.

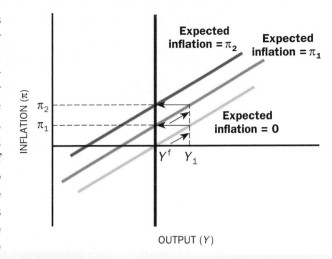

Figure 20.6

SHORT-RUN INFLATION ADJUSTMENT CURVES AND INFLATION EXPECTATIONS

Increases in output above potential lead to higher inflation for a given expected rate of inflation. Suppose expected inflation is initially equal to zero and the economy is at potential output Y^f. The SRIA curve is labeled "Expected inflation = 0." If output increases to Y_1, inflation rises to π_1. If workers and firms now expect an inflation rate of π_1, the SRIA curve shifts up, increasing the inflation rate associated with any given output. If output were to remain at Y_1, inflation would rise to π_2. The SRIA curve therefore shifts up again as expectations adjust to the new, higher rate of inflation. Inflation will be stable only when output is equal to potential.

---

[1]Expectations are called *adaptive* if they respond to recent experience. Adaptive expectations are also called *backward-looking,* since they respond to actual past experience. *Forward-looking expectations* respond to anticipated future developments.

Thinking Like an Economist

DISTRIBUTIONAL EFFECTS OF INFLATION AND UNEMPLOYMENT

Inflation and cyclical unemployment impose macroeconomic costs on the economy. Each does so by affecting the lives of millions of individuals. However, not everyone is affected equally. Even when cyclical unemployment reaches very high levels, as it did during the 1982 recession, only a small fraction of the total labor force bears the direct hardship of losing a job, and the burden does not fall evenly on different groups in the population. For example, unemployment rates differ significantly by race and age in the United States. Even during the long expansion of the 1990s, unemployment rates for blacks remained about double the overall rate and more than double the rate for whites (see figure). Young workers experience much higher rates of unemployment than do older workers. For young black workers, the unemployment rate exceeded 30 percent in 2003. The overall labor force has not experienced that level of unemployment since the Great Depression of the 1930s.

The figure shows three recessionary periods—1982–1984, 1990–1991, and 2001. All unemployment rates rise during recessions and fall during expansions. And as Christina and David Romer of the University of California, Berkeley, have recently documented, increases in unemployment are positively related to increases in the fraction of the population living in poverty.

The other macroeconomic problem—inflation—also influences the distribution of well-being in the economy, although its effects on the poorest households seem to be small. As we learned in Chapter 5, inflation, particularly if it is unexpected, redistributes wealth from creditors to debtors. Those who have borrowed funds are able to repay in dollars whose value has fallen as a result of inflation. Romer and Romer found, however, that inflation has little actual effect on the financial conditions of the poorest households. The reason for this is straightforward: the poor have few financial assets or liabilities.

SOURCE: Christina Romer and David Romer, "Monetary Policy and the Well-Being of the Poor," *Economic Review* (Federal Reserve Bank of Kansas City), 84 (1999): 21–49.

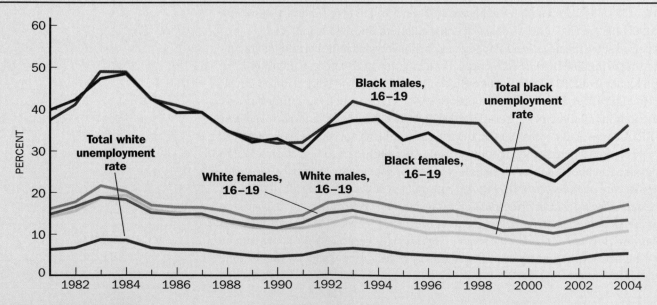

UNEMPLOYMENT RATES

SOURCE: *Economic Report of the President* (2004).

An important implication of this conclusion is a consensus belief about macro-economic policy: governments should not try to use macroeconomic policies to maintain the unemployment rate below the natural rate or output above potential. Expansionary policies will temporarily lower unemployment and boost income, but eventually unemployment returns to the natural rate. Thus, the policy question is whether the *temporary* fall in unemployment is worth the potential cost of higher inflation.

A key issue for policymakers is identifying the natural rate of unemployment and potential GDP in a dynamic economy. At one time, economists thought the natural rate was around 6 percent. Unemployment rates below that level were expected to lead to increases in the inflation rate. When the unemployment rate fell below 6 percent in 1995 and below 5 percent in 1997 without causing inflation to rise, economists needed to reassess their estimates. We will discuss shifts in the natural rate later in this chapter.

Wrap-Up

BASICS OF INFLATION ADJUSTMENT

Short-run inflation adjustment (SRIA) curve: shows the relationship between inflation and output *for given inflation expectations,* the higher that output is, relative to potential, the higher the inflation rate.

Expectations-augmented SRIA curve: the SRIA curve with expectations of inflation explicitly incorporated. The level of inflation associated with any level of output depends on expectations concerning inflation; the higher the inflationary expectations, the higher the level of inflation associated with any level of output. As inflationary expectations increase, the SRIA curve shifts up.

Case in Point

NOBEL VIEWS ON INFLATION AND UNEMPLOYMENT

Our understanding of the shifting relationship between unemployment and inflation owes much to the contributions of Milton Friedman and Robert Lucas, the 1976 and 1995 winners of the Nobel Prize in Economics. Friedman and Lucas are two of the giants of monetary economics. Friedman is most widely known for his emphasis on the role of monetary policy as a force in shaping the course of inflation and business cycles. He is best known to the lay public for his advocacy of free markets. Lucas is probably unfamiliar to most noneconomists, but like Friedman, he has made fundamental contributions to the study of money, inflation, and business cycles.

Milton Friedman, Nobel Laureate, 1976

During the 1960s, most economists believed that a stable Phillips curve allowed lower average unemployment rates to be achieved if one were willing to accept a permanently higher (but stable) rate of inflation. Friedman argued that such a trade-off could not persist. Expanding the economy to lower unemployment would lead to increases in nominal wages as firms attempted to attract additional workers. Firms would be willing to pay higher nominal wages if they expected prices for their output to be higher in the future owing to the economic expansion. Workers would recognize that inflation had increased, and would therefore demand more rapid wage increases. Inflation would not stabilize at a higher level but would continue to increase. Inflation would remain stable only when the economy returned to its natural rate of unemployment.

Most economists have followed Friedman in accepting that there is no long-run trade-off that would permanently allow lower unemployment to be traded for higher inflation. This acceptance can be attributed in part to the contributions of Lucas, who demonstrated the striking implications of assuming individuals formed their expectations rationally. He stressed the forward-looking nature of expectations. Expectations of a future economic expansion could immediately raise expectations of inflation, shifting up the Phillips curve. Inflation would rise without even a temporary decline in unemployment.

This chapter has shown how experiences with inflation lead individuals to revise their expectations concerning inflation, a change that shifts the short-run Phillips curve. But Lucas emphasized that workers in their wage bargains and firms in their price-setting behavior can also be forward-looking—they can anticipate inflation and thereby shift the short-run Phillips curve even before the inflation is actually experienced. For instance, if the government were to announce its intention to change its target for inflation, many individuals might adjust their inflation expectations.

These expectations-driven shifts can be both good news and bad news for the economy. On the one hand, inflation can pick up quite quickly—even when the economy has an unemployment rate above the natural rate, expectations that future inflation will be higher can push up inflation immediately. The good news is that inflation can be brought down quite quickly as well by this mechanism, without a period of painful unemployment.

Friedman argued that the growing evidence for the instability of the vintage Phillips curve for the 1960s was instrumental in forcing the profession to adjust its thinking. As Friedman put it, "The drastic change that has occurred in accepted professional views was produced primarily by the scientific response to experience that contradicted a tentatively accepted hypothesis—precisely the classical process for the revision of a scientific hypothesis."[2]

The insights of Friedman and Lucas continue to guide developments in macroeconomics. Their work on the links between inflation and unemployment has influenced the course of economic theory *and* the most practical of policy discussions. For example, Lucas's theory of rational expectations stresses the role of credibility in the conduct of monetary policy. This emphasis continues to have a major impact on policy discussions.

Robert Lucas, Nobel Laureate, 1995

[2]Milton Friedman, "Nobel Lecture: Inflation and Unemployment," *Journal of Political Economy* 185 (1977): 451–472.

SHIFTS IN THE NATURAL RATE

Though the *concept* of the natural rate of unemployment is well accepted, economists do differ in their judgments of the critical level of unemployment below which inflation increases. Because the natural rate itself may vary over time, our estimates of it are quite imprecise. In the late 1980s, most economists thought it was around 6 percent or slightly higher. As the unemployment rate fell to 5.6 percent in 1995, then to 5.4 percent in 1996, and eventually to 3.9 percent in 2000 without evidence that inflation was increasing, more and more economists believed the natural rate had decreased. Today, few economists believe the evidence is strong enough to yield a precise value; the best that can be done is to identify a range of plausible values. Most current estimates of the natural rate fall in the range of 5 to 5.5 percent.

Some of the changes in the natural rate are predictable. There is always some frictional unemployment, as people move from job to job. Such movements are more common among new entrants into the labor force; in the 1970s, these were numerous as the baby boomers reached working age and as more women began working outside the home. As a result, the natural rate increased. In the 1990s, these trends reversed themselves, partially accounting for the decline in the natural rate of unemployment. Government policies to help workers move quickly from one job to another may lower the natural rate. Similarly, because competitive pressures have increased and unionization has decreased, wages more frequently fall and are slower to rise. This change too has helped lower the natural rate.

Case in Point

THE BABY BOOMERS AND THE NATURAL RATE

The natural rate of unemployment is not a constant. One reason it changes is that the demographics of the labor force change over time. The prime example of the role of demographics is provided by the effect of the baby boomers.

We have focused on the overall unemployment rate, the fraction of the total civilian labor force that is unemployed. However, not all groups in the labor force experience the same unemployment rate. Teenagers, for example, have much higher unemployment rates than older workers. At the end of 2000, while the overall unemployment rate averaged only 4 percent, the rate for females sixteen to nineteen years old was 11 percent; for teenage males, over 13 percent. In contrast, the unemployment rates for older workers were much lower.

These differences in the unemployment experiences of different age groups have important implications for the total unemployment rate when the age distribution of the population is changing. The total unemployment rate is equal to a weighted average of the unemployment rates of different age groups. The weight placed on the unemployment rate of teenagers, say, will equal the number of teenagers in the labor force as a fraction of the total labor force. So if teenage workers represent 6 percent of the total labor force, as they did in 2000, the teenage unemployment rate will receive a weight of .06 (6 percent) in calculating the overall unemployment rate.

Because teenagers experience higher rates of unemployment, a change in the age distribution can alter the overall unemployment rate. This is exactly what happened in the 1960s, when the post–World War II baby boom generation started entering the labor force. Their entry boosted the natural rate; the same labor market conditions resulted in a higher measured overall unemployment rate because there were more young workers than previously. One recent estimate concluded that the baby boomers added 1.8 percent to the unemployment rate between 1959 and 1980. As boomers aged, they entered periods of life typically associated with low unemployment rates. This effect has cut almost 1.5 percent off the overall unemployment rate since 1980.

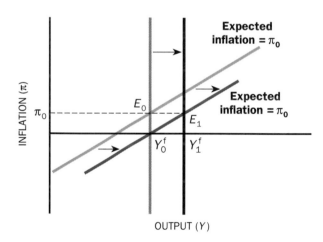

Figure 20.7

THE POSITION OF THE SRIA CURVE WILL SHIFT IF POTENTIAL GDP SHIFTS

An increase in the economy's potential GDP will shift the SRIA curve. In the figure, the economy is initially at point E_0 at full employment (output equals potential) and at an inflation rate of π_0 that is fully incorporated into expectations. If potential output rises from Y_0^f to Y_1^f, the SRIA curve then goes through the point E_1, where expected inflation and actual inflation are equal and output is at the new level of potential GDP.

SHIFTS IN POTENTIAL GDP

The inflation adjustment curve relates inflation to the state of the economy, measured by a comparison of actual output with potential output: the output gap. Positive output gaps—output levels above potential—accompany unemployment rates below the natural rate. Negative output gaps—output levels below potential—accompany unemployment rates above the natural rate. Just as measuring cyclical unemployment is difficult because the natural rate can shift, measuring the output gap is difficult because the economy's potential output level can shift.

Figure 20.7 shows the impact of an increase in potential output on the inflation adjustment curve. Initially, the economy's potential GDP is Y_0^f. Vertical lines are drawn at Y_0^f and Y_1^f to remind us that full-employment output does not depend on the inflation rate. If inflationary expectations are equal to π_0, the SRIA curve is positively sloped and goes through the point E_0. If potential increases to Y_1^f, the SRIA curve shifts to the right, going through the point E_1, since actual inflation and expected inflation are equal when the economy is at potential.

INFLATION SHOCKS

During 1973 and again in 1979, there were major increases in the price of oil. In 1973, supplies of oil to the United States were disrupted by the oil embargo imposed by the Organization of Petroleum Exporting Countries (OPEC) as a result of the 1973 Arab-Israeli War. The sharp increases in inflation caused by these oil price increases are clearly visible in Figure 20.1. As this experience suggests, other factors besides cyclical unemployment and expectations influence inflation.

The basic relationship between output and inflation that we summarized in the inflation adjustment curve started with the Phillips curve relationship between cyclical unemployment and wage increases. We then argued that wages and prices move in tandem, and thus the SRIA curve links cyclical unemployment and inflation. While Figure 20.3 shows that wages and prices generally move together, it also shows that inflation exceeded wage increases at the time of the oil price shocks. The oil price changes altered the relationship between wages and prices.

The reason is straightforward. Wages are a large part of the costs that firms face. But firms have other important costs as well, and the cost of the energy involved in producing is one of them. For a given increase in wages, prices will rise more as these other costs rise. The oil price hikes of the 1970s increased inflation relative to wages, as shown in Figure 20.3. Such events are called **inflation shocks,** and they produce temporary shifts in the SRIA curve. For given inflation expectations and output, a positive inflation shock increases the actual rate of inflation.

Some economists have argued that the late 1990s were a repeat of the 1970s but in reverse. That is, the United States was again hit by an inflation shock—but this time, a negative shock that temporarily shifted the SRIA curve down. Inflation was lower at each level of output. Put another way, we can say that inflation was lower at each level of cyclical unemployment. Two pieces of evidence are consistent with this interpretation. First, if we again look back to Figure 20.3, we see that just as inflation was pushed above the rate of wage increases by the positive inflation shocks of the 1970s, so during the 1990s inflation fell below wage increases. Second, at the end of the 1990s, unemployment plummeted. In April 2000, for example, the overall jobless rate fell to 3.9 percent, the lowest level since 1970. Despite this evidence of tight labor markets, inflation had not increased, as the SRIA curve would imply should happen. This stability, too, might indicate that the economy was experiencing a negative inflation shock.

Fundamentals of Inflation

CYCLICAL UNEMPLOYMENT

Movements in cyclical unemployment cause fluctuations in the rate of wage growth relative to productivity growth. In tight labor markets, wages will rise more rapidly; in periods of high unemployment, wage growth will slow and wages may decline. These fluctuations in firms' wage costs are passed through into prices and lead to fluctuations in the rate of inflation. As a consequence, fluctuations in the output gap will be positively associated with fluctuations in the rate of inflation.

EXPECTATIONS

Wage and price decisions will be influenced by the expectations about inflation that are held by individuals and firms. If higher inflation is expected, wage growth will rise, leading to an increase in actual inflation. This happens because workers and firms are concerned with real wages, and nominal wages must increase faster to maintain real wages when inflation is higher.

INFLATION SHOCKS

Factors such as oil price changes that affect the cost of production will lead to fluctuations in the rate of inflation. When oil prices increase, firms pass the higher cost on to consumers by raising prices.

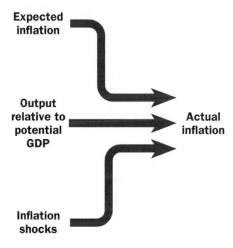

Combining the Aggregate Demand–Inflation and Inflation Adjustment Curves

The SRIA curve summarizes the impact of cyclical unemployment and the output gap—the difference between output and potential GDP—on inflation for given inflation expectations. The aggregate demand–inflation curve developed in Chapter 13 summarizes the short-run impact of inflation on real interest rates, aggregate expenditures, and equilibrium output. Putting the two together enables us to understand the factors that determine both output *and* inflation in the short run.

Equilibrium in the short run occurs where the ADI and SRIA curves intersect. Figure 20. 8 adds the ADI curve to Figure 20.7. The initial SRIA curve is drawn for an expected inflation rate equal to π_0. In the situation depicted, the short-run equilibrium occurs at point E_1 with output equal to Y_1 and inflation equal to π_1. Two aspects of this short-run equilibrium are important to note. First, the economy is producing at an output level above potential (Y^f). Second, the inflation rate π_1 is greater than people had expected.

The economy will not remain at point E_1, however, because inflation is now higher than people had expected. Inflation expectations will rise. As we learned in this chapter, a rise in inflation expectations causes the SRIA curve to shift up. As the SRIA curve shifts up, the economy's equilibrium moves along the ADI curve (shown by the arrow). Inflation continues to rise and output falls. This movement along the ADI curve involves rising interest rates. As inflation expectations rise, so does actual inflation. In response to rising inflation, the Fed raises interest rates and aggregate expenditures fall. Equilibrium output declines toward the full-employment level. Eventually, full-employment output is reached at an inflation rate of π_2. At this point, equilibrium output is equal to Y^f (so the economy is on its ADI curve) and both actual inflation and expected inflation are equal to π_2 .

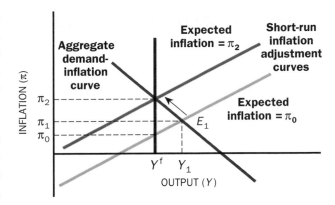

Figure 20.8

COMBINING THE ADI AND SRIA CURVES

The economy's short-run equilibrium is at the point where the ADI and SRIA curves intersect: E_1, in this figure. At E_1 output is above potential and inflation exceeds expected inflation. As people revise upward their expectations of inflation, the SRIA curve shifts up. Eventually, output returns to Y^f at an inflation rate equal to π_2. At that point, output is equal to potential and inflation is equal to expected inflation.

SECURING OUR ECONOMIC FUTURE

THE WHITE
CONFERENCE ON THE

BRIAN WESBURY   MARY FARRELL   MARY

THE S
OF
OUR ECO

Learning Goals

In this chapter, you will learn

1 Why economists disagree about the impact of government deficits

2 Why economists disagree about the usefulness of macroeconomic stabilization policies

3 What the main debates over the goals of monetary policy are

Chapter 21

CONTROVERSIES IN MACROECONOMIC POLICY

P arts Two and Three provide the tools you can use to analyze many important macroeconomic policy debates. You have learned how monetary and fiscal policy affect the economy, and how economic disturbances can lead to fluctuations in output, employment, and inflation. Much of the analysis represented positive economics—we asked what the impact of a policy action would be without asking whether the policy was good or bad. Now we need to apply the tools we have gained to questions of normative economics: What are good policies? How should policies be designed and implemented? What sorts of policymaking institutions seem to produce good policies? And we will use what we have learned to understand some of the most important current controversies in macroeconomics.

Three controversies will constitute the focus of this chapter. The huge increase in the U.S. federal budget deficit over the past few years has worried most economists, but some argue that these deficits are not cause for concern. So the first controversy we will discuss can be summarized in a simple question: Do fiscal deficits matter? A second controversy centers on the role of macroeconomic stabilization policies. Some economists have argued that any discussion of macroeconomic policies to help stabilize the economy is misguided. They either view the costs of business cycles as too small to worry about or believe that attempts to use monetary and fiscal policy to stabilize business cycles will actually make the economy more unstable. The question here is, Should governments attempt to stabilize the economy? Finally, the appropriate goals of monetary policy are a matter of debate. In many countries, governments have passed legislation to make price stability or low inflation the sole goal of monetary policy. In the United States, in contrast, the Federal Reserve has a mandate to keep inflation low *and* promote full employment; moreover, neither of these objectives is quantified. Many economists have called on the Federal Reserve to formally establish a numerical target for the rate of inflation. Alan Greenspan has opposed such a move, while other members of the Federal Open

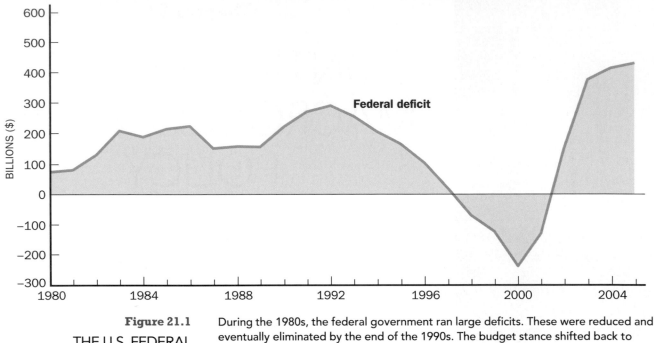

Figure 21.1

THE U.S. FEDERAL
BUDGET DEFICIT

During the 1980s, the federal government ran large deficits. These were reduced and eventually eliminated by the end of the 1990s. The budget stance shifted back to deficits after 2001.

SOURCE: *Economic Report of the President* (2005).

Market Committee (FOMC) have supported it. This issue gives us a third question: Should the Fed target inflation?

Do Deficits Matter?

The budget of the U.S. federal government deteriorated rapidly between 2000 and 2004. In 2000, the federal budget had a $236 billion surplus; by 2004, the deficit was $520 billion, equal to about 4.5 percent of GDP. Figure 21.1 shows the big swings in the federal budget picture over the past twenty-five years. By the end of the 1990s, the United States appeared to have solved its budget problems after the large deficits that began in the 1980s. Through a blend of tax increases and restrictions on spending growth, the deficit had been eliminated and replaced by a surplus. And looking into the future, the Congressional Budget Office produced budget projections showing huge surpluses for the first decade of the twenty-first century.

Beginning in 2001, several events combined to push the budget back into deficit. First, the economic recession that began in 2001 reduced incomes and thereby reduced the government's tax receipts, since most tax revenues are linked to income and spending. This cyclical factor was only temporary, however. By 2002, the economy was growing again; by 2004, the lingering effects of the recession on tax revenues were gone. But other factors continue to have an impact. Fulfilling campaign promises made before the 2000 election, President George W. Bush succeeded in shepherding a large tax cut through Congress in 2001. The September 11, 2001, terrorist attacks on the United States led to substantial increases in military expenditures. And the expiration in 2002 of the "pay-as-you-go" rule introduced in the 1990s removed a significant restraint on government spending.

But if we focus just on the current deficit, we will miss the big picture as far as the federal budget is concerned. Because of the aging of the American population, health care (Medicare and Medicaid) and Social Security payments are expected to grow significantly as a fraction of GDP. If huge deficits are to be avoided, either the generous benefits of current programs will have to be reduced or large tax increases will be necessary.

But should we care about these deficit forecasts? Does it matter whether the government pays for its expenditures by raising enough tax revenue or instead simply borrows? Despite the big increase in the deficit, some commentators have claimed that deficits are unimportant to the overall health of the economy. To understand their arguments, it will be helpful to briefly review the traditional view on the impact of deficits.

DEFICITS AND THE TRADITIONAL VIEW

In Chapter 7, the full-employment model was expanded to include government spending and taxing. We learned that a government deficit reduces national saving. When the government runs a deficit, spending more than it receives in revenue, it must borrow in the capital market, thereby reducing the amount of saving available for private investment. Figure 21.2A depicts the effect of a fiscal deficit on the capital market in a closed economy. The deficit increases the equilibrium real interest rate, and reduces the equilibrium level of private investment spending by crowding out private investment spending. Over time, lower levels of investment reduce incomes as the economy accumulates less capital. Thus, the analysis of Chapter 7 concluded that deficits do matter.

Reducing the deficit or actually running a surplus has the opposite effect (see Figure 21.2B). It enables the real interest rate to fall, stimulating private investment and thus promoting economic growth and better future living standards.

But is this always the case? Do deficits always reduce future income? We saw in Chapter 8 that in one case—the small open economy—deficits do not affect the interest rate or investment. For such an economy, the supply curve of saving is horizontal, at the interest rate set by the global world capital market. A fiscal deficit results in borrowing from abroad—a capital inflow— without changing the interest rate. Private investment is not crowded out, as would be the case in a closed economy. Instead,

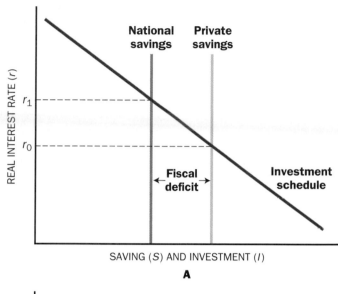

SAVING (S) AND INVESTMENT (I)

A

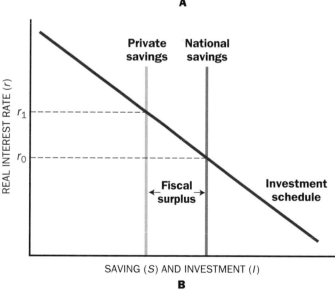

SAVING (S) AND INVESTMENT (I)

B

Figure 21.2

THE GOVERNMENT BUDGET AND THE CAPITAL MARKET IN A CLOSED ECONOMY

A budget deficit reduces national savings, leading to a higher equilibrium real interest rate and lower investment, as depicted in panel A. A surplus has the opposite effect, as illustrated in panel B.

the country must pay some of its national income each year to foreign investors as interest on its borrowing. A surplus in a small open economy would have the opposite effect, leading to a capital outflow.

That an increase in the fiscal deficit leaves private investment in the small open economy unaffected might suggest that it has no long-term consequences for economic growth. After all, since investment has not changed, the economy's future stock of capital is not reduced (as would happen in a closed economy with a deficit). Remember, though, that borrowing from abroad is what keeps the level of investment from being crowded out in the small open economy—it has a capital inflow. This borrowing will need to be repaid in the future to the foreign investors, and that repayment will render some of the income produced by the economy's capital stock unavailable to domestic residents.

ECONOMIC CONSEQUENCES OF DEFICITS AND SURPLUSES

Those holding the traditional view conclude that deficits reduce future income, either because lower private investment spending leads to a smaller stock of capital or because foreign borrowing must be repaid. This analysis is incomplete, however, focusing only on the costs of government borrowing. A complete evaluation of the government's budget must also consider the purposes to which the borrowed funds are put.

As we noted in Chapter 7, economists have traditionally assessed the wisdom of government and individual borrowing by the same criterion: the purpose for which the money is used. Just as it makes sense for individuals to borrow for purchases that will be put to long-term use (a house, a car) or will lead to future gains (e.g., a higher-paying job made possible by an advanced degree), so too countries appropriately borrow to finance projects that will be used for many years (a road, a school, industrial development). Similarly, taking on more debt than can be comfortably paid off or borrowing to cover this year's expenses creates real problems for both individuals and countries.

In the United States, concern is growing that most government borrowing today (as was true in the 1980s) is not being used for investment projects that will raise future incomes. The expenditures now projected to boost future deficits are mainly in the areas of Social Security and health care. Some health care spending can be viewed as an investment, making individuals (and thus the economy) more productive by improving their health. However, most goes to the elderly, who are no longer in the labor force; these payments, like those from Social Security, are used to finance consumption spending.

HOW FUTURE GENERATIONS ARE AFFECTED BY GOVERNMENT DEBT

As a result of past borrowing, the U.S. government currently owes over $5 trillion, or roughly $17,000 for every man, woman, and child in the nation. By borrowing rather than raising taxes to finance its expenditures, it has shifted the burden of reduced consumption to future taxpayers. During World War II, the U.S. government borrowed money rather than raise taxes by the full amount necessary to finance the war effort. Suppose that the bonds it issued were purchased by forty-year-old workers. Then, thirty years later, after those forty-year-olds retire, the government decides to pay off the bonds by raising taxes on those currently in the labor force. In effect, the government is transferring funds from these younger workers to those (now retired) who were working during the war. Thus, part of the cost of the war is borne by the generation who entered the labor force *after* the war. The lifetime consumption of those who purchased the bonds is little affected. The war (to the extent it is financed by debt, or government bonds) affected the form of their savings, which might otherwise have been put into stocks or bonds issued by firms, but not the total amount they have available to spend over the course of their lives.

Because deficits will force the government eventually to raise tax revenues or cut expenditures to repay its borrowing, they serve to shift resources from one generation to another. By reducing taxes today and running a deficit, the government enables current taxpayers to benefit at the expense of future taxpayers who will have to repay the debt.

ALTERNATIVE VIEWS

The discussion so far represents the current dominant views—which, according to some economists, overstate the burden of the debt on future generations. They give two different reasons for their belief.

The "Debt does not matter because we owe it to ourselves" Argument It used to be argued that the United States' fiscal deficit does not matter because we simply owe the money to ourselves. The budget deficit was compared to the effect on a family's wealth of one member borrowing from another. The borrower may be better off and the lender worse off, but the indebtedness really makes little difference to the family as whole. Financing government expenditures by debt, it was argued, could lead to a transfer of resources between generations, but this transfer would still keep all the buying power in the hands of U.S. citizens.

This argument is wrong on three counts. First, even if we owe the money to ourselves, the debt affects investment and thus future wages and productivity, as discussed in Chapter 7. Second, today we do not owe all the money to ourselves. The United States financed part of its deficits by borrowing abroad and becoming indebted to foreign investors. The consequences of spending beyond one's means are the same for a country and a family. Eventually the price of the consumption binge has to be paid—by future generations, in the case of a national spending spree. And third, simply to pay interest on the debt requires high levels of taxes; and taxes introduce distortions into the economy, discouraging work and saving (though economists disagree over the *quantitative* significance of this effect).

Ricardian Equivalence Some economists, most notably Robert Barro of Harvard University, argue that deficits will not raise real interest rates or lower investment. Barro bases his argument on an analysis originally developed by David Ricardo, an eighteenth-century English economist. Ricardo noted that when the government cuts taxes and runs a deficit, it must borrow to finance its expenditures. The government will need to raise taxes in the future to pay back what it has borrowed. If households correctly perceive that a tax cut today means higher taxes tomorrow, they will save any current windfall in order to ensure that they have the resources needed to pay the higher taxes in the future. According to Barro, even if they expect higher taxes to take effect after they are no longer alive, current taxpayers care enough about their children that they will pass on what they gain from any tax cut; this bequest will give their children the wealth that is needed to pay the higher taxes. On this account, private saving rises by the full amount of the tax cut. When private saving increases by the same amount that public saving has fallen, national saving is unchanged. The equilibrium real interest rate is unaffected, as is investment.

This argument does highlight an important fact. Governments must pay for their expenditures; if they cannot cover them with today's revenues, they will have to increase tax revenues in the future. Borrowing is equivalent to taxing, in this view—hence, the name *Ricardian equivalence.* But Ricardo himself ultimately rejected the view that deficits do not matter; and most economists today point out that the evidence does not support Barro's theoretical claim. During the 1980s and early 1990s, when the fiscal deficits were huge, private saving actually declined rather than increased. Today, private saving has not increased, although enormous deficits are projected for the future. Proponents of Ricardian equivalence do not find this evidence conclusive, arguing that a deficit may not lead individuals to save more if they believe that in the future the government will cut expenditures rather than raise taxes.

Wrap-Up

CONSEQUENCES OF GOVERNMENT DEFICITS

1. Issuing bonds reduces national saving, raises the real interest rate, and makes future generations worse off.
2. Foreign indebtedness may increase, reducing future standards of living.

The Goals of Macroeconomic Policy

The goals of macroeconomic policy in the United States are spelled out in the Full Employment and Balanced Growth Act of 1978, more commonly known as the Humphrey-Hawkins Act. It mandated the federal government to "promote full employment and production, increased real income, balanced growth, a balanced Federal budget, adequate productivity growth, proper attention to national priorities, achievement of an improved trade balance[,] . . . and reasonable price stability." The Humphrey-Hawkins Act set specific "interim" goals for unemployment (4 percent) and inflation (3 percent). These were ambitious targets: in 1978, actual unemployment was 6.1 percent and inflation was 9 percent. Over the next five years, unemployment averaged just under 8 percent, twice the interim goal of 4 percent, and inflation averaged 8.5 percent. Neither of the basic objectives of macroeconomic policy—low unemployment and low inflation—was achieved. At other times, the economy has managed to enjoy low unemployment and high growth with low inflation. In 2000, for instance, unemployment averaged 4 percent while inflation was 3.3 percent.

Our basic model, developed in Part Two, predicts that the economy tends to return to full employment; but at full employment, the rate of inflation can be either high or low. Policymakers should aim both to stabilize the economy around full employment (i.e., stabilize output around potential GDP) and to maintain an average inflation rate that is low and stable.

Yet even when average inflation is low, policymakers must continually make trade-offs. Consider the situation faced by the Federal Reserve in 2000. Unemployment, which in 1998 and 1999 had fallen to its lowest levels in almost thirty years, continued to remain well below previous estimates of its natural rate—the unemployment rate associated with full employment. Was it only a matter of time before inflation increased? Or had the natural rate of unemployment fallen, allowing lower rates of unemployment to be sustained without fear of inflation? If the Fed raised interest rates too soon, it might hasten the end of the boom unnecessarily; if it waited too long, inflation might increase. The Fed did raise interest rates in 2000; and by the end of the year, there were signs the economy was slowing. In January 2001, the Fed reversed course and cut interest rates as it moved to forestall a recession. The Fed faced the opposite situation in the spring and summer of 2004. Employment growth was finally beginning to pick up, but so was inflation. Should the Fed keep interest rates low to promote job growth? Or should it raise rates to head off an upsurge in inflation?

Economists differ in how they evaluate the trade-offs that policymakers face. A key to understanding their various positions is recognizing that unemployment and inflation affect different groups. Low-wage workers and other disadvantaged groups are the most likely to benefit from policies that stress low unemployment, and to bear the costs of high unemployment if inflation increases and must then be reduced. Since these workers have little savings, they bear little of the direct costs of inflation. The costs of *unanticipated* increases in inflation typically fall most heavily on those who hold long-term bonds—and who see the value of those bonds decrease as nominal interest rates rise, as happens when inflation increases. Unanticipated increases in inflation may also affect workers if their pension funds are invested in long-term bonds.

Because the costs of unemployment and inflation are not borne equally by all, it is not surprising that different groups take different positions in policy debates. To make economic policy—an exercise in normative economics—one must have both an understanding of how the economy operates (the role of positive economics) and a set of values to guide choices when they arise. Very often, economists reach different policy conclusions even when they share the same model of the economy. This outcome is to be expected, since each economist will evaluate the relative costs and benefits of policies differently. But a perhaps more fundamental question splits many economists—should governments even attempt to intervene to stabilize the macroeconomy? Or do such attempts simply worsen economic performance?

THE NONINTERVENTIONIST PERSPECTIVE

Those who share the view that government should not intervene to stabilize the economy differ in their reasons. Some believe that the economy is efficient, leaving little for the government to add. Others believe that government actions are ineffective, while still others argue that they do have significant effects but often simply make matters worse. We now take a closer look at each of these perspectives.

Real Business Cycle Theory: Intervention Is Unnecessary Intervention is clearly unnecessary if the economy always operates efficiently at full employment. Real business cycle theorists, led by Ed Prescott of the Arizona State University, attribute the economy's fluctuations to external shocks, such as the 1973 and 1979 oil price increases, or to shifts in the economy's underlying productivity, as may have occurred in the late 1990s. More importantly, these theorists believe that markets adjust quickly—prices and wages are sufficiently flexible that full employment will be rapidly restored—and certainly in less time than it would take for government to recognize a problem, act, and have an effect. According to real business cycle theorists, the fluctuations we observe are not signs that output is deviating from potential; instead, they argue that potential GDP fluctuates, with wages and prices adjusting to ensure that all markets clear.

Since the economy is at full employment, government need worry only about keeping inflation low and stable. The central bank just needs to set a low target for inflation and ensure that it is achieved.

New Classical Macroeconomics: Intervention Is Ineffective Some noninterventionists, while not claiming that all fluctuations are efficient, still argue that the government cannot affect output even in the short run. If the government attempts to expand the economy, shifting the aggregate demand–inflation (ADI) curve to the right, all market participants recognize that higher inflation will result. So price- and wage-setting behavior and expectations adjust immediately in anticipation of the higher inflation, and the short-run inflation adjustment (SRIA) curve shifts up, leaving the economy with higher inflation and no expansion in real output.

The new classical view also argues that inflation can be reduced without leading to higher unemployment. By reducing its inflation target, the monetary authority shifts the ADI curve to the right. If market participants are convinced that the inflation target has been reduced, they will immediately adjust their wage and price behavior, and lower inflation is achieved at no cost.

The new classical economists, led by Robert Lucas of the University of Chicago, strongly advance the view that predictable and systematic macroeconomic policies are largely ineffective in influencing real output and employment.

Intervention Is Counterproductive Some noninterventionists accept that government policies can affect the economy, and they may see shortcomings

Thinking Like an Economist
TRADE-OFFS AND CHOICES

When economists analyze the decisions of individual households making consumption purchases, they focus on two aspects. First, what are the choices available to a given household? These are defined by the household's income and the prices of the different goods it could purchase. With limited income, buying more of one thing means buying less of something else—the household faces trade-offs. Second, what are the preferences of the household? Faced with the same possibilities, different individuals will make different choices because they vary in what they like to do or consume.

Economists use this same perspective to analyze actions by economic policymakers. First, they focus on the trade-offs.

In the case of cyclical unemployment and inflation, they ask what the short-run trade-offs are—if unemployment is reduced slightly, how much will inflation rise over, say, the next year? And they need to understand the long-run trade-offs. Will the reduction in unemployment be only temporary? Once the policymakers understand the trade-offs, they can assess the costs and benefits of the different options and decide on the actual policies they want to implement. A policymaker who believes inflation is very costly will make different choices than one who sees its costs as less significant. Even if they agree about the way the economy behaves, differences in preferences will lead to differences in policy recommendations.

in markets, but they have little confidence in the ability of governments to improve macroeconomic performance. Indeed, some believe that intervention is counterproductive, for two reasons.

First, they recognize that there are important *lags* that make policymaking difficult. It takes time for the government to recognize a problem—and the lags in getting data, revisions in preliminary data, and the often conflicting information available can leave policymakers in great uncertainty as they try to assess the state of the economy. And after a problem is recognized, more time is needed before action can be taken. The Federal Open Meeting Committee of the Federal Reserve meets frequently, but fiscal policy actions may require congressional approval, which can easily take many months to secure. Finally, there are time lags between when a policy action is taken and when it has an impact on the economy. Interest rate changes by the Fed, for example, take six months or more to significantly affect output and even longer to influence inflation. Lags by themselves would not be a problem if the government could accurately forecast. But everyone, including government economists, sees the future with a cloudy crystal ball.

Because of these lags, the action may no longer be appropriate by the time its effects are fully realized. Expansionary policies may finally take effect just as the economy is already recovering, thereby encouraging inflation. Or contractionary policies designed to slow inflation might affect the economy just as it is starting to enter a recession, worsening the subsequent rise in unemployment.

Second, critics of strong interventionist policies argue that there are systematic political reasons why interventionists are often misguided. Politicians want the economy to expand before an election. They might boost government spending to overheat the economy, winning gains in employment before the election but incurring costs, in terms of higher inflation, that show up only after the election. In recent years, many countries have attempted to reduce the influence of elected politicians on monetary policy for just this reason.

Rules Versus Discretion Critics of intervention claim that historically, whether because of politically motivated decisions or simply because of the lags described earlier, government has actually exacerbated the economy's fluctuations. When the government attempts to dampen a boom, its policies aimed at reducing demand take effect just as the economy is weakening, reinforcing the downward movement. Conversely, when the government attempts to stimulate the economy, the increase in demand kicks in as the economy is strengthening on its own, thereby igniting inflation. Critics of government action such as Milton Friedman thus conclude that better outcomes would result if policies were based on simple **rules** rather than on the **discretion** of the government policymakers. Friedman proposed that the government should expand the money supply at a constant rate rather than actively tailor monetary policy to economic events in the hopes of stabilizing the economy. According to Friedman and others, by sticking to rules, the government would eliminate a major source of uncertainty and instability in the economy—uncertainty about future government policies.

A second argument for rules stresses the importance of commitment. A government might promise to keep inflation low. But as an election nears, politicians might be tempted to try to expand the economy a bit to improve their reelection chances, even though this action will lead to lower unemployment only temporarily while leaving the economy with higher inflation. Knowing that the government will face this temptation, individuals will not believe the initial promise to be steadfast; they will anticipate higher inflation in the future. As we learned in Chapter 20, a rise in inflation expectations increases current inflation. Lack of credible commitment to a low-inflation policy may result in higher-than-desired inflation without even a temporary gain of lower unemployment.

The uncertainty about whether a government will actually carry out a promised course of action is called the problem of **dynamic inconsistency.** This problem arises in many contexts. A city may promise to keep taxes low in order to attract a new shopping mall. Once the mall is built, however, the city may find it an irresistible source of tax revenues, despite earlier promises. Anticipating this change of course, the developers may decide not to build the mall in the first place.

For another example of dynamic inconsistency, consider the case of a final exam. Because its purpose is to provide students with an incentive to study the course material, teachers almost always think it good policy to announce a scheduled final exam. By the morning of the exam, it is too late to influence whether students have studied or not—the only thing a teacher has to look forward to is grading all those exams. So it makes sense to cancel the test. But if students anticipate this reprieve, they will not study, and announcing that there will be an exam will no longer have any effect. Few teachers cancel final exams, because they know that if they do it once, their future students will not prepare for an exam they expect to be canceled. The teacher has a *reputation* to protect. Similarly, the desire to maintain a reputation for doing what they promise can help governments fulfill their promises.

THE INTERVENTIONIST PERSPECTIVE

The case for intervention is based on two key beliefs. First, economic fluctuations are not simply the efficient response of the market to shifts in productivity, as the real business cycle theorists argue. Instead, wages do not adjust quickly enough to maintain a balance between labor supply and labor demand, and therefore declines in aggregate expenditures lead to cyclical unemployment. Second, the period of excessive unemployment can persist for a long time. In contrast, the underlying assumption of the noninterventionists is that markets adjust quickly, making cyclical unemployment a short-term affair at worst. While the process of wage and price adjustment alone may eventually bring the economy back to full employment, interventionists believe that this adjustment can be speeded up by appropriate policy interventions. They believe that macroeconomic policies can help stabilize the overall economy.

Today, the leading school of thought among economists who believe that government can and should design policies to stabilize the economy is called *New Keynesianism*. These economists share John Maynard Keynes's view that unemployment may be persistent and that though market forces may restore the economy to full employment, these forces often work so slowly that government action is required. The new Keynesian theorists differ from older Keynesian analysts in their emphasis on microeconomics—for instance, like many real business cycle and new classical economists, they believe that theories of aggregate behavior should be based on theories of the individual households and firms that make up the economy—and in their emphasis on the important role played by expectations about the future. But they also have identified a variety of reasons, such as costs of adjustment and imperfections of information, why markets do not adjust quickly to disturbances. Because markets may be slow to adjust, macroeconomic policies may be needed to help stabilize the economy in a timely fashion.

Wrap-Up

SCHOOLS OF THOUGHT ON MACROECONOMIC POLICY

Noninterventionists

Real business cycle theorists believe fluctuations in economic activity are due to external shocks and that markets respond quickly and efficiently. Government intervention has no useful role to play.

New classical economists think that the scope for government intervention is limited because wages and prices adjust quickly and because the private sector will adjust in anticipation of policies in ways that offset the impacts of the policies.

Others believe that even though markets adjust slowly, discretionary macroeconomic policies make matters worse rather than better because of the long and uncertain lags in determining the need for policy actions, in implementing policy changes, and in affecting the economy.

Interventionists

New Keynesian economists generally accept that policies can have no long-run effect on GDP or the natural rate of unemployment because wages, prices, and expectations eventually adjust, but they think markets respond slowly, so periods of cyclical unemployment can persist. Discretionary macroeconomic policy can be effective, and governments should design built-in stabilizers that can help make the economy less volatile.

Should the Federal Reserve Target Inflation?

Compared to our global financial system today, the financial structure of the country was vastly different in 1913, when the Federal Reserve was established. Its role has therefore evolved over time. The original intention of Congress, as laid out in the 1913 Federal Reserve Act, was that the Fed should prevent financial panics and bank runs. Only in the post–World War II era, after the experience of the Great Depression, have governments recognized that they bear a responsibility for preventing economic fluctuations. Accordingly, today the Fed's goal in conducting monetary policy is to promote low inflation, general economic stability, and sustainable economic growth.

An important lesson from the full-employment model examined in Part Two is that monetary policy is the chief determinant of inflation. Central banks, through their policies that affect reserve supply and the money supply, can control the *average* rate of inflation. This does not mean that inflation can be closely controlled month to month, or even year to year, but over longer time periods a central bank can exercise considerable control over the average level of inflation that the economy experiences. For this reason, in recent years most central banks have accepted that one of their primary responsibilities is to maintain low average inflation.

Monetary policy can also have important effects on two other macroeconomic goals—low (and stable) unemployment and economic growth. However, according to the full-employment model, neither the economy's potential GDP nor the unemployment rate at full employment depends on the money supply. They rest instead on household decisions about how much labor to supply in the marketplace, firms' decisions about how many workers to hire, and the economy's capital stock and technology—factors that do not vary with the absolute level of prices or the number of pieces of paper (green or any other color) that make up the money supply. Put in terms of our short-run model of Part Two, the level of potential GDP does not depend on the position of the central bank's policy rule.

This implication of the full-employment model is important. If full employment corresponds to an unemployment rate of, say, 5 percent, then the Fed cannot push the unemployment rate down to 4 percent and keep it there. It can do so temporarily, but as wages and prices adjust to restore labor market equilibrium, unemployment will return to 5 percent. The mechanisms that ensure this return to full employment are discussed in detail in Chapter 15. If monetary policy cannot succeed in keeping the unemployment rate below its full-employment level, then its appropriate goals are to contribute to economic stability by ensuring that full employment is maintained and by keeping inflation low. In this way, monetary policy ensures that the economy can experience sustainable economic growth.

To achieve the goals of full employment and low inflation, the Fed can pursue two types of policies. First, it can engage in **countercyclical policies**—policies designed to keep the economy at full employment by smoothing out fluctuations in the economy. If a recession begins, the Fed can try to stimulate the economy to move unemployment quickly back to its full-employment level. As we learned in Chapter 13, however, the economy can be stabilized around full employment with low inflation or with high inflation, since the full-employment output level does not depend on the average rate of inflation. Second, in addition to its countercyclical policies, the Fed must ensure that its actions are consistent with maintaining a low average rate of inflation. Central banks might try to stabilize the economy at full employment without keeping average inflation low. Alternatively, they might keep inflation low on average without helping to stabilize the economy at full employment. Most central banks, including the Fed, try to undertake policies that achieve both goals.

INFLATION TARGETING AND POLICY TRADE-OFFS

If the goal of monetary policy is to help stabilize the economy at full employment while still ensuring that inflation remains low, how should this policy actually be implemented? In recent years, central banks in many countries (including Canada, New Zealand, Mexico, England, Israel, and Sweden) have adopted **inflation targeting** as a framework for carrying out monetary policy. As might be expected of any approach used by such a diverse group of countries, its exact application has varied greatly. Inflation targeting generally involves the central bank publicly defining its policy goals solely in terms of keeping the inflation rate within a narrow range around a low average level. For example, New Zealand, which was the first to use inflation targeting to guide monetary policy, set a target for inflation of 0 to 2 percent. Under a law passed in 1989, the governor of the Reserve Bank of New Zealand (New Zealand's "Alan Greenspan") could be fired if inflation went above 2 percent.[1]

Many economists have called on the Federal Reserve to adopt a formal policy of inflation targeting. Among the most prominent advocates has been Ben Bernanke, chairman of President George W. Bush's Council of Economic Advisors and formerly a member of the Federal Reserve Board of Governors and professor of economics at Princeton University. Among the most prominent opponents of inflation targeting has been Alan Greenspan, chair of the Board of Governors. Supports of inflation targeting argue that the Fed, under Alan Greenspan, has behaved like an inflation targeter, so it might as well be honest and adopt a formal inflation target. Others worry that establishing a formal target for inflation on which the Fed's performance

---

[1]The target range has since been changed to 1 to 3 percent.

could be judged would reduce its flexibility to meet unforeseen future economic developments.

The Pros Supporters of inflation targeting cite three chief advantages.

Inflation targeting focuses on what the Fed can achieve Currently, the Fed has multiple goals. A 1977 congressional amendment to the Federal Reserve Act stipulated that they include promoting "maximum" sustainable output and employment and "stable" prices. The goal of stable prices is normally translated into a goal of low and stable inflation. The Fed's multiple aims concern both areas that it can control (such as average inflation) and matters that it can affect in the short run but not in the long run (such as output and employment). That it has multiple goals adds to the difficulty of holding the Fed accountable for its policy decisions. By establishing a formal target for inflation, the Fed would focus on an objective it can control and thereby increase its accountability. Opponents argue that by focusing only on inflation, the Fed would become less accountable for the effects of its policies on output and employment.

It enhances credibility Price- and wage-setting decisions depend on how much inflation individuals expect. If people begin to anticipate higher inflation, then actual inflation will start to increase, forcing the central bank to raise interest rates to lower aggregate demand and hold inflation in check. Inflation will remain low and stable only if individuals believe that the central bank is committed to keeping inflation low. Thus, the credibility of a central bank's policy is crucial, and it may be bolstered if a formal target for inflation is adopted. Opponents argue that credibility is earned by implementing policies that maintain low inflation—central banks cannot gain it by simply announcing an inflation target.

It institutionalizes good policy Many economists worry that U.S. monetary policy is too dependent on the abilities of whoever happens to be the chair of the Board of Governors. Policy under Alan Greenspan has been very successful, but other chairmen in the past have been less talented. Proponents of inflation targeting argue that its adoption would institutionalize good policy and help make policy less reliant on any one individual. By promoting continuity in policy, it would also serve to reduce the uncertainty that often accompanies a new chair's arrival. Formally targeting inflation would provide a framework for decisions that could guide future policymakers, thereby reducing the risk of policy mistakes that lead to inflation. Opponents also want to ensure the continuation of good policies, but they worry that inflation targeting will not necessarily achieve that aim.

The Cons Those who argue against inflation targeting cite three chief disadvantages.

Inflation targeting promotes one goal over other equally important goals of monetary policy The Federal Reserve is often described as now having a dual mandate: it should be concerned both with keeping inflation low *and* with helping to stabilize the economy at full employment. Achieving these two goals is viewed as consistent with promoting economic growth. Adopting a formal inflation target would elevate one goal at the expense of the other. While proponents argue that inflation targeting is consistent with actively stabilizing output around full employment, they argue that if the Fed is held accountable for achieving its inflation target, it will inevitably pay less attention to other goals.

Inflation targeting reduces flexibility Adopting a formal inflation target would reduce the Fed's flexibility in responding to new economic challenges. Supply shocks may require that the Fed allow inflation to increase temporarily in order to limit the economic contraction that would be needed to prevent its rise. A formal inflation target might limit the ability of the Fed to make such trade-offs, since its performance would be judged only on whether it maintained inflation at its target. Proponents of inflation targeting argue that in practice, most central banks with formal targets establish ranges for inflation—for example, the Riksbank, Sweden's central bank, has a target inflation rate of 2 percent, plus or minus 1 percentage point—which enable the central bank to let inflation rise temporarily if necessary to limit fluctuations in real output.

If it ain't broke, don't fix it Most commentators agree that the United States has enjoyed the benefits of good monetary policy over the past twenty years. Given this record of good performance, why change? Proponents of inflation targeting argue that its adoption would help ensure that these good policies continue into the future.

Case in Point

FED POLICY STATEMENTS—BALANCING POLICY GOALS

In 1999, the U.S. economy continued to expand and unemployment remained at historically low levels. The Fed was concerned that this strong growth would lead to higher inflation. The chief uncertainty was whether the low unemployment reflected a fall in the natural rate of unemployment. If it had fallen, then unemployment could remain low without a risk of inflation increasing; if not, then a continuation of actual unemployment below the natural rate would lead to a buildup in inflationary pressures over time. In the latter case, the Fed would want to raise interest rates to gradually slow the economy down.

During the summer, the Fed began to lean toward increasing interest rates. At their meeting on May 18, 1999, the FOMC members decided not to change interest rates, but they provided a clear signal that they were likely to raise rates soon. After the meeting, the Fed released the following statement:

> While the FOMC did not take action today to alter the stance of monetary policy, the Committee was concerned about the potential for a buildup of inflationary imbalances that could undermine the favorable performance of the economy and therefore adopted a directive that is tilted toward the possibility of a firming in the stance of monetary policy. Trend increases in costs and core prices have generally remained quite subdued. But domestic financial markets have recovered and foreign economic prospects have improved since the easing of monetary policy last fall. Against the

background of already-tight domestic labor markets and ongoing strength in demand in excess of productivity gains, the Committee recognizes the need to be alert to developments over coming months that might indicate that financial conditions may no longer be consistent with containing inflation.

By the time of their next meeting (on June 30), the FOMC members decided it was time to boost interest rates. After their meeting, they issued the following statement:

> The Federal Open Market Committee today voted to raise its target for the federal funds rate 25 basis points to 5 percent.[2] Last fall the Committee reduced interest rates to counter a significant seizing-up of financial markets in the United States. Since then much of the financial strain has eased, foreign economies have firmed, and economic activity in the United States has moved forward at a brisk pace. Accordingly, the full degree of adjustment is judged no longer necessary.
>
> Labor markets have continued to tighten over recent quarters, but strengthening productivity growth has contained inflationary pressures.
>
> Owing to the uncertain resolution of the balance of conflicting forces in the economy going forward, the FOMC has chosen to adopt a directive that included no predilection about near-term policy actions. The Committee, nonetheless, recognizes that in the current dynamic environment it must be especially alert to the emergence, or potential emergence, of inflationary forces that could undermine economic growth.

The Fed continued to increase the funds rate target through early 2000. By December 2000, there were signs the economy was slowing quickly, and a change in policy was needed to prevent it from heading into a recession. Acting between its normally scheduled meetings, the FOMC cut the funds rate target by half a percentage point on January 3, 2001. After the action, the FOMC released the following statement:

> The Federal Open Market Committee decided today to lower its target for the federal funds rate by 50 basis points to 6 percent. . . .

---

[2]A basis point is a hundreth of a percent, so a 25 basis point increase is a 0.25 percent increase—in this case, from 4.75 percent to 5 percent.

These actions were taken in light of further weakening of the sales and production, and in the context of lower consumer confidence, tight conditions in some segments of financial markets, and high energy prices sapping household and business purchasing power. Moreover, inflation pressures remain contained. . . .

CONSEQUENCES OF INFLATION TARGETING

Even a central bank that has adopted a formal inflation target still must make important policy choices. We can use the ADI framework to understand these policy trade-offs. Figure 21.3A shows two monetary policy rules. For both, the central bank's target for the inflation rate is π^T and the full-employment equilibrium real interest rate is r^*. When the economy is at full employment and inflation is on target, the nominal interest rate set by the central bank will be $i^* = r^* + \pi^T$. The policy rule labeled A is steeper than the one labeled B. If policy is set using rule A, a rise in inflation leads the central bank to boost interest rates by a larger amount than it would

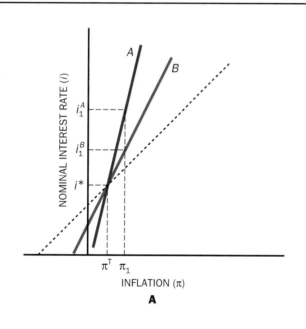

A

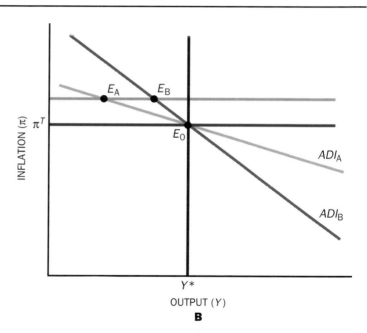

B

Figure 21.3

THE POLICY RULE AND
FLUCTUATIONS

The way the central bank responds to inflation affects the slope of the ADI curve, and this in turn has important effects on how the economy responds to disturbances. Panel A shows two policy rules. Under rule A, changes in inflation lead to larger changes in the real interest rate than is the case under rule B. If inflation rises from π^T to π_1, the nominal interest rate is increased to i_1^A under rule A and only to i_1^B under rule B. Since as a result the real interest rate changes more under rule A, a change in inflation has a bigger impact on aggregate demand than with rule B. As a consequence, the ADI curve with rule A is flatter than the one under rule B (see panel B). An inflation shock, as in panel B, leads to a bigger fall in output under rule A. Output will vary more and inflation less with rule A than with rule B.

when using the rule given by B. Panel B shows the ADI curves under the two different policy rules, ADI_A and ADI_B. The full-employment equilibrium is at point E_0.

Suppose the economy is hit by a temporary inflation shock that increases inflation, as shown in panel B. An oil price increase or a rise in inflationary expectations would have this effect. If the central bank's behavior is described by the policy rule A, the economy moves to a new short-run equilibrium at point E_A. If the central bank's behavior is described by the policy rule B, the economy moves to a new short-run equilibrium at point E_B. Under policy rule A, output declines more than under policy rule B. The sharper decline in output will put greater downward pressure on inflation, leadng inflation to return to the target more quickly. In the face of inflation shocks, the economy will experience more stable inflation and less stable output and employment under policy rule A than under policy rule B. If the central bank responds less aggressively to inflation (as under rule B), it lets inflation fluctuate more but succeeds in keeping output and employment more stable. This is the trade-off between output stability and inflation stability that confronts the central bank.

In practice, because of the lags between a change in interest rates and their effects on the economy, central banks must be forward-looking, basing interest rate adjustments on expectations about future inflation. By responding aggressively to changes in expected inflation (a steep policy rule), monetary policy will limit inflation fluctuations, but the cost will be greater instability in real output and employment when the inflation adjustment curve shifts. By responding less aggressively, monetary policy will cause inflation to fluctuate more when the inflation adjustment curve shifts, but output and employment will be more stable.

Price Level Targeting The 1977 amendment to the Federal Reserve Act established "stable prices," not stable inflation, as one of the Fed's goals. Under a policy of keeping inflation at a low rate, say, 2 percent per year, the average level of prices continues to rise from year to year. If the price level rises more rapidly in one year, a policy of inflation targeting aims to reduce the inflation rate back to its target level. In contrast, a policy of **price level targeting** would try to cause prices to actually fall to bring the average level of prices back to its targeted level.

The difference between inflation targeting and price level targeting is illustrated in Figure 21.4. The figure assumes the target inflation rate is zero but that in period 2 a temporary shock pushes inflation up to 2 percent for one period, as depicted by the blue line in panel A. Under inflation targeting, the inflation rate is brought back to zero. For the sake of simplicity, it is assumed that this occurs in period 3. Panel B shows what happens to the price level: it jumps to a higher level in period 2 and then remains permanently higher. Policy brings inflation back to zero, but no attempt is made to return prices to their initial level.

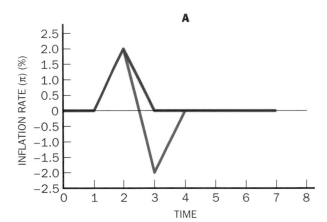

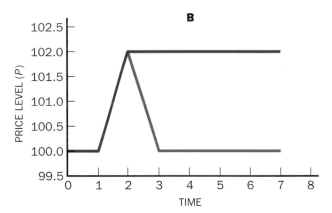

Figure 21.4

INFLATION TARGETING VERSUS PRICE LEVEL TARGETING

The blue line in panel A shows the rate of inflation as initially equal to zero. In period 2, there is a positive inflation disturbance, and inflation jumps to 2 percent. Under a policy of inflation targeting, the central bank tries to bring inflation back down to zero (shown in the figure as occurring in period 3). The behavior of the price level under this policy is shown in panel B. The temporary increase in inflation leaves the price level permanently higher than before.

Under a policy of price level targeting, the central bank would try to bring the price level back to its initial value, as shown by the green line in panel B. For the price level to fall, inflation must be negative, as shown in panel A by the green line.

CENTRAL BANK MANDATES

The formal policy goals of the Fed have evolved over time. In fact, the 1913 Federal Reserve Act that created the Federal Reserve System did not establish any specific macroeconomic goals. Instead, the chief hope was that the Fed would ensure an end to the financial crises that the United States had suffered periodically. The Great Depression of the 1930s and the high inflation rates experienced during the 1970s affected what we now consider to be the goals of monetary policy. A 1977 amendment to the Federal Reserve Act provides that the Fed "shall maintain long run growth of the monetary and credit aggregates commensurate with the economy's long run potential to increase production, so as to promote effectively the goals of maximum employment, stable prices, and moderate long-term interest rates." (See "The Goals of U.S. Monetary Policy," by John Judd and Glenn Rudebusch, *FRBSF Economic Letter*, January 29, 1999, at www.frbsf.org/econrsrch/wklyltr/wklyltr99/el99-04.html.) These goals involve measures of economic performance that are based both on the behavior of real economic activity (full employment, increased real income, growth, trade balance) and on the behavior of the general level of prices (stable prices).

Until recently, most other countries were similar to the United States in listing goals such as high employment, high growth, and low inflation or stable prices as the objectives to be pursued by monetary policy. But while there has been little debate in the United States over the legislated goals assigned to the Fed, the same has not been true elsewhere. The high inflation rates of the 1970s led many countries to rethink the goals of monetary policy. They have changed their laws to assign their central bank a more focused objective. Usually,

this involves establishing low inflation or price stability as the primary, or in some cases the sole, objective of monetary policy. New Zealand was the first country to move in this direction. After the country suffered years of poor inflation performance, the legislation governing New Zealand's central bank (the Reserve Bank of New Zealand) was revised in 1989. The new legislation states, "The primary function of the Bank is to formulate and implement monetary policy directed to the economic objective of achieving and maintaining stability in the general level of prices." Other goals, such as high employment or growth, are not mentioned.

Monetary policy for the member countries of the European Economic and Monetary Union is conducted by the European Central Bank, which came into existence January 1, 1999. As in New Zealand, the governing legislation for the bank specifies that price stability is the primary objective of monetary policy. Again, unlike in the United States, unemployment considerations are not explicitly named among the policy objectives of the European Central Bank.

The full-employment model implies that monetary policy plays an important role in determining the average rate of inflation but can do little about the economy's average rate of unemployment. From this perspective, it is perhaps not surprising that many countries have established low inflation or stable prices as the central bank's primary policy objective. In the short run, however, monetary policy actions can have important effects on real economic activity and employment. In Chapter 15 we saw how the actions of the central bank help achieve the twin goals of maintaining low (and stable) inflation and maintaining full employment.

The green lines in the figure illustrate what happens under price level targeting. The inflation shock pushes the price level higher, but now policy acts to return the price level to its initial level. This requires *deflation*—prices must actually fall.

Few central banks have adopted price level targeting. The deflation needed to get the price level back on target after a positive inflation shock would require a costly recession and a period of high unemployment.[3]

---

[3]While no central bank has adopted price level targeting as a formal policy, the appendix to this chapter shows how our basic model can be modified to deal with the case of a price level target.

Deflation and a Zero Nominal Interest Rate During the 1970s and early 1980s, inflation seemed an intractable problem. Most countries succeeded in eventually reducing inflation, but only at the cost of significant increases in unemployment. Today, the situation is quite different. The average inflation rate in the United States was just over 3 percent in 2004.

In many countries, concern over inflation has been replaced by worries that prices will fall—deflation. In Japan, prices declined each year from 1999 to 2003. Japan also has been suffering a decade-long recession, its worst of the postwar era. The last significant deflation in the United States occurred in the 1930s during the Great Depression.

Monetary policy faces a new problem in stimulating the economy when prices are falling during a recession. To stimulate the economy, the central bank should lower interest rates. Suppose the real interest rate needed to restore full employment is 1 percent, and suppose falling prices lead people to expect deflation to continue at 2 percent. What nominal interest rate will the central bank need to target to achieve a real interest rate of 1 percent? The real rate is the nominal interest rate minus expected inflation, so

$$\text{1 percent} = \text{required nominal interest rate} - (-2 \text{ percent}),$$

since the expected rate of inflation is –2 percent—that is, an expected deflation. If we rearrange this equation, the necessary nominal interest rate would be

$$\text{required nominal rate} = \text{1 percent} - \text{2 percent} = -1 \text{ percent!}$$

So a *negative* nominal interest rate would be necessary. But here is where the problem arises. Nominal interest rates cannot be less than zero. If the nominal interest rate were negative, you could borrow $100 today, pay back the $100 in a year, and receive an interest payment from the lender! If the nominal rate were –1 percent, after one year you would receive $1 from the lender. Given these conditions, everyone would try to borrow as much as they could. After all, if you could borrow $1 billion and just put it under your bed for a year, you would receive 1 percent, or $10 million, from the lender. Since everyone would try to borrow, and no one would want to lend, supply and demand would not balance in the capital market. A negative nominal interest rate cannot be an equilibrium.

The central bank can push the nominal interest rate down to zero but no lower. Thus, if the public expects a 2 percent deflation, the real interest rate cannot go below 2 percent—which might not be low enough to get the economy out of its recession. This is the situation the Bank of Japan faced at the end of the 1990s. Nominal interest rates were down to zero. Because the Bank of Japan continued to indicate that its real concern was ensuring that inflation did not reappear, people continued to expect falling prices, and the real interest rate remained too high.

Under these circumstances, what can a monetary authority do? One option is to announce a higher target for inflation. Suppose it announces that it will aim for 0 to 2 percent inflation. If as a result people start to expect some inflation, say, 1 percent, the real rate of interest falls from 2 percent to –1 percent (zero nominal rate–1 percent expected inflation). The promise to deliver some inflation helps stimulate the economy.

Deflations often have been associated with tough times, times of economic stagnation and high unemployment. When prices fall, the dollars a borrower must repay are worth more than the dollars that were borrowed. Much as unexpected inflation redistributes wealth from lenders to borrowers, so conversely, unexpected deflation benefits lenders at the expense of borrowers. During the 1870s and the 1930s, falling wages and prices for farm products hit borrowers hard, particularly farm families. Periods of deflation also have been associated with financial and banking crises. As the prices they receive for their products fall, many firms are unable to repay their loans. If they are forced into bankruptcy, the banks that have loaned money will not be repaid; they may also become bankrupt, leading to further disruptions in credit and economic activity.

Credibility Notions of credibility and reputation play a large role in discussions of monetary policy. It is easy to see why when we think about the problem of disinflation. As we have learned, policies to reduce inflation cause output to decline and unemployment to rise. Eventually, the economy returns to full employment with lower inflation, but the cost, in terms of cyclical unemployment, of reducing inflation can be quite significant. Many economists have argued that the cost of disinflation will be much smaller if the central bank announces in advance its plans to reduce inflation and if the central bank has credibility. If people expect lower inflation, the IA curve shifts down quickly, reducing the extent to which unemployment must exceed its natural rate to get inflation down.

Central banks with a reputation for delivering on their promises will have an easier time reducing inflation should it ever get too high. Many advocates of inflation targeting argue that setting explicit inflation goals, and meeting them, will build credibility for a central bank. It then will be better able to help stabilize the economy at full employment. Should unemployment fall below the natural rate, people will know that the monetary authority will keep inflation from getting out of control. Inflation expectations will remain stable, and actual inflation will not increase much. In contrast, if people are not sure about the monetary authority's commitment to low inflation, an economic expansion will raise concerns about higher future inflation. Inflation expectations will rise and actual inflation will start to increase more quickly.

DEMAND VERSUS SUPPLY DISTURBANCES AND POLICY TRADE-OFFS

Our discussion of inflation targeting and the interaction between fiscal and monetary policy illustrates an important insight. When the economy experiences disturbances that shift the inflation adjustment curve—such as oil price increases, temporary shifts in productivity, or shifts in inflation expectations—policymakers face a critical trade-off. They can try to keep output and employment stable, but doing so causes inflation to fluctuate more. Alternatively, policymakers can try to keep inflation stable,

e-Insight
e-TIME AND MACROECONOMIC POLICY

As the U.S. economy boomed during the late 1990s, economists speculated on how the business cycle would be affected. There has been less discussion of the impact the new information-based economy will have on macroeconomic policy. Policymakers will be affected if the economy now responds more rapidly to changing conditions.

Fluctuations in inventory investment, which have been a major factor in several previous business cycles, may in the future be limited by the new information technologies that enable firms to manage inventories better. In earlier business cycles, a slowdown in sales caused inventories to build up, as decisions about production could not be based on real-time sales information. The rising level of unsold inventories then triggered large cuts in production. Today, with access to almost instantaneous information on sales, production, and inventories, managers can fine-tune their production levels, avoiding the types of fluctuations seen in the past. By providing managers with information more rapidly, new technologies speed their responses to changing economic conditions.

Though businesses may benefit from being able to respond more quickly to changing economic conditions, policymakers may have less time to react and may therefore find themselves unable to anticipate economic developments in time to adjust policy. Because there is a lag between changes in policy and their effect on the economy, policymakers need to be forward-looking. In the case of monetary policy, the Federal Reserve would like to raise interest rates *before* inflation increases and lower rates *before* economic growth slows. If economic adjustments occur more quickly now, policymakers may be harder pressed to react in time. Thus, at the end of 2000, the sudden slowing of the U.S. economy caught policymakers by surprise. The Federal Reserve reacted with a half-point interest rate cut on January 3, 2001, *after* the slowdown began.

In the past, interest rate cuts by the Fed have taken twelve to eighteen months to have their peak impact on the economy. While the new economy may give the Fed less time to react, it remains to be seen whether it also shortens the lag between changes in policy and their impact on the economy.

Instantaneous computer tracking enables managers to avoid both inventory shortages and unnecessary inventory buildups.

but doing so leads to bigger swings in output and employment. Even though they would like to keep the economy stable at full employment and low inflation, policymakers must choose which goal to focus on—they cannot achieve both.

Policymakers do not face this same fundamental trade-off when the economy experiences disturbances that shift the ADI curve, such as shifts in fiscal policy, changes in spending decisions by households or firms, or economic fluctuations in other countries that affect net exports. If the ADI curve shifts to the left, threatening a recession, policymakers should engage in expansionary policies to offset the disturbance and keep the economy at full employment. In doing so, they also keep inflation stable. By offsetting disturbances that affect aggregate expenditures, policymakers can succeed in stabilizing both employment *and* inflation. It is not necessary to trade off one goal for another.

This is not to say that making policy decisions in response to demand disturbances is easy. The problem of lags and the difficulties of forecasting still apply. An example is provided by the Asian financial crisis of the late 1990s. It was widely predicted that this would reduce U.S. net exports and slow the U.S. economy down. The impact on U.S. output and inflation could be minimized if the Fed adopted a more expansionary policy. But the Fed had to decide how much more. Should the nominal interest rate be cut by 1 percent? 2 percent? And when? If fiscal policy should turn more contractionary, the full-employment real rate of interest would fall, but by how much? And how quickly would the fiscal contraction lead to a decline in spending? In principle, the central bank can offset the impacts of shifts in aggregate demand, such as fiscal policy, and keep both employment and inflation stable. In practice, policymakers are not able to fine-tune the economy to this extent. The key lesson, though, is that the choices between policy goals when supply shocks occur are much tougher than those faced when demand shocks occur.

Review and Practice

SUMMARY

1. The traditional view of government deficits argues that deficits reduce national saving, raise the equilibrium real interest rate, and crowd out private investment spending. The result is less capital and lower incomes in the future. The burden of government deficits falls on future generations.

2. Under Ricardian equivalence, individuals understand that deficits today mean higher taxes in the future. Those in the private sector increase their saving in anticipation of the higher future taxes. Thus, national saving does not fall and deficits do not matter.

3. Those who criticize active policy intervention to stabilize the economy argue that markets adjust quickly, making unemployment only short-lived. Attempts by government to intervene are not only unnecessary but largely ineffective, since they are offset by actions of the private sector. And to the extent that they do have effects, such policies often exacerbate fluctuations, because there are long lags, because the government has limited information, and because political pressures lead it to overheat the economy before elections.

4. Critics of discretionary policy believe that the government should tie its hands by using fixed rules. Discretionary policies may be inconsistent over time, leading to worse outcomes than occur when government follows predictable rules. Critics of fixed rules argue that by embracing them government gives up an important set of instruments and that fixed rules never work well because they fail to respond to the ever-changing structure of the economy.

5. The proponents of inflation targeting in the United States argue that it will make the Fed more accountable, increase the credibility of the Fed's low inflation policy, and institutionalize good policies.

6. Opponents of inflation targeting argue that it elevates one goal of monetary policy at the expense of other goals, limits Fed flexibility, and is unnecessary.

7. Aggregate supply shocks require policymakers to balance the goals of full employment and stable inflation. To achieve one goal, the other must be sacrificed. Aggregate demand shocks create no inherent conflict between these goals.

8. Disturbances such as oil price changes or shifts in inflationary expectations force policymakers to face a trade-off between stabilizing unemployment and stabilizing inflation. If the central bank adjusts interest rates more aggressively to changes in inflation, it can make inflation more stable, but output and employment will fluctuate more.

KEY TERMS

rules
discretion
dynamic inconsistency
countercyclical policies
inflation targeting
price level targeting

REVIEW QUESTIONS

1. Why might a government budget deficit reduce the economy's future stock of capital?

2. Suppose the government cuts taxes. If households save all of their tax cut, will the real interest rate and investment be affected? Explain.

3. What is meant by Ricardian equivalence?

4. How do inflation and unemployment affect different groups differently, and how do these differences affect views on macroeconomic policy?

5. Why do some economists argue that interventions to reduce economic fluctuations are either ineffective or counterproductive?

6. What is meant by dynamic inconsistency? Give at least two examples of policies that are dynamically inconsistent.

7. Why do some economists argue that interventions to reduce economic fluctuations are effective and productive?

8. What are the pros and cons of inflation targeting?

9. What trade-off between average unemployment and average inflation do policymakers face? What trade-off

between fluctuations in unemployment and fluctuations in inflation do policymakers face?

10. What is the difference between a policy of inflation targeting and a policy of price level targeting?

PROBLEMS

1. Suppose the government cuts taxes. Using a supply and demand analysis of the capital market, explain what the impact of the tax cut will be on the equilibrium real interest rate at full employment.

2. Suppose the government's budget is currently in balance but the government is projected to run a large deficit in the future because of large projected increases in spending. Assume Ricardian equivalence is true. How will these projected deficits affect current national saving if households expect that taxes will be raised in the future? How will the current equilibrium real interest rate and investment be affected?

3. Assume the economy is currently at full employment with an inflation rate of 2 percent. The government embarks on a major new expenditure program that increases aggregate expenditures (assume that full-employment output and the natural rate of unemployment are unaffected).
   (a) If the central bank's policy rule remains unchanged, what will be the short-run and long-run effects on output and inflation of this change in fiscal policy? What will be the long-run effects on the real interest rate at full employment?
   (b) Suppose the central bank's policy rule adjusts to reflect the change in the full-employment real interest rate. Will this alter the short-run or long-run effects of the fiscal expansion?

4. If you were in the position of the Fed in early 2001, with unemployment around 4 percent and inflation low but with signs the economy was starting to slow, would you have lowered interest rates? Why or why not? Does your answer depend on whether your estimate of the natural rate of unemployment is 4 percent or 6 percent?

5. "If expectations adjust quickly to changes in economic circumstances, including changes in economic policy, then it is easy to start an inflationary episode. But under the same conditions, it is also easy to stop inflation." Discuss. If true, what implications might this finding have for economic policy?

6. Assume that two members of the FOMC agree that the Fed's goals are to maintain full employment while ensuring low inflation, but one member (call this member W) believes that the costs of unemployment make it a much more pressing problem than inflation, while the other (member H) holds the opposite beliefs. For each of the following disturbances, will member W want the Fed to raise or lower interest rates? What about H? In which cases will the two agree? In which cases will they disagree?
   (a) An increase in business confidence
   (b) The development of new technologies that increase productivity
   (c) An increase in government purchases
   (d) An increase in inflation expectations

7. Suppose the economy is at full employment but inflation is viewed as too high. Consider the following two scenarios:
   (a) The central bank has great credibility. The central bank announces a policy of disinflation, and the public believes the announcement. Inflationary expectations fall immediately.
   (b) The central bank has no credibility. The central bank announces a policy of disinflation but the public is skeptical that the bank will actually follow through with it. The public's inflationary expectations fall only if they see actual inflation coming down.

Discuss the likely unemployment consequences of reducing inflation in each of these two scenarios. In which case will the sacrifice ratio (the unemployment cost of reducing inflation) be higher? Explain why.

Appendix: Price Level Targeting

Almost all central banks focus on inflation, not the price level, and they implement monetary policy through their control of a nominal interest rate. Some economists have advocated forms of price level targeting in which the central bank would try to keep the price level constant rather than simply keep inflation low. Although this type of price level targeting is not practiced by any central bank, many traditional textbooks treat central banks as if their chief concern were the level of prices. The approach we have followed—one that focuses on inflation and the policy response to inflation—can easily be modified to deal with the case of a central bank that targets the price level.

Under a policy of targeting the price level, the central bank will increase the nominal interest rate whenever the price level rises and lower the nominal interest rate whenever the price level falls. The objective in either case is to affect the real interest rate and aggregate expenditures. Rather than leading to the negative relationship between inflation and aggregate expenditures represented by our ADI curve, a policy of price level targeting will lead to a negative relationship between the price level and aggregate expenditures. This relationship, shown in Figure 21.5, is usually called an *aggregate demand curve*.

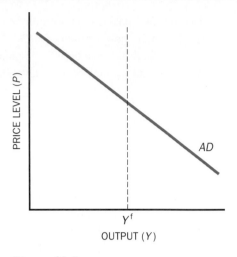

Figure 21.5

THE AGGREGATE DEMAND CURVE

If the central bank adjusts the interest rate whenever the price level deviates from its target level, the ADI curve is replaced with a relationship between the price level (P) and aggregate expenditures called the aggregate demand (AD) curve. If P increases, the central bank increases the interest rate, leading to a reduction in aggregate expenditures. Changes in fiscal policy or shocks to consumption, investment, or net exports shift the aggregate demand curve in the same way they would shift the ADI curve. An increase in government purchases, for instance, shifts the AD curve to the right.

Learning Goals

In this chapter, you will learn

1 About the principal investment alternatives available for your savings

2 The important characteristics of each of these investment options

3 Why some assets yield higher rates of return than others

4 Whether it is possible to "beat the market"

5 Some of the basic rules for intelligent investing

Chapter 22

A STUDENT'S GUIDE TO INVESTING

The 1990s saw a tremendous rise in the value of the stock market—it seemed as if almost every day some new company was selling shares to the public and creating new billionaires overnight. This picture all changed abruptly in 2000 when the stock market collapsed, causing millions to see their paper wealth disappear. The ups and downs of the stock market are often taken as key signals of the economy's health, and the swings of the financial market that we have seen during the past ten years are nothing new. When Alexander Hamilton, as the first U.S. secretary of the treasury under President George Washington, set up the first market for the new government's bonds in 1791, prices skyrocketed by more than 1,000 percent in the first month of trading before collapsing in value.

But what can economics tell us about the stock market and how it behaves? And what can economics tell us about how you should invest your money? Every decision to save is accompanied by a decision about what to do with the savings. They might go under the mattress, but usually savings are invested—most often in bank accounts, the stock or bond market, or the real estate market. These financial opportunities can be thought of as enticements to defer consumption—to save. Broadly speaking, an **investment** is the purchase of an asset in the expectation of receiving a return. For the economy as a whole, **real investment** must be distinguished from **financial investment.** Real investment includes the purchase of new factories and machines; it is the investment that is part of aggregate expenditures. Financial investment is the purchase of financial assets such as stocks and bonds that are expected to generate income or to appreciate in value.

This chapter examines financial investment. It first takes up the major alternatives available to savers and discusses the characteristics of those that are important to investors. From these characteristics, we can establish a simple theory to explain how the prices of financial assets such as stocks and bonds are determined. We can use what we learn about the characteristics of investment alternatives and the theory of asset prices to develop some strategies for intelligent investing.

Investment Alternatives

Savers wishing to invest are offered a range of possibilities. The choices they make depend on the amount of money they have to invest, their motivations to save, their willingness to bear risk, and such personal characteristics as age and health. Of the seemingly endless array of destinations for one's money, five are most important: bank deposits, including certificates of deposit (CDs); housing; bonds; stocks; and mutual funds. In making choices among them, investors focus on four characteristics: return, risk, tax liability, and liquidity.

BANK DEPOSITS

A *bank savings account* (or a similar account) offers three advantages: it pays interest, it allows easy access to the money in it, and it offers security. Even if the bank goes bankrupt, the federal government, through the Federal Deposit Insurance Corporation (FDIC), insures its deposits of up to $100,000.

As savings increase, the value of a higher interest rate also increases. A **certificate of deposit (CD),** which specifies an interest rate on money deposited in a bank for a preset length of time, is as safe as an ordinary bank account and yields a slightly higher return. The drawback of a CD is that withdrawals of money before the preset time has expired are subject to a penalty. The ease with which an investment can be turned into cash is called its **liquidity.** Perfectly liquid investments can be converted into cash speedily and without any loss in value. CDs are less liquid than standard saving accounts.

HOUSING

Two-thirds of American households invest by owning their own homes. Making this investment is far riskier than putting money into a savings account or a CD. Home prices usually increase over time, but not always, and recently the rate of increase has varied widely in different parts of the country. For example, over the past ten years, house prices have gone up almost 530 percent in Massachusetts but only 75 percent in Oklahoma. Prices may rise rapidly in one year, then remain flat or even fall in other years. Most families borrow most of the funds needed to purchase a house, and the owner bears the risk, since she is responsible for paying back the loan regardless of the market price of the house.

Housing as an investment has two other attributes—one attractive and one unattractive. On the positive side, property taxes and the interest on the loan used to purchase the house are generally tax deductible, and for most homeowners the capital gains escape taxation altogether. On the negative side, housing is usually fairly illiquid. If you try to sell your house quickly, on average you will receive less than if you have more time to make the sale. Moreover, the costs of selling a house are substantial, often more than 5 percent of the value of the house—in any case, more than the costs of selling stocks and bonds.

CALCULATING INTEREST RATES

The Federal Reserve Banks of New York and Chicago have Web sites that explain how interest rates are calculated. Their addresses are www.ny.frb.org/education/calc.html#calc and www.chicagofed.org/consumer_information/abcs_of_figuring_interest.cfm.

BONDS

Bonds are a way for corporations and government to borrow. The borrower—whether a company, a state, a school district, or the U.S. government—promises to pay the lender (the purchaser of the bond, or investor) a fixed amount in a specified number of years. In addition, the borrower agrees to pay the lender each year a fixed return on the amount borrowed. Thus, if the interest rate on a ten-year bond is 10 percent, a $10,000 bond will pay the lender $1,000 every year, and $10,000 at the end of ten years. The date on which a loan or bond is to be paid in full is called its *maturity*. Bonds that mature within a few years are called *short-term bonds;* those that mature in more than ten years are called *long-term bonds.* A long-term government bond may have a maturity of twenty or even thirty years.

Bonds may seem relatively safe, because the investor knows what amounts will be paid. But consider a corporate bond that promises to pay $10,000 in ten years and pays $1,000 every year until then. Imagine that an investor buys the bond, collects interest for a couple of years, and then realizes that he needs cash and wants to sell the bond. There is no guarantee that he will get $10,000 for it. He may get more and he may get less. If the market interest rate has fallen to 5 percent since the original bond was issued, a new $10,000 bond now would pay only $500 a year. Clearly, the original bond, which pays $1,000 a year, is worth considerably more. Thus, a decline in the interest rate leads to a rise in the value of bonds; and by the same logic, a rise in the interest rate leads to a decline in the value of bonds. This uncertainty about market value is what makes long-term bonds risky.[1]

Even if the investor holds the bond to maturity, that is, until the date at which it pays the promised $10,000, there is still a risk, since he cannot know for sure what $10,000 will purchase ten years from now. If the general level of prices increases at

---

[1]The market price of the bond will equal the percent discounted value of what it pays. For instance, a 3-year bond that pays $10 per year each of 2 years and $110 at the end of the 3rd year has a value of

$$\frac{10}{1+r} + \frac{10}{(1+r)^2} + \frac{110}{(1+r)^3},$$

where r is the market rate of interest. We can see that as r goes up, the value of the bond goes down, and vice versa.

a rate of 7 percent over those ten years, the real value of the $10,000 will be just one-half what it would have been had prices remained stable during that decade.[2]

Because of the higher risk caused by these uncertainties, long-term bonds must compensate investors by paying higher returns, on average, than comparable short-term bonds. And because every corporation has at least a slight chance of going bankrupt, corporate bonds must compensate investors for that higher risk by paying higher returns than government bonds. These higher returns more than compensate for the additional bankruptcy risk, according to economic research. That is, if an investor purchases a very large number of good-quality corporate bonds, the likelihood that more than one or two will default is very small, and the overall return will be considerably higher than the return from purchasing government bonds of the same maturity (the same length of time until they come due).

Some corporate bonds are riskier than others—that is, there is a higher probability of default. These bonds must pay extremely high returns to induce investors to take a chance on them. When Chrysler appeared to be on the verge of bankruptcy in 1980, Chrysler bonds were yielding returns of 23 percent. Obviously, the greater a firm's debt, the more likely it is to be unable to meet its commitments, and the riskier are its bonds. Especially risky bonds are called *junk bonds;* the yields on such bonds are much higher than those from a financially solid firm, but the investor must take into account the high probability of default.

SHARES OF STOCK

Those with savings might also choose to invest in shares of corporate stock. When people buy shares in a firm, they literally own a fraction (a share) of the total firm. Thus, if the firm issues 1 million shares, an individual who owns 100 shares owns 0.01 percent of the firm. Investors choose stocks as investments for two reasons.

First, firms pay some fraction of their earnings—their receipts after paying workers, suppliers of materials, and all interest due on bank and other loans—directly to shareholders. These payments are called **dividends.** On average, firms distribute one-third of earnings as dividends; the remainder, called **retained earnings,** is kept for investment in the company. The amount of a dividend, unlike the return on a bond, depends on a firm's earnings and on what proportion of those earnings it chooses to distribute to shareholders.

In addition to receiving dividends, those who invest in stocks hope to make money by choosing stocks that will appreciate in value and that can then be sold at the higher price. The increase in the realized price of a share (or any other asset) is called a **capital gain.** (If the asset is sold at a price below that at which it was purchased, the investor realizes a *capital loss.*)

Shares of stock are risky for a number of reasons. First, the earnings of firms vary greatly. Even if firms' dividends are the same, differences in profits will lead to differences in retained earnings, and these will be reflected in the value of the shares. In addition, the stock price of a company depends on the beliefs of investors

---

[2]If prices rise at 7 percent a year, with compounding, the price level in 10 years is $(1.07)^{10}$ times the level it is today; $(1.07)^{10}$ is approximately equal to 2—thus prices have doubled.

regarding the prospects of the economy, the industry, and that particular firm. Loss of faith in any one of these could lead to a drop in the stock price. Thus, an individual who has to sell all his shares because of some medical emergency might find they have declined significantly in value. Even if the investor believes that the shares will eventually return to a higher value, he may be unable to wait.

Shares of stock are riskier than corporate bonds. When a firm goes bankrupt and must pay off its investors, the law requires bondholders to be paid off as fully as possible before shareholders receive any money at all. As a result, a bondholder in a bankrupt company is likely to be paid some share of her original investment, while a shareholder may receive nothing. But over the long run, shares of stock have yielded very high returns. While corporate bonds yielded on average an annual real rate of return of 2 percent in the period from 1926 to 2003, shares of stock in the same period yielded a real return of nearly 10 percent.

MUTUAL FUNDS

A **mutual fund** gathers funds from many different investors into a single large pool of funds, with which it can then purchase a large number of assets. A *money market mutual fund* invests its funds in CDs and comparably safe assets.

The advantage of a money market mutual fund is that it offers both higher rates of interest than bank accounts and high liquidity. The fund managers know that most individuals will leave their money in the account, and some will be adding money to the account as others pull money out. They are thus able to put a large proportion of the fund in certificates of deposits and still not have to pay the penalties for early withdrawal. In this way, money market mutual funds give investors the easy access to their funds associated with banks, while providing them the higher return associated with CDs.

Money market mutual funds may also invest their customers' money in short-term government bonds, called **Treasury bills,** or **T-bills.** Treasury bills are available only in large denominations ($10,000 or more). They promise to repay a certain amount (their face value, say, $10,000) in a relatively short period, less than 90 or 180 days, and investors buy them at less than their face value. The difference between the amount paid and the face value becomes the return to the purchaser.

With most money market mutual funds, you can even write a limited number of checks a month against your account. The major disadvantages of mutual funds are that they may require that you maintain a high minimum balance in your account and they may not be insured by the federal government. However, some money market funds invest only in government securities or government-insured securities, making them virtually as safe as bank accounts.

Other mutual funds invest in stocks and bonds. Typically, they buy stock or bonds in dozens, sometimes hundreds, of different companies. Investors recognize the advantage of **diversification**—of not putting all their eggs in the same basket. If you put all your savings into a single stock and that firm has a bad year, you'll suffer a large loss. If you own stock in two companies, losses in one company may offset gains in the other. Mutual funds, in effect, allow much broader diversification. Of course, if the whole stock market does badly, a stock mutual fund will suffer too. When stocks go down, bonds often go up, so some mutual funds invest in both stocks and bonds. Others invest in risky ventures that, if successful, promise high returns; these are sometimes referred to as "growth" funds. There are many other specially designed mutual funds, and together they are enormously popular. For most investors, the first foray into the bond or stock market is through the purchase of a mutual fund.

Desirable Attributes of Investments

Table 22.1 sets forth the various investment opportunities we have described, with a list of their most important attributes. In surveying the broad range of investment opportunities available, individuals must balance their personal needs against what the different investment options have to offer. The ideal investment would have a high rate of return, be low risk, and be exempt from tax. Unfortunately, as economists always like to point out, investors face trade-offs. You can only expect to get more of one desirable property—say a higher expected return—at the expense of another, such as safety. To understand what is entailed in these trade-offs, we need to take a closer look at each of the principal attributes of investments.

EXPECTED RETURNS

First on the list of desirable properties are high returns. As we have noted, returns have two components: the interest (on a bond), dividend payment (on a stock), or rent (on real estate) and the capital gain. For instance, if you buy some stock for $1,000, receive $150 in dividends during the year, and at the end of the year sell the stock for $1,200, your total return is $150 + $200 = $350 (a rate of return of 35 percent). If you sell the stock for only $900, your total return is $150 − $100 = $50 (a rate of return of 5 percent). If you sell it for $800, your total return is a *negative* $50 (a rate of return of −5 percent).

Internet Connection

INDEX FUNDS

Many mutual funds are designed to follow the return of a market index, such as the Standard and Poor's (S&P) 500 index. Standard and Poor's Web site at www.spglobal.com pro- vides the latest information on the performance of their indexes. If you follow the links on the left side of the page, you will find a primer on the mathematics of calculating market indexes

Table 22.1

ALTERNATIVE INVESTMENTS AND HOW THEY FARE

Investment	Expected returns	Risk	Tax advantages	Liquidity
Banking savings accounts	Low	Low	None	High
CDs (certificates of deposit)	Slightly higher than savings accounts	Low	None	Slightly less than savings accounts
Houses	High returns from mid-1970s to mid-1980s; in many areas, negative returns in late 1980s, early 1990s, high returns since late 1990s	Used to be thought safe; viewed to be somewhat riskier now	Many special tax advantages	Relatively illiquid; may take long time to find "good buyer"
Federal government long-term bonds	Normally slightly higher than T-bills	Uncertain market value next period; uncertain purchasing power in long run	Exempt from state income tax	Small charge for selling before maturity
Corporate Bonds	Higher return than federal bonds	Risks of long-term federal bonds plus risk of default	None	Slightly less liquid than federal bonds (depends on corporation issuing bond)
Stocks	High	High	Capital gains receive tax preference if stocks held for more than 1 year	Those listed on major exchange are highly liquid; others may be highly illiquid
Mutual Funds	Reflect assets in which funds are invested	Reflect assets in which funds are invested; reduced risk from diversification	Reflect assets in which funds are invested	High
T-bills	About same as CDs	Low	Exempt from state income tax	Small charge for selling before maturity

Few assets offer guaranteed returns. If the stock market booms, a stock share might yield 20 percent; but if the market drops, the total return might be zero or even negative. To compare two alternative investment options, we apply the concept of **expected returns.** The expected return on an asset is the single number that takes into account both the various possible returns per dollar invested and the chances that each of those possibilities will occur. If there is a one-in-four chance (a 25 percent probability) a stock will yield a 20 percent return over the next year,

INVESTING IN THE NEW ECONOMY

Investors worry about risk. Risk can be reduced by *diversification,* that is, by not putting all your eggs in one basket. Dividing investments among a large number of securities lowers the risk because the value of some may go up when the value of others goes down. In spite of the distinct advantages of risk diversification, many individuals own relatively few securities. One of the reasons is that it is costly to buy and sell different stocks. As a result, individuals have increasingly turned to mutual funds. Mutual funds are financial intermediaries that buy large numbers of securities. Transactions costs are lowered because the securities are bought in bulk. But nothing is free in life. Mutual fund managers have to make a living, and they too charge transaction fees. These costs are substantially lower than if the individual tried to buy an equally diversified portfolio on her own, but they can be considerable nonetheless. Mutual funds have significant tax disadvantages as well. For instance, say you buy shares in a mutual fund in January 2000. In February 2000, the mutual fund sells some shares that it purchased ten years ago, and records a large capital gain.

Then the value of the fund decreases—perhaps because it was a high-technology fund, and technology shares plummeted in April 2000. At the end of the year you may think you have incurred a loss. But the IRS will still insist you pay a tax as if you had a capital gain, because you owned shares in the mutual fund at the time the capital gain was realized. This may seem grossly unfair—you are worse off, yet you have to pay a tax as if you were better off—but that is the way the tax law works.

The new economy has opened up new possibilities for individuals to diversify without large transaction costs. At least one new economy firm (FOLIO*fn*) is offering to allow investors to trade large numbers of stock for a single monthly fee, *with no marginal costs.* This arrangement enables individuals to obtain a highly diversified portfolio, to avoid the transaction costs of mutual funds, and to avoid the tax disadvantages of mutual funds. Like all innovations, it will take time for it to penetrate throughout the economy; but if successful, it may revolutionize how individuals—especially small investors—invest their money.

a one-in-two chance (a 50 percent probability) the return will be 5 percent, and a one-in-four chance (a 25 percent probability) the return will be zero, the expected return on the stock is 7.5 percent (.25 × 20 percent + .5 × 5 percent + .25 × 0 percent).

PG&E EMPLOYEES LEARN WHY DIVERSIFICATION IS IMPORTANT

In January 2001, Pacific Gas & Electric Company (PG&E), a major supplier of electricity to northern California, quite suddenly found itself facing bankruptcy. Under California's utility deregulation statutes, PG&E was prohibited from raising its prices to consumers but had to pay market prices for the electricity it purchased to deliver to them. When skyrocketing demand and energy shortages in the West led to record energy prices, PG&E quickly ran out of cash. Wall Street was equally quick to respond. PG&E's stock price plummeted from $31.64 on September 11, 2000, to

A crowd protests rate hikes by the California utility PG&E, which were made in an effort to fend off bankruptcy.

$10.19 in January 2001. The utility's bonds were downgraded to the lowest echelons of the junk bond range, indicating that Wall Street thought there was little chance that bondholders would be repaid or receive interest. PG&E suspended dividends on its stock, laid off workers, and hired bankruptcy lawyers to assess its options.

For some PG&E employees, the energy crisis that put at risk the booming California economy carried a double threat. Workers were clearly in danger of losing jobs. But more than 80 percent of PG&E's workers were also shareholders who owned stock through the company's retirement plan. PG&E for years had contributed stock one-for-one when employees purchased company stock for their individual 401(k) retirement accounts. Employees had the option of selling the PG&E stock and replacing it with other assets, but not everyone took advantage of the chance to diversify. When PG&E stock lost two-thirds of its value, these workers' 401(k) retirement plans followed suit. Though their pensions and 401(k) could not be seized by a bankruptcy court, workers whose 401(k) plans were heavily invested in PG&E stock had no protection from the risk that stock prices would nosedive.

Longtime employees who failed to diversify out of PG&E stock to obtain a more balanced portfolio saw their dreams of early retirement and a secure old age vanish. When asked why so many employees were overinvested in PG&E stock, one employee replied that people believed in the company that had provided a good living for them (and in some cases, their parents) for most of their lives. The sudden collapse of PG&E underscores the importance of diversification to minimize (though not avoid entirely) the risk of holding individual stocks.[3]

An important first lesson in investment theory is as follows: *If there were no differences between assets other than the ways in which they produce returns (interest, dividends, etc.), then the expected returns to all assets would be the same.* Why? Suppose an asset offered an expected return of 10 percent while all others offered 6 percent. Investors, in trying to buy the higher-yielding asset, would bid more for it, thereby pushing up its price. As the price rose, the expected return would decline. The upward pressure would continue until the expected return declined to match the level of all other investments.

In fact, for different assets the expected returns per dollar invested differ markedly from one another, because return is affected by a number of other important attributes. These include risk, tax considerations, and liquidity (the ease with which an asset can be sold).

RISK

Most of us do not like the risk that accompanies most future-oriented economic activity. We might spend a few dollars on some lottery tickets or occasionally play the slot machines, but for the most part we try to avoid or minimize risks. Economists say that individuals are *risk averse* and their behavior displays **risk aversion.**

A prime consideration for any investor, therefore, is the riskiness of any investment alternative. Bank accounts, in this regard, are safe. Since government deposit insurance was instituted in the 1930s after the bank failures that occurred during the Great Depression, no one in the United States has lost money in an insured bank account. But investments in housing, stocks, and bonds and most other investments involve risk. The return may turn out to be substantially lower, or higher, than initially expected.

Historically, stocks have yielded a higher average return than bonds, but stocks are riskier—prices on the stock market fluctuate, and they can do so quite dramatically. On the single day of October 19, 1987, stock prices on the New York Stock Exchange fell by 508 points, a drop in value of 23 percent.

Panel A of Figure 22.1 shows the closing monthly value of the Dow Jones industrial average, an index of stock prices that is based on the prices of shares in major companies. Today, thirty companies are included in the index, which was revised in 1999 to include such firms as Microsoft and Intel. Because the index has grown so much since 1928, the 1929 stock market crash barely shows up in the figure. Though the index fell in value almost 13 percent on October 28, 1929, this was a decline of only 38 points—well within the typical range of daily fluctuations in the market today. The

---

[3]Based on an article by Jennifer Bjorhus, "PG&E's 'Family' Falling Apart," *San Jose Mercury News,* January 22, 2001, p. 1.

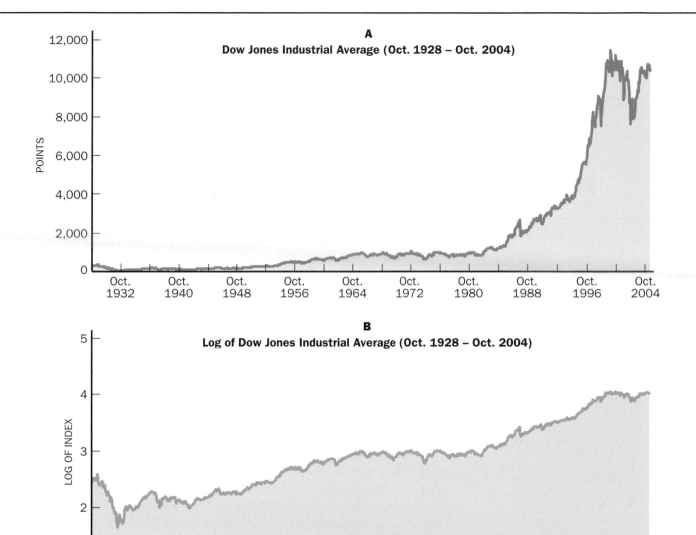

Figure 22.1

STOCK MARKET INDICES

Panel A shows the closing monthly value of the Dow Jones industrial average, an index of stock prices that is based on the prices of shares in major companies. Panel B plots the natural log of the Dow Jones index so that percentage changes in the level of stock prices can be seen more clearly.

largest one-day drop occurred on October 27, 1997, when the Dow Jones index lost 554 points.

The percentage change in the level of stock prices can be seen more clearly by plotting the natural log of the Dow Jones index (panel B). Here, the magnitude of the 1929 crash clearly stands out. The 1929 crash was not simply a one-day drop—three of the five biggest percentage daily declines over the 1900–2000 period occurred in late October and early November of 1929. The record for the largest percentage drop on a single day is held by December 12, 1914, when the market lost 24 percent of its value. Second is October 19, 1987, when the market fell 23 percent. The stock

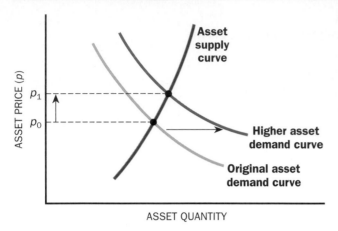

Figure 22.2

EFFECTS OF DIFFERENCES IN RISK

Lowering risk shifts the demand curve for the asset to the right, increasing the equilibrium price and lowering the average return.

market decline between August 2000 and March 2001 shows up clearly in panel A.

While the New York Stock Exchange is by far the largest stock market in the world, there are others, and in recent years the Nasdaq market has grown in importance. The Nasdaq stock market, created in 1971, is heavily weighted toward the new technology companies. The stocks of Microsoft and Intel, for example, are traded on the Nasdaq market, not the New York Stock Exchange. The addition of Microsoft and Intel to the Dow Jones index in 1999 marked the first time that companies traded on the Nasdaq market, and not the New York Stock Exchange, were included in the index.

Both the Dow Jones index and the Nasdaq index show a tendency to rise over time—leading to capital gains for those who hold stock—but both also show the ups and downs that occur over shorter periods. It is these fluctuations in value that make investing in stocks risky.

Risk can never be avoided completely, and it has been said that financial markets are the places where risk is bought and sold. We can see the effects of changes in risk in Figure 22.2. A reduction in the riskiness of an asset makes it more desirable, thereby shifting the demand curve for the asset to the right. In the short run, the supply of an asset is inelastic. Even in the longer run, supply is likely not to be perfectly elastic. Accordingly, as illustrated in the figure, the price of the asset goes up, from p_0 to p_1. Accompanying the increase in price is a reduction in the return per dollar invested.

An asset that is less risky will have a higher demand. The higher demand will lead to a higher price and lower return. Therefore, the expected return will be lower on assets that are safer. Economists say such desirable assets sell at a *premium,* while assets that are riskier sell at a *discount.* Still, market forces ensure that assets of comparable risk must yield the same expected returns.

TAX CONSIDERATIONS

Since different assets are treated differently in the tax code, tax considerations are obviously important in choosing a portfolio. After all, individuals care about after-tax returns, not before-tax returns. Investments that face relatively low tax rates are said to be *tax-favored.*

State and municipal bonds illustrate this point. These bonds yield a lower return than do corporate bonds of comparable risk and liquidity. So why do people buy them? The answer is that the interest on bonds issued by states and municipalities is generally exempt from federal tax. The higher your income, the more valuable this tax exemption is, because your tax savings are greater the higher your tax *rate* (which tends to increase with income). The higher demand for these tax-exempt bonds from high-income investors drives up their price, thereby driving down the return received on the bonds. We can expect the return to decline to the point at which the after-tax return for high-income individuals is at most only slightly higher than for an ordinary taxable bond of comparable risk.

Investing in housing, particularly a house to live in, is another tax-favored form of investment enjoyed by most Americans. Most homeowners can deduct their real estate taxes and the interest payments on their mortgage when calculating their income for tax purposes. In addition, the capital gain from owning the house is not taxed until the house is sold. Even then, the capital gain (up to $500,000 for a married couple) from the sale is not taxed at all. If the tax advantages of home ownership were ever withdrawn, we could expect housing prices to decline precipitously in the short run (in which supply is inelastic), as illustrated in Figure 22.3. It is not likely that tax preferences for housing will be suddenly removed, however, because most voters own houses, and politicians are loathe to anger such a large number of their constituents.

LIQUIDITY

The fourth important attribute to consider is liquidity. An asset is liquid if the costs of selling it are very low. A bank account is completely liquid (unless the bank goes bankrupt), because you can turn it into cash at virtually no charge by writing a check. Corporate stock in a major company is fairly liquid, because the costs of selling at a well-defined market price are relatively small.

In the basic competitive model, all assets are assumed to be perfectly liquid. There is a well-defined price at which anything can be bought and sold; any household or

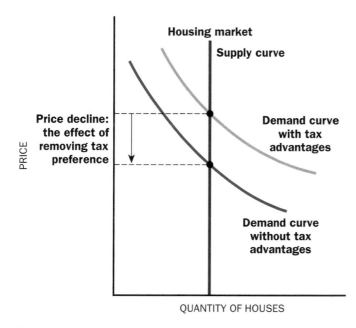

Figure 22.3

EFFECT OF REMOVING TAX PREFERENCES FOR HOUSING

Removing tax preferences for housing will shift the demand curve for housing down, and this will, in the short run (with an inelastic housing supply), cause marked decreases in the price of housing.

firm can buy or sell as much as it wants at that price; and the transaction is virtually without cost. But these assumptions are not always met: the costs of selling or buying an asset are often significant. As noted above, for instance, the costs of selling a house can be 5 percent or more of the house's value. At times, even municipal bonds have been fairly illiquid. The prices at which such bonds could be bought and sold have been known to differ by more than 20 percent.

Expectations and the Market for Assets

Gardeners today find shocking the price of tulip bulbs in early-seventeenth-century Holland, where one bulb sold for the equivalent of $16,000 in today's dollars. The golden age of tulips did not last long, however; and in 1637, prices of bulbs fell by more than 90 percent. Dramatic price swings for assets are not only curiosities of history. Between 1973 and 1980, the price of gold rose from $98 to $613, or by 525 percent; then, from 1980 to 1985, it fell to $318. Between 1977 and 1980, the price of farm land in Iowa increased by 40 percent, only to fall by more than 60 percent from 1980 to 1987. On October 19, 1987, stock values on the U.S. stock market fell by half a trillion dollars—almost 25 percent. Even a major war would be unlikely to destroy one-fourth of the U.S. capital stock in a single day. But there was no war or other external event to explain the 1987 drop.

How can the basic demand and supply model explain these huge price swings? If asset prices depend on the four basic attributes discussed above—expected return, risk, tax treatment, and liquidity—how can demand curves, or supply curves, shift so dramatically as to cause these large price movements?

The answer lies in the critical role that expectations play in the market for assets. Assets such as gold, land, or stocks are long-lived; they can be bought at one date and sold at another. For this reason, the price that individuals are willing to pay for them today depends not only on today's conditions—the immediate return or benefit—but also on some expectation of what tomorrow's conditions will be. In particular, the demand for an asset will depend on what the asset is expected to be worth in the future.

To see how expectations concerning future events affect *current* prices, consider a hypothetical example. People suddenly realize that new smog-control devices will, ten years from now, make certain parts of Los Angeles much more attractive places to live than they are today. As a result, future-oriented individuals will think that ten years from now the price of land in those areas will be much higher, say $1 million an acre. But, they also think, nine years from now it will already be widely recognized that in one short year an acre will be worth $1 million. Hence, nine years from now investors will be willing to pay almost $1 million for the land—even if, at that date (nine years from now), the smog has not yet been eliminated. In that case, these same individuals think, eight years from now investors will realize that in one short year the price will rise to almost $1 million and will pay close to that amount. Working backward like this makes it apparent that if people are confident land is going to be much more valuable in ten years, its price rises today.

Thinking Like an Economist

THE DISTRIBUTION OF WEALTH AND OWNERSHIP OF ASSETS

Although America is a very wealthy society, that wealth is distributed unevenly among American families. The chart shows median family net worth in 2001, classified by 2001 income percentiles. The median income of the 20 percent of families with the lowest incomes was $10,300, and the median net worth of these families was just $7,900. That means that half of the families in this income group had net worth less than $7,900. For families in the top 10 percent of income earners, median family income was $169,600, and median net worth was $833,600.

Not only is less wealth possessed by poor families than by high-income families, but the types of financial and nonfinan-cial assets held by families also differ by income. Wealthy families are more likely to own stocks and bonds, to hold mutual funds, and to have retirement accounts. The value of holdings of nonfinancial assets—cars, homes, nonresidential property, and businesses—varies widely by income as well. High-income families tend to have greater holdings in cars, residential property, and other property than do families with lower incomes, but the biggest difference across income categories is in the ownership of businesses. The median value of business equity held by the 10 percent of families with the highest 2001 income was $239,500, compared with holdings of $54,400 for the 10 percent of families with the next highest incomes.

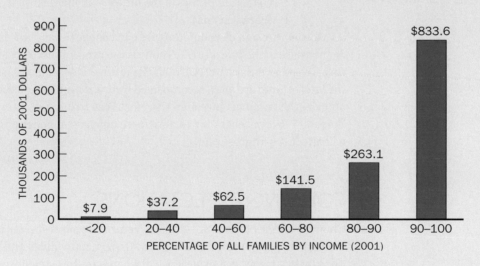

MEDIAN NET WORTH BY INCOME PERCENTILE

Thus, while changes in tastes or technology or incomes or the prices of other goods *today* could not account for some of the sharp changes in asset values described at the start of this section, changes in expectations concerning any of these variables in the future will have an effect *today* on the demand. Markets for assets are linked together over time. An event that is expected to happen in ten or fifteen or even fifty years can have a direct bearing on today's market.

To evaluate the effects of expected future prices on an asset's current price, the concept of present discounted value, introduced in Chapter 3, is important. By

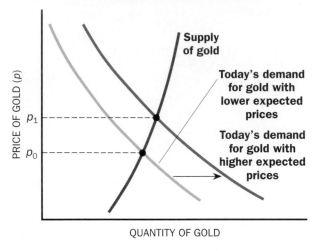

Figure 22.4

HOW EXPECTATIONS CAN SHIFT DEMAND

Expectations that the price of an asset like gold will rise in the future can cause the demand curve to shift to the right, thereby raising the current price.

calculating the present discounted value, we can measure and compare returns anticipated in the future. Demand today for an asset will depend on the present discounted value that it is expected to fetch when sold in the future.

Present discounted values can change for two reasons. First, they can change because of a change in the expected price of an asset at the time one anticipates selling it. This type of change is illustrated in Figure 22.4. That such expectations of future prices can be quite volatile helps explain the volatility of asset prices. Investors in seventeenth-century Holland were willing to pay enormous prices for tulip bulbs because they expected to be able to sell the bulbs at even higher prices. Such price increases that are solely based on the expectation that prices will be higher in the future—and not based on increases in the actual returns yielded by the asset—are called **asset price bubbles.** Prices continue to rise as long as everyone expects them to rise. Once people believe that the rise will stop, the current price crashes. The tremendous increase in stock prices in the United States during the 1990s led many to worry that it was a bubble that would eventually crash. Others pointed to increased productivity that promised higher corporate profits in the future—an increase in the actual returns that stocks can pay.

Second, present discounted values can change because the interest rate changes. An increase in the interest rate reduces the present discounted value of the dollars that investors expect to receive in the future. This is one reason why increases in the interest rate are often accompanied by drops in share prices on the stock market, and vice versa. Smart investors therefore seek to forecast interest rates accurately. So-called Fed watchers try to anticipate changes in Federal Reserve policies that will affect the interest rate.

FORMING EXPECTATIONS

Changes in expectations about future returns or interest rates thus can be reflected in large changes in asset prices today. In part, individuals and firms form expectations by looking at past experience. If a company has steadily grown more valuable, investors may come to expect that pattern to continue. If the Federal Reserve acts to slow the economy by raising interest rates every time inflation rates increase, people come to expect inflation to be followed by higher interest rates.

Psychologists and economists have studied how individuals form expectations. Sometimes people are *myopic,* or short-sighted. They expect what is true today to be true tomorrow. The price of gold today is what it will be tomorrow. Sometimes they are *adaptive,* extrapolating events of the recent past into the future. If the price of gold today is 5 percent higher than it was last year, they expect its price next year to be 5 percent higher than it is today.

When people make full use of all relevant available data to form their expectations, economists say that their expectations are *rational.* The price of gold rises during an inflationary period, but the price of gold also goes down when inflation subsides. Thus, if a person knows that economic analysts are predicting lower inflation, she will not expect the gold price increases to continue. Even when individuals form their expectations rationally, they will not be right all the time. Sometimes they will be overly optimistic, sometimes overly pessimistic (although in making their decisions, they are aware of these possibilities). But the assumption of rational expectations is that on average they will judge correctly.

The 1970s was a decade when adaptive expectations reigned. Many investors came to expect prices of assets such as land and housing to continue to rise rapidly. The more they invested, the more money they made. The idea that the price of a house or of land might fall seemed beyond belief—even though history is full of episodes (most recently in Japan during the 1990s) when such prices fell dramatically. The weak real estate markets of the 1980s in many regions reminded investors of the importance of incorporating historical data in forming expectations.

But in this, as in all types of fortune-telling, history never repeats itself exactly. Since the situation today is never precisely like past experience, it is never completely clear which facts will be the relevant ones. Even the best-informed experts are likely to disagree. When it comes to predicting the future, everyone's crystal ball is cloudy.

Efficient Market Theory

The demand for any asset depends on all four of its basic attributes—average return, risk, tax treatment, and liquidity. In a well-functioning market, there are no bargains to be had: you get what you pay for. If some asset yields a higher average return than most other investments, it does so because that asset has a higher risk, is less liquid, or receives less favorable tax treatment.

That there are no bargains does not mean the investor's life is easy. He still must decide what he wants, just as he does when he goes into a grocery store. Figure 22.5 shows the kind of choices he faces. For the sake of simplicity, we ignore liquidity and tax considerations and focus only on average returns and risk. The figure shows the opportunity set in the way that is usual for this case. Because "risk" is bad, to get less risk we have to give up some average returns. That is why the trade-off has a positive slope. We can see that assets with greater risk have a higher average return. Point A represents a government T-bill—no risk but low return. Point B might represent a stock or mix of stocks of average riskiness; point C, a stock or mix of high risk. A very risk-averse person might choose A; a less risk-averse person, B; a still less risk-averse person, C.

The theory that prices perfectly reflect the characteristics of assets—there are no bargains—is called the **efficient market theory.** Since much of the work on efficient market theory has been done on publicly traded stocks, our discussion centers on them. The lessons can be applied to all asset prices, however.

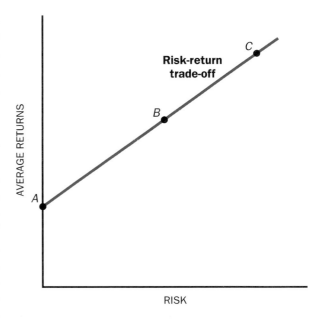

Figure 22.5

THE RISK-RETURN TRADE-OFF

To get a higher expected return, an investor must accept more risk.

EFFICIENCY AND THE STOCK MARKET

Most people do not think they can wander over to the racetrack and make a fortune. They are not so skeptical about the stock market. They believe that even if they themselves cannot sit down with the *Wall Street Journal* or browse an online broker's site and pick out all the best stocks, someone who studies the stock market for a living could do so. But economists startled the investment community in the early 1960s by pointing out that choosing successful stocks is no easier—and no harder—than choosing the fastest horses.

The efficient market theory explains this discrepancy in views. When economists speak of an efficient market, they are referring to one in which relevant information is widely known and quickly distributed to all participants. To oversimplify a bit, they envision a stock market where all investors have access to *Barron's* and *Fortune* magazines or to one of the many Internet sites devoted to providing good information about businesses, and where government requires businesses to disclose certain information to the public. Thus, each stock's expected return, its risk, its tax treatment, and so on will be fully known by all investors. Because participants have all the relevant information, asset prices will reflect that knowledge.

But it turns out that this broad dissemination of information is not only unrealistic but also unnecessary for the stock market to be efficient. Economists have shown that efficient markets do not require that *all* participants have information. If enough participants have information, prices will move as if the whole market had the information. All it takes is a few people knowledgeable enough to recognize a good deal (bad deal), and prices will quickly be bid up (or down) to levels that reflect complete information. And if prices reflect complete information, then even uninformed investors, purchasing at current prices, will reap the benefit; while they cannot "beat the market," neither do they have to worry about being "cheated" by an overpriced security.

You cannot beat an efficient market any more than you can beat the track. You can only get lucky in it. All the research done by the many big brokerage houses and individual investors adds up to a market that is in some respects like a casino. This is the irony of the view, held by most economists, that the stock market is an efficient one. If you are trying to make money in an efficient stock market, it is not enough to choose companies that you expect will be successful in the future. If you expect a company to be successful and everyone else also expects it to be successful, given the available information, then the price of the shares in that company will already be high. The only way to make abnormally high profits on stock purchases is to pick companies that will surprise the market by doing better than is generally expected. There are always such companies—the problem is to identify them before everyone else! When Microsoft shares first became available to the public in March 1968, they sold for 19 cents. By 2000, those shares were worth $58 dollars each. Early investors in technology stocks made enormous returns because technology firms did better than anyone had initially expected. Because of the success of many of these companies during the late 1990s, whenever a new one would "go public"—sells shares to the public for the first time—the price would often jump immediately to a very high level. The initial public offering of Google in 2004 exemplified this phenomenon. An investor buying the stock at high market prices can expect to earn only a normal level of profit. Of course, the trick is to know when to sell stocks before everyone else also decides it is time to sell. In 2000, the prices of technology stocks dropped dramatically. Today, shares of Microsoft trade for around $27 each.

The one exception is not really an exception because it involves trading with knowledge that other stock market participants do not have. *Inside traders* are individuals who buy and sell shares of companies for which they work. Studies show that their inside knowledge does in fact enable them to obtain above-average returns. Federal law requires inside traders to disclose when they buy and sell shares in their own company. People who may not have the inside knowledge but imitate the stock market behavior of the insiders also do slightly above average. The law also restricts the ability of insiders to share their information with outsiders and profit from their extra knowledge, and it exacts penalties for violations. After Ivan Boesky made untold millions trading on insider information in the 1980s, he paid large fines and even served time in jail. More recently, Martha Stewart spent five months in jail for obstructing an investigation into possible insider trading.

Because prices in an efficient market already reflect all available information, any price changes are a response to *unanticipated* news. If it was already known that something good was going to occur—for instance, that some new computer model better than all previous computers was going to be unveiled—the price of the firm's stock would reflect this knowledge (it would be high) before the computer actually hit the market. Investors might not know precisely how much better than its competitors the new computer was, and hence they could not predict precisely by how much future earnings were likely to rise. They would make an estimate. The market will reflect the average of these estimates. When the new computer is introduced, there is some chance that it will be better than this average, in which case the price will rise further. But there is also a chance that it will not be quite as good as this average estimate, in which case the price will fall, even though the computer is in fact better than anything else on the market. In the latter case, the "surprise" is that the computer is not as good as the market anticipated.

Since tomorrow's news is, by definition, unanticipated, no one can predict whether it will cause the stock price to rise or to fall. In an efficient stock market, prices will move unpredictably, depending on unexpected news. When a stock has an equal chance of rising or falling in value relative to the market as a whole, economists say that its price moves like a **random walk.** Figure 22.6 shows a computer-generated random walk, giving an idea of how unpredictable such a path is.

The phrase *random walk* conjures up the image of a drunk who rambles down the street with generally unstable—and unpredictable—movements. So too with the stock market. Although the level of all stock prices drifts upward, whether any particular stock will do better or worse than that average is unpredictable. If the stock market is indeed a random walk, it is virtually impossible for investors to beat the market. You can do just as well by throwing darts at the newspaper financial page as you can by carefully studying the prospects of each firm. The only way to do better than the market, on average, is to take greater risks; but taking greater risks also betters your chance of doing worse than the market.

The randomness of the market has one important consequence: *some* individuals are going to be successful. This is bad news for people who want to believe that their insights, rather than luck, are what has enabled them to beat the market.

EFFICIENT MARKETS OR RANDOM NOISE?

While most economists agree there is little evidence that individuals can consistently beat the market, even when they spend considerable money on information, they disagree over how to interpret this finding. Some see it as evidence of the efficiency of the market, as we have seen. But other economists view it as evidence of nothing more than the market's randomness. Those in the latter group point out that large changes in stock market prices often seem to occur in the absence of any "news" of sufficient magnitude to account for these changes. For example, there are usually ten or fifteen days in the year when the stock market changes by more than 2 percent—a very large change for a single day—without any obvious news-related explanation.

The famous economist John Maynard Keynes compared predictions of the stock market to predictions of the winner of a beauty contest in which what one had to decide was not who was most beautiful, but who the judges would think was the most beautiful. If investors suddenly "lose confidence" in a particular stock or in the whole stock market, or if they believe others are losing confidence, share prices may fall dramatically.

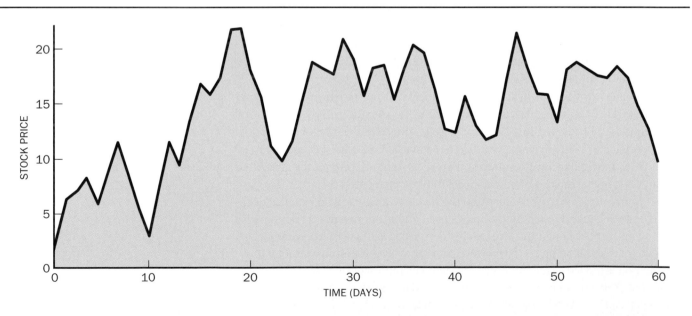

Figure 22.6

A COMPUTER-GENERATED RANDOM WALK

The series plotted here can be thought of as the closing price for a stock over 60 consecutive trading sessions. There is no predicting at the end of each day whether the stock will close higher or lower in the next day.

Strategies for Intelligent Investing

So far, we have investigated major investment alternatives available to those who save, some of the important attributes of each, and the ways in which their prices reflect these attributes. If you are lucky enough (have enough money) to be considering some of these alternatives, keep in mind the following four simple rules. These rules will not tell you how to make a million by the time you are twenty-five, but they will enable you to avoid the worst pitfalls of investing.

1. *Know the attributes of each asset, and relate them to your personal situation.* Each asset has characteristic returns, risk, tax treatment, and liquidity. In making choices among different assets, your attitude toward each of these attributes should be *compared with the average attitudes reflected in the marketplace.* Most individuals prefer safer, tax-favored, more liquid assets. That is why those assets sell at a premium (and produce a correspondingly lower average return). Are you willing to pay the amount required by the market for the extra safety or extra liquidity? If you are less risk averse than average, you will find riskier assets attractive. You will not be willing to pay the higher price— and accept the lower return—for a safer asset. And if you are confident that you are unlikely to need to sell an asset quickly, you will not be willing to pay the premium that more liquid assets require. If you are putting aside money for tuition next year, on the other hand, you probably will want to choose a relatively liquid asset.

2. *Give your financial portfolio a broad base.* In choosing among financial assets, you need to look not only at each asset separately but also at all of your assets together. A person's entire collection of assets is called her **portfolio.** (The portfolio also includes liabilities—what she owes—but consideration of these would take us beyond the scope of this chapter.) This rule is seen most clearly in the case of risk. One of the ways you reduce risk is by diversifying your investment portfolio. When a portfolio is well-diversified, it is extremely unlikely that something will go wrong with all the assets simultaneously. An investor with a diversified portfolio must still worry about events such as recessions or changes in the interest rate, which will tend to make all stocks go up or down. But events that primarily affect one firm will have a small impact on the overall holdings.

   Many mutual funds claim more than just diversification: they claim that their research and insight into markets enable them to pick winners. Our discussion of efficient markets casts doubt on these claims. Many other mutual funds do no research, claim no insights, and do nothing more than provide portfolio diversification. These are called *index funds.* There are several measures of the average price of stocks in the market. For instance, the Standard & Poor's (S&P) 500 index is the average price of 500 stocks chosen to be representative of the market as a whole. Other indexes track prices of various categories of stocks, such as transportation, utilities, or high technology. Index funds link their portfolio to these stock market indexes. Thus, there are a number of index funds that buy exactly the same mix of stocks that constitute the S&P 500 index. Naturally, these index funds do about as well as—no better and no worse than—the S&P 500 index, after a small charge for managing the fund is taken into account.

Because the index funds have low expenses, particularly in comparison with funds that are trying to outguess the market, they yield higher average returns to their investors than other funds with comparable risk.

3. *Look at* all *the risks you face, not just those in your financial portfolio.* Many people may be far less diversified than they believe. For example, consider someone who works for the one big company in town. She owns a house, has a good job, and has stock in the company, money in the bank, and a pension plan. But if that single company goes broke, she will lose her job, the value of her stock will fall, the price of her house is likely to decline as the local economy suffers, and even the pension plan may not pay as much as expected.

4. *Think twice before you think you can beat the market!* Efficient market theory delivers an important message to the personal investor. If an investment adviser tells you of an opportunity that beats the others on all counts, don't believe him. The bond that will produce a higher than average return carries with it more risk. The bank account that has a higher interest rate has less liquidity. The dream house at an unbelievable price probably has a leaky roof. The tax-favored bond will have a lower return—and so on. Efficient market theory, as we have seen, says that information about these characteristics is built into the price of assets, and hence built into the returns. Basically, investors can adjust the return to their portfolios only by adjusting the risk they face. Burton Malkiel, author of the best-selling book *A Random Walk Down Wall Street,* applies this theory to personal investment: "Every investor must decide the trade-off he or she is willing to make between eating well and sleeping well. The decision is up to you. High investment returns can be achieved only at the cost of substantial risk taking."[4]

---

[4]7th ed. (New York: Norton, 1999), p. 281.

Review and Practice

SUMMARY

1. Investment options for individuals include putting savings in a bank account of some kind or using them to buy real estate, bonds, or shares of stock or mutual funds.
2. Returns on investment can be received in four ways: as interest, dividends, rent, and capital gains.
3. Assets can differ in four ways: in their average returns, their riskiness, their treatment under tax law, and their liquidity.
4. By holding assets that are widely diversified, individuals can avoid many of the risks associated with specific assets, but not the risks associated with the market as a whole.
5. Today's price of an asset is influenced by expectations of the asset's price in the future. Expectation of a higher price in the future will cause the asset's price to rise today.
6. Asset prices can be very volatile because expectations about future returns can shift quickly.
7. The efficient market theory holds that all available information is fully reflected in the price of an asset. Accordingly, changes in price reflect only unanticipated events and, therefore, are random and unpredictable.
8. There are four rules for intelligent investors: (1) evaluate the characteristics of each asset and relate them to your personal situation; (2) give your financial portfolio a broad base; (3) look at all the risks you face, not just those in your financial portfolio; and (4) think twice before believing you can beat the market.

KEY TERMS

investment
real investment
financial investment
certificate of deposit (CD)
liquidity
dividends
retained earnings
capital gain

mutual fund
Treasury bills (T-bills)
diversification
expected returns
risk aversion
asset price bubbles
efficient market theory
random walk
portfolio

REVIEW QUESTIONS

1. Suppose an investor is considering two assets with identical expected rates of return. What three characteristics of the assets might help differentiate the choice between them?
2. List the principal alternative forms of investment that are available. What are the returns on each called? Rate them in terms of the characteristics described in Question 1.
3. True or false: "Two assets must have equal expected returns." If we modify the statement to read "Two assets that are equally risky must have equal expected returns," is the statement true? Explain your answer.
4. If you found out that several company presidents were buying or selling stock in their own companies, would you want to copy their behavior? Why or why not?
5. What is the efficient market theory? What implications does it have for whether you can beat the market? Does it imply that all stocks must yield the same expected return?
6. Why do economists expect the market to be efficient?
7. What alternative interpretations are given to the observation that individuals cannot, even by spending considerable money on information, consistently beat the market?
8. List and explain the four rules for intelligent investing.
9. True or false: "A single mutual fund may be a more diversified investment than a portfolio of a dozen stocks." Explain.

PROBLEMS

1. Imagine a lottery in which 1 million tickets are sold at $1 apiece, and the winning ticket receives a prize of $700,000. What is the expected return to buying a ticket in this lottery? Will a risk-averse person buy a ticket in this lottery?

2. Would you expect the rate of return on bonds to change with their length of maturity? Why or why not?

3. Why might a risk-averse investor put some money in junk bonds?

4. Would you predict that
   (a) the before-tax return on housing would be higher or lower than the before-tax return on other assets?
   (b) investors would be willing to pay more or less for a stock that has a high return when the economy is booming and a low return when the economy is in a slump than they would pay for a stock whose returns follow just the opposite pattern?
   (c) an investment with low liquidity would sell at a premium or at a discount compared with a similar investment with higher liquidity?

5. Imagine a short-term corporate $1,000 bond that promises to pay 8 percent interest over three years. This bond will pay $80 at the end of the first year and the second year, and $1,080 at the end of the third year. After one year, however, the market interest rate has increased to 12 percent. What will the bond be worth to an investor who is not too concerned about risk at that time? If the firm appears likely to go bankrupt, how will the expected return on this bond change?

6. The golfer Lee Trevino once said: "After losing two fortunes, I've learned. Now, when someone comes to me with a deal that's going to make me a million dollars, I say, 'Tell it to your mother.' Why would a stranger want to make me a million?" Explain how Trevino's perspective fits the efficient market theory.

GLOSSARY

absolute advantage: a country has an absolute advantage over another country in the production of a good if it can produce that good more efficiently (with fewer inputs)

adaptive expectations: expectations that respond or adapt to recent experience

aggregate consumption function: the relationship between aggregate consumption and aggregate income

aggregate demand-inflation curve: the curve that shows the negative relationship between inflation and spending

aggregate expenditures schedule: the relationship between *aggregate expenditures* and national income for a given *real rate of interest*

aggregate expenditures: total spending on goods and services produced in the economy (consumption plus investment plus government purchases plus net exports)

appreciation: a change in the *exchange rate* that enables a unit of currency to buy more units of foreign currencies

asset price bubbles: asset price increases that are based solely on the expectation that prices will be higher in the future, and not based on increases in the actual returns yielded by the asset

automatic stabilizer: expenditure that automatically increases or tax that automatically decreases when economic conditions worsen, and therefore tends to stabilize the economy automatically

balance of trade: a country's *exports* minus its *imports* (net exports)

basic competitive model: the model of the economy that pulls together the assumptions of self-interested consumers, profit-maximizing firms, and perfectly competitive markets

basic trade identity: net *exports* plus *capital inflows* equals zero

beggar-thy-neighbor policies: restrictions on imports designed to increase a country's national output, so-called because they increase that country's output while simultaneously hurting the output of other countries

bilateral trade: trade between two parties

boom: a period of time when resources are being fully used and *GDP* is growing steadily

borrowed reserves: the *reserves* that banks have borrowed from the discount window of the Federal Reserve

budget constraints: the limitations on consumption of different goods imposed by the fact that households have only a limited amount of money to spend (their budget); the budget constraint defines the opportunity set of individuals, when the only constraint that they face is money

business cycle: fluctuations in real economic activity around the economy's average growth path

capital deepening: an increase in capital per worker

capital gain: the increase in the value of an asset between the time it is purchased and the time it is sold

capital goods: the machines and buildings firms invest in, with funds obtained in the *capital market*

capital goods investment: investment in machines and buildings (to be distinguished from investments in inventory, research and development, or training [human capital])

capital inflows: money from abroad that is used to buy investments, to be deposited in U.S. banks, to buy U.S. government bonds, or to be lent in the United States for any reason

capital market: the various institutions concerned with raising funds and sharing and insuring risks, including banks, insurance markets, bond markets, and the stock market

capital outflows: money from the United States that is used to buy foreign investments or foreign government bonds, to be deposited in foreign banks or lent in foreign countries for any reason

causation: the relationship that results when a change in one variable is not only correlated with but actually produces a change in another variable; the change in the second variable is a consequence of the change in the first variable, rather than both changes being a consequence of a change in a third variable

central bank: the government institution responsible for monetary policy

central planning: the system in which central government bureaucrats (as opposed to private entrepreneurs or even local government bureaucrats) determine what will be produced and how it will be produced

certificate of deposit (CD): an account in which money is deposited for a preset length of time and yields a slightly higher return to compensate for the reduced liquidity

circular flow: the way in which funds move through the capital, labor, and product markets between households, firms, the government, and the foreign sector

commercial policies: policies directed at affecting either *imports* or *exports*

comparative advantage: a country has a comparative advantage over another country in one good as opposed to another good if its relative efficiency in the production of the first good is higher than the other country's

consumer price index: a price index in which the basket of goods is defined by what a typical consumer purchases

correlation: the relationship that results when a change in one variable is consistently associated with a change in another variable

countercyclical policies: policies designed to keep the economy at *full employment* by smoothing out fluctuations

countervailing duties: duties (*tariffs*) that are imposed by a country to counteract subsidies provided to a foreign producer

crowding out: a decrease in private investment resulting from an increase in government expenditures

currency board: a system in which the exchange rate between the local currency and foreign currency is fixed by law

cyclical unemployment: the increase in unemployment that occurs as the economy goes into a slowdown or *recession*

deflation: a persistent decrease in the general level of prices

demand: the quantity of a good or service that a household or firm chooses to buy at a given price

demand curve: the relationship between the quantity demanded of a good and the price, whether for an individual or for the market (all individuals) as a whole

demand deposits: deposits that can be drawn upon instantly, like checking accounts

depreciation: (a) the decrease in the value of an asset; in particular, the amount that capital goods decrease in value as they are used and become old; (b) a change in the *exchange rate* that enables a unit of one currency to buy fewer units of foreign currencies

depression: a strong downward fluctuation in the economy that is more severe than a *recession*

devaluation: a reduction in the rate of exchange between one currency and other currencies under a fixed exchange-rate system

developed countries: the wealthiest nations in the world, including western Europe, the United States, Canada, Japan, Australia, and New Zealand

diminishing returns: the principle that says that as one input increases, with other inputs fixed, the resulting increase in output tends to be smaller and smaller

discount rate: the interest rate charged on *borrowed reserves*

discretion: the ability to make explicit policy decisions in response to macroeconomic conditions

discretionary action: deliberate policy changes by the government, often used to indicate policy actions not constrained by past commitments

discretionary spending: government expenditures that are decided on an annual basis

disposable income: the amount of income a household has after paying taxes

distribution: the allocation of goods and services produced by the economy

diversification: spreading one's wealth among a large number of different assets

dividends: that portion of corporate profits paid out to shareholders

dollarization: abandonment of the domestic currency in favor of the U.S. dollar

dual economies: separations in many *less developed countries (LDCs)* between impoverished rural sectors and urban sectors that have higher wages and more advanced technology

dumping: the practice of selling a good abroad at a lower price than at home, or below costs of production

dynamic inconsistency: the problem of whether a government will actually carry out a promised course of action

efficiency wage: the wage at which total labor costs are minimized

efficient market theory: the theory that all available information is reflected in the current price of an asset

entitlements: programs that provide benefits automatically to individuals meeting certain criteria (such as age)

equilibrium: a condition in which there are no forces (reasons) for change

equilibrium price: the price at which demand equals supply

equilibrium quantity: the quantity demanded and supplied at the *equilibrium price,* where demand equals supply

European Union: an impotant regional trade bloc that now covers most of Europe

excess reserves: *reserves* that banks hold beyond what is legally required

exchange: the act of trading that forms the basis for markets

exchange rate: the rate at which one currency (such as dollars) can be exchanged for another (such as euros, yen, or pounds)

expansions: periods in which *real GDP* is growing

expected returns: the average return—a single number that combines the various possible returns per dollar invested with the chances that each of these returns will actually be paid

export-led growth: the strategy that government should encourage exports in which the country has a *comparative advantage* to stimulate growth

exports: goods produced domestically but sold abroad

federal funds market: the market through which banks borrow and lend *reserves*

federal funds rate: the interest rate on overnight interbank loans

Federal Open Market Committee (FOMC): the committee of the Federal Reserve System that sets monetary policy

final goods approach: measuring GDP by adding up all sales of final goods

financial investments: investments in stocks, bonds, or other financial instruments; these investments provide the funds that allow investments in *capital goods*

fiscal deficit: the gap between the government's expenditures and its revenues from sources other than additional borrowing

fiscal surplus: the amount by which government tax revenues exceed expenditures

fixed exchange rate system: an *exchange rate* system in which the value of each currency is fixed in relation to other currencies

flexible or **floating exchange rate system:** a system in which *exchange rates* are determined by market forces, the law of supply and demand, without government interference

flows: variables such as the output of the economy per year; stocks are in contrast to flows; flows measure the changes in stocks over a given period of time

fractional reserve system: the system of banking in which banks hold a fraction of the amount on deposit in *reserves*

free trade: trade among countries that occurs without barriers such as *tariffs* or *quotas*

frictional unemployment: unemployment associated with people moving from one job to another or moving into the labor force

full employment: a situation in which the demand for labor equals the supply of labor

full-employment deficit: what the deficit would be if the economy were at *full employment*

full-employment level of output: the level of output that the economy can produce under normal circumstances with a given stock of plant and equipment and a given supply of labor

GDP deflator: a weighted average of the prices of different goods and services, where the weights represent the importance of each of the goods and services in *GDP*

globalization: the closer integration of the countries of the world—especially the increased level of trade and movements of capital—brought on by lower costs of transportation and communication

Great Depression: the prolonged, worldwide period of severe economic *recession* during the 1930s

green revolution: the invention and dissemination of new seeds and agricultural practices that led to vast increases in agricultural output in *less-developed countries (LDCs)* during the 1960s and 1970s

gross domestic product (GDP): the total money value of all final goods and services produced within a nation's borders during a given period of time

human capital: the stock of accumulated skills and experience that makes workers productive

imperfect competition: any market structure in which there is some competition but firms face downward-sloping demand curves

imperfect information: a situation in which market participants lack information (such as information about prices or characteristics of goods and services) important for their decision making

implicit labor contract: an unwritten understanding between employer and employees that employees will receive a stable wage throughout fluctuating economic conditions

import function: the relationship between imports and national income

imports: goods produced abroad but bought domestically

incentives: benefits, or reduced costs, that motivate a decision maker in favor of a particular choice

income approach: the approach to calculating GDP that involves measuring the income generated to all of the participants in the economy

income effect: the reduced consumption of a good whose price has increased that is due to the reduction in a person's buying power, or "real" income; when a person's real income is lower, normally she will consume less of all goods, including the higher-priced good

income per capita: total income divided by the population

income-expenditure analysis: the analysis that determines equilibrium output by relating *aggregate expenditures* to income

industrialized countries: see *developed countries*

infant industry argument: the argument that industries must be protected from foreign competition while they are young, until they have a chance to acquire the skills that will enable them to compete on equal terms

infinite elasticity: the situation that exists when any amount will be demanded (supplied) at a particular price, but nothing will be demanded (supplied) if the price increases (declines) even a small amount

inflation: the rate of increase of the general level of prices

inflation adjustment line: a line showing the current rate of *inflation;* used with the inflation-adjustment curve to determine the equilibrium level of output

inflation shocks: events that produce temporary shifts in the SRIA curve

inflation targeting: policies designed to stabilize the economy through countercyclical policies while ensuring that average inflation remains low

information: the basis of decision making that can affect the structure of markets and their ability to use society's scarce resources efficiently

inside lag: the time it takes to recognize that there has been a change in the economy and decide on the appropriate policy response; in the United States, the inside lag for fiscal policy is normally assumed to be longer than the inside lag for monetary policy

interest-rate parity condition: a condition assuming perfect capital mobility where *expected returns* are equal across countries in equilibrium

inventory investment: firms' investment in raw materials or output on hand

investment: from the national perspective, an increase in the stock of capital goods or any other expenditure designed to increase future output; from the perspective of the individual, any expenditure designed to increase an individual's future wealth, such as the purchase of a share in a company (since some other individual is likely selling the share, that person is disinvesting, and the net investment for the economy is zero)

investment function: the relationship between the level of *real investment* and the value of the real interest rate; also called the investment schedule

labor force participation rate: the fraction of the working-age population that is employed or seeking employment

labor market: the market in which the services of workers are bought and sold

labor turnover rate: the rate at which a firm's workers quit to look for other jobs

land reform: the redistribution of land by the government to those who actually work the land

large open economy: an economy open to international trade and capital flows that is large enough, relative to the global economy, that its domestic conditions affect world levels of interest rates or incomes

law of supply and demand: the law in economics which holds that, in equilibrium, prices are determined so that demand equals supply; changes in prices thus reflect shifts in the *demand* or *supply curves*

less-developed countries (LDCs): the poorest nations of the world, including much of Africa, Latin America, and Asia

liquidity: the ease with which an investment can be turned into cash

loanable funds market: the market in which the supply of funds is allocated to those who wish to borrow; equilibrium requires that saving (the supply of funds) equals investment (the demand for funds)

long run: a length of time sufficient to allow wages and prices to fully adjust to equilibrate supply and demand

M1, M2, M3: measures of the money supply: M1 includes currency and checking accounts; M2 includes M1 plus savings deposits, *CDs,* and money market funds; M3 includes M2 plus large-denomination savings deposits and institutional money-market *mutual funds*

macroeconomics: the top-down view of the economy, focusing on aggregate characteristics

marginal benefits: the extra benefits resulting, for instance, from the increased consumption of a commodity

marginal cost: the additional cost corresponding to an additional unit of output produced

marginal propensity to consume: the amount by which consumption increases when income increases by a dollar

marginal propensity to import: the amount by which imports increase when income increases by a dollar

marginal propensity to save: the amount by which savings increase when income increases by a dollar

marginal revenue: the extra revenue received by a firm for selling one additional unit of a good

market clearing price: the price at which supply equals demand, so there is neither excess supply nor excess demand

market demand curve: the total amount of a particular good or service demanded in the economy at each price; it is calculated by "adding horizontally" the individual *demand curves;* that is, at any given price, it is the sum of the individual demands

market economy: an economy that allocates resources primarily through the interaction of individuals (households) and private firms

market supply curve: the total amount of a particular good or service that all the firms in the economy together would like to supply at each price; it is calculated by "adding horizontally" the individual firms' *supply curves* (that is, it is the sum of the amounts each firm is willing to supply at any given price)

medium of exchange: an item that can be commonly exchanged for goods and services throughout the economy

microeconomics: the bottom-up view of the economy, focusing on individual households and firms

monetary policy rule: the systematic relationship between the central bank's setting of policy and the variables that it reacts to, such as *inflation, cyclical unemployment,* or the *output gap*

money: any item that serves as a medium of exchange, a store of value, and a unit of account

money multiplier: the amount by which a new deposit into the banking system (from the outside) is multiplied as it is loaned out, redeposited, reloaned, etc. by banks

multilateral trade: trade between more than two parties

multiplier: the amount equilibrium output increases when the *aggregate expenditures schedule* shifts by a dollar

mutual fund: a fund that gathers money from different investors and purchases a range of assets; each investor then owns a portion of the entire fund

national saving: the combined saving of a country's private and public sectors

natural rate of unemployment: the unemployment rate when the economy is at *potential GDP* and *cyclical unemployment* is zero

net capital inflows: total *capital inflows* minus total *capital outflows*

neutrality of money: the idea that changing the money supply has no real effects on the economy, which is a basic implication of the full-employment model

newly industrialized countries (NICs): nations that have recently moved from being quite poor to being middle-income countries, including South Korea, Taiwan, Singapore, and Hong Kong

nominal GDP: the value of *gross domestic product* in a particular year measured in that year's prices

nominal rate of interest: the percentage return on a deposit, loan, or bond; the nominal rate of interest does not take into account the effects of *inflation*

nonborrowed reserves: the difference between *total reserves* and *borrowed reserves;* the Federal Reserve affects the level of nonborrowed reserves through *open-market operations*

nondiscretionary spending: expenditures that are determined automatically, such as interest payments and expenditures on entitlements

normative economics: economics in which judgments about the desirability of various policies are made; the conclusions rest on value judgments as well as facts and theories

North American Free Trade Agreement (NAFTA): the agreement between Canada, the United States, and Mexico that lowered trade and other barriers among the countries

Okun's law: the relationship between the output gap and cyclical unemployment first identified by Arthur Okun; according to Okun's law, *cyclical unemployment* of 1 percent is associated with a negative *output gap* of approximately 2 percent

open economy: an economy that is actively engaged in international trade

Open Market Desk: where the purchase or sale of government bonds by the Federal Reserve actually takes place

open-market operations: *central banks'* purchase or sale of government bonds in the open market

operating procedures: the manner in which a *central bank* chooses to implement monetary policy

opportunity cost: the cost of a resource, measured by the value of the next-best alternative use of that resource

opportunity set: a summary of the choices available to individuals, as defined by *budget constraints* and *time constraints*

output gap: the percentage deviation of actual GDP from potential

outside lag: the time lag between when a policy action is undertaken and when it has an impact on the economy; the outside lag for fiscal policy is normally assumed to be shorter than the outside lag for monetary policy

outsourcing: the move by U.S. firms to import goods and services these firms formerly produced in the United States

Pareto efficient: a resource allocation is said to be Pareto efficient if there is no rearrangement which can make anyone better off without making someone else worse off

peaks: the point in a business cycle where real output reaches its maximum level

perfect competition: a situation in which each firm is a price taker—it cannot influence the market price; at the market price, the firm can sell as much as it wishes, but if it raises its price, it loses all sales

perfectly mobile capital: capital that responds quickly to changes in returns in different countries

Phillips curve: the trade-off between unemployment and inflation such that a lower level of unemployment is associated with a higher level of inflation

plant and equipment investment: purchases by firms of new *capital goods*

portfolio: an individual's entire collection of assets and liabilities

positive economics: economics that describes how the economy behaves and predicts how it might change—for instance, in response to some policy change

potential GDP: a measure of what the value of GDP would be if the economy's resources were fully employed

present discounted value: how much an amount of money to be received in the future is worth right now

price elasticity of demand: the percentage change in quantity demanded of a good as the result of a 1 percent change in price (the percentage change in quantity demanded divided by the percentage change in price)

price elasticity of supply: the percentage change in quantity supplied of a good as the result of a 1 percent change in price (the percentage change in quantity supplied divided by the percentage change in price)

price-level targeting: a rarely adopted policy designed to achieve a stable price level

price system: the economic system in which prices are used to allocate scarce resources

private property: ownership of property (or other assets) by individuals or corporations; under a system of private property, owners have certain *property rights,* but there may be legal restrictions on the use of property

producer price index: a price index that measures the average level of producers' prices

product market: the market in which goods and services are bought and sold

production possibilities curve: a curve that defines the *opportunity set* for a firm or an entire economy and gives the possible combinations of goods (outputs) that can be produced from a given level of inputs

property rights: the rights of an owner of private property; these typically include the right to use the property as she sees fit (subject to certain restrictions, such as zoning) and the right to sell it when and to whom she sees fit

protectionism: the policy of protecting domestic industries from the competition of foreign-made goods

quantity equation of exchange: the equation $MV = PY,$ which summarizes the relationship between the amount of money individuals wish to hold and the dollar value of transactions

quotas: limits on the amount of foreign goods that can be imported

quota rent: profits that result from the artificially created scarcity of *quotas* and accrue to firms that are allocated the rights to import

random walk: a term used to describe the way the prices of stocks move; the next movement cannot be predicted on the basis of previous movements

real exchange rate: *exchange rate* adjusted for changes in the relative price levels in different countries

real GDP: the real value of all final goods and services produced in the economy, measured in dollars adjusted for *inflation*

real investment: the investment that is part of *aggregate expenditures,* such as the purchase of new factories and machines

real rate of interest: the real return to saving, equal to the nominal rate of interest minus the rate of *inflation*

real wage: the dollar, or nominal, wage corrected for changes in prices

recession: two consecutive quarters of a year during which GDP falls

repurchases (RPs): Federal Reserve open-market transactions that involve a combined sale of a government security and an agreement to repurchase it at a future date, perhaps the next day

reserves: funds held by banks in the form of vault cash or in deposits with the Federal Reserve

residential investment: households' purchases of new homes

retained earnings: that part of the net earnings of a firm that is not paid out to shareholders, but retained by the firm

risk aversion: the avoidance of bearing risk

rules: automatic adjustments of policy in response to macroeconomic conditions

scarcity: term used to describe the limited availability of resources, so that if no price were charged for a good or service, the *demand* for it would exceed its *supply*

seasonal unemployment: unemployment that varies with the seasons, such as that associated with the decline in construction in winter

sharecropping: an arrangement, prevalent in many *less-developed countries (LDCs)* in which a worker works land, giving the landowner a fixed share of the output

short run: a length of time during which wages and prices do not fully adjust to equilibrate *supply* and *demand*

short-run aggregate production function: the relationship between output and employment in the short run, that is, with a given set of machines and buildings

short-run inflation adjustment curve: positively sloped curve that shows the rate of *inflation* at each level of output relative to *potential GDP,* for a given expected rate of inflation

small open economy: an economy open to international trade and capital flows but whose domestic conditions are too small relative to the global economy to affect world levels of interest rates or incomes

stagflation: the phenomenon of high cyclical unemployment coupled with high inflation

sticky prices: prices that do not adjust or adjust only slowly toward a new equilibrium

sticky wages: wages that are slow to adjust in response to a change in labor market conditions

stocks: variables like the capital stock or the money supply stock, that describe the state of the economy (such as its wealth) at a point of time; they are contrasted by *flows*

store of value: something that can be accepted as payment in the present and exchanged for items of value in the future

strategic trade theory: the theory that protection can give a country a strategic advantage over rivals, for instance by helping reduce domestic costs as a result of economies of scale

structural unemployment: long-term unemployment that results from structural factors in the economy, such as a mismatch between the skills required by newly created jobs and the skills possessed by those who have lost their jobs in declining industries

substitution effect: the reduced consumption of a good whose price has increased that is due to the changed *trade-off,* the fact that one has to give up more of other goods to get one more unit of the high-priced good; the substitution effect is associated with a change in the slope of the *budget constraint*

sunk costs: costs that have been incurred and cannot be recovered

supply: the quantity of a good or service that a household or firm would like to sell at a particular price

supply curve: the relationship between the quantity supplied of a good and the price, whether for a single firm or the market (all firms) as a whole

supply shocks: unexpected shifts in the aggregate supply curve, such as an increase in the international price of oil or a major earthquake that destroys a substantial fraction of a country's capital stock

surplus of labor: a great deal of unemployed or underemployed labor, readily available to potential employers

sustainable development: development that is based on sustainable principles; sustainable development pays particular concern to environmental degradation and the exploitation of natural resources

tariffs: taxes imposed on imports

theory: a set of assumptions and the conclusions derived from those assumptions put forward as an explanation for some phenomena

time constraints: the limitations on consumption of different goods imposed by the fact that households have only a limited amount of time to spend (twenty-four hours a day); the time constraint defines the opportunity set of individuals if the only constraint that they face is time

total factor productivity (TFP): the part of economic growth that cannot be explained by increases in capital or labor

total factor productivity analysis: the analysis of the relationship between output and the aggregate of all inputs; total factor productivity growth is calculated as the difference between the rate of growth of output and the weighted average rate of growth of inputs, where the weight associated with each input is its share in GDP

total reserves: the sum of *borrowed* and *nonborrowed reserves,* as controlled directly by the Fed

trade creation: new trade that is generated as a result of lowered *tariff* barriers

trade deficit: the excess of *imports* over *exports*

trade diversion: trade that is diverted away from outside countries as a result of lowering *tariffs* between the members of a trading bloc

trade-offs: the amount of one good (or one desirable objective) that must be given up to get more of another good (or to attain more of another desirable objective)

Treasury bills (T-bills): short-term government bonds that are available only in large denominations

trough: the point during a *recession* at which real output reaches its lowest level

unemployment rate: the ratio of the number of people seeking employment to the total labor force

unit of account: something that provides a way of measuring and comparing the relative values of different goods

value added: the value added in each stage of production is the difference between the value of the output and the value of the inputs purchased from other firms

velocity: the speed with which money circulates in the economy, defined as the ratio of income to the money supply

World Trade Organization (WTO): the organization established in 1995 as a result of the Uruguay round of trade negotioations; replacing GATT, it is designed to remove trade barriers and settle disputes

zero elasticity: the situation that exists when the quantity demanded (or supplied) will not change, regardless of changes in price

CREDITS

INDEX

industrialized countries, 433
industry, defined, 84
inefficiencies, production possibilities curve
   and, 32
inequality, in LDCs, 436–37
infant industry argument, 385–86, 440
infinite elasticity, 75, 80
inflation, 7–9, 11–12, 117–28, 213, 214–20
   adjustment and, 260–61, 458–70
   aggregate demand and, 297–320
   alternative measures of, 125–27
   American experience with, 127–28
   central banks and, 350–53, 356–57
   changing expectations and, 463–65
   costs of, 117–19
   currency and, 118–19, 120–21, 411–12
   distributional effects and, 464
   exchange rates and, 418–19, 421–23
   expectations of, 458, 462–65, 470
   Fed and, 297–98, 308–9, 311, 316–17,
      475–76, 481, 486–87
   full employment and, 297–98, 299, 306–9,
      311, 458
   full-employment model and, 481
   government policies toward, 297–305, 481
   hyper-, 120–21
   indexing and, 118–19
   industrialized economies and, 457–58
   interest rates and, 347–57, 418–19
   lenders and, 118
   measurement of, 122–27
   monetary policy and, 261–64, 299–305,
      330–31, 486–97
   overstatement of, 124
   perceived costs of, 117–19
   Phillips curve and, 459–61
   quality improvements and, 125
   rate of, 117, 260, 308–12, 315–18, 459
   real costs of, 117–19
   real rate of interest and, 79–80, 347–49
   sufferers from, 118–19
   taxpayers and, 118
   unanticipated, 481
   uncertainty and, 119, 120–21
   and unemployment trade-off, 7–8, 261,
      264, 336–37, 457–73, 481–82, 483
   variability, 457
   Volcker victory over, 8, 308–9, 311
inflation adjustment curve, 312–18, 470–71
inflation adjustment line, 306–7, 318
inflation shocks, 313, 458, 468–69, 470
inflation stability-output stability trade-off,
   337
inflation targeting, 262, 263, 355–56, 475–76,
   486–97
   consequences of, 491–95
   pros and cons of, 488–89
inflation tax, 119

information:
   choices and, 12, 17–18, 41–42
   economic, 255, 520–22
   imperfect, 18, 45–46, 47
   real-time, 496
   technologies, 386, 496
injections, spending stream and, 143, 147,
   162
inputs, 19
inside lag, 358, 359
inside traders, 521
insourcing, 443–45
institutional infrastructure, 449–50
interactions and comparative advantage,
   373–74
interdependence and international trade,
   365–68
   costs and benefits of, 374–75
interest rate parity, 422
interest rates:
   cut of January 3, 2001, 351
   as discount rate, 237, 238, 326
   foreign, 420–21
   inflation and, 347–57, 418–19
   investment and, 145–46, 281–82
   monetary policies and, 11, 238, 299–305,
      329–31, 344–59, 496
   nominal, 79–80, 281, 300–303, 330–31,
      347–49, 494–95
   in open economy, 177–79
   present discounted value and, 76–79
   prices and, 518
   prime, 345–46
   real, see real interest rates
   savings decision and, 75–80, 144–47
intermediate outputs, 97, 99, 100
international financial crisis, 10, 396,
   408–9, 410–12, 441, 497
international financial system, 395–414
   deficit in, 163
   foreign exchange market and, 395–403,
      409–12
International Monetary Fund, 163, 427, 441,
   450
international trade, 180–90, 365–93
   aggregate expenditures and, 284–88
   balance of trade in, 285
   choices and, 13, 15–17
   cooperation and, 387–91
   costs and benefits of, 374–75
   fair competition in, 379–80
   in full-employment model, 175–76
   interdependence and, 365–68, 374–75
   and marginal propensity to import, 286,
      287–88
   open economy and, 176–79, 427
   policies, 375–80, 390–91
   protectionism and, 380–87

regional trading blocs and, 389–90
   see also exports; imports; trade; trade
      deficit
Internet:
   barter and, 228
   labor market and, 140
   United States' comparative advantage in,
      372
Internet connections:
   auction markets, 15
   banking information, 237
   Beige Book, 346
   Bureau of Economic Analysis, 97
   business cycles, 250
   consumer price index and, 124
   economic growth, 198
   Economic Report of the President, 340
   The Economists' Voice, 36
   Federal Open Market Committee, 318
   foreign exchange rates, 423
   index funds, 508
   inflation calculator, 125
   money facts, 218
   Nobel Prize, 467
   trade data, 181
   World Bank's development goals, 434
interventionists, 485–86
inventories, 272
   build up of, 283
   investment and, 280, 282–83
   production-facilitating function of, 282–83
investing, a student's guide, 503–26
   alternatives, 504–8
   desirable attributes of, 508–16
   efficient market theory and, 519–22
   expectations and, 516–19
   strategies for intelligent, 523–24
investment, investments, 280–84, 304–5
   attributes of, 508–16
   bonds, 505–6, 512, 514
   in capital goods, 145
   in capital markets, 82, 145–46
   determinants of, 145–46, 283
   diversification and, 507, 510–12, 523–24
   efficient market theory and, 519–22
   expected returns on, 78, 145–46, 281,
      508–12, 516–19
   financial, 145, 503
   foreign, 400–403, 422
   in full-employment model, 162
   government and crowding out, 159, 161
   India's Silicon Valley and, 444–45
   interest rates and, 145–46, 281–82
   in inventories, 280, 282–83
   liquidity of, 515–16
   market risks and, 282
   mutual funds, 221, 227, 507–8, 510, 523–24
   "new economy" and, 352–53, 510